Voices of the Confederate Navy

ALSO BY R. THOMAS CAMPBELL
AND FROM MCFARLAND

*Confederate Naval Cadet:
The Diary and Letters of Midshipman Hubbard T. Minor,
with a History of the Confederate Naval Academy* (2007)

*Confederate Naval Forces on Western Waters:
The Defense of the Mississippi River
and Its Tributaries* (2005; paperback 2011)

Voices of the Confederate Navy

Articles, Letters, Reports and Reminiscences

Edited by R. Thomas Campbell

McFarland & Company, Inc., Publishers
Jefferson, North Carolina, and London

The present work is a reprint of the illustrated case bound edition of Voices of the Confederate Navy: Articles, Letters, Reports and Reminiscences, *first published in 2008 by McFarland.*

LIBRARY OF CONGRESS CATALOGUING-IN-PUBLICATION DATA

Campbell, R. Thomas.
Voices of the Confederate Navy : articles, letters,
reports and reminiscences / edited by R. Thomas Campbell.
p. cm.
Includes bibliographical references and index.

ISBN 978-0-7864-7724-1
softcover : acid free paper ∞

1. Confederate States of America. Navy — History — Sources.
2. United States — History — Civil War, 1861–1865 — Personal narratives, Confederate.
3. United States — History — Civil War, 1861–1865 — Naval operations.
4. United States — History — Civil War, 1861–1865 — Riverine operations.
5. Confederate States of America. Navy — Biography — Anecdotes.
6. Confederate States of America. Navy — Officers — Biography — Anecdotes.
7. Sailors — Confederate States of America — Biography — Anecdotes.
I. Campbell, R. Thomas, 1938–
E596.V65   2013   973.7'82 — dc22   2007035262

BRITISH LIBRARY CATALOGUING DATA ARE AVAILABLE

© 2008 R. Thomas Campbell. All rights reserved

No part of this book may be reproduced or transmitted in any form or by any means, electronic or mechanical, including photocopying or recording, or by any information storage and retrieval system, without permission in writing from the publisher.

On the cover: clockwise from center, Commander Isaac N. Brown; Captain George N. Hollins; the USS *Water Witch* (courtesy Naval Historical Center); Captain Duncan N. Ingraham (courtesy Scharf, *History of the Confederate States Navy*)

Manufactured in the United States of America

*McFarland & Company, Inc., Publishers
Box 611, Jefferson, North Carolina 28640
www.mcfarlandpub.com*

Contents

Preface	1
"The Confederate States Navy," by 1st Lt. William H. Parker, CSN	3
I. The James River & Hampton Roads, Virginia	7
II. Eastern North Carolina	30
III. Charleston, South Carolina	62
IV. Savannah, Georgia	83
V. Columbus, Georgia	96
VI. Mobile, Alabama	104
VII. New Orleans, Louisiana	119
VIII. Louisiana Waters	139
IX. Mississippi River	153
X. Galveston, Texas	190
XI. Confederate Cruisers	206
XII. Torpedo Bureau	259
XIII. Blockade Runners	279
XIV. The CSN in Europe	300
XV. The Marine Corps	322
XVI. The Naval School	327
Some Final Thoughts	355
Bibliography	357
Index	359

Preface

The task of researching, studying, and writing about the naval exploits of the Confederacy for more than fifteen years has been an interesting, rewarding, and sometimes exhausting experience. Collected during this period were many essays and reminiscences written by Southern naval participants of the war. These narratives range from both the fond and the painful memories written by veterans who may, forty or fifty years after the "Late Unpleasantness," be approaching senility, to the carefully worded report of an officer claiming a victory or the loss of his ship. They lend information and color for us as we try to understand and appreciate just what these naval heroes of the South faced during this momentous period in our nation's history.

During the war, Confederate naval officers for the most part were punctual in submitting official reports to the Navy Department. When an action was completed, the commander of that naval district and the commander of the naval squadron that was involved submitted their reports to the Navy Department in Richmond. Individual ship commanders submitted their reports to the squadron commander, and these reports were most often forwarded on to the department as well. At least this was how it was supposed to work. As the war progressed and the Trans-Mississippi Department was effectively cut off from the rest of the Confederacy, reporting became more difficult. The official naval reports became less and less numerous, particularly during the last year of the war. This is understandable as the loss of places such as Mobile, Savannah, Wilmington, and finally Charleston essentially reduced the naval forces of the Confederacy in 1865 to a six-mile stretch of river below Richmond.

One of the greatest calamities for the researcher and the naval historian is that upon the evacuation of Richmond, Virginia, in April of 1865, the majority of these records in the Navy Department files located in the Mechanic's Building on Main Street went up in flames when that building burned. What records were carried away were eventually burned at Charlotte, North Carolina, because of a fear of retaliation by United States forces. This is unfortunate, but not an insurmountable problem, for many of the originators retained copies of their reports. When the United States Navy Department began the compilation of the *Official Navy Records* in 1884, the compilers asked former Confederate naval commanders to supply copies of personal correspondence with the pledge that they would be returned after inclusion in the work. With the generous cooperation of these Southern commanders, the *Official Records of the Union and Confederate Navies in the War of the Rebellion* today consists of approximately thirty percent Confederate records. In this work, some of these preserved records have been used.

Examples of Confederate navy writings are scattered across the South in various state and local archives. These writings include personal letters, diaries, journals, official reports, and production records of ships and ordnance. Notable among these repositories are the National Archives in Washington, D.C., and the Southern Historical Collection at the University of North Carolina in Chapel Hill. For the serious researcher, these archives are an invaluable tool in understanding the nature of the naval war.

Several Confederate naval commanders wrote their memoirs after the war. Most notable of these are Raphael Semmes, *Memoirs of Service Afloat*; William H. Parker, *Recollections of a Naval Officer 1841–1865*; Arthur Sinclair, *Two Years on the* Alabama; James D. Bulloch, *The Secret Service of the Confederate States in Europe*; James I. Waddell, *C.S.S. Shenandoah*; John M. Kell, *Recollections of a Naval Life Including the Cruises of the* Sumter *and* Alabama; and James M. Morgan, *Recollections of a Rebel Reefer*. A few of these Southern naval veterans were excellent writers. Semmes' account of his escape from New Orleans with the CSS *Sumter* is a classic and is included in this collection.

In 1887, Midshipman J. Thomas Scharf published his magnificent work, *History of the Confederate States Navy*. Even thought it contains some flaws, it is a monumental work that has yet to be surpassed. When no "voice" seemed to exist for a particular engagement, I have referred to Scharf's book for at least a brief overview of the event. Reprinted from his work are several selections, including his chapter on the Confederate States Marine Corps.

Some of the most interesting and informative narratives, however, appear in the *Southern Historical Society Papers*, a 52-volume work that began publication in 1869 and ended in the 1950s. The society solicited reminiscences and analyses of war experiences from Confederate veterans, some of whom had served in the navy. Several writings from this source are included here.

Another source of personal narratives is the *Century Magazine* that began publication in the United States by the Century Company of New York in 1881. It ceased publication in 1930, but during its lifetime solicited input principally from Union and Confederate officers. The series of articles between 1884 and 1887 were later incorporated into a four-volume set entitled *Battles and Leaders of the Civil War*. Many interesting naval accounts are found in this work.

Another interesting but less reliable source for the researcher is the old *Confederate Veteran* magazine, published by the United Confederate Veterans from 1893 to 1932. It, too, solicited input from Southern veterans, and even printed obituaries of many when they died, which were very useful in researching a veteran's life after the war.

In producing this collection, all of the above sources, along with a few others, have been relied upon. One word of caution here: many of these essays were written long after the war and sometimes are lacking in accuracy. Because these naval veterans were eager to tell their side of the conflict, it was only natural that they remembered the positive and forgot the negative. In addition, certain thoughts or rumors became implanted in their minds and over the years transcended "fact." This is especially true of the reminiscences published in *Confederate Veteran*, for it began production twenty-eight years after the end of the conflict. In order to arrive at a fair and balanced assessment of any given engagement, other sources including Union reports should be consulted. For this reason, this editor has attempted to present a blend of after-war writings and actual reports written during the conflict.

The veterans who wore the navy gray are all gone now. All we have are their words that speak to us from the written page. It is only through these accounts that we can ever hope to understand the courage that they displayed and the hardships and trials that these individuals faced. A selection of these writings assembled as they are in this work, truly become the voices of the Confederate navy.

R. Thomas Campbell
Fall, 2007

"The Confederate States Navy"
BY 1ST LT. WILLIAM H. PARKER, CSN

Confederate Military History (Atlanta: Confederate Publishing Company, 1899), 12:3–7

On the 11th day of March, 1861, the delegates from the seceded States, in session at Montgomery, Ala., adopted the "Constitution for the provisional government of the Confederate States of America," and this Constitution, as well as the one afterward adopted as "the permanent Constitution of the Confederate States," empowered Congress to "provide and maintain a navy," and made the President commander-in-chief of the army and navy.

South Carolina seceded December 20, 1860, and was followed by Mississippi, January 9, 1861; Florida, January 10, 1861; Alabama, January 11, 1861; Georgia, January 19, 1861; Louisiana, January 26, 1861, and Texas, February 1, 1861.

As the different States seceded, many of the officers of the United States navy belonging to those States resigned their commissions and offered their services to the Confederacy. Although many of these officers were informed by Mr. Gideon Welles, the secretary of the United States navy, that their names were "dropped from the rolls," and up to the present time they are marked on the official documents as "dismissed," yet, as a matter of fact, when they resigned their commissions the President could not, in accordance with the custom of the navy, do otherwise than accept them. The right of an officer to resign has never been disputed, unless the officer is at the time under arrest and liable to charges. Many examples could be cited to establish this point; but it is not necessary, as the Congress of the United States passed in 1861 an act to the effect that officers resigning would not be considered out of the service until their resignations were accepted by the President. This act is as follows:

> Any commissioned officer of the navy or marine corps who, having tendered his resignation, quits his post or proper duties without leave, and with intent to remain permanently absent therefrom, prior to due notice of the acceptance of such resignation, shall be deemed and punished as a deserter. Passed August 5, 1861.

The necessity for passing such an act proves the point just stated. Before 1861 the waiting for an acceptance of a resignation was simply an act of courtesy.

The Southern army officers were better treated. All resignations from the army were accepted. But many navy officers, in consequence of this spiteful and illegal action on the part of Secretary Welles, are now marked on the official list as "dismissed"(not a pleasant thing for their descendants to contemplate (for which no atonement can ever be made these officers. It is only one of the many sacrifices of the Confederate navy. The Naval Academy Association of Alumni, with a higher sense of honor and justice than Mr. Welles manifested, ignores this action of his in dismissing officers. It cordially admits these officers to membership, though officers legally dismissed are not admitted.

According to Col. J. Thomas Scharf's valuable history of the Confederate States navy, the statistics show that by June 3, 1861, of 671 officers from the South, 321 had resigned and 350 still remained in the United States navy. As the war progressed, however, many more Southern officers resigned.

Whatever has been said or written since that time of the action of the Southern officers, it is unquestionably true that it was the general belief of the Southern officers in the navy in 1861, that allegiance was due the State, and that when that State seceded, she withdrew her army and navy officers. It was, indeed, rather a matter of surprise to the better classes, even at the North, when a Southern officer failed to resign and join his friends and relatives at home. This action on the part of the naval officers who resigned must, and eventually will, stand forth as one of the most sublime instances in history of abnegation and devotion to principle.

In spite of all the censures in the Northern papers at that time and since, such as the talk of "bad faith, ingratitude, and treason," the fact remains that these officers (educated by their States, not at a royal or imperial academy, but at a United States academy) recognizing the right of a State to secede, heroically threw up their commissions, and offered their services to the States that claimed them. This sacrifice on the part of the Southern naval officers has never been properly appreciated. While at the close of the war the statesman returned to the Senate, the lawyer to his briefs, the doctor to his practice, the merchant to his desk, and the laborer to his vocation, the naval officer was utterly cast adrift. He had lost his profession, which was that of arms. The army officer was in the same category. Here it may be as well to explain to the general reader (too apt to confound the naval officer with the mere seaman) that the profession of a naval officer is precisely that of an army officer. They are both military men. So far as the profession goes, there is no difference between a lieutenant in the navy and a lieutenant of dragoons. One maneuvers and fights on shipboard, the other on horseback.

But there was this difference: The Southern officers of the United States army who came South were raised to high rank; young lieutenants, and even cadets, attained the rank of major or brigadier-general, and the close of the war left them with a national reputation. Far otherwise was it with the Southern naval officers. Men who, like Rousseau, Forrest and Tatnall, had commanded squadrons, could now only aspire to command a few converted river steamers; while commanders and lieutenants of many years' service were risking their reputations in command of canal boats. They came out of the war with the rank they had first, for there were few promotions. Under the circumstances, this was unavoidable; but it should be borne in mind by the present generation.

These officers with unparalleled devotion cast their lot with their people. No class of men had less to do with bringing the war about, and no men suffered more. At the close of the war they had literally lost all save honor (and there was much honor). But the coming of peace found these gentlemen unknown, and almost unhonored. Yet they have stood shoulder to shoulder since the war with nothing but their "wants, infirmities and scars to reward them;" they have felt the "cold hand of poverty without a murmur, and have seen the insolence of wealth without a sigh," and not one of them has cried, Peccavi!

Some of the Southern officers were at the beginning of the war in command of United States vessels on foreign stations. Upon being ordered home, they honorably carried their ships to Northern ports, and then, throwing up their commissions, joined the South. And what was before the Confederate naval officer? A nation with absolutely no navy, and with almost no facilities for building one! Professor Soley, assistant secretary of the navy under President Harrison, says in his work "The Blockade and the Cruisers":

> Except its officers, the Confederate government had nothing in the shape of a navy. It had not a single ship of war. It had no abundant fleet of merchant vessels in its ports from which to draw reserves. It had no seamen, for its people were not given to seafaring pursuits. Its only shipyards were Norfolk and Pensacola. Norfolk, with its immense supplies of ordnance and equipment was indeed valuable; but though the 300 Dahlgren guns captured in the yard were a permanent acquisition, the yard itself was lost when the war was one-fourth over. The South was without any large force of skilled mechanics, and such as it had were early summoned to the army. There were only three rolling-mills in the country, two of which were in Tennessee; and the third, in Alabama, was unfitted for heavy work. There were hardly any machine shops that were prepared to supply the best kind of workmanship; and in the beginning the only foundry capable of casting heavy guns was the Tredegar iron works [at Richmond, Va.], which, under the direction of Commander Brooke, was employed to its fullest capacity. Most deplorable of all deficiencies, there were no raw materials except the timber that was standing in the forests. Under these circumstances no general plan of naval policy on a large scale could be carried out, and the conflict on the Southern side became a species of partisan, desultory warfare.

In spite of all these difficulties, so plainly stated by Professor Soley, we shall see that the Southern navy was nevertheless built; and, incredible as it now appears, the South constructed during the war a fleet of ironclad vessels which, had they been assembled in Chesapeake bay, could have defied the navy of any nation in Europe. They were not seagoing vessels; but in smooth water the navy of Great Britain, at that time, could not have successfully coped with them.

I

The James River &
Hampton Roads, Virginia

1. The CSS *Virginia*

The executive officer of the ironclad *Virginia*, Catesby ap R. Jones, was one of the Confederacy's most highly respected naval officers. Born on April 12, 1821, in Frederick County, Virginia, Jones had established a solid career in the United States Navy after having been appointed to that service as an acting midshipman in 1836. He resigned his lieutenant's commission on April 17, 1861, and the next day was appointed a captain in the Virginia Navy. In June he was transferred to Confederate service with the rank of lieutenant, and later, after the Battle of Hampton Roads, he was promoted to commander. Jones is best known for his capable handling of the *Virginia* as her executive officer, and also for his command of that vessel during the history-making engagement with the USS *Monitor*. Perhaps his greatest achievement, however, albeit less known, was as superintendent of the Selma Naval Ordnance Works in Selma, Alabama, from May 9, 1863, until the end of the war. Most of the heavy naval ordnance used by the Confederate Navy during the latter half of the war came from Jones' foundry in Selma. Ironically, after the war, on June 29, 1877, Jones was shot and killed on a dusty Selma street by an enraged man whose child had had an altercation with one of Jones' children. The selection below was evidently written shortly before he was murdered. (Mabry, *A Brief Sketch of the Career of Captain Catesby ap R. Jones*.) [RTC]

"Services of the Virginia (Merrimac)" by
Commander Catesby ap R. Jones, CSN

Southern Historical Society Papers, Volume XI, January 1883, pp. 65–74

(The following deeply interesting narrative of the gallant and accomplished executive officer of the *Virginia* was prepared for our Society not long before his lamented death. It will be found to dispose of most conclusively the claim of the *Monitor* for prize money.)

When on April 21st, 1861, Virginia took possession of the abandoned navy-yard at Norfolk, they found that the *Merrimack* had been burnt and sunk. She was raised; and on June 23d following, the Hon. S. R. Mallory, Confederate Secretary of the Navy, ordered that she should be converted into an iron-clad, on the plan proposed by Lieutenant John M. Brooke, C. S. Navy.

The hull was 275 feet long. About 160 feet of the central portion was covered by a roof of wood and iron, inclining about thirty-six degrees. The wood was two feet thick; it consisted of oak plank four inches by twelve inches, laid up and down next the iron, and two courses of pine; one longitudinal of eight inches thickness, the other twelve inches thick.

The intervening space on top was closed by permanent gratings of two-inch square iron two and one-half inches apart, leaving openings for four hatches, one near each end, and one forward and one abaft the smokestack. The roof did not project beyond the hull. There was no knuckle as in the *Atlanta*, *Tennessee* and our other ironclads of later and improved construction. The ends of the shield were rounded.

Commander Catesby ap R. Jones (Naval Historical Center).

The armor was four inches thick. It was fastened to its wooden backing by one and three-eights inch bolts, countersunk and secured by iron nuts and washers. The plates were eight inches wide. Those first made were one inch thick, which was as thick as we could then punch iron. We succeeded soon in punching two inches, and the remaining plates, more than two-thirds, were two inches thick. They were rolled and punched at the Tredegar Works, Richmond. The outside course was up and down, the next longitudinal. Joints were broken where there were more than two courses.

The hull, extending two feet below the roof, was planted with one-inch iron; it was intended that it should have been three inches.

The prow was of cast iron, wedge-shape, and weight 1,500 pounds.

It was about two feet under water, and projected two feet from the stem, it was not well fastened.

The rudder and propeller were unprotected.

The battery consisted of ten guns, four single-banded Brooke rifles and six nine-inch Dahlgren's shell guns. Two of the rifles, bow and stern pivots, were seven-inch, of 14,500 pounds; the other two were 6.4-inch (32 pounds caliber) of 9,000 pounds, one on each broadside. The nine-inch gun on each side nearest the furnaces was fitted for firing hot-shot. A few nine-inch shot with extra windage were cast for hot shot. No other solid shot were on board during the fight.

The engines were the same the vessel had whilst in the United States Navy. They were radically defective, and had been condemned by the United States Government. Some changes had been made, notwithstanding which the engineers reported that they were unreliable. They performed very well during the fight, but afterwards failed several times, once whilst under fire.

There were many vexations delays attending the fitting and equipment of the ship. Most of them arose from the want of skilled labor and lack of proper tools and appliances. Transporting the iron from Richmond also caused much delay; the railroads were taxed to supply the army.

The crew, 320 in number, were obtained with great difficulty. With few exception they were volunteers from the army; most of them were landsmen. Their deficiencies were as much as possible overcome by the zeal and intelligence of the officers; a list of them is appended. In the fight one of the nine-inch guns was manned by a detachment of the Norfolk United Artillery.

The vessel was by the Confederate called *Virginia*. She was put in commission during the last week of February, but continued crowded with mechanics until eve of the fight. She was badly ventilated, very uncomfortable, and very unhealthy. There was an average of fifty or sixty at the hospital, in addition to the sick-list on board.

The Flag-Officer, Franklin Buchanan, was detained in Richmond in charge of an important bureau, from which he was only relieved a few days before the fight. There was no captain, the ship was commissioned and equipped by the Executive and Ordnance Officer, who had reported for duty in November. He had by special order selected her battery, and was also made responsible for its efficiency.

A trial was determined upon, although the vessel was in an incomplete condition. The lower part of the shield forward was only immersed a few inches, instead of two feet as was intended; and there was but one inch of iron on the hull. The port shutters, &c., were unfinished.

The *Virginia* was unseaworthy, her engines were unreliable, and her draft, over twenty-two feet, prevented her from going to Washington. Her field of operation was therefore restricted to the bay and its immediate vicinity; there was no regular concerned movement with the army.*

The frigates *Congress* and *Cumberland* temptingly invited an attack. It was fixed for Thursday night, March 6th, 1862; the pilots, of whom there were five having been previously consulted. The sides were slushed, supporting that it would increase the tendency of the projectiles to glance. All preparation were made, including lights at obstructions. After dark the pilots declared that they could not pilot the ship during the night. They had a high sense of their responsibility. In justice to them it should be stated that it was not easy to pilot a vessel of our great draft under favorable circumstances, and that the difficulties were much increased by the absence of lights, buoys, &c., to which they had been accustomed.

The attack was postponed to Saturday, March 8th. The weather was favorable. We left the navy yard at 11 AM, against the last half of the flood tide, steamed down the river past our batteries through the obstructions, across Hampton Roads, to the mouth of James river, where off Newport News lay at anchor the frigates *Cumberland* and *Congress*, protected by strong batteries and gunboats. The action commenced about 3 PM by our firing the bow-gun† at the *Cumberland*, less than a mile distant. A powerful fire was immediately concentrated upon us from all the batteries afloat and ashore. The frigates *Minnesota*, *Roanoke* and *St. Lawrence* with other vessels, were seen coming from Old Point. We fired at the *Congress* on passing, but continued to head directly for the *Cumberland*, which vessel we had determined to run into, and in less than fifteen minutes from the firing of the first gun we rammed her just forward of the starboard fore chains. There were heavy spars about her bows, probably to ward off torpedoes, through which we had to break before reaching the side of the ship. The noise of the crashing timbers was distinctly heard above the din of battle. There was no sign of the hole above water. It must have been large, as the ship soon commenced to careen. The shock to us on striking was slight. We immediately backed the engines. The blow was not repeated. We here lost the prow, and had the

---

There was, however, an informal understanding between General Magruder, who commanded the Confederate forces on the Peninsula, and the Executive, to the effect that General Magruder should be kept advised by us, in order that his command might be concentrated near Hampton when our attack be made. The movement was prevented in consequence of a large portion of the command having been detached just before the fight.

†*It killed and wounded ten men at the after pivot gun of the* Cumberland. *The second shot from the same gun killed and wounded twelve men at her forward pivot gun. Lieutenant Charles C. Simms pointed and fired the gun.*

stem slightly twisted. The *Cumberland** fought her guns gallantly as long as they were above water.

She went down bravely, with her colors flying. One of the shells struck the still of the bow-port and exploded; the fragments killed two and wounded a number. Our after nine-inch gun was loaded and ready for firing, when its muzzle was struck by a shell, which broke it off and fired the gun. Another gun also had its muzzle shot off; it was broken so short that at each subsequent discharge its port was set on fire. The damage to the armor was slight. Their fire appeared to have been aimed at our ports. Had it been concentrated at the water-line we could have been seriously hurt, if not sunk. Owing to the ebb tide our great draft we could not close with the *Congress* without first going up steam and then turning, which was a tedious operation, besides subjecting us twice to the full fire of the batteries, some of which we silenced.

We were accompanied from the yard by the gunboats *Beaufort*, Lieutenant-Commander W. H. Parker, and *Raleigh*, Lieutenant-Commander J. W. Alexander. As soon as the firing was heard up James river, the *Patrick Henry*, Commander John R. Tucker, *Jamestown*, Lieutenant Commander J. N. Barney, and the gunboat *Teaser*, Lieutenant-Commander W. A. Webb, under command of Captain John R. Tucker, stood down the river, joining us about o'clock. All these vessels were gallantly fought and handled, and rendered valuable and executive service.

The prisoners from the *Congress* stated that when on board that ship it was seen that we were standing up the river, that three cheers were given under the impression that we had quit the fight. They were soon undeceived. When they saw us heading down stream, fearing the fate of the *Cumberland*, they slipped their cables, made sail, and ran ashore bows on. We took a position off her quarter, about two cables' length distant, and opened a deliberate fire. Very few of her guns bore on us, and they were soon disabled. The other batteries continued to play on us, as did the *Minnesota*, then aground about one and one-half miles off. The *St. Lawrence* also opened on us shortly after. There was great havoc on board the *Congress*. She was several times on fire. Her gallant commander, Lieutenant Joseph B. Smith,[†] was struck in the breast by the fragment of a shell and instantly killed. The carnage was frightful. Nothing remained but to strike their colors, which they did. They hoisted the white flag, half-masted, at the main and at the spanker gaff. The *Beaufort* and *Raleigh* were ordered to burn her. They went alongside and secured several of her officers and some twenty of her men as prisoners. The officers urgently asked permission to assist their wounded out of the ship. It was granted. They did not return. A sharp fire caused the tugs to leave. A boat was sent from the *Virginia* to burn her, covered by the *Teaser*. A fire was opened on them from the shore, wounding Lieutenant Minor and others. We replied to this outrage with hot shot and incendiary shell. Her crew escaped by boats, as did that of the *Cumberland*. Canister and grape would have prevented it; but in neither case was any attempt made to stop them, though it has been otherwise stated, possibly from our firing on the shore or at the *Congress*.

We remained near the *Congress* to prevent her recapture. Had she been retaken, it might have been said that the Flag Officer permitted it, knowing that his brother[§] was an officer of that vessel.

A distant and unsatisfactory fire was at times had at the *Minnesota*. The gunboats also engaged her. We fired canister and grape occasionally in reply to musketry from the shore, which had become annoying.

**She was a sailing frigate of 1,726 tons, mounting two ten-inch pivots and twenty-two nine-inch guns. Her crew numbered 376; her loss in killed and wounded was 121.*

[†]*His sword was sent by flag of truce to his father, Admiral Joseph Smith.*

[§]*One of the sad attendants of civil war-divided families was here illustrated. The Flag-Officer's brother was Paymaster of the* Congress. *The First and Second Lieutenants had each a brother in the United States army. The father of the Fourth Lieutenant was also in the United States army. The father of the Midshipmen was in the United States navy.*

About this time the Flag Officer was badly wounded by a rifle ball, and had to be carried below. His bold daring and intrepid conduct, won the admiration of all on board. The Executive and Ordnance officer, Lieutenant Catesby ap R. Jones, succeeded to the command.

The action continued until dusk, when we were forced to seek an anchorage. The *Congress* was riddled and on fire. A transport steamer was blown up. A schooner was sunk and another captured.

We had to leave without making a serious attack on the *Minnesota*, Ground, and also at the *St. Lawrence*.* The latter frigate fired at us by broadsides, not a bad plan for small calibers against iron-clads, if concentrated. It was too dark to aim well. We anchored off our batteries at Sewell Point. The squadron followed.

The *Congress*† continued to burn; "she illuminated the heavens, and varied the scene by the firing of her own guns and the flight of balls through the air," until shortly after midnight, "when her magazine exploded, and a column of burning matter appeared high in the air, to be followed by the stillness of death," [extract from report of General Mansfield, U. S. A.] One of the pilots chanced about 11 PM, to be looking in the direction of the *Congress*, when there passed a strange looking craft, brought out in bold relief by the brilliant light of the burning ship, which he at once proclaimed to be the Ericsson. We were therefore not surprised in the morning to see the *Monitor* at anchor near the *Minnesota*. The latter ship was still aground. Some delay occurred from sending our wounded out of the ship; we had but one serviceable boat left. Admiral Buchanan was landed at Sewell Point.

At eight AM we got under way, as did the *Patrick Henry*, *Jamestown* and *Teaser*. We stood towards the *Minnesota* and opened fire on her. The pilots were to have placed us half-a-mile from her, but we were not at any time nearer than a mile. The *Monitor*§ commenced firing when about a third of a mile distant. We soon approached, and were often within a ship's length; once while passing we fired a broadside at her only a few yards distant. She and her turret appeared to be under perfect control. Her light draft enabled her to move about us at pleasure. She once took position for a short time where we could not bring a gun to bear on her. Another of her movements caused us great anxiety; she made for our rudder and propeller, both of which could have been easily disabled. We could only see her guns when they were discharged; immediately afterward the turret revolved rapidly, and the guns were not again seen until they were again fired. We wondered how proper aim could be taken in the very time the guns were in sight. The *Virginia*, however, was a large target and generally so near that the *Monitor*'s shot did not often miss. It did not appear to us that our shell had any effect upon the *Monitor*. We had no solid shot.

Musketry was fired at the look-out holes. In spite of all the care of our pilots we ran ashore, were we remained over fifteen minutes. The *Patrick Henry* and *Jamestown*, with great risk to themselves, started to our assistance. The *Monitor* and *Minnesota* were in full play on us. A small rifle-gun on board the *Minnesota*, or on the steamer alongside of her, was fired with remarkable precision.

When we saw that our fire made no impression on the *Monitor*, we determined to run into her if possible. We found it a very difficult feat to do. Our great length and draft, in a comparatively narrow channel, with but little water to spare, made us sluggish in our movements, and hard to steer and turn. When the opportunity presented all steam was put on; there was not, however, sufficient time to gather full headway before striking. The blow was given with the board wooden stem, the iron prow having been lost the day before. The *Monitor* received the blow in such a manner as to weaken its effect, and the damage

---

*A sailing frigate of fifty guns and 1,726 tons.
†A sailing frigate of 1,867 tons, mounting fifty guns. She had a crew of 434, of whom there were 120 killed and missing.
§She was 173 feet long and 41 feet wide. She had a revolving circular iron turret eight thick, nine feet high and twenty feet inside diameter, in which were two eleven-inch guns. Her draft was ten feet.

was to her trifling. Shortly after an alarming leak in the bows was reported. It, however, did not long continue.

Whilst contending with the *Monitor*, we received the fire of the *Minnesota*,* which we never failed to return whenever our guns could be brought to bear. We set her on fire and did her serious injury, though much less than we then supposed. Generally the distance was too great for effective firing. We blew up a steamer alongside of her.

The fight had continued over three hours. To us the *Monitor* appeared unharmed. We were therefore surprised to see her run off into shoal water where our great draft would not permit us to follow and where our shell could not reach her. The loss of our prow and anchor, and consumption of coal, water, &c., had lightened us so that the lower part of the forward end of the shield was awash.

We for some time awaited the return of the *Monitor* to the Roads. After consultation it was decided that we should proceed to the navy yard, in order that the vessel should be brought down in the water and completed. The pilots said if we did not then leave that we could not pass the bar until noon of the next day. We therefore at 12 PM quit the Roads and stood for Norfolk. Had there been any sign of the *Monitor*'s willingness to renew the contest we would have remained to fight her. We left her in the shoal water to which she had withdrawn, and which she did not leave until after we had crossed the bar on our way to Norfolk.

The official report says: "Our loss is two killed and nineteen wounded. The stem is twisted and the ship leaks; we have lost the prow, starboard anchor, and all the boats; the armor is somewhat damaged, the steam-pipe and smoke-stack both riddled, the muzzles of two of the guns shot away. It was not easy to keep a flag flying; the flag-staffs were repeatedly shot away; the colors were hoisted to killed or wounded in the fight with the *Monitor*. The only damage she did was to the armor. She fired forty-one shots. We were enabled to receive most of them obliquely. The effect of a shot striking obliquely on the shield was to break all the iron, and sometimes to displace several feet of the outside course; the wooden backing would not be broken through. When a shot struck directly at right angles, the wood would also be broken through, but not displaced. Generally the shot were much scattered; in three instances two or more struck near the same place, in each causing more of the iron to the displaced, and the wood to bulge inside. A few struck near the water-line. The shield was never pierced; through it was evident that two shots striking in the same place would have made a large hole through everything."

The ship was docked; a prow of steel and wrought iron attached, and a course of two-inch iron on the hull extending in length 180 feet. Want of time and material prevented its completion. The damage to the armor was repaired; wrought-iron port shutters were fitted, &c. The rifle guns were supplied with bolts of wrought and children iron. The ship was brought a foot deeper in the water, making her draft 23 feet.

Commodore Josiah Tattnall relieved Admiral Buchanan in command. On the 11th of April he took the *Virginia* down to Hampton Roads, expecting to have a desperate encounter with the *Monitor*. Greatly to our surprise, the *Monitor* refused to fight us. She closely hugged the shore under the guns of the fort, with her steam up. Hoping to provoke her to come out, the *Jamestown*† was sent in, and captured several prizes, but the *Monitor* would not budge. It was proposed to take the vessel to York river, but it was decided in Richmond that she should remain near Norfolk for its protection.

Commodore Tattnall commanded the *Virginia* forty-five days, of which time there were

---

She was a screw frigate of 3,200 tons, mounting forty-three guns of eight, nine and ten-inch caliber. She fired 145 ten-inch, 349 nine-inch, and 35 eight-inch and shell, and 5,567 pounds of powder. Her draft was about the same as the Virginia.

†*French and English men-of-war were present. The latter cheered our gunboat as she passed with the prizes.*

only thirteen days that she was not in dock or in the hands of the navy-yard. Yet he succeed in impressing the enemy that we were ready for active service. It was evident that the enemy very much overrated* our power and efficiency. The South also had the same exaggerated idea of the vessel.

On the 8th of May a squadron, including the *Monitor*, bombarded our batteries at Sewell Point. We immediately left the yard for the Roads. As we drew near, the *Monitor* and her consorts ceased bombarding, and retreated under the guns of the forts, keeping beyond the range of our guns. Men-of-war from below the forts, and vessels expressly fitted for running us down, joined the other vessels between the forts. It looked as if the fleet was about to make a fierce onslaught upon us. But we were again to be disappointed. The *Monitor* and the other vessels did not venture to meet us, although we advanced until projectiles from the Rip Raps fell more than half a mile beyond us. Our objects, however, was accomplished; we had put an end to the bombardment, and we returned to our buoy.

Norfolk was evacuated on the 10th of May. In order that the ship might be carried up the James river, we commenced to lighten her, but ceased on the pilots they could not take her up. Her shield was then out of water; we were not in fighting condition. We therefore ran her ashore in the bight of Craney Island, landed the crew, and set the vessel on fire. The magazine exploded about half-past four on the morning of the 11th of May, 1862. The crew arrived at Drewry's Bluff the next day, and assisted in defeating the *Monitor*, *Galena*, and other vessels on the 15th of May.

Commodore Tattnall was tried by court-marshal for destroying the *Virginia*, and was "honorably acquitted" of all the charges. The court stated the facts, and their motives for acquitting him. Some of them are as follows: "That after the evacuation of Norfolk, west over on James river became the most suitable position for her to occupy; that while in the act of lightening her for the purpose of taking her up to that point, the pilots for the first time declared their inability to take her up.... That when lightened she was made vulnerable to the attacks of the enemy.... The only alternative, in the opinion of the court, was to abandon and burn the ship then and there, which, in the judgment of the court, was deliberately and wisely done."

LIST OF OFFICERS OF THE C. S. IRON-CLAD *VIRGINIA*, MARCH, 8TH, 1862.

Flag-Officer—Franklin Buchanan. Lieutenants—Catesby ap. R. Jones, Executive and Ordnance officer; Charles C. Simms, R. D. Minor (flag), Hunter Davidson, J. Taylor Wood, J. R. Eggleston, Walter Butt. Midshipmen—Foute, Marmaduke, Littlepage, Craig, Long, and Roots. Paymaster—James Semple. Surgeon—Dinwiddie Phillips. Assistant-Surgeon—Algernon S. Garnett. Captain of Marines—Reuben Thom. Engineers—H. A. Ramsey, Acting Chief; Assistants—Tynan, Campbell, Herring, Jack and White. Boatswain—Hasker. Gunner—Oliver. Carpenter—Lindsey. Clerk—Sinclair.

2. The CSS *Beaufort*

The *Beaufort*, a screw tug of 85 tons, was built at Wilmington, Delaware, in 1854 and named the *Caledonia*. Upon the secession of Virginia she was armed with a single pivot gun on the bow and commissioned as *Beaufort* in the North Carolina navy. Run through the Dismal Swamp Canal to Albemarle Sound enroute to New Bern, she engaged the USS *Albatross* across the sand dunes of the Outer Banks in an inconclusive battle.

---

*Some of the Northern papers estimated her to be equivalent to an army corps.

When North Carolina's vessels were incorporated into Confederate service, Lieutenant Parker became her commander. Under Parker she participated in the Battle of Roanoke Island on February 7 and 8, 1862, and narrowly escaped destruction at Elizabeth City two days later by retreating up the Dismal Swamp Canal to Norfolk. She then acted as a tender to the CSS *Virginia*, and that is where Parker picks up her story. (Civil War Naval Chronology 1861-1865, pp. VI-203-VI-204.)

William Howell Parker was born in New York City on October 8, 1826, and had entered the U.S. Navy in 1841 at the tender age of 15. He was graduated from the U.S. Naval Academy in 1847, and taught at the naval school from 1853 to 1857, and again from 1860 to 1861. Parker was assistant professor of mathematics at Annapolis when the Southern states began to secede, and when Virginia left the Union he resigned his commission and offered his services to his adopted state. He was appointed a first lieutenant in the Confederate navy on June 10, 1861. After commanding the *Beaufort* at Roanoke Island, Elizabeth City, and the Battle of Hampton Roads, he was assigned as executive officer on the ironclad CSS *Palmetto State* at Charleston. Later, Lieutenant Parker became the first, last, and only commandant of the Confederate States Naval Academy. (Scharf, *History of the Confederate States Navy*, p. 773.) [RTC]

The Battle of Hampton Roads by 1st Lt. William H. Parker, CSN

Recollections of a Naval Officer 1841–1865, Chapter XXIII, pp. 270–282

About the 6th of March, 1862, the *Merrimac* [In his writings, Parker always refers the *Virginia* using it's old Federal name, *Merrimac*. RTC] being ready to go out, the Norfolk papers published an article to the effect that she was a failure, and would not be able to accomplish anything. It was intended, of course, to deceive the enemy, who we knew regularly received our papers. The Federal squadron then in Hampton Roads, consisted of the following vessels, viz.: the *Congress* and *Cumberland*, lying off Newport News; and the *Minnesota*, *Roanoke* and *St. Lawrence*, at anchor below Old Point. There were also at Old Point the store-ship *Brandywine*, the steamers *Mt. Vernon* and *Cambridge*, and a number of transports and tugs; these, however, took no part in the subsequent engagement. The *Congress* was a sailing frigate of 1867 tons, mounting 50 guns, principally 32-pounders, and a crew of 434 men; the *Cumberland* was a large corvette (a razee) of 1700 tons, mounting 22 nine-inch guns, and a crew of 376 men; the *Minnesota* was a steam frigate of 3200 tons, mounting 43 guns, of 9-inch and 11-inch caliber, and a crew of about 600 men. The *Roanoke* was similar to the *Minnesota*, and the *St. Lawrence* to the *Congress*.

Newport News is 6½ miles from Old Point and 12 miles from Norfolk. It is on the left bank of the James river, and above Old Point. The enemy had a large number of guns mounted there to protect the mouth of the river, and it had a large garrison. At Seawell's Point, 3½ miles from Old Point, the Confederates had a powerful battery to protect the entrance to the Elizabeth River. It also, in a measure, commanded the approach to Newport News; but the main ship channel is at a distance of 2 or 2½ miles from it. At Seawell's Point was mounted the only 11-inch gun we had in the Confederacy.

Everything being ready, it was determined by Commodore Buchanan to make the attack on the 8th of March. The night before, he sent for me and gave me my final orders. The last change made in our signal-books was that if the Commodore's flag was hoisted under number "one," it meant "sink before you surrender." Mr. Hopkins, who had formerly been my pilot, came on board the *Beaufort* as a volunteer, and Midshipman Ivy Foreman, of North Carolina, reported to me as volunteer aid. They both rendered excellent service the next day.

At 11 AM, March 8, 1862, the signal was made to sail, and the *Beaufort* cast off from the wharf in company with the *Merrimac* and *Raleigh*, and stood down the harbor. The weather was fair, the wind light, and the tide half flood; the moon was nine days' old. Nearly every man, woman and child in the two cities of Norfolk and Portsmouth were at the same time on their way to Seawell's Point, Craney Island and other points, where they could see the great naval combat which they knew was at last to take place. Some went by land, others by water. All the batteries were manned; all work was suspended in public and private yards, and those who were forced to remain behind were offering up prayers for our success. A great stillness came over the land.

Flag Officer Forrest who commanded the station, accompanied by all the officers of the navy yard went down with us in the *Harmony*

1st Lt. William H. Parker (Scharf, *History of the Confederate States Navy*).

as far as Craney island, 4½ miles below Norfolk. Everything that would float, from the army tug-boat to the oysterman's skiff, was on its way down to the same point loaded to the water's edge with spectators. As we steamed down the harbor we were saluted by the waving of caps and handkerchiefs; but no voice broke the silence of the scene; all hearts were too full for utterance; an attempt at cheering would have ended in tears, for all realized the fact that here was to be tried the great experiment of the ram and iron-clad in naval warfare. There were many who thought that as soon as the *Merrimac* rammed a vessel she would sink with all hands enclosed in an iron-plated coffin. The least moved of all, were those who were about to do battle for the "Cause" they believed in. On board the *Merrimac* the officers and men were coolly employed in the multifarious duties that devolved upon them, while the men of the *Beaufort* and *Raleigh* were going into battle with the same careless insouciance they had exhibited in the battles of Roanoke Island and Elizabeth City.

The James river squadron, consisting of the *Patrick Henry*, *Jamestown* and *Teaser*, under the command of Captain [John R.] Tucker, had been previously notified by Commodore Buchanan that the *Merrimac* would go out on the 8th, and Tucker was directed to come down the river as close to Newport News as he deemed prudent, so as to be ready to dash by the batteries and join our division when the action commenced. The commodore could not have given the order to a better man—eager to engage the enemy, Tucker, the most chivalric and bravest of men, ably seconded by his gallant captains, Nicholas Barney, Webb, and Rochelle, was only too ready to fly the Confederate flag in Hampton Roads. At daylight that morning he was at anchor off Smithfield Point—some ten miles above Newport News—and in full view of the enemy, as afterwards reported by Lieutenant George Morris who, in the absence of her commander, fought the *Cumberland*. As we got down towards the mouth of the Elizabeth River, about 12.30 PM, the *Beaufort* took a line from the port bow of the *Merrimac* to assist her in steering—being very near the bottom she steered very badly. Mr. Cunningham, one of her pilots, came on board at the same time by order of Commodore Buchanan. This gave the *Beaufort* three pilots; the *Merrimac* remained with three, and the *Raleigh* with one. We turned up the James River. The *Congress* and *Cumberland* were lying off Newport News and were riding to the last of the flood tide. They had their "washed clothes" up at the time we saw them, I remember, which shows how entirely unexpected our appearance was—In fact the captain of the *Cumberland*, Commander William C. Radford, was at this time on board the frigate *Roanoke* below Old Point attending a court-martial. Lieutenant George Morris was left in command, and the ship could not have been better fought by any officer of the U. S. Navy.

The *Cumberland* was lying at anchor just above Newport News, and the *Congress* abreast the Point. As soon as our vessels turned up the James River the enemy saw that our attack would be made upon the frigates, lying off Newport News, and the two ships there commenced getting ready to receive it.

At 1.30 PM we cast off the line from the *Merrimac*, and all three vessels steamed for the enemy, the *Beaufort* maintaining her position on the port bow of the *Merrimac*; and exactly at 2 PM we fired the first gun of the day, and at the same time hoisted the battle flag we had used at Roanoke Island at the mast-head. This flag resembled the French flag—it was, I think, the colors reversed. It was devised by Commodore Lynch and was used by his squadron. I had not thought of referring the matter to Commodore Buchanan; but I determined to hoist it "for luck," and I will not deny that I had some superstition in connection with it. The men were all for hoisting it, and that decided me. I do not wonder that Captain Marston of the *Roanoke* said in his report: "It was the impression of some of my officers that the rebels hoisted the French flag."

The *Merrimac* now hoisted the signal, "close action," and from that time until the surrender of the *Congress* she made no signal, nor did she answer one. I mention this particularly as it caused me to consider that I must use my own judgment during the battle only recollecting to obey the signal for close action—and I know that other officers commanding gunboats thought as I did.

The fire of the *Cumberland* on the *Merrimac* was so heavy while it lasted that it was impossible for a man to stand on her upper deck and live—so perhaps was the fire of the *Congress*. I only mention the fact stated; and I have no recollection of seeing a man on the deck of the *Merrimac* from the beginning of the fight until after the *Congress* surrendered. During the afternoon, in the heat of the action, the *Raleigh* came alongside me and her commander, Lieutenant Alexander, told me the carriage of his gun was disabled and he could not fire a shot. He said he could not get his signals answered by the *Merrimac*, and wanted to know what he should do. I directed him to return to Norfolk. This is in corroboration of what I have said above. Fortunately Alexander repaired the damage and did not have to leave the fight.

As we approached the enemy, firing and receiving their fire, the *Merrimac* passed the *Congress* and made for the *Cumberland*—which vessel was either just turning to the ebb tide, or had her broadside sprung across the channel. The *Beaufort* and *Raleigh* engaged the *Congress* and shore batteries, and the firing became fast and furious. I took up a position on the port quarter of the *Congress* and used the rifled gun with effect. The *Merrimac* rammed the *Cumberland*, striking her just forward of the starboard fore channel—firing and receiving a heavy fire in return—and stove her bow in so completely that she at once commenced to go down. As she took the bottom she turned over on her beam-ends. She made a gallant defense, her crew fighting their guns to the last, and went down with her colors flying. This was at 2.40 PM precisely. Boats went off from Newport News to save the drowning men. The *Merrimac* reversed her engines immediately upon ramming the *Cumberland*, and had some difficulty in extricating herself—indeed her bow sunk several feet. When free, she proceeded a short distance up the river to turn round, having done which she stood for the *Congress*.

As soon as the *Congress* observed the fate of her consort she slipped her cable, set her fore-topsail flying, and with the assistance of a tug, ran on shore below Newport News. At this time I observed the James River Squadron coming gallantly into action; they were under a very heavy fire while passing the Newport News batteries, but got by without receiving much damage. All of our vessels now directed their fire upon the *Congress*. I took up a position on her starboard quarter and kept it until she surrendered. The fire on this unfortunate ship was perfectly terrific. She returned it with alacrity, principally from her stern guns, and was assisted by the batteries on shore.

We saw now the frigates *Minnesota*, *Roanoke* and *St. Lawrence* coming up from Old Point to the assistance of the *Congress*, towed by powerful tugs. They were under a heavy fire from the batteries on Seawell's Point as they passed, and received some damage. The *Minnesota* received a rifle-shot through her mainmast, "crippling it," according to her captain's report. Strange to say all three of these vessels ran aground; the *Minnesota* about one and a half miles below Newport News, the *St. Lawrence* farther down, and the *Roanoke* below her again. The *Minnesota* was near enough to take part in the engagement and the *St. Lawrence* fired a few broadsides. The *Roanoke* and *St. Lawrence* were soon pulled off by the tugs and made the best of their way back to Old Point. They took no farther part in the battle. The *Minnesota* remained aground. The *Congress* made a gallant defense and did not surrender until one hour and twenty minutes after the sinking of the *Cumberland*. Her decks were running with blood, and she bore the brunt of the day. At 4 o'clock she hoisted a large white flag at her mainmast head, and as it went up, Midshipman Mallory in charge of our bow-gun, waved his cap and exclaimed: "I'll swear on the Bible that we fired the last gun!" So the *Beaufort* fired the first and last gun in this memorable battle. When I saw the white flag, I immediately lowered a boat, and sent Midshipman Mallory and Foreman with a boat's crew of three men to take possession of the prize and bring her commander on board the *Beaufort*. As the boat approached the *Congress* a marine at the gangway leveled his piece, and threatened to fire; but Mallory told him he was ordered to board the vessel, and was "bound to do it," and pulled alongside. He and his companions got on board, and Midshipman Foreman hauled down the colors and brought them to me.

The firing having ceased, the *Merrimac* signaled me to come within hail, which I did. Commodore Buchanan then ordered me to "go alongside the *Congress*, to take the officers and wounded men prisoners, to permit the others to escape to the shore, and then to burn the ship." I went alongside her in the *Beaufort*, at the port gangway, and sent an officer to direct her commander to come to me, at the same time sending my men aboard to help to get the wounded men to the *Beaufort*. I did not think it proper to leave my vessel myself as I had but two young and inexperienced midshipmen with me, and I saw an enemy's gunboat not very far off. In a few minutes Lieutenant Austin Pendergrast came down the side of the *Congress* accompanied by an officer whom I took to be the purser or surgeon of the ship. It proved to be Captain William Smith who had been in command until a few days before, when he had been relieved by Lieutenant Joseph B. Smith. Lieutenant Smith was killed in the action, which left Pendergrast in command. Captain Smith was acting as a volunteer; but this I learned afterwards. These two officers landed on the hurricane deck of the *Beaufort* where I was standing, and surrendered the ship. As they were without sidearms I thought it proper to request them to return to their ship and get them. This they did, though Pendergrast delivered to me a ship's cutlass instead of the regulation sword. I now told Pendergrast my orders and asked him to get his officers and wounded men on board as quickly as possible as I wanted to burn the ship. He said there were 60 wounded men on board the frigate and begged me not to burn the vessel. I told him my orders were peremptory. While we were engaged in this conversation the wounded men were being lowered into the *Beaufort*, and just then the *Raleigh* came alongside me. Lieutenant [James L.] Tayloe came on board and said Captain Alexander had sent him to me for orders. I directed him to take the *Raleigh* to the starboard side of the *Congress* and assist in getting off the wounded men. I had scarcely given him the order when a tremendous fire was opened on us from the shore by a regiment of soldiers—Medical Director, Shippen says it was the 20th Indiana. The firing was from artillery as well as small arms. At the first discharge every man on the deck of the *Beaufort*—save Captain Smith and Lieutenant Pendergrast—was either killed or wounded. Four bullets passed through my clothing; one of which carried off my cap cover and eye glass, and another slightly wounded me in the left knee, precisely in the spot where my friend Fauntleroy had accidentally wounded me at the siege of Vera Cruz. Lieutenant Pendergrast now begged me to hoist the white flag, saying that all his wounded men would be killed. I called his attention to the fact that they were firing on the white flag which was flying at his mainmast head directly over our heads. I said I would not hoist it on the *Beaufort*; in fact I did not feel authorized to do so without consulting Commodore Buchanan. I said: "Tell your men to stop firing;" he replied: "They are a lot of volunteers and I have no control over them." This was evident. The lieutenant then requested permission to go on board the *Congress* with Captain Smith and assist in getting the wounded down. This I assented to; in the first place, I was glad to have their assistance; and secondly, I would not have been willing to confine them in my cabin at a time when the bullets were going through it like hail—humanity forbade it; I would not have put a dog there.

I now blew the steam-whistle, and my men came tumbling on board. The fire of the enemy still continuing from the shore, I cast off from the *Congress* and steamed ahead so that I could bring my bow gun to bear. I had no idea of being fired at any longer without returning it, and we had several deaths to avenge. We opened fire, but could make little impression with our single gun upon the large number of men firing from entrenchments on shore. The sides and masts of the *Beaufort* looked like the top of a pepper-box from the bullets, which went in one side and out at the other. Being much encumbered with the prisoners, five of whom were wounded, and having no medical officer on board, I ran alongside the steamer *Harmony* and delivered them to Flag Officer Forrest. They consisted of Master's Mate Peter Hargous and 25 men. We then steamed immediately back and joined the other vessels in the attack on the *Minnesota*, which vessel was still on shore. The air seemed to be full of shot and shell from this time till some time between 7 and 8 PM, when we hauled off in obedience to signal, and anchored between Seawell's Point and Craney island. Dr. Herbert Nash kindly came off from the latter post and attended to the wants of the wounded on the *Beaufort*.

At midnight the *Congress* blew up. According to the report of Lieutenant Pendergrast she had been on fire from the beginning of the action; and Medical Director Shippen, who from his station would be likely to know, says: "We were on fire in the sick-bay, in the main-hold, and under the ward-room near the after-magazine. Some of these fires were extinguished, but the most dangerous one, that near the after-magazine, was never extinguished, and was the cause of the explosion, which, during the following night, blew the ship to pieces."

The results of this day's operations were the total destruction of the frigate *Congress* and corvette *Cumberland*, and the partial crippling of the frigate *Minnesota*. The loss in killed and drowned on board the *Cumberland*, as reported by her commander, was 121; and the surgeon reports 14 wounded, which makes 135 casualties. I find it difficult to ascertain from Lieutenant Pendergrast's report how many men the *Congress* lost in all. He gives the total number of killed and missing as 136; he then deducts 26 wounded, taken on shore, which leaves 110. If there were 60 wounded men when I went alongside, as he said (and this number was certainly not exaggerated), and if he sent 26 on shore, these, with the 5 I had, would account for 31; which leaves 29 unaccounted for, or still on board; and there is reason to fear that some wounded men were left on board to be consumed by the flames, who would have been taken off by the *Beaufort* and *Raleigh*, under the flag of truce, had they not been fired upon by the troops on shore. The fire of these troops killed their own wounded men as they were being lowered over the side, and rendered it impossible for us to continue the work. The *Raleigh* did not take a man on board from the *Congress*. The *Minnesota* lost 3 killed and 16 wounded, and there were some casualties reported among the other vessels. From what I can gather, I think the loss in the Federal fleet in killed, drowned, wounded and missing amounted to nearly 400 men.

On our side the *Merrimac* lost 21 in killed and wounded; the *Patrick Henry*, 14; the *Beaufort*, 8; the *Raleigh* had Lieutenant Tayloe and Midshipman Hutter killed, how many men I do not know; nor have I any information as to the number of killed and wounded in the *Teaser*. The *Jamestown* had no casualties. Our total loss, however, did not exceed 60.

> Lieutenant Parker is grossly mistaken on the number of casualties. According to numerous sources the *Virginia* had 2 killed and 6 wounded. Lieutenant James L. Tayloe and Midshipman William C. Hutter were from the *Raleigh*, but were onboard the *Beaufort* when killed. Therefore, Parker's figure of 8 for the *Beaufort* is correct, but Tayloe and Hutter should be counted as the *Raleigh's* casualties. The *Patrick Henry* had 7 injured. Total Confederate casualties appear to be approximately twenty-seven. [RTC]

On the *Merrimac*, Commodore Buchanan and his flag lieutenant, Robert D. Minor, were wounded. Captain Webb, of the *Teaser*, and Alexander of the *Raleigh*, received slight wounds, but not enough to disable them. Lieutenant Tayloe and Midshipman Hutter fell at the first murderous discharge from the shore, while the *Raleigh* lay alongside me; in fact, I had just assisted Mr. Tayloe to step over to the hurricane deck of the *Raleigh*, after giving him his orders, when he was shot. They were both killed under the flag of truce. Their loss was deeply felt by their comrades. Young and full of promise, it did indeed seem hard that they should fall at the end of a battle in which they had rendered such gallant service. Commodore Buchanan and Lieutenant Minor were sent to the Naval Hospital at Norfolk on the morning of the 9th, and the command of the squadron devolved upon Captain John R. Tucker, of the *Patrick Henry*. He did not leave his own vessel, however, and Lieutenant Catesby ap R. Jones succeeded to the command of the *Merrimac*.

The result of this day's battle—which was to revolutionize the navies of the world, as showing the power of the ram and ironclad—has immortalized the name of the *Merrimac*; this all will concede. But in all descriptions of this battle the *Merrimac* has so completely overshadowed her consorts that if they are alluded to at all it is in a light way; and the gunboats are frequently denominated tugs. Indeed the people on both sides formed such extravagant notions concerning the *Merrimac* that they seemed to think that from that time forward a gun could do no damage unless mounted upon an iron-clad vessel. The Confederate accounts of the battle were full of the *Merrimac*, the fire from her guns, etc.,—and but little was said of the smaller vessels whose fire was equally effective. Justice to those who served in these vessels and especially to those who died upon their decks, requires that I should establish this fact. As Campbell sings:

> And yet, amidst this joy and uproar,
> Let us think of them that sleep,
> Full many a fathom deep,
> By thy cold and stormy steep, Elsinore,

premising that it is difficult to make anyone at the present day understand what absurd and ridiculous men-of-war our gunboats really were. The magazine and boiler being above the waterline, and the hull of one-fourth inch iron, or one inch planking, a man serving in one of them stood a chance of death in four forms: he could be killed by the enemy's shot, (this was the legitimate form); he could be drowned by his vessel being sunk, (this might also be called a legitimate form); he could be blown up by a shot exploding the magazine, or he could be scalded to death by a shot passing through the boiler—the last two methods I always considered unlawful, and (strange as it may appear) strongly objected to!

To prove the services of the wooden vessels in the battle of Hampton Roads I shall quote only the Federal accounts. The italics are mine. The Secretary of the Navy, Hon. Gideon Welles, in his report of 1862 says:

"Having thus destroyed the *Cumberland*, the *Merrimac* turned again upon the *Congress*, which had in the meantime been engaged with the smaller rebel steamers [the *Beaufort* and *Raleigh*,] *and after a heavy loss*, in order to guard against such a fate as that which had befallen the *Cumberland*, had been run aground. The *Merrimac* now selected a raking position astern of the *Congress*, *while one of the smaller steamers poured in a constant fire on her starboard quarter. Two other steamers of the enemy also approached from James river firing upon the unfortunate frigate with precision and severe effect.*" The *Minnesota*, which had also got aground in the shallow waters of the channel, became the special object of attack, and the *Merrimac* with the *Yorktown* and *Jamestown* bore down upon her. The *Merrimac* drew too much water to approach very near; her fire was not therefore particularly effective. The other steamers selected their positions, *fired with much accuracy, and caused considerable damage to the Minnesota.*" Captain G. Van Brunt who commanded the *Minnesota* corroborates the above. Lieutenant Pendergrast who commanded the *Congress* in his report says: "After passing the *Congress*, she (the *Merrimac*) ran into and sank the United States sloop-of-war *Cumberland*. *The smaller vessels then attacked us killing and wounding many of our crew.* At 3.30 the *Merrimac* took a position astern of us at a distance of about 150 yards and raked us fore and aft with shells, *while one of the smaller steamers kept up a fire on our starboard quarter. In the meantime the Patrick Henry and Thomas Jefferson [Jamestown], rebel steamers, approached us from up the James River firing with precision and doing us great damage.*"

I think I have quoted enough to show that the wooden vessels bore an important part in this battle, and will only add that when Midshipman Mallory first boarded the *Congress*, Lieutenant Pendergrast asked him the name of my vessel and said that a shot from her went into the starboard quarter of the *Congress* and, traversing the whole length of the gun deck, went out of the port bow. We took from the *Congress* 16 navy revolvers, 8 Minie rifles, 20 Sharp's rifles, and 10 cutlasses, which I believe is about all that was saved from her by either side. And here I will stop to say that we made a mistake in not trying to get the *Congress* afloat and towing her up to Norfolk. I thought of doing it at the time the *Raleigh* came to me; but my orders to burn her were imperative and I did not feel at liberty to try it. She went on shore at half tide and I think could have been pulled off at the next high water.

We had to regret the loss of Jack Robinson, the captain of our gun. Poor fellow! he was faithful to the last. When I first sent my men on board the *Congress* to assist the wounded, I saw him standing, with his arms folded, at the breech of his gun, and demanded to know why he had not obeyed the order. "Why captain," said he, pointing to a gunboat nearby, "they can come and take you while we are gone." "Never mind that," said I, "I want your help here." He went, and I observed soon returned and took up his former position. He was killed at the first fire from the shore by a rifle ball passing through his body. In getting him below he suffered so much I had him taken to the cabin and laid upon my bed. We had no surgeon or medical stores, but that did not matter in his case as his wound was mortal. After the battle I went to see him and asked him what I could do for him. He said he would like a cup of tea and a pair of clean socks, which were given him. He died at 8 o'clock, quietly and resignedly; not the first sailor I have seen die in the same way.

Yet, though the worms gnaw his timbers and his vessel's a wreck, When he hears the Last Whistle, he'll spring up on deck.

3. Battle of Trent's Reach

During the year 1864, the Union Navy had advanced its ironclads up the James River as far as Trent's Reach where they had constructed a barricade of logs, chains, and sunken ships. Hundreds of large caliber guns, Confederate and Federal, now lined the river with the Federals controlling areas north and east, and the Southern forces arranged along a line south and west of the river.

In early January of 1865, the Union fleet in the lower James had been greatly reduced. Most of the warships had been sent to reinforce the massive attack that was about to take place on Fort Fisher at Wilmington, North Carolina. Secretary Mallory constantly urged Captain John K. Mitchell, commander of the James River Squadron, to take the offensive and attempt to capture Grant's huge supply base at City Point, Virginia. If this could be accomplished, the Federal Army of the Potomac might be compelled to withdraw its troops from in front of Petersburg. Only one U. S. ironclad remained below Trent's Reach, the double-turreted USS *Onondaga*, along with a few wooden gunboats.

The Confederate forces consisted of three ironclads, *Virginia II*, *Richmond*, and *Fredericksburg*; the wooden gunboats *Hampton*, *Beaufort*, *Torpedo*, and *Nansemond*; the torpedo boats *Wasp*, *Scorpion*, and *Hornet*; and the armed tender *Drewry*. The Confederate navy, Mallory stressed, would never again enjoy such superiority once the Federal vessels returned. (Campbell, *Sea Hawk of the Confederacy: Lt. Charles W. Read and the Confederate Navy*, pp. 144-145.)

On the dark night of January 23, Mitchell made the attempt to pass the obstructions and attack the enemy. Below is his report. [RTC]

Trent's Reach, Detailed Report by
Captain John K. Mitchell, CSN

Official Records Navy, Series I, Volume XI, pp. 669–673

C. S. FLAGSHIP *VIRGINIA II*,
James River Squadron, below Chaffin's Bluff, *February 3, 1865*

SIR: On the 25th ultimo I had the honor to report to you the return of this squadron to its present anchorage, with a brief notice of the unfortunate failure of the enterprise and the reason for relinquishing the, attempt of its prosecution beyond Trent's Reach.

On the evening of the 23d ultimo, the squadron moved down from its present anchorage soon after dark, consisting of the ironclad *Fredericksburg* leading, with the gunboat *Hampton* and torpedo boat *Hornet* secured alongside; the *Virginia*, ironclad, next with the gunboat *Nausemond*, tug *Torpedo*, and torpedo boat *Scorpion* secured alongside, and the ironclad *Richmond* last, with the gunboats *Drewry* and *Beaufort* and the torpedo boat *Wasp* secured alongside.

In this order they passed the fire of the enemy's batteries and sharpshooters on Signal Hill and vicinity, which opened upon them in Devil's Reach and continued until they had passed the Dutch Gap. On arriving in Trent's Reach, the *Virginia* and the *Richmond* anchored, at 10:40 PM, about half a mile above the obstructions, in 5 fathoms of water, with a kedge by the stern. The *Fredericksburg* proceeded at once near to the obstructions at the north channel, while a sounding and reconnoitering party in charge of Lieutenant C. W. Read examined them. He soon after reported the obstructions practicable on the removal of a spar which was anchored diagonally across a gap between two sunken bulks, about two-thirds from No. 3 hulk to No. 2, counting from the north bank. While the moorings of this spar were being cut, in company with Lieutenant C. W. Read, I sounded the chancel about two cables' length below the obstructions. We did not find less than 2½ fathoms water; a slight freshet in the river probably raised it about a foot above its ordinary level.

At 1 AM (24th) I went on board the *Fredericksburg* and immediately after she passed through the obstructions with the loss of her port outriggers for torpedo defenses by their coming in contact with No. 2 hulk.

After seeing the *Fredericksburg* through, I directed a light to be placed on the obstructions to guide the squadron through, arid returned to the *Virginia* at 1:45 AM To my inexpressible mortification I found her aground; ineffectual efforts were made with the aid of gunboats and kedges to get her afloat. At 3:30 o'clock it was reported to me that the *Richmond*, *Drewry*, and torpedo boat *Scorpion* also were aground. The ironclads had been anchored in 5 fathoms water by the stern with kedges and were unfortunately allowed to drag unobserved aground. The reports of the commanding officers of those vessels explain the circumstances of their grounding.

The tide having been at ebb for some hours, and it therefore being impossible to get the vessels afloat before the next flood, I directed the wooden vessels and torpedo boats to take up their anchorage before daylight opposite Battery Dantzler, under cover of a wooded point of land, which would secure them from the observation of the enemy, or at least afford some protection from his fire.

The *Fredericksburg* was now recalled and ordered to take up a position above the *Richmond* to cover, if practicable, the grounded vessels with her broadside.

As anticipated, at daylight the enemy's batteries and sharpshooters on the south side of Trent's Reach, that had been firing upon the squadron without effect from the time of its arriving in the reach, were now enabled to take deliberate aim. Their fire (the nearest about 800 yards) was chiefly directed at the *Richmond* and the *Drewry*, lying close together and in line. At 7:10 AM a shell exploded the magazine of the *Drewry*, blowing her to pieces and covering the deck of the *Richmond* with the fragments. Fortunately, for fear of such a disaster, the crew had been taken on board of the *Richmond* about 15 minutes before the explosion took place, and were thus all saved except two, who were killed, having gone to the torpedo boat *Scorpion*, lying alongside of the *Drewry*. The *Scorpion* was badly damaged by the explosion and was not brought off when the *Richmond* floated, but she subsequently drifted off with the high tide down to the obstructions, where she fell into the hands of the enemy a day or two after.

The first night after the return of the squadron to its present anchorage a party was sent to recover the *Scorpion*, if possible, but the approach to her was guarded by an enemy's gunboat above the obstructions, and our boats could not proceed.

After blowing up the *Drewry* the enemy concentrated the fire of his batteries upon the *Virginia*, and about 10:30 AM a double turreted monitor and a double ender appeared in the lower part of the reach and opened fire at the distance of about 1,600 yards upon the *Virginia*. About this time the *Virginia* and the *Richmond* commenced floating, and by 12:15 PM rounded the point above and anchored with the rest of the squadron. The *Richmond* received little or no damage, but the *Virginia* was struck upward of 70 times, many of them blows from the heaviest rifle projectiles and 2 from the monitor; one of the latter, probably a XV-inch solid shot and another, a rifle 200-pounder; the effect of the last two broke and crushed in the iron, the wooden backing, clamp, stanchions on port side of shield, and on the port quarter made a hole entirely through, 2 feet by 2½ in diameter. The splinter netting no doubt prevented many casualties, only 1 being killed and 2 wounded. The monitor fired about 7 times before we passed from her sight. The *Virginia* received much other damage in shield, deck, beams, and carlines, knuckle forward, port lanyards, a gun-deck beam, and in the starting of bolts and armor plates in various parts of the vessel. The smokestack was so badly cut up and the exhaust pipe cut in two as to allow the steam to escape on the spar and gun decks, but it did not prevent the raising of steam. A small Rodman projectile entered her open port quarter port, striking its side, broke a clamp of the forward gun (8-inch rifle), and, passing through the cheek of the carriage, exploded, wounding Lieutenant W. P. Mason and 7 men. None of the enemy's projectiles actually penetrated her shield. The 2 boat howitzers mounted on her shield deck were struck and disabled from indentations.

During the whole time while aground neither the *Richmond* nor the *Virginia* could get a gun to bear upon the enemy. The latter, in rounding head upstream obtained one shot at the monitor with her XI-inch, which was observed to take effect upon her. During the afternoon the monitor retired down the river below the Dutch Gap and disappeared from sight toward Varina.

Although our force was diminished by the loss of the *Drewry* and 1 torpedo boat, and the disabling of another, and the *Virginia* considerably damaged, yet, as her battery, except the 2 howitzers, was not materially injured, preparations and dispositions were at once made to move down the river as early in the night as the tide would serve.

Soon after dark the enemy exhibited a brilliant Drummond light on the south side of Trent's Reach, near the obstructions, which, illuminating the reach, would enable him to direct his fire almost as well at night as by day.

At 9 PM the squadron was underway, the *Virginia* leading, down Trent's Reach, when her pilots (Messrs. Edward Moore and Samuel Wood) declared it was impossible to direct the movements of the shill in consequence of the escape of the steam on deck from the damaged exhaust pipe and smokestack, together with the dazzling effect of the Drummond light. The squadron was at once brought to and efforts made by Chief Engineer H. X. Wright to remedy the trouble complained of, in which he only partially succeeded by diminishing somewhat the escape of steam on the upper deck, while it was rendered more dense on the gun deck.

A council of war was called, composed of Commander Kell, of the *Richmond*, Lieutenant Commanding John W. Dunnington, of the *Virginia*, and Lieutenant Commanding F. E. Shepperd, of the *Fredericksburg*, who advised the return of the squadron to its anchorage below Chaffin's Bluff for the following reasons, viz: The escape of steam on deck and the Drummond light blinding the pilots, the loss of the gunboat *Drewry* and a torpedo boat, and the disabling of another and the gunboat *Hampton*, and the enemy being now fully apprised of our movements diminished so much our prospects of success as to render it advisable to abandon the enterprise. Entertaining the same views, I at once made the necessary dispositions to return that night, in reverse order, sending the *Hampton*, disabled by having a piece of chain wound round her propeller, ahead, towed by the *Nansemond* and the *Torpedo*.

At 2:45 AM of the 25th the squadron started back and ran the gantlet of the enemy's batteries and sharpshooters from Battery Garnett to near the head of Devil's Reach. No serious damage appears to have been sustained by any of the vessels, although the *Virginia* was struck several times with heavy projectiles, nor were there any casualties, though exposed to showers of Minié balls, upward of 800 reported as having been picked up on the deck of the *Hampton*. The *Virginia*, the rear vessel of the line, reached her anchorage at 7:30 AM.

The leak of the *Virginia* is now about twice the quantity it was previous to the late movement, having increased from about 2 to about 4 inches in 12 hours.

The *Fredericksburg* since her return leaks badly, requiring the almost incessant working of the ship's pumps to keep her free, making, as she does, from 2 to 3 inches per hour. The ship received a hard blow from a projectile on the fantail forward, which carried away the chain cable and caused the loss of an anchor, but this blow of itself it is scarcely possible could have caused so considerable a leak. Pilots Parrish and Barnes state that they felt the vessel's bottom strike something as she passed through the obstructions and one of them saw pieces of timber rise to the surface alongside; if they are not mistaken, the leak may be traced to this cause.

Secretary of the Navy, Stephen R. Mallory (Library of Congress).

The safe passage of the squadron twice over the beds of the torpedoes, placed by Lieutenant Kennon, C. S. Navy, at Bishop's and at Howlett's, shows that they must have been washed away by the late high freshet or that they are harmless. If the enemy has torpedoes placed, they were rendered harmless from similar causes, or, if electric, our movement must have been so unexpected as to find him unprepared to use them.

A demonstration was made against the enemy's right by General Pickett, and our batteries keeping up a fire on those of the enemy, operated, no doubt, for our benefit, although the enemy's batteries in Treat's Reach were steadily and continuously directed against our vessels while exposed to their fire.

Our first-class pilots have given cause for complaint. Lieutenant Commanding Shepperd complains much of his, on board of the *Fredericksburg*; Lieutenant Commanding C. W. Read complains of Mr. Wood, of this ship, and the *Richmond* and the *Virginia*, being allowed to drag aground after being anchored in 5 fathoms water, is well calculated to keep commanding officers ever anxious for the safety of their vessels, and distrustful of the success of any movement depending upon the skill, coolness, and courage of their pilots. The *Virginia* in going down on the 23d passed so near the south bank as to run the *Torpedo*, lashed to her starboard side, aground, and in coming up on the morning of the 25th she (the *Virginia*), when the fire of the enemy had ceased, was run aground and remained fast for twenty minutes or more near the head of Devil's Reach.

In passing Cox's Landing the *Torpedo*, having been crowded into the south bank, and remaining aground, Lieutenant Commanding W. R. Butt was sent to the *Nansemond* to haul her off, but having tried without success and reported it impracticable, Lieutenant Commanding W. H. Wall was sent with the *Drewry* to perform the service. Much to his credit he got her afloat, and though not; requiring much effort, yet he was exposed to a heavy fire of the enemy's sharpshooters, and brought her safely to the squadron after she had been abandoned by her commanding officer, Lieutenant T. P. Bell, with all her crew except

Acting Master P. W. Smith, who, with two men, bravely remaining steadfast to his duty, is worthy of special notice. A letter from Lieutenant T. P. Bell, explanatory of his conduct on the occasion, is herewith enclosed; it is not satisfactory to me, and I submit that his conduct be made the subject of investigation.

I am gratified in stating that the commanding officers seconded me with their best efforts, and from their reports of our late movements under the fire of the enemy, the officers and men of their respective commands exhibited the skill and courage the occasion called for. I take pleasure in bearing testimony to the good conduct of my staff, Flag Lieutenant C. J. Graves, Midshipman F. S. Kennett, and my secretary, J. W. Daniel.

Enclosed are the reports of Commander J. M. Kell, of the *Richmond*; Lieutenants Commanding J. W. Dunnington, of the *Virginia*; F. E. Shepperd, of the *Fredericksburg*; W. H. Wall, of the ill-fated gunboat *Drewry*; J. W. Alexander, of the gunboat *Beaufort*; W. R. Butt, of the gunboat *Nansemond*; J. D. Wilson, of the gunboat *Hampton*; C. W. Read, of the steam torpedo boats *Scorpion*, *Hornet*, and *Wasp*; Acting Master P. W. Smith, of the tug *Torpedo*, and of Fleet Surgeon W. D. Harrison, of the casualties, which make a total of 5 killed and 14 wounded.

A copy of the opinion of the council of war held on the evening of the 24th, near Howlett's, is also enclosed. From the examination of the obstructions and the north channel in Trent's Reach, though hastily made, I felt reasonably assured that, but for the unfortunate grounding of the two ironclads, *Virginia* and *Richmond*, the whole squadron would have passed below that night, and, as the enemy was unprepared for the movement, there was every reason to indulge the hope that it would have been successful. As the result has proved so unfortunate for the public interests, I invite the closest scrutiny into the manner of conducting the enterprise committed to me.

I am, very respectfully, your obedient servant,

JNO. K. MITCHELL,
Flag-Officer, James River Squadron.

Hon. S. R. MALLORY,
Secretary of the Navy, Richmond, Va.

4. Overland Expedition

The failure of the James River Squadron to force its way downstream and attack the huge Federal supply base at City Point was a bitter disappointment. To make matters still worse, Lieutenant Charles Read had lost two of his three torpedo boats. No doubt he was convinced that if Mitchell had acted swiftly upon his report that the obstructions had been washed away, the ironclads and his torpedo boats could have raised havoc with the Federals. Maybe, just maybe, the destruction of the supply base at City Point would have necessitated the withdrawal of the massive army in blue that encircled Richmond and Petersburg. But now with the fall of Fort Fisher, the enemy's ironclads would soon return, and it would be impossible to launch another attack with any hope of success.

Read had a plan, however, that just might reverse the desperate situation. No official record of Read's expedition, if one was ever written, is known to have survived, but history is indebted to Master W. Frank Shippey, the commander of the small gunboat CSS *Raleigh* who had been assigned to the mission. Shippey kept a log during the expedition, and he wrote of the many dangers and frustrations that they encountered. (Campbell, *Southern Thunder: Exploits of the Confederate States Navy*, pp. 159-162.) [RTC]

"A Leaf from my Log-Book" by
Master W. Frank Shippey, CSN

Southern Historical Society Papers, Volume XII, 1884, pp. 416–421

The gray dawn of a frosty morning in February, 1865, broken upon a party of about one hundred officers and men in the uniform of the Confederate States navy, assembled at Drewry's Bluff, on the banks of the James River, Virginia. The morning was very cold, and as the men were formed in two ranks and their arms and equipment carefully inspected by the officers, it was easy to see that stern work and great danger was to be encountered, by the unusual attention given to this inspection, and the expression, half serious, half reckless, that characterized the men who, in those stirring times, were familiar with dangers and hardships. After some little delay in arranging preliminaries, the little command moved off in the direction of Petersburg, then invested by Grant's army. The situation at this time was gloomy and the hearts of the bravest had begun to fail. The enemy was pushing hard, and our brave army, reduced by sickness, death and disability, had diminished to a mere handful, to face the overwhelming numbers of our well-fed, well-clothed and well-equipped foe. Every effort had been made to compel the enemy to fall back, but without success. Grant's army then held the lower James River, his base of supplies being at City Point, and the heavy Federal monitors lay at anchor there, protected from an attack of our navy by obstructions in the river. Our ironclads and gunboats inactive at Chaffin's Bluff; officers and men restless under their forced inactivity and eager to try their strength against the enemy's fleet and share the laurels being won by our more fortunate brother officers who were upon blue water.

If we could gain possession of the river and hold it Grant would be compelled to fall back, as City Point would no longer furnish him a base and the James River an avenue of supplies, and to effect this object, the possession of the river at City Point, it was decided to make an effort to blow up the Federal ironclads, clear a passage for our fleet and force the abandonment of City Point, or compel Grant to fall back or bring his supplies from Norfolk. To drive him back would have necessitated an army equal in numbers to his own and a fearful cost of life.

Under these conditions Lieutenant Charles W. Read, of the navy, organized an expedition whose object was to carry boats, fitted with torpedoes, on wheels, and, turning Grant's left, strike boldly across the country in his rear, cross the Blackwater [River], and launch our boats in the James above their anchorage at Hampton Roads, capture some passing tugs, fix our torpedoes on them, ascend the river and strike the largest monitors at City Point. The larger monitors once destroyed, our fleet could easily scatter the wooden gunboats, and the James River would be open from Richmond to Hampton Roads. The expedition was a hazardous one from its incipiency, the enemy having declared their determination to show no mercy to prisoners taken on torpedo service. We had to operate in rear of Grant's army—a handful of men, with an army of one hundred and fifty thousand between us and our friends—and every man on the expedition fully understood and appreciated the danger we ran. If we were successful in reaching the James River our dangers would have but just commenced, as we would have to board and capture an unsuspicious craft, of whose fitness for our purpose we would have to judge from appearances at long range; the capture might attract attention of the men-of-war and make us the captured instead of the captors, or, our plan discovered, we would have a long way to retreat in order to reach a place of safety. Added to these difficulties, the weather was very cold, the roads rough, and the path before us a terra incognito. Surely to face such dangers and hardships, even though success did not crown our effort, deserves a mention in history, and I am not aware that anything had been written in relation to this expedition, which, if successful, would have crowned each one of those engaged in it with laurels as undying as those that deck the brows of the heroes of Thermopyle. I suppose that the modesty of the principal actor, the brave Read, forbade his publishing an account of the expedition which was, through the treachery of one of our most trusted men, a failure; but reverses and failures, as well as grand successes, should be chronicled, as evidences of the spirit that animated our men and the willingness to embark in almost hopeless undertakings, literal forlorn hopes, without the stimulus or the excitement of battle or the probabilities of a name on the roll of honor.

The expedition was composed of Lieutenant C. W. Read, Lieutenant W. H. Wall, Master W. F. Shippey, Passed Midshipmen Scott and Williamson, and Lieutenant of Marine Crenshaw, a Surgeon from the fleet (whose name, I regret to say, I cannot now recall) and about ninety seamen and marines. The officers and sailors were armed with skip's cutlasses and revolvers, and the marines with rifles. The boats were placed in chocks on four wagon wheels, torpedoes, poles and gear inside, and each drawn by four mules. One, Lewis, a volunteer officer of the Navy, had been sent ahead to reconnoiter, and was to meet us at the ford of the Blackwater and pilot us to the James. How he fulfilled his engagements will be shown in the sequel. This man Lewis was mate of an American ship lying in Norfolk harbor at the time of the secession of Virginia, and had left his ship to join the Confederates, had served faithfully in the army, been wounded at Bull Run, transferred to the Navy and commissioned an acting lieutenant, and was considered worthy of trust and confidence.

Our first day's march brought us to General Anderson's headquarters, the right of our army, where were encamped that night, and, breaking camp early the following morning, we struck out from our picket line to gain the old Jerusalem plank road—our party being reinforced by two young English gentlemen, guests of General Anderson, who thought they would "like to see the fun." A short distance outside of our lines we had our first alarm, running up nearly face to face with a column of the enemy coming up to attack our troops on the right. By a "change of base" we managed to dodge them, and they passed on, paying little heed to us, who they doubtless supposed to be a picket post, and soon the firing in our rear told us that the "ball had opened." We passed on our way, well assured that the fight going on behind would serve to attract attention from us and favor our march. We knew not what proportions the battle would assume or what would be the result, nor felt we much uneasiness, for was not one, Lee, and his brave boys in gray there to attend to them? Of our two volunteers, I never heard more, but suppose they found their way back to General Anderson's headquarters, as they were mounted and had only to follow the retreating cavalry pickets.

We were now fairly embarked on our expedition, pushing our way through the enemy's country and separated from our friends by his army.

Our march was in three detachments, the advance under Read and Ward, about one hundred yards ahead of the wagon train; Crenshaw, with his marines, about the same distance in rear of them, and Shippey commanding the centre, with the wagon train. Fortunately we met no stragglers or foraging parties of the enemy, and were not disturbed, and after a good day's march, we bivouacked in good spirits and very tired. The following day's march was without incident worthy of mention, an occasional false alarm or seeking the cover of woods of screen us from chance observers. Indeed, we were out of the line of travel, the Federals did all their business at City Point, and there was little more to attract anyone to this part of the country than to the Siberian deserts.

During the night the weather turned very cold, and our poor, tired fellows lay close to the fires. I have to laugh yet to think of poor Williamson's sky-rocket feat. He was lying close to a fire, and as I passed about midnight I saw that his coat-tail was on fire, and called him somewhat hurriedly from a sound sleep. He started up and rushed wildly through the woods,

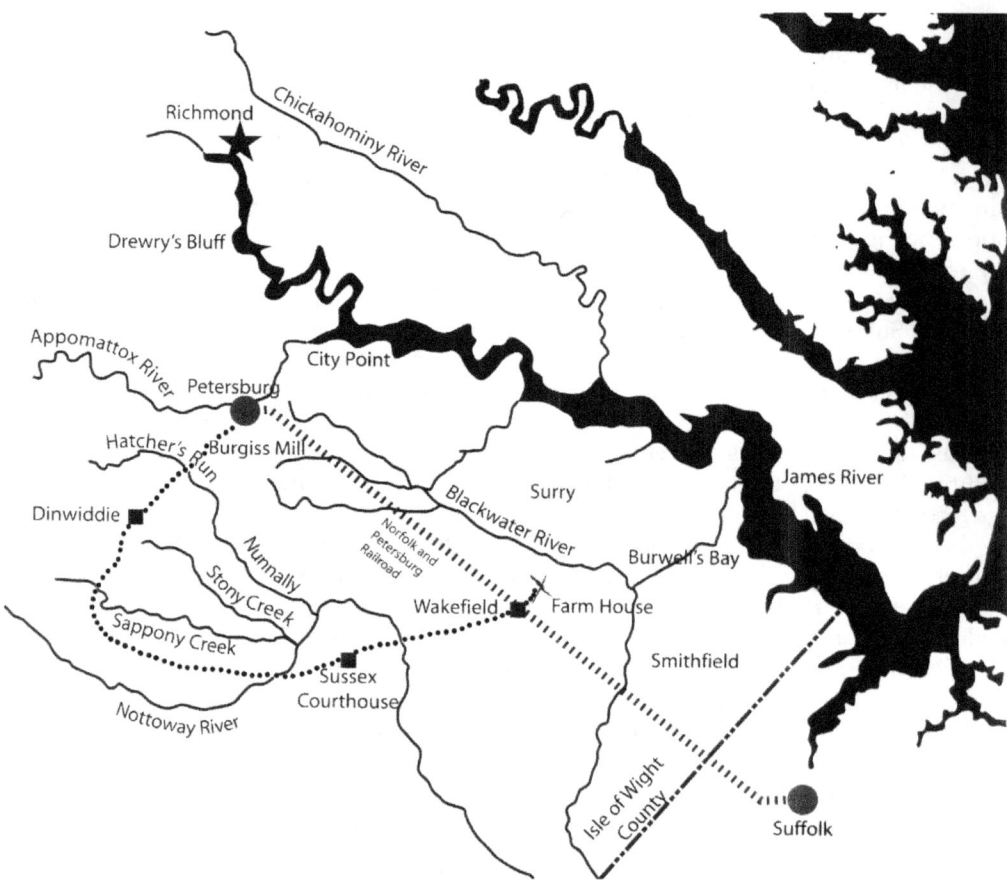

Map of the Overland Expedition (courtesy of *Civil War Historian* magazine).

the fiery tail streaming out behind, and for awhile all efforts to stop him were futile, but we finally succeeded in capturing him, extinguishing the fire with the loss of one skirt of his coat. He afterwards cut off the other skirt and made it more uniform.

The following morning we took up our march in the face of a storm of sleet, and we had to stop after a few hours, the sleet being so blinding that our mules could not make headway, besides the road being frozen and slippery. We took shelter in an old deserted farm-house only a few miles from our rendezvous on the Blackwater, once, doubtless, the happy home of some Southern family, now changed into the rude scenes of a soldiers' bivouac.

While resting and "thawing out" here by the warmth of bright fires in big fireplaces, impatiently awaiting the breaking up of the storm and anxious to continue our journey, a young man in gray uniform came in and informed us that our plan had been betrayed and that Lewis was at the ford to meet us, accordingly to promise, but accompanied by a regiment of Federals lying in ambuscade and awaiting our arrival, when they were to give us a warm reception. Had it not been for the storm and our having to take shelter we would have marched into the net spread for us, and most likely all have been killed, or suffered such other worse punishment as a court-martial should inflict.

This young man had been a prisoner of war at Fort Monroe, and from his window heard the conversation between Lewis and the Yankee officer, in which the former betrayed us, and the plan to capture the whole party, and having perfected his plans of escape, resolved to put them in execution that night, and, if possible, frustrate his designs by giving us information of his treachery.

After a hurried council of war it was decided that we should go back about a mile and find a hiding place in the woods, efface our tracks, and remain concealed, while Lieutenant Read should make a reconnaissance to satisfy himself that things were as bad as had been reported, and if indeed we would have to return to Richmond without accomplishing our object. Accordingly we hitched up and filed out into the road and took it back, and when we thought we had gone a safe distance turned into the woods and camped—Read taking leave of us, disguised, and saying he would rejoin us the next day, when if he did not by sunset we were to conclude he was captured and make our way back to Richmond. The night passed drearily away, the weather being very cold and we afraid to make fires for us, as we had no doubt they would be seen as soon as they discovered we were not going into their trap, and the following day though but a short winter one, seemed endless, so great was our anxiety for our leader, who had thrust his head into the lion's jaws. At length, about 4 PM, Read made his appearance in camp, cool and collected as ever, and told us that what we had heard was true, and gave orders to hitch up, form line, and retreat. The enemy's cavalry was already scouring the country in search of us and every road of retreat was guarded. We marched by night, avoiding main roads, and during the following day halted and concealed ourselves in the woods.

Headed off at one turn, we took another and pursued our way resolved to sell our lives dearly, should the enemy fall upon us. Every path now seemed guarded, and our retreat apparently cut off, when an old gentleman in citizens clothes and a "stove-pipe," hat on, who had joined us as guide, determined to take us through the water of the Appomattox River, and thus "take roundings" on them. There was a horse-shoe bend in the river, which, by fording, we could pass through between their pickets and reach our picket-lines This was decided upon, and our guide lead off and marched us to the ford. It was not a pleasant prospect, that of taking water with the thermometer hanging around freezing point, but it was better than falling in the hands of Yankees, so of the two evils we chose the least. My teeth chatter yet to think of that cold wade through water waist deep, covered with a thin coat of ice, but we passed it successfully, wagons, and all, and then double-quicked to keep from freezing; our clothes freezing stiff on us as we came out of the water.

We had now the inside track of our pursuers, and leaving them waiting for us to march up one of the many roads they had so well guarded, made our way back towards our lines, which we reached safely without loss of a man, wagon or mule.

The results accomplished by this expedition were nothing, but I have thought it worthy of a place in history, because of the effort.

Of the hardships of such a trip only those who have experienced them can judge, and I will not even attempt to paint those we encountered. Our flag waved in the James River two months after the events I have endeavored to describe, but of the hundred and one men who composed this expedition, fully seventy-five were in the Naval Hospital, in Richmond, suffering from the effects of their Winter march, on the sad day on which we turned our backs upon that city.

II

Eastern North Carolina

1. The Mosquito Fleet

Federal naval forces had forced their way into Pamlico Sound, North Carolina, in August of 1861, and were now threatening to attack the Southern fortifications on Roanoke Island. State and Confederate authorities were both fearful that if Roanoke Island fell, all of the eastern part of the state would be in jeopardy.

Here is Lieutenant Parker's account of the fighting in February of 1862 at Roanoke Island, and two days later at Elizabeth City. The "Mosquito Fleet," given that name derisively because of the small size of its vessels, was commanded by Captain William F. Lynch. [RTC]

Roanoke Island & Elizabeth City, NC by Commander William H. Parker, CSN

Recollections of a Naval Officer 1841–1865, Chapters XX and XXI, pp. 242–260

On the 24th of December I was sent by Commodore Lynch by rail to Newbern to appraise a small steamer bought by him for the Navy. I found Newbern in an excited state, fearing an attack from Hatteras, and the scene of constant alarms. Only the night of my arrival I was sent for by the colonel in command to whom I had offered my services, and informed that they had signaled from one of the posts below that the enemy was coming up the river. While we were waiting further news a captain came in and requested to be relieved from the command of a battery on the river. He said he knew nothing about guns, and if the enemy was coming up he wished to be relieved. He proposed that I should take his place. This did not look well, but I suppose it was an isolated case. Newbern made a good defense when the time came for it.

Upon my return to Norfolk I found the *Beaufort* nearly ready. Mr. Hopkins, my pilot, left me here and I secured another. Mr. Bain relieved Mr. Byrd as my clerk, and Lieutenant [John H.] Johnson joined as executive officer. Johnson, who was from Fredericksburg, was a classmate of mine. He had been engaged in a duel, as second, while at the Naval Academy and was dismissed, as I have before mentioned. He went in 1848 to California, and though afterwards reinstated in the Navy declined to return. He told me he was living on his ranch in California when he heard of the secession of Virginia, and that he turned the key in his door and left for home. He left me after the battle of Elizabeth City and was ordered to New Orleans. After the fall of that city he went to Wilmington where he was drowned while going to the assistance of a blockade runner. He was a very modest man, but a most determined and courageous one—every inch a gentleman he was as cool a man under fire as I ever saw.

About the middle of January I proceeded in the *Beaufort* to join the squadron at Roanoke Island. This island, which lies on Croatan Sound between Pamlico and Albemarle Sounds, was garrisoned by a regiment of North Carolina troops, in command of Colonel [Henry M.] Shaw. The district was commanded by General Henry A. Wise, and his brigade was ordered to assist in the defense of the island. His brigade, as far as I have been able to find out, was distributed between Elizabeth City and Nag's Head. Nag's Head, which is abreast of Roanoke Island, on the sea shore, about three miles across, was General Wise's head-quarters. Why General Wise when he was ordered to the command did not establish his headquarters on Roanoke Island, and order all his troops and artillery there, was what I have never been able to discover. Nag's Head itself could have been rendered untenable by the fire of one Federal gunboat.

Three forts had been constructed on the island to protect the channel. The upper one was on Weir's Point and was named Fort Huger. It mounted twelve guns, principally 32-pounders of 33 cwt., and was commanded by Major John Taylor, formerly of the Navy. About 13½ miles below, on Pork Point, was Fort Bartow; it mounted seven guns, five of which were 32-pounders of 33 cwt., and two were rifled 32-pounders. This fort, which was the only one subsequently engaged in the defense, was in charge of Lieutenant B. P. Loyall, of the Navy. Between these two points was a small battery. On the main land opposite the island, at Redstone Point, was a battery called Fort Forrest. The guns, which were 32-pounders, were mounted on the deck of a canal-boat which had been hauled up in the mud and placed so that the guns would command the channel. The channel itself was obstructed a little above Fort Huger by piling. It was hoped that these batteries, with the assistance of Commodore Lynch's squadron, would be able to prevent the enemy's ships from passing the island. The great mistake on our part was in not choosing the proper point at which to dispute the entrance to the Sound. The fortifications and vessels should have been at the "marshes," a few miles below, where the channel is very narrow. I do not know who was responsible for the selection of the points fortified as I was not at the island when ground was first broken.

The squadron under Commodore Lynch consisted of the *Seabird* (flagship), Captain McCarrick; *Curlew*, Captain Hunter; *Ellis*, Captain Cooke; *Appomattox*, Captain Simms; *Beaufort*, Captain Parker; *Raleigh*, Captain Alexander; *Fanny*, Captain Tayloe, and *Forrest*, Captain Hoole. Of these vessels the *Seabird* and *Curlew* were side-wheel river steamboats; the *Seabird* of wood and the *Curlew* of iron. The others were screw tug-boats, built for the canal, and were similar to the *Beaufort*. The *Appomattox* and perhaps the *Fanny* were wooden—the others of quarter-inch iron. Each mounted one 32-pounder rifled gun, except the *Seabird* which had a smooth-bore forward and a 30-pounder Parrott gun aft. In addition we had a fine large schooner called the *Black Warrior*, armed with two 32-pounders and commanded by Lieutenant Harris.

The expedition under General Burnside and Flag Officer Goldsborough was assembling at

Captain William F. Lynch (Bandann Brothers, Baltimore).

Hatteras Inlet, and although we did not know positively that it was not intended to attack Newbern yet the chances were in favor of Roanoke island. About the 1st of February the *Curlew* and *Raleigh* were sent to Hatteras, and upon their return reported the enemy nearly ready to move. The commodore now held a council of war to determine whether the vessels should dispute the advance of the enemy's ships at the "marshes," or assist in the defense in conjunction with the forts. It was decided to adopt the latter plan, though some of the captains favored the first. The majority thought it better not to divide our forces at the eleventh hour.

It was at nine o'clock on the morning of February 6th, 1862, that the enemy's fleet made its appearance. It consisted according to the report of Flag Officer [Louis M.] Goldsborough, of the *Stars and Stripes, Louisiana, Hetzel, Underwriter, Delaware, Commodore Perry, Valley City, Commodore Barney, Hunchback, Southfield, Morse, Whitehead, Lockwood, Brincker, Seymour, Ceres, Putnam, Shawsheen* and *Granite*. These vessels were armed with 100-pounder rifled, 80-pounder rifled, 30-pounder rifled, 20-pounder rifled, 12-pounder rifled, and 9-inch, 8-inch and 6-inch smooth bore guns. Some of them carried four guns each. Their number of guns, exclusive of the *Commodore Perry*, and *Commodore Barney*, was forty-eight; if these two vessels carried three guns each, the total number of guns opposed to us was fifty-four. The enemy's fleet was accompanied by a large number of transports bearing the troops of General (Ambrose) Burnside; and it was evidently his plan to silence our batteries—particularly the one at Pork Point—and land the troops under the protection of the guns of the ships.

The weather at the time the enemy made his appearance was cold, gloomy and threatening, and about 10 AM we observed that he had anchored below the "marshes." We had gotten underweigh and formed line abreast, in the rear of the obstructions, and we remained underweigh all day, as the weather was too thick to see very far, and we did not know at what moment the ships might commence the attack. The galley fires were out, and we could have no cooking done, and as the weather was cold with a drizzling rain at intervals, we passed considerably more than one mauvais quart d'heure!

About 4 in the afternoon Captain Simms in the *Appomattox* was sent down to reconnoiter. He went very close to the enemy, but was not fired at. Flag Officer Goldsborough says in his allusion to it: "She met with no opposition from us simply because we were not unwilling that she should accomplish her wishes." I presume he wanted us to know what we were to expect the next day. Simms gave a very correct report of the number of men-of-war in the fleet; the number of transports was what "no fellow could find out;" there were too many to count. At sunset, as we saw no disposition on the part of the enemy to move, we anchored and all hands went to supper. We kept guard boats out during the night to avoid a surprise. After getting something to eat I went on board the *Seabird* to see Commodore Lynch. I found him in his dressing gown sitting quietly in his cabin reading Ivanhoe. He expressed great pleasure at seeing me and said he had thought of signaling me to come aboard, but knew I must be very tired and he did not wish to disturb me; and I must say for the commodore that I never served under a man who showed more consideration for the comfort of his officers and men. We talked for a long time of what the next day would probably bring forth, and our plans for defense, &c. We neither of us believed that we would be successful, nor was there a naval officer in the squadron who thought we would. The force opposed to us both naval and military was too overwhelming. Ten thousand men to our two thousand on land, and nineteen vessels and 54 guns to our eight vessels with 9 guns on the water. After talking some time on the subject, we insensibly got upon literature. Lynch was a cultivated man and a most agreeable talker. He had made some reputation in the navy by his book upon the Dead Sea exploration.* We commenced

---

*Navy Lieutenant William F. Lynch led an American scientific and exploring expedition to the Jordan River and the Dead Sea in 1847–49. See W. F. Lynch, Narrative of the United States Expedition to the River Jordan and the Dead Sea (1852).

on Scott's novels, naturally, as he held one of the volumes in his hand; incident after incident was recalled and laughed over, and I never spent a more delightful evening. We were recalled to our senses by the ship's bell striking 8 (midnight). I jumped up exclaiming that I did not know it was so late and that I had not intended keeping my gig's-crew up so long. The commodore's last words to me at the gangway were: "Ah! if we could only hope for success;" "but," said he: "come again when you can." For my own part I looked upon it as an adieu and not an au revoir; for I had made up my mind that it would be death or a prisoner before the next day's sun had set; but as I rowed back to my vessel I thought what strangely constituted and happily constituted beings we are after all. Here were two men looking forward to death in less than 24 hours—death, too, in defeat not victory—and yet able to lose themselves in works of fiction. Well may Scott be called the Wizard of the North! Unknown to ourselves it must be as Campbell writes: "Hope springs eternal in the human breast!"*

At daylight the next morning the *Appomattox* was dispatched to Edenton, and as she did not return till sunset and the *Warrior* did not take any part in the action, this reduced our force to seven vessels and eight guns. At 9 AM we observed the enemy to be underweigh and coming up, and we formed "line abreast" in the rear of the obstructions. At 11.30 the fight commenced at long range. The enemy's fire was aimed at Fort Bartow and our vessels, and we soon became warmly engaged. The commodore at first directed his vessels to fall back in the hope of drawing the enemy under the fire of Forts Huger and Forrest; but as they did not attempt to advance, and evidently had no intention of passing the obstructions, we took up our first position and kept it during the day. At 2 PM the firing was hot and heavy, and continued so until sunset. Our gunners had had no practice with their rifled guns, and our firing was not what it should have been. It was entirely too rapid and not particularly accurate. Early in the fight the *Forrest* was disabled in her machinery, and her gallant young captain (Lieutenant Hoole) badly wounded in the head by a piece of shell. She got in under Fort Forrest and anchored. Some time in the afternoon, in the hottest of the fire, reinforcements arrived from Wise's brigade, and were landed on the island. The Richmond Blues, Captain O. Jennings Wise, were, I think, part of this force.

Pork Point battery kept up a constant fire on the fleet, and the enemy could not silence it. The garrison stood to their guns like men, encouraged by the spirited example of their instructor, Lieut. B. P. Loyall. Forts Huger and Forrest did not fire, the enemy being out of range; but the small battery between Pork Point and Weir's Point fired an occasional gun during the day. Towards 4 o'clock in the afternoon a shot or shell struck the hurricane-deck of the *Curlew* in its descent, and went through her decks and bottom as though they had been made of paper. Her captain, finding she was sinking, started for the shore, and as he passed me, hailed; but I could not make out what he said, and he being a very excitable fellow (the North Carolinians called him Tornado Hunter) I said to Johnson that I thought there was nothing the matter with him. "Oh, yes there is," said J., "look at his guards." And sure enough he was fast going down. I put after him in the *Beaufort*, but he got her ashore in time. Hunter put his vessel ashore immediately in front of Fort Forrest, completely masking its guns, and we could not fire her for fear of burning up the battery, which, as I have said, was built on an old canal boat. As it turned out, it did not much matter. To show what an excitable fellow Hunter was, he told me afterward that during the fight this day he found to his surprise that he had no trousers on. He said he could never understand it, as he had certainly put on a pair in the morning. I told him I had heard of a fellow being frightened out of his boots, but never out of his trousers. Poor Hunter; he served gallantly during the war, and was second in command at the battle of Sailors Creek, where he was made a prisoner. He dropped dead as he was taking an evening walk, a few years after.

*Sir Walter Scott was known as the Wizard of the North. Campbell is, of course, Thomas Campbell, op. cit.

We in the *Beaufort* did our best in maintaining our position, and I had reason to be proud of the way in which every officer and man performed his duty. Johnson as staunch as the mainmast, the two midshipmen full of zeal, and my clerk, Mr. Bain, standing by me on the hurricane deck coolly taking notes of the fight. The first shell that exploded over us scattered the pieces over our decks. Midshipman Mallory, a youth of 14, brought some of the pieces to me with much glee; he looked upon the whole proceeding as great fun. Poor boy! he met with a sad end at last. After serving with me in three engagements he was ordered to the gunboat *Chattahoochee* at Columbus, Ga., and lost his life by the explosion of her boiler. He was from Hampton and was an honor to his birth-place; had he lived and had the opportunity he would have become a great naval officer. My men worked their gun coolly and deliberately, and as the captain of it, Jack Robinson, was an English man-of-wars man, trained on the gunnery ship *Excellent*, I think we did some good firing. My gunner's mate, John Downard, was also from the same ship and knew his duties thoroughly. Both of these men had the Crimean medal. I must not forget to mention my engineer, Mr. Hanks, who was always ready with his engine.

About 4 PM I observed that the enemy's troops were landing to the southward of Pork Point [at Ashby Harbor] under the guns of a division of their fleet, and could not perceive that any successful resistance was being made to it. A little after sunset the firing ceased on both sides, and as we felt sure the enemy would not attempt to pass the obstructions by night as he had declined to attempt them by day we ran in and anchored under Fort Forrest. We lit our galley fires, and as we had been fighting all day were glad enough to get something to eat. Upon the whole I was rather surprised to find myself alive, and congratulated myself upon having one night more before me. I directed my steward to serve out the cabin stores to the men and let them have a good supper that was about what I thought of what would be the result of the next day's fight.

During the afternoon when the battle was at its height I ordered the engineer to send me all the men he could spare from the fire-room to work at the gun; one of the men sent up was my green coal-passer, who evidently did not like the appearance of things on deck. However he went to the side tackles of the gun as ordered; after awhile a shell bursting overhead I called to the men to lie down, and when it was over I ordered them to jump up and go at it again. All promptly obeyed but the coal-passer, who still lay flat on his stomach. "Get up," I called to him from the hurricane deck just above him: he turned his head like a turtle and fixed his eye on me, but otherwise did not move. "Get up," I said, "or I will kill you," at the same time drawing a pistol from my belt and cocking it. He hesitated a moment and then sprang to the gun, and behaved well during the rest of the engagement. As I went aft to my cabin after the battle, my steward being busy forward, I called to the engineer to send a man to make a fire in my stove. I had just seated myself before it when who should come in but my friend the coal-passer—he kneeled down in front of me and commenced blowing up a fire. Knowing that the man had not the slightest idea of the discipline of a man-of-war, and wishing to encourage him, I remarked, "Well, my man! I am glad you did your duty so well at the gun after I spoke to you." He blew awhile, and then looking back he said: "I tell you what, captain, I was mighty skeered;" "but," said he after another blow, "I saw you were going to kill me so I thought I mout as well take my chances with the enemy." After a few minutes more blowing, he said: "I warn't much skeered after that; it's all in getting used to it, Cap." Well, I thought, you have got at the philosophy of it, after all.

I do not remember our loss in the squadron in this day's engagement; but Lieutenant Hoole was dangerously wounded, and lost an eye, and Midshipman Camm of the *Ellis* lost an arm.

Soon after we anchored signal was made by the flag ship for the captains to report on board. Upon my entering the cabin I was informed by Commodore Lynch that we must retreat from Roanoke Island. Much surprised and mortified, I asked why, and was told that the vessels generally were out of ammunition. A council was held as to whether the vessels should retreat to Norfolk through the Chesapeake and Albemarle Canal, or go to Elizabeth City on the Pasquotank River. We would have saved the vessels by going to the former place, but the commodore's orders were to do his utmost to defend the waters of North Carolina; so we decided to go to the latter, where it was understood a fort had been built to protect the town. Elizabeth City was the terminus of the Dismal Swamp Canal, and we hoped to get ammunition that way from Norfolk in time to act in conjunction with the fort. I was sent to Roanoke Island to communicate all this to Colonel Shaw, and confess did not relish my mission. It looked too much like leaving the army in the lurch; and yet to have remained without ammunition would have been mere folly. I took an officer on shore with me who had gotten on board the *Seabird* somehow—probably he had come in the *Appomattox* from Edenton—he had just been released from a northern prison, and here he was going to meet the same fate again, as we all knew—but he did what he considered his duty. I think he was a Major Dinwiddie,—a noble fellow, whatever his name.

I met Colonel Shaw at his quarters, and stated the facts in relation to the vessels, and then returned to the *Beaufort*. All lights were now extinguished, and the squadron got underweigh for Elizabeth City, the *Seabird* taking the *Forrest* in tow. It was one of the darkest nights I ever knew, and as none of the vessels showed a light it was difficult to avoid a collision. My pilot got confused early in the evening and I had to do the best I could alone; and, considering I had but a faint idea of where Elizabeth City was, I did remarkably well. We fell in with some vessels carrying reinforcements to the island on our way—I think it was Green's battalion and the *Beaufort* had the credit of colliding with them. This was not true, however,—for while I was speaking one of the schooners, another of our gunboats carried away her head booms.

I anchored in the mouth of the Pasquotank River some time during the night, and the next morning went to Elizabeth City, where I found the remainder of the squadron. This was on Saturday, February 8th.

Elizabeth City is on the Pasquotank River, twelve miles from its mouth. The river here is very narrow and on the right bank, at Cobb's Point, some two or three miles below, was a battery of four 32-pounder smooth-bore guns. The fort, as it was called, was a wretchedly constructed affair and not by any means a credit to the engineer officer who built it. I afterwards met this officer. He acknowledged that it was badly done; he said that when the citizens of Elizabeth City applied to General Huger to have a battery put up to protect the town, he was sent to do it. He thought that "Elizabeth City was the last place the Federals would attack," and slighted his work. It shows how uncertain war is, and how important discipline is.

The magazine of this fort resembled an African ant-hill more than anything else, and had its door fronting the river, and was of course entirely exposed. The guns were good enough, but they were badly mounted—only one could be trained to fire across the river, the others looked down the channel. We found at Elizabeth City General Henningsen with one or more batteries of light artillery, and after our arrival the militia were called out, and some of them were sent into the fort. We learned that the Dismal Swamp canal was out of order, and vessels could not pass through. Commodore Lynch sent Captain Hunter by express to Norfolk for ammunition, and men to repair the canal.

We could hear firing in the direction of Roanoke Island until about noon of this day; it then ceased and we knew the island had fallen. We felt sure Elizabeth City would be the next place attacked, and the commodore appointed me to concert a plan of defense with General Henningsen.

My idea was to land the guns of the vessels and mount them on shore, not together, but distributed on both sides of the river, and to place Henningsen's guns in pits or behind temporary embankments in the same way. By this method the enemy, after getting up with the fort, would have been brought under a very heavy cross fire, and his vessels being of light construction Henningsen's guns would have done them as much damage as our large cannon. The infantry were to seek the best cover they could find and act as sharpshooters along the bank of the river, which was not two hundred yards wide. But there not appearing to be time enough to make this disposition of our guns, it was decided that the schooner *Black Warrior* should be put over on the left bank of the river a little below the fort, and the remainder of the squadron which now consisted of the *Seabird, Ellis, Appomattox, Beaufort, Raleigh* and *Fanny*, should form line abreast across the channel, opposite the fort, and that Henningsen's artillery should be held in reserve. After making these dispositions Commodore Lynch started in the *Seabird* on the 9th for Roanoke island to reconnoiter, and took the *Raleigh* with him. During the afternoon of this day the *Beaufort* towed to the mouth of the canal a schooner loaded with quartermaster's stores; she eventually got to Norfolk with her very valuable cargo. About sunset Commodore Lynch returned in the *Seabird* having been chased by the enemy's vessels, which anchored at the mouth of the river about ten miles below the fort at 8 PM. The *Raleigh* was either sent to Norfolk via the C. and A. canal, or she escaped in that direction while being chased.

The enemy's squadron consisted of fourteen vessels, mounting 33 guns; to oppose which we had six vessels, mounting 8 guns, and the guns of the fort. The *Curlew* had been left at Roanoke Island, where she was burned by her crew. The *Forrest* was hauled up on the ways at Elizabeth City, and the *Raleigh* was probably in Norfolk. Commodore Stephen C. Rowan was in command of the Federal vessels, and we knew him to be a dashing officer.

We anchored abreast the fort in our position, and spent most of the night in dividing the ammunition, so that each vessel should have an equal share. I passed the evening talking over matters with the commodore, and we both concluded that affairs looked blue. The canal being out of order, escape was impossible in that direction, and nothing remained but to fight it out. I went back to the *Beaufort* about two o'clock in the morning and sent for Johnson to give him directions for the next morning. After telling him to give the men breakfast before daylight and then to have everything ready for action, and to call me as soon as he saw the enemy getting underweigh, I went to my cabin and threw myself on my berth "all standing." I really believe I did not take off my sword and pistol; and I know I did not remove my cap. I never was so tired in my life. For more than a week I had not had my clothes off, had had but little sleep, and been in a constant state of excitement. I soon dropped off, and in less than a minute (as it seemed to me) Johnson called me to say the enemy was underweigh and coming up.

"Have the men had their breakfast?" said I. "Yes, sir," said Johnson. "Is the gun cleared away and ready for action?" "Yes, sir," he replied, "the men are at their quarters, the fires are out, the magazine is opened, and we are all ready for battle." "Very well," I answered; and Johnson went forward. I fell back on my pillow and commenced to moralize: how delightful, thought I, 'twould be to be on shore in the woods where I can hear the birds welcoming the rising sun:

> The breezy call of incense-breathing morn,
> The swallow twittering from the straw-built shed,

and all that sort of thing; here are these confounded fellows coming up to break the peace when I so particularly wish to remain quiet; why will men fight, and before breakfast, too; why not lead a life of peace? why not—. "Look here, Captain," said Johnson, "the enemy is right on top of us!" I sprang up and bade adieu to my moralizing. Upon reaching the hurricane-deck I think I saw the relieved expression of my men. I had not thought of it before, but my non-appearance had given rise to some anxiety.

The enemy were coming up at full speed and our vessels were underweigh ready to abide the shock when a boat came off from the shore with the bearer of a dispatch for me; it read: "Captain Parker with the crew of the *Beaufort* will at once take charge of the fort—Lynch." "Where the devil," I asked, "are the men who were in the fort?" "All run away," said the messenger. And so it was; they had recollected that:

> Souvent celui qui demeure,
> Est cause de son meschef, &c.
> Roughly translated, this is: He who hesitates is lost.

and had taken to their heels. The enemy's vessels were by this time nearly in range, and we were ready to open fire. I did not fancy this taking charge at the last moment, but there was no help for it, so I put the men in the boats with their arms and left the *Beaufort* with the pilot, engineer and two men on board. I directed the pilot to slip the chain and escape through the canal to Norfolk if possible, otherwise to blow the steamer up rather than be captured. He "cut out," as Davy Crockett says, accordingly. While pulling ashore the officers and men were engaged in tearing some sheets into bandages to be used for the wounded men: a cheerful occupation under the circumstances! but it was one of the delights of serving in these gunboats that no surgeons were allowed. All the wounded had to be sent to the flag ship for treatment. Upon getting into the fort I hastily commenced stationing the men at the guns, and as quickly as possible opened fire upon the advancing enemy. Some of the officers and men of the *Forrest* made their way to us upon learning that the militia had fled. I must not forget to say that the engineer officer who had been sent from Richmond for service in the fort remained bravely at his post. He asked me to report this fact in case he was killed. He was a Prussian, and I think his name was Heinrich. He was not the engineer who built the fort. I found Commodore Lynch on shore; his boat had been cut in two by a shot and he could not get off to his ship, as he informed me, and he furthermore said I was to command the fort without reference to his being there; that if he saw an opportunity to get off to the *Seabird* he should embrace it.

The enemy's vessels came on at full speed under a heavy fire from our vessels and the fort. The fire from the latter was ineffectual. The officers and men were cool enough; but they had not had time to look about them. Everything was in bad working order, and it was difficult to train the guns. Just before we commenced to fire two of my men brought a man to me and said in the most indignant manner: "Captain here's a man who says he don't want to fight!" The idea of one of the *Beaufort*'s not wanting to fight seemed to irritate them exceedingly. I looked and beheld my poor cook trembling before me. The men held him up by the collar, for his legs refused to do duty. He was a delicate-looking Spaniard and, poor fellow, could speak very little English. He had been captured in a prize and had shipped in the *Beaufort* for the want of something better to do. He knew nothing about the war and cared less. In the fight at Roanoke he had been stationed in the magazine, and as it was pitch dark there had fondly imagined himself in a safe place; but it was different here in the broad daylight. "Que diable allait-il faire Bans cette galere!" Falling on his knees before me, he could only say: "captain, me no wantee fight," which he kept repeating. Poor fellow, I thought, I don't wantee fight either—at least, not until after breakfast. "Put him in the magazine," said I, recalling his former station, and thought no more about him. But he was to be my bite noir that day, for in the heat of the battle two of Henningsen's horsemen brought him to me between them. He had fled from the magazine, and they had captured him. He was in an exceedingly limp condition; but I said, as before, "put him in the magazine," which was done. He got away again, however, and beat us all to Norfolk—and that's saying a good deal.

Commodore Rowan's steamers did not reply to our fire until quite close, and without slackening their speed they passed the fort and fell upon our vessels. They made short work of them! The *Seabird* was rammed and sunk by the *Commodore Perry*. The *Ellis* was captured after a desperate defense, in which her gallant commander, James Cook, was badly wounded. The schooner *Black Warrior* was set on fire and abandoned, her crew escaping through the marshes on their side of the river. The *Fanny* was run on shore near the fort and blown up by her commander, who with his crew escaped to the shore. Before the *Ellis* was captured some of her officers and men attempted to reach the shore among them, Midshipman Wm. C. Jackson, a handsome youth of 17—he was to have joined my ship the next day. He was shot in the water while swimming on shore. I do not blame the enemy for this—it was unavoidable but it was a melancholy affair. He was taken on board the U. S. steamer *Hetzel* and received every attention. He died at 10 PM the same day, and was buried on shore. Captain Simms, of the *Appomattox* kept up a sharp fire from his bow gun until it was accidentally spiked; and he then had to run for it. He had a howitzer aft which he kept in play; but upon arriving at the mouth of the canal he found his vessel was about two inches too wide to enter; he therefore set her on fire, and she blew up. The *Beaufort* got through to Norfolk.

We in the fort saw this work of destruction going on without being able to prevent it. As soon as the vessels passed the fort we could not bring a gun to bear on them, and a shot from them would have taken us in reverse. A few rounds of grape would have killed and wounded all the men in the fort, for the distance was only a few hundred yards. Seeing this, I directed Johnson to spike the guns, to order every man to shoulder his musket, and then to take down the flag. All this was promptly and coolly done, and upon the fact being reported to me by Johnson, I pointed to some woods in our rear and told him to make the best of his way there with the command. All this time Commodore Lynch had stood quietly looking on, but without uttering a word. As his command had just been destroyed under his eyes, I knew pretty well what his feelings were. Turning to him I said: "Commodore, I have ordered the fort evacuated." "Why so, sir?" he demanded. I pointed out the condition of affairs I have just stated, and he acquiesced. Arm in arm we followed the retreating men. The enemy had by this time turned their attention from the ships to the fort and commenced firing shot and shell in our direction.

We had to cross a ploughed field, and we made slow progress. I wished very much that the commodore was twenty years younger. I felt that instead of a slow walk, a sharp run would have been better exercise—more bracing, as it were. We had nearly reached the woods when I met my two men, Robinson and Downard, posting back in great haste. They took their hats off when they saw me and looked a little sheepish. "Were you not ordered into the woods?" I inquired. "Yes, sir," answered they. "Then where are you going?" I demanded. "Come back to look for you, sir," said Robinson. They had missed me in the woods, and fearing I had been killed or wounded were going back to carry me off! And here was my first lieutenant, Johnson, aiding and abetting them! As soon as we struck the road we procured a guide, and as we had to pass Elizabeth City which was now in possession of the enemy, we hurried up for fear of being taken prisoners. We had observed that some of the vessels carried troops—In fact there was a Rhode Island regiment present—and we expected they would land and intercept us. The officers and men of the *Fanny* and *Forrest*, and stragglers from the other vessels, reported to me and I found I was, next to the commodore, the senior officer on shore. I soon got the commodore off in a buggy, and I begged him to make the best of his way to Richmond. It was the most extraordinary-looking vehicle I ever laid my eyes on, and I felt sure it would cause a sensation in Richmond if the commodore's report did not.

2. Small Boat Attack

Ever since the Federals had captured Roanoke Island in February of 1862, and had occupied Albemarle Sound, Pamlico Sound, and most of the eastern shore of North Carolina, they had extended their fortifications to include the principal rivers and towns several miles inland. One North Carolina town whose occupation by the enemy was particularly objectionable was New Bern. Located at the confluence of the Neuse and Trent Rivers, New Bern had been heavily fortified by the Federal occupying troops, and it continued to provide a base for foraging expeditions against the citizens of the area. In addition, Federal excursions that had destroyed a gunboat being built at Tarboro and almost destroyed the ironclad *Neuse* being built at White Hall the previous December illustrated the dangers that lurked in eastern North Carolina. More importantly, New Bern was only 45 miles from the all-important Wilmington and Weldon Railroad over which passed most of the supplies for Lee's army in Virginia. If the Union forces from New Bern should attack and cut this railroad line, it would become almost impossible to adequately supply the Army of Northern Virginia. (Shingleton, *John Taylor Wood: Sea Ghost of the Confederacy*, p. 90.)

With Lee's army about to enter winter quarters, it was believed that enough troops could be temporarily spared and sent to North Carolina. If this force attacked New Bern from the land side, coupled with a surprise naval attack from the river, Confederate authorities believed that the town could be recaptured.

As preparation for the recapture of New Bern, President Davis sent Commander John Taylor Wood on an inspection tour of eastern North Carolina. Upon arriving there, Wood found that neither the *Albemarle* nor the *Neuse* would be ready in time. By spring, any troops dispatched from Lee's army would be needed for the coming campaigns in Virginia and would have to be returned. If the two ironclads could not be available, the only other option was to capture one or more of the enemy's gunboats and use them to attack the fortifications around New Bern while the army attacked from the land side. To accomplish this, Wood planned on staging a surprise night attack employing a force of sailors and marines in small boats. (Shingleton, pp. 91–92.)

Surgeon Daniel B. Conrad accompanied the expedition and after the war wrote this report for the *Southern Historical Society Papers*. [RTC]

"Capture of the USS Underwriter" by Surgeon Daniel B. Conrad, CSN

Southern Historical Society Papers, Volume XIX, January 1891, pp. 93–100

In January, 1864, the Confederate naval officers on duty in Richmond, Wilmington and Charleston were aroused by a telegram from the Navy Department to detail three boats' crews of picked men and offices, who were to be fully armed, equipped and rationed for six days; they were to start at once by rail for Weldon, North Carolina, reporting on arrival to Commander J. Taylor Wood, who would give further instructions.

So perfectly secret and well-guarded was our destination that not until we had all arrived at Kingston, North Carolina, by various railroads, did we have the slightest idea of where we were going or what was the object of the naval raid. We suspected, however, from the name of its commander, that it would be "nervous work," as he had a reputation for boarding, capturing and burning the enemy's gunboats on many previous occasions.

Embarking one boat after another on the waters of the Neuse, we found that there were ten of them in all, each manned by ten men and two officers, every one of whom were young, vigorous, fully alive and keen for the prospective work. Now we felt satisfied that it was going to be hand-to-hand fighting; some Federal gunboat was to be boarded and captured by us, or we were to be destroyed by it.

Sunday afternoon, February 1, 1864, about 2 o'clock, we were all quietly floating down the narrow Neuse, and the whole sunny Sabbath evening was thus passed, until at sunset we landed on a small island. After eating our supper, all hands were assembled to receive instructions. Commander Wood, in distinct and terse terms, gave orders to each boat's crew and its officers just what was expected of them, stating that the object of the expedition was to, that night, board some one of the enemy's gunboats, then supposed to be lying off the city of Newbern, now nearly sixty miles distant from where we then were by water. He said that she was to be captured without fail. Five boats were to board her on either side simultaneously, and then when in our possession we were to get up steam and cruise after other gunboats. It was a grand scheme, and was received by the older men with looks of admiration and with rapture by the young midshipmen, all of whom would have broken out into loud cheers but for the fact that the strictest silence was essential to the success of the daring undertaking.

In concluding his talk, Commander Wood solemnly said: "We will now pray;" and thereupon he offered up the most touching appeal to the Almighty that it has ever been my fortune to have heard. I can remember it now, after the long interval that has elapsed since then. It was the last ever heard by many a poor fellow, and deeply felt by every one.

Then embarking again, we now had the black night before us, our pilot reporting two very dangerous points where the enemy had out pickets of both cavalry and infantry. We were charged to pass these places in absolute silence, our arms not to be used unless we were fired upon, and then in that emergency we were to get out of the way with all possible speed, and pull down stream in order to surprise and capture one of the gunboats before the enemy's pickets could carry the news of our raid to them.

In one long line, in consequence of the narrowness of the stream, did we pull noiselessly down, but no interrupting pickets were discovered, and at about half past three o'clock we found ourselves upon the broad estuary of Newbern bay. Then closing up in double column we pulled for the lights of the city, even up to and close in and around the wharves themselves, looking (but in vain) for our prey. Not a gunboat could be seen; none were there. As the day broke we hastened for shelter to a small island up stream about three miles away, where we landed upon our arrival, dragged our boats into the high grass, setting out numerous pickets at once. The remainder of us, those who were not on duty, tired and weary, threw ourselves upon the damp ground to sleep during the long hours which must necessarily intervene before we could proceed on our mission.

Shortly after sunrise we heard firing by infantry. It was quite sharp for an hour, and then it died, away. It turned out to be, as we afterwards learned, a futile attack by our lines under General Pickett on the works around Newbern. We were obliged to eat cold food all that day, as no fires were permissible under any circumstances; so all we could do was to keep a sharp lookout for the enemy, go to sleep again, and wish for the night to come.

About sundown one gunboat appeared on the distant rim of the bay. She came up, anchored off the city some five miles from where we were lying, and we felt that she was our game. We began at once to calculate the number of her guns and quality of her armament, regarding her as our prize for certain.

As darkness came upon us, to our great surprise and joy, a large launch commanded by Lieutenant George W. Gift, landed under the lee of the island. He had been, by some curious circumstance, left behind, but with his customary vigor and daring impressed a pilot, and taking all the chances came down the Neuse boldly in daylight to join us in the prospective fight. His advent was a grand acquisition to our force, as he brought with him fifteen men and one howitzer.

We were now called together again, the orders to each boat's crew repeated, another prayer was offered up, and then, it being about nine o'clock, in double column we started directly for the lights of the gunboat, one of which was distinctly showing at each mast-head. Pulling slowly and silently for four hours we neared her, and as her outlines became distinct, to our great surprise we were hailed man-of-war fashion, "Boat, ahoy!" We were discovered, and, as we found out later, were expected and looked for.

This was a trying and testing moment, but Commander Wood was equal to the emergency. Jumping up, he shouted: "Give way hard! Board at once!" The men's backs bent and straightened on the oars, and the enemy at the same moment opened upon us with small arms. The long, black sides of the gunboat, with men's heads and shoulders above them could be distinctly seen by the line of red fire, and we realized immediately that the only place of safety for us was on board of her, for the fire was very destructive. Standing up in the boat with Commander Wood, and swaying to and for by the rapid motion, were our marines firing from the bows, while the rest of us, with only pistol in belt, and our hands ready to grasp her black sides, were all anxious for the climb. Our coxswain, a burly, gamy Englishman, who by gesture and loud word, was encouraging the crew, steering by the tiller between his knees, his hands occupied in holding his pistols, suddenly fell forward on us dead, a ball having struck him fairly in the forehead. The rudder now having no guide, the boat swerved aside, and instead of our bows striking at the gangway, we struck the wheelhouse, so that the next boat, commanded by Lieutenant Loyall, had the deadly honor of being first on board. Leading his crew, as became his rank, duty and desire, he jumped and pulled into the gangway—now a blazing sheet of flame, and being nearsighted, having lost his glasses, stumbled and fell prone upon the deck of the gunboat, the four men who were following close up on his heels falling on top of him stone dead, killed by the enemy's bullets; each one of the unfortunate fellows having from four to six of them in his body, as we found out later. Rising, Lieutenant Loyall shook of his load of dead men, and by this time we had climbed up on the wheelhouse, Commander Wood's long legs giving him an advantage over the rest of us; I was the closest to him, but had nothing to do as yet, except to anxiously observe the progress of the hand-to-hand fighting below me. I could hear Wood's stentorian voice giving orders and encouraging the men, and then, in less than five minutes, I could distinguish a strange synchronous roar, but did not understand what it meant at first; but it soon became plain: "She's ours," everybody crying at the top of their voices, in order to stop the shooting, as only our own men were on their feet.

I then jumped down on the deck, and as I struck it, I slipped in the blood, and fell on my back and hands; rising immediately, I caught hold of an officer standing near me, who with an oath collared me, and I threw up his revolver just in time to make myself known. It was Lieutenant Wilkinson, who the moment he recognized me, exclaimed: "I'm looking for you doctor; come here." Following him a short distance in the darkness, I examined a youth who was sitting in the lap of another, and in feeling his head I felt my hand slip down between his ears, and to my horror, discovered that his head had been cleft in two by a boarding sword in the hands of some giant of the forecastle. It was Passed Midshipman Palmer Sanders, of Norfolk. Directing his body, and those of all the other killed, to be laid out aft on the quarter deck, I went down below, looking for the wounded in the wardroom, where the lights were burning, and found half a dozen with slight shots from revolvers. After having finished my examination, a half an hour and elapsed, and when ascending to the deck again I heard the officers of the various corps reporting to Commander Wood; for immediately after the capture of the vessel, according to the orders, the engineers and firemen had been sent down to the engine-room to get up steam, and Lieutenant Loyall as executive officer, with a number of seamen had attempted to raise the anchor, cast loose the cable which secured the ship to the wharf just under the guns of Fort Stephenson, while the marines in charge of their proper officers were stationed at the gangways guarding the prisoners. The lieutenants, midshipmen and others manned the guns, of which there were six eleven-inch, as it was the attention to convert her at once into a Confederate man-of-war, and under the captured flag to go out to sea, to take and destroy as many of the vessels of the enemy as possible. But all our well-laid plans were abortive; the engineers reported the fires out, and that it would be futile to attempt to get up steam under an hour, and Lieutenant Loyall, too, after very hard work, reported it useless to spend any more time in trying to unshuckle the chains, as the ship had been moored to a buoy, unless he could have hours in which to perform the work. Just at this moment, too, to bring things to a climax, the fort under which we found that we were moored bow and stem, opened fire upon us with small arms, grape and solid shot; some of those who had escaped having reported the state of affairs on board, and this was the result.

In about fifteen minutes a solid shot or two had disabled the walking-beam, and it then became evident to all that we were in a trap, to escape from which depended on hard work and strategy. How to extricate ourselves in safety from the thus far successful expedition, was the question; but events proved that our commander was equal to the emergency.

Very calmly and clearly he directed me to remove all dead and wounded to the boats, which the several crews were now hauling to the lee side of the vessel, where they would be protected from the shots from the fort. The order was soon carried out by willing hands. They were distributed as equally as possible. Each boat in charge of its own proper officer, and subjected under that heavy fire to that rigid discipline characteristic of the navy, manned by their regular crews, as they laid in double lines, hugging the protected lee of the ship as closely as possible, it was a splendid picture of what a body of trained men can be under circumstances of great danger.

After an extended search through the ship's decks, above and below, we found that we had removed all the dead and wounded, and then, when the search was ended, reported to Captain Wood on the quarter-deck, where, giving his orders where the fire from the fort was very deadly and searching, he called up four lieutenants to him, to whom he gave instructions as follows: two of them were to go below in the forward part of the ship, and the other two below in the after part, where from their respective stations they were to fire the vessel, and not to leave her until her decks were all ablaze, and then at that juncture they were to return to their proper boats and report.

The remainder of us were lying on our oars while orders for firing the ship were being carried out; and soon we saw great columns of red flames shoot upward out of the forward hatch and ward-room, upon which the four officers joined their boats. Immediately, by the glare of the burning ship, we could see the outlines of the fort with its depressed guns, and the heads and shoulders of the men manning them. As the blaze grew larger and fiercer their eyes were so dazzled and blinded that every one of our twelve boats pulled away out into the broad estuary safe and untouched. Then we well realized fully our adroit and successful escape.

Some years after the affair I met one of the Federal officers who was in the fort at the time, and he told me that they were not only completely blinded by the flames, which prevented them from seeing us, but were also stampeded by the knowledge of the fact that there were several tons of powder in the magazine of the vessel, which when exploded would probably blow the fort to pieces; so, naturally, they did not remain very long after they were aware that the ship had been fired. This all occurred as we had expected. We in our boats, at a safe distance of more than half a mile, saw the *Underwriter* blow up, and distinctly heard the report of the explosion, but those at the fort, a very short distance from the ship, sought a safe refuge, luckily for them.

Fortunately there was no casualities at this stage of the expedition. I boarded the boat in my capacity as surgeon, attending to the requirements of those who demanded immediate aid, and I witnessed many amusing scenes; for among the prisoners were some old men-of-war's men, former shipmates of mine in the Federal navy years before, and of the other officers also. Their minds were greatly relieved when I made known to them who their captors were, and that their old surgeon and other officers were present, and as a natural consequences they would be treated well.

Continuing to pull for the remainder of the night, we sought and found by the aid of our pilot, a safe and narrow creek, up which we ascended, and at sunrise hauled our boats up on a beach, there we carefully lifted out our wounded men, placed them under the shade of trees in the grass, and made them as comfortable as possible under the circumstances. Then we laid out the dead, and after carefully washing and dressing them, as soon as we had partaken of our breakfast, of which we were in so much need, all hands were called, a long pit was dug in the sand, funeral services were held, the men buried and each grave marked. We remained there all that day recuperating, and when night came again embarked on our return trip; all through that night and the four succeeding ones, we cautiously pulled up the rapid Neuse, doing most of our work in the darkness, until when nearing Kingston we could with impunity pull in daylight.

Surgeon Daniel B. Conrad (Virginia Historical Society, Richmond, Virginia).

Arriving at Kingston, the boats were dragged up the hill to the long train of gondola cars which had been waiting for us, and then was presented an exhibition of sailors' ingenuity. The boats were placed upright on an even keel lengthwise on the fact cars, and so securely lashed by ropes that the officers, men, even the wounded, seated and laid in them as if on the water, comfortably and safely made the long journey of a day and two nights to Petersburg. Arriving, the boats were unshipped into the Appomattox River, and the entire party floated down it to City Point where it debouches into the James. It was contemplated that when City Point was reached to make a dash at any one Federal gunboat, should there be the slightest prospect of success; but learning from our scouts, on our arrival after dark, that the gunboats and transports at anchor there equaled of the number of our own boats at least, we had to abandon our ideas of trying to make a capture, and were compelled to hug the opposite banks very closely, where the river is nearly four miles wide, and in that manner ship up the James pulling hard against the current. By the next evening we arrived, without any further adventure, at Drury's Bluff, where we disembarked; our boats shown as mementos of the searching fire we had been subjected to—for they all were perforated by many minnie balls, the white wooden plugs inserted into the holes averaging fourteen to each boat engaged; they were all shot into them from stem to stern lengthwise.

Among the many incidents that occurred on the trip there were to which left a lasting impression on my mind, and to this day they are as vivid as if they had happened yesterday. As we were stepping into the boats at the island that night, the lights of the gunboat plainly visible from the spot on which we stood, a bloody, serious action inevitable, several of the midshipmen, youth-like, were gaily chatting about what they intended to do—joyous and confident, and choosing each other for mates to fight together shoulder to shoulder—when one of them who stood near me in the darkness made the remark, as a conclusion as we were taking our places in the boats: "I wonder, boys, how many of us will be up in those stars by to-morrow morning?" This rather jarred on the ears of we older ones, and looking around to see who it was that had spoken, I recognized the bright and handsome Palmer Sanders. Poor fellow, he was the only one who took his flight, though many of the others were severely wounded.

On our route down to Kingston by rail we were obliged to make frequent stops for wood and water, and at every station the young midshipmen swarmed into the depots and houses, full of their fun and deviltry, making friends of the many pretty girls gathered there, who asked all manner of questions as to this strange sight of boats on cars filled with men in a uniform new to them.

The young gentlemen explained very glibly what they were going to do—"to board, capture and destroy as many of the enemy's gunboats as possible." "Well, when you return," replied the girls, "be sure that you bring us some relics—flags, &c." "Yes, yes; we'll do it," answered the boys. "But what will you give us in exchange?" "Why, only thanks, of course." "That won't do. Give us a kiss for each flag—will you?"

With blushes and much confusion, the girls consented, and in a few moments we were off and away on our journey again. On the return trip the young men, never for an instant forgetting the bargain they had made, manufactured several miniature flags. We old ones purposely stopped at all the stations we had made coming down in order to see the fun. The young ladies were called out at each place, and after the dead were lamented, the wounded in the cars cared for, then the midshipmen brought out their flags, recalled the promises made to them, and demanded their redemption. Immediately there commenced a lively outburst of laughter and denials, a skirmish, followed by a slight resistance, and the whole bevy were kissed seriatim by the midshipmen, and but for the whistle of train warning them away, they would have continued indefinitely.

3. The CSS *Albemarle*

The naval disasters that besieged North Carolina during the years 1861 and 1862 had prompted Secretary Mallory to change his thinking concerning Southern shipbuilding. The navy secretary had always felt that the armored vessel was the only viable means to successfully counter the naval strength of the United States. Initially he and others at the Navy Department had emphasized large ironclad gunboats such as the *Virginia*, *Louisiana*, and *Arkansas* operating in conjunction with smaller wooden gunboats. Mallory had envisioned that these behemoths, in addition to defending the major seaports, would take to the sea and wreak havoc among the Union blockade. European-built cruisers, meanwhile, were to make war upon the Northern merchant service. With their deep draft, low freeboard, and heavy weight of armor, however, these large ironclads had not proven seaworthy. Now, with their loss, coupled with the alarming disasters in North Carolina, others in the department were urging Mallory to pursue a different course.

Heeding advisors such as Constructor John L. Porter and Commander John M. Brooke, Mallory determined to abandon the construction of wooden gunboats, except for those well under way or nearing completion, and to concentrate instead on smaller, light-draft, iron-plated gunboats. Hopefully, the armored warships that were currently being contracted for in Europe could eventually attack and destroy the blockade. With this new policy in mind, the Navy Department sought reliable shipbuilders who could produce, in home waters, the needed ironclads within the shortest possible time. By the summer of 1862, contracts had been negotiated for the construction of two ironclads at Wilmington, one on the Neuse River opposite White Hall, one at Tarboro on the Tar River, and another near Halifax on the Roanoke River. This last vessel would eventually be commissioned as the CSS *Albemarle*.

The building, launching, and committing to battle of the *Albemarle* under the most primitive conditions is a story unparalleled. The *Albemarle* was known as "the ironclad that was built in a cornfield," because that is precisely where she was constructed. Even more remarkable was her builder, Gilbert Elliott. In charge of the entire construction project, Elliott was only nineteen years of age when the ironclad's keel was laid. Her captain, Commander James W. Cooke, was a North Carolinian who, although badly wounded, had fought desperately refusing to surrender until overpowered during the struggle for Roanoke Island in February of 1862. Together, these two men, along with the *Albemarle*, would fill a magnificent page in the journal of Confederate naval history. At the request of the editors of *Century Magazine* in 1888, Elliott penned the following to explain the construction and engagements of the CSS *Albemarle*. (Campbell, *Storm Over Carolina: The Confederate Navy's Struggle for Eastern North Carolina*, pp. 100–101, 115.) [RTC]

"The Career of the Confederate Ram Albemarle" by 1st Lt. Gilbert Elliott, CSA

The Century Magazine, Volume 36, Issue 3, July 1888, pp. 420–427

During the spring of 1863, having been previously engaged in unsuccessful efforts to construct war vessels, of one sort or another, for the Confederate Government, at different points in eastern North Carolina and Virginia, I undertook a contract with the Navy Department to build an iron-clad gun-boat, intended, if ever completed, to operate on the waters of Albemarle and Pamlico Sounds. A point on the Roanoke River, in Halifax County, North Carolina, about thirty miles below the town of Weldon, was fixed upon as the most suitable for the purpose. The river rises and falls, as is well known, and it was necessary to locate the yard on ground sufficiently free from overflow to admit of uninterrupted work for at least twelve months. No vessel was ever constructed under more adverse circumstances. The shipyard was established in a cornfield, where the ground had already been marked out and planted for the coming crop, but the owner of the land was in hearty sympathy with the enterprise, and aided me then and afterwards, in a thousand ways, to accomplish the end I had in view. It was next to impossible to obtain machinery suitable for the work in hand. Here and there, scattered about the surrounding country, a portable sawmill, blacksmith's forge, or other apparatus was found, however, and the citizens of the neighborhoods on both sides of the river were not slow to render me assistance, but cooperated, cordially, in the completion of the ironclad, and at the end of about one year from the laying of the keel, during which innumerable difficulties were overcome by constant application, determined effort, and incessant labor, day and night, success crowned the efforts of those engaged in the undertaking.

Seizing an opportunity offered by comparatively high water, the boat was launched, though not without misgivings as to the result, for the yard being on a bluff she had to take a jump, and as a matter of fact was "hogged" in the attempt, but to our great gratification did not thereby spring a leak.

The plans and specifications were prepared by John L. Porter, Chief Constructor of the

Confederate Navy, who availed himself of the advantage gained by his experience in converting the frigate *Merrimac* into the ironclad *Virginia* at the Gosport Navy Yard.

The *Albemarle* was 152 feet long between perpendiculars; her extreme width was 45 feet; her depth from the gun-deck to the keel was 9 feet, and when launched she drew 6½ feet of water, but after being ironed and completed her draught was about 8 feet. The keel was laid, and construction was commenced by bolting down, across the center, a piece of frame timber, which was of yellow pine, eight by ten inches. Another frame of the same size was then dovetailed into this, extending outwardly at an angle of 45 degrees, forming the side, and at the outer end of this the frame for the shield was also dovetailed, the angle being 35 degrees, and then the top deck was added, and so on around to the other end of the bottom beam. Other beams were then bolted down to the keel, and to the one first fastened, and so on, working fore and aft, the main-deck beams being interposed from stem to stern. The shield was 60 feet in length and octagonal in form. When this part of the work was completed she was a solid boat, built of pine frames, and if calked would have floated in that condition, but she was afterwards covered with 4-inch planking, laid on longitudinally, as ships are usually planked, and this was properly calked and pitched, cotton being used for calking instead of oakum, the latter being very scarce and the former almost the only article to be had in abundance. Much of the timber was hauled long distances. Three portable saw-mills were obtained, one of which was located at the yard, the others being moved about from time to time to such growing timber as could be procured.

1st Lt. Gilbert Elliott (Clark, North Carolina Regiments).

The iron plating consisted of two courses, 7 inches wide and 2 inches thick, mostly rolled at the Tredegar Iron Works, Richmond. The first course was laid lengthwise, over a wooden backing, 16 inches in thickness, a 2- inch space, filled in with wood, being left between each two layers to afford space for bolting the outer course through the whole shield, and the outer course was laid flush, forming a smooth surface, similar to that of the Virginia. The inner part of the shield was covered with a thin course of planking, nicely dressed, mainly with a view to protection from splinters. Oak knees were bolted in, to act as braces and supports for the shield.

The armament consisted of two rifled Brooke guns mounted on pivot-carriages, each gun working through three port-holes, as occasion required, there being one port-hole at each end of the shield and two on each side. These were protected by iron covers lowered and raised by a contrivance worked on the gun-deck. She had two propellers driven by two engines of 200-horse power each, with 20-inch cylinders, steam being supplied by two flue boilers, and the shafting was geared together.

The sides were covered from the knuckle, four feet below the deck, with iron plates two inches thick.

The prow was built of oak, running 18 feet back, on center keelson, and solidly bolted, and it was covered on the outside with iron plating, 2 inches thick and, tapering off to a 4-inch edge, formed the ram.

The work of putting on the armor was prosecuted for some time under the most disheartening circumstances, on account of the difficulty of drilling holes in the iron intended for her armor. But one small engine and drill could be had, and it required, at the best, twenty minutes to drill an inch and a quarter hole through the plates, and it looked as if we would never accomplish the task. But "necessity is the mother of invention," and one of my associates in the enterprise, Peter E. Smith, of Scotland Neck, North Carolina, invented and made a twist-drill with which the work of drilling a hole could be done in four minutes, the drill cutting out the iron in shavings instead of fine powder.

For many reasons it was thought judicious to remove the boat to the town of Halifax, about twenty miles up the river, and the work of completion, putting in her machinery, armament, etc., was done at that point, although the actual finishing touches were not given until a few days before going into action at Plymouth.

Forges were erected on her decks, and black-smiths and carpenters were kept hard at work as she floated down the river to her destination.

Captain James W. Cooke, of the Confederate Navy, was detailed by the department to watch the construction of the vessel and to take command when she went into commission. He made every effort to hasten the completion of the boat. He was a bold and gallant officer, and in the battles in which he subsequently engaged he proved himself a hero. Of him it was said that "he would fight a powder magazine with a coal of fire," and if such a necessity could by any possibility have existed he would, doubtless, have been equal to the occasion.

In the spring of 1864 it had been decided at headquarters that an attempt should be made to recapture the town of Plymouth. General Hoke was placed in command of the land forces, and Captain Cooke received orders to cooperate. Accordingly Hoke's division proceeded to the vicinity of Plymouth and surrounded the town from the river above to the river below, and preparation was made to storm the forts and breastworks as soon as the *Albemarle* could clear the river front of the Federal war vessels protecting the place with their guns.

On the morning of April 18, 1864, the *Albemarle* left the town of Hamilton and proceeded down the river towards Plymouth, going stern foremost, with chains dragging from the bow, the rapidity of the current making it impracticable to steer with her head downstream. She came to anchor about three miles above Plymouth, and a mile or so above the battery on the bluff at Warren's Neck, near Thoroughfare Gap, where torpedoes, sunken vessels, piles, and other obstructions had been placed. An exploring expedition was sent out, under command of one of the lieutenants, which returned in about two hours, with the report that it was considered impossible to pass the obstructions. Thereupon the fires were banked, and the officers and crew not on duty retired to rest.

Having accompanied Captain Cooke as a volunteer aide, and feeling intensely dissatisfied with the apparent intention of lying at anchor all that night, and believing that it was "then or never" with the ram if she was to accomplish anything, and that it would be foolhardy to attempt the passage of the obstructions and batteries in the day-time, I requested permission to make a personal investigation. Captain Cooke cordially assenting, and Pilot John Luck and two of the few experienced seamen on board volunteering their services, we set forth in a small lifeboat, taking with us a long pole, and arriving at the obstructions proceeded to take soundings. To our great joy it was ascertained that there was ten feet of water over and above the obstructions. This was due to the remarkable freshet then prevailing; the proverbial "oldest inhabitant" said, afterwards, that such high water had never before been seen in Roanoke River. Pushing on down the stream to Plymouth, and taking advantage of the shadow of the trees on the north side of the river, opposite the town, we watched the Federal transports taking onboard the women and children who were being sent away for safety, on account of the approaching bombardment. With muffled oars, and almost afraid to breathe, we made our way back up the river, hugging close to the northern bank, and reached the ram about 4 o'clock, reporting to Captain Cooke that it was practicable to pass the obstructions provided the boat was kept in the middle of the stream. The indomitable commander instantly aroused his men, gave the order to get up steam, slipped the cables in his impatience to be off, and started down the river. The obstructions were soon reached and safely passed, under a fire from the fort at Warren's Neck which was not returned. Protected by the ironclad shield, to those on board the noise made by the shot and shell as they struck the boat sounded no louder than pebbles thrown against an empty barrel. At Boyle's Mill, lower down, there was another fort upon which was mounted a very heavy gun. This was also safely passed, and we then discovered two steamers coming up the river. They proved to be the *Miami* and the *Southfield*.

The two ships were lashed together with long spars, and with chains festooned between them. The plan of Captain Flusser, who commanded, was to run his vessels so as to get the *Albemarle* between the two, which would have placed the ram at a great disadvantage, if not altogether at his mercy; but Pilot John Luck, acting under orders from Captain Cooke, ran the ram close to the southern shore; and then suddenly turning toward the middle of the stream, and going with the current, the throttles, in obedience to his bell, being wide open, he dashed the prow of the *Albemarle* into the side of the *Southfield*, making an opening large enough to carry her to the bottom in much less time than it takes to tell the story. Part of her crew went down with her.

The chain-plates on the forward deck of the *Albemarle* became entangled in the frame of the sinking vessel, and her bow was carried down to such a depth that water poured into her port-holes in great volume, and she would soon have shared the fate of the *Southfield*; had not the latter vessel reached the bottom, and then, turning over on her side, released the ram, thus allowing her to come up on an even keel. The *Miami*, right alongside, had opened fire with her heavy guns, and so close were the vessels together that a shell with a ten-second fuse, fired by Captain Flusser, after striking the *Albemarle* rebounded and exploded, killing the gallant man who pulled the lanyard, tearing him almost to pieces. Notwithstanding the death of Flusser, an attempt was made to board the ram, which was heroically resisted by as many of the crew as could be crowded on the top deck, who were supplied with loaded muskets passed up by their comrades below. The *Miami*, a powerful and very fast side-wheeler, succeeded in eluding the *Albemarle* without receiving a blow from her ram, and retired below Plymouth, into Albemarle Sound.

Captain Cooke having successfully carried out his part of the program, General Hoke attacked the fortifications the next morning and carried them; not, however, without heavy loss, Ransom's brigade alone leaving 500 dead and wounded on the field, in their most heroic charge upon the breastworks protecting the eastern front of the town. General Wessells, commanding the Federal forces, made a gallant resistance, and surrendered only when further effort would have been worse than useless. During the attack the *Albemarle* held the river front, according to contract, and all day long poured shot and shell into the resisting forts with her two guns.

On May 5, 1864, Captain Cooke left the Roanoke River with the *Albemarle* and two tenders, the *Bombshell* and *Cotton Plant*, and entered the Sound with the intention of recovering, if possible, the control of the two Sounds, and ultimately of Hatteras Inlet. He proceeded about sixteen miles on an east-north-easterly course, when the Federal squadron, consisting of seven well-armed gun-boats, the *Mattabesett, Sassacus, Wyalusing, Whitehead, Miami, Commodore Hull,* and *Ceres,* all under the command of Captain Melancton Smith, hove in sight, and at 2 o'clock that afternoon approached in double line of battle, the *Mattabesett* being in advance. They proceeded to surround the *Albemarle*, and hurled at her their heaviest shot, at distances averaging less than one hundred yards. The *Albemarle* responded effectively, but her boats were soon shot away, her smoke-stack was riddled, many iron plates in her shield were injured and broken, and the after-gun was broken off eighteen inches from the muzzle, and rendered useless. This terrible fire continued, without intermission, until about 5 PM, when the commander of the double-ender *Sassacus* selected his opportunity, and with all steam on struck the *Albemarle* squarely just abaft her starboard beam, causing every timber in the vicinity of the blow to groan, though none gave way. The pressure from the revolving wheel of the *Sassacus* was so great that it forced the after deck of the ram several feet below the surface of the water, and created an impression on board that she was about to sink. Some of the crew became demoralized, but the calm voice of the undismayed captain checked the incipient disorder, with the command, "Stand to your guns, and if we must sink let us go down like brave men."

The *Albemarle* soon recovered, and sent a shot at her assailant which passed through one of the latter's boilers, the hissing steam disabling a number of the crew. Yet the discipline on the *Sassacus* was such that, notwithstanding the natural consternation under these appalling circumstances, two of her guns continued to fire on the *Albemarle* until she drifted out of the arena of battle. Two of the fleet attempted to foul the propellers of the ram with a large fishing-seine which they had previously procured for the purpose, but the line parted in paying it out. Then they tried to blow her up with a torpedo, but failed. No better success attended an effort to throw a keg of gunpowder down her smoke-stack, or what was left of it, for it was riddled with holes from shot and shell. This smoke-stack had lost its capacity for drawing, and the boat lay a helpless mass on the water. While in this condition every effort was made by her numerous enemies to destroy her. The unequal conflict continued until night. Some of the Federal vessels were more or less disabled, and both sides were doubtless well content to draw off. Captain Cooke had on board a supply of bacon and lard, and this sort of fuel being available to burn without draught from a smoke-stack, he was able to make sufficient steam to get the boat back to Plymouth, where she tied up to her wharf covered with wounds and with glory.

The *Albemarle* in her different engagements was struck a great many times by shot and shell, and yet but one man lost his life, and that was caused by a pistol-shot from the *Miami*, the imprudent sailor having put his head out of one of the port-holes to see what was going on outside.

Captain Cooke was at once promoted and placed in command of all the Confederate naval forces in eastern North Carolina. The *Albemarle* remained tied to her wharf at Plymouth until the night of October 27, 1864, when Lieutenant William B. Cushing, of the United States Navy, performed the daring feat of destroying her with a torpedo. Having procured a torpedo-boat so constructed as to be very fast, for a short distance, and with the exhaust steam so arranged as to be noiseless, he proceeded, with a crew of fourteen men, up the Roanoke River. Guards had been stationed by the Confederate military commander on the wreck of the *Southfield*, whose top deck was then above water, but they failed to see the boat. A boom of logs had been arranged around the *Albemarle*, distant about thirty feet from her side. Captain Cooke had planned and superintended the construction of this arrangement before giving up the command of the vessel to Captain A. F. Warley. Cushing ran his boat up to these logs, and there, under a hot fire, lowered and exploded the torpedo under the *Albemarle*'s bottom, causing her to settle down and finally to sink at the wharf. The torpedo-boat and crew were captured; but Cushing refusing to surrender, though twice called upon so to do, sprang into the river, dived to the bottom, and swam across to a swamp opposite the town, thus making his escape; and on the next night, after having experienced great suffering, wandering through the swamp, he succeeded in obtaining a small canoe, and made his way back to the fleet.

The river front being no longer protected, and no appliances for raising the sunken vessel being available, on October 31 the Federal forces attacked and captured the town of Plymouth.

[The following notes are from the editor of *The Century Magazine*. RTC]

The *Miami* carried six 9-inch guns, one 100-pounder Parrott rifle, and 24-pounder smoothbore howitzer, and the ferry-boat *Southfield* five 9-inch, one 100-pounder Parrott, and one 12-pounder howitzer.—EDITOR.

Of the officers and men of the *Southfield*, seven of the former, including Acting Volunteer Lieutenant C. A. French, her commander, and forty-two of her men were rescued by the *Miami* and the other Union vessels; the remainder were either drowned or captured.—EDITOR.

The following admirably clear and succinct account of the fight is given by Acting Master William N. Wells, of the *Miami*, in his report of April 23 to Admiral Lee:

"The siege commenced Sabbath afternoon, April 17, by an artillery fire upon Fort Gray. Early in the morning of April 18, between the hours of 3 and 5, the enemy tried to carry by storm Fort Gray, but were repulsed. In the afternoon of the 18th heavy artillery opened fire upon the town and breastworks. Then the fight became general. Up to this time the gun-boats *Southfield* and *Miami* were chained together in preparation to encounter the ram. They were then separated. The *Southfield*, moving up the river, opened fire over the town. The *Miami*, moving down the river, opened a cross-fire upon the enemy, who were charging upon Fort Williams. The firing, being very exact, caused the enemy to fall back. After three attempts to storm the fort, at 9 o'clock the firing ceased from the enemy, they having withdrawn from range. Commander Flusser dispatched a messenger to General Wessells to learn the result of the day's fight. The messenger returned at 10 PM, having delivered the message, and bearing one from General Wessells to Commander Flusser, stating that the fire from the naval vessels was very satisfactory and effective—so much so that the advancing columns of the enemy broke and retreated; also desired that the *Miami* might be kept below the town to prevent a flank movement by the enemy. At 10:30 PM, steamer *Southfield* came down and anchored near. At 12:20 AM, April 19, the *Southfield* came alongside to re-chain the two steamers as speedily as possible; the ram having been seen by Captain Barrett, of the *Whitehead*, and reported by him as coming down the river. At 3:45 AM the gun-boat *Ceres* came down, passing near, giving the alarm that the ram was close upon her. I immediately hastened to acquaint Commander Flusser of the information. He immediately came on deck, and ordered both vessels to steam ahead as far as possible and run the ram down. No sooner than given was the order obeyed. Our starboard chain was slipped and bells rung to go ahead fast. In obedience to the order, the steamers were in one minute moving up the river, the ram making for us. In less than two minutes from the time she was reported, she struck us upon our port bow near the water-line, gouging two planks nearly through for ten feet; at the same time striking the *Southfield* with her prow upon the starboard bow, causing the *Southfield* to sink rapidly. As soon as the battery could be brought to bear upon the ram, both steamers, the *Southfield* and *Miami*, commenced firing solid shot from the 100-pound Parrott rifles and 11-inch Dahlgren guns; they making no perceptible indentations in her armor. Commander Flusser fired the first three shots personally from the *Miami*, the third being a ten-second Dahlgren shell, 11-inch. It was directly after that fire that he was killed by pieces of shell; several of the gun's crew were wounded at the same time. Our bow hawser being stranded, the *Miami* swung round to starboard, giving the ram a chance to pierce us. Necessity required the engine to be reversed in motion to straighten the vessel in the river, to prevent going upon the bank of the river, and to bring the rifle gun to bear upon the ram. During the time of straightening the steamer the ram had also straightened, and was making for us. From the fatal effects of her prow upon the *Southfield* and of our sustaining injury, I deemed it useless to sacrifice the *Miami* in the same way."

The Union fleet had 32 guns and 23 howitzers, a total of 55.—EDITOR.

The upper section alone of the smoke-stack has 114 holes made by shot and shell.—G. E.

The *Albemarle* was subsequently raised and towed to the Norfolk Navy Yard, and after being stripped of her armament, machinery, etc., she was sold, Oct. 15, 1867, to J. N. Leonard & Co., for $3,200—EDITOR.

4. The CSS *Raleigh*

With the disasters that befell eastern North Carolina in 1861 and 1862, Wilmington and the Cape Fear region were included in the plan to build warships that could defend the inland waters of the state. While much confidence was placed in the forts down river, especially Fort Fisher (then under hurried construction), it was acknowledged that a naval force would be necessary in the event the Federals were able to force their way up river.

When the contracts were negotiated for the *Albemarle*, the *Neuse*, and the unnamed ironclad on the Tar River, contracts were also signed for two ironclads to be constructed at Wilmington.

One of these vessels was built at the shipyard of James Cassidey, a native of Massachusetts who had been building boats at his yard at the foot of Church Street for almost twenty years. On behalf of the Confederate Navy, Cassidey began work on a "Richmond" class ironclad and in the spring of 1864 the CSS *Raleigh* was finally completed. On April 30, 1864, she was commissioned with First Lieutenant J. Pembroke Jones of Virginia appointed as her commander. Jones had seen service on the James River at Richmond and at Savannah where he had commanded the floating battery *Georgia* and the Richmond class ironclad *Savannah*. (Campbell, *Storm Over Carolina: The Confederate Navy's Struggle for Eastern North Carolina*, pp. 184, 192.)

On May 6, 1864, The *Raleigh*, under Jones, descended the Cape Fear River and engaged six Federal blockaders off New Inlet. Midshipman Scharf in his book, *History of the Confederate States Navy*, gave a brief description of this engagement. [RTC]

"North Carolina Waters" by
Midshipman J. Thomas Scharf, CSN

History of the Confederate States Navy, Chapter XV, pp. 414–415

Wilmington continued to resist all efforts for her capture, until exhaustion had weakened the grasp which no Federal effort had been able during four years to unwrench. But, while the forts resisted successfully assault after assault, and blockade runners eluded all the watchfulness of the squadrons, the same fatality seemed to follow Confederate naval vessels at Wilmington, that had destroyed the vessels whenever they displayed their colors in battle.

At half-past seven o'clock on the night of May 6th, 1864, the iron-clad *Raleigh*, Lieut. Pembroke Jones commanding, bearing the broad pennant of Flag-officer Lynch, with the *Yadkin* and *Equator*, two small river steamers, steamed out of, New Inlet, Cape Fear River, convoying several blockade runners and in quest of the enemy. The *Raleigh* steamed directly for the U. S. steamer *Britannia*, with the evident purpose of running her down. The intention was discovered in time, but the *Britannia* narrowly escaped being injured from her shot and shell. When the *Britannia* discovered the *Raleigh* she made signals to the Federal fleet of approaching danger, and fired several shots without effect at the advancing ram. Several blockaders, whose stations were convenient, stood for the scene, thinking that it was a blockade-runner trying to escape. When the *Raleigh* got within 600 yards of the *Britannia* she began firing, the first shot putting out the *Britannia's* binnacle light, and the next going over her starboard paddle box. The *Britannia* then burned a blue light when the *Raleigh* fired again. The *Britannia* in her efforts to elude the *Raleigh* changed her course three times, until she passed the buoy and got into shallow water, where she burned several Coston signals for assistance from the Federal fleet. The *Raleigh* then changed her course and steering northeast, about midnight, ran for the U. S. Steamer *Nansemond*. The Federal vessel challenged the *Raleigh* a third time, and then ran off and opened fire with her after-howitzer. The *Raleigh* immediately replied by a shot, which passed over and near the *Nansemond's* walking beam, the *Raleigh* at this time not being over 500 yards distant. Several shots were exchanged on both sides until the *Nansemond* got out of range. Near daylight the *Raleigh* sighted the U. S. steamer *Howquah*, which put to sea with all speed after firing twenty shot and shell. The *Raleigh* returned the fire with her bow gun, one shell going through the *Howquah's* smoke-stack. At daylight the *Nansemond, Mount Vernon, Howquah, Britannia, Kansas, Niphon* and the entire Federal fleet came upon the scene of action, when the *Raleigh* and her consorts returned up the river. The ill-fated luck of the Confederate vessels overtook the *Raleigh* as she crossed the bar. She stuck and "broke her back."

1st Lt. J. Pembroke Jones (Virginia Historical Society, Richmond, Virginia).

Extract from the Report of the Secretary of the
Navy of the Confederate States, November 5, 1864

Official Records Navy, Series I, Volume X, pp. 24–25

On the 7th of May last, Flag-Officer William F. Lynch, in command of the ironclad *Raleigh*, crossed the Wilmington Bar and attacked the enemy's fleet, driving his vessels to sea. In returning to port, his ship got ashore and was fatally injured, her guns, equipments, iron, etc., being saved. A court of enquiry was ordered upon the disaster, whose report is annexed.

Report of the court of enquiry in the case of the loss of the C. S. S. *Raleigh*, in Cape Fear River:

AT WILMINGTON, N.C., *June 6, 1864.*

The court having inquired into all the facts connected with the loss of the C. S. S. *Raleigh* in the waters of North Carolina, leave the honor to report the same, together with our opinion upon the points in which it is required by the precept.

In the opinion of the court, the loss of the *Raleigh* can not be attributed to negligence or inattention on the part of anyone on board of her, and every effort was made to save said vessel. We further find that the *Raleigh* could have remained outside the bar of Cape Fear River for a few hours with apparent safety, but, in the opinion of the court, it would have been improper; and, in view of all the circumstances, "her commanding officer was justified in attempting to go back into the harbor when he did."

It is further the opinion of the court that the draft of water of the *Raleigh* was too great, even lightened as she had been on this occasion, to render her passage of the bar, except under favorable circumstances, a safe operation, particularly as her strength seems to have been insufficient to enable her to sustain the weight of armor long enough to permit every practicable means of lightening her to be exhausted.

GEORGE N. HOLLINS,
Captain and President.

J.W.B. GREENHOW, *Surgeon and Judge-Advocate.*

5. Fort Fisher and Wilmington

Robert Watson was from Key West, Florida, and at the beginning of the war he served in the Florida Coast Guard before that unit was incorporated into Co. K, 7th Florida Regiment. He participated in the Battle of Chickamauga and the Siege of Chattanooga, and along with other members of Company K, attempted to resist the Federal onslaught against Missionary Ridge on November 25, 1863. He then joined his company in the disastrous and headlong retreat to Dalton, Georgia. On March 3, 1864, he and seventeen other members of Company K were transferred to the Confederate Navy.

Watson and several others from his company were assigned to the crew of the Confederate ironclad CSS *Savannah* at Savannah, Georgia, where he served until that ship was destroyed by the Confederates to avoid capture upon the approach of Sherman's army from the west. The crew was marched to Charleston, South Carolina, and then to the defenses at Wilmington, North Carolina. Watson served at Fort Fisher and Battery Buchanan during the second attack and bombardment by the massive Federal fleet in January of 1865. Before the fall of the fortification, his detachment was withdrawn to Fort Buchanan and then across the river, thereby escaping capture.

Watson kept a journal throughout the war; it was one of the few to have survived from an enlisted man. Here are his entries from December 29, 1864, when he arrived at Wilmington, until February 22, 1865, when the city was evacuated. (Campbell [editor], *Southern Service on Land & Sea, The Wartime Journal of Robert Watson, CSA/CSN,* p. xiii.) [RTC]

Diary Entries of Seaman Robert Watson, CSN

December 29, 1864, to February 22, 1865

Thursday December 29

At 7 PM stopped at Flemington, N. C., ½ hour. This place is 34 miles from Wilmington where we arrived at 12 m., got on a ferryboat and crossed over to the navy yard, cleaned out a room and put up a stove. The room contains bunks enough for us all, very cold day.*

Friday December 30

Very cold day. Washed my clothes and just as I wrung them out we were ordered to pack up to go to the Battery Buchanan. Started at 1 PM in a small tugboat and arrived at the battery at 5 PM, landed in boats and had to wade ashore, water very cold. The quarters are small and badly crowded, scarcely room to turn around. Spread our blankets on the floor and slept very well.

Saturday December 31

Cold and clear. This place is called Confederate Point. It is a low, sandy place, water brackish, sand blowing over everything. The battery is a fine one, it mounts 2 eleven inch Brooke smoothbores and 2 ten inch Columbiards [sic] and 1 six pounder howitzer. There is a great deal of humbugging in boats, they are moored off all day and hauled up at night. The water is very shoal about this place and everything that is brought here we have to wade out to the boats and carry it on shore. I went over to Fort Fisher in the afternoon. The men in the fort all busy repairing and strengthening the works. The ground was covered with shell of all sizes, many of them unexploded. On Christmas day the Yankee fleet threw about 30,000 shells at the fort. They burnt all the quarters but did not injure the works much. 2 guns burst and several were dismounted. Our loss small. Fort Fisher is a large and strong work. Rain all the afternoon and night. We have to sleep on the floor and are so crowded that we can scarcely find room to lie. Our food is badly cooked, consequently have not enough to eat. The bread is made without salt or yeast and is as heavy as stone, the beef boiled, and coffee is slops. This day one year ago, I was at Dalton, Ga. and felt confident that the war would be over and I be at home today, but alas am sadly disappointed and God only knows when this cruel and unnatural war will end. I am afraid that it will not end during Lincoln's administration. This ends the year 1864 and I pray to Almighty God that I may be at home this time next year.

Sunday, January 1, 1865

New Years day. Very cold and on guard, 1 iron clad biscuit and a cup of weak coffee for breakfast and 1 iron clad biscuit and a small piece of boiled beef for dinner and 1 biscuit and a cup of slops for supper. Pretty rough fare for New Year's Day. Austin Williams and 5 marines took a boat and went to the Yankees during the night. Some of them were on guard when they deserted. As soon as they were missed the long roll was beat and the roll called to find out who were missing. Williams was one of the *Savannah's* crew. They got off clear.

---

*Watson joined the Confederate force defending the port of Wilmington from attack by sea. The force was scattered in a series of forts and fortifications along the Cape Fear River, of which the most powerful was Fort Fisher. Shortly before Christmas, while Watson was in Charleston, a combined Union army and navy expedition mounted an attack on Fort Fisher. The attack failed, but when Watson arrived, it was apparent that a second one was imminent. Battery Buchanan was located a few hundred yards down river from Fort Fisher. [RTC]

Monday, January 2

Came off guard at 9½ AM and at 10 AM all hands fell in for drill. Our crew were told to look on and see how the guns were worked, but we gained no information for the men were very poorly drilled. They drilled about ¾ of an hour then fell in and marched to quarters where we broke ranks. I did not get any sleep last night and was kept busy all day. When a man comes off guard he is not excused from duty that day.

Tuesday, January 3

I asked Lieut. Arledge to allow the *Savannah's* crew to mess together as it was very unpleasant for us to mess with a lot of "tar heels." He consented and I went to work and made a mess chest. In afternoon took a lot of beef and vegetables on shore and carried them up to the bomb proof and hauled up the boats. Very cold all night.

Wednesday January 4

Went to work on officer's quarters. The tools consist of 2 old broken saws, 1 hatchet, and 2 hammers. Very cold day.

Seaman Robert Watson (courtesy Jann O'Flynn).

Thursday January 5

Pleasant day. All work on building all day.

Friday January 6

Worked part of forenoon. Began to rain at 11 AM, and continued to blow and rain very hard all night.

Saturday January 7

Blowing very hard all day and very cold. At work all day.

Sunday January 8

Started our mess today. I made a swinging table for the mess. Cold but pleasant.

Friday January 13

Have been at work on officer's quarters since last date. Roll call at 4 AM and ammunition given out for small arms. At sunrise the enemy opened fire on Fort Fisher.* At 12 m. we were ordered to Fort Fisher to reinforce it. Double quicked up to the fort, the shell bursting around us in large numbers but did us no damage. We manned three guns and commenced firing at 1 PM and continued till dark when both parties ceased fire. The Yankees had been firing on the fort all day with 3 monitors and the *Ironsides*, but at 4 PM they brought the whole fleet to bear and kept up a terrific fire until dark. Fortunately none of our men were hurt except Lieut. Hudgins who was slightly wounded in the mouth with a fragment of shell, and several of us were knocked down with sand bags. We were all nearly buried in sand several times. This was caused by shell bursting in the sand. When-

---

*This is the beginning of the second attack on Fort Fisher. Approximately 8,000 Union troops were landed on January 13th under the cover of a naval bombardment. [RTC]

ever one would strike near us in the sand it would throw the sand over us by the cart load. All quiet through the night and very cold. Got no sleep for we were on the lookout all night for an infantry attack. Fired our guns every 15 minutes along the beach with canister. Very dark.

Saturday January 14

At daylight we fell in and marched back to Battery Buchanan. Marched in quick time and got a drink of whiskey on arrival, got breakfast and turned in and just as I fell asleep we were ordered to fall in and go back to Fort Fisher. The Yankees saw us, for they shelled us furiously all the way but did us no injury. We got through safe and manned the same guns we had yesterday. I was at a 6.4 inch Brooke rifle and made some excellent shots. We ceased firing at dark but the enemy kept up a severe fire all night. They seemed to direct their whole fire at our 3 guns for we were the only ones that did them any injury. Our shot and shell would strike the monitors and *Ironsides** and break in pieces and of course did them no injury, but the wooden vessels did not fare so well for several of them had to haul off. Their shell bursting among us very often, but fortunately none of us were injured. After dark a company of soldiers came in our gun chambers and had not been there 15 minutes before two of them were wounded, one mortally. We all suffered very much with cold and want of sleep. Skirmishing on our left between our pickets and the Yankee pickets. They are reported to be in large force up the beach on our left. Our pickets drove theirs back.

Sunday January 15

At daylight we went back to Battery Buchanan, took a drink, got breakfast and turned in, the Yankee fleet keeping up a heavy bombardment all the time and many of their shells exploding near our quarters. One man had a leg cut off and the other broken, he was asleep in the guard tent at the time. At 11 AM turned out and got dinner and all hands were ordered to pack up and go to the battery for the fleet had moved to the right and near us. The shelling was terrific. At 3½ PM, the Yankee infantry advanced on Fort Fisher and were repulsed three times but on the 4th charge they gained a footing on the left of the works. Unfortunately all the guns of the left were disabled, if this had not been the case they never would have gained a footing, but our men fought them bravely until after dark with musketry and contested every inch of ground. The slaughter was great. As soon as we saw that the enemy had gained a footing and planted their hateful flag on the left of the works we knew that the fort was lost and Captain [Robert T.] Chapman had all hands mustered, the roll called, and he then informed us that the fort was lost and that it was useless for him to keep us here to be taken prisoners or slaughtered, that we could fight the battery for some time and probably do the enemy some damage but that we could not hold it for any length of time. He then ordered us in the boats and we had to wade out to them up to our waists in water to get into them and just as we started he ordered us to await for orders. Our battery then opened fire on the left of Fort Fisher with one 11 inch and one 10 inch gun, the other two guns would not bear. Continued shelling until 8 PM. At 10 PM we were ordered to go across the river to Battery Lamb. We were very glad to leave for we were nearly frozen as our clothes were wet and it was a very cold night. The shells were bursting very near us all the time. Stopped at Battery Lamb ½ hour and started for Wilmington. I and several of my shipmates marched about four miles, halted, built a fire and turned in after drying our clothing. Slept well. Lieut. Hudgins was captured while trying to get into

---

**The USS New Ironsides was the most powerful and formidable armored warship in the U.S. Navy. She weighed 4,120 tons and carried twenty heavy guns. The Ironsides had been heavily damaged by a torpedo attack of the CSS David outside of Charleston, South Carolina on October 5, 1863. Out of action for almost two years, she was now repaired and participating in the attack on Fort Fisher. [RTC]*

the boat. The Yankees threw up thousands of rockets when they gained possession of Fort Fisher. The sight was magnificent.*

Monday January 16
Turned out at daylight and marched till 3 PM when three of us stopped at a house and got some corn bread and meat for the small sum of $30.00 from a Negro. We were very hungry for we left the battery with nothing to eat. This was the fault of the officers who I am sorry to say were all intoxicated. There was a large quantity of provisions in the fort which fell into the hands of the enemy. After eating the corn dodger and meat we proceeded a little farther and camped for the night. We got some rice and bacon from a Negro and gave him a pair of pants in exchange, cooked and ate it and turned in. Very cold all night.

Tuesday January 17
Started at daylight and arrived at Wilmington at 11 AM, very tired and sore, drew a pair of shoes and went to the navy yard and were ordered to hold ourselves in readiness to leave for a battery somewhere on the river. Drew some rations and remained there all day and night. Got but little sleep for a lot of the men came in drunk and kept up a noise all night and the place is overrun with lice. They were running over and biting me all night. I should not say lice for it is vulgar, the proper name for them is "soldier bugs."

Wednesday January 18
Turned out at daylight and got breakfast and packed up ready for a start. At 1 PM all hands fell in and went to Fort Campbell.† I and 2 more remained behind and started with the provision wagon at 4 PM, arrived at sunset. This battery mounts 1 eight inch smooth bore, 1 eighteen pounder, 1 twenty-four, and 2 thirty-two pounders, all smooth bore. The quarters are old leaky shanties, not half room enough for us, 6 of us slept out doors.

Thursday January 19
Turned out at daylight and got breakfast, on guard, pleasant day. Cannonading all day down the river. All hands were ordered to hold themselves ready to fight at a moments warning for we expected the enemy up the river every minute. In the afternoon a flat came down with two 9 inch Dahlgren guns. All hands except the guard worked on them getting them ashore, knocked off at midnight. I came off post at midnight and had just turned in when one of the sentinels fired his gun. The guard turned out, etc. but it was a false alarm, some animal in the woods no doubt.

Friday January 20
I came off guard at 8 AM and went to work carrying pine logs to slide the guns on. Worked all day and succeeded in getting the guns up the hill at 10 PM when we knocked off, all hands wet for it had been raining all the time and I have no clothes except what I have on. Turned in my wet clothes and slept well.

Saturday, January 21
Went to work on the guns at daylight, raining and cold. Worked about 2 hours and got breakfast, turned to again and got the guns to the battery knocked off at 11½ AM, raining and cold all day. I was on guard at night. This is pretty hard to work all day and stand guard at night. Had another false alarm at night.

The fall of Fort Fisher was a fatal blow for the Confederacy. Except for Galveston, in far off Texas, no Southern ports remained open for blockade runners. Union forces consisted of over 8,000 troops and fifty-nine warships mounting a total of 627 guns. The Federals lost approximately 1,070 soldiers and sailors in the attack, while Confederate losses were roughly 500. 1,500 Confederates were taken prisoner. [RTC]

†*Fort Campbell was located on the south side of the Cape Fear River guarding the lower passage known as Old Inlet. It was eight miles below Fort Fisher. [RTC]*

Sunday January 22
Came off guard at 8 AM and went to work getting another gun from the beach to the battery and dismounted two guns in the battery. Worked all day, rained at night.

Monday January 23
On guard, washed some of my clothes. Have to pull off part of what I have on and wash them and after they dry wash the others for I have but one suit. Raining all night. The sentinel on post fired his gun and the guard turned out, fake alarm. The fool heard a coon and thought it was a man crawling up to him. He was very frightened, he is a N. C. conscript.

Tuesday January 24
Came off guard at 8 AM, pleasant day, not much to do, washed clothes in forenoon. The Negroes are at work making an earthwork for a 30-pounder Parrot gun. Cannonading down the river.

Wednesday January 25
Cold and clear and plenty of work.

Thursday January 26
On guard, very cold and clear. Yankees reported landing below. Quiet through the night.

Friday January 27
Came off guard at 8 AM and took a drink of whiskey. Pleasant day. Drill at gun in morning and with some small arms in the afternoon. Officers all drunk and drilling us for their amusement. If these things continue much longer I shall certainly desert and go to some other command, for I am heartily sick of it. Some of the men killed a fine cow in the afternoon. This is done on the sly, but the officers know all about it and get some of the meat.

Saturday January 28
Very cold day. Some of the boys killed a fine hog. We have to steal meat or starve. No drill today, for a wonder.

Sunday January 29
Cold and clear, on guard. Took a stiff horn of whiskey and a fine breakfast of beef steak and hog head. Officers fiddling, dancing, and drinking whiskey all day and nearly all night. Shameful conduct for officers, the whiskey is sent for the men but they drink 9/10 of it themselves. The men are allowed 1 gill per day and they only give half a gill to the guard, the balance of the men get none. All quiet through the night.

Monday January 30
A fine clear day, came off guard at 8 AM and got [page torn] full of whiskey. Target practice at 10 AM. Our gun [page torn] shooting in the battery and knocked the cross down. It is a 9 inch Dahlgren on ship's broadside carriage.

Tuesday January 31
I am mess cook for this week. Drill battery in morning and infantry drill in afternoon. A boat loaded with poultry and vegetables came to our landing and asked such an enormous price that our boys took nearly everything from them. Our mess got a bag of potatoes, two geese and one chicken. Complaint was made to our commanding officers and at dress parade he requested that all that had a hand in it would step out and acknowledge it and remarked that they would only have to pay for the things. 15 or 20 men stepped out

and their names taken down. I think that this will be the last of it. Had a fine supper poultry and vegetables. Very cold night

Wednesday February 1, 1865
Cold and clear, drill in the battery in morning. Sixteen men went to town to work.

Thursday February 2
Pleasant day, drill in morning.

Monday February 6
I got through cooking last night, very disagreeable work for there is scarcely any cooking utensils. Heavy shelling for the last three days down the river. Drill in morning in battery and skirmish drill in the afternoon. Drew one pr. pants, 2 pr. cotton drawers, 2 cotton shirts, and 2 plugs tobacco, and 2 lbs. soap.

Tuesday February 7
Drill in morning and at skirmish drill in afternoon. I was detailed for guard in the morning but was excused as I had the cleanest gun. Rain all day. The guard fired at a boat and brought her to. There were four men in her who were trying to get to the Yankees. They were sent to jail.

Wednesday February 8
Very cold all day. In the morning Seth Cleveland who has been our pursers steward, and who has held that position ever since the war began, was triced up with his hands behind him. He fought manfully and it took three men and two officers to do it. He did nothing worthy of such punishment. It seems that he had to go down yesterday to get provisions. There is an ambulance here for that purpose but when it started a lot of officers half drunk jumped in and ordered Seth to walk. It was raining very hard at the time and he would not go, so the comdg. officer asked him why he did not. He told him that he had the itch very bad and was afraid to get wet as he was using sulphur. The officer told him that he would put another man in his place in the morning, so this morning he appointed a man who declined. [page torn] Seth was then ordered to keep his old place and refused to take it back, consequently he was triced up. I mention this to show how we are treated. The officers are intoxicated all the time and put on more airs than a commodore would. A Foraging party went across the river and killed 3 hogs, 1 sheep, and 5 geese. Our men got some of the pork which was an old boar. Drill with small arms in the afternoon.

Thursday February 9
I went to town and sold 15 undershirts and drawers for $180.00 and bought 100 lbs. corn meal at $1.00 per lb. and 1 lb. soda for $15.00. There are 15 men in our mess and each man put in a garment, for we are short of breadstuff. Got back to camp at five o'clock PM

Friday February 10
On guard. Cold and clear.

Saturday February 11
Came off guard at 8 AM. Target practice in battery in the afternoon. Fired three shots from each gun. Enemy shelling our forces from below.

Sunday February 12
Pleasant day, not much to do.

Monday 13th
On guard and very cold. At 1 AM while I was on post I heard something coming through the woods and when it came in sight it looked like two men. I hailed three times and was

about to fire my gun when I discovered that it was a mule. The officer of the guard came running to find out what I was hailing and in crossing the ditch the plank broke and he fell in. This amused me for the balance of my watch.

Tuesday February 14
Came off guard at 8 AM. Cold and windy all day. Battalion drill in afternoon. Rain through the night.

Wednesday February 15
Raining all the forenoon, our quarters leak like a sieve.

Thursday February 16
On guard, pleasant weather. In the afternoon Tom King was put under guard for refusing to whip a boy. The boy refused to black one of the officer's shoes and he ordered him to be whipped, but as Tom refused to whip him he was put under arrest also.

Friday February 17
Came off guard at 8 AM. Worked all the afternoon carrying lumber to build a house. Blowing very hard all day and part of the night. At 9 PM, just as I fell asleep, the alarm was given that the Yankees were landing below us. All hands went to quarters and 27 of us went out as pickets, remained there until 11 PM when we were relieved by some soldiers and we went to bed. Our officers did not know as much about posting us as a lot of old women, we were scattered all about in the woods and had the Yankees attacked us we would have shot our own men. All quiet the balance of the night.

Saturday February 18
Pleasant day, all hands busy on earthworks. Drill in morning. The enemy still shelling Fort Anderson, they have been at it for several days.*

Sunday February 19
Pleasant day. In the afternoon about 40 Yankee launches came up the river. Only one of our guns, a 30 pounder Parrot, would bear on them and soon drove them back. I think they were sounding the channel and dragging for torpedoes.

Monday February 20
At 10 AM 9 Yankee gunboats came up the river and at 3 PM they opened fire on us. Our Parrot gun opened on them in return it being the only gun that would bear on them. The third shell the Yankees threw came very near killing me and several more. Fortunately we had put up a lot of sand bags in the morning which saved us but we were buried in sand. Several shells exploded near our gun and one struck the platform and tore it all to pieces. Ceased fire at dark and we worked nearly all night repairing damages with sand bags. Very cold.

Tuesday February 21
All hands at work strengthening the fort with sand bags. At 4 PM the Yankees came in line and opened on us and continued till dark. They shelled us very heavily but did us but little injury. Our 8-inch shell gun was dismounted, and while trying to mount it the gunner was badly hurt by the gun falling on him.

Wednesday February 22
At 1 AM an officer came around and turned us out and ordered us to pack up and take everything that we wished to carry with us and not to make any noise. We did so and fell

---

*Fort Anderson was approximately five miles up river from Fort Fisher. [RTC]

in and stood in lines about ½ hour, then marched quietly off to a hollow about 400 yards from the battery and waited there about 1 hour. It was bitter cold and I thought that my feet would freeze. Started and marched through the city of Wilmington, not a word spoken for the Yankees were very close to us, in fact we afterwards found out that they were in the city when we passed through, but we went though the back part of the city and they were in the city front. Marched without resting till 10 AM when we rested for one hour then started and crossed a pontoon bridge at N. E. River, halted and took a good sleep, when our skirmishers commenced fighting and we were ordered to fall in and formed in line of battle. Remained in lines for ½ hour when we were ordered to go to Goldsborough. Marched to the depot and found that the train had left. We built fires and just as they were burning nicely we were ordered to fall in and marched on the railroad to Burgaw. Arrived there about 4 AM and turned in feeling dreadful tired and sore for we had marched 27 miles.

III

Charleston, South Carolina

1. The CSS *Palmetto State*

The keel for the ironclad *Palmetto State* was laid in 1862 at the Cameron & Company shipyard at Charleston. Shortly afterwards, the construction of the *Chicora* was begun by James Eason, the owner of Charleston's largest iron foundry. Both ironclads encountered the usual delays and frustrations in constructing armored warships in the Confederacy, but both were finally completed by October of 1863.

Prior to the launching of the *Palmetto State*, First Lieutenant John Rutledge was sent from Richmond to take command. Rutledge had commanded the gunboat CSS *Lady Davis* at the battle of Port Royal, South Carolina, in November of 1861, and he was most likely very knowledgeable with the engines on the *Palmetto State*, for they had been removed from the *Lady Davis*. Lieutenant Parker was assigned as his executive officer.

The Charleston Squadron at that time was under the overall command of Captain Duncan N. Ingraham. In consultations with General P. T. G. Beauregard, it was decided to attack the Federal blockaders lying off the port of Charleston. On the night of January 31, 1863, this attack took place, and below is Parker's account. (Campbell, *Southern Fire: Exploits of the Confederate States Navy*, pp. 95–113.) [RTC]

"The Attack on the Union Blockading Squadron off Charleston, SC" by Commander William H. Parker, CSN

Recollections of a Naval Officer, 1883, pp. 308–324

The *Palmetto State* was an iron-clad on the plan of the *Merrimac*, except that her ends were not submerged, and her side plating was turned down at the water's edge, making what we called a knuckle, and very strong. I think her plating was of four and a half inches of iron. Her roof, or upper deck, and her ends outside the shield were covered on top with two inches of iron, and her hatchways were covered with heavy iron gratings. Her pilot house, which was heavily armored, was abaft the smoke stack. Her armament consisted of an 80-pounder Brooke rifle gun forward, a 60-pounder rifle gun aft, and two 8-inch shell guns in broadside—four guns in all. Her engines always worked well, and under favorable circumstances she would go seven knots per hour, though her average speed was about six. She drew fourteen feet of water, and worked and steered well. The *Chicora* was similar in all respects, except that she had but 4-inch iron, I think. These two vessels were built at private ship-yards in Charleston, and great rivalry existed between them as to which should turn out the best ship. Both were well-built, creditable vessels. All their arrangements were good, magazines, shell-rooms, quarters, etc., all admirably arranged.

When these two vessels had been in commission a short time, they were fine specimens of men-of-war and would have done credit to any navy. They were well officered and manned. Their drill at both great guns and small arms was excellent, and the discipline perfect. They were the cleanest iron-clads, I believe, that ever floated, and the men took great pride in keeping them so. Their fire drill was good, as I have reason to remember, for the *Palmetto State* caught fire one morning in the fore-hold, adjoining the magazine. I was dressing at the time, when I heard a running about, and immediately became conscious that "something was the matter." I hurried on my coat, and just then heard the cry: "There's fire in the magazine!" Thinks I to myself, "if that be the case we will very soon hear of it," as Lord Howe once said under similar circumstances. I sprang up on the deck and had the fire-bell rung, and every man and officer went promptly to his station. The fire-party went below, and discovered the place of fire, and in fifteen minutes it was suppressed.

Speaking of a fire so near the magazine, I was some years after this placed in a situation so very peculiar, that I may be pardoned for introducing it here. I doubt if ever a man found himself in the same situation: After the war I entered the service of the Pacific Mail Steamship Company, and for six years commanded one of their steamers running between San Francisco and Panama. July 1st, 1873, I left Panama for San Francisco in the steamship Montana, with about fifty cabin and four hundred steerage passengers, and a large freight. All went well until the evening of the seventh day, when I found myself 130 miles from Acapulco, Mexico, which place I expected to reach the next morning at 8. It was a dark night and raining at intervals, but there was not much wind. The ship was well clear of the Tartar Shoal and there was nothing to cause any uneasiness. I remained up, as was my custom, until midnight, and then gave the second mate, who had the mid-watch, the written orders for the night. I turned in, and was soon asleep. I was awakened by the officer of the deck calling me. Upon my replying, he said in a calm manner: "Captain Parker, the ship is on fire." "What time is it?" I asked. "Twenty minutes past three," he replied. I then asked where the ship was on fire, and he told me it was in the forward store-room, where I knew the oils and paints were kept. He asked if he should ring the fire-bell, but I told him no; I thought we might extinguish it without letting the passengers know anything about it. All this time I was rapidly dressing, as may well be imagined, and in a minute from the time I was called I was out on deck. As soon as I reached it I saw the smoke coming up the fore-hatch, and the steerage passengers rushing up in great alarm. I ordered the fire-bell rung, stopped the engine, and turned the ship so as to bring the wind aft. The men were well drilled and soon every man was at his station. The steerage passengers were all sent aft on the hurricane deck, and made to sit down flat on deck; officers were placed over them and they remained quietly so until the fire was extinguished. The cabin passengers remained in the saloon in charge of the purser and doctor. We soon had eight good streams of water forward, and I scuttled the deck in several places over the store-room, and put the pipes down. Two or three pipes were turned down the open hatchway, but the fumes arising from the burning paints were so stifling that the men could not remain more than a few minutes at a time. There was no flinching on their part, however,-quite the contrary; as soon as a man was hauled up, half-suffocated, others were eager to take his place. After working some fifteen minutes in this way, seeing that the flames were apparently getting the advantage of us, and knowing that if the hurricane deck caught fire we would burn up very rapidly, I sent for the second mate and boatswain and directed them to lower the boats near the water's edge, but to allow no one to get into them. We carried about one hundred pounds of powder in a copper tank, in the magazine, which was just under the store-room. It could be filled with water by turning a cock. Sending for the first officer I told him to drown the magazine. He replied in a low tone, that it was useless to do so, as the powder had not been returned to the magazine, but was in the store-room.

"Do you mean to say," said I, "that it is in the fire?" "Yes, sir," said he, "it is."

I reflected. If it became known that the powder was in the store-room there would be a stampede; if, on the other hand, it exploded and blew the bows of the ship out, there would necessarily be great loss of life. I stuck to my original resolution to put the fire out. I had always impressed it upon my crew that if my ship caught fire, it must be put out. I had no faith in the custom of putting on all steam and heading for the shore. I knew that that of itself caused a panic; that, moreover, the fire was fanned up and swept aft, endangering the lives of the cabin passengers; and that the boats could not be lowered with the ship running at full speed. My idea was that if the passengers had to be put in the boats, it could be better done eight miles from the shore than in the breakers after the ship grounded.

So I spoke but a few words to my men now. I said, "We are men enough to handle this fire, and we must do it." They wanted no encouragement, and at the end of an hour we had it under. As soon as a man could breathe in the store-room, the powder-tank was passed up to me. It was so hot you could not put your bare hand upon it. My first impulse was to order the mate to throw it overboard; but I thought for a moment, and then directed him to put it in his state-room. I knew it would not explode then, and as we had gotten so well out of the scrape, determined to take the matter coolly. The steerage passengers were now sent forward again, given a cup of coffee, and advised to turn in for a morning nap. We started the engine ahead at 5 o'clock, and at 9 made fast to our buoy at Acapulco. We poured an immense quantity of water into the ship during the fire, but as we kept the donkey-engine at work pumping it out as it ran aft, our cargo was not damaged.

On this occasion I had a Chinese crew, with a Chinese boatswain. The leading men, quarter-masters and firemen were white, and they showed the others the example. It shows what effect that will have,—for the Chinese were the only ones engaged in putting out the fire who knew the powder was in the store-room. Yet they stuck to their posts. The first officer, whose duty it was to see that the powder was kept in the magazine, had been very negligent of his duty. He would have been dismissed the service had it not been for his courageous conduct during the fire. I reported to the agent, that although he had neglected his duty in the case—probably through forgetfulness—yet he had exhibited during the fire the highest traits of an officer, and I thought he should be retained. As for the conduct of the passengers, I never knew which deserved the most credit—they or my crew. The cause of the fire was spontaneous combustion, probably from oiled rags in the paint-room.

To return to the *Palmetto State*. One drill I introduced on board her, to which I attached much importance. Every officer and man had his appointed port or hatch to escape by in case of the vessel's suddenly sinking—say by the explosion of a torpedo. The first men who reached the deck immediately took off the iron gratings, without waiting to be told. At the order, "clear the ship," all hands would assemble on the roof in less than a minute. We never went to general quarters that I did not try this; and as I say, in less than a minute, the men from the magazine, shell-room, fire-room, everywhere, would be out on deck. There were a good many sailor-men in our crew, and we managed to put them in uniform and keep them provided with clothing. Occasionally we got a man from the army,—and we kept a bathing arrangement on the wharf, where all recruits were bathed and their clothes well boiled before being allowed to come on board, for obvious reasons. Both vessels were painted a pale blue or bluish-grey, the blockade runners having demonstrated that it was the most difficult to be distinguished. Before going into action we greased the shield with slush, as the *Merrimac* had done at Hampton Roads. Our officers in the *Palmetto State* were: Captain John Rutledge; Lieutenants Parker, Porcher, Shryock and Bowen; Surgeon Lynch; Paymaster Banks; Engineer Campbell; Master Chew; Midshipmen Cary, Sevier and Hamilton. We had a good boatswain and gunner, and a crew of about 120 men.

The *Palmetto State* bore the flag of Commodore Duncan L. Ingraham, who commanded the station. He was known as the hero of the Koszta affair. Koszta was a Hungarian refugee, who, when in the United States in 1850, had declared his intention of becoming an American citizen, and went through the preliminary forms. June 21, 1853, being in Smyrna, he was seized by a boat's crew from the Austrian brig *Huzzar*. Captain Ingraham, who was present in the sloop-of-war *St. Louis*, of 20 guns, demanded his release by a certain time, and prepared to attack the *Huzzar* on the 2nd of July. Koszta was then given up, and he afterwards returned to the United States. Captain Ingraham was much commended by his Government for his prompt and decisive action. He entered the U. S. Navy in 1812, being then but nine years of age. He served in the frigate *Congress*, under Captain Smith. He told me that they were at sea 9 months without going into port. They made a few prizes,

Captain Duncun N. Ingraham (Scharf, *History of the Confederate States Navy*).

but were not fortunate enough to fall in with any of the British frigates. It was considered an unlucky cruise, and the *Congress* got the name of being an unlucky ship. Commodore Ingraham commanded the brig *Somers* until just before the war with Mexico. During the war he served for a time on Commodore Conner's Staff. He was a delicate-looking man, of intelligence and culture, and bore the reputation of being a brave and good officer. He is still living.

By January, 1863, the vessels being all ready, we commenced to think of making some demonstration, and it was decided to attack the fleet off Charleston on the night of the 30th. The enemy's fleet off the harbor on that night consisted of the *Housatonic, Mercedita, Keystone State, Quaker City, Augusta, Flag, Memphis, Stettin, Ottawa* and *Unadilla*. Of these, the *Housatonic, Ottawa* and *Unadilla* were, I think, the only regularly-built men-of-war; the others being converted merchant steamers,—some paddles, the others screws. Captain Taylor, of the *Housatonic*, was the senior officer of the blockading force. Admiral Dupont, who commanded the station, was at this time at Port Royal with the iron-clad *New Ironsides*, the frigate *Wabash* and the steamships *Susquehanna, Canandaigua* and some others.

About 10 PM, January 30th, Commodore Ingraham came on board the *Palmetto State*, and at 11.30 the two vessels quietly cast off their fasts and got underweigh. There was no demonstration on shore, and I believe few of the citizens knew of the projected attack. Charleston was full of spies at this time, and everything was carried to the enemy. It was nearly calm, and a bright moonlight night,—the moon being 11 days old. We went down very slowly, wishing to reach the bar of the main ship channel, 11 miles from Charleston, about 4 in the morning, when it would be high water there. Commander Hartstene (an Arctic man who rescued Kane and his companions), was to have followed us with several unarmed steamers and 50 soldiers to take possession of the prizes; but, for some reason they did not cross the bar. We steamed slowly down the harbor and, knowing we had a long night before us, I ordered the hammocks piped down. The men declined to take them, and I found they had gotten up an impromptu Ethiopian entertainment. As there was no necessity for preserving quiet at this time the captain let them enjoy themselves in their own way. No men ever exhibited a better spirit before going into action; and the short, manly speech of our captain convinced us that we were to be well commanded under any circumstances. We passed between Forts Sumter and Moultrie—the former with its yellow sides looming up and reflecting the moon's rays-and turned down the channel along Morris Island. I presume all hands were up in the forts and batteries watching us, but no word was spoken. After midnight the men began to drop off by twos and threes, and in a short time the silence of death prevailed. I was much impressed with the appearance of the ship at this time. Visiting the lower deck, forward, I found it covered with men sleeping in their pea-jackets peacefully and calmly; on the gundeck a few of the more thoughtful seamen were pacing quietly to and fro, with folded arms; in the pilot-house stood the Commodore and Captain, with the two pilots; the midshipmen were quiet in their quarters (for a wonder), and aft I found the lieutenants smoking their pipes, but not conversing. In the wardroom the surgeon was preparing his instruments on the large mess-table; and the paymaster was, as he told me, "lending him a hand."

As we approached the bar, about 4 AM, we saw the steamer *Mercedita* lying at anchor a short distance outside it. I had no fear of her seeing our hull; but we were burning soft coal, and the night being very clear, with nearly a full moon, it did seem to me that our smoke, which trailed after us like a huge black serpent, must be visible several miles off. We went silently to quarters, and our main-deck then presented a scene that will always live in my memory. We went to quarters an hour before crossing the bar, and the men stood silently at their guns. The port-shutters were closed, not a light could be seen from the outside, and the few battle-lanterns lit cast a pale, weird light on the gun-deck. My friend Phil. Porcher, who commanded the bow-gun, was equipped with a pair of white kid gloves, and had in his mouth an unlighted cigar. As we stood at our stations, not even whispering, the silence became more and more intense. Just at my side I noticed the little powder-boy of the broadside guns sitting on a match-tub, with his powder-pouch slung over his shoulder, fast asleep, and he was in this condition when we rammed the *Mercedita*. We crossed the bar and steered directly for the *Mercedita*. They did not see us until we were very near. Her captain then hailed us, and ordered us to keep off or he would fire. We did not reply, and he called out, "You will be into me." Just then we struck him on the starboard quarter, and dropping the forward port-shutter, fired the bow gun. The shell from it, according to Captain [Henry S.] Stellwagen who commanded her, went through her diagonally, penetrating the starboard side, through the condenser, through the steam-drum of the port boiler, and exploded against the port side of the ship, blowing a hole in its exit four or five feet square. She did not fire a gun, and in a minute her commander hailed to say he surrendered. Captain Rutledge then directed him to send a boat alongside. When I saw the boat coming I went out on the after-deck to receive it. The men in it were half-dressed, and as they had neglected to put the plug in when it was lowered, it was half full of water. We gave them a boat-hook to supply the place of the plug, and helped to bail her out.

Lieutenant T. Abbott, the executive officer of the *Mercedita*, came in the boat. I conducted him through the port to the presence of Commodore Ingraham. He must have been impressed with the novel appearance of our gun deck; but his bearing was officer-like and cool. He reported the name of the ship and her captain, said she had 128 souls on board and that she was in a sinking condition. After some delay Commodore Ingraham required him to "give his word of honor, for his commander, officers and crew, that they would not serve against the Confederate States until regularly exchanged." This he did—it was a verbal parole. He then returned to his ship.

In the meantime the *Chicora*, under her dashing commander, had passed us and had become warmly engaged, and we in the *Palmetto State* were most impatient to be off. We were ready to exclaim with Horace:

> Fen whilst we speak, the envious Time
> Doth make swift haste away;
> Then seize the Present, use thy Prime,
> Nor trust another Day.

We rammed the *Mercedita* at 4.30 AM, and lost much valuable time while the commodore was deciding what to do with her officers and men. Our chance for making a great success lay in taking advantage of the darkness. We knew that when day came the enemy would see they were contending with iron-clads, and would refuse battle and we with our inferior speed could not force it. We finally stood out to the eastward and engaged the *Quaker City*, *Memphis*, and some other vessels, as they came up, but they sheered off as soon as they felt the weight of our metal. When day broke I got a chance to get up on the spardeck. I first looked astern for the *Mercedita*, and not seeing her, asked our pilot where she was. He said she must have sunk; and that was the general impression on board; but I knew she was not in deep water, and seeing no masts sticking up, "I had my doubts."

The fact is we did not ram her quite hard enough. The panic on board her caused by the shell from our bow-gun was at first so great that they thought she was sinking. One boiler being emptied caused her to heel over, I suppose; but as we stood out to engage the enemy to the eastward, they got matters to rights, and finally went off to Port Royal where she arrived safely. (But this we learned afterwards).

Tucker, in the *Chicora*, as we rammed the *Mercedita*, passed us to starboard and soon became warmly engaged with the *Keystone State*, which vessel came gallantly into action, with the intention to run the *Chicora* down. She soon received so much damage as to cause her to surrender by striking her colors.

As related to me by the officers of the *Chicora* the next day, the *Keystone State* struck her flag and they were about lowering a boat to take possession of her. Lieutenant Bier, the executive officer, observed that she was moving off by working her off wheel and called Captain Tucker's attention to it. The lieutenants begged the captain to renew the fire; but he not expecting any deception or treachery hesitated to fire on a ship with her colors down; and in a little while Captain [William E.] Leroy who commanded the *Keystone State* hoisted his colors again, renewed his fire and escaped. He was soon after taken in tow by the U. S. steamer *Memphis* and carried to Port Royal.

Captain Tucker in his official report, dated the same day, in relation to this matter says: "We then engaged a schooner-rigged propeller and a large side-wheel steamer, partially crippling both, and setting the latter on fire, causing her to strike her flag. At this time the latter vessel, supposed to be the *Keystone State*, was completely at my mercy, I having a raking position astern distant some 200 yards. I at once gave the order to cease firing upon her, and directed Lieutenant Bier, first lieutenant of the *Chicora*, to man a boat and take charge of the prize; if possible to save her, if that was not possible to rescue her crew. While the boat was in the act of being manned I discovered that she was in the act of endeavoring to escape by working her starboard wheel, the other being disabled. Her colors being down I at once started in pursuit and renewed the engagement. Owing to her superior steaming qualities she soon widened the distance to some two hundred yards. She then hoisted her flag and commenced firing her rifled gun; her commander by this faithless act placing himself beyond the pale of civilized and honorable warfare."

In his official report to Admiral Dupont, dated same day, Captain Leroy does not mention the fact of his having struck his colors; but an extract from the log of his vessel says: "About 6.17 AM a shell entering on the port side forward of the forward guard destroyed the steam chimneys, filling all the forward part of the ship with steam. The port boiler emptied of its contents, the ship gave a heel to starboard nearly down to the guard, and the water from the boiler, and two shot holes under water led to the impression the ship was filling and sinking, a foot and a half water being reported in the hold. Owing to the steam men were unable to get supplies of ammunition from forward. Ordered all boats ready for lowering. Signal books thrown overboard, also some small arms. The ram being so near, and the ship helpless, and the men being slaughtered by almost every discharge of the enemy, I ordered the colors to be hauled down, but finding the enemy were still firing upon us directed the colors to be re-hoisted, and resume our fire from the after battery."

The vessels in our vicinity having put off under all steam to the southward, our two vessels stood to the northward and eastward to meet the vessels coming from that direction. We exchanged a few shots with the *Housatonic* at very long range, but she soon also withdrew. Commodore Ingraham in his report says: "I then stood to the northward and eastward, and soon after made another steamer getting underweigh. We stood for her and soon after fired several shots at her, but as we had to fight the vessel in a circle to bring the different guns to bear, she was soon out of our range. In this way we engaged several vessels, they keeping at long range, and steering to the southward. Just as the day broke we made a large steamer (supposed to be the *Powhatan*) on the starboard bow, with another steamer in company, which had just got underweigh. They stood to the southward under full steam, and opened their batteries upon the *Chicora*, which was some distance astern of us. I then turned and stood to the southward to support the *Chicora*, if necessary, but the enemy kept on his course to the southward. I then made signal to Commander Tucker to come to an anchor, and led the way to the entrance to Beach channel, where we anchored at 8.45 AM, and had to remain seven hours for the tide, as the vessels cannot cross the bar except at high water." The commodore took the *Housatonic* to be the *Powhatan*—the *Powhatan* was at Port Royal that day.

We anchored off Sullivan's island, as the commodore says; the enemy's ships had all gone off to the eastward, and southward and eastward. It was useless to pursue with our inferior speed,—and they very wisely declined fighting iron-clads with wooden ships. The enemy's ships went off to the southward and eastward, and there they remained, hull down, for the remainder of the forenoon; their masts could be seen by using the spyglass. The *Housatonic* and some others some time during the afternoon took up a position more to the eastward, but remained a long distance off.

Soon after we anchored some of the foreign consuls were brought off to show them that the blockade had been raised, and General Beauregard and Commodore Ingraham issued a proclamation to that effect, I thought the "proclamation" ill-advised. The fact is that during the entire war the southern people attached too much importance to the recognition of the Confederacy by the English Government. Many thought that a recognition amounted to a declaration of war against the United States, and that England and France would become our allies. Entirely too much sentiment was wasted on this subject....

At 4 PM we got underweigh and returned to Charleston by the Beach channel, and were honored with salutes from Forts Moultrie, Beauregard and Sumter, and the acclamations of the citizens of Charleston: but I candidly confess I did not participate in the general joy. I thought we had not accomplished as much as we had a right to expect. As we entered the harbor, the Federal vessels closed in towards their old stations and resumed the blockade. It would not have been prudent for us to remain outside the bar during the night, as in case of a blow the vessels would have foundered. As to the proclamation in regard to the blockade being broken, I looked upon it as all bosh. No vessels went out or came in during the day, except our own river boats. Our only chance of any great success lay in a surprise under cover of the night. After ramming the *Mercedita*, we should have remained a little outside and near her with the *Chicora*; then, as the enemy's vessels came up in succession, we should have captured them: which it is reasonable to suppose we would have done. When a vessel struck, she should have been directed to run in and anchor near the *Mercedita*. By adopting this plan I think we would have retained the *Mercedita* and *Keystone State*, and probably have captured in addition the *Quaker City, Augusta* and *Memphis*. By that time daylight would have revealed to the other ships "what manner of men" they were contending against, and the fight would have ended. We could have sent our prizes in by the main ship channel, and returned ourselves in the afternoon by either channel. I am constrained to say that this was a badly managed affair on our part, and we did not make the best use of our opportunity.

2. The CSS *David*

The account of Confederate torpedo activity at Charleston during the war is a fascinating story. It was here, amid the strangulation of the blockade and the determination of the Southern forces to break that blockade, that the concept of underwater warfare grew to fruition. Long before the advent of the self-guided, powered torpedoes that were used in World War I and World War II, the Confederates took their torpedoes to the side of the enemy by mounting them on a long pole attached to a row-boat or steamer. The torpedo was then carried into the side of the enemy's vessel by the torpedo boat itself with about as mach danger to the attacker as it was to the enemy. The final development of this method was the sleek and fast steam-driven "David" type torpedo boats built at Charleston.

Commander William T. Glassell was a leading proponent of this method of attack. Although he was born in Virginia, he was appointed from the state of Alabama when he entered Confederate service. Glassell had served as a lieutenant in the U. S. Navy and was in China when the Southern states seceded. In the following account submitted to the *Southern Historical Society Papers*, he explains what happened to him when he returned to the United States, and then proceeds to describe his torpedo activities at Charleston. (Scharf, *History of the Confederate States Navy*, p. 754.) [RTC]

"Reminiscences of Torpedo Service in Charleston Harbor" by Commander William T. Glassell, CSN

Southern Historical Society Papers, 1877, Volume IV, p. 225–235.

[The following interesting paper was sent us through the Secretary of the South Carolina Historical Society. In a note accompanying the paper the author says that while he has written from memory, and without official reports to refer to, he believes he has given the facts in the order of their occurrence.]

I had served, I believe faithfully, as a lieutenant in the United States navy, and had returned from China on the United States steamer *Hartford* to Philadelphia, some time in 1862, after the battles of Manassas and Ball's Bluff had been fought. I was informed that I must now take a new oath of allegiance or be sent immediately to Fort Warren. I refused to take this oath, on the ground that it was inconsistent with one I had already taken to support the Constitution of the United States. I was kept in Fort Warren about eight months, and then exchanged as a prisoner of war, on the banks of the James river. Being actually placed in the ranks of the Confederate States, I should think that even Mr. President Hayes would now acknowledge that it was my right, if not my duty, to act the part of a belligerent.

A lieutenant's commission in the Confederate States navy was conferred on me, with orders to report for duty on the iron-clad *Chicora* at Charleston. My duties were those of a deck officer, and I had charge of the first division.

On the occasion of the attack upon the blockading squadron (making the attack at night), if I could have had any influence, we should not have fired a gun, but trusted to the effect of iron rams at full speed. It was thought, though, by older and perhaps wiser officers, that this would have been at the risk of sinking our iron-clads together with the vessels of the enemy. I have ever believed there was no such danger to be apprehended; and if there was, we had better have encountered it, than to have made the fruitless attempt which we did, only frightening the enemy and putting them on their guard for the future.

It was my part, on that memorable morning, to aim and fire one effective shell into the *Keystone State* while running down to attack us, which (according to Captain LeRoy's report), killing twenty-one men and severely wounding fifteen, caused him to haul down his flag in token of surrender.

The enemy now kept at a respectful distance while preparing their iron-clad vessels to sail up more closely. Our Navy Department continued slowly to construct more of these rams, all on the same general plan, fit for little else than harbor defense. The resources of the United States being such that they could build ten iron-clads to our one, and of a superior class almost invulnerable to shot or shell, I had but little faith in the measures we were taking for defence.

Mr. Frank Lee, of the Engineers, was employed constructing torpedoes to be placed in the harbor, and called my attention to the subject. It appeared to me that this might be made an effective weapon to use offensively against the powerful vessels now being built. An old hulk was secured and Major Lee made the first experiment, as follows: A torpedo made of copper, and containing thirty or forty pounds of gunpowder, having a sensitive fuze, was attached by means of a socket to a long pine pole. To this weights were attached, and it was suspended horizontally beneath a row-boat, by cords from the bow and stern—the torpedo projecting eight or ten feet ahead of the boat, and six or seven feet below the surface. The boat was then drawn towards the hulk till the torpedo came in contact with it and exploded. The result was the immediate destruction of the old vessel and no damage to the boat.

I was now convinced that powerful engines of war could be brought into play against iron-clad ships. I believed it should be our policy to take immediate steps for the construction of a large number of small boats suitable for torpedo service, and make simultaneous attacks, if possible, before the enemy should know what we were about. The result of this experiment was represented to Commodore Ingraham. I offered all the arguments I could in favor of my pet hobby. Forty boats with small engines for this service, carrying a shield of boiler-iron to protect a man at the helm from rifle-balls, might have been constructed secretly at one-half the cost of a clumsy iron-clad. The Commodore did not believe in what he called "new-fangled notions." I retired from his presence with a feeling of grief, and almost desperation, but resolved to prove at least that I was in earnest. I got row-boats from my friend, Mr. George A. Trenholm, and at his expense equipped them with torpedoes for a practical experiment against the blockading vessels at anchor off the bar.

Commodore Ingraham then refused to let me have the officers or men who had volunteered for the expedition, saying that my rank and age did not entitle me to command more than one boat. I was allowed, some time after this, to go out alone with one of these boats and a crew of six men, to attack the United States ship *Powhatan* with a fifty-pound torpedo of rifle-powder attached to the end of a long pole, suspended by wires from the bow and stern, beneath the keel of the boat, and projecting eight or ten feet ahead, and seven feet below the surface.

I started out with ebb-tide in search of a victim. I approached the ship about 1 o'clock.

The young moon had gone down, and every thing seemed favorable, the stars shining over head and sea smooth and calm. The bow of the ship was towards us and the ebb-tide still running out. I did not expect to reach the vessel without being discovered, but my intention was, no matter what they might say or do, not to be stopped until our torpedo came in contact with the ship. My men were instructed accordingly. I did hope the enemy would not be alarmed by the approach of such a small boat so far out at sea, and that we should be ordered to come alongside. In this I was disappointed. When they discovered us, two or three hundred yard distant from the port bow, we were hailed and immediately ordered to stop and not come nearer. To their question, "What boat is that?" and numerous others, I gave evasive and stupid answers; and notwithstanding repeated orders to stop, and threats to fire on us, I told them I was coming on board as fast as I could, and whispered to my men to pull with all their might. I trusted they would be too merciful to fire on such a stupid set of idiots as they must have taken us to be.

Commander William T. Glassell (courtesy of Orange Public Library).

My men did pull splendidly, and I was aiming to strike the enemy on the port-side, just below the gangway. They continued to threaten and to order us to lay in our oars; but I had no idea of doing so, as we were not within forty feet of the intended victim. I felt confident of success, when one of my trusted men, from terror or treason, suddenly backed his oar and stopped the boat's headway. This caused the others to give up apparently in despair. In this condition we drifted with the tide past the ship's stern, while the officer of the deck, continuing to ply me with embarrassing questions, gave order to lower a ship's boat to go for us.

The man who backed his oar had now thrown his pistol over-board, and reached to get that of the man next to him for the same purpose. A number of men, by this time, were on deck with rifles in hand. The torpedo was now an encumbrance to retard the movements of my boat.

I never was rash, or disposed to risk my life, or that of others, without large compensation from the enemy. But to surrender thus would not do. Resolving not to be taken alive till somebody at least should be hurt, I drew a revolver and whispered to the men at the bow and stern to cut loose the torpedo.

This being quickly done, they were directed quietly to get the oars in position and pull away with all their strength. They did so. I expected a parting volley from the deck of the ship, and judging from the speed with which the little boat traveled, you would have thought we were trying to outrun the bullets which might follow us. No shot was fired. I am not certain whether their boat pursued us or not. We were soon out of sight and beyond their reach; and I suppose the captain and officers of the *Powhatan* never have known how near they came to having the honor of being the first ship ever blown up a by a torpedo boat.

I do not think this failure was from any or want of proper precaution of mine. The man who backed his oar and stopped the boat at the critical moment declared afterwards that he had been terrified so that he knew not what he was doing. He seemed to be ashamed of his conduct, and wished to go with me into any danger. His name was James Murphy, and he afterwards deserted to the enemy by swimming off to a vessel at anchor in the Edisto River.

I think the enemy must have received some kind from spies, creating a suspicion of torpedoes, before I made this attempt. I got back to Charleston after daylight next morning, with only the loss of one torpedo, and convinced that steam was the only reliable motive power.

Commodore Tucker having been ordered to command the naval forces at Charleston, torpedoes were fitted to the bows of iron-clad rams for use should the monitors enter the harbor.

My esteemed friend, Mr. Theodore Stoney, of Charleston, took measures for the construction of the little cigar-boat *David* at private express; and about this time I was ordered off to Wilmington as executive officer to attend to the equipment of the iron-clad *North Carolina*. She drew so much water it would have been impossible to get her over the bar, and consequently was only fit for harbor defence.

In the meantime, the United States fleet, monitors and *Ironside*, crossed the bar at Charleston and took their comfortable positions protecting the army on Morris Island, and occasionally bombarding Fort Sumter.

The *North Carolina* being finished, was anchored near Fort Fisher. No formidable enemy was in sight, except the United States steamer *Minnesota*, and she knowing that we could not get out, had taken a safe position at anchor beyond the bar to guard one entrance to the harbor. I made up my mind to destroy that ship or make a small sacrifice in the attempt. Accordingly, I set to work with all possible dispatch, preparing a little steam tug which had been placed under my control, with the intention of making an effort. I fitted a torpedo to her bow so that it could be lowered in the water or elevated at discretion.

I had selected eight or ten volunteers for this service, and would have taken with me one row-boat to save life in case of accident. My intention was to slip out after dark through the passage used by blockade-runners, and then to approach the big ship from seaward as suddenly and silently as possible on a dark night, making such answer to their hail and question as occasion might require, and perhaps burning a blue light for their benefit, but never stopping till my torpedo came in contact and my business was made known.

I had every thing ready for the experiment, and only waited for a suitable night, when orders came requiring me to take all the men from the *North Carolina* by railroad to Charleston immediately. An attack on that city was expected. I lost no time in obeying the order, and was informed, on arriving there, "my men were required to reinforce the crews of the gun-boats, but there was nothing in particular for me to do." In a few days, however, Mr. Theodore Stoney informed me that the little cigar boat built at his expense had been brought down by railroad, and that if I could do anything with her he would place her at my disposal On examination I determined to make a trial. She was yet in an unfinished state. Assistant-Engineer J. H. Tomb volunteered his service, and all the necessary machinery was soon fitted and got in working order, while Major Frank Lee gave me his zealous aid in fitting on a torpedo. James Stuart (alias Sullivan) volunteered to go as firemen, and afterwards the service of J. W. Cannon as pilot were secured. The boat was ballasted so as to float deeply in the water, and all above painted the most invisible color, (bluish.) The torpedo was made of copper, containing about one hundred pounds of rifle powder, and provided with four sensitive tubes of lead, containing explosive mixture; and this was carried by means of a hollow iron shaft projecting about fourteen feet ahead of the boat, and six or seven feet below the surface. I had also an armament on deck of four double-barrel shotguns, and as many navy revolvers; also, four cork life-preservers had been thrown on board, and made us feel safe.

Having tried the speed of my boat, and found it satisfactory, (six or seven knots an hour,) I got a necessary order from Commodore Tucker to attack the enemy at discretion, and also one from General Beauregard. And now came an order from Richmond, that I should proceed immediately back to rejoin the *North Carolina*, at Wilmington. This was too much! I never obeyed that order, but left Commodore Tucker to make my excuses to the Navy Department.

The 5th of October, 1863, a little after dark, we left Charleston wharf, and proceeded with the ebb-tide down the harbor. A light north wind was blowing, and the night was slightly hazy, but starlight, and the water was smooth. I desired to make the attack about the turn of the tide, and this ought to have been just after nine o'clock, but the north wind made it run out a little longer.

We passed Fort Sumter and beyond the line of picket-boats without being discovered. Silently steaming along just inside the bar, I had a good opportunity to reconnoiter the whole fleet of the enemy at anchor between me and the camp-fires on Morris' Island.

Perhaps I was mistaken, but it did occur to me that if we had then, instead of only one, just ten or twelve torpedoes, to make a simultaneous attack on all the iron-clads, and this quickly followed by the egress of our rams, not only might this grand fleet have been destroyed, but the 20,000 troops on Morris' Island been left at our mercy. Quietly maneuvering and observing the enemy, I was half an hour more waiting on time and tide. The music of drum and fife had just ceased, and the nine o'clock gun had been fired from the admiral's ship, as a signal for all unnecessary lights to be extinguished and for the men not on watch to retire for sleep. I thought the proper time for attack had arrived.

The admiral's ship, *New Ironsides*, (the most powerful vessel in the world,) lay in the midst of the fleet, her starboard side presented to my view. I determined to pay her the highest compliment. I had been informed, through prisoners lately captured from the fleet, that they were expecting an attack from torpedo boats, and were prepared for it. I could, therefore, hardly expect to accomplish my object without encountering some danger from riflemen, and perhaps a discharge of grape or canister from the howitzers.

My guns were loaded with buckshot. I knew that if the officer of the deck could be disabled to begin with, it would cause them some confusion and increase our chance for escape, so I determined that if the occasion offered, I would commence by firing the first shot. Accordingly, having on a full head of steam, I took charge of the helm, it being so arranged that I could sit on deck and work the wheel with my feet. Then directing the engineer and firemen to keep below and give me all the speed possible, I gave a double-barrel gun to the pilot, with instructions not to fire until I should do so, and steered directly for the monitor. I intended to strike her just under the gang-way, but the tide still running out, carried us to a point nearer the quarter. Thus we rapidly approached the enemy. When within about 300 yards of her a sentinel hailed us: Boat ahoy! boat ahoy! repeating the hail several times very rapidly. We were coming towards them with all speed, and I made no answer, but cocked both barrels of my gun. The officer of the deck next made his appearance, and loudly demanded, "What boat is that?" Being now within forty yards of the ship, and plenty of headway to carry us on, I thought it about time the fight should commence, and fired my gun. The officer of the deck fell back mortally wounded (poor fellow), and I ordered the engine stopped. The next moment the torpedo struck the vessel and exploded. What amount of directed damage the enemy received I will not attempt to say. My little boat plunged violently, and a large body of water which had been thrown up descended upon her deck, and down the smoke-stack and hatchway.

I immediately gave orders to reverse the engine and back off. Mr. Tomb informed me then that the fires were put out, and something had become jammed in the machinery so that it would not move. What could be done in this situation? In the mean time, the enemy recovering from the shock, beat to quarters, and general alarm spread through the fleet. I told my men I thought our only chance to escape was by swimming, and I think I told Mr. Tomb to cut the water-pipes, and let the boat sink.

Then taking one of the cork floats, I got into the water and swam off as fast as I could.

The enemy, in no amiable mood, poured down upon the bubbling water a hailstorm of rifle and pistol shots from the deck of the Ironsides, and from the nearest monitor. Sometimes they struck very close to my head, but swimming for life, I soon disappeared from their sight, and found myself all alone in the water. I hoped that, with the assistance of flood-tide, I might be able to reach Fort Sumter, but a north wind was against me, and after I had been in the water more than an hour, I became numb with cold, and was nearly exhausted. Just then the boat of a transport schooner picked me up, and found, to their surprise, that they had captured a rebel.

The captain of this schooner made me as comfortable as possible that night with whiskey and blankets, for which I sincerely thanked him. I was handed over next morning to the mercy of Admiral Dahlgren. He ordered me to be transferred to the guard-ship *Ottowa*, lying outside the rest of the fleet. Upon reaching the quarter-deck of this vessel, I was met and recognized by her Commander, William D. Whiting. He was an honorable gentleman and high-toned officer. I was informed that his orders were to have me put in irons, and if obstreperous, in double irons. I smiled, and told him his duty was to obey orders, and mine to adapt myself to circumstances—I could see no occasion to be obstreperous.

I think Captain Whiting, felt mortified at being obliged thus to treat an old brother officer, whom he knew could only have been actuated by a sense of patriotic duty in making the attack which caused him to fall into his power as a prisoner of war. At any rate, he proceeded immediately to see the admiral, and upon his return I was released, on giving my parole not to attempt an escape from the vessel. His kindness, and the gentlemanly courtesy with which I was treated by other officers of the old navy, I shall ever remember most gratefully. I learned that my fireman had been found hanging on to the rudder-chains of the Ironsides and taken on board. I had every reason to believe that the other two, Mr. Tomb and Mr. Cannon, had been shot or drowned, until I heard of their safe arrival in Charleston.

I was retained as a prisoner in Fort La Fayette and Fort Warren for more than a year, and learned while there that I had been promoted for what was called "gallant and meritorious service."

What all the consequences of this torpedo attack upon the enemy were is not for me to say. It certainly awakened them to a sense of the dangers to which they had been exposed, and caused them to apprehend far greater difficulties and dangers than really existed should they attempt to enter the harbor with their fleet. It may have prevented Admiral Dahlgren from carrying out the intention he is said to have had of going in with twelve iron-clads on the arrival of his double-turreted monitor to destroy the city by a cross-fire from the two rivers. It certainly caused them to take many precautionary measures for protecting their vessels which had never before been thought of. Possibly it shook the nerve of a brave admiral and deprived him of the glory of laying low the city of Charleston. It was said by officers of the navy that the iron-clad vessels of that fleet were immediately enveloped like women in hoop-skirt petticoats of netting, to lay in idle admiration of themselves for many months. The *Ironsides* went into dry-dock for repairs.

The attack also suggested to officers of the United States Navy that this was a game which both sides could play at, and Lieutenant Cushing bravely availed himself of it. I congratulate him for the eclat and promotion he obtained thereby. I do not remember the date of my exchange again as a prisoner of war, but it was only in time to witness the painful agonies and downfall of an exhausted people, and the surrender of a hopeless cause.

I was authorized to equip and command any number of torpedo boats, but it was now too late. I made efforts to do what I could at Charleston, till it became necessary to abandon that city. I then commanded the iron-clad *Fredericksburg* on James River, until ordered by Admiral Semmes to burn and blow her up when Richmond was evacuated. Leaving Richmond with the admiral, we now organized the First Naval Artillery Brigade, and I was in command of a regiment of sailors when informed that our noble old General, R. E. Lee, had capitulated. Our struggle was ended.

All that is now passed, and our duty remains to meet the necessities of the future. After the close of the war I was offered a command and high rank under a foreign flag. I declined the compliment and recommended my gallant old commander, Commodore J. R. Tucker, as one more worthy and competent than myself to fill a high position.

In conclusion let me say: I have never regretted that I acted in accordance with what appeared to be my duty. I was actuated by no motive of self-interest, and never entertained a feeling of hatred or personal enmity against those who were my honorable opponents. I have asked for no pardon, which might imply an acknowledgment that I had been either traitor or rebel. No amnesty has been extended to me.

Bear in mind, loyal reader, these facts: I had been absent nearly two years. No one could have lamented the beginning of the war more than I did. It had been in progress nearly six months when I came home from sea. I had taken no part in it, when on my arrival in Philadelphia, only because I could not truthfully swear that I felt no human sympathy for my own family and for the friends of my childhood, and that I was willing to shed their blood and desolate their homes; and because I would not take an oath that would have been a lie, I was denounced as a traitor, thrown into prison for eight months, and then exchanged as a prisoner of war.

I may have been a fool. I supposed or believed that the people of the south would never be conquered. I hardly hoped to live through the war. Though I had no intention of throwing my life away, I was willing to sacrifice it, if necessary, for the interests of a cause I believed to be just. I was more regardless of my own interests and those of my family than I should have been. A large portion even of my paper salary was never drawn by me. Nearly every thing I had in the world was lost—even the commission I had received for gallant and meritorious conduct, and I possess not even a token of esteem from those for whom I fought to leave, when I die, to those I love.

But the time has arrived when I think it my duty to grant pardon to the government for all injustice and injury I have received. I sincerely hope that harmony and prosperity may yet be restored to the United States of America.

3. The CSS *H. L. Hunley*

In the approaching winter of 1863, the harbor of Charleston, South Carolina, was a beehive of naval activity. Steamers, torpedo boats, and the ungainly, smoke-snorting ironclads of the Confederate navy were a common sight. On many evenings, those who braved the occasional exploding Federal artillery shells noticed a very strange looking craft in the harbor. It usually rested with its dark iron hull barely awash in the harbor waters. Toward sundown, eight men, one an officer, would clamber onto the craft and disappear below. Another officer, standing in an open hatchway, would cast off the lines and then he, too, would vanish within. Slowly, the strange craft would ease into the channel and begin to make its way out of the anchorage. No protruding sail or smokestack could be discerned; its upper surface was barely visible above the water. Two entrance hatches, one forward and one aft, were all that interrupted the sleek lines of the black silhouette. A small metal spar jutted from the upper part of the bow, and from it stout lines led into the water evidently carrying the load of something very heavy and sinister beneath the surface. Gently rising and falling with the swells of the outgoing tide, the mysterious vessel glided silently out toward the cold green waters of the Atlantic Ocean. Soon the cigar-shaped craft would be lost in the gathering darkness. Only the lapping of the swells against the pilings and the monotonous pace of the sentry broke the quietness of the night.

If all went well, early daylight would find the vessel back at the wharf where it would be rocking gently in the wake of passing boats. On two occasions, however, it had not returned (at least not by its own power). It had taken several days for divers to locate the sunken craft. When she was finally raised from the harbor floor and the hatches opened, a morbid and hellish sight greeted the curious. Her crew had died a frantic and terrifying death.

In spite of these failures, little did the few observers realize that they were historic witnesses to what would become the world's first successful submarine. Forerunner of all the great and fearsome undersea craft to come in a later century, this historic vessel was the Confederate submarine CSS *H. L. Hunley*. Built in Mobile, Alabama, and later shipped by rail to Charleston, the *Hunley* became the first underseas craft to actually sink an enemy warship.

One of the soldiers placed on detached duty in Mobile was a young sandy-bearded British-born mechanical engineer by the name of William H. Alexander. A lieutenant in the 21st Alabama Infantry Regiment, Alexander had enlisted in Company B, commanded by Captain Charles Gage, at the beginning of hostilities. After sustaining heavy causalities at the Battle of Shiloh, the 21st Alabama was sent to Mobile where Alexander was ordered to the machine shop owned by Thomas Park and Thomas B. Lyons.

Alexander was instrumental in the construction and operation of both the *American Diver* and the *H. L. Hunley*. He served as the second officer on the latter, but fortunately for posterity, was called away prior to the *Hunley*'s last mission. As a consequence, his life was spared, and he wrote the following account about the *Hunley* after the war. (Campbell, *Gray Thunder, Exploits of the Confederate States Navy*, pp. 156–169.)

Recent excavations of the raised vessel have revealed some errors and omissions in Alexander's essay of 1902, but his article for the *Southern Historical Society Papers* still gives us a valuable insight into the construction and operation of the world's first successful submarine. [RTC]

"The Work of Submarine Boats" by Lt. William H. Alexander, CSA

Southern Historical Society Papers, Volume XXX, 1902, pp. 164–174

Visitors to the Spanish Fort, says the *New Orleans Picayune*, may still see, half submerged in the weeds and flowers growing on the bank of bayou St. John, a rusty vessel of curious shape. It is built of iron, about twenty feet long, and besides a propeller at the stern, is adorned on either side by strangely-shaped board metal fins. This boat is, or ought to be, one of the most interesting relics of the Civil war. It was, as stated in the accompanying narrative, built during the war by Captain Hunley as a submarine torpedo-boat, and though never used in battle is the prototype of the vessel which subsequently destroyed the Federal cruiser *Housatonic*. Although within recent years a great deal has been written and stated about submarine war ships, the fact remains that these Confederate boats are the only ones which have ever successfully endured the test of actual combat. The narrative printed herewith is the first complete account of the building of these remarkable craft and of the experiments which were made with them.

The Narrative

Having often read what purported to be a history of the Confederate submarine torpedo-boat *Hunley* and its operations, the accounts in every instance containing much of error, I have decided to write out the facts in regard to this boat and her career.

Shortly before the capture of New Orleans by the United States troops, Captain Hunley (not Hunley), Captain James McClintock and Baxter Watson were engaged in building a submarine torpedo-boat in the New basin of that city. The city falling into the hands of the Federals before it was completed, the boat was sunk, and these gentlemen came to Mobile. They reported, with their plans, to the Confederate authorities here, who ordered the boat to be built in the machine shops of Parks & Lyons, Mobile, Ala.

The writer was a member of Company B, State Artillery, Twenty-first Alabama Regiment, Captain Charles Gage, and was detailed to do government work in these shops.

Messrs. Hunley, McClintock and Watson were introduced to me by Parks & Lyons, who gave me orders to carry out their plans as far as possible.

We built an iron boat. The cross section was oblong, about 25 feet long, tapering at each end, 5 feet wide, and 6 feet deep. It was towed off fort Morgan, intending to man it there and attack the blockading fleet outside, but the weather was rough, and with a heavy sea the boat became unmanageable and finally sank, but no lives were lost.

We decided to build another boat, and for this purpose took a cylinder boiler which we had on hand, 48 inches in diameter and 25 feet long (all dimensions are from memory).

We cut this boiler in two, longitudinally, and inserted two 12-inch boiler-iron strips in her sides; lengthened her by one tapering course fore and aft, to which were attached bow and stern castings, making the boat about 30 feet long, 4 feet wide, and 5 feet deep. A longitudinal strip 12 inches wide was riveted the full length on top. At each end a bulkhead was riveted across to form water-ballast tanks (unfortunately these were left open on top); they were used in raising and sinking the boat. In addition to these water tanks the boat was ballasted by flat castings, made to fit the outside bottom of the shell and fastened thereto by "Tee" headed bolts passing trough stuffing boxes inside the boat, the inside end of bolt squared to fit a wrench, that the bolts might be turned and the ballast dropped, should the necessity arise.

In connection with each of the water tanks there was a sea-cock open to the sea to supply the tank for sinking; also a force pump to eject the water from the tanks in the sea for raising the boat to the surface. There was also a bilge connection to the pump. A mercury gauge, open to the sea, was attached to the shell near the forward of the end of the propeller shaft. On each end of this shaft, outside of the boat, castings, or later fins, five feet long and eight inches wide, were secured. This shaft was operated by a lever amidships, and by raising or lowering the ends of these fins, operated as the fins of a fish, changing the depth of the boat below the surface at will, without disturbing the water level in the ballast tanks.

The rudder was operated by a wheel, [since discovered as a lever, RTC] and levers connected to rods passing through stuffing boxes in the stern castings, and operated by the captain or pilot forward. An adjusted compass was placed in front of the forward tank. The boat was operated by manual power, with an ordinary propeller. On the propeller shaft there were formed eight cranks at different angles; the shaft was supported by brackets on the starboard side, the men sitting on the port side turning on the cranks. The propeller shaft and cranks took up so much room that it was very difficult to pass fore and aft, and when the men were in their places this was next to impossible. In operation, one half of the crew had to pass through the fore hatch, the other through the after hatchway. The propeller revolved in a wrought iron ring or band, to guard against a line being thrown in to foul it. There were two hatchways—one fore and one aft—16 inches by 12, with a combing 8 inches high. These hatches had hinged covers with rubber gasket, and were bolted from the inside. In the sides and ends of these combings glasses were inserted to sight from. There was an opening made in the top of the boat for an air box, a casting with a close top 12 by 18 by 4 inches, made to carry a hollow shaft. This shaft passed through stuffing boxes. On each end was an elbow with a 4-foot length of 1½ inch pipe, and keyed to the hollow shaft; on the inside was a lever with a stop-cock to admit air.

The torpedo was a copper cylinder holding a charge of ninety pounds of explosive, with percussion and friction primer mechanism, set off by flaring triggers. It was originally intended to float the torpedo on the surface of the water, the boat to dive under the vessel to be attacked, towing the torpedo with a line 200 feet after her, one of the triggers to touch the vessel and explode the torpedo, and in the experiments made in the smooth water of Mobile river on some old flatboats these plans operated successfully, but in rough water the torpedo was continually coming too near the rough boat. We then rigged a yellow-pine boom, 22 feet long and tapering; this was attached to the bow, banded and guyed on each side. A socket on the torpedo secured it to the boom.

Two men experienced in handling the boat, and seven others composed the crew. The first officer steered and handled the boat forward, and the second attended to the after-tank and pumps and the air supply, all hands turning on the cranks except the first officer. There was just sufficient room for these two to stand in their places with their heads in the hatchways and take observations through the lights of the comings.

All Hands Aboard

All hands aboard and ready, they would fasten the hatch covers down tight, light a candle, then let the water in from the sea into the ballast tanks until the top of the shell was about three inches under water. This could be seen by the water lever showing through the glasses in the hatch combings. The seacocks were then closed and the boat put under way. The captain would then lower the lever and depress the forward end of the fins very slightly, noting on the mercury gauge the depth of the boat beneath the surface; then bring the fins to a level; the boat would remain and travel at that depth. To rise to a higher level in the water he would raise the lever and elevate the forward end of the fins, and the boat would rise to its original position in the water.

If the boat was not under way, in order to rise to the surface, it was necessary to start the pumps, and lighten the boat by ejecting the water from the tanks into the sea. In making a landing, the second officer would open his hatch cover, climb out and pass a line to shore. After the experience with the boats in Mobile bay the authorities decided that Charleston harbor, with the monitors and blockaders there would be a better field for this boat to operate in, and General Maury had her sent by rail to General Beauregard at Charleston, S. C. Lieutenant John Payne, Confederate States navy, then on duty at Charleston, S. C., volunteered with eight others of the navy to take the boat out. The crew were about ready to make their first attack; eight men and gotten aboard, when a swell swamped the boat, drowning the eight men in her. The boat was raised, Lieutenant Payne and eight others again volunteering. She was about ready to go out, when she was swamped the second time. Lieutenant Payne and two of the crew escaped, but six men were drowned in her.

General Beauregard, then turned the boat over to a volunteer crew from Mobile, known as the "Hunley and Parks crew." Captain Hunley and Thomas Parks (one of the best of men), of the firm of Parks & Lyons, in whose shop the boat had been built, were in charge, with Messrs. Brockbank, Patterson, McHugh, Marshall, White, Beard, and another, as the crew, and until the day this crew left Mobile it was understood that the writer of this was to be one of them, but on the eve of that day Mr. Parks prevailed on the writer to let him take his place. Nearly all the men had some experience in the boat before leaving Mobile, and were well qualified to operate her.

After the boat had been made ready again Captain Hunley practiced the crew diving and rising again on many occasions, until one evening, in the presence of a number of people on the wharf, she sank and remained sunk for some days, thus drowning her crew of nine men, or a total up to this time of three different crews, or twenty-three men.

Lieutenant George E. Dixon, like myself, was a mechanical engineer, and belonged to the same regiment, the Twenty-first Alabama. He had taken great interest in the boats while building, and during their operations in Mobile River, and would have been one of the "Hunley and Parks" crew had there been a vacancy. As soon as the news that the boat had been lost again was verified, we discussed the matter together and decided to offer our services to General Beauregard, to raise and operate the boat for the defense of Charleston harbor.

General Pierre G. T. Beauregard (Library of Congress).

Our offer was accepted and we were ordered to report to General Jordan, chief of staff. The boat was raised, and the bodies were buried in the cemetery at Charleston. A monument with suitable inscription marks the spot. There had been much speculation as to the cause of the loss of the boat, for there could have been no swamping as in the other two cases, but the position in which the boat was found on the bottom of the river, the condition of the apparatus discovered after it was raised and pumped out, and the position of the bodies in the boat, furnished a full explanation for her loss. The boat, when found, was lying on the bottom at an angle of about 35 degrees, the bow deep in the mud. The holding-down bolts of each cover had been removed. When the hatch covers were lifted considerable air and gas escaped. Captain Hunley's body was forward, with his head in the forward hatchway, his right hand on top of his head (he had been trying, it would seem, to raise the hatch cover). In his left hand was a candle that had never been lighted, the sea cock on the forward end, or *Hunley's* ballast tank, was wide open, the cock-wrench not on the plug, but lying on the bottom of the boat. Mr. Parks' body was found with his head in the after hatchway, his right hand above his head. He also had been trying to raise his hatch cover, but the pressure was too great. The sea cock to his tank was nearly empty. The other bodies were floating in the water. Hunley and Parks were undoubtedly asphyxiated, the others drowned. The bolts that held the iron keel ballast had been partially turned, but not sufficient to release it.

Anxious Moments

In the light of these conditions, we can easily depict before our minds, and almost as readily explain, what took place in the boat during the moments immediately following its submergence. Captain Hunley's practice with the boat had made him quite familiar and expert in handling her, and this familiarity produced at this time forgetfulness. It was found in practice to be easier on the crew to come to the surface by giving the pumps a few strokes and ejecting some of the water ballast, than by the momentum of the boat operating on the elevated fins. At this time the boat was under way, lighted through the dead-lights in the hatch-ways. He partly turned the fins to go down, but thought, no doubt, that he needed more ballast and opened his sea cock. Immediately the boat was in total darkness. he then undertook to light the candle. While trying to do this the tank quickly flooded, and under great pressure the boat sank very fast and soon overflowed, and the first intimation they would have of anything being wrong was the water rising fast, but noiselessly, about their feet in the bottom on the boat. They tried to release the iron keel ballast, but did not turn the keys quite far enough, therefore failed.

The water soon forced the air to the top of the boat and into the hatchways, where Captains Hunley and Parks were found. Parks had pumped his ballast tank dry, and no doubt Captain Hunley had exhausted himself on his pump, but the had forgotten that he had not closed his sea-cock.

We soon had the boat refitted and in good shape, reported to General Jordan, chief of staff, that the boat was ready again for service, and asked for a crew. After many refusals and much dissuasion General Beauregard finally assented to our going aboard the Confederate States navy receiving ship *Indian Chief*, then lying in the river, and secure volunteers for a crew, strictly enjoining upon us, however, that a full history of the boat in the past, of its having been lost three times and drowning twenty-three men in Charleston, and full explanation of the hazardous nature of the service required of them, was to be given to each man. This was done, a crew shipped, and after a little practice in the river we were ordered to moor the boat off Battery Marshall, on Sullivan's Island. Quarters were given us at Mount Pleasant, seven miles from Battery Marshall. On account of chain booms having been put around the *Ironsides* and monitors in Charleston harbor to keep us off these vessels, we had to turn our attention to the fleet outside. The nearest vessel, which we understood to be the United States frigate *Wabash*, was about twelve miles off, and she was out objective point from this time on.

In comparatively smooth water and light current the *Hunley* could make four miles an hour, but in rough water the speed was much slower. It was winter, therefore necessary that we go out with the ebb and come in the with the flood tide, a fair wind, and dark moon. This latter was essential to our success, as our experience had fully demonstrated the necessity of occasionally coming to the surface, slightly lifting the hatch-cover, and letting in a little air. On several occasions we came to the surface for air, opened the cover, and heard the men in the Federal picket boats talking and singing. Our daily routine, whenever possible, was about as follows:

Leave Mount Pleasant about 1 PM, walk seven miles to Battery Marshall on the beach (this exposed us to fire, but it was the best walking), take the boat our and practice the crew for two hours in the Back bay. Dixon and myself would then stretch out on the beach with the compass between us and get the bearings of the nearest vessel as she took her position for the night; ship up the torpedo on the boom, and, when dark, go out, steering for the vessel, proceed until the condition of the men, sea, tide, wind, moon, and daylight compelled out return to the dock; unship the torpedo, put it under guard at Battery Marshall, walk back to quarters at Mount Pleasant, and cook breakfast.

Terrible Difficulties

During the months of November and December, 1863, through January and the early part of February, 1864, the wind held contrary, making it difficult, with our limited power, to make much headway. During this time we went out on an average of four nights a week, but on account of the weather, and considering the physical condition of the men to propel the boat back again, often, after going out six or seven miles, we would have to return. This we always found a task, and many times it taxed our utmost exertions to keep from drifting out to sea, daylight often breaking while we were yet in range. This experience, also our desire to know, in case we struck a vessel (circumstances required our keeping below the surface), suggested that while in safe water we make the experiment to find out how long it was possible to stay under water without coming to the surface for air and not injure the crew.

It was agreed by all hands, to sink and let the boat rest on the bottom, in the Back bay, off Battery Marshall, each man to make equal physical exertion in turning the propeller. It was also agreed that if any one in the boat felt that he must come to the surface for air, and he gave the word "up," we would at once bring the boat to the surface.

It was usual, when practicing in the bay, that the banks would be lined with soldiers. One evening, after alternately diving and rising many times, Dixon and myself and several of the crew compared watches, noted the time and sank for the test. In twenty-five minutes after I had closed the after manhead and excluded the outer air the candle would not burn. Dixon forward and myself aft, turned on the propeller cranks as hard as we could. In comparing our individual experience afterwards, the experience of one was found to have been the experience of all. Each man had determined that he would not be the first to say "Up." Not a word was said, except the occasional, "How is it," between Dixon and myself, until it was as the voice of one man, the word "up" came from all nine. We started the pumps, but I soon realized that my pump was not throwing. From experience I guessed the cause of the failure, took off the cap of the pump, lifted the valve, and drew out some seaweed that had choked it.

During the time it took to do this the boat was considerably by the stern. Thick darkness prevailed. All hands had already endured what they thought was the utmost limit. Some of the crew almost lost control of themselves. It was a terrible few minutes, "better imagined than described." We soon had the boat to the surface and the manhead opened. Fresh air! What an experience! Well, the sun was shining when we went down, the beach lined with soldiers. It was now quite dark, with one solitary soldier gazing on the spot where he had seen the boat until he saw me standing on the hatch coming, calling to him to stand by to take the line. A light was struck and the time taken. We had been on the bottom two hours and thirty-five minutes. The candles ceased to burn in twenty-five minutes after we went down, showing that we had remained under water two hours and ten minutes after the candle went out.

The soldier informed us that we had been given up for lost, that a message had been sent to General Beauregard at Charleston that the torpedo boat had been lost that evening off Battery Marshall with all hands.

We got back to the quarters at Mount Pleasant that night, went over early next morning to the city (Charleston) and reported to General Beauregard the facts of the affair. They were all glad to see us.

After making a full report of our experience, General Rains, of General Beauregard's staff, who was present, expressed some doubt of our having stayed under water two hours and ten minutes after the candle went out. Not that any of us wanted to go through the same experience again, but we did our best to get him to come over to Sullivan's Island and witness a demonstration of the fact, but without avail. We continued to go out as often as the weather permitted, hoping against hope, each time taking greater risks of getting back. On the last of January we interviewed the Charleston pilots again, and they gave it as their opinion that the wind would hold in the same quarter for several weeks.

On February 5, 1864, I received orders to report in Charleston to General Jordan, chief of staff, who gave me transportation and orders to report at Mobile, to build a breech loading repeating gun. This was a terrible blow, both to Dixon and myself, after we had gone through so much together. General Jordan told Dixon he would get two men to take my place from the German artillery, but that I was wanted in Mobile. It was thought best not to tell the crew that I was to leave them. I left Charleston that night and reached Mobile in due course. I received from Dixon two notes shortly after reaching Mobile, one stating that the wind still held in the same quarter, etc., the other telling the regrets of the crew at my leaving and their feelings towards me; also that he expected to get men from the artillery to make my place. These notes, together with my passes, etc., are before me as I write. What mingled reminiscences they bring!

Two Volunteers

Soon after this I received a note from Captain Dixon, saying that he had succeeded in getting two volunteers from the German artillery, that for two days the wind had changed to fair, and he intended to try and get out that night. Next came the news that on February 17 the submarine torpedo boat *Hunley* had sunk the United States sloop-of-war *Housatonic* outside the bar off Charleston, S. C. As I read I cried out with disappointment that I was not there. Soon I noted that there was no mention of the whereabouts of the torpedo boat. I wired General Jordan daily for several days, but each time came the answer, "No news of the torpedo boat." After much thought, I concluded that Dixon had been unable to work his way back against wind and tide, and had been carried out to sea. I held this opinion until I read the account of the sinking of the *Housatonic*, by an officer of that vessel, published in the Army and Navy Journal, and afterwards the finding of the torpedo boat on the bottom with the wreck of the *Housatonic*. The plan was to take the bearings of the ships as they took position for the night, steer for one of them, keeping about six feet under water, coming occasionally to the surface for air and observation, and when nearing the vessel, come to the surface for final observation before striking her, which was to be done under her counter, if possible.

The account of the sinking of the *Housatonic* by the submarine torpedo boat, as given in the Army and Navy Journal, by one of the officers of that vessel, says: "It occurred February 17, 1864, at 8:45 PM, about two and a half miles off Charleston bar. It was moonlight, with little wind, or sea. The lookout observed something moving in the water, the chain was slipped, and the engines backed when the crash came, the ship sinking in three minutes after being struck."

After the close of the war, the government divers working on the wreck of the *Housatonic*, discovered the torpedo boat with the wreck [this has since turned out to be untrue. RTC]. With this data the explanation of her loss is easy. The *Housatonic* was a new vessel on the station, and anchored closer in than the *Wabash* and others. On this night the wind had lulled, with but little sea on, and although it was moonlight, Dixon, who had been waiting so long for a change of wind, took the risk of the moonlight and went out. The lookout on the ship saw him when he came to the surface for his final observation before striking her. He, of course, not knowing that the ship had slipped her chain and was backing down upon him, then sank the boat a few feet, steered for the stern of the ship and struck. The momentum of the two vessels brought them together unexpectedly. The stern of the ship was blown off entirely. The momentum carried the torpedo boat into the wreck. Dixon and his men, unable to extricate themselves, sinking with it.

W. A. ALEXANDER.
Mobile, Ala., June, 1902.

IV

Savannah, Georgia

1. The CSS *Atlanta*

The ironclad *Atlanta* began life as the *Fingal*, a merchant steamship built in Scotland in 1861. In November of that year, Commander James D. Bulloch ran the blockade off Savannah with the *Fingal* containing a cargo of badly needed weapons and military supplies for the Confederate armies. After unloading this valuable cargo, several attempts were made to leave the port, but Union forces had closed the exits from Savannah, preventing the *Fingal*'s further use as a blockade runner. The steamer was then purchased by the Confederate government, and the brothers Nelson and Asa F. Tift were contracted with to convert her into an ironclad. Commissioned as the CSS *Atlanta*, she made her first appearance as a Confederate warship in mid–1862.

In the spring of 1863, Commander William A. Webb was sent to Savannah to take command. Webb had great confidence in the ship and he was determined "to do something" with her. Two efforts to attack Federal warships that were blockading the coast and rivers leading to Savannah were made. The first, in early 1863, was thwarted by the failure of a steam valve which caused the engine to immediately shut down. A new valve had to be manufactured in Columbus, and that took two weeks. On June 15, 1863, Webb tried again, targeting the blockaders in Wassau Sound. There, on June 17, the Atlanta encountered the USS *Nahant* and the USS *Weehawken*. The *Atlanta*, unfortunately for Webb, ran aground, and unable to bring her guns to bear in the ensuing brief battle, was overwhelmed by the *Weehawken*'s superior firepower and forced to surrender.

Commander Webb, along with his crew, was taken prisoner and sent to Fort Warren where he was confined until September 24, 1864. After his parole and return to the Confederacy, he wrote the following report on the loss of the *Atlanta*. (Melton, "First and Last Cruise of the CSS *Atlanta*," pp. 4–9, 44–46.) [RTC]

Official Report of
Commander William A. Webb, CSN

Official Records Navy, Series I, volume XIV, pp. 290–292

RICHMOND, VA., *October 19, 1864*

SIR: I most respectfully submit the following report of the C. S. S. *Atlanta's* movements and subsequent capture:

On the evening of June 15, 1863, at 6 PM, I got underway and left Thunderbolt, Wassaw [Wilmington] River, to save the tide which enabled the ship to go over the lower obstructions. At 8 PM I came to anchor and was occupied the entire night coaling. On the evening of the 16th about dark, I proceeded down the river to a point of land which would place me [with]in 5 or 6 miles of the monitors, at the same time concealing the ship from their view, ready to move on them at early dawn the next morning.

At 3:30 AM on the 17th, the tide then being a quarter flood, and everything favorable, I got underway with the hopes of surprising the enemy. They made no move indicating a knowledge of my approach until I was within a mile or a mile and a half, steering for them under full steam. When we reached within three-fourths of a mile of them the *Atlanta* touched the bottom. I immediately informed the pilots of the fact, and ordered the engines to be backed, but it was fully fifteen minutes before she was in motion, though the tide was rising fast. As soon as the ship was well afloat, I ordered the engines to go ahead, with the hopes of turning her more into the channel, but she could not obey her helm, from the fact of the flood tide being on her starboard bow, and her bottom so near the ground. She was consequently forced upon the bank again. During this time the U. S. monitor *Weehawken*, being in motion and making for us, I ordered Lieutenant Barbot to open fire on her, thinking this would arrest her course and cause her to engage at the distance then between us; but on she came, unheeding my fire. In the meantime the *Atlanta* floated again, still, however, refusing to mind her helm from the same cause as before stated, and was thus forced again on the bank.

Commander William A. Webb (Wikipedia Free Encyclopedia).

Whilst afloat, I was confident of success, as I felt confidence in my torpedo, which I knew would do its work to my entire satisfaction, should I but be able to touch the *Weehawken*, she then being but 200 yards off, steering for me.

Captain John Rodgers evidently knew the *Atlanta* was aground, as she had not approached him since he discovered her, and he held his fire up to this close range, I firing when I could obtain sight on him.

At this juncture the *Weehawken* fired simultaneously her XV and XI inch guns, the shot from the latter passing over me, but the shot from the XV-inch gun striking our shield on a line above the port shutter, nearly abreast the pilot house, driving the armor through, tearing away the woodwork inside 3 feet wide by the entire length of the shield, causing the solid shot in the racks and everything movable in the vicinity to be hurled across the deck with such force as to knock down, wound, and disable the entire gun's crew of the port broadside gun in charge of Lieutenant Thurston (Marine Corps) and also half of the crew at Lieutenant Barbot's bow gun, some men being injured more or less.

The next shot was from her XI-inch gun which struck her knuckles, not however breaking the iron, which is there but 2 inches, and doing no damage except starting the waterways.

The next and third shot striking us was from her XV-inch gun and struck the starboard side port shutter of Master Wragg's gun at a considerable angle (the *Weehawken* then being nearly on our quarter), breaking the shutter in half, ripping up the armor and throwing the fragments inside, and wounding and disabling for a time, half of the gun's crew.

The last shot fired was also a XV-inch, which struck the port corner of the pilot house, cutting the top off and starting the entire frame to its foundation, at the same time wounding two of the pilots very severely.

All this time we were hard and fast aground. The tide did not rise high enough for an hour and a half to float the ship, and seeing the effects of the *Weehawken's* shot, and the position she and the monitor *Nahant* had assumed on each quarter of the *Atlanta*, where my guns could not be brought to bear on them, to save life I was induced to surrender.

The action lasted from five minutes of 5 to half past 7 AM. I could only fire seven shots, and my aim was necessary very imperfect, owing to the want of lateral motion to my guns. The *Weehawken* fired six times.

I cannot speak too highly of the officers and crew under my command. They all displayed those qualities which are inherent in brave men, combining coolness with perfect obedience, though the majority of the crew were from the mountains of Georgia and had but a limited idea of a ship of war.

Accompanying this report I transmit the surgeon's report of casualties.

Hoping you will grant me a court of enquiry, to inquire into the circumstances attending the loss of the C. S. S. *Atlanta* at an early day,

I have the honor to be, yours, with great respect,

W.A. WEBB,
Commander, C.S. Navy.

Hon. S.R. MALLORY,
Secretary Navy, Confederate States of America.

2. The USS *Water Witch*

In late 1863, Midshipmen Hubbard T. Minor and John D. Trimble were rotated from the Naval School on the *Patrick Henry* to the Savannah Squadron where they were assigned to the ironclad CSS *Savannah*. For some time Confederate authorities at the Georgia city had observed a handsome seagoing side-wheel steamer used by the Federals as one of their blockading vessels. She was the USS *Water Witch*, a 378-ton gunboat mounting four cannon and engaged in patrolling the many sounds and marshes that surrounded Savannah. Lately it was observed that she consistently anchored every night in Ossabaw Sound. Plans were laid for her capture by Flag Officer William W. Hunter, commander of the Savannah Squadron, and First Lieutenant Thomas P. Pelot, commander of the floating battery, CSS *Georgia*. Pelot was assigned to lead this dangerous mission with First Lieutenant Joseph Price appointed as his second in command. (Campbell, *Academy on the James, The Confederate Naval School*, pp. 97–98.)

Midshipman Minor kept a diary during the war and the following is his account of the attack and capture of the USS *Water Witch*. [RTC]

"The Capture of the USS Water Witch" by Midshipman Hubbard T. Minor, CSN

Confederate Naval Cadet, *The Diary and Letters of Midshipman Hubbard T. Minor with a History of the Confederate Naval Academy*

On the Morning of Tuesday May 31st 1864, an expedition, under the command of Lieutenant Thomas P. Pelot, left Fort Jackson in the Savannah River. The total number of men composing the expedition, officers & men included, was one hundred & thirty-one. Of those was a Negro man named Moses Dallas, the only pilot along. There were seven boats, all of which were taken in tow by the C. S. Steamer *FireFly*. The officers, with the exception of the coxswains, & men going on board of the steamer in this way it went through Augustine Creek into Thunderbolt, both as far as the Island of Hope where the steamer was left to return to the city. There the boats were formed into two columns, the officers according to their rank commanding the highest numbered boats. Boat No. 1, commanded by Mr. Pelot led the port column. Boat No. 2, commanded by Lieutenant Price led the starboard column. Boats No. 3, No. 5 & No. 7, commanded respectively by Midshipman Minor, Boatswain Seymour, & Master's Mate [John A.] Rosler, followed each other in the port column, & boats No. 4 & No. 6, respectively commanded by Midshipman Trimble & Master's Mate [Hamilton] Golder, followed in succession in the starboard column. In Lieutenant Pelot's boat No. 1 was Master's Mate [Thaddeus S.] Grey, Engineers [George W.] Caldwell & [James L.] Fabian, & the pilot by name [of] Moses [Dallas]. In Midshipman Minor's boat No. 3 was Master's Mate [Arthur C.] Freeman, in Boatswain Seymour's boat No. 5 was Master's Mate [A. H. E. W.] Barclay, in Master's Mate Golder's boat No. 6 was Assistant Surgeon [C. Wesley] Thomas, & in Master's Mate Rosler's boat No. 7 was Assistant Surgeon [William C.] Jones.

The columns being thus formed were kept so, as far as practicable, until the expedition had passed through the Skidaway Narrows & come to Battery Beaulieu in the Vernon River. Here Mr. Pelot learned that the vessel he had intended to attack, if possible at night, had only on this evening gotten up steam & gone out, but as one remained in the neighborhood all the time, he determined to remain until morning & then reconnoiter. Should he be unable to discover a vessel in Ossabaw Sound, it was his intention to go into St. Catherine's Sound where he was sure to find one. It was now about 8:30 PM, & as the men needed not the boats, all headed for shore where Mr. Pelot had already gone & the men went into camp for the night after supper. All but the watches paid a visit to dreamland, & I trust sweet was the sleep of many.

When the morning of Wednesday June 1st came clear & bright, Lieutenant Pelot took his boat & a picked crew, & accompanied by Lieutenant Price & Assistant Surgeon Thomas, went out on a reconnaissance leaving Midshipman Minor in charge of the camp. During the whole of this day the men remained in camp & kept their good spirits, & these latter were added to by the good mess of turnip salad they enjoyed with their hard bread & salt beef for dinner. The salad was tendered to Midshipman Minor early in the morning by the courteous Captain [Cornelius R.] Hanleiter, commanding at Battery Beaulieu, & that officer had appreciation enough for the salad & the motive that promoted the offer to accept it on behalf of his officers & men. At about 7:30 Lieutenant Pelot returned having left Lieutenant Price, Assistant Surgeon Thomas, & one of his boat's crew on a point of land near the vessel he had discovered [in order] to watch her movements. After supper Midshipman Minor was ordered to have all hands called to muster & then after all were found present Mr. Pelot addressed them. In his short speech he said that they had discovered a vessel & would board her that night, that he expected every man to do his duty & felt confident that they would do so. He also called their attention to the low muttering of the thunder that could be plainly heard & told them that it was an indication that God was with them for the thunder indicated a dark night which could be nothing but favorable to their enterprise. When he was done speaking the men gave him three hearty cheers, & then Midshipman Minor was ordered to go to work & launch the boats, which for fear of discovery by the enemy, had been hauled up on shore & concealed.

Early in the morning at about 8:30 the boats were all launched & manned. When the officers stepped into their respective boats, & amid three cheers from the men & officers of the battery, were pulled down Vernon River towards, Ossabaw Sound where we came to the point where Mr. Price had been left. Mr. Pelot went ashore & brought Mr. Price, Dr. Thomas, & the man with them to their respective boats. It was now about 11:30 & too early to proceed for the enemy was not a great way off, as far as Mr. Pelot could judge, so we returned up the river a little way & the noses of all of the boats were stuck into the marsh, & all of the officers were acquainted with the portion of the vessel they were to board & men appointed in each boat to go to different portions of the vessel where they should have gotten on board. Mr. Pelot intended to board the furthest portion of the vessel on the left side going, & the remaining boats of the port column were to board just behind him & each other respectively. The order on the right side was to be the same, Mr. Price taking the furthest portion from him going on that side & the other boats boarding respectively just after him & each other.

At 12:30 the boats once more put off & were pulled for a long time towards where the enemy was supposed to be. They pulled about but saw no vessel. At this the men became much annoyed & soon it was found that the sea was not far, for the surf could be plainly heard. It was now about 3:30 & necessary that all possible speed should be made to get back, for the enemy had been evidently passed during the night & must be re-passed before it was light. At about 4:30 it was found that the point of land upon which Mr. Price & party had been left was near us, so Mr. Pelot took Boatswain Seymour & a man named Osburn in his boat & put them ashore with some rations to watch the vessel during the day when it should arrive. Mr. Barclay now had charge of Mr. Seymour's boat & with the rest returned toward Battery Beaulieu where they all arrived at about 8 AM of the morning, Thursday, June 2nd 1864, & went ashore & into camp as before but it was deemed unnecessary to haul the boats out of the water so they remained anchored out in the river. At breakfast time it was discovered that the rations were exhausted so Mr. Pelot ordered Midshipman Minor to go up & see Captain Hanleiter & ask him to let him have 20 lbs. of bacon which he would return. The courteous captain sent the bacon & the men had a good meal having some meal sent out in time for dinner from Savannah by wagon.

When supper again was over all were called to muster & Mr. Pelot told the men that he did not think it necessary to say anything more to them. The men responded with cheers & said that "they were in for it." At about 8 PM, the boats were again manned & put off down the river but this time no cheers came from the men of the battery but they stood and watched us in silence. That day the enemy's vessel had taken such a position to be seen from the bomb proof with glasses of the battery & when we put off this time some perhaps thought that many were doomed to return no more as they went away. When near the point where Mr. Seymour had been left, Mr. Pelot again went ashore & brought him & Osburn over to their boat. Mr. Seymour had discovered the vessel we had been looking at during the day from the bomb proof & by picking out her position on the chart found her to be in 40 feet of water & Moses said that he knew where she was that she was laying just in the spot he thought she was during the day. Mr. Seymour being in his boat, we again put off & went through Hell Gate & up to the east for a short distance when the boats were again stuck in the marsh & silence preserved. This night the order of attack was somewhat changed, it being decided best for Mr. Pelot to board the nearest portion to him going on the left side, & Midshipman Minor the furthest. The other two boats were to board one just forward of the wheel & the other just aft. The order on the right side was the same, Mr. Price boarding the portion on that side going & Midshipman Trimble the furthest. Mr. Golder was to board between the two anywhere he could. It was now about 12:30, so the boats again put off & were pulled in columns towards the west.

It was a favorable night for it was very dark & every now & then the lightening lit up the waters all around us & there was not much fear of our again passing the vessel without seeing her. Our boats were riding silently on, apparently through a sea of fire, & at about 2 AM, we discovered a light which we supposed to be that of a vessel, as nearer we

The USS *Water Witch* (Naval Historical Center).

came by the lightning's flash we discovered the vessel we were in search of. When discovered she bore about 2 points off our starboard bows distant over a thousand yards. As closer we came the lightening discovered her plainly to us while our boats being white washed were not so easily discovered. When with in three hundred yards all seemed to be asking God, as I know I was, to prosper our undertaking, to shield us from harm, & to make us do our duty. When within 80 yards they hailed. When Moses answered, "Runaway Negros," but the chivalric Lieutenant Pelot shouted almost in the same voice, "We are Rebels, give way boys!" All of the boats except the two last in the port column were well up & gave way with a will. The two boats in advance on the port column touched the ship about the same time & the men were on board some seconds before those of the starboard column as the starboard column had to describe arcs of circles while those of the port ran across the chords of same arcs. Mr. Pelot was said to be the first man on board & did not live long after getting there for he was shot directly through the heart. The fight lasted not more than ten or 15 minutes & in it we lost, besides Mr. Pelot, 5 brave & good men & among them our pilot. All of the boats but Nos. 5 & 7 boarded where they were ordered, & these two did not board at all. Mr. Price & Midshipman Minor were wounded early in the fight but both remained on duty. At the death of Mr. Pelot, Mr. Price became commander & Midshipman Minor executive officer. After much confusion, a great deal of it occasioned by the loss of our pilot, we got underway, & after getting aground three times anchored safely on Saturday evening June 3rd off Battery Beaulieu.

When we came up we had a boat pennant flying above the stars & stripes & we met with hearty cheers from all the assembled spectators. Were it my place to mention the gallant deeds of the members of this expedition I know of nothing that would give me more pleasure. I must say that all who boarded the vessel merit honor for so doing & none but gallant men dare do such things. Had we not lost our pilot we would have gotten up to Beaulieu without the loss of the provisions which were thrown overboard to lighten the vessel the last time we got aground. Our capture proved to be the U.S. Steamer *Water Witch*, [a] side wheel of [378] tons & a crew of 68 men & officers, Lieutenant [Austin] Pendergrast, commanding.

3. The CSS *Savannah*

A key defensive position on the coast of the Confederacy was Savannah, Georgia. The capture of Fort Pulaski on Cockspur Island on April 11, 1862, had effectively eliminated Savannah as a port of entry for blockade runners. Nevertheless, the city itself, an important manufacturing and communication center, remained under Confederate control. Additional Federal advances from the sea were contained by Fort Jackson and the ships of the Savannah Squadron. These vessels included the ironclad CSS *Savannah*, the ironclad CSS *Georgia*, two wooden gunboats, the CSS *Isondiga*, and the CSS *Sampson*. Transferred from the 7th Florida Regiment on March 3, 1864, Robert Watson was assigned to the *Savannah*.

By December 1864, time was running out for the Georgia city, for General Sherman's forces were threatening to envelope the city from the west. As the ominous war clouds spread toward Savannah, Watson continued faithfully to record his activities as a seaman onboard the CSS *Savannah*. (Campbell [ed.], *Southern Service on Land & Sea: The Wartime Journal of Robert Watson, CSA/CSN*, pp. 98–164.) [RTC]

Diary of Seaman Robert Watson, CSN
Southern Service on Land & Sea; The Wartime Journal of Robert Watson, pp. 136–145

Thursday December 1, 1864

At work all day on shore making gun racks, etc,

Friday December 2

Repairing boat cradles and making gun racks.

Saturday December 3

Went to work on the steamer *Resolute* repairing her wheels, 13 arms and 11 buckets being broken. Have to live on board her till the work is done, sorry for it, for I dislike to be shifting about among strangers. Went on board the Ram at night.

Sunday December 4

Got my things ready to take to the *Resolute*, took breakfast and dinner at the Ram. General muster at 9½ AM it being the first Sunday in the month. Got on board at 4 PM and got supper.

Friday December 9

Have been at work steady since last date, got through tonight. Great excitement in the city, the Yankees reported near the place expect an attack on the city in the morning, bringing provisions, etc. on board the *Resolute* until 1AM, made such a noise that I could not sleep. Quite cold all night.

Saturday December 10

At 3 AM took my things on the wharf and cast off the *Resolute*'s lines. She and the *Samson* went up the river. Commodore Hunter went in the latter. I remained on the wharf until 7 AM, when I went on board the Ram. Cold damp morning. Got up steam in afternoon and started down the river but turned back and came to anchor again. Rain through the night. Fighting near the city all day.*

---

*General Sherman's army, after leaving Atlanta, had cut a path of destruction across Georgia and had then arrived in front of the outer land defenses of Savannah. Confederate General William J. Hardee's gray-clad army was dug in, but their lines were long and they numbered only 10,000.

Sunday December 11

After breakfast got up steam and went down the river and anchored off Fort Jackson. Very cold and blowing hard all day and night, fighting near the city all day. Our cavalry crossing the river all day to the Carolina side to prevent a flank movement I suppose.

Monday December 12

Very cold all day. Cannonading still going on. At 9½ PM all hands were called and hauled anchor short and turned in again at 10½ PM, but I was unable to sleep on account of the noise. Our boats were going and coming from town all night. Steam up all night. At 12 midnight all hands were called again and hammocks lashed and stowed away. Hove up anchor and started up, what is called the back river, did not go far when we ran aground, the tide being too low for us to go any farther. The crew were then told to cook bread for the next day as it was likely that we would be fighting all day and no fire is allowed while the magazine is opened. Our mess cook being on liberty I acted in his place and cooked breakfast and all the flour the mess had.

Tuesday December 13

At 5¼ AM, quarters were beat and all hands rushed to their quarters, cast loose and ran in guns in a hurry, remained at quarters about ¾ of an hour and then ate breakfast. Heavy cannonading all day. At night our 2 boats from the *Georgia* went on an expedition up the river and returned at 11 PM They went inside the enemy's lines but were not discovered.

Wednesday December 14

A very pleasant day. Heavy cannonading all day. All hands washing clothes in forenoon. Received the unpleasant intelligence that Fort McAllister was taken by the Yankees.* At 10 PM armed boats were called away. Our two boats were manned and went up the river. They were fired at by the Yankee pickets but nobody was hurt. They returned at 4 AM.

Thursday December 15

A warm pleasant day. 10 men were sent up town to work on pontoons. I did not go as the carpenters mate is sick and I am doing his duty. I went to the city in the dingy to carry some officers. Returned at 9 PM and stood watch till midnight. Our armed boats were away all day and returned in the night. Picket fighting all night.

Friday December 16

I was at work nearly all day in the engine room. Foggy all day and night. Cannonading still going on.

Saturday December 17

Foggy morning but cleared off in forenoon and had a pleasant day. At work repairing whale boat, finished at 3½ PM General Beauregard came to Screven's Ferry where we are lying and one of our four boats took him up to the city.† Our men still working on the pontoons.§ Very foggy night, ringing the bell all night. At 8 PM by some mistake of the quartermaster, the gong was beat for quarters and all hands turned out and ran to their quarters in a hurry. Turned in again and slept sound all night.

---

*The fall of Fort McAllister enabled Sherman to establish contact with the Federal fleet.
†Confederate General Pierre G. T. Beauregard was responsible for the defenses of the South Carolina and Georgia coasts.
§When General Beauregard visited Savannah he asked General Hardee what plans had been laid in case the city had to be evacuated. None had been made, Hardee replied, because he was relying upon the navy gunboats to ferry his troops safely to the South Carolina shore of the Savannah River. Beauregard, not satisfied with this, ordered Hardee to immediately begin construction of a pontoon bridge over the river.

Sunday December 18
Foggy morning, all quiet in front.

Tuesday December 20
Hard at work making wooded shutters for the ports. The captain talks of running out and going to Charleston S. C., fear it will be a dangerous undertaking for the river is full of torpedoes and if we should escape them we would have the whole Yankee fleet to contend with. All hands up nearly all night packing up for we are afraid that we will have to burn the Ram and march to Charleston.

Wednesday December 21
At 3 AM the two new Rams and Navy Yards and Fort Jackson were set on fire, also the gunboat *Isondiga* was fired at 7 AM, and the pontoon bridge destroyed.* The Yankee flag was hoisted on the Marine Barracks at 7 AM, and shortly afterwards they hoisted one on Fort Jackson. At 9 AM the steamer *Swan* was fired. At 10½ AM the Yankees opened fire on us from the city. We were not slow in returning the compliment but with what effect I cannot say. The Yankees made excellent shots, nearly every one struck our sides or smoke stack. One shell went down the smoke stack and rested on the grating but did not explode. They ceased fire at 11½ AM, but commenced shelling again at 4 PM and continued till after dark. We got the Ram ready for firing during the afternoon. Coffee, sugar, bread, etc. were given to the men by the wholesale. At dark the crew then left in boats by divisions and landed at Screven's Ferry, South Carolina. The Ram was then set on fire. The Capt. and 1st Lieut. were the last to leave her. I was in the boat that took them on shore. The steamer *Firefly* was then fired and we took up our lines of march and camped at midnight, all hands very tired. The Ram blew up at 20 minutes after 11 PM. We were about 8 miles from the ferry when we heard the explosion, it was terrific, it lit the heavens for miles, we could see to pick up a pin where we were and the noise was awful. She had in her 7½ tons of powder and several hundred shells. Cloudy and cold all day and night. The roads were lit up for miles by the fires from the burning vessels and houses. All our troops left Savannah 24 hours before we did. Met a few cavalry on the road.

Thursday December 22
At 2 AM we were ordered to fall in and marched to Hardeeville, S.C. I and a few more arrived at 7 AM feeling very tired and sore. The rest of the boys came straggling in during the forenoon. We built shelters of pine limbs and leaves and got a lot of firewood expecting a stay all night but at dark we got on a train of platform cars and started for Charleston. We were stowed so close that we did not have room to sit so we were jammed and screwed up very uncomfortable. It was bitter cold. In crossing Pocotaligo bridge [South Carolina] over Broad River the Yankees threw about 20 shells at us but fortunately did not hit us although they bursted over and around us. Running all night very slow and stopping very often.

Friday December 23
On the cars all day, bitter cold. Arrived in Charleston at dark, built fires, cooked supper, took a couple of drinks of whiskey and turned in. Slept well.

Saturday December 24
A fine morning, rather cold. Had a good wash, ate breakfast and felt much refreshed. At 10 AM we packed up and went on board the ship *Indian Chief*. She is the receiving ship and full of lice and very dirty. Got on board at 1 PM. She had on board 60 men who do noth-

---

One of these was the uncompleted ironclad CSS Milledgeville *which had been launched only the month before. The other unnamed "ram" was probably still on the stocks.*

ing but guard duty in boats. Drew 1 days ration of pork and bread, got supper and dinner at dark. Slept on the deck for there was not berths enough for all.

Sunday December 25

Christmas day. Turned out at 6 AM, very cold. We were ordered to hold ourselves in readiness to leave at moments warning. 20 men were sent to the Ram *Charleston*, all the balance except the *Savannah's* crew went to James Island.* I went in a boat to carry a lot of officers and marines, head wind and tide, miserable old leaky boat, very slow. In coming back we were hailed and brought to at Castle Pinckney and had the same trouble over again, finally started and got on board the *Indian Chief* at 10 PM tired and wet, put on my only suit of clothes and turned in. This ends Christmas day. The poorest one I ever spent.

Monday December 26

Scrubbing decks in the morning. After breakfast I went in a boat to James Island to carry some marines, remained there a short time and got back to the ship at 1 PM None of us have been allowed any liberty since we've been here, none of the men on this station get liberty. Took in some provisions in the afternoon. We are hoisting and lowering boats, the ship is a perfect humbug. Foggy all day and night.

Tuesday December 27

Weighed one anchor and cleared chain, it being foul. In the afternoon the captain of the Ram *Charleston* came on board and called for 18 volunteers for his vessel. I stepped out with the number, but as some of the men he wanted were on shore he said he would call next day and call for volunteers. It is rumored on board that the most of us will go to Wilmington, N. C. 300 lbs. of meat is ordered to be cooked. All our men that went to James Island came on board in the afternoon. In the evening a lot more of our men were sent to different vessels. My chum Alfred Lowe was among the number, but I went to Lieut. [William E.] Hudgins and asked him to send me in another man's place as I did not wish to be separated from my friend as we had left home together and I had never been separated since. He said that he wanted me to go with him but that he would not separate us so he sent another man in Alf's place.

Wednesday December 28

Rainy morning. At 12 all hands were mustered and 74 men sent to the Ram *Columbia*† and some to the Ram *Charleston*, the balance of us are to go to Wilmington, N. C. At 1 PM we went on shore and got into some old dirty box cars and started at 2 PM. Drew 2 days rations of bread and meat before starting. Stopped at Florence, S. C. 1 hour. Here we changed cars, very cold. Got into passenger cars here and was comfortable the rest of the day.

Thursday December 29

At 7 PM stopped at Flemington, N. C., ½ hour. This place is 34 miles from Wilmington where we arrived at 12 m., got on a ferryboat and crossed over to the navy yard, cleaned out a room and put up a stove. The room contains bunks enough for us all, very cold day.§

The CSS Charleston was the flagship of the Charleston Squadron. The 180-foot ironclad was armed with six guns, and had entered service early in 1864. Her captain was Commander Isacc N. Brown.

†*The ironclad CSS Columbia was 216 feet long and mounted six guns. She was launched late in 1864.*

§*Watson joined the Confederate force defending the port of Wilmington from attack by sea. The force was scattered in a series of forts and fortifications along the Cape Fear River, of which the most powerful was Fort Fisher. Shortly before Christmas, while Watson was in Charleston, a combined Union army and navy expedition mounted an attack on Fort Fisher. The attack failed, but when Watson arrived, it was apparent that a second one was imminent. Battery Buchanan was located a few hundred yards down river from Fort Fisher.*

Friday December 30

Very cold day. Washed my clothes and just as I wrung them out we were ordered to pack up to go to the Battery Buchanan. Started at 1 PM in a small tugboat and arrived at the battery at 5 PM, landed in boats and had to wade ashore, water very cold. The quarters are small and badly crowded, scarcely room to turn around. Spread our blankets on the floor and slept very well.

Saturday December 31

Cold and clear. This place is called Confederate Point. It is a low, sandy place, water brackish, sand blowing over everything. The battery is a fine one, it mounts 2 eleven inch Brooke smoothbores and 2 ten inch Columbiards [sic] and 1 six pounder howitzer. There is a great deal of humbugging in boats, they are moored off all day and hauled up at night. The water is very shoal about this place and everything that is brought here we have to wade out to the boats and carry it on shore. I went over to Fort Fisher in the afternoon. The men in the fort all busy repairing and strengthening the works. The ground was covered with shell of all sizes, many of them unexploded. On Christmas day the Yankee fleet threw about 30,000 shells at the fort. They burnt all the quarters but did not injure the works much. 2 guns burst and several were dismounted. Our loss small. Fort Fisher is a large and strong work. Rain all the afternoon and night. We have to sleep on the floor and are so crowded that we can scarcely find room to lie. Our food is badly cooked, consequently have not enough to eat. The bread is made without salt or yeast and is as heavy as stone, the beef boiled, and coffee is slops. This day one year ago, I was at Dalton, Ga. and felt confident that the war would be over and I be at home today, but alas am sadly disappointed and God only knows when this cruel and unnatural war will end. I am afraid that it will not end during Lincoln's administration. This ends the year 1864 and I pray to Almighty God that I may be at home this time next year.

Official Report of Commander Thomas W. Brent, CSN, Destruction of the CSS Savannah

Official Navy Records, Series I, Volume 16, pp. 483–485

CHARLESTON, S. C., *December 24, 1864.*

SIR: I enclose the copy of a dispatch I received from the Secretary of the Navy., dated Richmond, December 14. The original, which I retain, is dated Charleston, December 15, and forwarded to you by General Beauregard, with the request that Lieutenant-General Hardee would have it deciphered and transmitted. I enclose a copy of a letter dated December 17, I received from the office of orders and detail, at Hardeeville. I was most anxious to carry out the instructions of the Department in relation to the escape of the vessels from Savannah after its occupation by the enemy, and with this view was making preparations to put the *Savannah* in a fit condition for sea. I directed Lieutenant McAdam, Provisional Navy C.S., the officer who laid the torpedoes, to remove with all possible dispatch those that obstructed the passage to sea by the way of Turner's Rocks. In his report, dated the 20th, he states that he immediately proceeded to the C.S.S. *Savannah*, where he was furnished with two boats and their crews, but after every endeavor he found that with all the appliances at his command, grapnels, etc., he was unable with the motive power of boats to remove any one of them, the anchors to which they are attached being too firmly embedded in the sand. The steam tender *Firefly* towed the boats. Finding it impossible, with the means at my command, before the time fixed upon for the evacuation of the city, to remove the torpedoes, I determined that it would not be proper to attempt the passage of the river in that direction, and the passage by the North Cannel was effectually obstructed. Under these circumstances it did not seem to me possible to carry out the instructions of the Department in regard to taking the *Savannah* to sea and fighting her way into this or some other port. As to the *Isondiga*, she was a very inferior vessel in speed and her magazine was very much exposed.

I therefore thought her best chances of escape would be to attempt to go up the river if a passage could be found not commanded by the enemy's batteries. The *Water Witch* was burned on the 19th, after consultation with the commanding general and by his advice, to prevent her falling into the hands of the enemy. In a conference I had with Generals Beauregard and Hardee a few days before the evacuation the plan was fixed upon that the *Savannah* should attempt to get to sea by Wassaw Sound, and the *Isondiga* and *Firefly* up the river. This proved to be impracticable, principally on account of the torpedoes, as before stated. General Hardee requested me to remain after the evacuation of the city until Thursday night, the 22d instant, to protect valuable stores at Screven's Ferry, and which could not be sooner removed, and informing me that Major-General Wheeler had been directed to keep in constant communication with me to inform me of the movements of the enemy, and if those movements should render my position unsafe that I should be advised by General Wheeler. I was happy to have it in my power to render very important service in the construction of pontoon bridges with detachments of the crew of the *Savannah* and *Georgia*, under Boatswain McCalla. On the morning of the 21st the enemy, in possession of the city, opened upon the ship a well-directed fire of field artillery from the bluff near the gas works. I was unable to give my guns sufficient elevation to reach them when I returned the fire. On the evening of the 21st Captain Quirk [Manning J. Kirk?], the commanding officer, and having charge of the transportation at Screven's Ferry, informed me that he intended evacuating that night by 8 o'clock, and asking me if I could land my command by that time. The city and commanding positions being in, possession of the enemy, every outlet of escape closed except that by Screven's Ferry, and my supply of provisions getting short, I considered it my duty to destroy my ship to prevent her from falling into the hands of the enemy, and to save the officers and crew. Accordingly, at about 7:30 PM, the ship was fired, having previously landed her officers and crew, except the firing party under charge of the, executive officer, Lieutenant Hudgins. I left with the last boat. Upon landing at Screven's Ferry, the wharf there was fired, and the *Firefly*, which was alongside of it.

I then proceeded with the officers and men in a march of about 18 miles to Hardeeville. Nothing was saved except what was carried about the person, and no transportation could be obtained from the army except a wagon to carry the sick, who could not march. On the morning of the 22d I arrived with my command at Hardeeville, where I received by the hands of Lieutenant Ingraham, Provisional Navy C.S., the letter from the Navy Department referred to at the commencement of this letter. It was then too late to carry out the order of the Department, even had it been in my power to do so. I found at Hardeeville Lieutenant Dalton, with the officers and crew of the *Isondiga*, which he had burned on account of her getting ashore above the pontoon bridge in Back River, after the enemy had possession of the city, and whilst he was coming down the river to communicate with me. His report will be enclosed if ready before the closing of this dispatch.

Upon application to Lieutenant-General Hardee, I obtained transportation for the officers and crews of the vessels to this place, leaving Hardeeville on the evening of the 22d and arriving here on the night of the 23d. I immediately reported to Flag-Officer Ingraham, through whom the sick were sent to the naval hospital, and on the following morning to Flag-Officer Tucker, who placed the officers and crew on board the receiving ship. On the 24th I telegraphed my arrival to the Navy Department and am awaiting orders. On yesterday, the 25th, Flag-Officer Tucker asked me to place 100 men under Lieutenant Dalton, principally composed of the crews of the *1sondiga* and *Georgia*, with the marines of the *Savannah*, under Lieutenant Pratt, to reinforce Fort Johnson, threatened with an attack by the enemy. The rest of the command, consisting of about 300 men under Lieutenant Hudgins of the *Savannah*, were kept in readiness if required. I send this under charge of Third Assistant Engineer T. O. McClosky, with orders to report to you. I have transmitted a copy of this report to the Navy Department.

I am, sir, very respectfully, your obedient servant,

THOS. W. BRENT,
Commander

Lieutenant General William J. Hardee (Miller, Photographic History of the Civil War).

V

Columbus, Georgia

1. The CSS *Chattahoochee*

The CSS *Chattahoochee* was a twin screw steamer with a schooner rig that was built from 1862 to 1863 at Saffold, Georgia, by David S. Johnston and William O. Saffold. The steamer was armed with a 9-inch smoothbore aft, a rifled 32-pounder forward, and four 32-pounders in broadside. Commander Catesby ap R. Jones supervised her construction, and he commissioned the vessel on January 1, 1863. Jones commanded the *Chattahoochee* until February 4, when he was succeeded by First Lieutenant John J. Guthrie. The gunboat operated on the Chattahoochee and Apalachicola Rivers between Columbus, Georgia, and Apalachicola, Florida, which was blockaded by Federal warships.

On May 27, 1863, the *Chattahoochee* prepared to sail from her anchorage at Blountstown, Florida, in an attempt to recapture the Confederate schooner *Fashion* that had been seized by Federal forces on the Apalachicola River. As steam was being raised, the boiler exploded.

First Lieutenant Augustus McLaughlin, commander of the Confederate Navy Yard at Columbus, wrote several letters to his friend and former commander of the *Chattahoochee*, Catesby ap R. Jones, giving the sad and graphic details of the disaster. These letters were later included in the *Official Navy Records* (Turner, *Navy Gray: A Story of the Confederate Navy on the Chattahoochee and Apalachicola Rivers*, pp. 99–107.) [RTC]

"Boiler Explosion!"
Letters to Commander Catesby ap R. Jones, CSN, from
1st Lt. Augustus McLaughlin, CSN
Official Records Navy, Series I, Volume XVII, pp. 869–872

COLUMBUS, GA, *June 1, 1863.*

MY DEAR JONES: I hasten to inform you of the sad accident which happened on board the *Chattahoochee,* and as the quickest method I enclose the account furnished the newspaper by Gift, who, though not on board at the time, came up on the *Young* with the wounded. Young Mallory is badly hurt and his recovery considered doubtful. The statements as to how the accident occurred are very conflicting. Some say that the steam gauge had been out of order the day previous. At the time of the explosion it was showing only 7 pounds of steam. Others say that pumping water in the boiler, the water at the time being low, was the cause. She was at anchor and only waiting for steam to be reported to get underway. Mr. Fagan at the time was sick, though had just gone into the engine room. He was the only one on board having any knowledge of the engines. The gunner is at the vessel with most of the crew. The medical officers have moved their effects to Chattahoochee. Captain Guthrie is here. I will write you again soon.

       Yours, truly,

       A. McLAUGHLIN.

Commander C. ap R. JONES, C. S. Navy.

     NAVAL STATION, COLUMBUS, GA., *June 15, 1863*.

 MY DEAR JONES: Your letter of the 8th has just reached me, enclosing a letter to Gift. As he has left here permanently with orders to Mobile, I have done as you directed, opened the document and forwarded the letters of recommendation, through Pembroke Jones, at Savannah, with a request that he will hand them to the men. I will go on to explain and endeavor to furnish you with all the information connected with the lamentable accident which happened to the ill-fated steamer. The accounts, such as we get, are most conflicting, but Gift, having taken an active part in placing the information before the public, I think, has prevented the matter from being as freely discussed as would otherwise have been the case.

 The only officers on board at the time were Guthrie, Midshipmen Craig, Mallory, and Gibbs, Golder, Dr. Ford, and the gunner, and the engineers, whose names have already appeared in print with the exception of Third Assistant H. (?) Blanc, of New Orleans, who, not being on duty, escaped uninjured. The vessel had started for the obstructions, and had gone but 20 miles when it was found there was not sufficient water on the bar to admit of her crossing. The vessel was anchored. The next morning it was ascertained that the river had swollen, when orders were given to raise steam, and, as near as I can learn, they commenced firing up at or near 10 o'clock with wood. At 12 m., when the relief came down (which, by the way, accounts for the number of deaths), the steam gauge was showing 7 pounds of steam. It is now understood that it was out of order the day previous. A discussion now arose with regard to the quantity of water in the boiler. Mr. Fagan, the senior engineer, being at the time in his bunk with a chill, hearing the dispute, and fearing from the length of time since the fires had been started that something was wrong, hastened to the engine room and was descending the ladder when the explosion took place. Curiosity had taken the pilot to the engine room, and some think it was he who started the pump. The explosion was instantaneous with the starting of the pump. Guthrie, at the time, was in his cabin. There is some difference of opinion about the time of his arrival on deck. Otherwise I do not hear of his name being mentioned, except by Dr. Ford, who speaks of his administering baptism to those who had been wounded and were about to die.

 It being reported that an explosion of the magazine was imminent, caused a panic among the crew. Three, I believe, were drowned in trying to reach the shore. Among the number was a quartermaster by the name of Berry. No description, I am told, could possibly be given of the scene on the deck of the *Chattahoochee*, men running about frantic with pain, leaving the impression of their bleeding feet, and sometimes the entire flesh, the nails and all, remain behind them. The dead and wounded were taken on shore, where they remained until the next afternoon, most of the time a terrible storm raging. Finally they were taken on board the *Young* and reached Columbus on Sunday night, just five days after the accident. No attempt was made to dress the wounds until after their arrival here, which could not be avoided. Poor Mallory! I shall never forget his appearance. I would not have known him had be not spoken. His face, hands, and feet were scalded in the most terrible manner; he plead piteously to have his wounds attended to. I urged the doctor, who, by the way, was almost used up himself, to pay Mallory some attention. He then told me that he would have to wait for some assistance. He then said that Mallory could not live. You would have thought differently had you seen him. I could not make up my mind that he would die. When they first commenced to remove the cloths he was talking cheerfully, but the nervous system could not stand the shock. He commenced sinking and was a corpse before they had gotten half through. Duffy, the fireman, expired on the next day. You would have been surprised to have seen the effect produced on Mr. Craig and Golder, who were only slightly injured, Mr. Craig in the foot, Mr. Golder side of face, arm, and hand. They were so prostrated after their wounds were dressed that they were only roused by the use of stimulants. It seems almost useless to mention that they received all the attention that could possibly have been bestowed. The Home was literally besieged with ladies, and for one week the street in front of the Home was blocked up with vehicles of all descriptions. I really looked on with astonishment. The four worst cases were placed together in the room upstairs, directly in front of the steps. It was with the utmost difficulty that I could remain in the room sufficiently long to ascertain what was required and to see what service I could render, the atmosphere was so unpleasant, yet the ladies did not seem to notice it and remained at their post till the last.

1st Lt. Augustus McLaughlin (National Civil War Naval Museum).

Guthrie came up on the boat, bringing the guns, which, strange to say, he turned over to Major Humphreys, with a request that he would hold them subject alone to his order or that of the Secretary of the Navy. I immediately made a report of the affair. The Secretary, through the Office of Ordnance, replied promptly by telegraph, directing the guns and everything pertaining to them, as well as ship's stores, be turned over to me. The matter caused considerable talk among the people in town. It was not understood why naval guns should not have been placed under the control of naval officers. It does appear to me that Guthrie's conduct throughout the whole affair has been most singular. He has given leave of absence to some of his crew to visit a place in possession of the enemy, and some 13 of his men left him at Chattahoochee with the intention of not returning. Among the number was a man by the name of Lee, whom you will no doubt recollect. After placing the guns in charge of Major Humphreys he took his family and started for Chattahoochee, were [he] remained four or five days, when he again embarked for Columbus, bringing the crew, minus the 13 mentioned above. At that time I had in my possession a telegram from Richmond to Guthrie, directing him to send the crew to Savannah. He remarked he would turn them over to me, and I might do what I pleased with them, but he thought I had better wait for further instructions. As Guthrie appeared to be laboring under some bodily infirmity, I gave the men quarters in my mold room, and sent 40 of them the next day to Savannah. They arrived on the day the *Savannah* was put in commission. The men were all nicely dressed when they left here, and on their arrival at Savannah, being all straight and in good condition, were the cause of many remarks. It was certainly reflecting great credit to those who had organized and disciplined the crew. I felt proud of them. During their stay with me there was not one guilty of the slightest impropriety. Cronin (?), May, and Rosler expressed deep regret that they had not time to put a piece in the paper thanking the ladies for their many kindnesses, but said they would do so on their arrival at Savannah. The crew of the *Chattahoochee* will ever remember the latter and the paymaster. They would have been willing to have gone anywhere to have gotten rid of the vessel. Webb was exceedingly anxious to get hold of some of the men. He will have some of the landsmen; the remainder will remain on the *Savannah*, I ordered Dr. Jones and Midshipman Gibbs and Mr. Golder with the crew. They are now attached to the *Savannah*.

The 6.4-inch rifle belonging to the *Chattahoochee* I was directed to send to Charleston. It is to be double-banded and returned, to be used, I suppose, on the *Muscogee*. I am doing very well. The calkers have commenced to-day, and I am laying the spar deck. The engines are about being placed in position. I will keep you advised from time to time of the progress.

With kind regards to Simms, I remain, truly, yours,

A. McLAUGHLIN.

[Commander CATESBY ap R. JONES, C. S. Navy.]

COLUMBUS, GA., *December 26, 1863.*

MY DEAR JONES: The *Chattahoochee*, her officers and men, have been turned over to me. I have succeeded in having her towed to this place, and will commence work on her at once. She is not as badly damaged as I had supposed. The deck immediately over the boiler on the port side was raised by the explosion some 6 inches. Beyond that there has been no damage to the boiler. Mr. Warner has not had an opportunity to examine the boiler. From a casual observation he thinks she can soon be in running order; the machinery has not been injured. It has been to me still more a matter of surprise why that vessel should have been allowed to sink. A pine plug driven into the feed pipe, which had been blown off, would have been all that was necessary. She draws in her present condition 6 feet 3 inches aft, 5 feet 3 inches forward. Nearly all her outfit has been plundered, and in some instances sold and given away by those who were left in charge. Things were scattered around, some at the arsenal, Johnston's, and Eufaula. Johnston had the entire control in raising the vessel. After she was up she remained in charge of his Negroes. She has been stripped of everything that could be converted into money. The paymaster's clerk gave furlough to the men, some of which are still away. There was a regular communication kept up with Apalachicola by means of the dingy, which was at the disposal of Father Somebody, the Catholic priest. No doubt the enemy have been kept fully posted with regard to movements in the Confederacy, more particularly with matters on the river.

Guthrie has made one round trip on the *Advance*, a vessel belonging to the State of North Carolina. I was at Wilmington when he arrived. He seemed to be perfectly happy; says he has now established his reputation. I don't know why be did not continue on her. Crossan is out with her now. Guthrie has been spending some of his time at Eufaula, where he has purchased a house, and intends his family to reside there during the war.

Washington is here. He seems anxious to get detached. I hope he may. His conduct while down the river was shameful.

D. S. Johnston has taken a contract to build *Morino* a barge 90 feet long, 22 feet breadth of beam. The contract was closed on Sunday last. He pledged to have her ready by the 1st of January.

The *Muscogee* is all ready for launching. I am only waiting for the river, which, from present appearances, will not keep me waiting long. The internal arrangements are complete, with the exception of the magazine. I wish I could have the benefit of your advice in fitting it up.

I was pleased to hear that you had met with such success in casting guns. I hope you will be ready to furnish the *Muscogee* her battery. I am told it is the only chance. They are not doing much in Richmond, Governor Milton informs me that so soon as this vessel is ready for service, Apalachicola will be reoccupied. He expressed himself thoroughly disgusted with Morino and all his works. Morino wants to make a wagon road over the river, using the obstructions as a foundation. Old Milton says he will blow them all to the devil and open the river. He has already communicated with the President on the subject, who thinks favorably of it.

Hope soon to hear from you.

I remain, very truly, your friend,

A. McLAUGHLIN.

Commander CATESBY ap R. JONES

2. A Desperate Effort

As work progressed on raising the sunken wreck of the CSS *Chattahoochee*, First Lieutenant George W. Gift replaced Lieutenant Guthrie as her commander. Guthrie had been sent to command the blockade runner *Advance*. Gift was an energetic and courageous officer, and he convinced the Navy Department in Richmond that he could break the blockade at Apalachicola, Florida, by boarding and capturing one of the enemy's two blockaders at the mouth of the river. He then planned to attack and capture the second vessel, thus clearing the area of Federal warships. (Turner, *Navy Gray: A Story of the Confederate Navy on the Chattahoochee and Apalachicola Rivers*, pp. 188–195.)

Midshipman J. Thomas Scharf was part of this expedition and gave an account of it in his book *History of the Confederate States Navy*. [RTC]

An Account of a Desperate Effort at Apalachicola, Florida by Midshipman J. Thomas Scharf, CSN

History of the Confederate States Navy, Chapter XIX, pp. 618–622.

In the spring of 1864 [May], Lieut. Gift and his officers determined to make a desperate effort to capture one or more vessels blockading Apalachicola. At this time the coast was blockaded by the U. S. steamers *Somerset* and *Adela,* and the plans of the officers of the *Chattahoochee* were to board in small boats one of these vessels, man her and attempt to capture the other, and if successful, break the blockade, and run the vessels into Mobile or burn them. About seven boats were fitted with muffled oars, grapnels, incendiary materials, signal flags, lanterns, compasses, medical stores, provisions, etc., and manned by the officers and crew of the *Chattahoochee*, numbering about seventy men, and about twenty volunteers from Company F, Bouneau's battalion of Confederate soldiers. The officers and men were armed with rifles, muskets, shot-guns, revolvers and cutlasses, with over 1,000 rounds of ammunition. Everything being made ready, the boats proceeded down the Apalachicola River on their hazardous enterprise. Pilots having been secured, when the boats arrived in St. George's Sound, they proceeded across the bay to East Point, to await a dark night before making the attack. The officers of the party were: Lieut. Commanding,

George W. Gift; Passed Midshipmen, Samuel P. Blanc, Henry L. Vaughan, George W. Sparks; Midshipmen, J. Thomas Scharf, Wm. S. Hogue; Assistant Paymaster, Marshal P. Sotheron; Assistant Surgeon, Marcellus Ford; First Assistant Engineer, Loudon Campbell; Third Assistant Engineer, A. De Blanc; Master's Mate, Carman Frazee; Volunteers: Colonel D. P. Holland, aide to the Governor of Florida; Surgeon Cherry, first Georgia regulars; A. G. Sparks, Signal Officer, and Capt. Blunt, in command of the volunteers from Bouneau's battalion.

Midshipman J. Thomas Scharf (Scharf, *History of the Confederate States Navy*).

The expedition landed in the night at East Point, near the east pass of St. George's Sound, which the U. S. steamer *Adela* was blockading. The plan was to remain under cover at this point until a favorable dark or stormy night, when the party was to row to the blockading vessel, and attempt her capture by boarding. Lieut. Gift and his men waited patiently for a favorable opportunity to make the attack, but they were doomed to disappointment. The nights were clear and the sea smooth, and the dipping of the oars in the phosphorescent water emitted a luminous light which shone brightly some distance beyond. In the meantime the provisions of the party gave out, and it was necessary to secure a supply from the town. Intelligence was also received from the Confederate scouts, that information of the contemplated attack had been communicated to the enemy's vessels by Unionists in Apalachicola.

Under these circumstances Lieut. Gift determined to abandon the enterprise and push across the sound and hasten up the Apalachicola River, before the enemy knew of his departure.

The Confederates embarked in their boats with the intention of crossing the sound to Apalachicola, but, as a storm was approaching, only two of the boats—the one containing Lieut. Gift, Midshipman Scharf and the volunteer officers, and the other manned by ten soldiers—attempted to cross the sound, while the others hugged the shore. The latter party, under the command of Passed Midshipman De Blanc, reached the town in safety, while the boat containing the soldiers was swamped; but the men in it were rescued by Lieut. Gift, who was driven fifteen miles across the sound to St. George's Island. The storm raged for several hours, and the heavily laden boat of Lieut. Gift made vain efforts to reach the town, from which direction the wind was blowing a terrible gale. Lieut. Gift being taken suddenly ill, the command of his boat devolved upon Midshipman Scharf. At this time the boat was half filled with water, with seventeen men inside and ten men from the swamped boat hanging on the outside, and the sea washing over her. The boat was two miles from shore, and all expected every moment would be the last. Finding that it would be impossible to reach the town in the face of the storm, Midshipman Scharf informed Lieut. Gift that their only hope for safety was to turn round and go to sea before the wind. The commander instructed him to do what he thought best, and immediately Midshipman Scharf informed his men of his determination. There was great fear of swamping in the trough of the sea in turning, but having confidence in his judgment the crew were ready to obey his commands. He ordered the boat to be lightened, and all the guns, ammunition, baggage, lanterns, water-casks, etc., thrown overboard. Six of the nearly exhausted men were taken in from the outside and stowed in the bottom of the boat. When everything was ready the order was given and the boat was headed for the Gulf of Mexico as a large wave struck under her quarter, nearly lifting her out of the water. The four men, who were still hanging on the outside, having become nearly exhausted, were taken in the already over-laden boat, and the storm-driven Confederates proceeded to sea, hoping, if possible, to reach St. George Island off the coast. When the boat approached St. George Island the breakers were heard roaring over the beach, and the pilot gave up all hope of reaching the shore in safety. The men prepared to swim for their lives in the event of the boat being swamped by the breakers, by throwing off all surplus clothing. Fortunately, the boat passed through safely and reached the island, where the party remained for two days in a starving condition, sustaining life only by eating "palmetto cabbage," "alligators," oysters, etc.

In the meantime, the remainder of the boats reached Apalachicola in safety, and took up quarters in the town, to await intelligence from Lieut. Gift. The enemy meanwhile, receiving information of the dispersing of the expedition, landed a force and drove Midshipman DeBlanc and his command to the swamps. In his report, Lieut. Com. Wm. Budd of the U. S. steamer *Somerset*, West Pass, St. George's Sound, May 16th, 1864, said:

"I have the honor to report, that on the night of the 12th inst. I sent the light-draft boats of this vessel and of the U. S. schooner *Chambers* to land a detachment of troops under command of Lieut. Hunter, 110th New York Vols., a few miles below the town of Apalachicola. After landing the troops the officer in charge of the boats (Acting Ensign E. H. Smith) was instructed to proceed slowly along shore, so as to be in communication with them during their march and approach to the town, in the rear of which the whole force was to arrive at daybreak. Taking two launches from this ship, I arrived in front of the place about the same time, and discovered a force of about seventy or eighty of the enemy attempting to embark in boats from the upper end of the wharves. The rapid approach of the first launch caused them to abandon that project and retreat through the town, which movement was hastened by a couple of shells from our howitzer. They passed within a short distance of a portion of our troops under Lieut. Hunter, who unfortunately thought that they were part of his command, and permitted them to gain and escape by the up-river road without molestation. We followed them about two miles, but the density of the undergrowth and number of paths leading through the woods in all directions rendering any further pursuit unwise and futile, we returned to the boats.

"Ascertaining that the commanding officer of the expedition (George W. Gift, Lieutenant C. S. N.) was on the sound with about thirty men, I dispatched my boats and troops after him, but the swiftness of his boat and the approach of night enabled him to escape, having been chased by our first launch, under command of Acting Ensign C. H. Brantingham, who captured one of his small boats and three of his party. * * * We captured six of their boats (all they had except one), four prisoners, a quantity of small arms, (rifles, cutlasses, etc.) 1,000 rounds of ammunition, all their compasses, signal flags, blankets, haversacks, medical stores, etc. They abandoned everything. * * * Had it not been for the unfortunate mistake of the officer in command of our troops, we should have captured or destroyed the entire force."

In a subsequent report dated May 21st, 1864, he said

"I send down by the U. S steamer *Honduras*, as prisoners, Thomas McLean, Anthony Murray and James Anderson, citizens of Apalachicola. These men were engaged in active co-operation with the enemy when captured. McLean enacted the role of a scout or spy. Mistaking our troops for those of the enemy, he gave them information respecting my force and position in front of the town on the morning of the 13th inst. Murray and Anderson were acting as scouts for Gift, keeping open his communications and supplying him with provisions when he was absent from the main body of his command. When taken, they were carrying soldiers from the islands back to the main. Heretofore all of them have enjoyed immunity from us as citizens. Their local knowledge makes them dangerous to us and very useful to the enemy; for the latter they act as scouts, spies and pilots, and in this case they were caught in the act. They pretend to have been forced into Gift's service, but I know them well, and earnestly request that they will not be permitted to return to Apalachicola."

The enemy captured Andrew McCormick, Sergeant of Company F, Bouneau's battalion, Napoleon Terry and Louis Gay, privates, and Joseph Sire, Captain after-guard of the *Chattahoochee*.

Before Midshipman DeBlanc and his command retreated to the swamps, he sent Thomas McLean, Anthony Murray, and James Anderson, citizens of Apalachicola, with a supply of provisions to search the islands along the coast for Lieut. Gift and his two boats' crews. The relief party found the wrecked crews, and as soon as the storm abated they returned with them to Apalachicola, where they learned for the first time that their comrades had been driven from the town. Lieut. Gift then hastened up the river to avoid the enemy, who were searching the islands for him. He carried his boat some distance up the river, then sank it in a bayou and traveled over-land with his command until he joined the remainder of his party above the obstructions in the Apalachicola River.

Upon the abandonment of the river by the Confederates [April 16, 1865] the *Chattahoochee* was destroyed, together with the iron-clad gunboat *Columbus*, [*Jackson*] which had been building for a long time at Columbus, Ga., under the direction of Lieut. Andrew McLaughlin. A torpedo boat, nearly completed, was also destroyed at Columbus, together with the navy-yard, machine shops, etc.

VI

Mobile, Alabama

1. The CSS *Tennessee*

By the beginning of the American Civil War, Mobile, Alabama, was one of the most important deepwater ports in the South. When Admiral David G. Farragut's Union fleet captured New Orleans on April 25, 1862, Mobile took on an added importance to the Confederacy as the primary port on the Gulf for the exportation of cotton and the importation of essential war materials. While much faith was placed on the two forts guarding the entrance to Mobile Bay, Secretary Mallory knew that the forts plus a strong naval force was the only way the South could hope to prevent the loss of this important port.

In October of 1862, Confederate authorities entered into a contract with Henry D. Bassett, a Mobile shipbuilder, for the construction of an ironclad warship that would eventually be commissioned as the CSS *Tennessee*. Bassett was already busy building two ironclad floating batteries at Selma, Alabama, and the keel for the *Tennessee* was laid in the shipyard next to them. After the usual frustrating delays, she was launched in February of 1863, and the armored steamer *Baltic* towed her to Mobile where the *Tennessee*'s machinery and armament was installed.

She had taken a long time to complete, and had cost $883,880, but by the end of January 1864, the large ironclad was all but finished. At 9:00 AM on the morning of February 16, she was officially commissioned as the CSS *Tennessee*, and her officers were assigned and ordered aboard. (*Official Records Navy*, Series I, Volume XXI, p. 934.)

While Buchanan flew his flag from the ironclad as commander of the Confederate Mobile Squadron, the *Tennessee*'s captain was Commander James D. Johnston of Kentucky. Johnston had resigned from the U.S. Navy on April 10, 1861, and after seeing service at New Orleans, had been given command of the iron and cotton clad steamer *Baltic* at Mobile. By February of 1863, the *Baltic* had been declared unfit for service, and Buchanan, much impressed by Johnston's abilities, ordered him to command the *Tennessee*. (Symonds, *Confederate Admiral: The Life and Wars of Franklin Buchanan*, p. 200.)

On August 5, 1864, the expected storm broke, as Admiral Farragut's powerful fleet of four ironclad monitors and 14 wooden steamers began their push into Mobile Bay. In an article for *Century Magazine*, later incorporated into *Battles & Leaders of the Civil War*, Commander Johnston gave his account of the *Tennessee*'s epic battle. [RTC]

"The Ram Tennessee *at Mobile Bay*" by Commander James D. Johnston, CSN

Battles & Leaders of the Civil War, Volume IV, pp. 401–406

The Confederate naval forces at the time of Admiral Farragut's attack was commanded by Admiral Franklin Buchanan, of *Merrimac* fame, and consisted of the iron-clad ram *Ten-*

nessee, armed with four 6.4-inch rifled guns in broadside, and two 7-inch rifles, one at each end of the shield; the gun-boats *Morgan* and *Gaines*, carrying six guns each, chiefly of smaller caliber; and the *Selma*, carrying only four, making in all 22 guns. The entire force of officers and men was about 470. Admiral Farragut's fleet consisted of six first-class steam sloops of war, eight smaller sloops and gun-boats, and four monitors, two of which had double turrets. The total number of guns carried by these vessels was 159, and 33 howitzers; and the officers and crews numbered about 3000.

The hull of the *Tennessee* was constructed on a high bluff near the Alabama River, a short distance above the city of Selma, and all the timber used was cut in the immediate vicinity. She was 209 feet in length and 48 feet in breadth of beam. The shield for the protection of her battery and crew was 78 feet 8 inches long and 8 feet high above the deck, which at each end of the shield was only about 18 inches above the surface of the water when the vessel had been prepared for service. Sponsons of heavy timber projected about five feet from the sides in a line with the deck, extending seven feet below it, the lower edge of the shield covering the outer angle or apex of the sponsons. The sides of the shield were of yellow pine and white oak, 23 inches thick, placed at an angle of 33 degrees with the deck.

Commander James D. Johnston (Naval Historical Center).

When she was prepared for launching, I was ordered by Admiral Buchanan to charter two steamboats and proceed with them to Selma, to tow her down to Mobile, as soon as she was launched. I found on arrival at Selma that every preparation had been made for that purpose by the naval constructor in charge (Mr. Henry Pearce). She was immediately taken in tow by the steamboats and towed down to Mobile, to receive her machinery and battery, the latter having been cast at the Government foundry at Selma, under the superintendence of Commander Catesby ap Roger Jones, late commander of the *Merrimac*, who had acquired great distinction as an ordnance officer of the United States navy. The armor plating had been prepared at the rolling-mills of Atlanta, and was rapidly arriving. It consisted of plates of exceedingly tough and malleable iron seven inches wide, two inches thick and 21 feet long. Three layers of the 2-inch plates were bolted on the forward end of the shield as far as the after end of the pilot-house (which extended about two feet above the top of the shield), and from that point to the termination of the shield two plates of 2-inch and one of 1-inch were used.

While this tedious work was progressing, the machinery and guns were placed in position, and about the 1st of April, 1864, the vessel was ready to receive her crew. As executive officer of the station under the admiral, I had superintended the completion of the vessel, and by his request I was now selected for the command, being immediately afterward promoted to the grade of commander.

But as the draught of the vessel was over thirteen feet, and there were only nine feet of water on Dog River bar, at the mouth of the Mobile River, it became a serious problem to solve as to the means of floating her over this bar. Naval Constructor Thomas Porter conceived the idea building heavy camels or floats, to be made fast to the sides of the ram; the surfaces in contact with the ram to conform to the model of the hull; and the camels were to contain a sufficient weight of water to counterbalance in part the weight of the vessel. This plan was immediately adopted, but the timber for the purpose had yet to pass from the forest, through the saw-mill, some ten miles up the river, down to Mobile. Time was precious, and the newspapers were beginning to express the impatience of the people to see the powerful ram of which so much was expected taken down the bay to attack the blockading fleet. The camels were being constructed with all possible dispatch, but just as they were nearly ready they were totally destroyed by fire. Undaunted by this calamity, Admiral Buchanan, with his usual energy and pluck, soon had them rebuilt, and about the middle of May the *Tennessee*, drawing less than nine feet of water, was towed over the bar by two steamboats, one of which contained her coal, and the other her ammunition.

Her crew were employed during the passage down the bay in transferring these supplies, and by the time she reached a sufficient depth of water to float without the aid of the camels, she was quite prepared for action. But unfortunately it was now near midnight, and by the time the camels had been sent adrift, the tide had fallen so much that she was found to be hard and fast aground. Here was an insurmountable and most unlooked-for end to the long-cherished hope of taking the enemy by surprise, dispersing the blockading fleet, and capturing Fort Pickens, at the entrance of Pensacola Bay. Such was the work Buchanan had mapped out for the ram, and but for the fact that her presence in the bay was soon revealed by daylight, this attempt would certainly have been made.

When the tide rose sufficiently to float the ship, she was moved down to an anchorage near Fort Morgan, where she remained nearly three months, engaged in exercising the crew at their guns.

Having realized from the first that the running of the steering gear was very defective, I addressed a letter to the admiral soon after reaching our anchorage, suggesting certain necessary alterations therein, and he sent the naval constructor down from the city to make plans for the purpose; but before they could be perfected we were compelled to take the consequences of the defect, which proved to be disastrous.

On the evening of the 4th of August, 1864, it was plainly to be seen that the blockading fleet, which had recently been augmented by the arrival of the heavier wooden vessels and the monitors, was making preparations to attempt the passage of Forts Morgan and Gaines, situated on either side of the entrance to the bay, and to attack the Confederate squadron. Similar preparations were made by our vessels, which had been anchored just within the bay for nearly three months, in daily expectation of the impending encounter. During the night a blockade-runner entered the bay and was boarded by the executive officer of the *Tennessee*.

At about 6 o'clock on the morning of the 5th, the fleet was discovered to be underway toward the bay, the monitors on the right and the wooden vessels lashed together two and two, each of the heavier ships having a gun-boat lashed alongside. All the light spars had been sent down, leaving only the lower and top masts standing, while the boats had been hauled upon the beach at Sand Island just within the bar, on the morning previous.

All hands were immediately called on board the Confederate vessels, and after hurriedly taking coffee, the crew were set to work to slip the cable and buoy the anchor. This being done, they were assembled at their quarters for action, as the distance from the bar to the entrance of the bay is only about three miles, and the Federal vessels were already within range of the guns of Fort Morgan and were receiving its fire without damage.

As the leading monitor, the *Tecumseh*, reached the center of the channel between the forts, the *Tennessee* steamed out to meet her, but the speed of both vessels was so slow that the steam-sloops advanced beyond them, and the *Tennessee* was directed toward the leading ship, with the hope of reaching her in time to run into her broadside and sink her; but by slightly changing her course, and with her superior speed, the ship easily avoided the intended ramming, and seemed to fly up the bay. This was the admiral's flag-ship *Hartford*, and while she passed ahead of the ram, the *Brooklyn*, leading the other vessels of the fleet, passed astern and followed the admiral. I learned after the fight that her commander had obtained the admiral's permission to take the lead but an event occurred just after the *Tennessee* had moved down to the middle of the channel* which disconcerted him for a moment and caused him to stop his ship, thus compelling the admiral to take the lead himself. This event was the most startling and tragic of the day, causing the almost instantaneous loss of 93 lives. The monitor *Tecumseh* at her commander's special request, had been detailed to "take care of the *Tennessee*" and had reserved her fire until she had approached that vessel within a quarter of a mile, when she was suddenly struck by a torpedo, and disappeared beneath the water. But for the cheering of my men as they saw her sinking I should not have seen her go down. Twenty-one of her crew escaped from her, of whom four landed at Fort. Morgan.

Meantime the other vessels of the Confederate squadron were doing their duty faithfully by raking the enemy's ships as they advanced head on, and they killed and wounded a large number of men.

As soon as Admiral Buchanan realized that his enemy had escaped for the moment he ordered me to follow him up the bay; but meanwhile the lashings between each two vessels of the fleet had been cast off, and four gun-boats went immediately in pursuit of the three hastily improvised wooden vessels of our squadron. The *Selma* was speedily captured by one of these the *Metacomet*, after a gallant resistance, during which seven of her crew and her executive officer were killed, and her commander, Lieutenant P. U. Murphy, was slightly wounded. The *Gaines*, commanded by Lieutenant John W. Bennett, which was run ashore near Fort Morgan to prevent her from sinking, had received several shots below the water-line, and at night was burned by her own crew. The *Morgan*, Commander George W. Harrison, ran alongside the wharf at the fort to escape capture, and during the night passed safely through the enemy's fleet up to the city of Mobile. She afterward rendered good service in the defense of the city.

While this sort of by-play was in progress the heavier ships of the fleet, together with the monitors, steamed up the bay to a point about four miles above Fort Morgan, where they were in the act of anchoring when it was discovered that the ram was approaching with hostile intent. Upon this apparently unexpected challenge the fleet was immediately put in motion, and the heavier vessels seemed to contend with each other for the glory of sinking the daring rebel ram, by running themselves up on her decks, which extended some thirty feet at each end of the shield, and were only about eighteen inches above the surface of the water. So great was their eagerness to accomplish this feat that the *Lackawanna*, one of the heaviest steamers, ran bows on into the *Hartford*, by which both vessels sustained greater damage than their united efforts in this direction could have inflicted upon their antagonist.

Early in the action, the pilot of the *Tennessee* had been wounded by having the trap-door on the top of the pilot-house knocked down upon his head by a shot from one of the enemy's ships, which struck it on the edge while it was thrown back to admit of his seeing more clearly the position of the vessel. Thereafter I remained in the pilot-house, for the purpose of directing the movements of the ram.

The monitors kept up a constant firing at short range. The two double-turreted mon-

---

In this statement, Captain Johnston's chronology is undoubtedly at fault. The testimony of eye-witnesses makes it certain that the Brooklyn *had stopped before the sinking of the* Tecumseh. — EDITORS.

itors (*Chickasaw* and *Winnebago*) were stationed under the stern of the *Tennessee,* and struck the after end of her shield so repeatedly with 11-inch solid shot that it was found at the close of the action to be in a rather shaky condition. One of these missiles had struck the iron cover of the stern port and jammed it against the shield so that it became impossible to run the gun out for firing, and Admiral Buchanan, who superintended the battery during the entire engagement, sent to the engine room for a machinist to back out the pin of the bolt upon which the port cover revolved. While this was being done a shot from one of the monitors struck the edge of the port cover, immediately over the spot where the machinist was sitting, and his remains had to be taken up with a shovel, placed in a basket, and thrown overboard. The same shot caused several iron splinters to fly inside of the shield, one of which killed a seaman, while another broke the admiral's leg below the knee. The admiral sent for me, and as I approached he quietly remarked, "Well, Johnston, they've got me. You'll have to look out for her now. This is your fight, you know." I replied, "All right, sir. I'll do the best I know how."

While returning to the pilot-house I felt the vessel careen so suddenly as nearly to throw me off my feet. I discovered that the *Hartford** had run into the ram amidships, and that while thus in contact with her the Federal crew were using their small-arms by firing through the open ports. However, only one man was wounded in this way, the cause of all our other wounds being iron splinters from the washers on the inner ends of the bolts that secured the plating. I continued on my way to the pilot-house, and upon looking through the narrow peep-holes in its sides to ascertain the position of the enemy's ships, I discovered that the wooden vessels had mostly withdrawn from the action, leaving it to the monitors to effect the destruction of the ram at their leisure. At this time both of my most efficient guns had been placed in broadside, because both the after and forward port covers had been so effectually jammed against the shield as to block up the ports.

The steering apparatus had been completely destroyed, as it had been plainly visible on the after deck, and the smoke-stack had fallen, destroying the draught in such a degree as to render it impossible to keep steam enough to stem the tide, which was running out at the rate of over four miles an hour.

Realizing the impossibility of directing the firing of the guns without the use of the rudder, and that the ship had been rendered utterly helpless, I went to the lower deck and informed the admiral of her condition and that I had not been able to bring a gun to bear upon any of our antagonists for nearly half an hour, to which he replied: "Well, Johnston, if you cannot do them any further damage you had better surrender." With this sanction of my own views I returned to the gun-deck, and after another glance about the bay to see if there was any chance of getting another shot, and seeing none of the enemy's ships within range of our broadside guns, I went to the top of the shield and took down the boat-hook to which the flag had been lashed after having been shot away several times during the fight. While I was thus engaged repeated shots came from the enemy's vessels, but as soon as I returned to the gun-deck and had a flag of truce attached to the boat-hook the firing ceased. Having returned to the top of the shield, I saw one of the heaviest ships of the fleet approaching rapidly, apparently for the purpose of making another attempt to sink the ram. Seeing the flag of truce, the commander stopped his ship, but her momentum was too great to be overcome in the short intervening space, and she struck the ram on the starboard

---

**All the official reports show that the only contact between the Hartford and the ram was bows on, a glancing blow (see Report of the Secretary of the Navy, 1864, pp. 402, 407, and 410). Captain Johnston undoubtedly mistook the* Lackawanna *for the* Hartford. *Admiral Farragut in his report (ibid., p. 402) says:*

"*The* Lackawanna, *Captain Marchand, was the next vessel to strike her, which she did at full speed; but, though her stern was cut and crushed to the plank ends for the distance of three feet above the water's edge to five feet below, the only perceptible effect on the ram was to give her a heavy list." EDITOR.*

quarter, but without injuring it.* As she did so her commander hailed, saying: "This is the United States steamer *Ossipee*. Hello, Johnston, how are you? Le Roy—don't you know me? I'll send a boat alongside for you." The boat came and conveyed me on board the *Ossipee*, at whose gangway I was met by her genial commander, between whom and myself a lifelong friendship had existed. When I reached the deck of his ship, he remarked, "I'm glad to see you, Johnston. Here's some ice-water for you—I know you're dry; but I've something better than that for you down below." I thanked him cordially, but was in no humor for receiving hospitalities graciously, and quietly followed him to his cabin, where he placed a bottle of "navy sherry" and a pitcher of ice-water before me and urged me to help myself. Calling his steward, he ordered him to attend to my wishes as he would his own. I remained on board six days, during which time I was visited by nearly all the commanding officers of the fleet.

Within an hour after I was taken on board the *Ossipee* Admiral Farragut sent for me to be brought on board his flag-ship, and when I reached her deck he expressed regret at meeting me under such circumstances, to which I replied that he was not half as sorry to see me as I was to see him.

His flag-captain, Percival Drayton, remarked, "You have one consolation, Johnston; no one can say that you have not nobly defended the honor of the Confederate flag today." I thanked him, but gave all the honor due to its defense to Admiral Buchanan, who was the true hero of the battle; and when the disparity between the forces engaged is duly considered, I am constrained to believe that history will give him his just need of praise.

The casualties on board the *Tennessee* were two killed and nine wounded. Her armor was never penetrated, although she was under the heaviest fire for nearly four hours. One solid 15-inch shot struck her shield, at point-blank range, between two of the ports and caused an indentation of about twelve inches, but did not break the iron plating.† Her speed did not exceed six knots under full steam in slack water, owing to her heavy draught, which exceeded the original calculation by more than a foot. Her engine had been removed from, an old Mississippi River steamboat and adapted to a propeller, and its power was totally inadequate to the performance of the work expected of it.

After I left the *Tennessee* Admiral Buchanan was transferred to a small transport steamer and taken to the hospital in the navy yard at Pensacola, where he was accompanied by his own fleet surgeon, Dr. D. B. Conrad, and his aides. Five days after the admiral's departure I was transported to Pensacola and transferred to the receiving-ship *Potomac*, lying off the navy yard; but as soon as Admiral Farragut's fleet-surgeon, Dr. James C. Palmer, heard of my arrival he had me removed to the hospital, owing to the fact of my suffering at the time with a painful disease. On reaching the hospital I found myself placed in a room near to that occupied by Admiral Buchanan, and immediately adjoining that of Captain J. R. M. Mullany, who had commanded the steamer *Oneida* of the fleet, and had had the misfortune to have his left arm shot away during the action. I had known him long before the war, and called upon him at once to offer my condolence.

After remaining in the hospital about three weeks I was placed on board a small

---

This statement is not sustained by the official records of the fight. Admiral Farragut in his report says: "She [the ram] was at this time sore beset; the Chickasaw *was pounding away at her stern, the* Ossipee *was, approaching her at full speed, and the* Monongahela, Lackawanna, *and this ship [*Hartford*] were bearing down upon her." Here is direct mention of four wooden ships, and the* Brooklyn, Richmond, *and others were not out of the fight. EDITORS.*

†*The Board of Survey appointed by Admiral Farragut, and consisting of Captain T. A. Jenkins, Captain James Alden, Commander W.E. Le Roy, and Chief Engineer Thomas Williamson, reported in part as follows on the injuries received in the action, by the* Tennessee:

"*On the port side of the casemate the armor is also badly damaged from shot. On that side nearly amidship of the casemate, and between the two broadside guns, a 15-inch solid shot knocked a hole through, the armor and backing, leaving on the inside an undetached mass of oak and pine splinters, about three by four feet, and projecting inside of the casemate about two feet from the side. This is the only shot that penetrated the wooden backing of the casemate, although their are numerous places on the inside giving evidence of the effect of the shot" (Report of the Secretary of the Navy, 1864, p. 455).*

ordnance steamer in company with Lieutenant-Commanding Murphy, late of the *Selma*, with Lieutenants Bradford and Wharton of the *Tennessee*, accompanied by my servant (whom Admiral Farragut had kindly allowed me to retain), for transportation to the Brooklyn Navy Yard. We reached our destination after a pleasant passage of five or six days, and on arrival the commander of the steamer, Captain Tarbox, reported to Admiral Hiram Paulding, commandant of the yard. On returning to the steamer he informed me that he had obtained the admiral's permission to escort the party to the navy yard at Boston, and that it was his intention to take us all down to his home at Cape Ann to spend a few days with him before turning us over to the officer commanding Fort Warren, which was to be our abode until we were exchanged. We were all delighted at the prospect of this pleasing respite from prison life, and expressed our gratitude to the kind-hearted captain. But we were awakened early on the following morning by the announcement from the distressed captain, who had had a second interview with the admiral, that we were all to be placed in irons and conveyed to Boston by rail. We remonstrated gently against this unprecedented mode of treating prisoners of war, but to no purpose.

When we reached the wharf at Fort Warren, the commanding officer, Major A. A. Gibson, inquired the cause of our being in irons, and upon being informed that they were placed upon us by order of Admiral Paulding, he made the further inquiry whether or not we had been guilty of any rebellious conduct as prisoners of war; this being answered in the negative, he replied that he had never heard of such treatment, and that we could not be landed on the island until the irons were removed.

Soon after becoming settled in my new quarters I addressed a communication to the Secretary of the Navy inquiring whether or not he had authorized the action of Admiral Paulding, which was answered by Assistant-Secretary Fox, who disavowed the act, but excused it on the ground of repeated attempts of prisoners to escape.

An order for the exchange of all the prisoners in the fort had reached the commanding officer previous to our arrival, and after ten days we left for City Point on the steamer *Assyrian*. We naturally supposed that on our arrival at City Point we would be immediately forwarded to the landing on James River, at which exchanges were usually made. But when General B. F. Butler, whose lines were between us and that point, was advised of our presence he refused to allow us to pass through them, on account of President Davis' proclamation declaring him an outlaw. The Commissioner of Exchange informed General Grant of the fact and he came alongside the *Assyrian* with his steamer, and informed us that we should be forwarded to Richmond on the following day.

True to his promise he had us landed near Dutch Gap the next morning, whence we were conveyed in ambulances to Varina Landing, where we found a Confederate steamer awaiting us with the Federal prisoners on board. We soon exchanged places to the tune of "Dixie." After a delightful visit of five days at the house of Mrs. Stephen R. Mallory, the charming wife of the Secretary of the Confederate Navy, I was ordered to return to Mobile and report for duty under Commodore Ebenezer Farrand, who had succeeded Admiral Buchanan in command of that station.

2. The CSS *Gaines*

Lieutenant John W. Bennett resigned from the U. S. Navy on April 18, 1861, even though his home state of Maryland was forcibly prevented from seceding by the Lincoln government. He was granted a commission in the Confederate navy on June 20, and assigned to the cruiser CSS *Nashville* being fitted out at Charleston. Bennett served on the *Nashville* as it ran the blockade on October 21 on its way to England. Upon the ship's return to the Confederacy in February of 1862, he was assigned to command the gunboat CSS *Gaines* at Mobile, Alabama.

The *Gaines* was a sidewheel steamer of 863 tons and was hastily constructed at Mobile during 1861 and 1862 from unseasoned wood. She was partially covered with 2-inch iron plating to protect her machinery, and was armed with one 8-inch rifle and five 32-pounders. (Scharf, *History of the Confederate States Navy*, pp. 555–556.)

Lieutenant Bennett and the *Gaines* fought in the Battle of Mobile Bay, and several days after the battle he submitted his report to his commanding officer, Admiral Franklin Buchanan. [RTC]

Official Report of
1st Lt. John W. Bennett, CSN

Official Records Navy, Series I, Volume XXI, pp. 588–590

MOBILE, ALA., *August 8, 1864.*

SIR: I have the honor to submit a report of the part taken by the *Gaines*, under my command, in the action of the 5th instant, off Fort Morgan, and the circumstances which led to the beaching and abandonment of the ship.

The *Gaines* was geared for action about 6:20 AM, and in obedience to signal from the admiral to follow "his motions," waited for him to open upon the advancing enemy, advancing with four monitors in line mead and fourteen wooden vessels by twos, each large ship having a smaller one lashed to her port side, the whole forming one compact line of battle. As soon as the *Tennessee* delivered fire, the *Gaines*, having placed herself next the admiral, commenced at about 2,000 yards distance with her pivot guns, upon the leading wooden ships, supposed to be the *Hartford* and her consort, at about 6:50, as nearly as supposed determine, and continued to deliver a raking fire upon the leading wooden ships until their passage past the fort. She then made one circle to prevent too close action—as she was lying nearly in the track of the advancing fleet—and afterwards steered in nearly parallel lines with the enemy at distances gradually diminishing, until she was within at least 700 yards and engaging with her port guns. The enemy now being clear of the fort, was enabled to direct attention exclusively to our little squadron.

Early in the action a shell exploded near the steering wheel, wounding the two men stationed at it and cutting the wheel rope. The ship was then steered with the relieving tackles until the after wheel ropes could be rove. Shortly after this, it was reported that the forward magazine was filled with smoke and thought to be on fire. This, on examination, luckily proved a mistake. An XI-inch shot had entered the starboard bow, striking the deck above the magazine, had broken it in, and made so much dust that the gunner's mate, serving powder in that magazine, thought it smoke, and believed from the shock and dust that a shell had exploded and fired that part of the ship: He reported accordingly. This occasioned a short delay in the serving of powder to the forward division. The firemen of this division, with hose and buckets, went promptly to the spot, under the executive officer, and soon discovered the mistake. About this time the ship was subjected to a very heavy concentrated fire from the *Hartford*, *Richmond*, and others at short range as the enemy passed me. Nearly their whole fire seemed for a time to be directed at the *Gaines*. The after magazine was now discovered filling with water. I went below to examine it, and found much water had accumulated in it, and was rapidly increasing. Not being aware of any shot having entered near the water [in] that part of the ship, and being unable to see any damage upon inspection from the side which could have caused such a leak, I directed the executive officer, with the carpenter's mate, to get into a boat and make examination of the counter. He found a shot had broken in the outer planking under the port quarter about the water line, and which, from marks, seemed to have glanced below in the direction of the sternpost. This could not be stopped by reason of the impossibility of getting to it, because of the flare of the counter. As this break could not have caused all the water which flowed into the ship, I am of opinion that it was a shell which had caused the break and had probably exploded below water under the counter and had started the timbers near the sternpost; the ship had received a shock during the engagement which shook her from stem to stern, being much more violent than that of shot passing through. The bilge pumps were immediately worked, but there was no water in the engine room. Finding the magazine rapidly filled, also the after hold and shell room, with no water in the engine room, I caused the after bulkhead of the engine room to be knocked down so as to allow the flow of water to the bilge pumps. By this time the stern had settled some and the steering became difficult. Under these circumstances I determined to withdraw from action. The enemy's fleet had now passed.

Finding the ship would sink in a short time, and thinking I might be able to reach the shore, now about two or three miles distant, I withdrew from action and made the best of my way toward the fort, steering the ship principally with the side wheels, which position I reached without embarrassment from the enemy thanks to an opportune rain squall which shut me from view—and placed her bow upon the beach within 500 yards of Fort Morgan, about 9:30.

I am happy to state there was no confusion or panic under the circumstances of our position, but that every work was done with deliberation and without undue excitement. The ship delivered fire to the enemy at the moment of striking the shore.

At the time of beaching the magazine was nearly filled. I had caused all the powder to be removed to the cabin, the shells were removed as rapidly as possible, but not before many of them might become submerged. The usefulness of the ship having been destroyed by the enemy, I devoted myself and crew to the preservation of all valuable materiel, and I landed all the powder, shells, shot, gun equipment, etc., which I gave to the general commanding at Fort Morgan, to whom I thought they might be useful in the expected siege. The crew were then landed with their bags and blankets, muskets, cutlasses, and small-arms ammunition, and the ship abandoned at 12 o'clock, with her battle flags flying, and her stern settled as far as it could—about 2 fathoms. I did not spike the guns, because they could be secured by the fort, and could not to be taken by the enemy.

Having thus left my command, it became necessary to devise a retreat for my crew—they were not necessary to the fort, as I was informed when I offered their services. Already I had secured two boats belonging to the *Tennessee*—left by her at anchor—and with four boats from the Games—one having been destroyed by shot—I left the fort at 8 o'clock PM, and reached Mobile at 7 o'clock AM on the 6th with 129 officers and men, small arms, etc., and six boats, passed the enemy's fleet without observation, and reported myself and crew to the senior officer for further service. Not a man was lost by straggling, and I brought up the wounded. The dead were buried on the afternoon of the 5th in the fort's burial ground. We had only 2 killed and 3 wounded. The surgeon's report of casualties I herewith enclose.

Whilst running the gantlet up the bay I became apprehensive of capture or of being forced to land and make a march to Mobile. The *Morgan* was being chased by the enemy. As I knew it was her intention to pass near the eastern shore, and could see her approach us, I feared she might lead the enemy upon the boats. Under these circumstances I deemed it prudent to drop the signal book into the sea. I did so.

The officers and crew of the *Gaines* for about ten or fifteen minutes were subjected to a very heavy fire from the enemy at short distance, and I am proud to say stood it with great gallantry; there were two or three exceptional cases only. Without casting censure upon any by my silence, I can not withhold the expression of my thanks to Lieutenant Payne, Passed Assistant Surgeon Iglehart, Second Assistant Engineer Debois, Gunner Offutt, and Paymaster's Clerk Wilson (in charge of the supply of shells to the after division) for their examples of coolness and gallantry under the trying circumstances of this combat against an overwhelming force, and the influence it must have had among the crew, most of whom had never before been in action. Frequent interviews with these officers caused me to regard them with admiration.

The ship received seventeen shots in her hull and smokestack; of these only two can be said to have caused her any distress—that which caused the leak and the cutting of the wheel ropes.

As is usual and proper when a ship is lost, I beg the Department to order a court of enquiry to investigate the causes which led to the abandonment of the *Gaines*.

I am, very respectfully, your obedient servant,

1st Lt. John W. Bennett (Hartzler, *A Band of Brothers*).

J. W. BENNETT,
Lieutenant, Commanding.

Hon. S. R. MALLORY,
Secretary of the Navy, Richmond, Va.

3. The CSS *Morgan*

The CSS *Morgan*, an 863-ton sidewheel steamer, was similar to the CSS *Gaines* and was built at Mobile during 1861 and 1862. Various reports have her as being armed with anywhere from six to 10 guns. She was captained by Commander George W. Harrison who was born in the West Indies, but was appointed to Confederate service from Virginia after resigning from the U. S. Navy on April 17, 1861. Harrison commanded the steamers *Hampton* and *Jamestown* of the James River Squadron during 1862 before being transferred to Mobile and the CSS *Morgan*. (Moebs, *Confederate States Navy Research Guide*, p. 219.)

Admiral Buchanan sharply criticized the *Morgan*'s commander for his behavior at the Battle of Mobile Bay; however, in his report to the admiral, Harrison seems to justify his actions. [RTC]

Official Report of Commander George W. Harrison, CSN

Official Records Navy, series I, vol., XXI, pp. 583–585

C. S. S. MORGAN,
Mobile, October 1, 1864.

Sir: I respectfully address you this letter for the purpose of relating the particular part taken by this vessel in the action with the enemy's fleet on the 5th of August last.

The *Morgan*, as you must be aware, was on the extreme right of the Confederate line of battle as the enemy came up the channel from seaward by Fort Morgan, and was thus enabled from her position ahead of hire to deliver a very effective broadside raking fire into his leading vessel, which met with little or no response until the head of his column, said to be the *Hartford*, with a double-ender lashed to her western side, had approached to within about 600 yards of us, and having with others in the rear well entered the bay had obliged our line of battle to swing back by its right. The *Hartford* was then enabled to use her bow guns upon us; but as we kept for the most of the time on her starboard bow we could materially injure her, while she could inflict but small damage upon us. Our shell are reported to have several times struck, and one in particular from our forward pivot gun must have been considerably destructive (afterwards confirmed by a New Orleans account) as it struck her bulwarks forward and for a time silenced the gun mounted on her forecastle.

We maintained our excellent position until toward the close of the action with the *Hartford*, when we fell astern to her beam and the *Selma* shot ahead of us. At this time a broadside of missiles were thrown at us, but fortunately the greater part went over, only a few grapeshot striking us.

The enemy's fleet had now accomplished its purpose, being entirely within the bay and running up the "pocket" of deep water known as the "Lower Fleet." The *Tennessee*, owing to her slowness, was some distance astern following up its rear. The *Gaines* had been disabled and forced out of action and the course we were pursuing was taking us farther and farther away from

Admiral Franklin Buchanan (Naval Historical Center).

the peninsula which was our only place of refuge in case of being hard pressed, and thus the chances were continually increasing of our being cut off from all retreat by the enemy's gunboats, which I foresaw would soon be thrown off from the fleet in pursuit; so I sheered off to the starboard, the *Selma* doing the same, and (as I had anticipated) a double-ender, said to be the *Metacomet*, in a few moments after started off from the *Hartford* and soon overhauled and engaged in action with my vessel, while the *Selma*, on our port bow, continued her retreat (unfortunately for her) in a direction to cross the mouth of Bon Secours Bay and reach the eastern shore of Mobile Bay. After a short cannonading between us the *Metacomet* slipped off and steamed rapidly in pursuit of the *Selma*, seeing which and that my vessel would inevitably be cut off and captured by the two other vessels of the enemy now on their way to join in the pursuit if I suffered her to engage in a stern chase, which is always a long one, and knowing, furthermore, that with the coal dust on board, which was my only fuel, I could not possibly make steam enough to overtake two such fast vessels as the *Metacomet* and *Selma*, going off as they were at top speed, I deemed it best to turn the *Morgan's* bow directly in to shallower water, and in doing so we grounded on the long stretch of shoals which extends off from the land a little to the eastward of Navy Cove. We backed off, however, in a few minutes, and the *Selma* having by that time surrendered to the *Metacomet* and the other chasing gunboats having nearly reached them, I directed my vessel's course toward Fort Morgan, on approaching which we discovered a small Federal gunboat aground on the western side of the seaward channel about a mile and a half below the fort. I steamed down toward her and sent a boat with Lieutenant Thomas L. Harrison to burn her, which was accordingly done. She proved to be the *Philippi*, disabled by a shot from the fort and abandoned. Having performed this duty, we returned to the fort and made fast to the wharf.

A short time before proceeding on this affair of the burning, the *Tennessee*, about 4 miles distant from us, after a desperate contest with the enemy, been compelled, by being disabled (as we afterwards learned), to yield to an overwhelming force, and the *Morgan* was now the only vessel left of our little squadron. I felt exceedingly anxious to save her to the Confederacy by "running the gantlet" up the bay to Mobile, distant about 25 miles; but it seemed so impossible in a noisy, high-pressure steamer, making black smoke, to pass the enemy's fleet unobserved or to elude the vigilance of his gunboats, which were seen after the action to go up the bay, that I gave up the idea at one time as impracticable and made preparations to take to the boats, as the *Gaines* people intended to do when night should come. Upon reconsideration of the matter, however, I determined to make the effort, and having landed three-fourths of my provisions for the use of the garrison and thrown overboard my coal dust for the purpose of picking out all the lumps that could be found, as well as to lighten the vessel, I started at 11 PM of a starlight night upon an enterprise which no one on shore or afloat expected to be successful. Not only was this the universal opinion, but all letters and papers from the fort were sent in charge of Lieutenant Commanding Bennett in his boats, which were to go up along shore, nor would the two or three townspeople who happened to be down there take passage with us, preferring the longer and safer route by land. But fortune favored us, and although hotly pursued and shelled by the enemy's cruisers for a large portion of the way, we successfully reached the outer obstructions near Mobile at daybreak, having been struck but once slightly. We found the "gap" through the obstructions, much to our surprise, closed, and it was not until the afternoon that the gate was pulled sufficiently aside to allow us to enter. In the action down the bay we had the good luck to escape with but small damage. We were struck but six times, and only one of that number did any harm, and that entered the port wheelhouse and passed out of the starboard, destroying some muskets, boarding pikes, and stanchions in its progress over the deck. Only one person was wounded, and he slightly, by a splinter. I owe thus exemption from injury and loss, doubtless, in a great measure, to the excellent position I was enabled to keep, generally on the *Hartford*'s bow. The casualties, however, seem to have been small in all the vessels save the *Selma*.

The officers and men in their conduct afforded me much satisfaction, particularly as the most of them had never been under fire before, and I am a good deal indebted to my executive officer, Lieutenant Thomas L. Harrison (who had especial charge of the after division of guns, owing to an insufficiency of officers) for his hearty cooperation and assistance.

I have the honor to be, your obedient servant,

GEO. W. HARRISON,
Commander.

Admiral F. BUCHANAN.

P. S.—Besides the two other double-enders mentioned in the foregoing as having left the fleet after the *Metacomet* to join in the chase, there was a gunboat, also, which followed after a while.

It must be understood, with regard to the *Selma*, that she did not discontinue her retreat to engage the *Metacomet*, but that her fighting was done with her after gun, fired over her stern at the approaching vessel, and that she surrendered while the *Metacomet* was yet astern or had just got up.

Very respectfully, etc.,

GEO. W. HARRISON,
Commander.

4. The CSS *Selma*

The CSS *Selma* was a 320-ton side-wheel coastal steamer built at Mobile, Alabama, in 1856, where she carried the name *Florida*. She was taken over by the Confederate government in April of 1861, and converted to a warship, retaining the name *Florida*. She was well armed with two 9-inch and one 8-inch smoothbores, and one 6.4-inch rifle. As the *Florida* she served in the New Orleans, Lake Ponchartrain, and the Mississippi Sound area during the first year of the war under the command of First Lieutenant Charles W. Hays. (Moebs, *Confederate States Navy Research Guide*, p. 358)

On October 19, 1861, she successfully engaged the USS *Massachusetts* in Mississippi Sound, hitting the Union vessel with one well-placed shot. The Federal vessel's captain, Commander Melancton Smith, reported, "It entered the starboard side abaft the engine five feet above the water line, cutting entirely through 18 planks of the main deck, carried away the table, sofas, eight sections of iron steam pipe, and exploded in the stateroom on the port side, stripping the bulkheads of four rooms, and setting fire to the vessel." (*Official Records Navy*, Series I, Volume XVI, p. 749.)

With the commissioning of the cruiser *Florida*, the gunboat was renamed *Selma* in July of 1862, and First Lieutenant Peter U. Murphey was given her command. She constituted an important part of the Mobile Squadron and continued to operate in consort with the CSS *Morgan* and CSS *Gaines* in the Mobile Bay area. In February of 1863, she was sunk by a snag near Mobile, but was quickly repaired and returned to service.

Lieutenant Murphey was from North Carolina and had resigned from the U. S. Navy on April 21, 1861. He entered Confederate service on June 10, and was stationed at the Gosport Navy Yard at Portsmouth, Virginia, before being sent to Mobile. Murphey was severely wounded in the Battle of Mobile Bay where he was taken prisoner and carried to the U. S. Naval Hospital at Pensacola along with Admiral Buchanan. It was from his hospital bed at Pensacola that he wrote his official report. (Moebs, p. 244.) [RTC]

Official Report of
1st Lt. Peter U. Murphey, CSN

Official Records Navy, Series I, Volume XXI, pp. 587–588

PENSACOLA HOSPITAL, *August 15, 1864.*

Sir: The shattered state of my nervous system produced by the wound I received has prevented my making my report before this.

Between 5 and 6 o'clock on the morning of the 5th instant it was reported to me that a move was made by the fleet outside. I gave the order at once to get up steam, to weigh anchor, and to lash both securely and then to go to breakfast, and if we had time for the crew to clean themselves. The *Selma* was lying to the southward and eastward of the flagship and much nearer the shore. After the anchor was weighed, the steamer dropped down with the tide to the northward and eastward. While the crew were at breakfast, the engagement commenced, and many shots were fired by both sides before I went to quarters, but as soon as the crew were through with their breakfast and the decks were cleared up I went to quarters and stood slowly to the northward and westward under easy steam and nearly parallel with the vessels coming in, and as soon as I passed the stern of the *Tennessee* I opened on the enemy with all my guns and continued to fight, all of them for some time, when I perceived the *Metacomet* was towing the *Hartford*, the leading ship, when I gave the order to give her all the steam they could that I might get ahead and on the port side of her. My intention was perceived, and before I could get into the position I wanted the *Metacomet* cast off and gave chase. A constant fire had been kept up all the time, first at one and then at another, as the opportunity offered. Before the *Metacomet* had

1st Lt. Peter U. Murphey (author's collection).

cast off, my best gunner had been killed by a piece of shell, from the *Hartford*, I think, but several vessels were firing at me at the same time, and in a short while my next best gunner met the same fate. The fight was then with the *Metacomet* (carrying eight IX-inch Dahlgren and two 100-pounder Parrott guns), one of the fastest vessels in their squadron. She tried hard to rake me, which was prevented by good steering. The *Metacomet* being so much faster, soon came quite near, and firing one of her IX-Inch guns, killed 6 and wounded 7 men at the same gun, as well as disabling the gun itself. I had only been able to use two of the four guns which composed the battery of the *Selma* for some time, and the crew of No. 1 gun had just been sent aft to assist in working these two.

My first lieutenant, John H. Comstock, and Master's Mate Murray were both killed by the same shot, and I was wounded in the left arm after firing one or two shots more.

I perceived that the *Metacomet* was about to rake me with grape and shrapnel and that the *Port Royal*, of about the same class, was about to open on me also, and as I did not believe that I was justified in sacrificing more of my men in such an unequal contest, I gave the order, at about half-past 9 o'clock, to haul down the colors. My wound was bleeding fast, and I knew if I left the deck for one moment the vessel might be sunk. I had 8 killed and 7 wounded; my deck was a perfect slaughter pen when I surrendered.

I can not speak too highly of the officers and crew; not the least confusion occurred during the action. The wounded were taken below, and the men returned instantly to their quarters. The powder division was beautifully attended to; every charge and every shell were sent to the different guns without a single mistake. The enemy acknowledged great loss in killed and wounded inflicted on them by the *Selma*.

I am, sir, very respectfully, your obedient servant,

P. U. MURPHEY, C. S. Navy.

Admiral FRANKLIN BUCHANAN, C. S. Navy.

VII

New Orleans, Louisiana

1. The *Manassas* Attacks

The CSS *Manassas* was originally known as the *Enoch Train*. Built for service as an icebreaker and tow boat in Medford, Massachusetts, in 1855 by James O. Curtis, she was purchased and brought to New Orleans in 1859 and used there as a heavy tugboat. At that time she was a single decked two-masted steamer, 128 feet in length, 28 feet abeam, drawing twelve and one-half feet of water. Her twin engines each drove a single screw, and she was one of the most powerful tugs in the harbor. (Robinson, *The Confederate Privateers*, p. 156.)

Steamboat Captain John A. Stevenson acquired her for use as a privateer and fitted her out at Algiers, Louisiana, as an ironclad ram of radically modern design. Covered with 1½-inch iron convex plating, her hull projected only 2½ feet above the water. In order to give her ram an extra punch, a gun port was cut in the forward end of the shield. Here was mounted a 9-inch Dahlgren 32-pounder smoothbore gun that was obtained from the navy. It turned out that it was impossible to train or elevate and almost impossible to load. To enable her to ram enemy vessels, the *Enoch Train*'s bow was solidly filled with timbers for a length of twenty feet, and a cast iron ram was affixed to the bow below the water line. Fast moving, lying low in the water and a difficult target, she looked like a floating cigar and was described by Union intelligence as a "hellish machine." (*Civil War Naval Chronology*, p. VI-266.)

Commissioned as a Confederate privateer on September 12, 1861, and after a request that Stevenson cooperate with the navy squadron was rebuffed, the *Manassas* was seized by Captain George N. Hollins, commander of the Confederate squadron at New Orleans.

First Lieutenant Alexander F. Warley, a native of South Carolina, had resigned from the U. S. Navy on December 24, 1860, and was appointed to the Confederate navy on March 26, 1861. His first Confederate service was on the CSS *McRae* at New Orleans; however, when the *Manassas* was seized, he was given her command. After the war Warley wrote his account of the Battle of New Orleans and the part played by the CSS *Manassas*. (Moebs, *Confederate States Navy Research Guide*, pp. 271–272.) [RTC]

"The Ram Manassas *at the Passage of the New Orleans Forts" by 1st Lt. Alexander F. Warley, CSN*

Battles and Leaders of the Civil War, Vol., 2 pp. 89–91

JUST after the war I thought "bygones" had better be "bygones" and the stirring up of bitter memories was a thing to be avoided; now that so many years have passed, it seems to me almost impossible for one who was observant, and had good opportunities to observe, to tell all he believed he witnessed without in some way reflecting upon one or another of those in position who have gone to their rest and are no longer able to meet criticism.

But from the day of the veracious historian Pollard to the present one of Captain Kennon, no mention has been made of the vessel under my command on the night Admiral Farregut passed "the Forts," except in slighting, sneering, or untruthful statements.

There are only a few of those who were with me left, and I think it due to them and to the memory of those gone that I tell in as few words as I can what the *Manassas* did on the night in question.

The *Manassas* was made fast to the bank on the Fort St. Philip side above the forts, and had alongside of her a heavy steam-tug to enable her to be turned promptly down the river. On the evening before the attack I went on board of the Confederate steamer *McRae*, carrying some letters to put in the hands of my friend Captain Huger, and found him just starting to call on me, on the same errand. Both of us—judging from the character of the officers in the enemy's fleet, most of whom we knew—believed the attack was at hand, and neither of us expected support from the vessels that had been sent down to help oppose the fleet.

Before night all necessary orders had been given, and when at 3:30 AM the dash of the first gun was seen on the river below the forts, the *Manassas* was cut away from the bank, turned downstream, cast off from the tug, and was steaming down to the fleet in quicker time than I had believed to be possible.

The first vessel seen was one of the armed Confederate steamers. She dashed up the river, passing only a few feet from me, and no notice was taken of my hail and request for her to join me. The next vessel that loomed up was the United States steamer *Mississippi*. She was slanting across the river when the *Manassas* was run into her starboard quarter, our little gun being fired at short range through her cabin or ward-room. What injury she received must be told by her people. She fired over the *Manassas*, tore away, and went into the dark. While this was going on other vessels no doubt passed up, but the first I saw was a large ship (since known to have been the *Pensacola*). As the *Manassas* dashed at her quarter, she shifted her helm, avoided the collision beautifully, and fired her stern pivot-gun close into our faces, cutting away the flag-staff.

By that time the *Manassas* was getting between the forts, and I told Captain Levin, the pilot, that we could do nothing with the vessels which had passed, but we could go down to the mortar-fleet; but no sooner had we got in seeing range than both forts opened on us, Fort Jackson striking the vessel several times on the bend with the lighter guns. I knew the vessel must be sunk if once under the 10-inch guns, so I turned up the river again, and very soon saw a large ship, the *Hartford* [*Brooklyn*], lying across-stream. As I was not fired upon by her I thought then that her crew were busy fending off what I think now to have been a, burning pile-driver, and could not see the *Manassas* coming out of the dark. The *Manassas* was driven at her with everything open, resin being piled into the furnaces. The gun was discharged when close on board. We struck her fairly amidship; the gun recoiled and turned over and remained there, the boiler started, slightly jamming the Chief Engineer Dearning, but settled back as the vessel backed off. For any damage done to the *Hartford* [*Brooklyn*] her records must be consulted. Just then another steamer came up through the fog. I thought her the *Iroquois*, and tried to run into her, but she passed as if the *Manassas* had been at anchor.*

Professor J. Russell Soley, U.S.N., in a communication to the Editors, gives the following discussion of the question, Did the Manassas *ram the* Hartford *at the battle of New Orleans? "In the affirmative is the following testimony: (1) Captain Kautz, a lieutenant on board the* Hartford, *says that immediately after the* Hartford *went ashore she was struck by the fire-raft which was pushed up by the tug Mosher, and immediately after that event the* Manassas *struck her and turned her round so that she slid off the shoal. (2) Lieutenant Warley, commanding the* Manassas, *states that she struck the* Hartford. *He does not state that she struck the* Brooklyn. *In the negative is the following testimony : (1) Admiral Farragut makes no mention of*

Steaming slowly up the river,—very slow was our best,—we discovered the Confederate States steamer *McRae*, head up-stream, receiving the fire of three men-of-war. As the *Manassas* forged by, the three men-of-war steamed up the river, and were followed to allow the *McRae* to turn and get down to the forts, as she was very badly used up.

Day was getting broader, and with the first ray of the sun we saw the fleet above us; and a splendid sight it was, or rather would have been under other circumstances. Signals were being rapidly exchanged, and two men-of-war steamed down, one on either side of the river. The *Manassas* was helpless. She had nothing to fight with, and no speed to run with. I ordered her to be run into the bank on the Fort St. Philip side, her delivery-pipes to be cut, and the crew to be sent into the swamp through the elongated port forward, through which the gun had been used. The first officer, gallant

1st Lt. Alexander F. Warley (Naval Historical Center).

(continued) *being struck by a ram. His report says: 'I discovered a fire-raft coming down upon us, and in attempting to avoid it ran the ship on shore, and the ram* Manassas, *which I had not seen, lay on the opposite side of it and pushed it down upon us.' Farragut evidently mistook the* Mosher *for the* Manassas, *as it is a well-established fact that the* Mosher *shoved the raft against the* Hartford. *(2) Commander Richard Wainwright, commanding the* Hartford, *makes no mention in his detailed report of having been struck by any ram. He describes the incident of the fire-raft thus: 'At 4:15 grounded on shoal near Fort St. Philip, in the endeavor to clear a fire-raft which was propelled by a ram on our port quarter, setting fire to the ship.' Wainwright also makes the mistake of calling the* Mosher *a ram, but this only bears out the general opinion among the Union officers as to the character of all the Confederate vessels. (3) The report of James H. Conley, carpenter of the* Hartford, *stating in detail the damages sustained by the ship in the action, makes no mention of any injury which could have been inflicted by a ram. (4) It seems impossible that the* Manassas *should have struck such a blow to the* Hartford *as Warley describes and have left no traceable injury. (5) It is exceedingly improbable that the* Manassas *would have struck the* Hartford *under such advantageous circumstances as Captain Kautz describes (when the* Hartford *was ashore) and have had no effect other than to turn the* Hartford *round so that she slid off the shoal. (6) Commander Watson informs me that he thinks it is a mistake to suppose that the* Manassas *touched the* Hartford *at any time. He goes on to say: 'Farragut thought it was the* Manassas *which pushed the fire-raft against the* Hartford's *port side, while the Confederate reports state that this was done by a certain tug-boat. The admiral never, to my knowledge, entertained the idea, that such a blow as the* Manassas *is supposed to have given would have released the* Hartford's *bow. I believe that he ascribed her release to the backing of the screw as I did; I always understood him that way. (7) Mr. Herbert B. Tyson says, in a recent letter (Mr. Tyson was a midshipman and the navigator of the* Hartford *at this time, but has since left the service): 'I am satisfied the* Hartford *was never rammed at the battle of New Orleans. The nearest approach to her being rammed was when a Confederate craft pushed a fire-raft under her port quarter while she was aground under Fort St. Philip.' (8) Lieutenant Warley mentions only one vessel rammed by him in the description certainly answers for what happened in the attack on the* Brooklyn. *(9) In reference to the* Brooklyn *there is no possible question. Captain Craven's and Commander Bartlett's testimony is absolutely conclusive. (10) Lieutenant Warley must be mistaken in stating that Captain Mahan informed him that his vessel struck the* Hartford. *Mahan in his book [pp. ford by the* Manassas. *His statements are such that [76 and 77] does not mention any ramming of the* Hartford *he had supposed the* Manassas *rammed the* Hartford *he could not have omitted it. He says of the* Hartford: *'She toke the ground close under St. Philip, the raft lying on her port quarter, against which it was pushed by the tug* Mosher,' *adding in a footnote, 'As this feat has been usually ascribed to the* Manassas, *it may be well to say that the statement in the text rests on the testimony of the commander of the ram, as well as other evidence.' He closes his description of this episode by saying: 'Then working herself clear, the* Hartford *passed from under their fire.' Finally he gives a minute description of the ramming of the* Brooklyn *by the* Manassas."

Frank Harris, reported all the men on shore. We examined the vessel, found all orders had been obeyed, and we also took to the swamp.

I think our two attendants ran into each other. Harris said such was the case. At any rate I soon heard heavy firing,—some for our benefit, but most, I think, for the abandoned *Manassas*. I heard afterward that she was boarded, but, filling astern, floated off, on fire, and blew up somewhere below in the neighborhood of the mortar-fleet.

I have confined my remarks to the *Manassas*, and it is just that I should tell what the *Manassas* was,—a tow-boat boarded over with five-inch timber and armored with one thickness of flat railroad iron, with a complement of thirty-four persons and an armament of one light carronade and four double-barreled guns. She was very slow. I do not think she made at any time that night more than five miles an hour.

If on that occasion she was made to do less than she should have done, if she omitted any possible chance of putting greater obstructions in the track of the fleet, the fault was mine,—for I was trammeled by no orders from superior authority; I labored under no difficulty of divided counsel; I had not to guard against possible disaffection or be jealous about obedience to my orders.

I have finished, having endeavored to avoid personality even to omitting much in praise I could say of brother officers in the same fight, but not in any way connected with the *Manassas*.

Captain Squires, who commanded Fort St. Philip, informed me that his fort had fired seventy-five times at the *Manassas*, mistaking her for a disabled vessel of the enemy's floating down-stream. The *Manassas* was not struck once by Fort St. Philip.

The following are the only officers living, as far as I know, who were with me on the night referred to: Engineers George W. Weaver and T. A. Yensies, and Pilots Robert Levin and Robert Wilson.

2. The CSS *McRae*

In 1876 there appeared in the *Southern Historical Society Papers* an essay entitled "Reminiscences of the Confederate States Navy" by former First Lieutenant Charles W. Read. Born and raised in the Mississippi delta country, Read was graduated from the U.S. Naval Academy in 1860, at the bottom of his class. Upon the secession of his home state, he resigned his midshipman commission and was appointed acting midshipman in Confederate service on April 13, 1861. (Campbell, *Sea Hawk of the Confederacy: Lt. Charles W. Read and the Confederate Navy*, p. 15.)

In his article, Charles Read described in great detail his experiences during the war, from his first assignment at the beginning of the conflict to when he was ordered to the cruiser CSS *Florida*, where he reported on November 4, 1862. It is unfortunate that Read never submitted a second part to his "Reminiscences" that could have chronicled his remaining war experiences, for no other officer in the Confederate navy was involved in more engagements and hair-raising escapades than Charles Read. His account here, however, is selected from that portion of his "Reminiscences" that pertains to the CSS *McRae* at New Orleans.

The *McRae* was the former Mexican rebel screw sloop of 830-tons, *Marqués de la Habana*, that had been captured by the USS *Saratoga* in March of 1860. Berthed at New Orleans, she was purchased by the Confederate government on March 17, 1861, and fitted out with the intent of taking her to sea as a commerce raider. The Federal blockade of the lower Mississippi River prevented that, however, and she was retained as the flag ship of Captain George N. Hollins' New Orleans fleet. Armed with one 9-inch gun and six 32-pounders, the *McRae*, in Read's narrative below, has just returned from the upper river

"Reminiscences of the Confederate States Navy" by 1st Lt. Charles W. Read, CSN

Southern Historical Society Papers, Volume I, No. V, May 1876, pp. 341–347

The *McRae* arrived at the forts on the 16th of April, 1862, and anchored close into the bank just above Fort St. Phillip. The enemy's fleet was around the bend below Fort Jackson, and his mortar-boats were throwing about ten shells every minute in and around the forts. The river was obstructed by schooners anchored across the river, in line abreast, between the forts, and chains and lines were passed from vessel to vessel; but a passage was left open near each bank. The forts were well garrisoned and had a large number of the heaviest guns. There were six Montgomery rams, one Louisiana ram called the *Governor Moore*, the ram *Manassas* and the *McRae*, and also a number of fire-rafts and tow-boats—all on the Fort St. Phillip side of the river between that fort and the point above. On the 20th of April the large iron-clad *Louisiana*, mounting 16 guns of the largest and most approved pattern, arrived and anchored just above the obstructions. She was in command of commander McIntosh, of the navy. Captain Jno. K. Mitchell was placed in command of all the boats of the Confederate navy, viz: *Louisiana*, *Manassas* and *McRae*. The Montgomery rams were under the command of Captain Stevenson, the designer of the *Manassas*. The *Governor Moore*, of the Louisiana navy, was in charge of Lieutenant Kennon, formerly of the navy. Captain Mitchell endeavored to get control of everything afloat, but succeeded only in obtaining the consent of the other "naval" commanders to co-operate with him if they should think proper, but under no circumstances were they to receive or obey orders from any officer of the regular Confederate army.

The *Louisiana* was in an unfinished condition; several of her guns were unmounted, and a few could not be used on account of the carriages being too high for the ports. Her machinery was not all in, and as a steamer she was regarded as a failure; it was believed by competent engineers that she would not have power sufficient to enable her to stem the current of the Mississippi river during high water. Mechanics labored day and night to get the *Louisiana* ready, as Captain Mitchell designed to move on the enemy as soon as that vessel could be used as a steamer. General Duncan, who commanded the fortifications to the department, and Colonel Ed. Higgins, who commanded the forts, were both of the opinion that Captain Mitchell should drop the *Louisiana* below Fort St. Phillip and drive the enemy's mortar-boats out of range. The mortar shells had injured Fort Jackson somewhat, eight or ten guns having been rendered unserviceable. Fort St. Phillip was entirely uninjured, as but few shell could reach it. Captain Mitchell objected to placing the *Louisiana* in the position desired by the army officers, because he proposed to attack the enemy in a few days—that is, as soon as the *Louisiana* was ready, and he thought Fort Jackson could stand the mortars for that time; furthermore, he thought it was hazardous to place the *Louisiana* in mortar range, as she was not ironed on her decks, and as mortar shells fall almost perpendicularly, if one should strike her on deck it would probably sink her.

On the afternoon of April 23d I visited Fort Jackson, and with Colonel Higgins observed from the parapet of the fort the fleet below; their light spars had been sent down, and the ships were arranging themselves in lines ahead. We were both of the opinion that a move would be made on the forts the following night. So, when I returned on board the *McRae*, I directed the cable to be got ready for slipping and a man stationed to unshackle it at a moment's warning; one-half of the men to be on deck; steam to be up; the guns cast loose and loaded with 5-second shell. I remained on deck until after midnight, when, retiring to my room, I cautioned the officer of the deck to keep a bright lookout down the river and call me the moment anything came in sight. At 3 AM, I was called and informed that a steamer was coming up. In less than a minute the *McRae* was under way and her guns blazing at the approaching ships of the enemy. I saw the rams *Governor Moore* and *Stonewall Jackson* rushing for one of the Yankee steamers, but they were soon lost in the smoke, and I saw them no more. The commanders, officers and men of the Montgomery rams (except those of the *Stonewall Jackson*) deserted their vessels at the first gun and fled wildly to the woods. The enemy's gunboats were soon through the obstructions, and turning their attention to the Confederate flotilla made short work of it.

The deserted rams were set on fire and served as beacons through the darkness and smoke which hung over the river. On the *McRae* we had little trouble to find something to fire at, for as we were out in the river the enemy was on every side of us, and gallantly did our brave tars stand to their guns, loading and firing their guns as rapidly as possible. Our commander, Lieutenant Huger, was what we all expected—cool and fearless, and handled the *McRae* splendidly. One of the enemy's shell, fired from one of the howitzers aloft, went through our decks and exploded in the sail-room, setting the ship on fire; and as there was only a pine bulkhead of 2-inch boards between the sail-room and magazine, we were in great danger of being blown up. Just then one of the large sloops-of-war ranged alongside and gave us a broadside of grape and canister, which mortally wounded our commander, wounded the pilot, carried away our wheel ropes and cut the signal halyards and took our flag overboard. New tiller ropes were rove and soon we were at close quarters with a large steamer. Just after daylight, being close into the west bank of the river, about three miles above Fort Jackson, we found one of the Montgomery rams, the *Resolute*, ashore, with a white flag flying. I sent Lieutenant Arnold, with twenty men, to take charge of her and to open fire with her two heavy rifle pivots. At 7.30 AM we ceased firing, being at that time about four miles above the forts. In going around, to return to the batteries, our wheel ropes were again shot away, and the ship ran into the bank before her headway could be checked. Captain Mitchell sent one of the tugs to our assistance and we were soon afloat. At 8.30 we anchored near the *Louisiana*. While we were aground the ram *Manassas* was discovered floating helplessly down the river. I sent a boat to her, and ascertained that she was uninjured, but had her injection pipes cut, and that it would be impossible to save her.

It was afterwards ascertained that the enemy's fleet, consisting of twenty ships, under the command of Commodore Farragut, had endeavored to run by the forts; only thirteen succeeded in passing. The advance was made in two lines en echelon, and the steamers passed through the gaps in the line of obstructions near each bank. The guns of the forts, being mounted mostly in barbette, were silenced as soon and as long as the gun-boats were in canister range. The passages through which General Duncan thought the enemy could not pass were the very ones Farragut preferred; for, as his ships carried heavy guns, and plenty of them, it was his object to get within point-blank range, so as to drive the Confederates away from the barbette guns by keeping a steady rain of canister on them. Had the "Montgomery rams" fought, or towed the fire rafts out into the current, it is very doubtful if any of the gun-boats would have passed. One of the enemy's gun-boats, the *Veruna* was gallantly assaulted by the rams *Governor Moore* and *Stonewall Jackson* hung on to his enemy like an avenging fate, and did not quit him till he sunk him.

Every night, previous to the one the fleet passed, a fire-raft had been sent down below the obstructions, and burnt for the purpose of lighting up the river; but by a strange chance no raft was sent down that night. The importance of having the fire-raft below on the night has been exaggerated; for, after the firing commenced, the smoke was so dense along the river that a dozen fire-rafts would have done but little in showing the ships to the forts.

Captain Mitchell has been blamed by many for not placing the *Louisiana* in the position desired by General Duncan. Had the *Louisiana* been moored below Fort Saint Phillip there can be no doubt that she would have driven the mortar boats out of range of Fort Jackson. But by occupying that position she would have done nothing towards deterring Farragut in executing his bold move; and it is quite certain that she would not have been more serviceable against steamers under way in one place more than another. The day after the fleet passed the forts I was ordered by Captain Mitchell to transfer all the officers and men (except barely enough to run the vessel) from the *McRae* to the *Louisiana*, and to carry on board all the Confederate sick and wounded, and to proceed to New Orleans under a flag of truce. The *McRae* had been badly cut up in upper works and rigging during the action, besides having several large shots through her near the water-line, which caused her to leak badly; her smoke-stack was so riddled that it would scarcely sand, and the draft was so much affected that it was difficult to keep steam in the boilers.

1st Lt. Charles W. Read (author's collection).

I applied to Captain Mitchell for permission to take the *McRae's* crew, get the ram *Resolute* afloat, and at night to go down, ram one of the mortar fleet, and go on a raid on the coast of New England. The *Resolute* was well protected; had two large pivot guns, was full of coal and supplies, was a sea-going steamer, and was faster than any war vessel the enemy had. Captain Mitchell replied that my proposition would be considered. The following day the enemy's fleet at the quarantine attacked the *Resolute* and succeeded in planting a shell forward below the water line, which exploded and rendered her useless.

On the morning of the 26th the *McRae* started up the river under a flag of truce. At the quarantine I went on board the steamer *Mississippi*, and received permission from the commanding officer of the squadron to pass his lines with the cartel. On account of the condition of the *McRae's* smoke-stack we could get but a small head of steam, and consequently but slow progress against the strong current. We passed various floating wrecks, which told us too plainly of the destruction of our shipping at New Orleans. While we all deplored the loss of our rams and gunboats, and the successful advance of such a large number of formidable ships of the enemy, we confidently expected that the Confederate commanders at New Orleans would use our resources above in such a way as to make Farragut repent his bold undertaking; for we well knew that the iron-clad *Mississippi* had been launched at New Orleans and was nearly ready for service, and that the rest of Hollins' fleet and eight Montgomery rams, then above Memphis, could soon descended the rapid current of the Mississippi River; besides, the large number of river and ocean steamers on the river could have been readily and easily converted into rams and used successfully against Farragut's wooden fleet. The *Mississippi* was a most formidable iron-clad, with plenty of power, and was to mount twenty of the heaviest guns. She could have been ready for action within ten days after the enemy passed the forts. The lower forts were uninjured, and had six months' provisions, and were supported by the iron-clad battery *Louisiana*.

About 10 AM, April 27th, the *McRae* arrived in front of the city. Farragut's fleet was anchored in the stream abreast of New Orleans, and was treating for the surrender. Getting permission to land our wounded, the *McRae* was anchored at the foot of Canal Street, and all of our poor fellows were landed safely that afternoon. I went on shore to see our commander, Lieutenant Huger, carried to his residence, and returned on board about 6 PM. The donkey-engine had been going steadily since the fight, but having become disabled the water was rapidly gaining. I put the crew to work at the bilge-pumps. The steamer commenced dragging just after dark. All the chain was paid out, but she would not bring up; but getting in the eddy, near the Algiers shore, she swung around several times, striking once against one of the sunken dry docks, which caused the ship to make water more freely. The pumps were kept going until daylight next morning. The shot holes having got below the water, the steamer settled fast, and we were obliged to abandon her. The crew had hardly reached the shore when our good old ship went down. I went on board the enemy's flag-ship and reported the occurrence. On the 29th I had prepared to return to the forts in one of the small boats of the *McRae*, when, going to the mayor's office to get the flag-of-truce mail, I was astonished to learn that the forts had surrendered, and that the *Louisiana* had been blown up. I went down on the levy and met a number of the officers and men of the forts and gun-boats, and learned that the surrender had been brought about by a mutiny in Fort Jackson. Late on the night of the 27th the officers of that fort awoke to find that about two hundred of the garrison were under arms, had spiked some of the guns, and demanded that the very liberal terms offered the day previous by Commodore Porter, of the enemy's mortar fleet, be accepted. General Duncan and officers appealed to the men to stand by their colors and country; that the forts were in good condition and could hold out many months. But the mutineers were firm, and insisted on an immediate surrender. General Duncan then promised that the forts should be surrendered at daylight.

The men who thus deserted their country in her dark hour were mostly of foreign birth and low origin, and had been demoralized by the mortar shells, the contentions between the military and naval commanders, the discouraging tone of army officers conversations, and the liberal terms offered by Porter. So at early dawn a boat was sent down to inform the enemy that his terms would be accepted. Fort Saint Phillip, on the opposite side of the river, was entirely unhurt, and was well supplied and had a full garrison of true men. The *Louisiana* mounted sixteen heavy guns, and was invulnerable. Comment is unnecessary.

Before the fleet passed the forts I talked freely with the officers ashore and afloat, and but one of them would admit the bare possibility of the enemy's steamers being able to run the batteries. Colonel Edward Higgins (afterwards Brigadier-General and one of the most gallant soldiers in the Confederate army) told me on the afternoon of the 23d of April—the eye of the attack—that the fleet could pass at any time, and probably would pass that very night! When the *McRae* came down the river, in the summer of 1861, Duncan had command of the forts. I heard him say one day that all the vessels in the world could not pass his forts; that the forts had once driven back the fleet of Great Britain; and that at that time the forts were nothing compared to what they were in 1861. It did not seem to occur to Duncan that the English ships were sailing vessels, sailing against a strong current; that they were "crank and tall," and mounted 24-pounders, long-nines, and such like small ordnance. He was oblivious of the fact that modern war ships carried huge 11-inch pivots and 9-inch broadside guns, and that double stand of grape and canister were prescribed by the naval manual of the United States.

3. The Battle of New Orleans

The loss of New Orleans was a devastating blow for the Confederacy. One author who wrote a book on the subject aptly titled his work *The Night the War Was Lost*. Much recrimination followed the loss of the city. The navy blamed the army for surrendering the forts prematurely. The army blamed the navy for not positioning the *Louisiana* below the forts and for not driving away the Federal mortar boats. Stevenson's rams fled the scene, and powerful tow-boats that could have saved the unfinished CSS *Mississippi* by towing her up river also fled. In addition, everyone blamed the government in Richmond, particularly Secretary Mallory, for not appreciating the enormity of the impending crises, and therefore doing little to bolster the defenses. Certainly there was enough blame to go around.

It is evident that Mallory considered the threat from Union ironclads upriver around Island No 10 and New Madrid as more serious. Once the *Mississippi* and *Louisiana* were completed, he reasoned, they would be able to destroy Farragut's wooden fleet and raise the blockade of New Orleans. Admiral Farragut, however, did not wait for the Confederate ironclads to be completed. (Luraghi, *A History of the Confederate Navy*, pp. 89–110.)

Congress ordered an investigation, and in the midst of all this controversy, John K. Mitchell, commander of the naval forces at New Orleans, filed his official report. [RTC]

---

*Official Report of
Commander John K. Mitchell, CSN*

Official Navy Records, Series I, Volume XVIII, pp. 289–301

Greensboro, N. C., *August 19, 1862.*

SIR: I avail myself of the first opportunity to make to the Department a report of the engagement on the 24th April last, at Forts Jackson and St. Philip, on the Mississippi River, between the Confederate States naval forces under my command and those of the United States under Flag-Officer D. G. Farragut, in which the latter, being in overwhelming forces, succeeded in forcing the passage of the forts; and also, to report the subsequent events, resulting in the destruction of the C. S. S. *Louisiana*, by my order, on the unanimous recommendation of all the commissioned line officers present on the 28th of April last, and the surrender of the remaining forces under my command to the enemy on the same day.

On Sunday, April 20, I embarked on board the *Louisiana*, by order of Captain W. C. Whittle, commanding naval station at New Orleans, to assume the immediate command of the Confederate States naval forces operating near Forts Jackson and St. Philip, and proceeded at once down the river, arriving there the following morning and taking up a position below all the gunboats and just above the water battery of Fort St. Philip, securing the *Louisiana* to the bank of the river, with her bow downstream, within effective range of the remnants of the raft or chain obstructions, so that her three bow guns, one rifled 7-inch and two IX-inch shell, could be trained so as to command both banks of the river.

I waited at once on General J. K. Duncan, commanding the land defenses, informing him of my orders and plans and my desire to cooperate with him. The position taken by the *Louisiana* seemed to meet his approbation, and was the best, I conceive, that could, under the circumstances, have been taken, being just clear of the line of fire from the enemy's mortar boats, then playing night and day upon Fort Jackson and occasionally upon Fort St. Philip, and especially in view of the important fact of her being not only unprepared for an offensive movement against the enemy, but even for defense, in consequence of deficient motive power and some of her guns being mounted so as to render them unfit for service till shifted.

I deem it proper to state here particularly the condition of the *Louisiana* at this time. It was notorious that she was not ready for service when ordered to leave New Orleans; yet, in view of the bombardment then going on of Fort Jackson, and the apprehension that the enemy might, at any moment, run by the forts below, it was deemed advisable, under all the circumstances, for her to be sent down in her incomplete condition, to render what aid she could in the defense of the passage, in the conviction that her presence there might prevent the enemy's vessels coming up the river, while, if she remained at New Orleans, and the enemy should pass the forts, the *Louisiana* would be unable to save the city and must herself have inevitably fallen into his hands or been destroyed to prevent it.

The propellers, designed more to facilitate the steering of the *Louisiana* than to add materially to her direct motive power, were not ready; the railroad iron plating on the forecastle and on the forward hatch combings, as also the boiler plating on upper deck, was not all laid. Mechanics were, however, taken on board and carried down the river so that the work of finishing the vessel could be in progress while she was in position to render some aid against the approach or apprehended attack of the enemy. On leaving New Orleans a trial of the motive power with wheels only was made, which proved lamentably deficient, though a dangerous pressure of steam was used; and even after her two tenders were called alongside and used as tugs with all their power it was difficult to steer the vessel, and when pointed with her head upstream, she barely stemmed the current off the city. Her own rudders seemed to be utterly powerless to control her.

On the trial of the wheels it was found that the bulkheads around them leaked so badly that the deck was flooded aft, and for want of combings to the hatchways the water ran into the after magazine and shell room, making it necessary to stop the wheels. Calkers and carpenters were obtained from the city as soon as possible and set to work to repair these defects.

It was impossible to weigh her bower anchors after letting them go, owing to the short nip of the hawse pipes and having no capstan or other sufficient purchase, only a deck tackle being provided. It was still more difficult to purchase, secure, or use a stern anchor, as it seriously endangered the propellers, the two rudders, and the whole steering apparatus, which was complicated and much exposed to accident from being fouled by lines, contact with boats, vessels, etc., and to being disabled by grape or canister shot of an enemy. One of the two bowers (the lighter one) and the only stern anchor had to be slipped, and were lost in her operations near Fort St. Philip, owing to there being no adequate purchase to weigh them. It may not be out of place to state here that the iron protection of the *Louisiana* only came down to the water line, her sides at and below it being without any iron protection. The two tenders were not only indispensable as tugs, but also as quarters for officers and crew; the former were partly accommodated with a tent awning on the flat roof or upper deck. The gun or berth deck was sufficient for only about half the crew, and the want of ventilation would have rendered it almost uninhabitable with steam kept steadily up, especially over the boilers, where it would have been difficult, if not impossible, from the excessive heat, for the men to have remained any time at their guns.

The following vessels of the C. S. Navy I found at Fort St. Philip, viz:

Steamer *McRae*, Lieutenant Commanding Thomas B. Huger, with six light 32-pounder smoothbore broadside guns and one IX-inch shell gun, pivoted amidships, total seven. The steamer *Jackson*, Lieutenant Commanding F. B. Renshaw, two pivoted smoothbore 32-pounders, one forward and one aft. The iron-plated ram *Manassas*, Lieutenant Commanding A. F. Warley, one 32-pounder carronade in bow.

Launch No. 3, Acting Master Tilford, one howitzer, 20 men.
Launch No. 6, Acting Master Fairbanks, one howitzer, 20 men.

Also the following converted sea steamers into Louisiana State gunboats, with pine and cotton barricades to protect machinery and boilers, viz:

The *Governor Moore*, Commander Beverly Kennon, two 32-pounder rifle guns.
The *General Quitman*, Captain Grant, two 32-pounder guns.

All of the above steamers being converted vessels, were too slightly built for war purposes.

The following unarmed steamers belonged to my command, viz:

The *Phoenix*, Captain [Brown], tender to *Manassas*.
The *W. Burton*, Captain Hammond, tender to *Louisiana*.
The *Landis*, Captain Davis, tender to *Louisiana*.

The following unarmed steamers chartered by the Army were placed under my orders, viz:

The *Mosher*, Captain Sherman, a very small tug.
The *Belle Algerine*, Captain [Jackson], small tug.
The *Star*, Captain La Place, used as telegraph station.
The *Music*, Captain McClellan, tender to forts.

The two former were in bad condition, and were undergoing such repairs as could be made below, previous to the 24th.

On arriving below I delivered to Captain Stevenson written orders from Major-General M. Lovell, requiring him to place all the river defense gunboats under his command under my orders, which consisted of the following converted towboats, viz:

1. The *Warrior*, under the immediate command of Captain Stevenson.
2. The *Stonewall Jackson*, Captain Phillips.
3. The *Resolute*, Captain Hooper.
4. The *Defiance*, Captain McCoy.
5. The *General Lovell*, Captain [Paris].
6. The *R. J. Breckinridge*, Captain [Smith], joined the evening before the action.

All of the above vessels mounted from one to two pivot 32-pounders each, some of them rifled; their boilers and machinery were all more or less protected by thick, double, pine barricades, filled in with compressed cotton, which, though not regarded as proof against heavy, solid shot, shell, and incendiary projectiles, would be a protection from grape and canister; and ought to have inspired those on board with sufficient confidence to use their boats boldly as rams, for which they were in a good measure, prepared with flat bar-iron casing around their bows; in thus using them their own safety would be best consulted, as well as the best way of damaging the vessels of the enemy.

Captain Stevenson, on receiving General Lovell's orders, addressed me a communication to the effect that all the officers and crews of the vessels under his command had entered that service with the distinct understanding or condition that they were not to be placed under the orders of naval officers, and that, therefore, while willing to cooperate with my forces, he could receive no orders from me himself, nor allow any vessels of his command to do so; that he reserved to himself the right of obeying, or not, any orders I might issue. His attitude with respect to my authority was one of absolute independence of action and command, and very embarrassing in the face of the enemy. A copy of his communication was sent by me to General Duncan, and one through Captain W. C. Whittle to

General Lovell, informing them, at the same time, that the position assumed by Captain Stevenson relieved me from all responsibility for the conduct of the vessels under his command. Not knowing what moment an attack might be made by the enemy, I endeavored to agree upon a plan of cooperation with his forces by the arrangement of signals and concert of action, and the particular service to be performed by him, an endeavor which he himself seemed disposed zealously to second in many respects.

The night of the 20th April, on my way down in the *Louasiana*, the enemy's boats are said to have visited the raft obstructions and cut the chain. To prevent further injury to it, to break the night reconnaissances of the enemy, and to watch and report all his movements, I was unsuccessful in my efforts to get Captain Stevenson to employ one or two of his gunboats below the obstructions at night. Although favoring the idea, he seemed to have no confidence in the fitness of his commanders for the service, and I could not induce him to give the necessary orders to them. I had no suitable vessel for this duty under my command; the only one that would have answered, the *Jackson*, having been sent with *launch No. 3* five miles above to the Quarantine Station, at the request of General Duncan, to watch the enemy in that neighborhood and prevent his approach through any of the adjacent bayous and canals.

The interval between the arrival of the *Louisiana* at the forts on the 21st April, and the morning of the 24th, when the engagement commenced, was occupied in the organization of the force under my command and endeavors to arrange some concert of action with the river-defense gunboats, but as our chief hopes rested upon the completion of the *Louisiana*, our principal efforts were directed to getting her propellers ready, on which we worked night and day. All the other mechanical work was pushed with all our means, many of the guns having been mounted so as to be entirely unserviceable, being either too high or too low, had to be dismounted and shifted, a most tedious and laborious work, on account of the confined and cramped general arrangement of the gun deck, and its lumbered condition from the mechanical work in progress on board. To assist in the rearrangement of the guns, all the men that could be spared from the *McRae* were borrowed. The constant occupation of the crew and the condition of the gun deck prevented any systematic exercise at quarters. Every night however, the crews of those guns that could be used in the event of an attack by the enemy were required to sleep at their quarters, and every possible preparation made for immediate action, under the painfully adverse circumstances which rendered it expedient, if not necessary, that the *Louisiana* should be placed in position for battle, though so lamentably unprepared.

The deficiency in her complement was supplied by Captain T. H. Hutton's company of Crescent Artillery as volunteer artillerists, who joined the *Louisiana* at New Orleans, and a supernumerary force, consisting of a detachment of Lieutenant Dixon's artillery and one of Captain Ryan's sharpshooters, were received on board for temporary service from Fort St. Philip.

General Duncan proposed and urged upon me, the second or third day after my arrival below, to take up a new position with the *Louisiana* at the river bank just below Fort Jackson and under cover of its guns, from whence her fire could be opened with effect on the mortar fleet of the enemy, when at the same time the mechanics could go on with their work. This proposition I declined (and my action was sustained in a consultation with all the commanding officers of the naval vessels present) on the ground that:

1st. The battery of the *Louisiana* was not in a condition for service and that all her own crew proper, together with all the men that could be spared from the *McRae*, were constantly at work in rearranging it.
2d. That the completion of the propellers and other mechanical work in progress was indispensable to the efficiency of the vessel, and that it would be interrupted if she were placed under fire.

3d. And that placing the *Louisiana* in a position to receive the fire of the enemy, before her own battery could be served with effect, would be improperly hazarding not only her own safety, but the security of the passage between the forts, on which rested the possession of New Orleans.

On the afternoon of the 23d, the arrangement of the *Louisiana*'s battery, the work on her propellers and in other mechanical departments, had so far progressed as to encourage the hope and belief that the next day she might be moved to the position proposed by General Duncan. I accordingly made a reconnaissance of it and the enemy's mortar fleet, in consequence of which, I decided to move the *Louisiana* to it the next day or night as might be deemed proper, a plan for which was arranged with Captain Stevenson, who would assist with two of his gunboats which were particularly well adapted to this service from their batteries, as well as their being originally towboats, and the reported skill of their commanders in towing operations.

The correspondence between General Duncan and myself on this particular subject, as well as others, with my official papers generally, were burned during the engagement, or lost in the subsequent destruction of the vessel; copies of the former are probably in his possession and may be obtained from him if desired by the Department, which will tend to show, I think, that however much I appreciated and am willing to admit the importance of the proposed change of position for the *Louisiana*, her condition as to the state of her battery alone, independent of other weighty reasons, were sufficient to prevent its being made previous to the engagement of the 24th.

Late in the evening of the 23d a consultation was held by me with Commander McIntosh, Lieutenants Commanding Huger and Warley, and Captain Stevenson, in relation to the general aspect of affairs, and especially in relation to information received from General Duncan that the enemy, late in the afternoon, had placed small white flags on the river bank below Fort St. Philip, which he regarded as indicating an intention to take up a position with his fleet for cannonading Fort Jackson.

At this consultation with the commanding officers, verbal orders were given and arrangements made that, in the event of an attack at night, each commander would act at his discretion and make every effort to oppose the passage of the enemy; steam was to be kept up as usual, and all the vessels, whether armed or not, held in readiness for immediate action and movement. The river defense gunboats had each a fire boat secured to her, which were to be towed into the stream, fired, and turned adrift upon the enemy.

Captain Stevenson would also set adrift at stated hours of the night three or four fire rafts to keep the passage lighted, as requested by General Duncan. I also arranged with Captain Stevenson to aid the next day in connecting with chains a string of fire boats long enough, if possible, to extend entirely across the river, to be kept in constant readiness, to be towed into position and fired in the event of any serious attempt of the enemy to pass the forts, an arrangement which was originally designed in the preparation of the fire boats at New Orleans.

The evening of the 23d, the day before the action, the armed vessels under my command and those under Captain Stevenson were arranged in about the following close order on the, eastern bank of the river above the *Louisiana* near Fort St. Philip, viz:

1. The *Louisiana* with two tenders, unarmed.
2. The *Warrior*, Captain Stevenson.
3–4. River Defense gunboats.
5. The *McRae*.
6. *Governor Moore*, Louisiana State gunboat.
7. The *Manassas*, with unarmed tender *Phoenix*.
8–9-10. River Defense gunboats.

11. The *General Quitman*, Captain Grant, lay on the opposite side of the river above Fort Jackson.

Commander John K. Mitchell (Naval Historical Center).

Launch No. 6, Acting Master Fairbanks, was employed during the nights of the 22d and 23d to keep up a fire on the river bank below Fort St. Philip for the purpose of lighting up the river, as desired by General Duncan. My instructions to him on the 23d were very particular to keep up a good fire, to keep a vigilant lookout, and give the alarm by firing his howitzer and discharging rockets on discovering any suspicious movements of the enemy, not to leave his station before daylight, and to repel any attack of boats that might be made on him. I learned after the action that on discovering the movement of the enemy's vessels Mr. Fairbanks left his station, giving no alarm whatever, brought his launch up near the *Louisiana*, making no report of his movements, and, on the commencement of the action, he escaped with his crew to the swamp. After the action three of the crew returned to the *Louisiana*, making the foregoing statement of the cowardly, if not treacherous, conduct of Acting Master Fairbanks, of whom nothing has since been heard.

The engagement April 24, 1862

The first alarm or knowledge of the approach of the enemy was the sudden, heavy, and general cannonade about 3:30 o'clock AM on the 24th April between the two forts and the enemy's mortar fleet, sloops; and gunboats. All hands at once repaired to quarters with alacrity on board of the *Louisiana*. About ten or fifteen minutes after I had gained her deck the first vessel of the enemy was discovered coming up abreast of Fort St. Philip, on which she opened at once with her bow guns; other vessels of the enemy followed in rapid succession, all of which received as they came within range the fire of the *Louisiana's* three bow guns (one rifled 7-inch and two IX-inch shell) and three starboard broadside guns (one rifled 6-inch and two VIII-inch shell) which were all that could be brought to bear during the engagement, for, being moored to the river bank, all her stern and port beam guns were useless for the want of power to move her. The enemy moved up in two divisions, one on each shore, delivering their fire as they passed all our vessels, whether armed or only transports and tenders.

One of his heavy sloops was set on fire by one of the fire boats. It was, however, soon extinguished without doing her serious harm.

The small unarmed tug *Mosher*, Captain Sherman, it is said, while gallantly towing a fire boat against a heavy sloop of war, was instantly sunk by her broadside, with what loss of life I have been unable to learn.

The night was calm and pleasant but so dark, though starlight, that it was impossible to observe or direct the movements of our own vessels. In such a night conflict it must necessarily be somewhat of a melee. The *McRae* and the *Manassas* were in the stream in time to run the gantlet of the enemy's fleet and were no doubt skillfully and gallantly handled. The *McRae* burst her IX-inch pivot shell gun during the action and was badly and seriously cut up, though not actually disabled; her escape from utter annihilation was miraculous, considering her slight construction. The *Manassas* dealt two or more blows against heavy ships of the enemy; but, it is feared, with little effect, as she was comparatively light and deficient in motive power. Having followed the enemy around the first point above, and being hard pressed by two of his heaviest ships, she was run ashore, her supply pipes cut, and abandoned by her officers and crew, who were fired upon by the pursuing enemy with grape and canister shot while escaping to the swamp. She subsequently floated off, and, drifting down the river, sank below the two forts.

The *McRae*, after following the enemy above the point, returned to her position near the *Louisiana* soon after daylight. Only a hurried verbal report was received from Lieutenant C. W. Read, who succeeded to the command after the fall of her able and heroic commander, Lieutenant Thomas B. Huger, mortally wounded, in the unequal contest in which he was engaged. The early separation of the *McRae* after the action, in sending her with a flag of truce to carry our wounded to New Orleans, and her inability to return, prevented a written report being made to me by Lieutenant Read, which, I presume, must have been made subsequently to the Department. I feel confident that that gallant officer has vindicated himself from the charge of having violated his flag of truce, made by a scandalous enemy, in consequence of the sinking of the *McRae* off New Orleans.

The enemy returned the fire of the *Louisiana* in passing with grape, canister, and shell, but without serious damage to her hull. No one was injured under deck, no projectiles having entered through ports or otherwise, the only casualties being on deck caused by splinters from the light barricade for sharpshooters, which was somewhat cut up. One of the enemy's heaviest sloops, supposed to be the *Hartford*, delivered her fire while almost, if not in actual contact with the *Louisiana*. Two of his XI-inch shells struck the forward part of the roof, crushing the railroad iron plating about two-thirds their diameter, and then broke into fine fragments; solid shot or heavy rifle projectiles, under similar circumstances, would, in all probability, have easily pierced the roof. While in actual contact with the *Louisiana* stern, the *Hartford* received the fire of her three bow guns, the projectiles from which must have passed through her.

The Louisiana State gunboat *Governor Moore*, Commander Beverly Kennon, appears, from his report, herewith enclosed, to have been well and bravely handled, and to whom the credit is chiefly, if not entirely, due for sinking the enemy's heavily armed gunboat *Varuna*, though his own boat was afterwards run on shore in a disabled condition and destroyed to prevent her falling into the hands of the enemy pressing upon him in superior force.

I respectfully refer the Department for details as to the part taken by this vessel to the full report of her commander, Commander B. Kennon, of the Louisiana Navy. Also to the report of Lieutenant Commanding A. F. Warley respecting the part taken by the ram *Manassas*, under his command; and to the report of Lieutenant Commanding John W Wilkinson, executive officer of the *Louisiana*, upon whom her command devolved after the fall (toward the close of the action, mortally wounded) of her lamented commander, Charles F. McIntosh, for his testimony as to the good conduct of the officers and men. The favorable reports made of the officers and crews of these two vessels by their respective commanders have my cordial approbation, and I can, from my own personal observation, bear testimony to the activity and good conduct of Commander McIntosh while gallantly discharging his duties in the most exposed part of the vessel on deck, as well as to his zeal and industry in the preparation of the *Louisiana* for service previous to the action.

What part the Louisiana State gunboat *General Quitman* took in the action I have been unable to learn, except the fact that she was destroyed.

The *Warrior*, the *Stonewall Jackson*, the *General Lovell*, and *R. J. Breckinridge*, all river defense gunboats, under the command of Captain Stevenson, were all destroyed by the enemy's fire or by their own crews to prevent their falling into his hands. Captain S., whom I saw after the battle, appeared to be greatly mortified at what he seemed to regard as a serious mismanagement of his vessels.

None of them appear to have made a real attempt to ram the enemy's vessels, for which they were designed and supposed to have been prepared, nor were they more successful in handling the fire boats, as not more than one or two appear to have been fired and turned adrift in accordance with the plan of action, nor did I learn that any attempt was made to tow them against the enemy's vessels.

The *Resolute* was discovered aground after the action, on the west bank of the river, a mile above Fort Jackson, abandoned by her crew. She was taken possession of by a party from the *McRae*, under the command of Lieutenant Arnold, who, while making efforts to get her afloat, she being very little injured, was attacked by one of the enemy's gunboats from above at long range, who succeeded in putting several rifle shot through the iron plating on the *Resolute's* bow below the water line, passing through or out of the opposite side, which it was impossible to repair.

The enemy's fire was gallantly returned from the *Resolute*, with what effect is unknown, as he soon after hauled off. To prevent her falling into the hands of the enemy, being exposed to an attack from his land as well as naval forces, the *Resolute* was burned, after removing as much of the property on board as practicable, the enemy's vessels then approaching for another attack.

The *Defiance* (river-defense gunboat), Captain McCoy, escaped without any material injury; what useful part, if any, she performed in the action, I did not learn. Her commander appeared to be drunk all day of the 24th, and would not render any satisfactory assistance to me, as requested, idling away his time in running about the river in our vicinity, apparently without useful purpose.

On the 26th of April Captain Stevenson turned her over to my command without any of her officers and crew, who refused to remain in her and went ashore. The *Defiance* had a smoothbore 32-pounder, pivoted aft, and being mounted on an army carriage, was probably almost useless, and I believe had not been fired during the action. Having no men to spare to man her she was kept ready for any exigency that might arise, and was finally destroyed on the 28th by cutting her supply pipes and sinking her, to prevent her falling into the hands of the enemy after the surrender of the forts and the burning of the *Louisiana*.

The *Jackson*, Lieutenant Commanding F. B. Renshaw, as she could offer no check to the enemy's progress, retired up the river on his approach to the Quarantine Station, where she was stationed with *launch No. 3* previous to the 24th. The latter fell into the bands of the enemy.

The steam tenders *W. Burton* and *Landis*, being badly damaged, were received into the service from their respective commanders, who left with their crews. This seemed the proper course for me to pursue, as, by the contracts, the Government took the war risks.

The tender *Phoenix* was destroyed in the action; also the steamers *Star* and *Belle Algerine*.

Pilot L. F. Huggins, of the *Louisiana*, was missing after the action, and his absence since has not been satisfactorily accounted for.

The only vessels that escaped to the city, I believe, were the gunboat *Jackson* and the transport *Diana*. All the others, except those heretofore named, were either destroyed by the enemy during the engagement or by their own crews to prevent their capture.

Not more than thirty or forty minutes appeared to be the duration of the conflict below the first point of the river, about a mile above Fort St. Philip, around which the enemy's vessels, to the number of twelve, at least, had all passed out of sight and beyond reach of our fire before it was fairly light.

The following is believed to be a correct list of the enemy's vessels that passed up by Forts Jackson and St. Philip during the engagement of the 24th April, mounting in the aggregate 184 guns, viz:

Name of steamer.	Number of guns.	
Hartford	28	First-class sloop.
Richmond	28	Do.
Brooklyn	28	Do.
Pensacola	28	Do
Mississippi	21	Do
Iroquois	10	Second-class sloop.
Oneida	10	Do
Varuna	11	Do
Cayuga	5	Do.
Pinola	5	Do.
Wissahickon	5	Do.
Winona	5	Do.

Many, if not all of the above vessels, were protected in the wake of their boilers and machinery by chain cables bighted up and down against their sides. Their passage of the forts was covered by the fire of many other vessels that remained below, as well as by their mortar fleet of twenty-one or more vessels mounting one mortar and two 32-pounders each. Any one of the above fine first-class steam sloops was more than a match for the entire force afloat opposed to them, not even leaving out the *Louisiana*, which, for the want of motive power, was no better than a floating battery, and having only six guns which could be brought to bear upon the enemy, and only then as his vessels passed their line of fire.

After the action the detachments from the forts of sharpshooters, under Captain Ryan, and of artillery, under Lieutenant Dixon, were returned. It gives me great pleasure to bear testimony to their good conduct and coolness under the fire of the enemy.

The mechanics employed on board of the *Louisiana* made their escape and did not return after the action. Some of them are supposed to have suffered from casualties, as they were much exposed on board of the tender *W. Burton*, where they were quartered. Efforts were, however, made with our own resources, and great credit is due to Second Assistant Engineer Youngblood, in charge, for his untiring exertions night and day to get the propellers ready for service, though little confidence was felt in their being of sufficient power with the wheels to enable the *Louisiana* to stem the current and to be handled with effect in the Mississippi. During the night of Sunday, the 27th, we had so far succeeded in operating the propellers that we expected early the next day to make a fair trial of them in connection with the paddle wheels, when, at daylight, an officer, sent by General Duncan, came on board to inform me that many of the garrison of Fort Jackson had deserted during the night, that serious disturbances had occurred, and that the disaffection of the men was believed to be general, on account of what appeared to them to have become the desperate character of the defense of the forts, and in consequence of this condition of affairs he, General Duncan, had dispatched a flag of truce to Commander Porter, commanding United States naval forces below, offering to surrender the two forts to him on the terms tendered by him the day before, but rejected by General Duncan.

I at once waited on General Duncan in Fort Jackson to learn from himself the particulars of his course. He informed me that in his offer to surrender the forts he had disclaimed all control over the forces afloat. This unexpected surrender of these important land defenses, seriously compromising the position and very safety of my own command, I expressed to General Duncan my deep regret that a previous knowledge of his intention to surrender had not been communicated to me, particularly as I expected early in the day to test the full power of the *Louisiana* under her propellers and wheels, and that if successful I might be able to achieve something against the enemy. It was, however, too late; the flag of truce had been dispatched and could not be recalled; but I informed General Duncan that in no event would the enemy be allowed to obtain possession of the *Louisiana*.

I at once returned on board and called a council, composed of Lieutenants John Wilkinson (commanding), W. H. Ward, A. F. Warley, W. C. Whittle, Jr., R. J. Bowen, [Thomas] Arnold, F. M. Harris, and George S. Shryock, the latter also acting as recorder, by whom, in consequence of the enemy having the entire command of the river above and below us with an overwhelming naval force, and who was in the act of obtaining the quiet and undisturbed possession of Forts Jackson and St. Philip, with all their material defenses intact, with ordnance, military stores, and provisions, thus cutting the *Louisiana* off from all succor or support, and her having on board not more than ten days' provisions, her surrender would be rendered certain in a brief period by the simple process of a blockade, and that, in the condition of her motive power and defective steering apparatus and the imminent danger of an attack, she was very liable to capture, it was unanimously recommended that the *Louisiana* be destroyed forthwith to prevent her falling into the hands of the enemy while it remained in our power to do so, first retiring to our tenders.

It was with the most painful regret that I yielded to what seemed an unavoidable necessity, and at once gave orders to Lieutenant Commanding Wilkinson to carry out the recommendation of the council and fire the *Louisiana*. He was aided by Lieutenants Ward, Whittle, Lee, and Shryock and Acting Chief Engineer Youngblood in this service, which was executed to my entire satisfaction, and these officers, with myself, were the last to leave the vessel, at which moment the flames were ascending the forward hatchway.

The vessel, after being fired and abandoned, broke adrift from the shore, and being caught in an eddy, blew up at about 10:45 AM, near the water battery of Fort St. Philip, in which one man was killed and one wounded by falling fragments.

The destruction of the vessel was complete, not less than 10,000 pounds of powder having exploded; the water being deep, the recovery of any ordnance or materials is regarded as impossible. *Launch No. 6* was burned with the *Louisiana*.

The enemy was in sight when this work was commenced and soon after anchored near Fort Jackson with several gunboats, from which, and the two forts, flags of truce were flying.

Having had no communication with the enemy, and not being in any manner whatever a party to the negotiation pending for the surrender of the forts, I of course had no flag of truce flying.

After abandoning the *Louisiana* I retired in her two tenders, the *W. Burton* and *Landis*, to the opposite or western shore to await events, throwing overboard all the small arms, knowing our surrender to be inevitable. As the enemy was in force above at the quarantine, and had his pickets extended across the country, all chance for escape by the levee or swamp was cut off, except for a few individuals in small parties. Several officers, however, availed themselves of my permission for all to land who chose to make an attempt to escape capture. Among them were Lieutenants R. J. Bowen, [Thomas] Arnold, George S. Shryock, and [Daniel] Pfister; Acting Masters G. W. Gift, S. S. Lee, James McBaker, H. D. Bremond,

Albert Hulse, and John Glass; Assistant Engineers N. P. Wilcox, James Durning, James Nolan, and James Riley; Midshipmen Chew and McDermott, and Master's Mate Beck. What portion of these officers succeeded in eluding the enemy and finally escaping I am not informed.

I can not omit here to make my acknowledgments of the cool, active, and zealous conduct of that intelligent officer, George S. Shryock, who served as my aid to my entire satisfaction.

About 4 o'clock PM Commander Porter having taken possession of the two forts, moved up with three of his gunboats, fired a shot over our tenders, which being unarmed, their flags were struck by my order. Possession was immediately taken of them, and all the officers except those of the Crescent Artillery—about 26—were transferred to the U. S. gunboat *Clifton*, Commander Baldwin; thence, on the 5th May, to the sailing transport *Fearnot* at Pilot Town; thence, on the 7th, to the frigate *Colorado* at anchor off southwest bar, where I found Captain Hutton and the other officers of the Crescent Artillery, and Commander B. Kennon and Lieutenant Haynes, late of the Louisiana State gunboat *Governor Moore*. From the *Colorado* the entire party was transferred, on the 9th, to the steam transport *Rhode Island*, from which all were landed and imprisoned in Fort Warren, Boston, on the 23d May last.

The following officers of my late command took the oath of allegiance to the United States after their surrender, thereby deserting to the enemy, viz: Samuel Jones, acting boatswain, who was left on board the *Clifton*, James Wilson, gunner; Virginius Cherr, carpenter; James Waters, third assistant engineer; and Theodore Hart, third assistant engineer, who were left at Fort Warren. With the above exceptions, all of the officers were returned to the Confederacy at Aiken's Landing on the 5th instant, except Captain Hutton and Lieutenant Dart, who obtained temporary paroles from the enemy to visit their families. Their arrival may therefore be looked for at an early day.

The crew of the *Louisiana* and the rank and file of the volunteer artillery serving on board were paroled at New Orleans.

I would here invite the attention of the Department to the correspondence (herewith enclosed) between Flag-Officer D. G. Farragut, the U. S. Secretary of the Navy, the Hon. Gideon Welles, and myself respecting the treatment of the officers of my command after surrender, from which it will be perceived that Commander Porter, by the suppression of some facts, the perversion and misrepresentation of others, in his report of the destruction of the *Louisiana* to Flag Officer Farragut, sought to make it appear that I had violated by that act a flag of truce and the laws of war, and that Flag-Officer Farragut, in his answer to my communication, willfully assumes false views of circumstances and events to justify and sustain the course of Commander Porter, through whose joint misstatements to their Navy Department the lieutenants of my command and myself became the victims of its injustice.

The course of Flag-Officer Farragut and that of Commander D. D. Porter in this matter shows them to be servile and degraded tools well fitted for carrying out the infamous policy of an unprincipled and despotic Government.

The correspondence in this connection, respecting the unjustifiable treatment of Commander B. Kennon, of the Louisiana State Navy, is also enclosed and commended to your notice....

[A list of included reports is omitted here — RTC]

The success of the enemy in forcing the passage of Forts Jackson and St. Philip below New Orleans, and the great disasters to the nation generally that followed that event, as well as to the naval forces late under my command, must very naturally suggest inquiries as to the conduct of those concerned and to whom the defenses were entrusted. I would, therefore, in forwarding this, my report, respectfully submit to the Department the propriety of ordering a court of enquiry in relation to the part performed by the Navy, so far as its operations were under my, control.

I have the honor to be, very respectfully, your obedient servant,

JNO. MITCHELL,
Commander, C. S. Navy.

Hon. S. R. MALLORY,
Secretary of the Navy, Richmond, Va.

VIII

Louisiana Waters

1. The CSS *J. A. Cotton*

Taking advantage of the high water in the spring of 1862, numerous civilian steamboats began leaving the city of New Orleans. Steaming north up the Mississippi River, many found their way into the Red River, which flows out of northwestern Louisiana and empties into the Mississippi about 75 miles above Baton Rouge. Just before the Red meets the "Father of Waters," the Atchafalaya River branches off from the Red and winds its way southward into the fabled bayou country of southern Louisiana. It finally flows into a body of water known as Berwick Bay, and from there it ultimately breaks through to the Gulf of Mexico some 90 miles west of New Orleans. Turning into the Atchafalaya during that spring rush to flee the Crescent City was the Southern steamboat *J. A. Cotton*, under the command of Mississippi riverboat captain Emelious W. Fuller.

Constructed at Jefferson, Indiana, and completed in early 1861, the *J. A. Cotton* was a typical side-wheel steamer of the period, weighing 549 tons, and was built specifically for the passenger and freight trade on the Louisiana bayous. Purchased by the Confederate Army in early 1862, she was one of several vessels that arrived in Berwick Bay after the exodus from New Orleans. (Moebs, *Confederate States Navy Research Guide*, p. 335.)

Her captain was a civilian, and according to Lieutenant General Richard Taylor, commander of the District of West Louisiana, "was a western steamboat man, and one of the bravest of a bold, daring class." After a brief stint in command of the armed tug *Music*, which had escaped the disaster at New Orleans, Fuller approached Major J. L. Brent, Chief of Artillery and Ordnance on General Taylor's staff, asking for the army's permission and help in converting the *Cotton* into a gunboat. Because of her light construction, Fuller suggested that she be armored with railroad iron for protection of her vital machinery. Brent, on behalf of the army agreed to the proposal and the conversion commenced.

Heavy timbers, backed by a layer of *cotton* bales, were fabricated into a partial casemate, which was designed to protect her boilers and engines from enemy fire. Once this was in place, a small quantity of railroad iron was tacked on, and a crew was recruited from volunteers among the army units in the area. Two 24-pounder smoothbores and a field piece supplied by Major Brent were mounted on the hurricane deck.

Near the end of October, Union Brigadier General Godfrey Weitzel advanced from New Orleans with a force of approximately 5,000 troops. Taken by steamers up the Mississippi to Donaldsonville, 60 miles above the city, his troops disembarked and began pushing south along the north bank of Lafourche River. The only Confederate troops in the area able to offer opposition were 500 men under the immediate command of Colonel Leopold L. Armant. With these troops and a four-gun battery, Colonel Armant made his stand along Lafourche.

At the little hamlet of Labadieville, a vicious skirmish occurred about ten miles north of the railroad that runs from Algiers opposite New Orleans to Brashear City on Berwick Bay. Overwhelmed by the large Federal force, their ammunition exhausted, and suffering many casualties, the small band of Confederates retreated west along the railroad to Berwick Bay and began crossing over to the village of Berwick City on the western shore.

To confront this enemy advance, Confederate Brigadier General Alfred Mouton began concentrating all available troops, including the remnants of Armant's demoralized men, on a line just west of Berwick Bay and astride the Bayou Teche (River). Assembling 1,300 men and ten guns, Mouton had earthworks constructed on either side of the Teche with the left flank resting on Grand Lake, and the right on the impassable bayou two thousand yards south of the Teche. Three floating bridges were thrown over the Teche in the rear to facilitate moving troops from one side of the bayou to the other; and to the front, pickets were maintained on the western shore of the bay. It was here on Saturday evening November 1, 1862, that Captain Fuller on the *J.A. Cotton* anchored in the bay saw ominous plumes of black smoke rolling over the trees to the south. (Taylor, *Destruction and Reconstruction*, pp. 141–143.) [RTC]

The Ordeal of the Gunboat J.A. Cotton *by Captain Emelious W. Fuller*

Official Records Navy, Series I, Volume XIX, pp. 335–337, 523–525

GUNBOAT *COTTON, November 7, 1862.*

Gen. A. Mouten, *Commanding Forces South of Red River*:

SIR: I embrace the first opportunity of making my report of the recent affairs between the *Cotton*, under my command, and the squadron of Federal gunboats that have occupied Berwick Bay.

On Saturday evening, November 1, smoke from the enemy's boats warned me of their near approach in such force that resistance at the bay was considered by me to be rashness. Acting upon your order, received but a few minutes previously, I immediately gave the necessary orders for leaving the bay. The steamers *Hart* and *Seger* were there at the time, also *Launch No. 1*, under the command of J. M. Rogers, who I had temporarily appointed to the position of acting master. My orders to the officers of those boats were to get immediately underway, the *Hart*, under the command of Lieutenant E. Montague, to proceed up to the Teche with a barge loaded with Government sugar in tow. This was safely done according to orders, with one exception. Lieutenant Montague at one time dropped his barge and returned, like a gallant soldier, to aid the *Cotton* in an unequal conflict. As soon as

Captain Emelious W. Fuller (Washington State University Library).

I could communicate to him my wishes he resumed his tow and proceeded safely to destination. *Launch No. 1* also obeyed the order given to her commander, and conveyed the launch up the lake [Grand] to a place near Indian Bend, from where he has since safely reported, and is now in position to render valuable service. The *Seger*, under the command of Acting Master I. C. Coons, disobeyed the order I gave of proceeding up the lake and turned up the Atchafalaya, and was ignobly abandoned to the enemy at a time when the *Cotton* was between the enemy and the *Seger*. The commanding officer has not since reported. I have been informed that he abandoned his men and proceeded as fast as possible to Saint Martinsville. Up to the present time the only reliable fact I have about the *Seger* is that it is in the hands of the enemy, prowling about Grand Lake and bayous in the vicinity; of the crew, nothing.

The enemy came into Berwick Bay on Saturday evening just at dark. As the *Cotton* was in range, having had to wait to get the other boats off, they immediately opened fire upon us and gave chase up the bay with three boats, continuing the fire which I did not return until rounding into the Atchafalaya, when one of our guns was brought to bear and we fired one shot, which sped straight to its mark, striking one of the Federal boats in her bow, breaking many timbers, and have since been informed that it killed 3 and wounded 5 men. The Federals continued to fire shot and shell at us from eighteen guns for about thirty minutes, when they gave up the chase. The *Cotton* came up to the Teche, turned bow down, and backed into it, keeping our teeth to the enemy. We backed up to the Turelier plantation, where we stopped for the night.

On Sunday morning, the 2d instant, I received orders to move the *Cotton* above Cornay's bridge, which I did as soon as possible. The bayou had some obstructions thrown across at that point, which I was ordered to defend until it got too hot for me and then to fall back, turn my boat across the bayou at the second bridge, and, if pursued, sink her.

On Monday, 2 PM, the four Federal boats, mounting twenty-seven guns, came up and opened fire upon us. They came up in full delay of about twenty minutes. One more adventuresome than the rest steadily steamed up the bayou; when in about 100 yards of the obstructions we gave her a plunging shot from each of our guns, which all struck near the water on the starboard quarter. The boat immediately ran her head up on shore, and was listed down so as to throw her guns out of use and ceased her fire, except occasionally from one gun on the bow. At this time but one of the enemy's boats fired with any vigor. When victory seemed to be within our reach, it was announced that we had no more cartridges, having fired the last one. Retreat was all that remained for us; but as we slowly backed up we had some sacks made by cutting off the legs from the pantaloons of some of our men, which we filled and returned the fire with as often as we could in that manner obtain a cartridge. This we continued until we were out of range and the enemy ceased their fire. We had to mourn the loss of one brave soldier killed by an accidental discharge of his gun, which severely wounded another. Another was accidentally wounded at another gun by the recoil of the carriage and has since died. One man was wounded by a piece of the enemy's shell. These are all the casualties that occurred. The boat sustained no perceptible damage.

On Tuesday morning we resumed our original position near the obstructions, the enemy having previously retired. We worked hard to improve the condition of our boat and got up some iron to shield the engines. Nothing occurred worthy of note during the day.

On Wednesday, the 5th instant, the enemy again opened fire upon us with four boats at about 10:30 o'clock. They fired from behind a point out of our range for about twenty minutes; then two of them steamed up into sight. We then immediately returned their fire, and with such effect that the enemy retired and abandoned the contest in fifty-five minutes from firing their first shot. The two boats that came into sight were badly damaged and their loss heavy; ours nothing, the only damage being a trifling break in the cabin roof. This day victory was clearly ours. The enemy retired from action badly discouraged, with severe loss. We were unhurt.

On Thursday the enemy came up and opened fire upon us, but took care not to come into sight. I did not return their fire. They threw shells at us for half an hour and retired without doing us any damage. Since that up to the present date they have not assailed us.

I can not close this report without returning thanks to officers and men. Where all did their duty gallantly it may seem invidious to mention particular names, yet I must particular mention the good conduct of O. S. Burdett, pilot, who, for two hours and a half, during the fierce combat on the 3d instant, maneuvered the boat with the utmost coolness; also the same gallant conduct on the 5th instant. Each of my lieutenants did his duty nobly and ably. Also F. G. Burbank, gunner, and privates F. D. Wilkinson and Henry Dorning deserve particular mention for their gallant conduct. But all did their duty well and are again ready to meet the enemy should they come up and try us again.

Respectfully, your obedient servant,

E. W. FULLER,
Captain, Commanding Gunboat *Cotton*.

General ALFRED MOUTON,
Commanding Forces South of Red River.

In January of 1863, General Weitzel again advanced his forces up the Bayou Teche. No report by Captain Fuller has survived, but a newspaper account was published in the *Official Navy Records* and is included here to complete the story of Captain Fuller and the *J. A. Cotton*. [RTC]

Extract from the Houston, *Texas Tri-Weekly Telegraph*, February 2, 1863

C. S. gunboat *J. A. Cotton*, burnt.

On the evening of the 13th instant a large Federal force was reported to be advancing both by land and water to attack our troops stationed about 12 miles below Franklin. The report proved to be correct, for at 6 o'clock PM they were encamped upon the plantation of J. Carpentier, and two of their much-dreaded gunboats were anchored below the obstructions at Cornay's bridge.

At about 8 o'clock AM on the morning of the 14th their intention was announced by a rapid firing from their gunboats, and it was evident that they had not come, as usual, to feel for our position, but to meet us face to face. Owing to the superior range of their guns, the batteries of the *Cotton* did not at first reply to their salutations; but as they neared the obstructions the deep thunder of our heavy guns trembled on the wind, and we knew that the game had ceased to be altogether on one side. For hours the roar of artillery was almost incessant, and the high wind which had been prevailing seemed frightened into silence.

It was evident in a very short time that our fire from the *Cotton* was telling seriously upon the enemy's vessels. The *Grey Cloud*, which was the first to attack, was discovered to have drifted broadside across the bayou, in which condition she remained, receiving broadside upon broadside without replying from her batteries. At this juncture the *Estrella* was seen to approach her and remain some time by her side. The *Estrella* then retired a short distance, keeping under cover of the *Grey Cloud* and took up a position which enabled her to throw her fire from behind the latter, whose shots thereafter were but few and ineffective.

Surely Providence was with us in this artillery duel. Our shots were frequently seen to plunge into their sides, at one time with such effect as to cause the crew of the *Grey Cloud* to abandon her gun decks, while the enemy's, though frequently striking us, inflicted no real damage whatever.

About 10 o'clock AM it was discovered that three regiments of the enemy's infantry were advancing in such a manner that their extreme left would flank the *Cotton*. These were supported by batteries of fieldpieces. Upon perceiving this, the *Cotton*'s springs were cut and the order given to back up the bayou to be in line with our land forces. The movements of the enemy were so rapid that they were soon upon the very banks of the bayou, firing volley after volley upon our gun decks, and sweeping the men from the batteries.

It was about this time that Lieutenant Stevens, of the Confederate Navy, fell, fighting like a hero, brave as a lion, and calm and immovable as the very statue of silence. The loss of such men, while deeply mourned by individuals, should clothe a whole nation in sadness. The monuments they merit are deep in the hearts of the people, more enduring than the shaft which pierceth to the clouds.

At this time, too, was wounded our brave captain of the *Cotton* [Fuller]. Shot through both arms, the purple tide of life gushing from his wounds, he stood like granite at his post, nor left it until his boat was moored in line with our advanced troops on land. He was then removed to the steamer *Gossamer*, to be transported to Franklin, and Lieutenant E. T. King assumed command.

The lieutenant, after the removal of the killed and wounded, directed the *Cotton* once more toward the scene of action. While advancing in this direction several batteries, which were concealed upon the banks, opened upon this boat with a heavy fire, almost every shot striking her. Her cabin was riddled with balls, but the iron over her machinery proved the efficacy of such a defense, for their shots made scarcely an impression upon it. It is certain that, for all practical purposes, the *Cotton* was as formidable after the engagement as if she had never sustained the fire of the enemy.

Finding that he could not reply with effect to the land batteries, and there being no support on shore, Lieutenant King returned to the position he had occupied when taking command. The loss of the *Cotton* is as follows:

Killed.- Lieutenant H. K. Stevens, C. S. Navy , Corporal V. Gautreau, privates J. A. Chesnut, O. A. Fleurot, J. Melancon.

Wounded.- Captain E. W. Fuller, in both arms; Lieutenant E. Montague, in the side; Sergeants F. De la Rue, J. Gautreau, in the side, and D. Como, in the hand. Privates J. C. Bishop and R. J. Hankins, in the foot; F. Devillier, J. A. Hickman, in the head.

Colonel MeWaters, of the Second Louisiana Cavalry, was also killed, near the residence of Colonel Bethel, and his remains have been taken to Alexandria for interment. We are unable to-day (Monday) to give a list of the killed and wounded of the land forces, but it was very trifling, not exceeding 10, it is believed, all told. Up to the present writing—Sunday, 1 o'clock PM—we are unable to learn the enemy's loss. This closes the history of the battle on the 14th.

Since that day there has been no fighting beyond occasional skirmishes. The enemy have retreated to Berwick Bay. What are their intentions for the future in regard to this, the fairest portion of our State? The red blaze of incendiarism, the smoldering ruins which mark their backward march, would seem to indicate that they are about to abandon this section and seek to leave cruel remembrances of their fanatical hate behind them. Among the houses destroyed on this side of the bayou we notice those of Colonel P. C. Bethel, Mr. A. A. Fuselier, and Mr. Numa Cornay.

Our forces were commanded by Brigadier-General Alfred Mouton, and those of the enemy by General Weitzel and Commander T. M. Buchanan, the latter of whom was killed. The Yankees, in the words of the brave Captain Fuller (the Paul Jones of the South), fought like tigers, and exhibited feats of great daring and bravery. They were in such close proximity to the *Cotton* that the word of command, "Oblique, march!" was distinctly understood when our battery, placed on her hurricane deck, let fly its missiles of death at their advancing columns, which were decimated by the unerring aim of our expert gunners.

The *Cotton*, which had become the pet and pride of our community; the *Cotton*, which had come to be regarded as personal property among us, is no more. After having fought with unparalleled success in more than one engagement all the gunboats the enemy could bring against her; baptized in blood that welled from the hearts of the noblest and the bravest in the land; invincible to her enemies, the idol of her friends, one stroke of the mighty pen has swept into annihilation what tempests of shot and shell and fire had failed to scathe. She now lies a gloomy wreck upon the water, though lost and abandoned, defiant in her loneliness, and still, as she was when afloat, a barrier to the advance of her foe.

Is there blame to be attached to anyone for this destruction of our means of defense? Can it be explained why there was no concert of action upon the part of our land and water forces? We are no warrior, nor do we seek to constitute ourselves a tribunal to attach censure to anyone; but surely where such tremendous effects are remarked there must have been causes for their production. Let the matter be thoroughly sifted by the constituted powers, and let those who are "weighed in the balance and found wanting" be placed among the lights of the community.

2. The CSS *Missouri*

By the beginning of the summer of 1863, Confederate naval operations on western waters had suffered serious setbacks. The *Louisiana* and *Mississippi*, along with numerous wooden gunboats, had been destroyed at New Orleans. Island No. 10, Fort Pillow, and Memphis had been lost. The River Defense Fleet had been more or less annihilated, and the *Arkansas* had been destroyed. Arkansas Post was lost, and with the White and Arkansas rivers essentially controlled by the Union Navy, the capitol at Little Rock was threatened. Only Vicksburg and Port Hudson on the Mississippi River remained as a link to the Trans-Mississippi Department, and only the Red River on the western side remained in Confederate hands.

It became evident to Confederate authorities in Richmond, and especially to naval secretary Stephen R. Mallory, that if Vicksburg fell, western Louisiana would be next. With this threat in mind, Mallory, in October of 1862, instructed First Lieutenant Jonathan H. Carter to contract for the construction of one or more ironclads on the Red River in western Louisiana. Mallory reasoned that if one or more formidable warships could be built along the Red, they could deter or perhaps even defeat any Federal push into western Louisiana.

Lieutenant Carter, a native of North Carolina and an 1846 graduate of the U. S. Naval Academy, traveled to Shreveport, Louisiana, and there contracted with Thomas Moore and John Smoker, two Red River steamboat captains, to build an "iron-clad steam gun boat." On December 10, 1862, Moore and Smoker acquired a lot on the river in Shreveport, and later that month the keel for their ironclad was laid.

The construction of the vessel, later named the CSS *Missouri*, proceeded rather well considering the many obstacles with which the builders were faced in obtaining materials and workmen in this remote part of the Confederacy. In spite of the difficulties, the *Missouri* was launched on April 14, 1863, and by the middle of June she was finished.

While the *Missouri* was designed to carry six guns, Carter was never able to acquire more than three. The feature that set the *Missouri* apart from other Confederate ironclads was her mode of propulsion. A large 22-foot paddle wheel was set in the aft portion of the casemate, eight feet of which projected above the roof of the casemate and was unprotected. (Campbell, *Confederate Naval Forces on Western Waters*, pp. 195–199.)

In a series of letters to Secretary Mallory, Lieutenant Carter reported on his successes and his many frustrations in attempting to effectively operate an armored warship so distant from the major theaters of war. Included here from his letter-book is a selection of his correspondence to the naval secretary beginning in 1864 until the end of the war. [RTC]

"Against All Odds"
Selection of Letters from 1st Lt. Jonathan H. Carter, CSN, to Secretary of the Navy Stephen R. Mallory

Letter book of Lt. Jonathan H. Carter,
War Records Branch, Record Group 45, National Archives

Naval Commandants Office.
Shreveport, La. Jan. 5th 1864

Hon. S. R. Mallory
Sec. of the Navy, Richmond, Va.

Sir:

I have the honor to report the condition of Naval affairs under my command in Western Louisiana. The steamer *Missouri* is now ready for service with three guns mounted; one 11 inch Dahlgren, one 9 inch Dahlgren, and one 32 pounder, as stated in a former letter. I am now awaiting the crew. Two officers are in Texas getting men.

The steamer *Webb* will be used as a ram, should an opportunity occur. The steamer *Cotton* will be used as a transport for stores and wood.

I have ordered Lieuts Grant and Crane, appointed for the war, to report to me for duty.

I shall be obliged to appoint several Assistant Engineers and Acting Masters, but I fear it will be impossible to procure good and. trusty men to serve (particularly as Engineers) for the Navy pay. So far, I have failed to get as many as are required. I do not know how I am to overcome this difficulty. I made known these facts to Comdr. Brent before he ordered the officers from this Station.

The draft for five hundred and eighty five thousand dollars ($585,000) payable to Asst. Paymaster A. A. Nelson, has not been paid by the C. S. Depository at this place, as he has received no notice from the Treasurer to pay it. I would be glad if orders could be sent for the payment of the draft.

I have appointed Mr. George R. Marsh a 3rd Assistant Engineer, and Mr. John Bunicum a 2nd Assistant Engineer, subject to the approval of the Navy Department. The appointment of the former bears date Dec. 15th 1863; the appointment of the latter, Jan. 5th 1864.

I would be glad if the Department will inform me whether Lieuts Grant and Crane draw pay from the date of their appointments or from the date of their acceptance.

I am very respectfully

Your obt. Servt.
J. H. Carter Lt. Comdg. Naval Defenses Western La.

P. S. Red river is low, but it is rising slowly. There will probably be enough water in a month for the *Missouri* to start down.

Naval Commandants Office
Shreveport, La. January 28th 1864.

Sir:

Lieut. J. L. Phillips, C. S. N. has reported to me for duty as commander of the C. S. Str. *Webb*, in obedience to an order from Adml. Franklin Buchanan approved by the Navy Department. He is accompanied by Passed Midsmn. E. J. McDermett and 1st & 2nd Asst Engrs. Benj Herring and Wm. Smith. Every facility in my power will be extended to Lieut. Phillips, the means at my command are very limited. Red River is now very low and it may be some time before anything can be done. In the mean time the river may be rafted and render it impossible to get out. Under such circumstances I can be of no service in Red River. In such an event, and when assured that I can be of no further service here, I would ask the Department to allow me to turn over the *Missouri* and other vessels to the Army, and move my command East of the Miss. River where we might be of more service. The propriety of such a step will of course depend entirely on circumstances.

The *Missouri* is ready for service with three guns. I experience great difficulty in getting a crew. Act. Master Musgrave has been in Texas some time trying to recruit men from the Army. He was sent with orders from Lieut. Genl. Smith to call for volunteers, and they should be transferred. Gen. Magruder refuses to allow the men to be transferred. Lieut. Crane in now in lower Louisiana, recruiting men from the Army there. Genl. Taylor has offered every facility and I hope to get men from him.

Lieut. Phillips having reported for the command of the *Webb*, I have ordered Lieut. A. D. Wharton to report to Adml. Buchanan at Mobile, for duty, and to notify the Department of his arrival at that place.

Third Asst. Eng. Wm. Flake, appointed by Comdr. T. W. Brent, has this day resigned in consequence of ill health. I have accepted his resignation, having the authority form Comdr. Brent to revoke all acting appointments made by him.

Since writing the foregoing I have received a letter from Genl. Taylor in which he refuses to allow me men until the *Missouri* goes to Alexandria. I will then be called into service with undisciplined men. Unless I can get the men and have them drilled, I will not be able to render efficient service.

I am very respectfully

Your obt. Servt.
J. H. Carter Lt. Comdg. Naval Defenses Western La.

To
Hon. S. R. Mallory
Sec. of the Navy, Richmond, Va.

Naval Commandants Office
Shreveport, La. March 9th 1864.

Sir:

Your letters of Dec. 29th/63 and Jany. 4th by the hands of Mr. Mead, Naval Constructor, have been received. In a few days I will leave here with Mr. Mead for Texas for the purpose of making the necessary examinations for the construction of the iron clad Torpedo boat. From my knowledge of the condition of this Department, and the scarcity of labor and material, such a vessel as the plan and specifications call for, cannot be built within fifteen months or two years, if at all, and at a cost of not less than one million of dollars. Confederate Money in Texas is at a discount of twenty for one. But the Department can rest assured that no effort on my part will be left undone to carry out its wishes; except discharging the duties of Paymaster and disbursing officer. Under no circumstances can I undertake that duty. The labor of superintending the work, collecting materials, and other outside duties will be sufficiently onerous. Should I find that the proposed vessel can be built, a Paymaster must be assigned. Asst. Paymaster McKean would be a proper person for that duty, and another paymaster could be assigned to the vessels on this river.

The *Missouri* is now ready with her officers and forty eight men on board and ammunition for her three guns. The river is rising slowly, and there may be water enough for her to go down. Full reports of the character and condition of the vessels under my command have been forwarded to the Department.

Since my last communication I have appointed the following officers; viz: F. P. Jones, 2nd Asst. Engr. appointed Feb. 19th, John W. Swift, 2nd Asst. Engr. appointed Feb. 19th and Anderson Claytor, 2nd Asst. Engr. appointed Feb. 29th. These appointments were made subject to the approval of the Navy Department.

I have employed the services of pilots at the rate of $250.00 per month after the vessels leave here and during the season of navigation; after which I have agreed to pay them $125.00 per month. These were the only terms on which pilots could be procured. I have Lieut. W. O. Crain, senior officer in charge of the vessel, here during my absence in Texas.

I am very respectfully

Your obt. Servt.
J. H. Carter Lt. Comdg. Naval Defenses Western La.

Honr. S. R. Mallory,
Secretary of the Navy, Richmond, Va.

Naval Commandants Office
Shreveport, La. April 4th 1864

Sir:

I have the honor to report that in obedience to your orders of Jany 4th by the hands of Mr. R. P. Meads, Naval Constructor, I left this place on the 17th of March in company with Mr. Meads and Mr. Robt. Grant, Master builder, to make the necessary examinations in regard to his building the iron clad Torpedo boats, according to the plans and specifications sent me. On my arrival at Henderson, Texas, en route to Houston a Telegram was handed me, stating that the enemy were in possession of Alexandria. Knowing that Red River was navigable at that time for the light draught gun-boats of the enemy, I deemed it proper to return to this place.

I directed Mr. Meads to proceed to Houston and consult with Maj. Gen. Magruder and report to me the result of his examination. I have as yet received no report from him, except a simple notice of his arrival at Houston. I have stated in a former letter that I considered it almost impossible to build an iron clad in Texas and I see no reason as yet to change my opinion. Machinery cannot be procured there unless manufactured, and the obstacles to be overcome in the manufacture of machinery are almost insufferable.

The enemy are in possession of Alexandria and the Lieut. Genl. Comdg. informs me that their gun-boats are above the falls. The river is now falling and if they attempt to come up far enough for me to reach them I hope to be able to strike them a blow. In the present stage of water, the *Missouri* cannot go far below this place. "Tones Bayou" is taking off more than half the water, rendering Red River proper, at this time navigable only for light draught boats. The enemy appears to be advancing from below, and we may expect warm work here in a short time.

I am Respectfully &c.

J. H. Carter Lt. Comdg. &c.

Hon. S. R. Mallory
Sec &c. Richmond

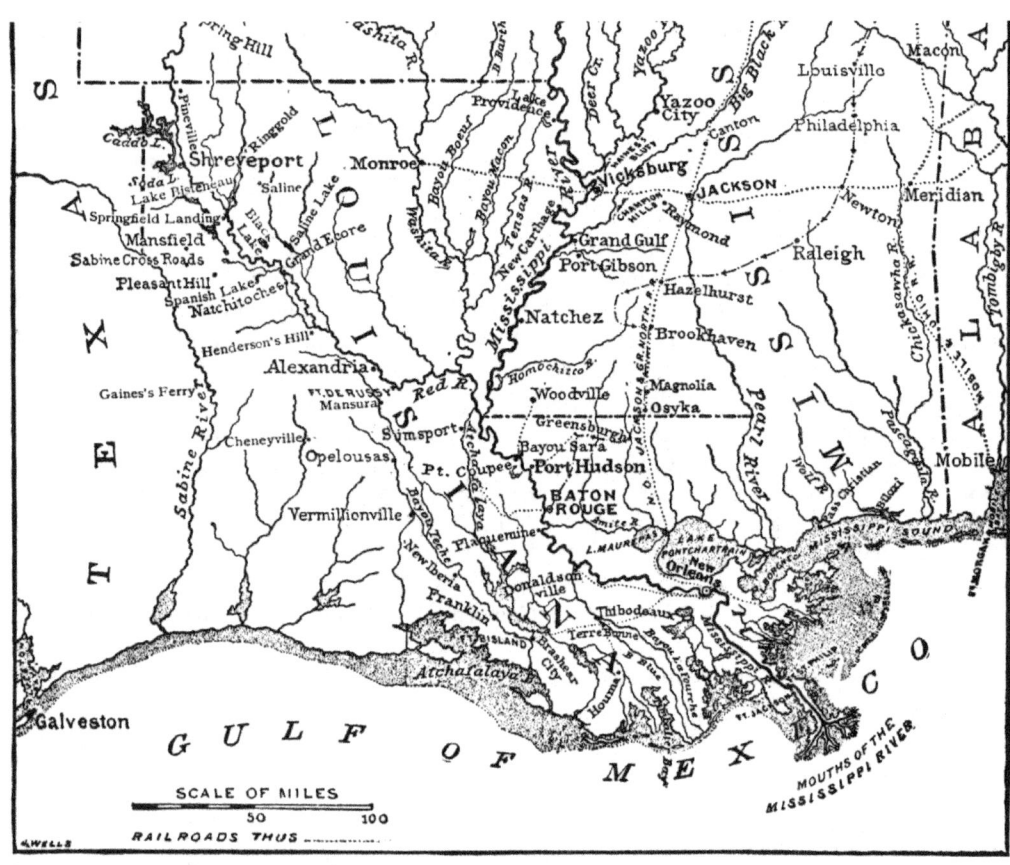

Map of the Red River Area (Johnson and Buel, Battles and Leaders of the Civil War).

Naval Commandant Office
Shreveport, La. April 25th 1864

Sir:

I have the honor to enclose the report of Mr. R. P. Meads, Naval Constructor, after a careful examination as to the means, facilities, &c. for the construction of an iron clad Torpedo boat at, or near Galveston, Texas.

All the carpenters, blacksmiths, &c. are employed in the Ordnance & Engineer Departments. The six ship-carpenters employed in the construction of the *Missouri*, have all left the country, except two. Maj. Williams, the engineering officer mentioned in your letter of Jany 4th has not reported. The necessary mechanical skill for putting up a rolling mill cannot be procured in this Department. The Nitre & Mining Bureau has been at work nearly a year and no rolling mill has as yet been put in operation. The chief of that Bureau informed me a few days since that he would have a small rolling mill in operation in three of or four months, but that the want of competent operatives greatly retarded the work. This mill is located in North Eastern Texas, some three hundred miles from Galveston, the only available point for building in Texas. Could iron be rolled at this mill within a reasonable time, transportation by wagons would be the only means of getting it to the place of construction. There is not transportation in this Department sufficient to meet the wants of the army. Taking all things into consideration, I deem it impracticable to build in Texas such a vessel as the plan and specifications require. I do not feel willing to commence the work unless there is a probability of its successful completion. The wood work of the vessel might be completed within a year, but iron and machinery can only be procured by importation. I have therefore directed Mr. Meads to return to Richmond.

I regret to state that I have had no opportunity to do anything with the *Missouri* in consequence of low water. The enemy attempted to reach this place both by land and water. On the 8th and 9th inst they were met by our forces near Mansfield and were driven back with heavy loss. Their gun boats returned as soon as they heard of the repulse of their land forces and they are now between Grand Ecore and Alexandria.

The future usefulness of the *Missouri* and the other vessels under my command will depend entirely on the river. If more active service could be had East of the Miss. river, I would be glad to cross. This however is for the Department to determine. The obstructions placed in Red River below Alexandria have been removed, partly by the action of the current and partly by the enemy. I fear that continued low water will prevent any active naval operations in Red River until next winter.

I am very respectfully

Your obt. Servt
J. H. Carter Lt. Comdg. Nav. Defenses West. La.

Hon. S. R. Mallory
Sec. of the Navy, Richmond Va.

P.S. Since writing the foregoing I have had an interview with Maj. Genl. Magruder who is now in Shreveport on the subject of building an iron clad vessel in the water of Texas. In his opinion, no ironclad can be built in Texas. The mere building of the vessel he thinks might possibly be done, but the iron for armor and machinery for driving cannot be had. He has had surveys made of the harbor of Galveston and Buffalo Bayou and no vessel drawing over five feet water built in Buffalo Bayou could get out. J.H.C.

Naval Commandants Office
Shreveport, La. Oct. 1st 1864

Sir:

I have the honor to acknowledge the receipt of your letter of Aug. 17th by the hands of Asst. Paymaster Hearn. As soon as Asst. Paymaster McKean can turn over the accounts of the Station he will be directed to proceed to Richmond. Your order for one hundred and fifty six thousand dollars ($156,000) has been received and the money drawn.

The docking of the *Missouri* has not yet been completed. This work has been very difficult and tedious, but I hope in a short time to have the work completed. The cost of this work is considerable, in consequence of the high prices of labor and material, and the depreciation of Confederate money. Additional funds will be required to carry on the operations of Navy Defenses in this Department during the coming winter.

At the solicitation of Genl. Smith I left this place on the 16th of August with twenty men and officers for the purpose of assisting in crossing the troops to the East side of the Mississippi river, and also to capture one of the enemy's gunboats; arrangements having been made, and reported to me, that would insure the capture. On the 4th of Sept. I reached the Mississippi River opposite the plantation of President Davis and watched the landing that night of the boat of the "tin clad" gun boat *Rattler*. After the landing of the men, eighteen in number, I attempted to take possession of the boat. In doing so it became necessary to fire on the boat-keepers as one of them was in the act of shooting Lieut. Larmour. The firing produced an alarm on board the steamer and before I could reach her she was under weigh. Lieut. Larmour was slightly wounded in the hand. If the firing had not occurred I am of the opinion that I would have captured the boat and with her I might have captured or destroyed several others. I returned to this place after an absence of one month. The crossing of the troops was abandoned as the enemy had been informed of the contemplated movement, and their gun boats were consequently very alert and vigilant. Surgeon Page will explain to you fully the object of my expedition and the causes of its failure.

I desire to call the attention of the Department to the frequency of the crime of desertion at this Station. It is out of my power to put a stop to the commission of this offense, as I am not authorized to order a General Court Martial for the punishment of the offenders and of course a Summary Court Martial can take no cognizance of a crime of such magnitude. If I possessed the power to order a General Court Martial, I have not a sufficient number of commissioned officers to constitute a Court, unless a Paymaster or Surgeon could be ordered to sit as a member of such a tribunal. I request instruction as to whether a Paymaster or Surgeon can be ordered to sit on a General Court Martial. As I cannot prevent desertion by the infliction of such punishments as are within my power I respectfully request that the Department will devise some means that will be effective in arresting the evil.

I have been requested by Genl. Smith, at the suggestion of Maj. Genl. Walker, Comdg. Dept. of Texas to either go myself, or send a competent Naval officer to take charge of the vessels at Galveston. These vessels have heretofore been under the command of Army officers, and I understand that Gen. Walker is anxious for a Naval officer to take command, as he does not deem them so efficient as they would be if otherwise manned and officered. I have no officer under my command suitable to take charge of the defenses of Red River, or Galveston, and I would ask that an officer be sent me to take charge of either this Station or Galveston.

I am very respectfully

Your obt. Servt.
J. H. Carter Lt. Comdg. Naval Defenses Western La.

Hon. S. R. Mallory
Secretary of the Navy, Richmond, Va.

Naval Commandants Office
Shreveport, La. Jan. 17th 1865

Sir:

Your letter of 12th ult. has been received. I am glad to learn that Surgeon Page is on his return to this place.

Preparations are being made to use torpedoes in Red River, but the sudden rises and falls, and the great quantity of drift wood render torpedoes very uncertain in the stream, as well as in the Mississippi. A torpedo boat is now in course of construction near Houston by the Engineer Department. She will probably be completed by spring.

Lieut. J. L. Phillips returned a short time since from Texas with a detachment of men for the *Missouri*. He differs with Acting Naval Constructor Meads in regard to the railroad iron in Texas. Lieut Phillips reports that there are large quantities of rail road iron in Texas, not laid down or in use. I think that with an efficient Naval Constructor and means sufficient, together with the facilities for running the blockade and thus obtaining material, a vessel of light draft might be built in the waters of Texas.

I have just received notice from Mr. Gray, Treasury Agent, Trans Miss. Depart. that funds to the amount of two hundred and twenty thousand ($220,000) dollar have been allotted, subject to my requisition. I find on examination that no appropriation has been made for "repairs of vessels." This is the heaviest outlay I have, and I would request that an appropriation for that purpose be ordered for immediate use.

I have had some difficulty in procuring a crew for the *Missouri* but it is now nearly complete and she is ready for active service. The enemy have, as yet, made no attempt to ascend Red River this winter, nor, so far as can be ascertained, have they made any preparations for that purpose.

I have appointed Wm. J. Fluery an Acting Gunner subject to your approval.

I enclose the reports of Capt. Lubbock Comdg. Marine Dept. of Texas, showing the number and character of the vessels in the waters of Texas. Some of these vessels might be rendered efficient.

Accompanying this is a communication from Acting Master Musgrave, stating his reasons for returning to this place after having been ordered to Wilmington. Since his return I have assigned him to duty on board the *Missouri*. The resignation of Lieut. Grant having been accepted, the services of Acting Master Musgrave are required on this Station.

Should the Department see fit to order the construction of a vessel in the waters of Texas, the Superintendent of construction should have cotton placed at his disposal, in order that material could be easily and cheaply procured.

I must again call your attention to the importance of providing for the punishment of deserters and other offenders. It is impossible to preserve proper discipline, as the punishment that is within my power is not sufficient to deter men from deserting.

I am very respectfully

Your obt. Servt.
J. H. Carter Lt. Comdg. Nav. Defenses Western La.

Hon. S. R. Mallory,
Secretary of the Navy, Richmond, V a.

C. S. Steamer *Missouri*
Alexandria, La. April 5th 1865.

Sir:

I have the honor to inform the Department that after consultation with General Smith & Buckner, I determined to move the *Missouri* from Shreveport to this place to act in conjunction with the facts. Before doing so however, it was the distinct understanding that the Lower Red River county was to be held by the land force; for should the river fall and the low country be abandoned by our troops, I should be compelled to destroy my vessel. I am satisfied that I can do good service here should the enemy advance by water, though one vessel against so large a force as the enemy would and could not resist long, but I will do all that can be done with the services at my command.

The *Missouri* is now in good order and has a crew that will be well drilled in a very short time. Some of the men I have recently received from the Army. I have had great difficulty in procuring men. The commanders of Regiments have repeatedly thrown every obstacle in my way. I am compelled to take wild Texans and men who never saw a gun or a ship.

I left Shreveport on the 23rd ult. and worked my way down this narrow and crooked river. There is no coal in the country and I was compelled to use wood; stopping at different plantations and having the wood cut. The performance of the *Missouri* exceeded my expectation. Her speed is much greater than I expected. She has made as much as ten miles per hour with a current of from two to three miles. Her machinery works well. I only regret that I have not half a dozen such vessels as the *Missouri*, but with only one I am compelled to act on the defensive.

Lieut. Chas. W. Read reported to me on the 1st inst. for the command of the *Webb*. I regret that Lieut. Phillips should have been relieved from the command of the *Webb* at this time as every arrangement was being made to make an effort to destroy the *Tennessee* and run the vessel to the sea. I very much doubt the success of such an attempt, yet I intended that Lieut. Phillips should make the effort. He came to this Department for the purpose of running the *Webb* into the Miss. River, but circumstances over which we had no control have heretofore prevented his going out. This Spring is the only time within two years that there has been sufficient water for the *Webb* to move. Lieut. Phillips is a gallant and meritorious officer, and I must again express my regret that the Department felt the necessity of relieving him. This action by the Department implies a want of confidence in the activity and energy of both Lieut. Phillips and myself. The Department cannot appreciate the difficulties under which I have to labor. I was on my way down to this place when Lieut. Read reported to me. I gave him letters to Genl. Smith and extended to him every assistance in my power. There is nothing in the way of Naval stores in this Department. I am dependent entirely on the Army for everything. I have not had the means to import stores &c.

Surgeon Page left Shreveport for Richmond on the 3rd of Oct. last, with dispatches, and with orders to return as soon as possible. At that time his services could be dispensed with as the sickly season was over. I have heard, though not officially, that he has been assigned to duty in Richmond. I have been without a surgeon since he left Shreveport and on my departure from that place I was compelled to call on Gen. Smith for a Medical officer. He kindly ordered one to report to me for temporary duty. I hope that the Department will appreciate the importance of directing a surgeon, at once, to report to me for duty.

I have appointed Charles Moore and Chester Bestwick Acting Carpenters in the Provisional Navy. These men are ship carpenters and their services are valuable to me. I have pursued this course as the best and most economical. This class of men cannot be enlisted in the Navy in this Department, and I have therefore been constrained to secure their services by appointment.

I have ordered Lieut. Phillips to Texas to take command of a Torpedo boat built near Galveston by the Engineer Department.

So far as I can ascertain no demonstrations are being made by the enemy in the Trans Miss. Dept.

I am very respectfully,

Your obt. Servt.
J. H. Carter Lt. Comdg. Naval Defenses Western La.

Hon. S. R. Mallory
Secretary of the Navy, Richmond, Va.

IX

Mississippi River

1. The CSS *Manassas*

Six months prior to the Battle of New Orleans, the CSS *Manassas* was involved in the first offensive naval engagement in the world by an iron-armored warship. This occurred on the night of October 12, 1861, when she rammed the USS *Richmond* at the "Battle" at the Head of the Passes below New Orleans.

The description of the *Manassas* and information on her commander, Alexander F. Warley, was previously covered in selection number one in Chapter VII.

Midshipman James Morris Morgan was born in New Orleans in 1845, and attended the U. S. Naval Academy prior to the war. He resigned from Annapolis on April 16, 1861, and was commissioned as acting midshipmen in Confederate service on June 8. In the following selection, Morgan, an officer at the time on the CSS *McRae* (which also participated in the attack at the Head of the Passes), describes the actions of the *Manassas* on that October night in 1861. (Campbell, *Gray Thunder: Exploits of the Confederate States Navy*, pp. 1–18.) [RTC]

"The Pioneer Ironclad" by Midshipman James Morris Morgan, CSN

Proceedings, Volume 43, No. 176, October, 1917

Most people generally prefer to gather their historical lore from popular rumor rather than to laboriously search official records for their facts. For instance; the public press at the present time (1916) is full of patriotic suggestions as to where a suitable place would be at which to enshrine and preserve for the admiration of future generations the once scrapped hull of the first (?) submarine boat, the one built by "Holland," the writers seemingly convinced that she was the original under-water craft despite the fact recorded in naval annals that 30 years or more before Holland designed her the Confederates not only built the little submarine *Hunley*, which bore the name of her inventor, but with her they sank the U. S. sloop-of-war *Housatonic* off Charleston, S. C., on February 17, 1864.

A similar erroneous idea prevails, among the misinformed, that the *Merrimac*, the famous adversary of the *Monitor*, was the first ironclad ever engaged in battle when she attacked the wooden frigate *Congress* and the sloop-of-war *Cumberland* in Hampton Roads in March, 1862, while the fact is indisputable that five months prior to that fight (October 12, 1861) the Confederate ironclad ram *Manassas* was engaged in an attack on the Federal fleet at the Head of the Passes of the Mississippi River, in which engagement she rammed the U. S. S. *Richmond* carrying twenty-two 9-inch guns (at that time).

There are two participants in that affair known to be still living [1917]. One of them is Captain H. H. Marmaduke and the other is the writer of this account; both of them were midshipmen on board of the Confederate flagship *McRae* at the time, and Marmaduke was severely wounded while on the *Merrimac* during the battle of Hampton Roads.

In 1861 Flag Officer George N. Hollins was ordered by the Confederate authorities to the command of the naval defenses on the Mississippi River. He had been a midshipman on the U. S. frigate *President* when she was captured by the British in 1812. In 1854 while in command of the U. S. S. *Cyane* he bombarded the Nicaraguan port of Greytown (San Juan). He laughingly described his experience by saying that "while some people wanted to have him court-martialed for his act, others thought he ought to be made president, and as his conduct on that occasion was becoming a political question, politicians settled the matter by getting him the command of a better ship, and having him sent as far as possible from temptation."

At the outbreak of the Civil War the commodore was in the Mediterranean flying his flag on the sidewheel frigate *Susquehanna*. He brought his ship home to a northern port, turned her over to the U. S. Government, resigned his commission, and went south. His first adventure in the Confederate service was to board the *St. Nicholas*, a steamer plying between Baltimore and Washington, and with several other southern sympathizers, register themselves as passengers, and then forcibly capture the boat as soon as she was fairly out in the stream. With the *St. Nicholas* he took several small prizes.

Lying at New Orleans in 1861 was an ocean-going tug called the *Enoch Train*. This boat had been purchased by a small company of speculators whose love of dollars was greater than their affection for the Confederacy. They caused the upper works of the tug to be removed and then had built a turtleback of 12-inch oak which completely covered her. This wooden protection was made the backing for a light armor of railroad iron, the "T" rails being dovetailed into each other and forming a metal protection about four inches thick and almost solid. She carried one 32-pounder mounted in her bows. The port was so small the gun could neither be elevated nor depressed, and as there was not sufficient room there were no traverses or other means of training the weapon except by the helm. The gun was only expected to be used at the moment of collision with an enemy vessel.

Midshipman James Morris Morgan (courtesy of Morgan P. Goldbarth).

When ready to be put into commission the *Enoch Train* was re-christened *Manassas*, and her patriotic owners proposed that the Confederate authorities enter into a contract to pay many thousands of dollars for each Federal warship destroyed. The Richmond Government refused the offer, and the ram, manned by a bad-mouthed set of toughs, lay idly at her anchor on the Algiers side of the river, opposite Jackson Square and the old St. Louis Cathedral.

The distance from the Passe a L'outre to the Southwest Pass of the Mississippi is some 27 miles, and the river has four principal mouths, widely separated from each other, necessitating a large number of war vessels to make an effective blockade. The Confederate cruiser *Sumter* had recently escaped to sea. To shorten the blockade line Flag Officer W. W. McKean, U. S. N., ordered Captain Pope to proceed up the Southwest Pass with the sloops-of-war *Richmond*, *Vincennes*, and *Preble*, and the gunboat *Water Witch*, and take possession of that part of the river immediately above the wide sheet of water known as "The Head of the Passes," and thus make it impossible for either the *McRae* (which cruiser was ready to put to sea) or any commercial blockade runner to get by, as the river was only about a mile wide where the fleet took up its station. New Orleans was in this way not only bottled up but the cork was squeezed in.

Commodore Hollins determined, if possible, to drive the Federal fleet away from their position of vantage, and to effect this purpose the only vessel he had under his command which bore the slightest resemblance to a war ship was a small bark-rigged steamer carrying seven guns called the *McRae*. This steamer under the name of *Marquis de la Habana*, and her consort, the *General Miramon*, was the property of General Miramon, a Mexican revolutionary leader. They were captured near Vera Cruz by the U. S. sloop-of war *Saratogo* in 1860 after quite a lively fight in which some 22 men were killed and wounded. The prizes were sent to New Orleans, the *Marquis de la Habana* under the command of Lieutenant R. T. Chapman, with instructions to deliver them into the custody of the United States Court and prefer the charge against them "that they belonged to an unrecognized revolutionary government and were pirates upon the high seas." In less than a year from that time Chapman was an officer on the Confederate cruiser *Sumter* "belonging to an unrecognized revolutionary government and (branded as) a pirate on the high seas."

The United States Court decided that the Mexican ships were unlawful prizes, but the decision was made too late to benefit their owners as the outbreak of the Civil War caught them at New Orleans. The *Marquis de la Habana* was immediately taken possession of by the Confederates who fitted her out as a commerce destroyer. But she never succeeded in getting to sea and finished her exciting career at the bottom of the Mississippi River when Admiral Farragut captured New Orleans.

Besides the *McRae*, with her seven guns, Commodore Hollins' flotilla (?) was composed of three side-wheel tow boats, the *Ivy*, *Calhoun*, and *Jackson*, and the screw river tug *Tuscarora*, each carrying two 32-pounders.

The commodore was a man of decided character, and he decided that he needed the ram *Manassas* in his business. A polite invitation to her owners that she be allowed to participated in the proposed adventure was contemptuously declined, but a little rebuff like that did not phase the "old salt" who knew what he wanted, and meant to have it, too. He informed the owners that he would take possession of the ram with or without their consent. They defied him. He had the *McRae*, with her crew at quarters ranged up alongside the *Manassas* whose crew, composed of some 30 odd men, were standing on the turtleback hurling defiances at the navy men whom they pretended to hold in the greatest contempt. The *McRae* lowered a boat manned by an armed crew of eight men under the command of Lieutenant A. F. Warley, (the same who afterwards commanded the ironclad *Albemarle* when Lieutenant Cushing, U. S. N., sunk her with a torpedo). The other officer in the boat was the writer of this account, who was at the time a midshipman in his 16th year, and very small for his age.

As the boat approached the ram her crew ceased their defiant billingsgate and stood on the turtleback in speechless, helpless, amazement. There was a makeshift Jacob's ladder over the armor, reaching from its apex to the waterline, and under orders, the small midshipman steered for it. Arriving alongside Mr. Warley ordered the midshipman to keep the boat's crew in their seats until he called for them, and then, revolver in hand, he lightly tripped up the ladder. The crew of braggarts, who had a few moments before hurled defiance at him, took to their heels and disappeared down a small hole forward which served the purpose of a hatchway. Mr. Warley followed them below and soon they scampered up on deck again through a similar hole aft, some of them being so badly scared that they jumped overboard and swam to shore which, fortunately, was not far away.

It was in this way that the first ironclad built in America became a part of the Confederate Navy.

The large Mississippi River flatboats were also commandeered. The boats, like Noah's Ark, were built without iron nails, their timbers being pinned together by wooden treenails. These boats when loaded with seasoned cordwood, pine knots, and barrels of turpentine, made very good fireships. Two very small tugs, the *Mosher* and another called the *Music*, furnished the motive power.

This Confederate armada (?), when ready, went down the river to Forts Jackson and St. Philip and waited there until near midnight of October 11, when it again started down stream to attack the United States fleet of three sloops-of-war and a gunboat, mounting in all, some 57 guns.

The night was very dark. The *Manassas* led the flotilla followed by the fireships. The *McRae* (the flagship) came next, and then the *Ivy* and *Tuscarora* in order. The powerful towboat *Jackson* had high-pressure engines and the noise, made by her escape pipes, could be heard for miles, necessitating that she remain far behind if a surprise attack was to be successful. The other tow-gunboat *Calhoun*, whose machinery was very much exposed, kept the *Jackson* company.

At 3:45 AM (October 12) a rocket went up from the *Manassas*. That was the agreed upon signal to let the Confederates know she had succeeded in ramming one of the ships of the Federal fleet. Instantly the broadsides of the big sloops-of-war shook the atmosphere and the fireships bursting into flames added to the grandeur of the spectacle.

The *Manassas* had struck the *Richmond* abreast the port forecastle, with the result that three planks of the wooden ship were stove in two feet below the water-line making a small hole some five inches in circumference. But the ram had done more mischief than this to herself. The *Richmond* had a coal schooner alongside which the pilot of the ram did not see, owing to the darkness of the night. The *Manassas* tore the schooner away from her fastenings and at the same time the latter's hawser shaved off the former's smokestacks even with her turtleback, causing the whole vessel to soon be filled with her own smoke, compelling her crew to seek air outside. Besides this disaster, the force of the impact, when she struck the solid wooden side of the big *Richmond*, had jarred her engines and boilers out of position and rendered them useless. In that condition she was carried by the current past the *Richmond* while under a terrific, but harmless fire. The ram lay so low in the water that the projectiles passed over her, and she helplessly drifted into the marsh grass growing on the muddy bank of the river where she was found at daylight by her consorts.

The fireships (?) had also floated harmlessly on to the marsh where they consumed themselves without having done the slightest damage to anything else. The captains of the tugs claimed that they did not have sufficient power to control their heavy tows while going down stream.

While the broadsides of the Federal ships were tearing holes through the air, the *McRae*, *Ivy*, and *Tuscarora* were being carried by a five-knot current toward them, and had they remained at their anchorage they would certainly have captured the *Manassas*, and most probably the rest of the Confederate flotilla, but fortunately for the latter, while the big guns of the sloop were roaring, they slipped their cables and made for the open sea via the Southwest Pass with the *Preble* leading, followed by the *Vincennes*, *Richmond*, and *Water Witch* in the order named; the sailing ships with all sail set, and helped by afresh and breeze. The Confederates followed at a respectful distance.

The *Preble* and *Water Witch*, being of lighter draft, passed over the bar and out into the

Gulf safely, but the heavier *Richmond* and *Vincennes* grounded, the *Vincennes* with her stern and the *Richmond* with her broadside pointing up stream.

The light-draft and speedy *Ivy*, under the command of Lieutenant Joseph B. Fry, formerly an officer of the U. S. Navy, quickly took advantage of the uncomfortable position in which the *Vincennes* found herself. Running down to within easy range, he commenced to throw shot at her cabin windows (after ports) in which there were two guns that should have been sufficient to destroy the *Ivy*, with her towering walking-beam and huge paddle-boxes making an ideal target, and besides, the *Ivy* could only use her forward gun.

The *McRae*, with the object of diverting the attention of the *Richmond* from the *Ivy*, engaged the heavy sloop at long range keeping under way, and making circles during the entire action, the little converted tug *Tuscarora* under the command Lieutenant Beverly Kennon, following the *McRae*, firing her two little guns with great rapidity.

While the action was going on the *Jackson* and *Calhoun* came down the pass and tied up at the pilot station, but neither of then fired a shot.

The action had not lasted two hours when the Confederates were astounded to see the crew of the *Vincennes* abandon their ship, and row over to the *Richmond* and *Water Witch*! Commodore Pope, in his official report of the affair says: "…we returned the fire from our port battery and rifled gun on the poop, our shot, falling short of the enemy, while their shell burst on all sides of us and several passed directly over the ship. At about 8:30, Commander Handy, of the *Vincennes*, mistaking my signal to the ships outside the bar "to get underway" for a signal for him to abandon his ship came on board the *Richmond* with all his officers and a large number of the crew, the remainder having gone to the *Water Witch*. Commander Handy before leaving his ship placed a lighted slow match at the magazine. Having waited a reasonable time for an explosion, I directed Commander Handy to return to his ship with his crew…."

Commodore Pope was mistaken about all of his shot "falling short" as many of them passed over the *McRae* and *Tuscarora*, and other projectiles from his ship threw so much spray over the *Ivy* that as soon as the *Vincennes* was abandoned, Commodore Hollins signaled the little "tow-gunboat" to withdraw, as the *Vincennes* was under the protection of the guns of the *Richmond* and it would have been useless to attempt to take possession of her, and thus ended the first fight in which an ironclad was ever engaged.

The news of the fight was first proclaimed a great victory by the citizens of New Orleans, but a newspaper admiral soon discovered that Commodore Hollins was much to blame in that he had not brought the whole United State fleet up to the city as prizes of war, this expert not taking into account the fact that the *Richmond* alone could have whipped the Gulf of Mexico full of just such craft as opposed the Confederate flotilla. Unfortunately for the commodore he had laid himself open to ridicule by a telegram he sent to the city which the following is a copy:

> Fort Jackson, 2 PM, Oct. 12. Last night I attacked the blockaders with my fleet. I succeeded, after a very short struggle, in driving them all aground on the Southwest Pass bar, except the *Preble*, which I sunk. I captured a prize (the coal schooner) from them, and after I got them fast on the sand I peppered them well. There were no casualties on our side. It was a complete success.

The *Manassas* having reported that she had rammed one of the warships, and the *Preble* not being in sight at daylight, it was taken for granted that she had been sunk.

The end of the *Manassas* was spectacular, to say the least. When Admiral Farragut passed the forts below New Orleans on the night of the 24th of April, 1862, the ram "ran amuck" through his fleet. She took the broadsides of his heavy ships one after the other and sometimes all together. Among others she rammed the *Brooklyn* and *Mississippi* (Admiral Dewey being the executive officer of the latter vessel), and she also had the temerity to tow a fire-ship alongside the *Hartford* and succeeded in setting the flagship on fire. Under a hail of shot she burst into flames and shortly afterwards went to the bottom of the "Father of Waters." The credit for her final destruction being awarded to the *Mississippi*.

It may be of interest to add to this account of "the affair at the Head of the Passes" that the Lieutenant Joseph B. Fry, who with the *Ivy* so daringly attacked the *Vincennes*, was the same man who was captured by the Spaniards (while he was in command of the blockade runner *Virginius*,) and so cruelly gone to death at Santiago, Cuba.

2. Island No. 10, Missouri

As the year 1862 dawned, Confederate authorities at New Orleans and Richmond were becoming increasingly concerned over the Federal buildup on the upper Mississippi River. With amazing speed, taking only three months during the winter, the Federals around St. Louis and Mound City had completed nine shallow-draft ironclads: the *Benton*, the *Carondelet*, the *Essex*, the *Louisville*, the *Mound City*, the *Cincinnati*, the *Cairo*, the *Pittsburg*, and the *St. Louis*, all under the command of Flag Officer Andrew H. Foote. All of these vessels, with the exception of the *Benton* (which was a stern-wheeler), were centerwheel boats of 500 tons built to the specifications of James B. Eads, a Missouri engineer and entrepreneur. Each had a rectangular casemate armored with two and one-half inches of iron plate that sloped 45 degrees fore and aft and 35 degrees on the sides. Armament varied, but usually consisted of ten or more heavy guns served by a crew of 250 men.

As Secretary Mallory studied the strategic situation in the west, he became evermore convinced that the real threat to New Orleans, and to the Confederacy as a whole, came not from the growing number of enemy warships at the mouth of the Mississippi, but from the powerful fleet of Captain Foote around Cairo, Illinois.

During this period, Columbus, Kentucky, had been evacuated by the Confederates on February 28, 1862, and all the troops and heavy guns conveyed to Island Number 10, so-called because it was the tenth island down the Mississippi River from Cairo, Illinois. With the arrival of Captain George N. Hollins' fleet from New Orleans, it was hoped that the Federal advance could be checked. (Campbell, *Confederate Naval Forces on Western Waters*, pp. 36–51.)

The CSS *McRae* was part of Hollins' Confederate fleet that supported the army at Island No. 10 and at New Madrid, Missouri. Midshipman James Morris Morgan, an officer on the *McRae*, wrote about the fighting in this area in his book, *Recollections of a Rebel Reefer*, published in 1917. [RTC]

"Island No. 10" by
Midshipman James Morris Morgan, CSN
Recollections of a Rebel Reefer, Chapter VIII, pp. 60–70

Here is a coronet for Confederate soldiers evidently written by an "unreconstructed rebel." It appears on a headstone in the Methodist Cemetery, St. Louis:

> Here lize a stranger braiv,
> Who died while fightin' the Suthern Confederacy to save
> Piece to his dust.
> Braive Suthern friend
> From iland 10

You reached a Glory us end.
We plase these flowrs above the stranger's hed,
In honer of the shiverlus ded.
Sweet spirit rest in Heven
Ther'l be know Yankis there.

When I returned to the *McRae*, I found great changes had occurred during my two weeks' absence. All idea of running the blockade and going to sea as a cruiser had been abandoned, and judging from my later experience in a "commerce destroyer" it was well that the intention had been abandoned, for with her limited coal capacity, and her want of speed owing to the small power and uncertain humor of her gear engines, it is doubtful if she would have lasted a month in that business.

I now found her much changed in outward appearance. The tall and graceful spars, with the exception of the lower masts, had disappeared. With the exception of Captain Huger, Sailing Master Read ("Savez"), and Midshipman Blanc, all of the line officers, whom I loved so dearly, were detached. Lieutenant Warley was to command permanently the *Manassas*; Lieutenant Eggleston and Midshipman Marmaduke were to join the *Merrimac* at Norfolk; Lieutenant Dunnington was to command the gunboat *Pontchartrain*; Midshipman Sardine Graham Stone was to go to the cruiser *Florida*; and Midshipman Comstock was to go to the gunboat *Selma*, on board of which he was cut in two by a shell at the battle of Mobile Bay; and I was appointed Aide-de-camp to Commodore Hollins, whose flagship the, *McRae* was to be.

Three river steamboats had been converted into men-of-war by having their luxurious cabins removed and their boilers protected by iron rails. They each carried four guns—three forward and one aft—and there had also been built (from designs by a locomotive roundhouse architect, I suppose) the most wonderful contraption that ever was seen afloat, called the *Livingston*. She carried six guns, three forward and three abaft the paddle-boxes, and she was almost circular in shape. She was so slow that her crew facetiously complained that when she was going downstream at full speed they could not sleep on account of the noise made by the drift logs catching up with her and bumping against her stern. These boats, with the *Ivy* and the tug *Tuscarora*, constituted our fleet.

Information reached us that a number of real ironclads which the Federal Government was building at St. Louis and on the Ohio River were completed and were about to come down the river.

The Confederates hastily fortified Island Number 10, a few miles above New Madrid, Missouri, and at the latter place had built two forts (Bankhead and Thompson). Our fleet was ordered to make all haste up the river to assist them in preventing the Federal fleet from coming down.

On the way up the river our first disaster happened, when on a dark and foggy night we rammed the plantation of Mr. Jefferson Davis, President of the Confederacy. For this heroic performance, it is needless to say, none of us were promoted, and we lay ingloriously stuck in the mud until we were pulled off by a towboat. Disaster number two came when we were passing Helena, Arkansas,—the *Tuscarora* caught fire and was destroyed.

Day after day, with our insufficient power and great draft, we struggled against the mighty current of the Mississippi, occasionally bumping into a mud bank and lying helpless there until we were pulled off. At the cities of Vicksburg and Memphis we received ovations. The dear people were very enthusiastic, and knowing nothing about naval warfare, they felt sure we could whip the combined fleets of the universe.

When we finally arrived at Island Number 10, we found a lively bombardment going on. It was, however, decided that we should drop down to New Madrid to assist in the defense of that city.

The winter of 1861–62 was a very cold and bleak one in that part of the country, and for several weeks the monotony of our lives was broken only by the sound of the distant booming of the guns at Island Number 10.

The *McRae* had been laid alongside the riverbank at the head of the main street of the town and the muzzles of her guns were just above the levee, thus giving us the whole State of Missouri for a breastwork.

Everything seemed to be very peaceful until one day a solitary horseman made his appearance galloping at full speed. He stopped when he arrived opposite the *McRae*, and shouted from the shore that he wanted to see Commodore Hollins. The commodore, who was standing on the deck, asked him what he wanted, and the excited cavalier shouted back: "I am General Jeff Thompson, the swamp fox of Missouri. There are a hundred thousand Yankees after me and they have captured one of my guns, and if you don't get out of this pretty quick they will be on board of your old steamboat in less than fifteen minutes!" Just then another man, apparently riding in a sulky, between the shafts of which was hitched a moth-eaten mule, appeared on the scene. On closer inspection it was discovered that he was sitting astride of a small brass cannon which was mounted on a pair of buggy wheels. This piece of ordnance was scarcely three feet long. The general gazed on it admiringly, and for our information sand: "That is a one-pounder—I invented it myself. The Yanks have got its mate, and if you don't get out of this they will hammer you to pieces with it." By this time there was great commotion in the two forts—seeing which General Jeff Thompson, nodding his head at the commodore, said, "So long!" and galloped away. That was the last we saw of him in that campaign.

As the gallant "swamp fox" disappeared in the distance, the gun's crew of his one-gun battery resignedly observed, "I can't keep up with Jeff "; and brought down his thong on the mule's bony back, and the poor beast leisurely walked away.

Above New Madrid a bayou emptied itself into the river. It meandered through a swamp for miles into the interior and was supposed to be impassable by troops, but General Pope and his thirty thousand men had accomplished the feat and taken New Madrid in the rear. His army was marching boldly up to our lines, and had they kept on they would have taken the place at once; but when the *McRae's* big nine-inch Dahlgren gun opened on them at long range, they stopped and proceeded to lay siege to it. It was evidently intended that they would take the place by regular approaches and the dirt commenced to fly while the artillery kept up a desultory fire.

The Confederate forts were situated at each end of the town and the flotilla of gunboats lay between them. Unfortunately the *McRae's* battery was the only one mounted at a sufficient height above the riverbank to fire over it. While at the same time using it for a breastwork; the other boats had to lie out in the stream where they were very much exposed to the enemy's fire.

Some three thousand raw recruits formed the garrisons and manned the trenches which connected the forts. The forts had been built with regard to commanding the river and were very weak on the land side.

Day by day the Union troops drew nearer and the firing increased in fury. Commodore Hollins sent me frequently with communications to General Bankhead, who commanded our land forces. One day, when the firing was particularly furious, I was sent with one of these missives and found General Bankhead on the firing line. Shells were bursting frequently in unpleasant proximity to where he was standing with his field-glasses pressed to his eyes. Just behind him stood several officers. I saluted the General and handed him the envelope. He told me to wait until he could send back an answer. As I joined the group of officers I distinctly heard a major say, "What a damned shame to send a child into a place like this!" The other officers must have noticed that my dignity was offended, for they spoke very kindly, but I could not get over the insult—it stuck in my gorge. I was so mad

I could hardly speak. Returning to the ship I at once consulted my friend, the first lieutenant, who was now Mr. Read ("Savez"), on the propriety of sending the major a challenge, but "Savez" soothed my wounded feelings by telling me that "the commodore would not approve of such action and anyhow I need not mind what the major said, as he was nothing but a damned soldier, and a volunteer at that, and of course did not know any better."

The enemy got to the river-bank below us and a new danger menaced us. They prevented our transports from coming up the stream. The levees were breastworks readymade, and day after day our gunboats had to go down to clear them out. We would be drifting down the apparently peaceful river, when suddenly a row of tall cottonwood saplings would make us a graceful bow and fall into the stream as a dozen or more field pieces poured a galling broadside into us. Of course, with our heavy guns we would soon chase them away, but only to have them reappear a mile above or below in a little while, and then the same thing had to be gone through again. Later they brought up some heavy guns and then we had some really good tussles with them.

Captain George N. Hollins (Natural Historical Center).

Our troops were forced back until they were under cover of the forts, leaving the space between, which was the abandoned town, to be protected by the guns of the *McRae*. I was standing by the commodore on the poop deck watching the firing when we saw a light battery enter the other end of the main street. Our nine-inch gun was trained on them, and when it was fired the shell struck the head of the column and burst in about the middle of the company. To see horses, men, and guns cavorting in the air was a most appalling sight. Flushed with success the officer in charge of the gun reloaded and tied another shot, when the gun exploded, the muzzle falling between the ship's side and the river-bank, while one half of the great breech fell on the deck beside its carriage. The other half went away up into the air and coming down struck the rail between the commodore and myself and cut the side of the ship, fortunately glancing out instead of inside. The commodore coolly remarked, "Youngster, you came near getting your toes mashed!"

We had a rough little steam launch, about twenty-five feet in length, which acted as a tender to the *McRae*, and as our gunboats were makeshift ones, they were not provided either with signals or any place to fly them from. I used this launch to convey to them the flag officer's orders. The commodore suspected that the enemy were fortifying the point above us which, if done, would have cut us off from communication with Island Number 10 which was making a heroic defense and preventing the Union ironclads from coming down and annihilating our little mosquito fleet. So he sent me on a reconnaissance, cautioning me to be careful and not approach too close to the point until I was satisfied there was no battery there.

The launch had no deck and consequently her little boiler and engine were all exposed to the weather. Her crew consisted of a fireman from the *McRae* and a sailor to steer her. I proceeded to the point keeping well out in the stream, but saw nothing suspicious. Being of a curious turn of mind I wanted to see what was around the river bend, so kept on. As we turned the point my helmsman exclaimed, "The *Tom Benton*!" The *Tom Benton* was the largest Union ironclad on the river and all ironclads were "Tom Bentons" to us. Sure enough, across the next bend we saw a column of black smoke, evidently issuing from the funnel of a steamer and we turned tail and ran for the *McRae* with all speed possible. As we passed the point, which I had previously satisfied myself was absolutely harmless, the small cottonwood trees fell into the river and a battery opened on us, one of the shells exploding as it struck the water, drenching us. But our noble craft kept on her way, the engineer by this time having tied down the safety-valve. Arriving within hailing distance of the flagship, I sang out *"Tom Benton* coming down, sir!" Commodore Hollins being on deck shouted back, "Come aboard, sir!" My chief engineer gasped out, "For God's sake, don't stop, sir; she will blow up!" We ran around the *McRae* while the officer of the deck, and it seemed to me everybody else, was shouting, "Come aboard!" The safety-valve by this time had been unlashed and she was blowing off steam, while the whirling engine was also using up as much of the surplus as possible as around and around we went, while the commodore was stamping on the deck and fairly frothing at the mouth. At last—it seemed to me an age—the engineer pronounced it safe to stop, and we went alongside the flagship. As I stepped on to the quarterdeck Commodore Hollins demanded to know why I had disobeyed his instructions and gone around the point. Hesitatingly I answered, "I thought, sir-" But I got no farther, as the commodore interrupted me with "You thought, sir! You dared to think, sir! I will have you understand I am the only man in this fleet who is allowed to think!" I was so badly scared that probably that awful interview with the commodore was the reason I was never afterwards so thoughtless.

The Federal ironclad, not knowing our weakness, after she had run by the Island Number 10 batteries in the night, was quietly waiting at her anchors for her consorts to do likewise before attacking us.

The houses of New Madrid interfered with our fire. They were just as their owners had left them when they fled in such haste that they had not time to move their furniture or belongings, and it had up to this time seemed a pity to destroy them, but now they had been riddled by shells and were very much in the way. The commodore sent for me one night and ordered me to take a detail of men and go ashore and set fire to the town. I begged him not to send me and told him the history of the place, and how in 1787 the King of Spain had given my great-grandfather, Colonel George Morgan, formerly of the Revolutionary Army, a grant of land comprising, according to Gayarre, in his history of Louisiana, some seventeen millions of acres, and how my ancestor had founded the city of New Madrid on it, and that it would be dreadful for me to have to destroy it. The old commodore simply remarked that it would be a singular coincidence and that it was all the more appropriate that I should destroy my ancestor's town.

I went ashore with a number of men all provided with matches and fat-pine torches. The wind was blowing toward the river and we sneaked along in the darkness until [we arrived at the last houses in the suburbs. I made my way out to a barn that was filled with straw and quickly set it on fire. A mass of flames instantly leaped many feet above the roof. The enemy pickets opened fire and we all fled toward the river. We succeeded in reaching the ship without the loss of a man. I had undone the work of my ancestors.]

We lay for several days at anchor near Tiptonville, expecting every moment that the Federal ironclads would come down and attack us, but they did not put in an appearance before we left. Nevertheless, we received a very unpleasant surprise one morning while we were at breakfast when the cottonwood trees on the opposite side of the river suddenly tumbled down and a long line of guns opened fire on us. We got up our anchors as quickly as possible and went into action, with the result that our flotilla suffered considerably. The first disaster happened when a shell burst in the pantry of the *Livingston* and smashed all of Commander Pinckney's beautiful chinaware of which he was very proud. The *General Polk* then received several shells in her hull on the water line and was run ashore to keep her from sinking, and the other boats were cut up considerably, but running close in to the masked batteries the grape and canister from our big guns caused the enemy to limber up and disappear. Commodore Hollins said "the campaign had taught him one thing and that was that gunboats were not fitted for chasing cavalry."

It was at Tiptonville that Commodore Hollins received a message from the senior naval officer at New Orleans begging him to bring his gunboats as quickly as possible, as it was certain that Admiral Farragut would soon try to dash by Forts Jackson and St. Philip. No one knew the danger better than the old commodore did. Ordering his flagship to follow, he went on board of the fast *Ivy* accompanied by his small aide, and we started at full speed for New Orleans.

3. Plum Point, Tennessee

By the end of April of 1862, those Confederate navy vessels that had constituted Commander Hollins' fleet at Island No. 10 had long since departed, and, with few exceptions, had either been captured or destroyed at the Battle of New Orleans. The only Southern naval force left to contest the relentless advance down the river by the Union ironclads was the ill-conceived and poorly organized "River Defense Fleet."

On January 9, 1862, the Confederate Congress had passed authorizations 344 and 350 which provided for a naval force of steamers at New Orleans to be operated by and under the control of the War Department. The laws as passed stated that these vessels were:

> "Not to be a part of the navy, for the acts intend a service on the rivers, and will be composed of the steamboat-men of the Western waters. The expedition is to be subject to the general command of the military chief of the department where it may be ordered to operate, but the boats will be commanded by steamboat captains and manned by steamboat crews, who will be armed with such weapons as the captains may choose, and the boats will be fitted out as the respective captains may desire.... Capts. Montgomery and Townsend have been selected by the President as two of those who are to command these boats...." [Scharf, *History of the Confederate States Navy*, pp. 249–250.]

The above action by the Confederate Congress was in reaction to the ominous news that kept reaching Richmond about the construction of the Union ironclads on the upper Mississippi.

By the first of May, eight rams of the River Defense Fleet from New Orleans had assembled at Fort Pillow. They were: the *Little Rebel* which was the flagship commanded by Captain Montgomery; the *General Bragg*, captained by William H. H. Leonard; the *General Sterling Price*, with First Officer J. E. Harthorne; the *General Sumter*, Captain W. W. Lamb; the *General Earl Van Dorn*, Captain Issac D. Fulkerson; the *General M. Jeff Thompson*, Captain John H. Burke; the *Colonel Lovell*, Captain James C. Delaney; and the *General Beauregard*, Captain James Henry Hurt. Five of the rams were armed with a varying assortment of 12- and 32-pounders, some rifled, some not. All were sidewheel steamers, except for the *Little Rebel* that was screw-driven, and all had reinforced bows intended for ramming.

On the night of May 9, 1862, Montgomery called a meeting of all steamboat captains aboard the flagship *Little Rebel*. There in Montgomery's cabin by the dim light of an old oil lantern, a battle plan was formulated. One by one the captains gave their assent to Montgomery's plan. In the hours long before daylight, they would form their rams in line astern. When the Federal mortar boat, which had been dropping its shells on Fort Pillow, opened fire at daybreak, they would charge up the river and attack the Union ironclad guarding the mortar boat. After ramming the ironclad, and, with a bit of luck, sinking the mortar barge by gunfire, they would then attack the Union vessels farther up river. It was a bold plan, and with a little courage — and some much-needed luck — they just might stampede Admiral Davis' entire fleet. (Campbell, *Confederate Naval Forces on Western Waters*, pp. 83–91.)

The following is Captain Montgomery's report to General Beauregard. [RTC]

"River Defense Fleet at Plum Point" by Captain James E. Montgomery

Official Records Navy, Series I, Volume XXIII, pp. 55–57

FLAG-BOAT LITTLE REBEL, *Fort Pillow, Tenn., May 12, 1862.*

SIR: I have the honor to report an engagement with the Federal gunboats at Plum Point Bend, 4 miles above Fort Pillow, May 10.

Having previously arranged with my officers the order of attack, our boats left their moorings at 6 AM, and proceeding up the river passed round a sharp point, which brought us in full view of the enemy's fleet, numbering eight gunboats and twelve mortar boats.

The Federal boat *Carondelet* [*Cincinatti*] was lying nearest us, guarding a mortar boat, that was shelling the fort. The *General Bragg*, Capt. W. H. H. Leonard, dashed at her; the *Carondelet* [*Cincinatti*], firing her heavy guns, retreated toward a bar where the depth of water would not be sufficient for our boats to follow. The *Bragg* continued boldly on under fire of nearly the whole fleet, and struck her a violent blow that stopped her further flight, then rounded down the river under a broadside fire and drifted until her tiller rope, that had got out of order, could be readjusted. A few moments after the *Bragg* struck her blow the *General Sterling Price*, First Officer J. E. Henthorne, ran into the same boat a little aft of her starboard amidships, carrying away her rudder, stern-post, and a large piece of her stern. This threw the *Carondelet*'s [*Cincinatti*] stern to the *Sumter*, Capt. W. W. Lamb, who struck her, running at the utmost speed of his boat.

The *General Earl Van Dorn*, Capt. Isaac D. Fulkerson, running, according to orders, in the rear of the *Price* and *Sumter*, directed his attention to the [USS] *Mound City*, at the time pouring broadsides into the *Price* and *Sumter*. As the *Van Dorn* proceeded, by skillful shots from her 32-pounder, W. G. Kendall, gunner, silenced a mortar boat that was filling the air with its terrible missiles. The *Van Dorn*, still holding on to the *Mound City's* amidships, in the act of striking, the *Mound City* sheered, and the *Van Dorn* struck her a glancing blow, making a hole 4 feet deep in her starboard forward quarter, evidenced by splinters left on the iron bow of the *Van Dorn*. At this juncture the *Van Dorn* was above four of the enemy's boats.

As our remaining boats, the *General M. Jeff. Thompson*, Capt. J. H. Burke; the *Colonel Lovell*, Capt. J. C. Delancy, and the *General Beauregard*, Capt. J. H. Hurt, were entering boldly into the contest in their prescribed order, I perceived from the flag-boat that the enemy's boats were taking positions where the water was too shallow for our boats to follow them, and, as our cannon were far inferior to theirs, both in number and size, I signaled our boats to fall back, which was accomplished with a coolness that deserves the highest commendation.

I am happy to inform you, while exposed to close quarters to a most terrific fire for thirty minutes, our boats, although struck repeatedly, sustained no serious injuries.

The CSS *General Bragg* (Naval Historical Center).

Our casualties were 2 killed and 1 wounded-arm broken.

General M. Jeff. Thompson was on the *General Bragg*; his officers and men were divided among the boats. They were all at their posts, ready to do good service should an occasion offer.

To my officers and men I am highly indebted for their courage and promptness in executing all orders.

On the 11th instant I went on the *Little Rebel* in full view of the enemy's fleet. Saw the *Carondelet* [*Cincinatti*] sunk near the shore and the *Mound City* sunk on the bar.

The position occupied by the enemy's gunboats above Fort Pillow offers more obstacles to our mode of attack than any other between Cairo and New Orleans. But of this you may rest assured, if we can get fuel, unless the enemy greatly increase their force, they will never penetrate farther down the Mississippi.

I am, with great respect, your obedient servant,

J. E. MONTGOMERY,
Captain, Commanding River Defense Service.

General G. T. BEAUREGARD,
Comdg. C. S. Army of the West.

4. Memphis, Tennessee

On May 30, 1862, Union forces captured Corinth, Mississippi, forcing the Confederate evacuation of all positions along the Mississippi River north of Vicksburg, including Fort Pillow and Memphis, Tennessee. On June 4, General Beauregard ordered all troops out of Fort Pillow and Memphis. About noon on the fifth of June, the River Defense Fleet, short on coal and missing many crew members, arrived at Memphis. The men of General Jeff Thompson's command, who had manned the muskets and heavy guns on the rams so well at Plum Point, had been sent ahead on a transport and were not on the rams.

Five steamers lay tied to the wharves and Montgomery seized them for their coal. With the army pulling out, the fate of Memphis was in the hands of the River Defense Fleet.

Brigadier-General M. Jeff Thompson (Johnson and Buel, Battles & Leaders of the Civil War).

The city, situated on a sloping fifty-foot bluff on the eastern side of the Mississippi River, was a scene of bedlam as military and city officials rushed to remove important war materials and destroy what could not be carried away. A pall of smoke blanked the city, particularly over the navy yard where the unfinished ironclad, CSS *Tennessee*, was on fire. At 10:00 PM that night, with Fort Pillow in Federal hands, Southern tugs posted as pickets reported the arrival of the Union fleet two miles above Memphis. One can suppose that the old oil lantern in the commodore's cabin once again burned late into the evening on the flagship *Little Rebel*.

The River Defense Fleet was about to make its last stand. No report of Captain Montgomery has been found; however, General M. Jeff Thompson penned a report to General Beauregard that described the action on June 6, 1862, opposite Memphis. (Campbell, *Confederate Naval Forces on Western Waters*, pp. 92–98.) [RTC]

Official Report of
Brig. Gen. M. Jeff Thompson, Missouri State Guards.

Official Records Navy, Series I, Volume XXIII, pp. 139–140

Grenada, Miss., June 7, 1862.

GENERAL: I am under the painful necessity of reporting to you the almost entire destruction of the River Defense Fleet in the Mississippi River in front of Memphis. I regret that I have to state I think the misfortune was occasioned by a misapprehension of orders or misinformation as to the surrounding circumstances.

The evacuation of Fort Pillow was, from all accounts, well and orderly conducted after once determined upon, but by some means my men were sent to Memphis on a transport instead of being placed on the gunboats. The circumstances which may have caused the evacuation of Fort Pillow did not surround Fort Randolph, and I am satisfied that, even with the few troops that were at Pillow, Randolph could have been held for several days, with a sure and safe retreat when necessary, if ever.

Our fleet, for want of coal, as represented, fell back to Memphis on the 5th, with the intention of returning to Island No. 40. The arrangements for this purpose were being made, but before 10 o'clock PM on the 5th the tugs which were on picket above the city reported the enemy's tugs in sight. This was discredited, but our boats anchored in the channel of the river, prepared for a battle.

At 12.30 AM on the 6th your telegram giving Commodore Montgomery and myself the joint command of the river defense was received. I immediately wrote a note to the commodore, enclosing your telegram and asking what I should do to cooperate with him. He requested two companies of artillery to be sent on board at daybreak. (All of my men were at the depot, awaiting transportation to Grenada.) I at once ordered the companies to hold themselves in readiness. At the dawn of day I was awakened with the information that the enemy were actually in sight of Memphis. I hurried on board to consult with Montgomery. He instructed me to hurry my men to Fort Pickering Landing and sent a tug to bring them to the gunboats, which were advancing to attack the enemy. I hastened my men to the place indicated, but before we reached it our boats had been either destroyed or driven below Fort Pickering, and I marched back to the depot to come to this place to await orders.

I saw a large portion of the engagement from the river banks, and am sorry to say that, in my opinion, many of our boats were handled badly or the plan of battle was very faulty. The enemy's rams did most of the execution and were handled more adroitly than ours—I think, however, entirely owing to the fact that guns and sharpshooters of the enemy were constantly employed, while we were almost without either. The *Colonel Lovell* was so injured that she sank in the middle of the river; her captain, James Delancy, and a number of others swam to shore. The *Beauregard* and *Price* were running at the *Monarch* (*Yankee*) from opposite sides when the *Monarch* passed from between them, and the *Beauregard* ran into the *Price*, knocking off her wheel and entirely disabling her. Both were run to the Arkansas shore and abandoned. The *Little Rebel*, the commodore's flag boat, was run ashore and abandoned after she had been completely riddled, and I am satisfied the commodore killed. The battle continued down the river out of sight of Memphis, and it is reported that only two of our boats, the *Bragg* and *Van Dorn*, escaped.

It is impossible now to report casualties, as we were hurried in our retirement from Memphis, and none but those from the *Lovell* escaped on the Tennessee side of the river. So soon as more information can be collected, I will report.

Yours, most respectfully,

M. JEFF THOMPSON,
Brigadier-General, Missouri State Guard.

General G. T. BEAUREGARD, C. S. Army,
Baldwyn, Miss.

5. Pursuit of the *Indianola*

In the spring of 1863, at a makeshift shipyard in Alexandria, Louisiana, the steamer *William H. Webb* was converted into an armored ram. The *Webb*, a 650-ton side wheel steamer with very powerful engines, had a remarkable top speed for her time.

During this period, the USS *Indianola* had passed the Confederate batteries on the Mississippi River at Vicksburg on February 13, 1863. The *Indianola* was an enormous ironclad. She was constructed at Cincinnati, Ohio, in late 1862, and commissioned on January 14, 1863. She was 175 feet long with a beam of 52 feet and was driven by four engines, two propelling enormous side wheels and two additional engines each driving a propeller. Her top speed was a reported six knots. On her forward deck, which was almost awash, was a sloping iron casemate housing two heavy 11-inch smoothbores on pivots which enabled them to fire forward as well as to the side. Between her wheels aft was another casemate housing two 9-inch smoothbores that covered her stern. Both casemates were inclined to 26½ degrees and were plated with three inches of iron. The *Indianola* was under the command of Lieutenant Commander George Brown. (Scharf, *History of the Confederate States Navy*, p. 362.)

After successfully passing the Vicksburg batteries, Brown steamed on down the Mississippi to the mouth of the Red River and proceeded to blockade that waterway for the next two days. While there, he received word that the Confederates had repaired the recently captured *Queen of the West*, and that she, along with the *Webb*, was about to descend the Red and attack the *Indianola*. Brown decided that discretion was the better determination, and on February 21, 1863, the *Indianola* raised anchor and started up the Mississippi.

The next day, February 22, four Confederate vessels rendezvoused on the Red about twenty miles below Fort Taylor. They included: the CSS *Webb*, commanded by a civilian, Captain Charles Pierce; the newly repaired CSS *Queen of the West*, commanded by another civilian, Captain James McCloskey; the *Grand Era*, (commander unknown); and the *Dr. Beatty*, commanded by Lieutenant Colonel F. Brand. All four Confederate vessels were under the command of Major Joseph L. Brent. (Campbell, *Confederate Naval Forces on Western Waters*, pp. 185–192.) [RTC]

Official Report of the Chase & Capture of the USS Indianola *by Major Joseph L. Brent, CSA*

Official Records Navy, Series I, Volume XXIV, pp. 402–407

FEBRUARY 25, 1863.

MAJOR: My last dispatch to you, exclusive of the telegraphic communication sent you last night, was from Natchez. The Federal ironclad *Indianola* had forty-eight hours start of us at Acklin's Landing; at Natchez she was less than twenty-five hours in advance.

We left Natchez on the evening of the 23d, and I found that we could easily overhaul the enemy in the morning of the 24th, but I determined not to do so, in order to bring him to an engagement at night, considering for many reasons that this time was eminent advantageous to us. We reached Grand Gulf before sunset, and there learned that he was only about four hours in advance of us. We were running more than 2 miles to his 1 the time required to overtake him could easily be calculated, so I determined to overtake and bring him to action at 9 o'clock that evening. We came up with him about 9:40, just above New Carthage, near the foot of Palmyra Island, and I immediately signaled the *Webb* to prepare for action. Our order of approach was as follows: The *Queen of the West* about 500 yards in advance of the *Webb*, and the *Beatty*, Lieutenant-Colonel F. B. Brand commanding (who, I wrote you, had joined us with a force and steamer fitted out from Port Hudson), 2 miles in the rear, and lashed to my tender, the *Grand Era*. The moon was partially obscured by a veil of white clouds, and gave and permitted just sufficient light for us to see where to strike with our rams and just sufficient obscurity to render uncertain the aim of the formidable artillery of the enemy.

We first discovered him when about 1,000 yards distant, hugging the eastern bank of the Mississippi, with his head quartering across and down the river. Not an indication of life was given as we dashed on toward him—no light, no perceptible motion of his machinery was discernible. We had also obscured every light, and only the fires of the *Era* could be seen, 2 miles back, where she was towing the *Beatty*. The distance between him and us had diminished to about 500 yards. We could clearly distinguish the long black line of his two coal barges, which protected his sides from forward of his bow to nearly abreast of his

The USS *Indianola* (Naval Historical Center).

wheels. The impatience of our men to open fire could be scarcely restrained, but I was too sensible of the vast advantage to be obtained by traversing the distance to be passed over without drawing the fire of his powerful guns. At last, when within about 150 yards of him, I authorized Captain James McCloskey to open fire, which he accordingly did with his two Parrott guns and one brass 12-pounder. At the second fire the 20-pounder Parrott gun was disabled by the blowing out of its vent piece. Our intention was to dash the bow of our boat in his larboard wheelhouse, just in the rear of the coal barge, but when about 150 yards from him he backed and interposed the barge between us and him. Our bow went crashing clear through the barge, and was not arrested until it shattered some of his timbers amidships and deeply indenting the iron plating of his hull. So tremendous had been the momentum of our attack that for nearly five minutes we could not disengage ourselves, but remained stuck fast. In this position our sharpshooters opened fire on every light and crevice that could be seen, but no living men were to be seen on the enemy's decks. While thus adhering to the enemy the *Webb* came dashing by us and plunged with terrific force just in the rear of his bow. Some few iron plates were loosened, but this blow of the *Webb* produced no serious external injury to the enemy. The prisoners since report that it disabled, by the jar, the starboard engine. Urged forward by the *Webb*, the *Indianola* swung away. One end of the coal barge that the *Queen* had cut in two sunk, and the other drifted down the current a little way and immediately sunk, and the *Queen*, finding herself free, immediately rounded upstream to add to the impetuosity of her next charge the additional power obtainable from the descending current of the river. As the *Webb* approached on her first charge the two XI-inch Dahlgren guns on the bow of the *Indianola* opened on her at 75 yards with solid shot, but fortunately she was untouched.

The vigor of her onset pushed the enemy around, and, carrying her forward, laid her across and under the very muzzle of these monstrous guns. Dashing safely around from this perilous position, the *Webb* swung on the starboard side of the enemy, between him and his coal barge, breaking the fastenings and setting the barge adrift.

The result of our first onset was to strip the *Indianola* of her coal barges, which protected her sides, and to injure her to some extent in her wheel, as was apparent from her subsequent want of rapidity and precision in her movements. As soon as the *Webb* swept away clear of the enemy, the *Queen of the West* swung round and again dashed upon him, who, this time with partial success, endeavored to break the force of the onset by presenting her bow to our blow; but his movements were too torpid and were not entirely successful, which tends to confirm the belief entertained by some that her machinery was injured by the first blow. The *Queen* struck a little in advance of amidships, but, as she was turning, the force of the blow glanced along his side and past his wheelhouse without inflicting any very serious damage. Just as the *Queen* swung clear of his stern he opened on her with his two aft IX-inch guns. One struck us on the shoulder and knocked off our cotton, and one on the starboard knocked away 10 or 12 bales of cotton, causing us to list over considerably, and another (a shell) entered our front porthole on the port side, passed out, and struck the chase of a brass 12-pounder gun, and exploded, killing 2 men, disabling 4, and disabling two pieces. This time the *Queen* swung around rapidly up the stream, and in a very brief interval again dashed on him striking a little to the rear of his starboard wheelhouse, crushing trough and shattering his framework and loosening some of his iron plates.

By this time the *Webb* had run upstream, turned, and came careering on, with a full head of steam, and struck him very nearly in the same place where the *Queen of the West* had before hit him. Through and through his timbers, crushing and dashing aside his iron plates, the sharp bow of the *Webb* penetrated as if it were going to pass entirely through the ship. As the *Webb* backed clear the *Indianola*, with all the speed she could raise, declined further fight, and ran down the river toward the bank, with the intention, as after appeared, of getting a line out, in order that the officers and crew might land and abandon their steamer, which was making water rapidly. In fact, a line was got out on land, but not fastened, and three of the crew effected their escape from the vessel, but were recaptured next day by the cavalry of Major Isaac F. Harrison. After the *Queen of the West* struck the *Indianola* the third time she was for some time almost unmanageable. She had listed so much over to the port side that one of her wheels was much the most raised out of the water. She was making water, and presented every appearance of sinking. Captain McCloskey righted her a little by throwing over cotton from his upper decks, and they were able to bring her round very slowly, but still she was brought up by her gallant commander for a further charge. While the *Webb* had her bow knocked off, her splendid machinery was unhurt and she quickly and gallantly bore up for her third charge. When bearing down and approaching the enemy, Captain Charles J. Pierce reports that he was hailed from the deck, announcing the surrender, and begging to be towed ashore, as he was sinking. Captain Pierce represents that he placed a line on board and commenced towing the *Indianola*, when the line parted. As the *Queen of the West* was running off from her last charge to make a circuit to obtain space to add increased momentum to her onset we encountered the *Dr. Beatty* (Lieutenant-Colonel Brand), who had cast off from the tender *Grand Era* and was hovering round to enter the fight when an opportunity offered.

The *Dr. Beatty* is a frail steamer, with but little power, and incapable of being used as a ram or of resisting the terrible fire to which we were exposed. She was crowded with nearly 250 gallant spirits, who volunteered from the forces at Port Hudson, and who had embarked in the *Beatty* with the resolution to fight the enemy by boarding her. We called out to them that the opportunity for boarding her had arrived, as it was apparent that the enemy was disabled and much demoralized. Lieutenant-Colonel Brand with his command gallantly bore away, approached the enemy, and gave, as I am informed by him, the command "Prepare to board," when he was greeted by a voice from the decks of the *Indianola*, announcing that she had surrendered and was in a sinking condition. Colonel Brand then boarded her upper deck and received the sword of Lieutenant-Commander Brown. This result must have been very gratifying to Colonel Brand, as it was obtained without the loss or injury of a single man of his command. Upon my reaching the deck, Colonel Brand most handsomely acknowledged that the capture was entirely due to the *Queen of the West* and the *Webb*. I have no doubt if it had been necessary that himself and his gallant command would have again demonstrated that nothing can resist the desperation of troops who regard not their own lives, but victory.

I immediately appointed Lieutenant Handy, of the *Webb*, as prize master. We found our prize a most formidable monster, mounting two XI-inch guns forward and two IX-inch guns aft, and all protected by splendid iron casemates, utterly impervious except to the heaviest artillery at the very shortest range. Her propelling power consisted of side-wheels and two screw propellers. She was filled with a most valuable cargo, embracing supplies of every kind. The officers and crew, amounting to over 100, fell into our hands as prisoners. Nothing shows more clearly how well protected were her men than the fact that our artillery, though they frequently fired at the range of 20 and 30 yards, utterly failed to injure her. Lieutenant Handy, of the *Webb*, fired his 32-pounder rifled gun so close to the casemates of the enemy that it actually enveloped both portholes in flames, and yet no injury was sustained. Our skillful and courageous sharpshooters fired deliberately at every onset.

Notwithstanding all these circumstances, the enemy lost but 1 man killed and none wounded. The *Webb* had but 1 man wounded, while the *Queen of the West* had 2 killed and 4 wounded.

The fire of the enemy was terrific. Their huge shot and shell came whizzing by us, directed wide of the mark in every instance, except the two shots that struck the *Queen* and one that passed through the bulwarks of the *Webb*, while the far-darting flames of their enormous guns almost licking our bows, and the loud thunder of their reports (heard as far as Vicksburg, 30 miles off), added unusual sublimity to the scene. The *Queen of the West* has some appearance of protection for her men—how feeble was manifested by the injury inflicted by one shot alone; but the men on the *Webb* were utterly without protection. The boilers were rudely surrounded by cotton, but her walking beams were entirely exposed. I think the annals of naval warfare may be safely challenged to produce an instance where a feeble craft was thrice precipitated upon the iron sides of a first-class. war steamer, mounting as heavy an armament as is to be found in the Western waters.

The heroic gallantry of both captains in rushing their steamers against the ironclad enemy in face of and against the muzzles of IX-inch and XI-inch guns can not be overestimated.

I am much indebted for the success that crowns this expedition to the skill and gallantry of my officers.

Captain McCloskey, commanding the *Queen of the West*, combined with the courage of the soldier the skill and aptitude that characterizes the sailor of our Western waters. Taking his position in the front of the steamer, by word and example, he cheered the men on to their duty and rallied them when disheartened. I reserve to him the mention of the names of the officers and men under him who merit special mention, but I feel compelled in one case to specify an example of heroic courage and skill as exhibited by Sergeant Edward Langley, of the Third Maryland Artillery. He had on the *Queen*, a detachment of 13 men of his artillery, and was placed in charge of the two Parrott guns. He himself took command of the 30-pounder gun in our bow, where he remained during the action, neither he nor his gallant comrades ever leaving their posts for a moment. While our bows were resting against the side of the *Indianola* he still manned and fired his gun, though he and his men were without the least covering or protection. In addition to this courage, the skill and judgment he showed in maneuvering his piece mounted on wheels within a most contracted space, is deserving of equal commendation.

Lieutenant T. H. Handy, of the Crescent Artillery, commanded the troops on the *Webb*.

He exhibited the greatest skill and courage in handling his command, and he himself in person manned and pointed his rifled 32-pounder gun. His report will disclose the names of such officers and men as merit special mention.

I learn from verbal report that Lieutenant H. A. Rice, of the Twenty-first [Thirty-first] Tennessee, on board of the *Webb*, served most efficiently and gallantly.

Acting Lieutenant Prather served his two fieldpieces, entirely unprotected, with most unshrinking courage, and was ably seconded by Mr. Charles Scholer, acting as captain of the guns.

Captain Charles J. Pierce, a civilian, commanded and controlled the movements of the *Webb*. It was he who selected the weak spots of the enemy, and with a steady hand and eye dashed the *Webb* against the *Indianola*.

Not only did the officers do their duty, but I have nothing but commendation for the private soldiers. Captain E. E. Carnes and Lieutenant Rice's company, of the Twenty-first [Thirty-first] Tennessee, and the detachment of Lieutenant R. S. Dulin, adjutant of Major James Burnet's battalion of Texans, were in the expedition of the *Queen* and *Webb*, and under fire they, as well as their gallant officers, comported themselves with courage and discipline.

On taking possession, we found our prize rapidly making water which we could not arrest. Seeing that she would sink, I did not wish that this should take place on the Western side of the river, and therefore made fast to her with two of the steamers and towed her over the river, when she sank in the water up to her gun deck, thus losing to us the greater part of the valuable stores that were in her hold.

Captain James W. Mangum, assistant adjutant-general of Brigadier-General J. C. Moore, being in Alexandria, accompanied the expedition as a volunteer and acted as my adjutant. He comported himself gallantly under fire, and throughout the expedition rendered me valuable service.

I herewith submit the report of Captain McCloskey, of the *Queen of the West*. He mentions favorably Captain Carnes and Lieutenant Henry Miller, of the Twenty-first [Thirty-first] Tennessee Volunteers; Lieutenant R. S. Dulin, adjutant of Major Burnet's battalion of Texans, and Captain T. H. Hutton, chief of artillery; Sergeant Edward Langley, acting as lieutenant in charge of the two Parrott guns and the volunteers; Captain C. H. White, slightly wounded, acting with great efficiency as ordnance officer; Captain Tank, Lieutenant Fisk, Lieutenant C. Stanmyer, and Lieutenant K. R. Hymans, quartermaster and commissary, who exhibited much energy. Lieutenants Stanmyer and Fisk were wounded at their pieces while gallantly acting as captains of artillery.

As I was on board the *Queen* during the action, the conduct of these gentlemen was under my own eye, and I cheerfully endorse the commendation of Captain McCloskey. Captain McCloskey also speaks highly of the intrepid promptness and skill of Pilots Z. Milligan, W. Melloy, Frank Fitrell, and N. Dunbar; also of the engineers (Messrs. J. R. Allyboy, E. Woods, J. Crawford, P. Montrose, and G. W. Daniel), and of the mate, Mr. W. H. Parker. Though the gentlemen were civilians, yet, knowing that the boat was well and skillfully handled, I have thought it a matter of justice to approve the endorsement of Captain McCloskey. He also speaks approvingly of the conduct of Assistant Surgeon Blanchard, who manifested much care and coolness, coming on the gun deck in the midst of the action and personally supervising the removal of the wounded.

Sergeant Magruder, of the Signal Corps, also deserves mention for having rendered very important services in the discharge of the responsible duties devolved upon him.

Captain Pierce, of the *Webb*, reports to me verbally that his pilots (Mr. Norman White, mate, and the Messrs. Elijah Trene, Frank Smith, Charles Oakey, and O. S. Burdett), and chief engineer (Hugh Derby), and the assistant engineers (George Marsh, Richard Stockton, J. E. Conklin, and William Kuvish), behaved themselves with the utmost gallantry and bravery, and discharged their duties with promptness and ability. I have no doubt that this is correct, from the skillful manner in which the *Webb* was handled while she was in action.

I am, major, yours, respectfully,

J. L. BRENT,
Major, Commanding Expedition.

Major E. SURGET,
Assistant Adjutant-General.

6. The CSS *Arkansas*

Construction of the ironclad CSS *Arkansas* was begun in a hastily constructed shipyard in Memphis, in October of 1861, along with her sister ship the *Tennessee*. (Still, *Iron Afloat, the Story of the Confederate Armorclads*, p. 62.) Both were designed by Chief Naval Constructor John L. Porter, and in late 1861 a contract was signed between the Confederate government and Memphis steamboat builder John T. Shirley for their construction. Both boats were 165 feet in length, 35 feet abeam, and drew 12 feet of water when fully loaded. An unusual characteristic of their design was a casemate that featured vertical sides instead of the slanted armor normally seen on all other Southern ironclads. Only the ends of the shield were slanted 35 degrees.

Shirley decided to concentrate first on the *Arkansas*, but due to the scarcity of supplies and the lack of skilled workers, construction soon fell behind schedule. With the fall of Island Number 10 on April 7, 1862, and the surrender of New Orleans on April 25, it was painfully evident that the unfinished *Arkansas* had to be moved to a place where she would be safe from the advancing Union forces. After much searching, a refuge was found. The unfinished ironclad was towed south down the Mississippi and then northeast up the Yazoo River to the little hamlet of Greenwood, Mississippi. Placed under the charge of Lieutenant Charles McBlair who had little interest in completing her, the unfinished warship was essentially abandoned. It was here at this backwater village that her captain, Isaac N. Brown found her when he arrived to relieve McBlair on May 29, 1862. (Still, *Iron Afloat, the Story of the Confederate Armorclads*, p. 62.)

Kentucky born Commander Brown proved to be one of the most capable and energetic officers in the Confederate Navy, and the following is his account of the building and operations of the CSS *Arkansas*. [RTC]

"The Confederate Gun-Boat *Arkansas*" by Commander Isaac N. Brown, CSN

Battles and Leaders of the Civil War, Volume VI, pp. 572–579

AFTER the Appomattox capitulation, the observance of which, nobly maintained by General Grant, crowns him as the humane man of the age, I took to the plow, as a better implement of reconstruction than the pen; and if I take up the latter now, it is that justice may be done to the men and the memory of the men of the *Arkansas*.

On the 28th of May, 1862, I received at Vicksburg a telegraphic order from the Navy Department at Richmond to "proceed to Greenwood, Miss., and assume command of the Confederate gun-boat *Arkansas*, and finish and equip that vessel without regard to expenditure of men or money." I knew that such a vessel had been under construction at Memphis, but I had not heard till then of her escape from the general wreck of our Mississippi River defenses. Greenwood is at the head of the Yazoo River, 160 miles by river from Yazoo City. It being the season of overflow, I found my new command four miles from dry land. Her condition was not encouraging. The vessel was a mere hull, without armor; the engines were apart; guns without carriages were lying about the deck; a portion of the railroad iron intended as armor was at the bottom of the river, and the other and far greater part was to be sought for in the interior of the country.

Taking a day to fish up the sunken iron, I had the *Arkansas* towed to Yazoo City, where the hills reach the river. Here, though we were within fifty miles of the Union fleets, there was the possibility of equipment. Within a very short time after reaching Yazoo City we had two hundred men, chiefly from the nearest detachment of the army, at work on the deck's shield and hull, while fourteen blacksmith forges were drawn from the neighboring plantations and placed on the bank to hasten the iron-work. Extemporized drilling-machines on the steamer *Capitol* worked day and night fitting the railway iron for the bolts which were to fasten it as armor. This iron was brought from many points to the nearest railroad station and thence twenty-five miles by wagons. The trees were yet growing from which the gun-carriages had to be made—the most difficult work of all, as such vehicles had never been built in Mississippi. I made a contract with two gentlemen of Jackson to pay each his own price for the full number of ten. The executive officer, Mr. Stevens, gave the matter his particular attention, and in time, along with the general equipment, we obtained five good carriages from each contractor.

Commander Isaac N. Brown (Naval Historical Center).

This finishing, armoring, arming, and equipment of the *Arkansas* within five weeks' working-time under the hot summer sun, from which we were unsheltered, and under the depressing thought that there was a deep channel, of but six hours' steaming between us and the Federal fleet, whose guns were within hearing, was perhaps not inferior under all the circumstances to the renowned effort of Oliver Hazard Perry in cutting a fine ship from the forest in ninety days. We were not a day too soon, for the now rapid fall of the river rendered it necessary for us to assume the offensive without waiting for the apparatus to bend the railway iron to the curve of our quarter and stern, and to the angles of the pilot-house. Though there was little thought of showing the former, the weakest part, to the enemy, we tacked boilerplate iron over it for appearance' sake, and very imperfectly covered the pilot-house shield with a double thickness of one-inch bar iron.

Our engines' twin screws, one under each quarter, worked up to eight miles an hour in still water, which promised about half that speed when turned against the current of the main river. We had at first some trust in these, not having discovered the way they soon showed of stopping on the center at wrong times and places; and as they never both stopped of themselves at the same time, the effect was, when one did so, to turn the vessel round, despite the rudder. Once, in the presence of the enemy, we made a circle, while trying to make the automatic stopper keep time with its sister-screw.

The *Arkansas* now appeared as if a small seagoing vessel had been cut down to the water's edge at both ends, leaving a box for guns amidships. The straight sides of the box, a foot in thickness, had over them one layer of railway iron; the ends closed by timber one foot square, planked across by six-inch strips of oak, were then covered by one course of railway iron laid up and down at an angle of thirty-five degrees. These ends deflected overhead all missiles striking at short range, but would have been of little security under a plunging fire. This shield, flat on top, covered with plank and half-inch iron, was pierced for 10 guns—3 in each broadside and 2 forward and aft. The large smoke-stack came through the top of the shield, and the pilot-house was raised about one foot above the shield level. Through the latter led a small tin tube by which to convey orders to the pilot.* The battery was respectable for that period of the war: 2 8-inch 64-pounders at the bows; 2 rifled 32s (old smooth-bores banded and rifled) astern; and 2 100-pounder Columbiads and a 6-inch naval gun in each broadside,—10 guns in all, which, under officers formerly of the United States service, could be relied on for good work, if we could find the men to load and fire. We obtained over 100 good men from the naval vessels lately on the Mississippi, and about 60 Missourians from the command of General Jeff Thompson. These had never served at great guns, but on trial they exhibited in their new service the cool courage natural to them on land. They were worthily commanded, under the orders of our first lieutenant, by Captain Harris.

Our officers were Lieutenants Stevens, Grimball, Gift, Barbot, Wharton, and Read, all of the old service, and Chief Engineer City, Acting Masters Milliken and Nicholls, of the Volunteer Navy, and Midshipmen Scales,† R. H. Bacot, Tyler, and H. Cenas. The only trouble they ever gave me was to keep them from running the *Arkansas* into the Union fleet before we were ready for battle. On the 12th of July we sent our mechanics ashore, took our Missourians on board, and dropped below Satartia Bar, within five hours of the Mississippi. I now gave the executive officer a day to organize and exercise his men.

The idea exists that we made "a run," or "a raid," or in some way an "attack by surprise" upon the Union fleet. I have reason to think that we were expected some hours before we came.

On Monday AM, July 14th, 1862, we started from Satartia. Fifteen miles below, at the mouth of Sunflower River, we found that the steam from our imperfect engines and boiler had penetrated our forward magazine and wet our powder so as to render it unfit for use. We were just opposite the site of an old saw-mill, where the opening in the forest, dense everywhere else, admitted the sun's rays. The day was clear and very hot; we made fast to the bank, head down-stream, landed our wet powder (expecting the enemy to heave in sight every moment), spread tarpaulins over the old saw-dust and our powder over these. By constant shaking and turning we got it back to the point of ignition before the sun sank below the trees, when, gathering it up, we crowded all that we could of it into the after magazine and resumed our way, guns cast loose and men at quarters, expecting every moment to meet the enemy.§

---

*In this action 68 shot-holes were made in the stack, and 4 minie-balls passed through the tin tube—I.N.B.

†Dabney M. Scales was from the Naval Academy at Annapolis; he distinguished himself afterward in the Shenandoah, and is now a prominent lawyer of Memphis.—I. N. B.

§A Federal letter relating to the Arkansas, and evidently press correspondence, was captured by Confederates at Greenville, Miss. It began by saying, "Last night at 10 o'clock [it seems to have been written on the day of the combat] two deserters from Grandpre's sharp-shooters at the Yazoo, who had stolen a skiff, came alongside the admiral's ship, the Hartford, and reported that the Arkansas had cut the raft and would be down at daylight to attack the fleet. Upon this a council of war was immediately [that night] called on board the Hartford," etc., etc. The same letter, bearing every internal evidence of truth and sincerity, went on to say,

I had some idea of their strength, General Van Dorn, commanding our forces at Vicksburg, having written to me two days before that there were then, I think he said, thirty-seven men-of-war in sight and more up the river. Near dark we narrowly escaped the destruction of our smoke-stack from an immense overhanging tree. From this disaster we were saved by young Grimball, who sprang from the shield to another standing tree, with rope's-end in hand, and made it fast. We anchored near Haynes' Bluff at midnight and rested till 3 AM, when we got up anchor for the fleet, hoping to be with it at sunrise, but before it was light we ran ashore and lost an hour in getting again afloat.

At sunrise we gained Old River—a lake caused by a "cut-off" from the Mississippi; the Yazoo enters this at the north curve, and, mingling its deep waters with the wider expanse of the lake, after a union of ten miles, breaks through a narrow strip of land, to lose itself finally in the Mississippi twelve miles above Vicksburg. We were soon to find the fleet midway between these points, but hid from both by the curved and wooded eastern shore. As the sun rose clear and fiery out of the lake on our left, we saw a few miles ahead, under full steam, three Federal vessels in line approaching. These, as we afterward discovered, were the iron-clad *Carondelet*, Captain Henry Walke,* the wooden gun-boat *Tyler*, Lieutenant William Gwin, and a ram, the *Queen of the West*, Lieutenant James M. Hunter. Directing our pilot to stand for the iron-clad, the center vessel of the three, I gave the order not to fire our bow guns, lest by doing so we should diminish our speed, relying for the moment upon our broadside guns to keep the ram and the *Tyler* from gaining our quarter, which they seemed eager to do. I had determined, despite our want of speed, to try the ram or iron prow upon the foe, who were gallantly approaching; but when less than half a mile separated us, the *Carondelet* fired a wildly aimed bow gun, backed round, and went from the *Arkansas* at a speed which at once perceptibly increased the space between us. The *Tyler* and ram followed this movement of the iron-clad, and the stern guns of the *Carondelet* and the *Tyler* were briskly served on us. Grimball and Gift, with their splendid sixty-fours, were now busy at their work, while Barbot and Wharton watched for a chance shot abeam. Read chafed in silence at his rifles. The whole crew was under the immediate direction of the first lieutenant, Henry Stevens, a religious soldier, of the Stonewall Jackson type, who felt equally safe at all times and places. I was on the shield directly over our bow guns, and could see their shot on the way to the *Carondelet*, and with my glasses I thought that I could see the white wood under her armor. This was satisfactory, for I knew that no vessel afloat could long stand rapid raking by 8-inch shot at such short range. We soon began to gain on the chase, yet from time to time I had to steer first to starboard, then to port, to keep the inquisitive consorts of the *Carondelet* from inspecting my boiler-plate armor. This gave the nearer antagonist an advantage, but before he could improve it he would be again brought ahead. While our shot seemed always to hit his stern and disappear, his missiles, striking our inclined shield, were deflected over my head and lost in air. I received a severe contusion on the head, but this gave me no concern after I had failed to find any brains mixed with the handful of clotted blood which I drew from the wound and examined. A moment later a shot from the *Tyler* struck at my feet, penetrated the pilot-house, and, cutting off a section of the wheel, mortally hurt, Chief Pilot Hodges and disabled our Yazoo River pilot, Shacklett, who was at the moment much needed, our Mississippi pilots knowing nothing of Old River. James Brady, a Missourian

---

(continued from previous page) *"At daylight [following the night council] the little tug which [Admiral] Davis had sent up the Yazoo as a lookout came down like a streak of lightning, screaming,' The Arkansas is coming! The Arkansas is coming!'"* and then follows the account of excitement and preparation. Now all this may have been only in the imagination of the correspondent, but there was a detachment of our sharp-shooters under Captain Grandpre at the raft, and we did cut and pass through it as stated. I. N. B.

The commander of the Carondelet *and I had been friends in the old navy and messmates on a voyage around the world:* I. N. B.

of nerve and equal to the duty, took the wheel, and I ordered him to "keep the iron-clad ahead." All was going well, with a near prospect of carrying out my first intention of using the ram, this time at a great advantage, for the stern of the *Carondelet* was now the objective point, and she seemed to be going slow and unsteady. Unfortunately the *Tyler* also slowed, so as to keep near his friend, and this brought us within easy range of his small-arms. I saw with some concern, as I was the only visible target outside our shield, that they were firing by volleys. I ought to have told Stevens to hold off Grimball and Gift from the iron-clad till they could finish the *Tyler*, but neither in nor out of battle does one always do the right thing. I was near the hatchway at the moment when a minie-ball, striking over my left temple, tumbled me down among the guns.

I awoke as if from sleep, to find kind hands helping me to a place among the killed and wounded. I soon regained my place on the shield. I found the *Carondelet* still ahead, but much nearer, and both vessels entering the willows, which grew out on the bar at the inner curve of the lake. To have run into the mud we drawing 13 feet (the *Carondelet* only 6), would have ended the matter with the *Arkansas*. The *Carondelet's* position could only be accounted for by supposing her steering apparatus destroyed.* The deep water was on our starboard bow, where at some distance I saw the *Tyler* and the ram, as if awaiting our further entanglement. I gave the order "hard a-port and depress port guns." So near were we to the chase that this action of the helm brought us alongside, and our port broadside caused her to heel to port and then roll back so deeply as to take the water over her deck forward of the shield. Our crew, thinking her sinking, gave three hearty cheers. In swinging off we exposed our stern to the *Carondelet's* broadside, and Read at the same time got a chance with his rifles.

The *Carondelet* did not return this fire of our broadside and stern guns. Had she fired into our stern when we were so near, it would have destroyed us or at least have disabled us.

Though I stood within easy pistol-shot, in uniform, uncovered, and evidently the commander of the *Arkansas*, no more notice was taken of me by the *Carondelet* than had been taken of my ship when, to escape running into the mud, I had exposed the *Arkansas* to being raked. Their ports were closed, no flag was flying, not a man or officer was in view, not a sound or shot was heard. She was apparently "disabled." We neither saw nor felt the *Carondelet* again, but turned toward the spiteful *Tyler* and the wary ram. As these were no longer a match for the *Arkansas*, they very properly took advantage of a speed double our own to gain the shelter of their fleet, the *Tyler* making good practice at us while in range with her pivot gun, and getting some attention in the same way from our bows. Under the ordinary circumstances of war we had just got through with a fair hour's work; but knowing what was ahead of us, we had to regard it in the same light as our Missouri militia did, as "a pretty smart skirmish."

On gaining the Mississippi, we saw no vessels but the two we had driven before us. While following these in the direction of Vicksburg I had the opportunity of inspecting engine and fire rooms, where I found engineers and firemen had been suffering under a temperature of 120 to 130. The executive officer, while attending to every other duty during the recent firing, had organized a relief party from the men at the guns, who went down into the fire-room every fifteen minutes, the others coming up or being, in many instances, hauled up, exhausted in that time; in this way, by great care, steam was kept to service gauge, but in the conflict below the fire department broke down.

The connection between furnaces and smoke-stack (technically called the breechings) were in this second conflict shot away, destroying the draught and letting the flames come out into the shield, raising the temperature there to 120, while it had already risen to 130 in the fire-room. It has been asked why the *Arkansas* was not used as a ram.

*Such was the fact.— Editors

The want of speed and of confidence in the engines answers the question. We went into action in Old River with 120 pounds of steam, and though every effort was made to keep it up, we came out with but 20 pounds, hardly enough to turn the engines.

Aided by the current of the Mississippi, we soon approached the Federal fleet—a forest of masts and smoke-stacks—ships, rams, iron-clads, and other gun-boats on the left side, and ordinary river steamers and bomb-vessels along the right. To any one having a real ram at command the genius of havoc could not have offered a finer view, the panoramic effect of which was intensified by the city of men spread out with innumerable tents opposite on the right bank. We were not yet in sight of Vicksburg, but in every direction, except astern, our eyes rested on enemies. I had long known the most of these as valued friends, and if I now had any doubts of the success of the *Arkansas* they were inspired by this general knowledge rather than from any awe of a particular name. It seemed at a glance as if a whole navy had come to keep me away from the heroic city,—six or seven rams, four or five iron-clads, without including one accounted for an hour ago, and the fleet of Farragut generally, behind or inside of this fleet. The rams seemed to have been held in reserve, to come out between the intervals. Seeing this, as we neared the head of the line I said to our pilot, "Brady, shave that line of men-of-war as close as you can, so that the rams will not have room to gather head-way in coming out to strike us." In this way we ran so near to the wooden ships that each may have expected the blow which, if I could avoid it, I did not intend to deliver to any, and probably the rams running out at slow speed across the line of our advance received in the smoke and fury of the fight more damage from the guns of their own men-of-war than from those of the *Arkansas*.

As we neared the head of the line our bow guns, trained on the *Hartford*, began this second fight of the morning (we were yet to have a third one before the day closed), and within a few minutes, as the enemy was brought in range, every gun of the *Arkansas* was at its work. It was calm, and the smoke settling over the combatants, our men at times directed their guns at the flashes of those of their opponents. As we advanced, the line of fire seemed to grow into a circle constantly closing.

The shock of missiles striking our sides was literally continuous, and as we were now surrounded without room for anything but pushing ahead, and shrapnel shot were coming on our shield deck, twelve pounds at a time, I went below to see how our Missouri backwoodsmen were handling their 100-pounder Columbiads. At this moment I had the most lively realization of having steamed into a real volcano, the *Arkansas* from its center firing rapidly to every point of the circumference, without the fear of hitting a friend or missing an enemy. I got below in time to see Read and Scales with their rifled guns blow off the feeble attack of a ram on our stern. Another ram was across our way ahead. As I gave the order, "Go through him, Brady!" his steam went into the air, and his crew into the river. A shot from one of our bow guns had gone through his boiler and saved the collision. We passed by and through the brave fellows struggling in the water under a shower of missiles intended for us. It was a little hot this morning all around; the enemy's shot frequently found weak places in our armor, and their shrapnel and minie-balls also came through our port-holes. Still, under a temperature of 120, our people kept to their work, and as each one, acting under the steady eye of Stevens, seemed to think the result depended on himself, I sought a cooler atmosphere on the shield, to find, close ahead and across our way, a large iron-clad displaying the square flag of an admiral. Though we had but little head-way, his beam was exposed, and I ordered the pilot to strike him amidships. He avoided this by steaming ahead, and, passing under his stern, nearly touching, we gave him our starboard broadside, which probably went through him from rudder to prow. This was our last shot, and we received none in return.

We were now at the end of what had seemed the interminable line, and also past the outer rim of the volcano. I now called the officers up to take a look at what we had just come through and to get the fresh air; and as the little group of heroes closed around me with their friendly words of congratulation, a heavy rifle-shot passed close over our heads, it was the parting salutation, and if aimed two feet lower would have been to us the most injurious of the battle. We were not yet in sight of Vicksburg, but if any of the fleet followed us farther on our way I did not perceive it.

The *Arkansas* continued toward Vicksburg without further trouble. When within sight of the city, we saw another fleet preparing to receive us or recede from us, below one vessel of the fleet was aground and in flames. With our firemen exhausted, our smoke-stack cut to pieces, and a section of our plating torn from the side, we were not in condition just then to begin a third battle; moreover humanity required the landing of our wounded terribly torn by cannon-shot-and of our dead.

We were received at Vicksburg with enthusiastic cheers. Immediate measures were taken to repair damages and to recruit our crew, diminished to one-half their original number by casualties, and by the expiration of service of those who had volunteered only for the trip to Vicksburg.

We had left the Yazoo River with a short supply of fuel, and after our first landing opposite the city-hall we soon dropped down to the coal depot, where we began coaling and repairing, under the fire of the lower fleet, to which, under the circumstances, we could make no reply. Most of the enemy's shot fell short, but Renshaw, in the *Westfield*, made very fine practice with his 100-pounder rifle gun, occasionally throwing the spray from his shot over our working party, but with the benefit of sprinkling down the coal dust. Getting in our coal, we moved out of range of such sharp practice, where, under less excitement, we hastened such temporary repairs as would enable us to continue the offensive. We had intended trying the lower fleet that evening, but before our repairs could be completed and our crew reinforced by suitable selections from the army, the hours of night were approaching, under the shadows of which (however favorable for running batteries) no brave man cares from choice to fight.

About sunset of the same day, a number of our antagonists of the morning, including the flag-ship *Hartford* and the equally formidable *Richmond*, were seen under full steam coming down the river. Before they came within range of the *Arkansas*, we had the gratification of witnessing the beautiful reply of our upper shore-batteries to their gallant attack. Unfit as we were for the offensive, I told Stevens to get under way and run out into the midst of the coming fleet. Before this order could be executed one vessel of the fleet sent a 160-pound wrought-iron bolt through our armor and engine-room, disabling the engine and killing, among others, Pilot Gilmore, and knocking overboard the heroic Brady, who had steered the *Arkansas* through our morning's work. This single shot caused also a very serious leak, destroyed all the contents of the dispensary (fortunately our surgeon, Dr. Washington, was just then away from his medicines), and, passing through the opposite bulwarks, lodged between the wood-work and the armor. Stevens promptly detailed a party to aid the carpenter in stopping the leak, while our bow and port-broadside guns were rapidly served on the passing vessels. So close were these to our guns that we could hear our shot crashing through their sides, and the groans of their wounded; and, incredible as it now seems, these sounds were heard with a fierce delight by the *Arkansas*'s people. Why no attempt was made to ram our vessel, I do not know. Our position invited it, and our rapid firing made that position conspicuous; but as by this time it was growing dark, and the *Arkansas* close inshore, they may have mistaken us for a water-battery. We had greatly the advantage in pointing our guns, the enemy passing in line ahead, and being distinctly visible as each one for the time shut out our view of the horizon. And now this busy day, the 15th of July, 1862, was closed with the sad duty of sending ashore a second party of killed and wounded, and the rest which our exhaustion rendered necessary was taken for the night under a dropping fire of the enemy's 13-inch shells.

During the following week we were exposed day and night to these falling bombs, which did not hit the *Arkansas*, but frequently exploded under water near by. One shell, which fell nearly under our bows, threw up a number of fish. As these floated by with the current, one of our men said: "Just look at that, will you? Why, the upper fleet is killing fish for the lower fleet's dinner!" In time we became accustomed to this shelling, but not to the idea that it was without danger; and I know of no more effective way of curing a man of the weakness of thinking that he is without the feeling of fear than for him, on a dark night, to watch two or three of these double-fused descending shells, all near each other, and seeming as though they would strike him between the eyes.

In three days we were again in condition to move and to menace at our will either fleet, thus compelling the enemy's entire force, in the terrible July heat, to keep up steam day and night. An officer of the fleet writing at this time, said: "Another council of war was held on board the admiral's [flag-ship] last night, in which it was resolved that the *Arkansas* must be destroyed at all hazards, a thing, I suspect, much easier said than done; but I wish that she was destroyed; for she gives us no rest by day nor sleep by night." We constantly threatened the offensive, and our raising steam, which they could perceive by our smokestack, was the signal for either fleet to fire up.

As the temperature at that season was from 90 to 100 in the shade, it was clear that unless the *Arkansas* could be "destroyed" the siege, if for sanitary reasons alone, must soon be raised.

The result of our first real attempt to resume the offensive was that before we could get within range of the mortar fleet, our engine completely broke down, and it was with difficulty that we regained our usual position in front of the city.

The timely coming of the iron-clad *Essex*, fresh from the docks, and with a new crew, enabled the Union commander to attack us without risk to his regular original blockading force. They could not have taken us at a more unprepared moment. Some of our officers and all but twenty-eight of our crew were in hospitals ashore, and we lay helplessly at anchor, with a disabled engine. I made known to the general commanding at Vicksburg the condition of our vessel, and with great earnestness personally urged him to give me, without delay, enough men to fight my guns, telling him that I expected an attack every hour. I was promised that the men (needed at the moment) should be sent to me the next day. The following morning at sunrise the *Essex*, Commodore William D. Porter, with the *Queen of the West*, no doubt the best ram of the Ellet flock (though as far as my experience went they were all ordinary sheep and equally harmless), ran down under full steam, regardless of the fire of our upper shore-batteries, and made the expected attack. We were at anchor and with only enough men to fight two of our guns; but by the zeal of our officers, who mixed in with these men as part of the guns' crews, we were able to train at the right moment and fire all the guns which could be brought to bear upon our cautiously coming assailants. With a view perhaps to avoid our bow guns, the *Essex* made the mistake, so far as her success was concerned, of running into us across the current instead of coming head-on with its force. At the moment of collision, when our guns were muzzle to muzzle, the *Arkansas*'s broadside was exchanged for the bow guns of the assailant; a shot from one of the latter struck the *Arkansas*'s plating a foot forward of the forward broadside port, breaking off the ends of the railroad bars and driving them in among our people; the solid shot followed, crossed diagonally our gun-deck, and split on the breech of our starboard after-broadside gun. This shot killed eight and wounded six of our men, but left us still half our crew. What damage the *Essex* received I did not ascertain, but that vessel drifted clear of the *Arkansas* without again firing, and after receiving the fire of our stern rifles steamed in the face and under the fire of the Vicksburg batteries to the fleet below. Had Porter at the moment of the collision thrown fifty men on our upper deck, he might have made fast to us with a hawser, and with little additional loss might have taken the *Arkansas* and her twenty men and officers. We were given time by the approaching ram to reload our guns, and this second assailant, coming also across instead of with the current, "butted" us so gently that we hardly felt the shock. The force of his blow was tempered to us no doubt by the effect of our three broadside guns, which were fired into him when he was less than fifty feet distant. Apparently blinded by such a blow in the face, he drifted astern and ran ashore under the muzzles of Read's rifles, the bolts from which were probably lost in the immense quantity of hay in bales which seemed stowed over and around him. Getting clear of the bank, the ram wore round without again attempting to strike the *Arkansas*, and steamed at great speed up the river, receiving in passing a second broadside from our port battery, and in the excitement of getting away neglecting the caution of his advance, he brought himself within range of our deadly bow guns, from which Grimball and Gift sent solid shot that seemed to pass through him from stem to stern. As he ran out of range he was taken in tow and was run up into the Davis fleet.

Thus closed the fourth and final battle of the *Arkansas*, leaving the daring Confederate vessel, though reduced in crew to twenty men all told for duty, still defiant in the presence of a hostile force perhaps exceeding in real strength that which fought under Nelson at Trafalgar. The conduct of our men and officers was on this occasion, as on every former trial, worthy of the American name. Moving quickly in a squad, from gun to gun, reloading, and running out each one separately, and then dividing into parties sufficient to train and fire, they were as determined and cheerful as they could have been with a full crew on board. The closeness of this contest with the *Essex* may be inferred from the circumstance that several of our surviving men had their faces blackened and were painfully hurt by the unburnt powder which came through our port-holes from the assailant's guns.

It was perhaps as much a matter of coal as of cannon, of health as of hostility, that the Union commanders had now to decide upon. If the *Arkansas* could not be destroyed, the siege must be raised, for fifty ships, more or less, could not keep perpetual steam to confine one little 10-gun vessel within her conceded control of six miles of the Mississippi River. It was, indeed, a dilemma, and doubtless the less difficult horn of it was chosen. Soon after our contribution to the *Essex*'s laurels, and between sunset and sunrise, the lower fleet started for the recuperative atmosphere of salt-water, and about the same time the upper fleet-rams, bombs, and iron-clads-steamed for the North. Thus was dissipated for the season the greatest naval force hitherto assembled at one time in the New World.

Vicksburg was now without the suspicion of an immediate enemy. I had taken, with my brave associates, for the last sixty days, my share of labor and watchfulness, and I now left them for four days, only, as I supposed, to sustain without me the lassitude of inaction. Important repairs were yet necessary to the engines, and much of the iron plating had to be refastened to her shattered sides. This being fairly under way, I called, Thursday PM, upon General Van Dorn, commanding the forces, and told him that, having obtained telegraphic permission from the Navy Department to turn over the command of the vessel temporarily to the officer next in rank, First Lieutenant Stevens, I would go to Grenada, Miss and that I would return on the following Tuesday AM by which time the *Arkansas*, I hoped, would be ready once more to resume the offensive. Almost immediately on reaching Grenada I was taken violently ill, and while in bed, unable, as I supposed, to rise, I received a dispatch from Lieutenant Stevens saying that Van Dorn required him to steam at once down to Baton Rouge to aid in a land attack of our forces upon the Union garrison holding that place. I replied to this with a positive order to remain at Vicksburg until I could join him; and without delay caused myself to be taken to the railroad station, where I threw myself on the mail-bags of the first passing train, unable to sit up, and did not change my position until reaching Jackson, 130 miles distant.

On applying there for a special train to take me to Vicksburg, I learned that the *Arkansas* had been gone from that place four hours.* Van Dorn had been persistent beyond all reason in his demand, and Stevens, undecided, had referred the question to a senior officer of the Confederate navy, who was at Jackson, Miss., with horses and carriages, furnished by Government in place of a flag-ship, thus commanding in chief for the Confederacy on the Mississippi, sixty miles from its nearest waters. This officer, whose war record was yet in abeyance, had attained scientific celebrity by dabbling in the waters of the Dead Sea, at a time when I was engaged in the siege of Vera Cruz and in the general operations of the Mexican war. Ignorant or regardless of the condition of the *Arkansas*, fresh from Richmond on his mission of bother, not communicating with or informing me on the subject, he ordered Stevens to obey Van Dorn without any regard to my orders to the contrary.

Under the double orders of two commanders-in-chief to be at Baton Rouge at a certain date and hour Stevens could not use that tender care which his engines required, and before they completed their desperate run of three hundred miles against time, the starboard one suddenly broke down, throwing the vessel inextricably ashore. This misfortune, for which there was no present remedy, happened when the vessel was within sight of Baton Rouge. Very soon after the *Essex* was seen, approaching under full steam. Stevens as humane as he was true and brave, finding that he could not bring a single gun to bear upon the coming foe, sent all his people over the bows ashore, remaining alone to set fire to his vessel; this he did so effectually that he had to jump from the stern into the river and save himself by swimming; and with colors flying, the gallant *Arkansas* whose decks had never been pressed by the foot of an enemy, was blown into the air.

7. St. Charles, Arkansas

In April of 1862, when Captain George N. Hollins took his naval force south to contest the expected Federal attack at New Orleans, he left behind several small gunboats to guard the various tributaries that flowed into the Mississippi. Two of these, the CSS *Pontchartrain* and the CSS *Maurepas*, were dispatched up the White River in Arkansas. The White, 685 miles long, flows into the Mississippi just above the mouth of the larger Arkansas River. After the loss of Memphis, Confederate engineers, concerned with defending the state and the capitol at Little Rock, had surveyed both rivers to determine the most suitable spots to build fortifications which, hopefully, would stop the advance of the enemy's ironclads. At Arkansas Post, 50 miles from the mouth of the Arkansas River, construction was begun on an earthen fortification later known as Fort Hindman. On the White, the most favorable spot appeared to be the bluffs that rose above the river near the hamlet of St. Charles.

Also during this period of time, a Federal land force under General Samuel R. Curtis had been pushing south out of Missouri into northern Arkansas. Harassed by numerous cavalry attacks by Confederate General Thomas C. Hindman and burdened with a long and tenuous supply line from St. Louis, Curtis had withdrawn to Batesville, Arkansas, on the White River. From there, believing that Hindman had received reinforcements from Texas, he pleaded with the federal command for help. As a result of his pleas, a Federal naval task force under Commander Augustus H. Kilty was formed consisting of the ironclads *Mound City* and *St. Louis*; the timberclads *Lexington* and *Conestoga*; and one armored tug. Attached to Kilty's expedition was a fleet of transports carrying the 46th Regiment of Indiana volunteers. On June 16, 1862, approximately 100 miles from the mouth of the

---

I was entirely cured by this intelligence, and immediately hurried to Pontchatoula, the nearest approach by rail to Baton Rouge, and thence arrived nearly in time to see the explosion of the Arkansas.— I. N. B.*

White River, at St. Charles, Confederate sailors and soldiers dug in to await the advance of Kilty's fleet.

Previous to the Federal fleet's arrival, First Lieutenant John W. Dunnington had placed in position two rifled 32-pounders from the *Pontchartrain*, and two 3-inch field pieces that he had found in the arsenal. Two rifled 3-inch guns and two 12-pounder brass guns had been landed from the *Maurepas*, and these were positioned 400 yards below the guns from the *Pontchartrain*. These lower guns were under the command of Midshipman Francis M. Roby. A small 12-pound howitzer was placed on the land-side to assist the 35 infantry soldiers under the command of Captain Williams, CSA. First Lieutenant Joseph Fry of the navy was in overall command of the fortification.

On the evening of the sixteenth, the federal ironclads advanced to within a few miles of the Confederate guns. Lieutenant Dunnington in his official report gives a comprehensive picture of the engagement at St. Charles. (Campbell, *Confederate Naval Forces on Western Waters*, pp. 98–101.) [RTC]

Official Report of
1st Lt. John W. Dunnington, CSN

Official Records Navy, Series I, Volume XXIII, pp. 199–201

C. S. Gunboat *Pontchartrain*
Little Rock, Ark., June 21, 1862.

GENERAL: As the senior officer in command of the naval forces, in the absence of Captain Fry, C. S. Navy, I beg leave to submit the following report of the engagement between our forces and the enemy's gunboats at St. Charles, on the morning of the 17th instant:

I reached St. Charles on Monday evening, 16th instant, about 6 PM, with the men I carried with me to work the two rifled 32-pounder cannon, which I had previously placed there in battery. I found our forces there under arms. The smoke of the enemy's gunboats was plainly seen from the bluff, and the pickets who had come in reported two gunboats, one tug, and two transports below advancing.

Owing to the unexpected approach of the enemy Captain Fry had not time to land his arms [guns], but immediately placed his vessel across the river above my battery of rifled guns, intending to resist their progress. Finding the enemy did not advance, after dark it was determined to sink the gunboat *Maurepas*, the transports *Eliza G.* and *Mary Patterson* in a line across the river.

The sinking of the gunboats was entrusted to Captain Leary.

Captain Fry, with his own crew, sank the *Maurepas*, remaining on board until the gun deck was submerged.

The blockading of the river was necessarily so hastily done that no ballast or weight could be placed in the transports. About daybreak the last vessel was sunk, and the river blockaded temporarily.

Supposing the enemy would make the attack at early daylight, one rifled Parrott gun and ammunition, in command of Midshipman Roby, was moved some 400 yards below the rifled battery and placed in position. The sailors who manned the different batteries were ordered to sleep within a few feet of their guns. Shortly after daylight, two rifled Parrott 8-pounder guns, that had been sent to the rear for want of ammunition, were brought up and placed in position near the guns commanded by Midshipman Roby. These three guns were manned by the crew from the *Maurepas*, and Captain Fry in person superintended the fighting of them. One 12-pounder howitzer from the *Maurepas*, manned also by the crew, was sent down the river to assist Captain Williams in checking the enemy's advance by land.

At 7 AM, on the morning of the 17th, the pickets reported the enemy getting up steam. At 8:30 they had advanced up the river to our lines, and two gunboats commenced throwing shell, grape, and canister among our troops on the right bank of the river. They advanced very slowly, attempting to find our heavy guns. When they arrived abreast of Captain Fry's rifled guns, they opened on his battery very rapidly for three-quarters of an hour, endeavoring to silence his guns. Failing to do so, they slowly moved up the river until they came within point-blank range of one of our rifled 32-pounders. The leading gunboat stopped to fight that gun, but finding the gun still farther up was firing at her, she moved up the river to get its position, and in so doing placed herself between the two guns and in point-blank range.

1st Lt. John W. Dunnington (author's collection).

The other gunboat, in obedience to signal, I suppose, came abreast of the lower battery and opened a brisk fire upon us. About this stage of the action, 10 AM, Captain Fry sent me word that the enemy were landing a large force below. All the available men that could be found were immediately sent to Captain Williams' assistance. At 10:30 a shot from the rifled 32-pounder farthest up the river penetrated the leading gunboat and either passed through her boilers, steam chest, or pipe, filling the entire vessel with steam, and causing all that were not killed or scalded with steam to jump into the river. The vessel was completely deserted, and drifted across the stream into the bank near Captain Fry's battery. He immediately hailed and directed their flag hauled down. They failing to do so, although the order was given by some of their own officers in hearing of our people, our own men were directed to shoot those in the water attempting to escape. The two rifled guns were immediately directed to fire upon the lower gunboat, which was still engaging us. She was struck several times and soon ceased firing, slowly dropping down the river, I think, materially damaged, as she made no effort to assist the boat we had blown up, or save their friend in the river. Near 11:30 Captains Fry and Williams came to my battery and told me the enemy had completely surrounded us; the battery of small rifled guns had been spiked, and our people were in retreat. I trained one of the rifled guns to take a last shot at the enemy, and as we fired their infantry appeared over the brow of the hill, about 50 yards distant, and opened on us with musketry. Captain Fry then proposed to make a stand with the sailors, and attempted to hold the guns, but they were only armed with single barreled pistols, which they had fired at the enemy in the water.

Nothing was now left but to save all the men we could, and, as the enemy had us under a cross fire, the men were ordered to retreat, the officers bringing up the rear, until scattered in the woods.

I had confined in single irons at my battery, six prisoners captured by Captain Fry at

Little Red River. Deeming it inexpedient to bring them away, and as Captain Fry told me he had no positive proof against them, I left them for the enemy.

The gallantry of Captains Fry and Williams was so conspicuous as to arouse general notice and remark. To my own officers and several of Captain Fry's who served with me, I am particularly indebted. Mr. William Smith, acting master; Mr. William Barclay, engineer; Midshipman Roby, who commanded one of the guns; Mr. W.L. Campbell and Doctor Addison, of the *Maurepas*, acted with great gallantry and displayed a coolness and courage unsurpassed by any one in the engagement.

To Colonel Belknap, one of the citizens of St. Charles, we are all indebted for the untiring energy and zeal with which he assisted before and during the action. He was always where he was needed, encouraging the men and assisting the officers. I am unable to furnish a list of killed and wounded, but do not, think the number exceeds 3 up to the time of the retreat. For the operations of the infantry I respectfully refer you to Captain Williams.

I herewith enclose a rough sketch of St. Charles and the surrounding country, including the position of our batteries and that of the enemy's gunboats.

I am sir, with great respect,

J. W. Dunnington,
Commanding Gunboat *Pontchartrain*.

Major General Hindman,
Commanding Trans-Mississippi District.

8. The CSS *Webb*

In mid-February of 1865, Lieutenant Charles W. Read — the same officer who had fought on the Mississippi in the *McRae* and then the *Arkansas* — presented a plan to the naval secretary. Read believed that it was still possible to hurt the enemy on the high seas. Lying at Shreveport, Louisiana, along with Lieutenant Carter's ironclad *Missouri*, was the Confederate ram CSS *Webb*. Read proposed taking the powerful steamer down the Red River, running the blockade at the mouth of the river, and then steaming south down the Mississippi. The Mississippi River was heavily patrolled by Federal gunboats; however, if he could reach the mouth of the river below New Orleans by stealth and deception, he would launch the *Webb* into the blue waters of the Gulf as a commerce raider. (Campbell, *Confederate Naval Forces on Western Waters*, pp. 208–209.)

Secretary Mallory gave his consent and Read traveled to Shreveport, Louisiana, taking command of the *Webb* on March 31, 1865. William Biggio, a quartermaster on the *Webb*, wrote an account of the expedition for the January 1914 edition of the *Confederate Veteran* magazine. [RTC]

"Running the Blockade on the Mississippi" by Quartermaster William Biggio, CSN

Confederate Veteran, Vol. XXII, No. 1, January 1914, pp. 22–23

The *W. H. Webb* was built in New York several years prior to the war for the New York Underwriters. She was of fine model and was employed for wrecking purposes and for assisting vessels in distress. She had two independent engines, two walking beams, thirty-five-foot wheels, and was the most powerful vessel of her size then extant. After being thus used for a few years, she was sold to Peter Marcy, of New Orleans, who used her as a low-bar towboat. These towboats were very powerful vessels, and the *Webb* was the strongest of all. When New Orleans was captured by Butler, the *Webb* was sent up to Red River by her owner for safe-keeping. Soon after reaching the Red River she came into the possession of the Confederates, and she was converted into a ram. She was accordingly strengthened and fitted up as such with an armament of one 32-inch swivel rifle in her bow, two nine-inch decoy guns, one on each side, and two 12-pounders aft. Thus equipped, the *Webb* was ready for work as a Confederate ram.

The first exploit of the *Webb* was to, sink the Federal gunboat *Indianola*, which had run the gantlet at Vicksburg and was the first blockade vessel at the mouth of Red River. While there the *Webb* ran into the *Indianola* one night and sent her to the bottom of the river. Shortly after this the *Webb* had another fight at Atchafalaya.

The *Webb's* exploits attracted the attention of the Confederate War Department, and the idea was conceived of bringing her to the Gulf, where she could work on a more effective scale. To bring her out was a desperate undertaking, as the Mississippi River was full of Federal gunboats, to say nothing of the blockade at the mouth of Red River. Capt. Charles Read, of the Confederate navy, already famous for his destruction of thirty-five merchantmen in the Atlantic Ocean, was selected as the proper man to get the *Webb* into the Gulf. He was accordingly sent from Richmond and arrived in Shreveport in March, 1865.

Captain Read immediately began the task of getting his vessel ready for the dangerous undertaking. His first work was to organize a crew, which was soon done. James Kelly and I being made quartermasters. The next work was the coaling of his vessel and placing on board two hundred and fifty tons of fat pine knots and a large amount of resin. The *Webb* was well provisioned and then moved down the river as far as Alexandria, where two hundred arid fifty bales of cotton were taken aboard for the protection of the pilot house and the machinery. The vessel was then white-washed, as a white vessel is not so easily seen at night.

While lying here [Alexandria] an incident occurred which would have made many an old sailor shake in his boots. No matter how safe and sound a vessel may be, there is an old superstition that rats will invariably desert her if disaster is ahead, and it seemed as if the last one deserted at daylight of the morning we were to start on our perilous journey.

After leaving Alexandria the *Webb* moved down the river about forty miles and then tied up. At this point a spar torpedo fastened to a 35-foot spar was attached to the bow of the boat. It was intended with this torpedo to blow up the *Manhattan* or one of the other large vessels lying at the mouth of Red River, provided it became necessary. After getting the spar satisfactorily arranged, the *Webb* moved again slowly down the river, the intention being to reach the mouth of the river just after dark. This was accomplished, and so far all plans had worked well.

In front of the *Webb*, only a few hundred yards distant, lay the Federal fleet of about six vessels. It was a little after eight o'clock in the evening on a starlit night in April when we first descried the enemy's vessels. All of our lights were concealed and we were running very slowly in order not to make much noise. We approached close enough to distinguish every vessel and were within five hundred yards of them before they discovered us. I was at the wheel and we had slowed up the vessel as much as possible preparatory to making the final run of the gantlet. The steam in the engines was very high, and the engineer called to the captain that he could not stand it much longer without blowing the vessel up. At this moment a rocket went up from the Federal fleet, and we knew that we had been discovered. Captain Read then yelled, "Let her go!" and I rang the fast bell. The engineer threw the throttle wide open, and the *Webb* fairly leaped and trembled. "Keep her for the biggest opening between them!" shouted the captain, and I did as commanded. By this time every whistle of the fleet was screaming, drums were beating, rockets were going up, and it seemed as if the very devil was to pay. I kept the *Webb* straight on her course, however, headed for the biggest opening, and before a gun was fired we had passed the blockade and had turned the bend and were making down the Mississippi River. We had run the gantlet and were now "between the devil and the deep blue sea." After we had gone down the river some distance the *Manhattan* fired a few shots, but did us no harm. Passing out of (the) Red River, and through the very jaws of death, it was only to encounter new and greater dangers before the Gulf could be reached.

After passing Hogg Point I looked back and saw two Federal gunboats following the *Webb*, but kept on her course, and soon left her pursuers in the distance. All the way from Red River to New Orleans Federal gunboats were supposed to be anchored in the river every five miles. As the *Webb* approached one of these boats she was signaled. The signal was answered by Kelly, who remained on deck uncovering lights. When the *Webb* was nearly on the gunboat, Kelly would run up any kind of a light, and the *Webb* would be past the Federal boat before the fraud could be detected. About fifteen miles below the mouth of Red River the *Webb* lowered a boat and sent a squad ashore to cut the telegraph wires. This operation was performed several times, and thus passed the first night after running the blockade at the mouth of Red River.

At daylight we were close to a gunboat lying in front of us at Donaldsonville. She ran up her signals and at the same time ran out her guns. We thought we were in for it, but fortunately it was nothing more than a drill, and the guns were run back in.

The signals of the Federal boats were duly answered by the *Webb*, flags being used in the daytime in the same manner that lights were used at night. We could have destroyed millions of dollars of property on our trip, but our sole object was to run the blockade. Determining to pass New Orleans as soon as possible, we made the best time we could down the river. About 1 PM, we reached New Orleans and found the Federal fleet lying at St. Mary's Market. We were all feeling good, thinking that everything was all right and that we were not expected. We reckoned wrong, however, for just as we got abreast of the *Lackawanna*, a 24-gun ship, her captain received news of our coming. Before he could get all his men to their quarters, however, we were right on him; in fact, so close that a rock could have been thrown from one boat to the other. In less time than it takes to tell it the *Lackawanna* gave a shot that went clear through the *Webb* abreast the forehatch four feet from the water's edge and landed in Algiers. After the first shot Captain Reed ordered Kelly to haul down the false colors and run up the colors of the Confederacy, as he expected to see the *Webb* sunk right there and he wanted her to go down with her own colors flying. After giving this order the captain walked to the side of the *Webb* nearest the firing and remained there until we passed. Pilot Tim West, an old Red River pilot, who was helping me handle the vessel, lay down on the deck and I was left alone at the wheel. The *Lackawanna's* first shot was followed by others. Her second shot was aimed at the pilot house, but struck a bale of cotton and glanced up, passing over the pilot house and doing no damage. The third shot went through the chimney guys of the *Webb* and did little harm. By this time we were turning the bend of the river just below New Orleans, and the firing from the *Lackawanna* ceased, her captain discovering that her shots were going straight into Algiers and doing great damage there. At the lower part of Algiers, and about the middle of the river, was a large vessel supposed to be the Federal gunboat *Hartford*. We tried to blow her up with our torpedo, but by some mistake the torpedo couldn't be fired in time; and the mistake, as it happened, was a fortunate one, for the vessel proved not to be the *Hartford*, but the *Fear Not*, loaded with fixed ammunition. Had we run into her with the torpedo as we intended, the chances are that no one on either vessel would have lived to tell the tale. When we got alongside the *Fear Not*, an odd incident occurred. A Federal was standing on the deck of the *Fear Not* with a lady. Price, one of the pilots of the *Webb*, picked

The Destruction of the CSS *Webb* (Naval Historical Center).

up a gun and was in the act of shooting the officer when Captain Read ordered him to desist. Price reluctantly obeyed, remarking as he laid down the gun that it was the first time he was ever ordered not to shoot a Yankee.

Seeing that the *Fear Not* would not molest us, our next thought was to get away, so down the river we went. Looking back, we saw the steamer *Hollyhock* coming after us. The *Hollyhock* was a low-bar towboat, fast and powerful, but not so large as the *Webb*. Our object was to keep ahead of her and this we did with little trouble. She chased us thirty-two miles down the river from New Orleans, when all of a sudden we ran right on top of the war sloop *Richmond*, a 24-gun ship, lying in the middle of the river. As we neared her we saw that she had both broadsides out.

The *Webb* was slowed up and Captain Read called all the officers in front of the pilot house and addressed them: "It's no use; it's a failure. The *Richmond* will drown us all, and if she does not the forts below will, as they have a range of three miles each way up and down the river, and they know by this time that we are coming. Had we passed New Orleans without being discovered, I would have cut the wires below the city and we could have reached the Gulf with little trouble. As it is, I think the only, thing left for us to do is to set fire to the *Webb* and blow her up." When the captain finished talking, not a word was spoken by any one, but every man bowed his head in respectful obedience. Captain Read then ordered the pilot and myself, who were at the wheel, to steer to the shore, and ordered the gunner to set the fires in all parts of the vessel with slow match and magazine. Hardly had the Captain finished his order when we made for the east bank of the river. We struck bottom fifty yards from the shore, running the *Webb's* nose out in four feet less water than she drew. Lifelines were then thrown over the bow on the boat to get overboard by, and everybody commenced to go ashore like rats leaving a ship. As soon as we got ashore, we struck out across a sugar plantation until we reached the back of it, where we hid from the enemy's view and yet could see the *Webb*.

In the meantime the *Hollyhock* steamed up to the *Webb* and tried to put out her fires with water hoses. She also rescued a man named Preston and a boy named Hyner, who had remained on the *Webb* and had made no effort to escape. The *Hollyhock* took from the *Webb* her flags and small arms and backed away. It was now about three o'clock in the afternoon, and from our position at the back of the farm we watched the boat burn. At length her magazine was reached and with an explosion that shook the waters far and near, the Confederate ram *Webb* came to her tragic end.

After the *Webb* had blown up, we divided into three parties, each party striking out for itself in the endeavor to get back into Confederate lines. The party I was with numbered twenty-two, and our first move was to get through the swamp to Pearl River, but failed. One of the parties, numbering about twenty-two, surrendered to the *Hollyhock*, that same evening. My party tramped about in the swamp until dark, when we went to a planter's house to get something to eat. This he gave us in a hurry in order to get rid of us as quickly as possible, for fear that the enemy would find us there and arrest him for harboring Confederates. That night we slept in the hayloft, contrary to his orders, and the next morning we went to another planter's for breakfast. Breakfast was served in short order, and we were then requested to move on. This we did, and we soon found ourselves on a public road, where we were captured by a company of cavalry.

We were then kept under guard for three days, while a detachment went out to search for the *Webb's* crew. Then we were marched to New Orleans and all over it like a circus train. As we passed windows ladies waved handkerchiefs and showered flowers upon us, while repulsive and frenzied Negroes danced around us in the street and amused themselves by spitting on us and kicking us. After being exhibited all over the city as so many wild animals, we were marched to the old Picayune Press and kept in confinement for two weeks, when we were exchanged.

We heard nothing of Captain Read and his party until about the time of our release, when we learned that a Federal gunboat picked them up and brought them to New Orleans as prisoners. Shortly after our release the surrender came and thus ended my occupation as a sailor in the Confederate navy.

X
Galveston, Texas

1. Battle of Galveston

On October 4, 1862, eight Federal warships sailed unmolested into the harbor of Galveston, Texas. While there were no Union troops on board the Federal vessels, the naval fleet under the command of Commodore William B. Renshaw effectively controlled the Texas port.

On November 29, 1862, Major General John Bankhead Magruder arrived to assume command of the Department of Texas. Acting on Magruder's orders, Commander William W. Hunter, CSN, made every effort to arm several of the boats on the Trinity River that had been purchased by the Confederate government. Two iron-strapped river steamers, which were being operated by the Texas Marine Department, were reasonably large and could carry a sizable boarding party. These two boats, the CSS *Bayou City* and the CSS *Neptune*, were moved to Harrisburg, Texas, on the Buffalo Bayou where workers built bulwarks of lumber and cotton bales. Two smaller vessels, the CSS *John F. Carr* and the CSS *Lucy Gwin*, were fitted out at Houston as transports.

Workers first stripped off the upper cabins and pilot house of the *Bayou City*, and cotton bales were stacked three tiers high. Another row, two bales high, backed these and provided a protected firing platform for sharpshooters. Boarding planks were constructed on each side of the boat and hoisted beside the smokestacks where they could be dropped instantly on an enemy vessel. Mounted on a pivot, and protruding ominously from among the cotton bales on the bow, was an old 32-pounder which had been reworked into a rifle. A company of cavalry, Colonel Thomas Green's 5th Texas, and a number of volunteers from Colonel Arthur Bagby's 7th Texas Cavalry, all went aboard as sharpshooters. From a distance the 165 foot *Bayou City*, under the command of Captain Henry S. Lubbock who held the rank of master in the Confederate Navy, now resembled an ironclad ram. (Scharf, *History of the Confederate States Navy*, p. 505.)

The *Neptune* sported two small 24-pounder howitzers, and she, too, was "armored" with cotton bales. Commanded by Captain William H. Sangster, the *Neptune* also carried her complement of sharpshooters, these being under the charge of Colonel Bayley of the 7th Texas Cavalry. The *Lady Gwinn* and the *John F. Carr* had cotton bales protecting their engines and machinery, but being designed to act as tenders, were otherwise unarmed. All the "Horse-Marines," as the men described themselves, were armed with Enfield rifles and double barrel shotguns. The Confederate naval force of approximately 250 men was under the command of one-time river boat captain, Major Leon Smith, who, records indicate, had also served in the Texas Navy during that republic's struggle for independence. (*Official Records Navy*, Series I, Volume XIX, p. 471.)

General Magruder was determined to retake Galveston, and his report on February 26, 1863, describes his successful attack, and also describes the naval action that took place in the harbor of Galveston. [RTC]

Report of the Battle of Galveston, Texas by Maj. Gen. J. Bankhead Magruder, CSA

Official Records Army, Series I, Volume XV, No. 21, pp. 211–220.

HDQRS. DIST. or TEXAS, *NEW MEXICO, AND ARIZONA*,
Galveston, *February 26, 1863.*

SIR: On my arrival in Texas I found the harbors of this coast in the possession of the enemy, from the Sabine River to Corpus Christi; the line of the Rio Grande virtually abandoned, most of the guns having been removed from that frontier to San Antonio, only about 300 or 400 men remaining at Brownsville. I resolved to regain the harbors if possible and to occupy the valley of the Rio Grande in force. The latter would be a very serious undertaking, on account of the scarcity of supplies in Mexico and the difficulty of transporting them across the desert from Eastern Texas. Having announced this determination as soon as I arrived on the Sabine, Captain A. R. Wier, of Cook's regiment of artillery, commanding a fort on that river, stepped forward and volunteered with his company to man a steamboat on the Sabine and to clear the Pass. This officer and this company had the honor to be the first volunteers for the desperate enterprise of expelling the enemy's fleets from our waters.

I remained a day or two in Houston, and then proceeding to Virginia Point, on the main-land, opposite to Galveston Island I took with me a party of 80 men, supported by 300 more, and passing through the city of Galveston at night I inspected the forts abandoned by our troops when the city was given up. I found the forts open in the rear, and taken in reverse by every one of the enemy's ships in the harbor. They were therefore utterly useless for my purposes. The railway track had been permitted to remain from Virginia Point to Galveston, and by its means I purposed to transport to a position near to the enemy's fleet the heavy gun hereinafter mentioned, and by assembling all the movable artillery that could be collected together in the neighborhood I hoped to acquire sufficient force to be able to expel the enemy's vessels from the harbor.

Meeting here Capt. Leon Smith, whom from my acquaintance with him in California I knew to be of great experience in steamboat management, I employed him in the quartermaster's department, placing him as a volunteer aide on my staff. I entrusted to his charge all the steamers on the Sabine River and in the bayous emptying into Galveston Bay, and at the same time directed that those on the Sabine should be fitted out forthwith. Learning subsequently that the enemy had landed at Galveston a considerable force (strength unknown), I directed Capt. Leon Smith, without delaying preparations on the Sabine, to fit up as gunboats the steamers *Bayou City* and *Neptune*, and to employ two others as tenders, for the purpose of supplying the larger vessels with wood. At the same time I received information that other Federal troops were on the way to Galveston. I therefore directed that the work on the last-mentioned steamer should be carried on night and day, and that captains and crews should be forthwith provided for them.

Fearing that the enemy might land troops at Galveston and fortify himself there, I determined to make the first attack at that point, with the object of destroying in detail his land forces as fast as they might arrive. Captain Wier, who had first volunteered, was therefore, with his company, ordered from the Sabine on board of the *Bayou City*. Captain Martin, commanding a company of cavalry, having arrived from New Iberia, La., volunteered his services, and was likewise assigned to duty on board the same steamer. When the boats designed for the Galveston expedition were nearly ready I called for volunteers from Sibley's brigade, then stationed in the neighborhood; under orders for Monroe, La. It is proper to state that I had previously ascertained that the services of these troops at Galveston would not delay a moment their departure for Louisiana, they being unable for want of transportation to move in that direction. This call was for 300 men. It was promptly responded to, Colonels Green and Bagby volunteering to lead the men of their respective regiments. After these officers had volunteered Col. James Reily, commanding the brigade, also offered to lead the troops from his command, but his services in that capacity were declined, as he was then the brigade commander. About 60 men of Reily's regiment likewise volunteered, but they did not accompany the expedition, having been ordered back to their regiment by Colonel Reily after having once reported to Colonel Green, who commanded the land forces on the steamers. In addition to these troops Lieutenant Harby, late captain in the revenue service of the United States, with a company of infantry acting as artillery, was ordered on board the *Neptune*. The men destined for the naval expedition were armed with Enfield rifles, which I had brought with me from Richmond, and with double-barrel shot-guns.

The enemy's fleet, then lying in the waters of Galveston, consisted of the *Harriet Lane*, carrying four heavy guns and two 24-pounder howitzers, commanded by Captain Wainwright, U.S. Navy; the *Westfield*, flag-ship of Commodore Renshaw, a large propeller, mounting eight heavy guns; the *Owasco*, a similar ship to the *Westfield*, mounting eight heavy guns; the *Clifton* a steam propeller, four heavy guns; the *Sachem*, a steam propeller, four heavy guns; two armed transports, two large barks, and an armed schooner. The enemy's land forces were stationed at the end of a long wharf and were crowded into large buildings immediately under the guns of the steamships. The approaches landward to this position were impeded by two lines of strong barricades, and communication with the shore was destroyed by the removal of portions of the wharf in front of the barricades. It thus became necessary for our storming parties to advance by wading through the water, and to enable them to mount on the end of the wharf fifty sealing ladders were constructed. As there were no breastworks or other protection for our artillery making the attack on the enemy's ships and land forces, my object was to bring to bear as heavy a fire of artillery as possible after reaching the wharves and other points selected for the purpose under cover of the night. I knew that the co operation of the cotton boats with the land forces would be extremely difficult to attain, the distance the former had to run being 30 miles. I therefore had not calculated with confidence on a success greater than that of the expulsion of the enemy's fleet from the harbor. If the desired co-operation should be secured the result would be immediately accomplished, and would be attended probably with the capture or destruction of some of the enemy's ships. If the co-operation should fail, I nevertheless felt satisfied that by throwing up entrenchments at the ends of the streets leading to the water I could gradually expel the fleet from the harbor. For this purpose entrenching tools in large quantities were prepared.

To attain the object in view I had at my disposal six siege pieces, the heaviest weighing 5,400 pounds. I also caused to be constructed a railroad ram, armed with an 8-inch Dahlgren and mounted on a railway flat. This flat and gun were carried by railway to a point within a few hundred yards of the *Harriet Lane*. A large quantity of cotton was transported in the same way, with the view of using it in making a breastwork for this gun should we not succeed in our object before daylight. In addition I had fourteen field pieces, some of them rifled and some smooth-bore. Three of the heaviest of the siege guns had to be transported 9 miles, the others 7 miles, between sunset, and 12 o'clock, under cover of the darkness and over very difficult roads.

A system of rapid communication with our gunboats by telegraph and otherwise having been established, it was arranged that the attack should take place at 12 midnight, the fire of our land batteries constituting the signal for the naval attack. Nevertheless I informed Commodore Smith, in command of the naval expedition, that I would attack the enemy's fleet whether gunboats made their appearance or not.

The key of the whole position was Fort Point, at the mouth of the harbor, 2 miles below the mouth of the town [?]. This fort was entirely open in the rear, thus affording no protection for our artillery against the enemy's vessels inside of the harbor. The attack from this point was entrusted to Captain S. T. Fontaine, of Cook's regiment artillery, supported by six companies of Pyron's regiment dismounted dragoons, under command of the gallant Colonel Pyron. Wilson's battery of six pieces was to attack the enemy from the center wharf; the railroad ram was sent to the upper wharf. The remainder of the artillery was manned from Cook's regiment and posted in eligible positions. Colonel [J. J.] Cook himself was entrusted with the command of the storming party of about 500 men, composed of details from Pyron's and Elmore's regiments and Griffin's battalion, and furnished with ladders to scale the wharf on which the enemy's land forces were barricaded. Brig. Gen. W. R. Scurry was placed in command of Pyron's regiment and of the remainder of Sibley's brigade, and Elmore's men, commanded by Lieutenant-Colonel [L. A.] Abercrombie, the latter acting as a support for the whole. Lieut. Col. J. H. Manly, of Cook's regiment, was ordered to Virginia Point to defend that work, which was our base of operations, and which was connected with Galveston Island by a railroad bridge 2 miles in length, open to the attack of the enemy.

Major General J. Bankhead Magruder (Library of Congress).

Leading the center assault in person, I approached within two squares of the wharves, at which point I directed the horses of the field pieces to be removed from them and placed behind some brick buildings for shelter from the anticipated discharges of grape and canister. After allowing the lapse of what turned out to be ample time for Captain Fontaine to reach and occupy his more distant position the guns were placed along a line of about 2½ miles, principally within the limits of the city. It having been agreed that the fire of the center gun should furnish signal for a general attack, I proceeded to carry out this portion of the plan by discharging the piece myself. The signal was promptly responded to by an almost simultaneous and very effective discharge along the whole line. The moon had by that time gone down, but still the light of the stars enabled us to see the Federal ships. The enemy did not hesitate long in replying to our attack. He soon opened on us from his fleet with a tremendous discharge of shell, which was followed with grape and canister. Our men, however, worked steadily at their guns under cover of the darkness. Colonel Cook now advanced with his storming party to the assault; his men, wading through the water and bearing with them their scaling ladders, endeavored to reach the end of the wharf on which the enemy were stationed. Colonel Cook was supported by Griffin's battalion and by sharpshooters deployed on the right and left, in order to distract the enemy's attention. A severe conflict took place at this point, our men being exposed to a fire of grape and canister and shell item the ships its well as of musketry from the land forces. The water was deep, the wharf proving higher than was anticipated, and the scaling ladders, as was reported to me by Colonel Cook, were found to be too short to enable the men to accomplish their object. After an obstinate contest the infantry were directed to cover themselves and fire from the buildings nearest this wharf, which was accordingly done.

The enemy's fire was deadly. The ships being not more than 300 yards from our batteries it, was extremely difficult to maintain the positions we had assumed, and some of the artillery-men were driven from their pieces. As daylight, which was now approaching, would expose these men still more to the enemy's fire, and as our gunboats had not yet made their appearance, I ordered the artillery to be withdrawn to positions which afforded more protection, but from which the fire could be continued on the adversary with greater advantage to us. Knowing Captain Fontaine to be in a position the most exposed of all I at the same time dispatched a staff officer with instructions to have his pieces likewise withdrawn. This order reaching Captain Fontaine's men before it was received by their captain, and the concentrated fire from the enemy's ships, but a few hundred yards distant, having increased in intensity, they were compelled to leave their pieces. They were, however, soon formed by Captain Fontaine in a position of greater security.

The delicate duty of withdrawing the pieces in the city from the close vicinity of the enemy was entrusted to Brigadier-General Scurry, who performed it with skill and gallantry. Preparations were then ordered for the immediate fortification and permanent occupation of the city. But at this moment, our fire still continuing, our gunboats came dashing down the harbor and engaged the *Harriet Lane*, which was the nearest of the enemy's ships, in the most gallant style, running into her, one on each side, and pouring on her deck a deadly fire of rifles and shot-guns. The gallant Captain Wainwright fought his ship admirably. He succeeding in disabling the *Neptune* and attempted to run down the *Bayou City*, but he was met by an antagonist of even superior skill, coolness, and heroism. Leon Smith, ably seconded by Capt. [Henry S.] Lubbock, the immediate commander of the *Bayou City*, and by her pilot, Captain McCormick, adroitly evaded the deadly stroke, although as the vessels passed each other he lost his larboard wheel-house in the shock. Again the *Bayou City*, while receiving several broadsides almost at the cannon's mouth, poured into the *Harriet Lane* a destructive fire of small-arms. Turning once more she drove her prow into the iron wheel of the *Harriet Lane*, thus locking the two vessels together. Followed by the officers and men of the heroic volunteer corps, Commodore Leon Smith leaped to the deck of the hostile ship, and after a moment of feeble resistance she was ours. The surviving officers of the *Harriet Lane* presented their swords to Commodore Leon Smith on the quarter-deck of the captured vessel. After the surrender the *Ownsee* passed alongside pouring into the *Harriet Lane* a broadside at close quarters, but she was soon forced to back out by the effect of our musketry.

Commodore Smith then sent a flag to Commodore Renshaw, whose ship had in the mean time been run aground, demanding the surrender of the whole fleet, and giving three hours' time to consider. These propositions were accepted by the commanding officer, and all the enemy's vessels were immediately brought to anchor, with white flags flying. Most of this time was occupied in attempting to get the *Harriet Lane* to the wharf in order to remove the wounded to a place of safety. The ships and boats were so much damaged that this was found to be almost impossible with the means at hand. Proceeding myself to the wharf I met one of my most distinguished and scientific staff officers, Maj. A.M. Lea, who informed me that on board the *Harriet Lane* he had found his son, the second in command, mortally wounded. He represented to me that there were other officers badly wounded, and urged me to delay, if possible, their removal. It now being within an hour of the expiration of the period of truce I sent another flag to Commodore Renshaw, whose ship was among the most distant, claiming all his vessels immediately under our guns as prizes, and giving him further time to consider the demand for the surrender of the whole fleet. This message was borne by Colonel Green and Captain Lubbock. While these gentlemen were on their way in a boat to fulfill their mission Commodore Renshaw blew up his ship and was himself accidentally blown up with it. They boarded the ship of the next in command, who dropped down the bay, still having them on board, and carried them some distance toward the bar, while still flying the white flag at the mast-head.

In the meantime General Scurry sent to know if he should fire at the ships immediately in his front at the expiration of the period of truce. To this I replied in the negative, as another demand under a flag of truce from me had been sent to the commodore. When the first period of truce expired the enemy's ships under our guns, regardless of the white flags still flying at their mast-heads, gradually crept off. As soon as this was seen I sent a swift express on horseback to General Scurry, directing him to open fire on them. This was done with so much effect that one of them was reported to have sunk near the bar and the *Owasco* was seriously damaged.

I forward a correspondence on this subject between Commodore Bell and myself. In this correspondence Commodore Bell states that the truce was violated by the firing of cannon and small-arms by our men on shore, as he had been informed. This is an error; not a gun or small-arm was discharged during the stipulated period or until the enemy's vessels were discovered to be creeping off out of the harbor. Commodore Leon Smith fired a heavy stern gun at the retiring ships with effect from the *Harriet Lane*. Jumping on board the steamer *Carr*, he proceeded to Bolivar Channel and captured and brought in the immediate presence of the enemy's armed vessels the two barks and schooner before spoken of. As soon as it was light enough to see the land force surrendered to General Scurry.

We thus captured one fine steamship, two barks, and one schooner. We ran ashore the flag-ship of the commodore, drove off two war steamers, and sunk another, as reported, all of the U.S. Navy, and the armed transports, and took 300 or 400 prisoners. The number of guns captured was fifteen, and, being found on Pelican Spit, a large quantity of stores, coal, and other material also was taken. The *Neptune* sank; her officers and crew, with the exception of those killed in battle, were saved, as were also her guns. The loss on our side was 26 killed and 117 wounded. Among the former was the gallant Captain Wier, the first volunteer for the expedition. The alacrity with which officers and men, all of them totally unacquainted with this novel kind of service, some of whom had never seen a ship before, volunteered for an enterprise so extraordinarily and apparently desperate in its character and the bold and dashing manner in which the plan was executed, are certainly deserving of the highest praise.

Although it may appear invidious to make distinctions, I nevertheless regard it as a duty to say that too much credit cannot be bestowed on Commodore Leon Smith, whose professional ability, energy, and perseverance amidst many discouraging influences were so conspicuously displayed in the preparation for the attack, while in its execution his heroism was sublime. In the latter he was most ably and gallantly seconded by Colonel Green, commanding the land forces serving on board of our fleet; by Captain Lubbock, commanding the *Bayou City*; by her pilot, Captain McCormick; Captain Wier, commanding the artillery; Captain Martin, commanding dismounted dragoons, and by the officers and men on board of that boat. Though in the case of the *Neptune* the result was not so favorable, her attack on the *Harriet Lane* was equally bold and dashing and had its weight in the capture. Colonel Bagby, commanding the land troops on board the *Neptune*; Captain Sangster; her pilots, Captains Swift and McGovern; Captain Harby, and the officers and crew of the ship, likewise deserve, as they have received, my thanks for their participation in this brilliant battle. The engineers, among whom Captain Seymour, of the *Bayou City*, and Captain Conner, of the *Neptune*, were distinguished by remarkable coolness, skill, and devotion in the discharge of their important duties.

In the land attack especially commendations are due to Brig. Gen. W. R. Scurry, Col. X. B. Debray, Major Von Harten, Cook's regiment of artillery; Captain Fontaine, Cook's regiment; Maj. J. Kellersberg, of the Engineer Corps; also to Colonels Cook, Pyron,

Lieutenant-Colonel Abercrombie, commanding Elmore's men; Major Griffin, Major Wilson, of the artillery; Captain Mason, Captain McMahan, and to the accomplished and devoted Lieutenant Sherman, who fell at his piece mortally wounded, and to Privates Brown and Shoppman, of Daly's company of cavalry, the latter of whom kept up the fire of one piece almost without assistance under the enemy's grape and canister.

The officers of my staff exhibited on this, as on previous occasions, conspicuous ability and gallantry. When some of the men were compelled to leave their pieces at one of the wharves nearest the enemy Major Dickinson, assistant adjutant-general, calling for volunteers, dashed down the street in order to withdraw the pieces. Whilst in the act of consummating this design he was badly wounded by a fragment of a shell striking him in the left eye, which unfortunately has lost its sight. Capt. E. P. Turner, assistant adjutant-general, likewise behaved with conspicuous gallantry. Lieuts. George A. Magruder and H. M. Stanard, my aides-de-camp, executed my orders with remarkable gallantry, promptness, and intelligence. These two officers have thus been distinguished in the battles of Bethel, Yorktown, Savage Station, and Malvern Hill. It is only just that I should commend them to the special consideration of the Government. Lieutenant Magruder volunteered for the service, and brought off in the most gallant manner some pieces which the men had been compelled to retire from. Lieutenant Stanard behaved with equal gallantry in the execution of orders, exposing himself to the enemy's fire. Lieutenant Colonel McNeill of Sibley's brigade, adjutant and inspector general, rendered distinguished service in carrying out my orders, as also did Lieutenant Carrington, of the same regiment, acting on my staff. Mr. Dennis Brashear, who has been in every battle in which I have been engaged, except that of Bethel, and served with great gallantry everywhere without pay or reward of any kind for more than a year, rendered important and most gallant services on this occasion. I am also under obligations to Lieutenant-Colonel Nichols, volunteer aide, whose ability and local knowledge were of great service in arranging the details of the attack. I likewise thankfully acknowledge the services of Judge P. W. Gray and the Hon. J. A. Wilcox, members of Congress from Texas, who, as volunteer aides, accompanied me to the front when the battle opened and remained with me during the continuance. The assistance of General [Thomas B.] Howard, of the Militia, and his adjutant-general, Major Tucker, residents of Galveston, was of great value, as was also that of Mr. E. W. Cave, volunteer aide, from Houston. Hon. M. M. Potter, of Galveston, was likewise conspicuous during the engagement for his activity and devotion.

I take this occasion to recommend to the special consideration of the President the conduct of Governor J. R. Baylor, of Arizona, who, though not in command of any troops nor attached to any staff, was conspicuous for his gallant conduct as a private, serving the guns during the hottest of the fire, and with his coat off working to place them in position during the night.

Lieutenant-Colonel Manly sustained the operations from Virginia Point with great ability and activity. Captain [W. J.] Pendleton, acting aide-de, camp, who accompanied the troops, proved himself to be an officer of very remarkable ability, energy, and devotion. Captain Stoy, assistant quartermaster, is also deserving of high commendation. Maj. J. B. Eustis, acting ordnance officer on my staff, assisted by Lieut. M. Hughes, of the artillery, performed admirably his difficult and important duties in the preparation for the attack. The former by my order remained in charge of his depot at Virginia Point, while the latter discharged gallantly his duties on the field. I likewise take pleasure in recognizing the efficient and gallant services of Major [O. M.] Watkins, in charge of conscript business, on my staff; of Colonel [C. G.] Forshey, of the Engineer Corps; of Capt. H. Pendleton, assistant quartermaster, who accompanied me to the front; and of Major [E. B.] Pendleton, chief commissary, on my staff, who discharged his important duties with gallant ability.

Lieutenants Stringfellow, Jones, and Hill, of the artillery, behaved with remarkable gallantry during the engagement, each of them volunteering to take charge of guns and personally directing the fire after the officers originally in charge of them had been wounded.

It would be improper to close this report without directing the particular attention of the Government to invaluable services rendered by Major B. Bloomfield, quartermaster, of my staff, and by Captain [E. C.] Wharton, assistant quartermaster at Houston. These officers, by their intelligence, energy, and activity proved themselves fully adequate to all the demands made upon them in the preparation of the means appropriate to their department, and contributed materially to the successful result of the expedition. Nor should I here omit to mention Captain [W. S.] Good, in command of ordnance. I commend him especially to the Chief of Ordnance and to the consideration of His Excellency the President.

Besides the names mentioned above I would call attention to the names of the officers and men reported by their respective commanding officers to have distinguished themselves by gallant and meritorious services. As it would have been imprudent to give full warning to the inhabitants of Galveston of my intention to attack the Federal fleet, lest information of the design might reach the enemy, as soon as the head of our column entered the suburbs of the town I directed the ambulances, in charge of one of my staff officers, to proceed to the Convent of Ursuline Nuns near that point, and place the conveyances at their disposal for their immediate removal to the houses provided for them. I also in like manner informed the foreign consuls and the mayor of the contemplated attack, and gave them time to move their families and the citizens most exposed to a place of safety. The noble women of the convent, while recognizing the courtesy extended to them, expressed a preference to remain and nurse the wounded, offering their building as a hospital. Many of the inhabitants left the houses most exposed to the enemy's fire, and I am happy to state that although many edifices were much injured and the town riddled by balls no casualty occurred among the citizens. The wounded of the enemy were conducted to the same hospital, and the same attentions were bestowed on them as if they had been our own men. Captain Wainwright and Lieutenant Lea, of the Federal Navy, were buried with masonic and military honors in the same grave; Major Lea, of the Confederate Army; father of Lieutenant Lea, performing the funeral services.

Having buried the dead, taken care of the wounded, and secured the captured property, my exertions were directed to getting the *Harriet Lane* to sea. The enemy's ships fled to New Orleans, to which place one of their steam transports was dispatched during the action. I knew that a large naval force might be expected to return in a few days. I therefore ordered the employment at high wages of all the available mechanics to repair the *Harriet Lane*, her main shaft having been dislocated and her iron wheel greatly disabled, so that the engine could not work. The United States flags were ordered to remain flying on the custom-house and at the mastheads of the ships, so as to attract into the harbor any of the enemy's vessels which might be bound for the port of Galveston. A line of iron buoys which we had established for the guidance of his ships in the harbor were displaced and so arranged as to insure their getting aground.

On the 3d of January, I being then on board of the *Harriet Lane*, a yawl-boat, containing several men, in command of a person named Thomas Smith, recently a citizen of Galveston, and who had deserted from our army, was reported alongside. He informed me that he was sent from the United States transport steamship *Cambria*, then off the bar, for a pilot, and that they had no idea of the occupation of the city by us. I forthwith ordered a pilot boat, under command of Captain Johnson, to bring in this ship, but through a most extraordinary combination of circumstances the vessel which contained E. J. Davis and many other apostate Texans, besides several hundred troops, and 2,500 saddles for the use of native sympathizers, succeeded in making her escape. The man Smith, who had, it is said, several times set fire to the city of Galveston before he deserted, had been known as Nicaraugua Smith, and was dreaded by every one. He returned to Galveston in order to act as Federal provost-marshal. His arrival produced much excitement, during which some one without orders sent a sailboat to Pelican Spit, now occupied by our troops, to direct the commanding officer there not to fire on our pilot boat, although she was under Yankee colors. The sail-boat thus sent was at once supposed to be destined for the Yankee transport. The pilot boat gave chase to her, and the guns from the shore opened on her within hearing of the ship.

Night coming on, I thought it surer, as the alarm might be taken, to capture her at sea before morning, but the *Harriet Lane* could not move, and our cotton gunboats could not live on the rough sea on the bar. Therefore one of the barks, the *Royal Yacht*, a schooner of ours, the pilot boat, and the *Leader*, a schooner loaded with cotton, which I had ordered to be sent to a foreign port, with a proclamation of the raising of the blockade at Galveston, were directed to be prepared and armed with light artillery. This was done by 2 o'clock the same night, our little fleet being manned by volunteers, under the command of Captain Mason, of Cook's regiment of artillery.

Unfortunately the wind lulled and none but the pilot-boat could reach the enemy's ship. The pilot-boat went out under the command of a gallant sailor, Captain Payne, of Galveston. The enemy's ship proved to be a splendid iron steamer, built in the Clyde. I had ascertained from her men taken ashore that she had only two guns, and they were packed on deck under a large quantity of hay, and I anticipated an easy conquest and one of great political importance, as this ship contained almost all the Texans out of the State who had proved recreant to their duty to the Confederacy and to Texas. The pilot-boat was allowed to get close to the ship, when the boat was hailed and the pilot ordered to come on board. Captain Payne answered that he thought there were rather too many men to trust himself to; whereupon he was directed to come on board or he would be fired into. He went on board as ordered, and soon after the steamer sailed in all haste seaward, leaving the pilot-boat and hands to return to us.

I am thus particular in this narration, as the friends of Captain Payne fear that he may meet with foul play from the enemy. I shall ascertain, through Commodore Bell, his fate, and act accordingly. Smith, the deserter, was tried regularly the next day before a general court-martial, and being convicted of deserting to the enemy, was publicly shot in Galveston in accordance with his sentence. The proceedings, which were formal in all respects, legal and regular, are forwarded.

At the time of these occurrences I received through Colonel [W. G.] Webb reliable information of an insurrection among the Germans in Colorado, Fayette, and Austin Counties, 800 being reported in arms to resist the conscript law and the State draft. I immediately ordered the Arizona brigade, with a section of artillery, to the disaffected region, declared martial law in these three counties, and had the ringleaders arrested and lodged in jail. The rest yielded, and tranquillity and obedience to the laws are now prevalent.

Major Webb contributed much by his personal activity and influence to produce these results, and I earnestly recommend him to the President for the appointment of assistant adjutant-general, with the rank of lieutenant-colonel, to be stationed in the disaffected regions, and to take charge of the business growing out of these affairs and those of the militia. He was an officer of the old Army, and colonel under General Taylor in the Mexican war.

The German ringleaders above mentioned have been turned over to the civil authorities for trial.

I have the honor to announce that the whole coast and islands are now in our possession and that the Rio Grande is strongly occupied.

I am, very respectfully, your obedient servant,

J. BANKHEAD MAGRUDER,
Major-general, Commanding.

General S. COOPER,
Adjutant and Inspector General, Richmond, Va.

2. Alabama vs. Hatteras

Northern newspapers, found on several prizes seized by the Confederate commerce raider CSS *Alabama*, had spelled out in great detail the plans for the sailing of a large Federal expeditionary force with the intent of invading Texas. This force, led by General Nathaniel P. Banks, consisted of 30,000 troops transported in 100 transports, and was scheduled to arrive off Union-held Galveston, according to the newspapers, on January 10, 1863. No Federal warships were being dispatched with the invading force, for Union authorities felt there was little danger of interference by Confederate naval forces. Captain Raphael Semmes, commander of the *Alabama*, planned to surprise the transports in a night attack, steam through their midst firing at every target, and then make his escape. (Campbell, *Gray Thunder: Exploits of the Confederate States Navy*, p. 96.)

On January 5, 1863, the *Alabama* left the pristine waters and island paradise of Las Arcas off the Yucatan and headed north. The selection below from Semmes' book *Memoirs of Service Afloat* details this endeavor and the resulting battle with the USS *Hatteras*. [RTC]

The Sinking of the USS Hatteras *by Captain Raphael Semmes, CSN*

Memoirs of Service Afloat (Baltimore: Kelly, Piet, 1869), pp. 540–550.

As has been mentioned to the reader, the Banks' expedition was expected to rendezvous at Galveston, on the 10th of January. On the 5th of that month we got under way from the Areas, giving ourselves five days in which to make the distance, under sail. Our secret was still perfectly safe, as only a single sail had passed us, whilst we lay at anchor, and she at too great a distance to be able to report us. We had an abundant supply of coal on board, the ship was in excellent trim, and as the sailors used to say of her, at this period, could be made to do everything but "talk." My crew were well drilled, my powder was in good condition, and as to the rest, I trusted to luck, and to the "creek's not being too high." The weather continued fine throughout our run, and on the 11th at noon having been delayed a day by a calm, we observed in latitude 28° 51' 45", and longitude 94° 55', being just thirty miles from Galveston. I now laid my ship's head for the Galveston light-house, and stood in, intending to get a distant sight of the Banks' fleet before nightfall, and then haul off, and await the approach of night, before I ran in, and made the assault.

I instructed the man at the mast-head, to keep a very bright look-out, and told him what to look out for, viz., an immense fleet anchored off a light-house. The wind was light, and the afternoon was pretty well spent before there was any sign from the mast-head. The look-out at length cried, "Land ho! sail ho!" in quick succession, and I already began to make sure of my game. But the look-out, upon being questioned, said he did not see any fleet of transports, but only five steamers which looked like ships of war. Here was a damper! What could have become of Banks, and his great expedition, and what was this squadron of steam ships-of-war doing here? Presently a shell, thrown by one of the steamers, was seen to burst over the city. "Ah, ha!" exclaimed I to the officer of the deck who was standing by me, "there has been a change of program here. The enemy would not be firing into his own people, and we must have recaptured Galveston, since our last advices." "So it would seem," replied the officer. And so it turned out. In the interval between our leaving the West Indies, and arriving off Galveston, this city had been retaken by General Magruder, assisted by a gallant seaman of the merchant service, Captain Leon Smith. Smith, with a couple of small river steamers, protected by cotton bags, and having a number of sharpshooters on board, assaulted and captured, or drove to sea the enemy's entire fleet, consisting of several heavily armed steamships.

The recapture of this place from the enemy changed the destination of the Banks' expedition. It rendezvoused at New Orleans, whence General Banks, afterward, attempted the invasion of Texas by the valley of the Red River. He was here met by General Dick Taylor, who, with a much inferior force, demolished him, giving him such a scare, that it was with difficulty Porter could stop him at Alexandria, to assist him in the defence of his fleet, until he could extricate it from the shallows of the river where it was aground. The hero of Boston Common had not had such a scare since Stonewall Jackson had chased him through Winchester, Virginia.

What was best to be done in this changed condition of affairs? I certainly had not come all the way into the Gulf of Mexico, to fight five ships of war, the least of which was probably my equal. And yet, how could I very well run away, in the face of the promises I had given my crew? For I had told them at the Areas islands; that they were, if the fates proved propitious, to have some sport off Galveston. Whilst I was pondering the difficulty, the enemy himself, happily, came to my relief; for pretty soon the look-out again called from aloft, and said, "One of the steamers, sir, is coming out in chase of us." The *Alabama* had given chase pretty often, but this was the first time she had been chased. It was just the thing I wanted, however, for I at once conceived the design of drawing this single ship of the enemy far enough away from the remainder of her fleet, to enable me to decide a battle with her before her consorts could come to her relief.

The *Alabama* was still under sail, though, of course, being so near the enemy, the water was warm in her boilers, and in a condition to give us steam in ten minutes. To carry out my design of decoying the enemy, I now wore ship, as though I were fleeing from his pursuit. This, no doubt, encouraged him, though, as it would seem, the captain of the pursuing ship pretty soon began to smell a rat, as the reader will see presently by his report of the engagement. I now lowered my propeller, still holding on to my sails, however, and gave the ship a small head of steam, to prevent the stranger from overhauling me too rapidly. We were still too close to the fleet, to think of engaging him. I thus decoyed him on, little by little, now turning my propeller over slowly, and now stopping it altogether. In the meantime night set in, before we could get a distinct view of our pursuer. She was evidently a large steamer, but we knew from her build and rig, that she belonged neither to the class of old steam frigates, or that of the new sloops, and we were quite willing to try our strength with any of the other classes.

At length, when I judged that I had drawn the stranger out about twenty miles from his fleet, I furled my sails, beat to quarters, prepared my ship for action, and wheeled to meet him. The two ships now approached each other, very rapidly. As we came within speaking distance, we simultaneously stopped our engines, the ships being about one hundred yards apart. The enemy was the first to hail. "What ship is that?" cried he. "This is her Britannic Majesty's steamer *Petrel*," we replied. We now hailed in turn, and demanded to know who be was. The reply not coming to us very distinctly, we repeated our question, when we heard the words, "This is the United States ship..." the name of the ship being lost to us. But we had heard enough. All we wanted to know was, that the stranger was a United States ship, and therefore our enemy. A pause now ensued—a rather awkward pause, as the reader may suppose. Presently, the stranger hailed again, and said, "If you please, I will send a boat on board of you." His object was, of course, to verify or discredit the answer we had given him, that we were one of her Britannic Majesty's cruisers. We replied, "Certainly, we shall be happy to receive your boat;" and we heard a boatswain's mate call away a boat, and could hear the creaking of the tackles, as she was lowered into the water.

Things were now come to a crisis, and it being useless to delay our engagement with the enemy any longer, I turned to my first lieutenant, and said, "I suppose you are all ready for action?" "We are," he replied; "the men are eager to begin, and are only waiting for the word." I then said to him, "Tell the enemy who we are, for we must not strike him in disguise, and when you have done so, give him the broadside." Kell now sang out, in his powerful, clarion voice, through his trumpet, "This is the Confederate States steamer *Alabama*!" and turning to the crew, who were all standing at their guns, the gunners with their sights on the enemy, and lock-strings in hand, gave the order, fire! Away went the broadside in an instant, our little ship feeling, perceptibly, the recoil of her guns. The night was clear. There was no moon, but sufficient star-light to enable the two ships to see each other quite distinctly, at the distance of half a mile, or more, and a state of the atmosphere highly favorable to the conduct of sound. The wind, besides, was blowing in the direction of the enemy's fleet. As a matter of course, our guns awakened the echoes of the coast, far and near, announcing very distinctly to the Federal Admiral Bell, a Southern man, who had gone over to the enemy, that the ship which he had sent out to chase the strange sail, had a fight on her hands. He immediately, as we afterward learned, got under way; with the *Brooklyn*, his flag-ship, and two others of his steamers, and came out to the rescue.

Our broadside was returned instantly; the enemy, like ourselves, having been on his guard, with his men standing at their guns. The two ships, when the action commenced, had swerved in such a way, that they were now heading in the same direction—the *Alabama* fighting her starboard-broadside, and her antagonist her port-broadside. Each ship, as she delivered her broadside, put herself under steam, and the action became a running fight, in parallel lines, or nearly so, the ships now nearing, and now separating a little from each other. My men handled their pieces with great spirit and commendable coolness, and the action was sharp and exciting while it lasted; which, however, was not very long, for in just thirteen minutes after firing the first gun, the enemy hoisted alight, and fired an off-gun, as a signal that he had been beaten. We at once withheld our fire, and such a cheer went up from the brazen throats of my fellows, as must have astonished even a Texan, if he had heard it. We now steamed up quite close to the beaten steamer, and asked her captain, formally, if he had surrendered. He replied that he had. I then inquired if he was in want of assistance, to which he responded promptly that he was, that his ship was sinking rapidly, and that he needed all our boats. There appeared to be much confusion on board the enemy's ship; officers and crew seemed to be apprehensive that we would permit them to drown, and several voices cried aloud to us for assistance, at the same time. When the captain of the beaten ship came on board to surrender his sword to me, I learned that I had been engaged with the United States steamer *Hatteras*, Captain Blake. I will now let Captain Blake tell his own story. The following is his official report to the Secretary of the Federal Navy:

UNITED STATES' CONSULATE,
KINGSTON, JAMAICA, *Jan. 21, 1863.*

SIR:-It is my painful duty to inform the Department of the destruction of the United States steamer *Hatteras*, recently under my command, by the rebel steamer *Alabama*, on the night of the 11th inst., off the coast of Texas. The circumstances of the disaster are as follows:

Upon the afternoon of the 11th inst., at half-past two o'clock, while at anchor in company with the fleet under Commodore Bell, off Galveston, Texas, I was ordered by signal from the United States flag-ship *Brooklyn*, to chase a sail to the southward and eastward. I got under way immediately, and steamed with all speed in the direction indicated. After some time the strange sail could be seen from the *Hatteras*, and was ascertained to be a steamer, which fact I communicated to the flag-ship by signal. I continued the chase and rapidly gained upon the suspicious vessel. Knowing the slow rate of speed of the *Hatteras*, I at once suspected that deception was being practiced, and hence ordered the ship to be cleared for action, with everything in readiness for a determined attack and a vigorous defence.

When within about four miles of the vessel, I observed that, she had ceased to steam, and was lying broadside and awaiting us. It was nearly seven o'clock, and quite dark; but, notwithstanding the obscurity of the night, I felt assured, from the general character of the vessel and her maneuvers, that I should soon encounter the rebel steamer *Alabama*. Being able to work but four guns on the side of the *Hatteras*—two short 32-pounders, one 30-pounder rifled Parrott gun, and one 20-pounder rifled gun—I concluded to close with her, that my guns might be effective, if necessary.

I came within easy speaking range—about seventy-five yards and upon asking, "What steamer is that?" received the answer, "Her Britannic Majesty's ship *Vixen*" I replied that I would send a boat aboard, and immediately gave the order. In the meantime, the vessels were changing positions, the stranger endeavoring to gain a desirable position for a raking fire. Almost simultaneously with the piping away of the boat, the strange craft again replied, "We are the Confederate steamer *Alabama*," which was accompanied with a broadside. I, at the same moment, returned the fire. Being well aware of the many vulnerable points of the *Hatteras*, I hoped, by closing with the *Alabama*, to be able to board her, and thus rid the seas of the piratical craft. I steamed directly for the *Alabama*, but she was enabled by her great speed, and the foulness of the bottom of the *Hatteras*, and, consequently, her diminished speed, to thwart my attempt when I had gained a distance of but thirty yards from her. At this range, musket and pistol shots were exchanged. The firing continued with great vigor on both sides. At length a shell entered amidships in the hold, setting fire to it, and, at the same instant—as I can hardly divide the time—a shell passed through the sick bay, exploding in an adjoining compartment, also producing fire. Another entered the cylinder, filling the engine-room and deck with steam, and depriving me of my power to maneuver the vessel, or to work the pumps, upon which the reduction of the fire depended.

With the vessel on fire in two places, and beyond human power, a hopeless wreck upon the waters, with her walking-beam shot away, and her engine rendered useless, I still maintained an active fire, with the double hope of disabling the *Alabama* and attracting the attention of the fleet off Galveston, which was only twenty-eight miles distant.

It was soon reported to me that the shells had entered the *Hatteras* at the water-line, tearing off entire sheets of iron, and that the water was rushing in, utterly defying every attempt to remedy the evil, and that she was rapidly sinking. Learning the melancholy truth, and observing that the *Alabama* was on my port bow, entirely beyond the range of my guns, doubtless preparing for a raking fire of the deck, I felt I had no right to sacrifice uselessly, and without any desirable result, the lives of all under my command.

To prevent the blowing up of the *Hatteras* from the fire, which was making much progress, I ordered the magazine to be flooded, and afterward a lee gun was fired. The *Alabama* then asked if assistance was desired, to which an affirmative answer was given.

The *Hatteras* was then going down, and in order to save the lives of my officers and men, I caused the armament on the port side to be thrown overboard. Had I not done so, I am confident the vessel would have gone down with many brave hearts and valuable lives. After considerable delay, caused by the report that a steamer was seen coming from Galveston, the *Alabama* sent us assistance, and I have the pleasure of informing the Department that every living being was conveyed safely from the *Hatteras* to the *Alabama*.

Two minutes after leaving the *Hatteras* she went down, bow first, with her pennant at the mast-head, with all her muskets and stores of every description, the enemy not being able, owing to her rapid sinking, to obtain a single weapon.

The battery upon the *Alabama* brought into action against the *Hatteras* numbered seven guns, consisting of four long 32-pounders, one 100-pounder, one 68-pounder, and one 24-pounder rifled gun. The great superiority of the *Alabama*, with her powerful battery and her machinery under the waterline, must be at once recognized by the Department, who are familiar with the construction of the *Hatteras*, and her total unfitness for a conflict with a regular built vessel of war.

The distance between the *Hatteras* and the *Alabama* during the action varied from twenty-five to one hundred yards. Nearly fifty shots were fired from the *Hatteras*, and I presume a greater number from the *Alabama*.

I desire to refer to the efficient and active manner in which Acting Master Porter, executive officer, performed his duty. The conduct of Assistant Surgeon Edward S. Matthews, both during the action and afterward, in attending to the wounded, demands my unqualified commendation. I would also bring to the favorable notice of the Department Acting Master's Mate McGrath, temporarily performing duty as gunner. Owing to the darkness of the night, and the peculiar construction of the *Hatteras*, I am only able to refer to the conduct of those officers who came under my especial attention; but from the character of the contest, and the amount of damage done to the *Alabama*, I have personally no reason to believe that any officer failed in his duty.

To the men of the *Hatteras* I cannot give too much praise. Their enthusiasm and bravery was of the highest order.

I enclose the report of Assistant Surgeon E. S. Matthews, by which you will observe that five men were wounded and two killed. The missing, it is hoped, reached the fleet at Galveston.

I shall communicate to the Department, in a separate report, the movements of myself and my command, from the time of our transfer to the *Alabama* until the departure of the earliest mail from this place to the United States.

I am, very respectfully, your obedient servant,

H. C. BLAKE,
Lieutenant Commanding.

Hon. GIDEON WELLES,
Secretary of the Navy, Washington.

Setting aside all the discourteous stuff and nonsense about "a rebel steamer," and a "piratical craft," of which Captain Blake, who had been bred in the old service, should have been ashamed, especially after enjoying the hospitalities of my cabin for a couple of weeks, the above is a pretty fair report of the engagement. I am a little puzzled, however, by the Captain's statement, that he could use but four guns on a side. We certainly understood from all the officers and men of the *Hatteras*, at the time, that she carried eight guns; six in broadside, and two pivots, just like the *Alabama*, the only difference between the two ships being, that the *Alabama*'s pivot guns were the heaviest.

There is another remark in the report that is quite new to me. I am informed, for the first time, that Captain Blake desired to board me. I cannot, of course, know what his intentions were, but I saw no evidence of such an intention, in the handling of his ship; and Captain Blake must himself have known that, in the terribly demoralized condition of his crew, when they found that they had really fallen in with the *Alabama*, he could not have depended upon a single boarder. What Captain Blake means by saying that his ship went down, with her pennant flying, I am at a loss, as every seaman must be, to understand. Did he not surrender his ship to me? And if so, what business had his pennant, any more than his ensign, to be flying? But this, I suppose, was a little clap-trap, like his expressions, "rebel," and "pirate," thrown in to suit the Yankee taste of the day. Indeed, nothing was more lamentable to me, during the whole war, than to observe how readily the officers of the old Navy, many of whom belonged to the gentle families of the land, and all of whom had been bred in a school of honor, took to the slang expressions of the day, and fell, pell-mell, into the ranks of the vulgar and fanatical rabble that was bounding on the war.

The officers of the Confederate States Navy, to say the least, were as much entitled to be regarded as fighting for a principle as themselves, and one would have thought that there would have been a chivalrous rivalry between the two services, as to which should show the other the most courtesy. This was the case, a thousand years ago, between the Christian and the Saracen. Did it result from their forms of government, and must democrats necessarily be vulgarians? Must the howling Demos devour everything gentle in the land, and reduce us all to the common level of the pot-house politician, and compel us to use his slang? Radicalism seemed to be now, just what it had been in the great French Revolution, a sort of mad-dog virus; every one who was inoculated with it, becoming rabid. The bitten dog howled incessantly with rage, and underwent a total transformation of nature. But our figure does not fit the case exactly. There was more method in this madness, than in that of the canine animal, for the human dog howled as much to please his master, as from rage. The size of the sop which he was to receive depended, in a great measure, upon the vigor of his howling.

Captain Raphael Semmes (Library of Congress).

But to return to the *Alabama* and the *Hatteras*. As soon as the action was over, and I had seen the latter sink, I caused all lights to be extinguished onboard my ship, and shaped my course again for the passage of Yucatan. In the meantime, the enemy's boat, which had been lowered for the purpose of boarding me, pulled in vigorously for the shore, as soon as it saw the action commence, and landed safely; and Admiral Bell, with his three steamers, passed on either side of the scene of action, the steamers having been scattered in the pursuit, to cover as much space as possible, and thus increase their chances of falling in with me. They did not find the *Alabama,* or indeed anything else during the night, but as one of the steamers was returning to her anchorage off Galveston, the next morning, in the dejected mood of a baffled scout, she fell in with the sunken *Hatteras*, the tops of whose royal masts were just above water, and from the main of which, the pennant—the night pennant, for the action was fought at night spoken of by Captain Blake, was observed to be flying. It told the only tale of the sunken ship which her consort had to take back to the Admiral. The missing boat turned up soon afterward, however, and the mystery was then solved. There was now as hurried a saddling of steeds for the pursuit as there had been in the chase of the young Locbinvar, and with as little effect, for by the time the steeds were given the spur, the *Alabama* was distant a hundred miles or more.

There was very little said by the enemy, about this engagement, between the *Alabama* and the *Hatteras,* as was usual with him when he met with a disaster; and what was said was all false. My own ship was represented to be a monster of speed and strength, and the

Hatteras, on the other hand, to be a tug, or river steamer, or some such craft, with two or three small guns at the most. The facts are as follows: The *Hatteras* was a larger ship than the *Alabama*, by one hundred tons. Her armament, as reported to us by her own people, was as follows: Four 32-pounders; two Parrot 30-pounder rifles; one 20-pounder rifle; and one 12-pounder howitzer—making a total of eight guns. The armament of the *Alabama* was as follows: Six 32-pounders; one 8-inch shell gun; one Blakeley rifle of 100 pounds—total, eight guns. There was, besides, a little toy rifle, a 9-pounder-on the quarter-deck of the *Alabama*, which had been captured from a merchant-ship, and which, I believe, was fired once during the action. The crew of the *Hatteras* was 108 strong; that of the *Alabama* 110. There was thus, as the reader sees, a considerable disparity between the two ships, in the weight of their pivot-guns, and the *Alabama* ought to have won the fight; and she did win it, in thirteen minutes—taking care, too, though she sank her enemy at night, to see that none of his men were drowned—a fact which I shall have occasion to contrast, by-and-by, with another sinking. The only casualty we had on board the *Alabama* was one man wounded. The damages to our hull were so slight, that there was not a shot-hole which it was necessary to plug, to enable us to continue our cruise; nor was there a rope to be spliced. Blake behaved like a man of courage, and made the best fight he could, ill supported as he was by the "volunteer" officers by whom he was surrounded, but he fell into disgrace with the Demos, and had but little opportunity shown him during the remainder of the war, to retrieve his disaster.

XI

Confederate Cruisers

1. The CSS *Sumter*

One of the most successful aspects of the Confederate navy during the American Civil War was the activities of her commerce-raiding cruisers. Faced with the reality of an inferior naval force that could never hope to challenge the United States Navy on anything approaching an equal footing, the Confederate government sought the most expedient way of damaging the Northern economy. During the war, more than half of all U. S. shipping disappeared from the world's oceans as Confederate raiders destroyed 110,000 tons of shipping and drove an additional 800,000 tons to foreign flags. As a result, American leadership in maritime commerce remained crippled until the advent of World War II.

The Confederacy accomplished this by commissioning seagoing cruisers to hunt down and destroy Northern-owned merchant ships and their cargoes. The Southern navy commissioned and put to sea eight cruisers during the war, the most renowned of these being three ships built in England: the *Florida*, the *Shenandoah*, and the *Alabama*. Several cruisers were converted from existing vessels that had been seized or purchased in home ports. The first of these "home-grown" cruisers to get to sea was the CSS *Sumter* out of New Orleans. (Campbell, *Gray Thunder: Exploits of the Confederate States Navy*, p. 74.)

The *Sumter* was originally the bark-rigged steamer *Habana* and was built at Philadelphia in 1859 for McConnell's New Orleans & Havana Line. Stranded at New Orleans when war came, she was purchased by the Confederate Navy Department, and Captain Raphael Semmes requested that he be given her command. (*Civil War Navy Chronology, 1861–1865*, p. VI–306.)

Raphael Semmes was born in Maryland on September 27, 1809, and had entered the United States Navy as a midshipman at the young age of sixteen. Living in Alabama at the time of that state's secession, he resigned his lieutenant's commission in the U. S. Navy and offered his services to the Confederacy. Destined to become one of only two Confederate admirals, Semmes was a prolific writer. His description in *Memoirs of Service Afloat* of the fitting out and escape of the CSS *Sumter* from New Orleans on June 30, 1861, ranks as a classic in Naval literature and is included here. [RTC]

"Preparation & Escape,"
Preparation of the Sumter *and Departure from New Orleans by*
Captain Raphael Semmes, CSN

Memoirs of Service Afloat Chapters X and XI, pp. 97–119

A GREAT change was apparent in New Orleans since I had last visited it. The levee in front of the city was no longer a great mart of commerce, piled with cotton bales, and supplies going back to the planter; densely packed with steamers, and thronged with a busy multitude. The long lines of shipping above the city had been greatly thinned, and a general air of desolation hung over the riverfront. It seemed as though a pestilence brooded over the doomed city, and that its inhabitants had fled before the fell destroyer. The *Sumter* lay on the opposite side of the river, at Algiers, and I crossed over every morning to superintend her refitment. I was sometimes detained at the ferry-house, waiting for the ferry-boat, and on these occasions, casting my eyes up and down the late busy river, it was not unfrequent to see it without so much as a skiff in motion on its bosom.

But this first simoom of the desert which had swept over the city, as a foretaste of what was to come, had by no means discouraged its patriotic inhabitants. The activity of commerce had ceased, it is true, but another description of activity had taken its place. War now occupied the thoughts of the multitude, and the sound of the drum, and the tramp of armed men were heard in the streets. The balconies were crowded with lovely women in gay attire, to witness the military processions, and the Confederate flag in miniature was pinned on almost every bosom. The enthusiasm of the Frenchman had been most easily and gracefully blended with the stern determination of the Southern man of English descent; the consequence of which was, that there was more demonstrative patriotism in New Orleans, than in any other of our Southern cities. Nor was this patriotism demonstrative only, it was deep and real, and was afterward sealed with some of the best Creole blood of the land, poured out, freely, on many a desperate battle-field. Alas! poor Louisiana. Once the seat of wealth, and of a gay and refined hospitality, thy manorial residences are deserted, and in decay, or have been leveled by the torch of the incendiary; thy fruitful fields, that were cultivated by the contented laborer, who whistled his merriment to his lazy plow, have been given to the jungle; thy fair daughters have been insulted, by the coarse, and rude Vandal; and even thy liberties have been given in charge of thy freedmen; and all this, because thou wouldst thyself be free!

I now took my ship actively in hand, and set gangs of mechanics at work to remove her upper cabins, and other top hamper, preparatory to making the necessary alterations. These latter were considerable, and I soon found that I had a tedious job on my hands. It was no longer the case, as it had been in former years, when I had had occasion to fit out a ship, that I could go into a navy-yard, with well-provided workshops, and skilled workmen ready with all the requisite materials at hand to execute my orders. Everything had to be improvised, from the manufacture of a water-tank, to the "kids, and cans" of the berth-deck messes, and from a gun-carriage to a friction-primer. I had not only to devise all the alterations but to make plans, and drawings of them, before they could be comprehended. The main deck was strengthened, by the addition of heavy beams to enable it to support the battery; a berth-deck was laid for the accommodation of the crew; the engine, which was partly above the water-line, was protected by a system of wood-work, and iron bars; the ship's rig was altered so as to convert her into a barkentine, with square-sails on her fore and main-masts; the officers' quarters, including my own cabin, were re-arranged; new suits of sails were made, and new boats constructed; hammocks and bedding were procured for the crew, and guns, gun-carriages, and ammunition ordered. Two long, tedious months were consumed in making these various alterations, and additions. My battery was to consist of an eight-inch shell gun, to be pivoted amid ships, and of four light thirty-two pounders, of thirteen cwt. each, in broadside.

The Secretary of the Navy, who was as anxious as myself that I should get to sea immediately, had given me all the assistance in his power, readily acceding to my requests, and promptly filling, or causing to be filled, all my requisitions. With the secession of Virginia we had become possessed of a valuable depot of naval supplies, in the Norfolk Navy Yard. It was filled with guns, shot, shell, cordage, and everything that was useful in the equipment of a ship, but it was far away from New Orleans, and such was the confusion along the different lines of railroad, that it was difficult to procure transportation. Commander Terry Sinclair, the active ordnance officer of the yard, had early dispatched my guns, by railroad, but weeks elapsed without my being able to hear anything of them. I was finally obliged to send a lieutenant in search of them, who picked them up, one by one, as they had been thrown out on the road-side, to make room for other freight. My gun-carriages I was obliged to have constructed myself, and I was fortunate enough to obtain the services of a very ingenious mechanic to assist me in this part of my duties Mr. Roy, a former employee of the Custom-House, within whose ample walls he had established his workshop. He contrived most ingeniously, and constructed out of railroad iron, one of the best carriages (or rather, slide and circle) for a pivot gun, which I have ever seen. The large foundry of Leeds & Co. took the contract for casting my shot, and shells, and executed it to my satisfaction.

Whilst all these various operations are going on, we may conveniently look around us upon passing events, or at least upon such of them as have a bearing upon naval operations. President Davis, a few days after the secession of Virginia, and when war had become imminent, issued a proclamation for the purpose of raising that irregular naval force, of which I have spoken in a previous page. Parties were invited to apply for letters-of-marquee and reprisal, with a view to the fitting out of privateers, to prey upon the enemy's commerce. Under this proclamation several privateers—generally light-draught river-steamers, with one or two small guns each—were hastily prepared, in New Orleans, and had already brought in some prizes captured off the mouths of the Mississippi. Even this small demonstration seemed to surprise, as well as alarm the Northern government, for President Lincoln now issued a proclamation declaring the molestation of Federal vessels, on the high seas, by Confederate cruisers, piracy. He had also issued a proclamation declaring the ports of the Confederacy in a state of blockade. The mouths of the Mississippi were to be sealed on the 25th of May.

The European governments, as soon as it became evident, that the two sections were really at war, took measures accordingly. Great Britain took the lead, and declared a strict neutrality between the combatants. It was of the essence of such a declaration, that it should put both belligerents on the same footing. This was apparently done, and the cruisers of both sections were prohibited, alike, from taking their prizes into British ports. I shall have something to say of the unequal operation of this declaration of neutrality, in a future part of these memoirs; for the present it is only necessary to state, that it acknowledged us to be in possession of belligerent rights. This was a point gained certainly, but it was no more than was to have been expected. Indeed, Great Britain could do nothing less. In recognizing the war which had broken out between the sections, as a war, and not as a mere insurrection, she had only followed the lead of Mr. Lincoln himself. Efforts had been made it is true, both by Mr. Lincoln, and his Secretary of State, to convince the European governments that the job which they had on their hands was a small affair; a mere family quarrel, of no great significance.

But the truth would not be suppressed, and when, at last, it became necessary to declare the Confederate ports in a state of blockade, and to send ships of war thither, to enforce the declaration, the sly little game which they had been playing was all up with them. A blockade was an act of war, which came under the cognizance of the laws of nations. It concerned neutrals, as well as belligerents, and foreign nations were bound to take notice of it. It followed that there could not be a blockade without a war; and it equally followed, that there could not be a war without at least two belligerent parties to it. It will thus be seen, that the declaration of neutrality of Great Britain was a logical sequence of Mr. Lincoln's, and Mr. Seward's own act. And yet with sullen, and singular inconsistency, the Northern Government has objected from that day to this, to this mere routine act of Great Britain. So much was this act considered, as a matter of course, at the time, that all the other powers of the earth, of sufficient dignity to act in the premises, at all, followed the example set them by Great Britain, and issued similar declarations; and the four years of bloody war that followed justified the wisdom of their acts.

We may now return to the equipment of the *Sumter*. A rendezvous had been opened, and a crew had been shipped for her, which was temporarily berthed on board the receiving ship, *Star of the West*, a transport-steamer of the enemy, which had been gallantly captured by some Texans, and turned over to the Navy. New Orleans was full of seamen, discharged from ships that had been laid up, and more men were offering themselves for service, than I could receive. I had the advantage, therefore, of picking my crew, an advantage which no one but a seaman can fully appreciate. My lieutenants, surgeon, paymaster, and marine officer had all arrived, and, with the consent of the Navy Department, I had appointed my engineers—one chief, and three assistants, boatswain, carpenter, and sailmaker. My provisions had been purchased, and were ready to be put on board, and my funds had already arrived, but we were still waiting on the mechanics, who, though doing their best, had not yet been able to turn the ship over to us. From the following letter to the Secretary of the Navy, inclosing a requisition for funds, it will be seen that my demands upon the department were quite moderate, and that I expected to make the *Sumter* pay her own expenses, as soon as she should get to sea.

NEW ORLEANS, May 14,1861.

SIR:-I have the honor to enclose, herewith, a requisition fur the sum of $10,000, which I request may be remitted to the paymaster of the *Sumter*, in specie, for use during my contemplated cruise. I may find it necessary to coal several times, and to supply my crew with fresh provisions, &c., before I have the opportunity of replenishing my military chest from the enemy.

The ammunition remained to be provided, and on the 20th of May, I dispatched Lieutenant Chapman to the Baton Rouge Arsenal, which had been captured a short time before, for the purpose of procuring it, under the following letter of instructions:

NEW ORLEANS, May 20, 1861.

SIR:-You will proceed to Baton Rouge, and put yourself in communication with the commander of the C. S. Arsenal, at that point, for the purpose of receiving the ammunition, arms, shot, shell, &c., that may be required for the supply of the C. S. steamer *Sumter*, now fitting for sea at this port. It is presumed that the proper orders (which had been requested) have been, or will be dispatched from Montgomery, authorizing the issue of all such articles, as we may need. Should this not be the case; with regard to any of the articles, it is hoped that the ordnance officer in charge will not hesitate to deliver them, as it is highly important that the *Sumter* should not be detained, because of any oversight, or informality, in the orders of the War Department. Be pleased to present the accompanying requisition to Captain Booth, the superintendent, and ask that it may be filled. The gunner will be directed to report to you, to accompany you to Baton Rouge, on this service.

The reader will thus perceive that many difficulties lay in the way of equipping the *Sumter*; that I was obliged to pick up one material here, and another there, as I could best find it, and that I was not altogether free from the routine of the "Circumlocution Office," as my requisitions had frequently to pass through many hands, before they could be complied with.

About this time, we met with a sad accident in the loss of one of our midshipmen, by drowning. He, with other young officers of the *Sumter*, had been stationed, temporarily, on board the receiving ship, in charge of the *Sumter*'s crew, whilst the latter ship was still in the hands of the mechanics. The following letter of condolence to the father of the young gentleman will sufficiently explain the circumstances of the disaster.

NEW ORLEANS, May 18, 1861.

SIR:-It becomes my melancholy duty to inform you, of the death, by drowning, yesterday, of your son, Midshipman John F. Holden, of the C. S. steamer *Sumter*. Your son was temporarily attached to the receiving ship (late *Star of the West*) at this place, whilst the *Sumter* was being prepared for sea, and whilst engaged in carrying out an anchor, in a boat belonging to that ship, met his melancholy fate, along with three of the crew, by the swamping of the boat, in which he was embarked. I offer you, my dear sir, my heartfelt condolence on this sad bereavement. You have lost a cherished son, and the Government a valuable and promising young officer.

W. B. HOLDEN, Esc., Louisburg, Tenn.

War had begun, thus early, to demand of us our sacrifices. Tennessee had not yet seceded, and yet this ardent Southern youth had withdrawn from the Naval Academy, and cast his lot with his section.

A few extracts from my journal will now, perhaps, give the reader a better idea of the progress of my preparations for sea, and of passing events, than any other form of narrative.

May 27th

News received this morning of the appearance, at Pass à L'Outre, yesterday, of the U. S. steamer *Brooklyn*, and of the establishment of the blockade. Work is progressing satisfactorily, and I expect to be ready for sea, by Sunday next.

News of skirmishing in Virginia, and of fresh arrivals of Northern troops, at Washington, en route for that State. The Federal Government has crossed the Potomac, in force, and thus inaugurated a bloody, and a bitter war, by the invasion of our territory. So be it-we but accept the gantlet, which has been flung in our faces. The future will tell a tale not unworthy of the South, and her glorious cause.

Monday, May 30th.

My patience is sorely tried by the mechanics. The water-tanks for the *Sumter* are not yet completed. The carriage for the 8-inch gun was finished, to-day, and we are busy laying down the circles for it, and cutting the holes for the fighting-bolts. The carriages for the 32-pounders are promised us, by Saturday next, and also the copper tanks for the magazine. Our ammunition, and small arms arrived, yesterday, from Baton Rouge. Besides the *Brooklyn*, at the Passes, we learn, to-day, that the *Niagara*, and *Minnesota*, two of the enemy's fastest, and heaviest steamships have arrived, to assist in enforcing the blockade, and to lie in wait for some ships expected to arrive, laden with arms and ammunition, for the Confederacy.

May 31st

The tanks are at last finished, and they have all been delivered, to-day. Leeds & Co. have done an excellent job, and I shall be enabled to carry three months' water for my crew. We shall now get on, rapidly, with our preparations.

Saturday, June 1st

Finds us not yet ready for sea! The tanks have all been taken on board, and stowed; the gun carriages for the 32s will be finished on Monday. The circles for the 8-inch gun have been laid down, and the fighting-bolts are ready for placing. On Monday I shall throw the crew on board, and by Thursday next, I shall, without doubt be ready for sea. We are losing a great deal of precious time. The enemy's flag is being flaunted in our faces, at all our ports by his ships of war, and his vessels of commerce are passing, and re-passing, on the ocean, in defiance, or in contempt of our power, and, as yet, we have not struck a blow.

At length on the 3rd of June, I was enabled to put the *Sumter*, formally, in commission. On that day her colors were hoisted, for the first time—the ensign having been presented to me, by some patriotic ladies of New Orleans—the crew was transferred to her, from the receiving ship, and the officers were ordered to mess on board. The ship was now hauled off and anchored in the stream, but we were delayed two long and tedious weeks yet, before we were finally ready. During these two weeks we made a trial trip up the river, some ten or twelve miles. Some of the principal citizens were invited on board, and a bright, and beautiful afternoon was pleasantly spent, in testing the qualities of the ship, the range of her guns, and the working of the gun-carriages; the whole ending by a collation, in partaking of which my guests were kind enough to wish me a career full of "blazing honors."

I was somewhat disappointed in the speed of my ship, as we did not succeed in getting more than nine knots out of her. There was another great disadvantage. With all the space I could allot to my coal-bunkers, she could be made to carry no more than about eight days' fuel. We had masts, and sails, it is true, but these could be of but little use, when the coal was exhausted, as the propeller would remain a drag in the water, there being no means of hoisting it. It was with such drawbacks, that I was to take the sea, alone, against a vindictive and relentless enemy, whose Navy already swarmed on our coasts, and whose means of increasing it were inexhaustible. But the sailor has a saying, that "Luck is a Lord," and we trusted to luck.

On the 18th of June, after all the vexatious delays that have been described, I got up my anchor, and dropped down to the Barracks, below the city a short distance, to receive my powder on board, which, for safety, had been placed in the State magazine. At 10.30 PM of the same day, we got up steam, and by the soft and brilliant light of a moon near her full, threw ourselves into the broad, and swift current of the Father of Waters, and ran rapidly down to the anchorage, between Fort Jackson, and Fort St. Philip, where we came to at 4 AM. In the course of the day, Captain Brand, an ex-officer of the old Navy, and now second in command of the forts, came on board to make us the ceremonial visit; and I subsequently paid my respects to Major Duncan, the officer in chief command, an ex-officer of the old Army. These gentlemen were both busy, as I found upon inspecting the forts, in perfecting their batteries, and drilling their men, for the hot work that was evidently before them. As was unfortunately the case with our people, generally, at this period, they were overconfident. They kindly supplied some few deficiencies, that still remained in our gunner's department, and I received from them a howitzer, which I mounted on my taffarel, to guard against boat attacks, by night.

I remained three days at my anchors between the forts, for the purpose of stationing, and drilling my crew, before venturing into the presence of the enemy; and I will take advantage of this lull to bring up some matters connected with the ship, which we have hitherto overlooked. On the 7th of June, the Secretary of the Navy—the Government having, in the mean time, removed to Richmond—sent me my sailing orders, and in my letter of the 14th of the same month, acknowledging their receipt, I had said to him: "I have an excellent set of men on board, though they are nearly all green, and will require some little practice, and drilling, at the guns, to enable them to handle them creditably. Should I be fortunate enough to reach the high seas, you may rely upon my implicit obedience of your instructions, 'to do the enemy's commerce the greatest injury, in the shortest time.'"

Here was a model of a letter of instruction—it meant "burn, sink, and destroy," always, of course, within the limits prescribed by the laws of nations, and with due attention to the laws of humanity, in the treatment of prisoners. The reader will see, as we progress, that I gave the "implicit obedience" which had been promised, to these instructions, and that if greater results were not accomplished, it was the fault of the *Sumter*, and not of her commander. In the same letter that brought me my sailing orders, the Secretary had suggested to me the propriety of adopting some means of communicating with him, by cipher, so that, my dispatches, if captured by the enemy, would be unintelligible to him. The following letter in reply to this suggestion, will explain how this was arranged:

"I have the honor to enclose herewith a copy of 'Reid's English Dictionary,' a duplicate of which I retain, for the purpose mentioned in your letter of instructions, of the 7th instant. I have not been able to find in the city of New Orleans, 'Cobb's Miniature Lexicon,' suggested by you, or any other suitable dictionary, with but a single column on a page. This need make no difference, however. In my communications to the Department, should I have occasion to refer to a word in the copy sent, I will designate the first column on the page, A, and the second column, B. Thus, if I wish to use the word 'prisoner,' my reference to it would be as follows: 323, B, 15; the first number referring to the page, the letter to the column, and the second number to the number of the word from the top of the column." By means of this simple, and cheap device, I was enabled, at all times, to keep my dispatches out of the hands of the enemy, or, in other words, prevent him from interpreting them, when I had anything of importance to communicate.

Before leaving New Orleans, I had, in obedience to a general order of the service, transmitted to the Navy Department, a Muster Roll of the officers, and men, serving on board the *Sumter*. Her crew, as reported by this roll, consisted of ninety-two persons, exclusive of officers. Twenty of these ninety-two persons were marines—a larger guard than was usual for so small a ship. The officers were as follows:

Commander—Raphael Semmes.
Lieutenants—John M. Kell; Robert T. Chapman; John M. Stribling; William E. Evans.
Paymaster—Henry Myers.
Surgeon—Francis L. Galt.
1st Lieutenant of Marines—B. Howell.
Midshipmen—William A. Hicks; Albert G. Hudgins; Richard F. Armstrong; Joseph D. Wilson.
Engineers—Miles J. Freeman; William P. Brooks; Matthew O'Brien; Simeon W. Cummings.
Boatswain—Benjamin P. Mecasky.
Gunner—Thomas C. Cuddy.
Sailmaker—W. P. Beaufort.
Carpenter—William Robinson.
Captain's Clerk—W. Breedlove Smith.

Commissions had been forwarded to all the officers entitled to receive them, and acting appointments had been given by me to the warrant officers. It will thus be seen, how formally all these details had been attended to. These commissions were to be our warrants for what we were to do, on the high seas.

And now the poor boon will be permitted to human nature, that before we launch our frail bark, on the wild sea of adventure, before us, we should turn our thoughts, homeward, for a moment.

"'And is he gone?'—on sudden solitude
How oft that fearful question will intrude!
'T was but an instant past—and here he stood!
And now! '—without the portal's porch she rushed,
And then at length her tears in freedom gushed;
Big, bright, and fast, unknown to her they fell;
But still her lips refused to send farewell!'
For in that word—that fatal word—howe'er
We promise—hope—believe—there breathes despair."

Such was the agony of many a fair bosom, as the officers of the *Sumter* had torn themselves from the embraces of their families, in those scenes of leave-taking, which more than any other, try the sailor's heart. Several of them were married men, and it was long years before they returned to the homes which they had made sad by their absence.

Semmes & His Officers on Board the *Sumter* (Naval Historical Center).

WHILST we were lying at our anchors between the forts, as described in the last chapter, Governor Moore of Louisiana, who had done good service to the Confederacy, by seizing the forts, and arsenals in his State, in advance of secession, and the Hon. John Slidell, lately returned from his seat in the Federal Senate, and other distinguished gentlemen came down, on a visit of inspection to the forts. I went on shore to call on them, and brought them on board the *Sumter* to lunch with me. My ship was, by this time, in excellent order, and my crew well accustomed to their stations, under the judicious management of my first lieutenant, and I took pleasure in showing these gentlemen how much a little discipline could accomplish, in the course of a few weeks. Discipline!—what a power it is everywhere, and under all circumstances; and how much the want of it lost us, as the war progressed. What a pity the officers of our army did not have their respective commands, encircled by wooden walls, with but a "single monarch to walk the peopled deck."

Just at nightfall, on the evening of the 21st of June, I received the following dispatch from the commanding officer of the forts:

CAPTAIN:—I am desired by the commanding officer to state, that the *Ivy*—this was a small tender of the forts, and letter-of-marque—reports that the *Powhatan* has left, in pursuit of two ships, and that he has a telegram from Pass à L' Outre, to the effect, that a boat from the *Brooklyn* had put into the river and was making for the telegraph station, where she was expected to arrive within a few minutes.

The *Powhatan* was blockading the Southwest Pass, and it was barely possible that I might get to sea, through this pass, if a pilot could be at once procured; and so I immediately ordered steam to be raised, and getting up my anchor, steamed down to the Head of the Passes, where the river branches into its three principal outlets. Arriving here, at half past ten PM I dispatched a boat to the light house, for a pilot; but the keeper knew nothing of the pilots, and was unwilling to come on board, himself, though requested. The night wore away, and nothing could be done.

The telescope revealed to us, the next morning, that the *Powhatan* had returned to her station. From the sullen, and unsatisfactory message, which had been returned to me, by the keeper of the light-house, I began to suspect that there was something wrong, about the pilots; and it being quite necessary that I should have one constantly, on board, to enable me to take advantage of any temporary absence of the enemy's cruisers, without having to hunt up one for the emergency, I dispatched the *Ivy*, to the pilots' station, at the Southwest Pass, in search of one. This active little cruiser returned in the course of a few hours, and reported that none of the pilots were willing to come on board of me! I received, about the same time, a telegraphic dispatch from the Southwest Pass, forwarded to me through Major Duncan, which read as follows

"Applied to the Captain of the Pilots' Association for a pilot for the *Sumter*. He requested me to state, that there are no pilots on duty now!" "So ho! sits the wind in that quarter," thought I—I will soon set this matter right. I, at once, sent Lieutenant Stribling on board the *Ivy*, and directed him to proceed to the Pilots' Association, and deliver, and see executed the following written order:

C. S. STEAMER *SUMTER*, HEAD OF THE PASSES,
June 22, 1861.

SIR:—This is to command you to repair on board this ship, with three or four of the most experienced pilots of the Bar. I am surprised to learn, that an unwillingness has been expressed, by some of the pilots of your Association, to come on board the *Sumter*; and my purpose is to test the fact of such disloyalty to the Confederate States. If any man disobeys this summons I will not only have his Branch taken from him, but I will send an armed force, and arrest, and bring him on board.

This order had the desired effect, and in the course of the afternoon, Lieutenant Stribling returned, bringing with him, the Captain of the Association, and several of the pilots. I directed them to be brought into my cabin, and when they were assembled, demanded to know the reason of their late behavior. Some stammering excuses were offered, which I cut short, by informing them that one of them must remain on board constantly, and that they might determine for themselves, who should take the first week's service; to be relieved at the end of the week, by another, and so on, as long as I should find it necessary. One of their number being designated, I dismissed the rest. The reader will see how many faithful auxiliaries, Admiral Farragut afterward found, in the Pilots' Association of the mouths of the Mississippi, when he made his famous ascent of the river, and captured its great seaport. Nor was this defection confined to New Orleans. The pilots along our whole Southern coast were, with few exceptions, Northern men, and as a rule they went over to the enemy, though pretending, in the beginning of our troubles, to be good secessionists. The same remark may be applied to our steamboat men, of Northern birth, as a class. Many of them had become domiciled in the South, and were supposed to be good Southern men, until the crucial test of self-interest was applied to them, when they, took deserted us, and took service with the enemy.

The object of the *Brooklyn's* boat, which, as we have seen, pulled into the telegraph station at Pass à L' Outre, just before we got under way from between the forts, was to cut the wires, and break up the station, to prevent intelligence being given me of the movements of the blockading fleet. I now resorted to a little retaliation. I dispatched an officer to the different light-houses, to stave the oil-casks, and bring away the lighting apparatus, to prevent the enemy's shipping from using the lights. They were of great convenience, not only to the ships employed on the blockade, but to the enemy's transports, and other ships, bound to and from the coast of Texas. They could be of no use to our own blockade-runners, as the passes of the Mississippi, by reason of their long, and tortuous, and frequently shifting channels, were absolutely closed to them.

The last letter addressed by me to the Secretary of the Navy, before escaping through the blockade, as hereinafter described, was the following:

C. S. STEAMER *SUMTER*, HEAD OF THE PASSES,
June 30, 1861

SIR:- I have the honor to inform the Department that I am still at my anchors at the "Head of the Passes"—the enemy closely investing both of the practical outlets. At Pass à L' Outre there are three ships, the *Brooklyn*, and another propeller, and a large side-wheel steamer; and at the Southwest Pass, there is the *Powhatan*, lying within half a mile of the bar, and not stirring an inch from her anchors, night or day. I am only surprised that the *Brooklyn*, does not come up to this anchorage, which she might easily do—as there is water enough, and no military precautions, whatever, have been taken to hold the position—and thus effectually seal all the passes of the river, by her presence alone; which would enable the enemy to withdraw the remainder of his blockading force, for use elsewhere. With the assistance of the *Jackson*, Lieutenant Gwathmey, and the *McRae*, Lieutenant Huger—neither of which has, as yet, however, dropped down—I could probably hold my position here, until an opportunity offers of my getting to sea. I shall watch, diligently, for such an opportunity, and have no doubt, that sooner or later, it will present itself. I found, upon dropping down to this point, that the lights at Pass à L' Outre, and South Pass had been strangely overlooked, and that they were still being nightly exhibited. I caused them both to be extinguished, so that if bad weather should set in—a gale from the south-east, for instance—the blockading ships, having nothing to "hold on to," will be obliged to make an offing. At present the worst feature of the blockade of Pass à L' Outre is, that the *Brooklyn* has the speed of me; so that even if I should run the bar, I could not hope to escape her, unless I surprised her, which with her close watch of the bar, at anchor near by, both night and day, it will be exceedingly difficult to do. I should be quite willing to try speed with the *Powhatan*, if I could hope to tun the gantlet of her guns without being crippled; but here again, unfortunately, with all the buoys, and other marks removed, the bar which she is watching is a perfectly blind bar, except by daylight. In the meantime, I am drilling my green crew, to a proper use of the great guns and small arms. With the exception of a diarrhea, which is prevailing, to some extent, brought on by too free use of the river water, in the excessive heat which prevails, the crew continues healthy.

Nothing in fact surprised me more, during the nine days I lay at the Head of the Passes, than that the enemy did not attack me with some of his light-draught, but heavily armed steamers, or by his boats, by night. Here was the *Sumter*, a small ship, with a crew, all told, of a little over a hundred men, anchored only ten, or twelve miles from the enemy, without a gun, or an obstruction between her and him; and yet no offensive movement was made against her. The enemy watched me closely, day by day, and bent all his energies toward preventing my escape, but did not seem to think of the simple expedient of endeavoring to capture me, with a superior force. In nightly expectation of an assault, I directed the engineer to keep the water in his boilers, as near the steam-point as possible, without actually generating the vapor, and sent a patrol of boats some distance down the Southwest Pass; the boats being relieved every four hours, and returning to the ship, at the first streaks of dawn. After I went to sea, the enemy did come in, and take possession of my anchorage, until he was driven away by Commodore Hollins, in a little nondescript ram; which, by the way, was the first ram experiment of the war. The reader may imagine the tedium, and discomforts of our position, if he will reflect that it is the month of June, and that at this season of the year, the sun comes down upon the broad, and frequently calm surface of the Father of Waters, with an African glow, and that clouds of that troublesome little insect the mosquito tormented us, by night and by day. There was no sleeping at all without the mosquito bar, and I had accordingly had a supply sent down for all the crew. Rather than stand the assaults of these little picadores, much longer, I believe my crew would have run the gantlet of the whole Federal Navy.

My diary will now perhaps give the reader, his clearest conception of the condition of things on board the *Sumter*, for the remaining few days that she is to continue at her anchors.

Tuesday, June 25th.—A sharp thunder-storm at half-past three AM, jarring and shaking the ship with its crashes. The very flood-gates of the heavens seem open, and the rain is descending on our decks like a cataract. Clearing toward ten o'clock. Both blockading ships still at their anchor's. The British steam sloop *Talon* touched at the Southwest Pass, yesterday, and communicated with the *Powhatan*. We learn by the newspapers, to-day, that the enemy has taken possession of Ship Island, and established a blockade of the Sound. The anaconda is drawing his folds around us. We are filling some shell, and cartridges to-day, and drilling the crew at the battery.

Wednesday, June 28th.—Cloudy, with occasional rain squalls, which have tempered the excessive heats. The *Ivy* returned from the city to-day, and brought me eighty barrels of coal. Sent the pilot, in the light-house keeper's boat, to sound the S. E. bar, an unused and unwatched outlet to the eastward of the South Pass—in the hope that we may find sufficient water over it, to permit the egress of the ship. The Federal ships are keeping close watch, as usual, at both the passes, neither of them having stirred from her anchor, since we have been at the "Head of the Passes."

Thursday, June 27th.—Weather sultry, and atmosphere charged with moisture. Pilot returned this afternoon, and reports ten and a half feet water on the S. E. bar. Unfortunately the *Sumter* draws twelve feet; so we must abandon this hope.

Saturday, June 29th.—A mistake induced us to expend a little coal, to-day, uselessly. The pilot having gone aloft, to take his usual morning's survey of the "situation," reported that the *Brooklyn* was nowhere to be seen! Great excitement immediately ensued, on the decks, and the officer of the watch hurried into my cabin with the information. I ordered steam to be gotten up with all dispatch, and when, in the course of a very few minutes, it was reported ready—for we always kept our fires banked—the anchor was tripped, and the ship was under way, ploughing her way through the turbid waters, toward Pass à L' Outre. When we had steamed about four miles down the pass, the *Brooklyn* was seen riding very quietly at her anchors, in her usual berth near the bar. Explanation: The *Sumter* had dragged her anchor during the night, and the alteration in her position had brought a clump of trees between her, and the enemy's ship, which had prevented the pilot from seeing the latter! With disappointed hopes we had nothing to do, but to return to our anchors, and watch and wait. In half an hour more, the sailors were lounging idly about the decks, under well spread awnings; the jest, and banter went round, as usual, and save the low hissing and singing of the steam, which was still escaping, there was nothing to remind the beholder of our recent disappointment. Such is the school of philosophy in which the seaman is reared. Our patience, however, was soon to be rewarded.

Early on the next morning, which was the 30th of June, the steamer, *Empire Parish*, came down from the city, and coming alongside of us, put on board some fresh provisions for the crew, and about one hundred barrels of coal, which my thoughtful, and attentive friend, Commodore Rousseau, had sent down to me. Having done this, the steamer shoved off, and proceeded on her trip, down Pass à L' Outre, to the pilots' station, and lighthouse. It was a bright Sunday morning, and we were thinking of nothing but the usual muster, and how we should get through another idle day. In the course of two or three hours, the steamer returned, and when she had come near us, she was seen to cast off a boat, which she had been towing, containing a single boatman—one of the fishermen, or oystermen so common in these waters. The boatman pulled rapidly under our stern, and hailing the officer of the deck, told him, that the Brooklyn had gone off in chase of a sail, and was no longer in sight. The crew, who had been "cleaning themselves," for Sunday muster, at once stowed away their bags; the swinging-booms were gotten alongside, the boats run up, and, in ten minutes, the steam was again hissing, as if impatient of control. The men ran round the capstan, in "doublequick," in their eagerness to get up the anchor, and in a few minutes more, the ship's head swung off gracefully with the current, and, the propeller being started, she bounded off like a thing of life, on this new race, which was to decide whether we should continue to stagnate in midsummer, in the marshes of the Mississippi, or reach those "glad waters of the dark blue sea," which form as delightful a picture in the imagination of the sailor, as in that of the poet.

Whilst we were heaving up our anchor, I had noticed the pilot, standing near me, pale, and apparently nervous, and agitated, but, as yet, he had said not a word. When we were fairly under way, however, and it seemed probable, at last, that we should attempt the blockade, the fellow's courage fairly broke down, and he protested to me that he knew nothing of the bar of Pass à L' Outre, and durst not attempt to run me over. "I am," said he, "a S. W. bar pilot, and know nothing of the other passes." "What," said I, "did you not know that I was lying at the Head of the Passes, for the very purpose of taking any one of the outlets through which an opportunity of escape might present itself, and yet you dare tell me, that you know but one of them, and have been deceiving me." The fellow stammered out something in excuse, but I was too impatient to listen to him, and, turning to the first lieutenant, ordered him to hoist the "Jack" at the fore, as a signal for a pilot. I had, in fact, resolved to attempt the passage of the bar, from my own slight acquaintance with it, when I had been a light-house inspector, rather than forego the opportunity of escape, and caused the Jack to be hoisted, rather as a matter of course, than because I hoped for any good result from it.

The *Brooklyn* had not "chased out of sight," as reported—she had only chased to the westward, some seven or eight miles, and had been hidden from the boatman, by one of the spurs of the Delta. She had probably, all the while, had her telescopes on the *Sumter*, and as soon as she saw the black smoke issuing from her chimney, and the ship moving rapidly toward the pass, she abandoned her chase, and commenced to retrace her steps.

We had nearly equal distances to run to the bar, but I had the advantage of a four-knot current. Several of my officers now collected around me, and we were discussing the chances of escape. "What think you of our prospect," said I, turning to one of my lieutenants, who had served a short time before, on board the *Brooklyn*, and knew well her qualities. "Prospect, sir! not the least in the world—there is no possible chance of our escaping that ship. Even if we get over the bar ahead of her, she must overhaul us, in a very short time. The *Brooklyn* is good for fourteen knots an hour, sir." "That was the report," said I, "on her trial trip, but you know how all such reports are exaggerated; ten to one, she has no better speed, if so good, as the *Sumter*." "You will see, sir," replied my lieutenant; "we made a passage in her, only a few months ago, from Tampico to Pensacola, and averaged about thirteen knots the whole distance."

Here the conversation dropped, for an officer now came to report to me that a boat had just shoved off from the pilots' station, evidently with a pilot in her. Casting my eyes in the given direction, I saw a whale-boat approaching us, pulled by four stout blacks, who were bending like good fellows to their long ashen oars, and in the stern sheets was seated, sure enough, the welcome pilot, swaying his body to, and fro, as his boat leaped under the oft-repeated strokes of the oars, as though be would hasten her already great speed. But more beautiful still was anther object which presented itself. In the balcony of the pilot's house, which had been built in the very marsh, on the margin of the river, there stood a beautiful woman, the pilot's young wife, waving him on to his duty, with her handkerchief. We could have tossed a biscuit from the *Sumter* to the shore, and I uncovered my head gallantly to my fair countrywoman. A few moments more, and a tow-line had been thrown to the boat, and the gallant young fellow stood on the horse-block beside me.

As we swept past the light-house wharf, almost close enough to touch it, there were other petticoats fluttering in the breeze, the owners of which were also waving handkerchiefs of encouragement to the *Sumter*. I could see my sailors' eyes brighten at these spectacles, for the sailor's heart is capacious enough to love the whole sex, and I now felt sure of their nerves, in case it should become necessary to tax them. Half a mile or so, from the light-house, and the bar is reached. There was a Bremen ship lying aground on the bar, and there was just room, and no more, for us to pass her. She had run out a kedge, and had a warp attached to it that was lying across the passage-way. The crew considerately slackened the line, as we approached, and in another bound the *Sumter* was outside the bar, and the Confederate flag was upon the high seas! We now slackened our speed, for an instant— only an instant, for my officers and men all had their wits about them, and worked like good fellows—to haul the pilot's boat alongside, that he might return to the shore. As the gallant young fellow grasped my hand, and shook it warmly, as he descended from the horse-block, he said, "Now, Captain, you are all clear; give her hell, and let her go!"

We had now nothing to do, but turn our attention to the enemy. The *Brooklyn*, as we cleared the bar, was about three and a half, or four miles distant; we were therefore just out of reach of her guns, with nothing to spare. Thick volumes of smoke could be seen pouring from the chimneys of both ships; the firemen, and engineers of each evidently doing their best. I called a lieutenant, and directed him to heave the log. He reported our speed to be nine, and a half knots. Loath to believe that we could be making so little way, through the yet turbid waters, which were rushing past us with great apparent velocity, I directed the officer to repeat the experiment; but the same result followed, though he had paid out the line with a free hand. I now sent for the engineer, and, upon inquiry, found that he was doing his very best—"though," said he, "there is a little drawback, just now, in the 'foaming' of our boilers, arising from the suddenness with which we got up steam; when this subsides, we may be able to add half a knot more."

The *Brooklyn* soon loosed, and set her sails, bracing them sharp up on the starboard tack. I loosed and set mine, also. The enemy's ship was a little on my weather quarter, say a couple of points, and had thus slightly the weather-gauge of me. As I knew I could lay nearer the wind than she; being able to brace my yards sharper, and had besides, the advantage of larger fore-and-aft sails, comparatively, stay-sails, trysails, and a very large spanker, I resolved at once to hold my wind, so closely, as to compel her to furl her sails, though this would carry me a little athwart her bows, and bring me perhaps a little nearer to her, for the next half hour, or so. A rain squall now came up, and enveloped the two ships, hiding each from the other. As the rain blew off to leeward, and the *Brooklyn* reappeared, she seemed fearfully near to us, and I began to fear I should realize the foreboding of my lieutenant. I could not but admire the majesty of her appearance, with her broad flaring bows, and clean, and beautiful run, and her masts, and yards, as taunt and square, as those of an old time sailing frigate. The stars and stripes of a large ensign flew out from time to time, from under the lee of her spanker, and we could see an apparently anxious crowd of officers on her quarterdeck, many of them with telescopes directed toward us. She had, evidently, I thought, gained upon us, and I expected every moment to hear the whiz of a shot; but still she did not fire.

I now ordered my paymaster to get his public chest, and papers ready for throwing overboard, if it should become necessary. At this crisis the engineer came up from below, bringing the welcome intelligence that the "foaming" of his boilers had ceased, and that his engine was "working beautifully," giving the propeller several additional turns per minute. The breeze, too, favored me, for it had freshened considerably; and what was still more to the purpose, I began to perceive that I was "eating" the *Brooklyn* "out of the wind"; in other words, that she was falling more and more to leeward. I knew, of course, that as soon as she fell into my wake, she would be compelled to furl her sails. This she did in half an hour or so afterward, and I at once began to breathe more freely, for I could still hold on to my own canvas. I have witnessed many beautiful sights at sea, but the most beautiful of them all was when the *Brooklyn* let fly all her sheets, and halliards, at once, and clewed up, and furled, in man-of-war style, all her sails, from courses to royals. We now began to gain quite perceptibly on our pursuer, and at half-past three, the chase was abandoned, the baffled *Brooklyn* retracing her steps to Pass à L'Outre, and the *Sumter* bounding away on her course seaward.

We fired no gun of triumph in the face of the enemy—my powder was too precious for that—but I sent the crew aloft, to man the rigging, and three such cheers were given for the Confederate flag, "that little bit of striped bunting," that had waved from the *Sumter*'s peak during the exciting chase, as could proceed only from the throats of American seamen, in the act of defying a tyrant—those cheers were but a repetition of many such cheers that had been given, by our ancestors, to that other bit of "striped bunting" which had defied the power of England in that olden war, of which our war was but the logical sequence. The reader must not suppose that our anxiety was wholly allayed, as soon as we saw the *Brooklyn* turn away from us.

We were, as yet, only a few miles from the land, and our coast was swarming with, the enemy's cruisers. Ship Island was not a great way off, and there was a constant passing to and fro, of ships-of-war between that island and the passes of the Mississippi, and we might stumble upon one of these at any moment. "Sail ho!" was now shouted from the mast head. "Where away!" cried the officer of the deck "Right ahead," said the lookout. A few minutes only elapsed, and a second sail was descried, "broad on the starboard bow." But nothing came of these specters; we passed on, seaward, without so much as raising either of them from the deck, and finally, the friendly robes of night enveloped us. When we at length realized that we had gained an offing; when we began to feel the welcome heave of the sea; when we looked upon the changing aspect of its waters, now darkening into the deepest blue, and breathed the pure air, fresh from the Gulf, untainted of malaria, and untouched of mosquito's wing, we felt like so many prisoners who had been turned loose from a long and painful confinement; and when I reflected upon my mission, to strike for the right! to endeavor to sweep from the seas the commerce of a treacherous friend, who had become a cruel and relentless foe, I felt, in full force, the inspiration of the poet:

> "Ours the wild life in tumult still to range,
> From toil to rest, and joy in every change.
> Oh, who can tell? Not thou, luxurious slave,
> Whose soul would sicken o'er the heaving wave;
> Not thou, vain lord of wantonness and ease,
> Whom slumber soothes not-pleasures cannot please;
> Oh, who can tell, save he whose heart hath tried,
> And danced in triumph o'er the waters wide,
> The exulting sense-the pulse's maddening play,
> That thrills the wanderer of that trackless way?
> ********************* * * * Death!
> Come when it will—we snatch the life of life;
> When lost—what reeks it—by disease or strife?

Let him who crawls, enamored of decay,
Cling to his couch, and sicken years away;
Heave his thick breath, and shake his palsied head;
Ours! the fresh turf, and not the feverish bed;
While gasp by gasp he falters forth his soul,
Ours, with one pang—one bound—escapes control.
His corpse may boast its wan and narrow cave,
And they who loathed his life, may gild his grave:
Ours are the tears, though few, sincerely shed,
When ocean shrouds and sepulchres our dead."

2. Arrest in Tangier

Paymaster Henry Myers, who hailed from Georgia, resigned from the U. S. Navy on February 1, 1861, and immediately offered his services to the Confederacy. He shipped on the cruiser *Sumter* and served on her until the vessel's arrival at Gibraltar in January of 1862. Unable to procure coal, Captain Semmes dispatched Myers across the Strait of Gibraltar to Morocco in search of the precious fuel. Myers later wrote of his "adventure" for the *Confederate Veteran*. (Semmes, *Memoirs of Service Afloat During the War Between the States*, pp. 332–333.) [RTC]

"Cruising with the Sumter" by Paymaster Henry Myers, CSN

Confederate Veteran, December 1923, pp. 452–454

Capt. Raphael Semmes, in command of the Confederate steamer *Sumter*, passed through the blockade of the Mississippi in July, 1861. After inflicting some damage to merchantmen in the Gulf and in South American waters, the vessel went to Southampton, England, followed closely by the United States steamer *Tuscarora*. From Southampton the *Sumter* went for the Straits of Gibraltar. After my resignation from the United States navy I had at once reported for duty, on the *Sumter* at New Orleans.

On January 4, 1862, the Confederate steamship *Sumter* arrived at Cadiz in a somewhat crippled condition. She had struck upon a rock in going into Maranham, Brazil, some months before, and was leaking badly. It was absolutely necessary that the ship be docked. We had been on a cruise of forty days before reaching Cadiz. Immediately on our arrival Captain Semmes opened a correspondence with the governor of the city. We were granted permission to remain, as it was shown that it was absolutely necessary for us to make repairs, and we were allowed to proceed to the naval dockyard.

The commander treated us with every respect and consideration, and hurried our repairs as rapidly as possible. As soon as the repairs were finished we returned to Cadiz. The governor was evidently timid, for he pelted Captain Semmes with so many official communications that at last, in disgust, Captain Semmes gave the order to "up anchor," and we steamed out of the harbor, followed by a government boat. The last I remember of our escort was an officer standing up and waving an envelope at us. No notice was taken of him, and we proceeded to Gibraltar. I mention these facts simply as a prelude to an episode in my life connected with my service as paymaster of the *Sumter*.

On our way into the harbor of Gibraltar we sighted an American vessel (the schooner *Neapolitan*, bound for Boston with a cargo of sulphur and fruit, which we burned in full sight of the town. This naturally created great excitement, and our vessel was the subject of much curiosity. As soon as we came to I was sent on shore to purchase (without funds) an anchor. When that cleverly-handled ship the *Iroquois* had tried to blockade us at Martinique and we ran for it, we had slipped our cable and lost our spare anchor. It was necessary, in so exposed a harbor as Gibraltar, that we should have another anchor. By good luck the first person I called upon in Gibraltar was a Scotch merchant. He proved a good friend, furnishing us with everything that we needed, except coal. Mr. Sprague, the American consul, who had been in Gibraltar for many years, and was deservedly respected, had used his influence in preventing our being furnished with coal. We remained at Gibraltar for more than a month before we received funds from Mr. Mason, one of our commissioners in England. We enjoyed our enforced stay at Gibraltar all the more because we had been on a most harassing cruise for many months. We were treated with marked hospitality by an English regiment, the Royal Prince of Wales Regiment, under the command of Lieutenant Colonel Dunn, and officered principally by Canadians. Colonel Dunn was said to have been one of the six hundred who rode "into the jaws of death" at Balaklava.

Immediately on receipt of funds, I was ordered to proceed to Cadiz, to purchase a cargo of coal and return to Gibraltar with it. I at once took passage in a small French steamer, which touched at Tangier. At Tangier I heard that a particular friend of mine, an English officer, was ill. I was glad of an opportunity of meeting him. We had been much together several years before on the Pacific station, when I was in the United States navy.

After spending an hour very pleasantly with him, recalling our younger days, I bade him good-by and started to return to the steamer which was to convey me to Cadiz. On reaching the Tangier boat landing, two swarthy Moors took their places on each side of me. I was seized by the wrists and turned toward the town. At first I could not realize the situation. Looking ahead, I saw a large man, evidently directing the movements of my captors. He was the American consul. He was gesticulating violently and indulging in a choice collection of oaths: "I'll teach you," he yelled, "to burn ships!" I was dragged along the streets. I attracted little attention, as I suppose such scenes were too common to create any excitement. I was at first carried into a stable, and across the narrow street was the consulate. After a while an old blacksmith, grizzled and grimed, proceeded with evident pleasure to rivet with horseshoe nails the heavy irons which manacled my ankles. Then I was informed I was to be put in the consulate for safekeeping.

At the door of the stable, just as I was going out, there stood a large swarthy man. Afterwards I learned that he was the interpreter to the legation. He extended his hand to me and grasped mine making me understand that he was a friend. He took me up in his arms, carrying me to the second story of the building, where I was to be kept a prisoner. Addressing me in French, he told me that means of communication would be found, and that, if I attempted an escape, I would be aided. With a view then of keeping up communication with my friend outside, I declined receiving food or anything else from the consul. My meals were sent me from an adjacent hotel. I was apparently not in good health. I, therefore, asked that a physician be sent for. An English physician came, and he gave me, in lieu of a prescription, a steel bow saw. It was to be used for cutting my irons off. My recovery was rapid, due to such a stimulus.

I at once set to work and sawed off the head of one of the nails. The manacle was a bar of rough iron, twelve or fourteen inches in length. There were holes in both ends, through which passed a ring fastened by this riveted nail. After cutting of one of the irons most unfortunately the saw broke and I could make no further use of it. I lashed the bar with a handkerchief to my leg. I was prepared for escape, though hampered. I had been informed that on a certain night parties would be under my window to receive me. That night happened to be a dark one, and, being on the alert, I heard the signals agreed upon.

During my imprisonment there were always six to eight guards in the next room. One of them was sitting in the doorway when I approached the window. I waited, a second signal, and then jumped out of the window. The distance to the ground was about eighteen feet. The ground was so hard, or the leap in the dark so uncertain, that on landing I burst my boot from toe to heel. To my great dismay, no one was there to assist me in my escape. I had jumped into an enclosed court. Seeing no way of exit, I climbed to the top of the adjoining Moorish house, which was only one story high, and, running along the roofs of several connecting houses, I made a second jump, thinking I would land in the street. I found myself in a Moorish court, with numerous cells opening into it. On attempting to enter one of the cells, women yelled and screamed, attracting the attention of the guard. I was recaptured and marched off to prison.

Paymaster Henry Myers (Naval Historical Center).

The guard, to show their zeal, showered blows upon me, one of the men, a very tall fellow, holding a sword point to my throat. The situation looked embarrassing. I soon discovered, however, that their anger was only simulated; as none of their blows hurt me. Once more my old friend, the blacksmith, made his appearance, and the irons were again riveted upon me.

After a week or ten days, a United States sloop of war, the *Ino*, came into port for the purpose of receiving me. She was commanded by a Captain Cressy, famous as having made an unusually quick voyage from New York to Australia in the early days of clipper ships. I was present when he made an official call on the consul, and felt assured that I could not expect any very generous treatment from him. On Captain Cressy's return to his ship, a body of about fifteen seamen was sent to take me on board. I suppose, as my capture was in violation of the neutrality laws of the port, a rescue might have been thought possible. On reaching the ship, I was placed between decks, and, to add to the indignities that had been heaped upon me, handcuffs were placed upon my wrists. My watch and my money were taken from me. Some time after, while a prisoner at Fort Warren, I communicated these facts to the Navy Department, and, through the instrumentality of Judge Wayne, one of the Supreme Court Judges, an old friend of my father's, they were returned.

We sailed for Cadiz, and I was prepared for a great deal of suffering. When off the harbor we met a four-masted schooner, the *Harvest Home*, loaded with salt and bound for Boston. I was transferred to the schooner. Although the sea was rough, I was compelled to go over the side of the ship manacled; hand and foot, and dropped into the boat which took me to the *Harvest Home*.

The voyage to Boston was a very stormy one. The old captain was a Maine man, with a warm sailor's heart. Although ordered to put me into the forecastle, he took me into his cabin, and I ate at his table. He took off my handcuffs. His treatment of me was in strong contrast to that of Captain Cressy. I hope the good old fellow is alive today, and I would have him know that his kindness to me I shall never forget. On reaching Boston I was delivered into the keeping of the United States marshal of the District of Massachusetts. I was taken to his office, where my irons were removed. A deputy marshal was sent out with me, and he purchased for me all that was necessary for my comfort. The Marshal's name I think, was Davis. He took me to the Tremont House, where, over a good dinner and a bottle of wine, he treated me as an officer and not as a pirate. He took my parole and left me, giving me the liberty of the city.

I walked about Boston unconscious of any trouble. After a short ramble, I returned to the hotel, where I slept the sleep of the just. In the morning, before daylight, some one awakened me. It proved to be the United States marshal. He said the night before there had nearly been a riot in the hotel. Parties who had had their ships burned by the *Sumter* expressed great indignation at my being treated in a humane way. Some had advocated the use of the nearest lamppost as a suitable ending of my career. More prudent counsels had, however, prevailed, and I was reserved for better things than an ornament to a street lamp. The marshal's office sent me in a carriage to the boat, which conveyed me to Fort warren, at that time commanded by Colonel Dimmick, of the 4th Artillery. A noble-hearted, gallant soldier was he, whose kind government of the prison won the affection and admiration of all who were in his keeping. He was strict in his discipline, yet extending to the prisoners every privilege consistent with their safety. The largest number of the prisoners had been captured at Fort Donelson. There were a few privateersmen and many Baltimoreans. I often recall with pleasure my social intercourse with these men. Among them were S. Teackle Wallace, Judge Parkins Scott, Mr. Charles Howard, his son Frank, Mr. Gatchell, Mayor Brown, and Harry Warfield. The monotony of prison life was relieved by books, cards, and other games. In the afternoons, when the weather permitted, hundreds would engage in football. During my stay no attempt was made by us to escape, not that that we were satisfied to remain prisoners, but there were too many chances against our being successful. After remaining at Fort Warren for four months, the joyful news came that there was to be an exchange, [although] saddened by the knowledge that the political prisoners form Baltimore were not included in the order.

My own hopes were dampened when I received a message to call at Colonel Dimmick's headquarters. I was informed that I was not included in the order, but that he would take the responsibility of sending me on to Fortress Monroe, where all the formalities of the exchange were to be carried out, and if the authorities at Washington desired to still retain me as a prisoner, I should then be informed of their decision. I felt some anxiety. I went through with the rest without any notice being taken of me. The passage from Fort Warren to Fortress Monroe was without incident or discomfort. A pleasing incident took place at Aiken, our point of debarkation on the James River. I had formed quite an intimacy with Colonel Waggaman, of the Louisiana regiment, who was captured at the Battle of the Wilderness, where he lost his sword. It was an heirloom and much prized by him. In some way he learned that his sword was at the War Department at Washington, and had had some correspondence in regard to it. While waiting to receive his baggage on board a steamboat lying at the landing, he noticed a general officer standing at the cabin door, resting a sword upon the deck. The Confederate colonel's eye traveled quickly from the point to the hilt of that sword. He recognized his own. Presently the United States officer informed him that he had been requested by General Meagher to return the sword to its former owner. The colonel's delight was great, for that sword had been handed down to him through several generations and had never been dishonored. That proved to me that all chivalry had not departed from the world, and that a soldier, though an enemy, recognized the fact that the most valued possession of a soldier was his untarnished sword.

I was fortunate in my intimacy with Colonel Waggaman, for his adjutant had procured an ambulance, and we were driven to Richmond, while most of the poor fellows had to travel on foot through the dust and mud.

In regard to my imprisonment at Tangier, Captain Semmes wrote: "A formal call was made in the British Parliament upon the Under Secretary for Foreign Affairs for an official statement of the facts, but it being rumored and believed soon afterwards that the prisoner had been released, no steps were taken by the British government, if any were contemplated, until it was too late."

3. The CSS *Alabama*

On August 1, 1861, Commander James D. Bulloch, Confederate naval agent in Europe, signed a contract with John Laird and Sons of Birkenhead across the Mersey from Liverpool for the construction of their 290th hull. The "290" eventually became the famous Confederate cruiser CSS *Alabama*. She was launched under the name *Enrica* to avoid British neutrality laws, and sailed for the Porta Praya in the Azores on July 29, 1862. There she was met by Captain Raphael Semmes and her other officers, fitted out as a cruiser, and commissioned on August 24.

Semmes' executive officer was First Lieutenant John M. Kell from Georgia, who had resigned from the U. S. Navy when his home state seceded. Kell was commissioned in the Confederate navy on March 26, 1861. He served on the cruiser *Sumter* in the same capacity as Semmes' executive officer, and the two developed a close and trusting relationship. After the war, Kell was asked by the editors of *Century Magazine* to write his account of the cruise of the *Alabama*. His essay was later incorporated into the *Battles & Leaders* series and is presented here. (Hearn, *Gray Raiders of the Sea*, p. 15.) [RTC]

"Cruise & Combats of the Alabama" by Commander John M. Kell, CSN

Battles and Leaders of the Civil War, Volume IV, pp. 600–614

The Confederate cruiser *Alabama* was built by the Lairds, of Birkenhead, England, for the Confederate States government. In the House of Commons the senior partner of the constructors stated "that she left Liverpool a perfectly legitimate transactions." Captain James D. Bulloch, as agent for the Confederacy, superintended her construction. As a "ruse" she was sent on a trial trip, with a large party of ladies and gentlemen. A tug met the ship in the channel and took off the guests, while the two hundred and ninetieth ship built in the Laird yard proceeded on her voyage to the island of Terceira, one of the Azores, whither a transport had preceded her with war material. Captain Raphael Semmes, with his officers, carried by the *Bahama*, met her there. Under the lee of the island, outside the marine league, we lashed our ships together, and made the transfer of armament and stores.

Arriving on Wednesday, August 20th, 1862, by Saturday night we had completed the transfer, and on Sunday morning, under a cloudless sky, upon the broad Atlantic, a common heritage, we put the *Alabama* in commission, by authority of the Confederate States Government. Thus empowered, we proceeded to ship such men from the crews of the several ships as were willing to sign the articles. Eighty men signed, and these formed the nucleus of our crew, the full complement being soon made up from the crews of our prizes. We then commenced our cruise of twenty-two months, during which she more successfully accomplished the work for which she was constructed than had any single ship of any nation in any age.

The *Alabama* was built for speed rather than battle. Her lines were symmetrical and fine; her material of the best. In fifteen minutes her propeller could be hoisted, and she could go through every evolution under sail without any impediment. In less time her propeller could be lowered; with sails furled, and yards braced within two points of a head-wind, she was a perfect steamer. Her speed, independent, was from ten to twelve knots; combined, and under favorable circumstances, she could make fifteen knots. When ready for sea she drew fifteen feet of water. She was barkentine-rigged, with long lower masts, which enabled her to carry an immense spread of lower canvas, and to lay close to the wind. Her engines were of three hundred horsepower, with a condensing apparatus that was indispensable. Since we lived principally upon provisions taken from

Commander John McIntosh Kell (Naval Historical Center).

our prizes, their water supply was never sufficient. Our condenser enabled us to keep the sea for long periods, as we had to seek a port only for coals.

Our armament consisted of eight guns: one Blakely 100-pounder rifled gun pivoted forward; one 8-inch solid-shot gun, pivoted abaft the mainmast; and six 32-pounders in broadside. Our crew numbered about 120 men and 24 officers. The commander, Captain Semmes, had been an officer of high standing in the old navy, had studied law, paying particular attention to the international branch, and had been admitted to the bar in Alabama, of which state he was a citizen. Thus he was eminently qualified for the position he was now called upon to assume. During the Mexican war he commanded the brig *Somers* in the blockade of Vera Cruz, and lost that unfortunate vessel in chase, during a norther, and narrowly escaped drowning. He afterward accompanied the army to the city of Mexico. The writer, his executive officer, had served twenty years in the old navy, and had accompanied every expedition of a warlike nature fitted out by the United States during that period. In the Mexican war, on the coast of California, I served ashore and afloat; then with the gallant Commodore Perry, in his expedition to Japan, and again in the Paraguay expedition. Our second lieutenant, R. F. Armstrong, from Georgia, and third lieutenant, J. D. Wilson, from Florida, came out with us in the *Sumter*. They were just from Annapolis, having resigned on the secession of their respective states. Both the father and the grandfather of our fourth lieutenant, Arthur Sinclair, Jr., of Virginia, had been captains in the United States navy. Our fifth lieutenant, John Lowe, of Georgia, had seen some service, and was a most efficient officer; our Acting Master, I. D. Bulloch, of Georgia, was a younger brother of Captain James D. Bulloch. A few months' active service gave confidence to the watch-officers of the ward-room, and it may safely be affirmed that older heads could not have filled their places with greater efficiency. The remainder of our ward-room mess was made up of our surgeon, Dr. F. L. Galt, of Virginia, also of the old service; Dr. D. H. Llewellyn, of Wiltshire,

England, who, as surgeon, came out in the ship when under English colors, and joined us as assistant surgeon. First Lieutenant B. K. Howell, of the Marine Corps, brother-in-law of President Davis, was from Mississippi, and Mr. Miles J. Freeman, our chief engineer, had been with us in the *Sumter*. The steerage mess was made up of three midshipmen (E. M. Anderson, of Georgia; E.A. Maffitt, of North Carolina, son of the captain of the Confederate States steamer *Florida*; and George T. Sinclair, of Virginia. The latter was afterward detached from the *Alabama* and made executive officer to Lieutenant Lowe on the *Tuscaloosa*, a tender that we captured and commissioned. Upon our arrival at Cherbourg, Sinclair came at once to join his old ship, having heard of the contemplated engagement. Accompanying him came also Lieutenant William C. Whittle, Jr., of Virginia, a gallant young son of Commodore W. C. Whittle of the old navy, and Lieutenant John Grimball, a South Carolinian, offering their services for any position during the engagement. They were not permitted to join us, on the ground that it would be a violation of French neutrality. The remainder of the steerage mess was made up of young master's mates and engineers, most of whom had come out with us in the *Sumter*.

The eleventh day after going into commission we captured our first prize, not one hundred miles from where we hoisted our flag. After working round the Azores for some weeks, with fine breezes, we shaped our course for Sandy Hook; but we encountered frequent gales off the Newfoundland banks, and on the 16th of October lost our main-yard in a cyclone. Being considerably shaken up, we decided to seek a milder latitude. Running down to the Windward Islands, we entered the Caribbean Sea. Our prizes gave us regularly the mails from the United States, from which we learned of the fitting out of the army under General Banks for the attack on Galveston and the invasion of Texas, and the day on which the fleet would sail; whereupon Captain Semmes calculated about the time they would arrive, and shaped his course accordingly, coaling and refitting ship at the Areas Keys. He informed me of his plan of attack, which was to sight the shipping off Galveston about the time that General Banks was due with his large fleet of transports, under the convoy perhaps of a few vessels of war. The entire fleet would anchor in the outer roadstead, as there is only sufficient water on the bar for light-draughts. All attention at such a time would be given to the disembarkation of the army, as there were no enemy's cruisers to molest them, our presence in the Gulf not being known. We were to take the bearing of the fleet, and, after the mid-watch was set and all was quiet, silently approach, steam among them with both batteries in action, slowly steam through the midst of them, pouring in a continuous discharge of shell to fire and sink them as we went; thus we expected to accomplish our work and be off on another cruise before the convoys could move.

But instead of sighting General Bank's fleet of transports we sighted five vessels of war at anchor, and soon after our lookout reported a steamer standing out for us. We were then under topsails only, with a light breeze, heading off shore, and gradually drawing our pursuer from the squadron. It was the *Hatteras,* and about dark she came up with us, and in an action of thirteen minutes we sank her. The action closed about twilight, when Captain Semmes, who always took his position on the weather horse-block, above the rail of the ship, to enable him to see all the surroundings, and to note the effect of our shot in action, or at exercise at general quarters, called to me and said, "Mr. Kell, the enemy has fired a gun to leeward; cease firing." We were then about seventy-five yards from the enemy, and could hear distinctly their hail, saying they "were fast sinking and on fire in three places, and for God's sake to save them." We immediately sent boats, and in the darkness took every living soul from her. These events occurred in the presence of the enemy's fleet, bearing the pennant of Commodore Bell with in signal distance. The *Hatteras* went down in a few minutes. She carried a larger crew than our own. Knowing that the Federal squadron would soon be upon us, every light on board ship was put under cover and we shaped our course for broader waters. During the night a fearful norther came sweeping after us, but under the circumstances it was a welcome gale. Hoisting our propeller, we crowded all the sail we could bear, and soon were out of harm's way. As Captain Blake of the *Hatteras* (whom I had known in the old service) came on deck, he remarked upon the speed we were making, and gracefully saluted me with, "Fortune favors the brave, sir!" I wished him a pleasant voyage with us; and I am sure he, with his officers and men, received every attention while on board the *Alabama*.

We paroled the officers and crew of the *Hatteras* at Kingston, Jamaica, and after repairing a few shot-holes and coaling ship, we passed on to our work in the South Atlantic, taking our position at the cross-roads of the homeward-bound East India and Pacific trade. After a few weeks of good work in that locality and along the coast of Brazil, we crossed over to the Cape of Good Hope, where we played "hide and seek" with the United States steamer *Vanderbilt*, whose commander, Charles H. Baldwin, had explained to Sir Baldwin Walker, the English Admiral of the station at Simon's Town, "that he did not intend to fire a gun at the *Alabama*, but to run her down and sink her." We were not disposed to try issues with the *Vanderbilt*; so one night about 11 o'clock, while it blew a gale of wind from the southeast, we hove anchor and steamed out of Simon's Bay. By morning we had made a good offing, and, setting what sail we could carry, hoisted our propeller and made a due south course. We ran down to the fortieth degree south latitude, where we fell in with westerly gales and bowled along nearly due east, until we shaped our course for the Straits of Java. Our long stretch across the Indian Ocean placed us in the China Sea, where we were least expected, and where we soon fell in with the China trade. In a few weeks we had so paralyzed the enemy's commerce that their ships were absolutely locked up in port, and neutrals were doing all the carrying trade. Having thus virtually cleared the sea of the United States flag, we ran down to Singapore, coaled ship, and then turned westward through the Straits of Malacca, across to India, thence to the east coast of Africa. Passing through the Mozambique Channel, we again touched at the Cape of Good Hope, and thence crossed to the coast of Brazil.

Our little ship was now showing signs of the active work she had been doing. Her boilers were burned out, and her machinery was sadly in want of repairs. She was loose at every joint, her seams were open, and the copper on her bottom was in rolls. We therefore set our course for Europe, and on the 11th of June, 1864, entered the port of Cherbourg, [France] and applied for permission to go into dock. There being none but national docks, the Emperor had first to be communicated with before permission could be granted, and he was absent from Paris. It was during this interval of waiting, on the third day after our arrival, that the *Kearsarge* steamed into the harbor, for the purpose, as we learned, of taking on board the prisoners we had landed from our last two prizes. Captain Semmes, however, objected to this on the ground that the *Kearsarge* was adding to her crew in a neutral port. The authorities conceding this objection valid, the *Kearsarge* steamed out of the harbor, without anchoring. During her stay we examined her closely with our glasses, but she was keeping on the opposite side of the harbor, out of the reach of a very close scrutiny, which accounts for our not detecting the boxing to her chain armor. After she left the harbor Captain Semmes sent for me to his cabin, and said: "I am going out, to fight the *Kearsarge*; what do you think of it?" We discussed the battery, and especially the advantage the *Kearsarge* had over us in her 11-inch guns. She was built for a vessel of war, and we for speed, and though she carried one gun less, her battery was more effective at point-blank range. While the *Alabama* carried one more gun, the *Kearsarge* threw more metal at a broadside; and while our heavy guns were more effective at long range, her 11-inch guns gave her greatly the advantage at close range. She also had a slight advantage in her crew, she carrying 163, all told, while we carried 149. Considering well these advantages, Captain Semmes communicated through our agent to the United States consul that if Captain Winslow would wait outside the harbor he would fight him as soon as we could coal ship.

Accordingly, on Sunday morning, June 19th, between 9 and 10 o'clock, we weighed anchor and stood out of the western entrance of the harbor, the French ironclad frigate *Couronne* following us. The day was bright and beautiful, with a light breeze blowing. Our men were neatly dressed, and our officers in full uniform. The report of our going out to fight the *Kearsarge* had been circulated, and many persons from Paris and the surrounding country had come down to witness the engagement. With a large number of the inhabitants of Cherbourg they collected on every prominent point on the shore that would afford a view seaward. As we rounded the breakwater we discovered the *Kearsarge* about seven miles to the northward and eastward. We immediately shaped our course for her, called all hands to quarters, and cast loose the starboard battery. Upon reporting to the captain that the ship was ready for action, he directed me to send all hands aft, and mounting a gun carriage, he made the following address:

"OFFICERS AND SEAMEN OF THE *ALABAMA*: You have at length another opportunity of meeting the enemy the first that has been presented to you since you sank the *Hatteras*! In the meantime you have been all over the world, and it is not too much to say that you have destroyed, and driven for protection under neutral flags, one-half of the enemy's commerce, which at the beginning of the war covered every sea. This is an achievement of which you may well be proud, and a grateful country will not be unmindful of it. The name of your ship has become a household word wherever civilization extends! Shall that name be tarnished by defeat? The thing is impossible! Remember that you are in the English Channel, the theater of so much of the naval glory of our race and that the eyes of all Europe are at this moment upon you. The flag that floats over you is that of a young Republic, which bids defiance to her enemy's whenever and wherever found! Show the world that you know how to uphold it! Go to your quarters."

In about forty-five minutes we were somewhat over a mile from the *Kearsarge*, when she headed for us, presenting her starboard bow. At a distance of a mile we commenced the action with our 100-pounder pivot-gun from our starboard bow. Both ships were now approaching each other at high speed, and soon the action became general with broadside batteries at a distance of about five hundred yards. To prevent passing, each ship used a strong port helm. Thus the action was fought around a common center, gradually drawing in the circle. At this range we used shell upon the enemy. Captain Semmes, standing on the horse-block abreast the mizzenmast with his glass in hand, observed the effect of our shell. He called to me and said: "Mr. Kell, use solid shot; our shell strike the enemy's side and fall into the water." We were not at this time aware of the chain armor of the enemy, and attributed the failure of our shell to our defective ammunition.

After using solid shot for some time, we alternated shell and shot. The enemy's 11-inch shells were now doing severe execution upon our quarter-deck section. Three of them successively entered our 8-inch pivot-gun port: the first swept off the forward part of the gun's crew; the second killed one man and wounded several others; and the third struck the breast of the gun-carriage, and spun around on the deck till one of the men picked it up and threw it overboard. Our decks were now covered with the dead and the wounded, and the ship was careening heavily to starboard from the effects of the shot-holes on her water-line.

Captain Semmes ordered me to be ready to make all sail possible when the circuit of fight should put our head to the coast of France; then he would notify me at the same time to pivot to port and continue the action with the port battery, hoping thus to right the ship and enable us to reach the coast of France. The evolution was performed beautifully, righting the helm, hoisting the head-sails, hauling aft the fore try-sail sheet, and pivoting to port, the action continuing almost without cessation.

This evolution exposed us to a raking fire, but, strange to say, the *Kearsarge* did not take advantage of it. The port side of the quarter-deck was so encumbered with the mangled trunks of the dead that I had to have them thrown overboard, in order to fight the after pivot-gun. I abandoned the after 32-pounder, and transferred the men to fill up the vacancies at the pivot-gun under the charge of young Midshipman Anderson, who in the midst of the carnage filled his place like a veteran. At this moment the chief engineer came on deck and reported the fires put out, and that he could no longer work the engines. Captain Semmes said to me, "Go below, sir, and see how long the ship can float." As I entered the ward-room the sight was indeed appalling. There stood Assistant-Surgeon Llewellyn at his post, but the table and the patient upon it had been swept away from him by an 11-inch shell, which opened in the side of the ship an aperture that was fast filling the ship with water.

It took me but a moment to return to the deck and report to the captain that we could not float ten minutes. He replied to me, "Then, sir, cease firing, shorten sail, and haul down the colors; it will never do in this nineteenth century for us to go down, and the decks covered with our gallant wounded." The order was promptly executed, after which the *Kearsarge* deliberately fired into us five shot.

I ordered the men to stand to their quarters and not flinch from the shot of the enemy; they stood every man to his post most heroically. With the first shot fired upon us after our colors were down, the quartermaster was ordered to show a white flag over the stern, which order was executed in my presence. When the firing ceased Captain Semmes ordered me to dispatch an officer to the *Kearsarge* to say that our ship was sinking, and to ask that they send boats to save our wounded, as our boats were disabled. The dingey, our smallest boat, had escaped damage. I dispatched Master's-mate Fullam with the request. No boats appearing, I had one of our quarter-boats lowered, which was slightly injured, and I ordered the wounded placed in her. Dr. Galt, the surgeon who was in charge of the magazine and shell-room division, came on deck at this moment and was at once put in charge of the boat, with orders to "take the wounded to the *Kearsarge*." They shoved off just in time to save the poor fellows from going down in the ship.

I now gave the order for every man to jump overboard with a spar and save himself from the sinking ship. To enforce the order, I walked forward and urged the men overboard. As soon as the decks were cleared, save of the bodies of the dead, I returned to the stern-port, where stood Captain Semmes with one or two of the men and his faithful steward, who, poor fellow! was doomed to a watery grave, as he could not swim. The *Alabama's* stern-port was now almost at the water's edge. Partly undressing, we plunged into the sea, and made an offing from the sinking ship, Captain Semmes with a life preserver and I on a grating.

The *Alabama* settled stern foremost, launching her bows high in the air. Graceful even in her death struggle, she in a moment disappeared from the face of the waters. The sea now presented a mass of living heads, striving for their lives. Many poor fellows sank for the want of timely aid. Near me I saw a float of empty shell-boxes, and called to one of the men, a good swimmer, to examine it; he did so and replied, "It is the doctor, sir, dead." Poor Llewellyn! He perished almost in sight of his home. The young midshipman, Maffitt, swam to me and offered his life-preserver. My grating was not proving a very buoyant float, and the whitecaps breaking over my head were distressingly uncomfortable, to say the least. Maffitt said: "Mr. Kell, take my life-preserver, sir; you are almost exhausted." The gallant boy did not consider his own condition, but his pallid face told me that his heroism was superior to his bodily suffering, and I refused it. After twenty minutes or more I heard near me some one call out, "There is our first lieutenant," and the next moment I was pulled into a boat, in which was Captain Semmes, stretched out in the stern-sheets, as pallid as death. He had received during the action a slight contusion on the hand, and the struggle in the water had almost exhausted him. There were also several of our crew in the, boat, and in a few moments we were alongside a little steam-yacht, which had come among our floating men, and by throwing them ropes had saved many lives. Upon reaching her deck, I ascertained for the first time that she was the yacht *Deerhound*, owned by Mr. John Lancaster, of England. In looking about I saw two French pilot-boats engaged in saving our crew, and finally two boats from the *Kearsarge*. To my surprise I found on the yacht Mr. Fullam, whom I had dispatched in the dingey to ask that boats be sent to save our wounded. He reported to me that our shot had literally torn the casing from the chain armor of the *Kearsarge*, indenting the chain in many places, which explained Captain Semmes' observation of the effect of our shell upon the enemy, "that they struck the sides and fell into the water."

Captain Winslow, in his report, states that his ship was struck twenty-five or thirty times, and I doubt if the *Alabama* was struck a greater number of times. I may not, therefore, be bold in asserting that had not the *Kearsarge* been protected by her iron cables, the result of the fight would have been different. Captain Semmes felt the more keenly the delusion to which he fell a victim (not knowing that the *Kearsarge* was chain-clad) from the fact that he was exceeding his instructions in seeking an action with the enemy; but to seek a fight with an iron-clad he conceived to be an unpardonable error. However, he had the satisfaction of knowing she was classed as a wooden gun-boat by the Federal Government; also that he had inspected her with most excellent glasses, and so far as outward appearances showed she displayed no chain armor. At the same time it must be admitted that Captain Winslow had the right unquestionably to protect his ship and crew. In justice to Captain Semmes I will state that the battle would never have been fought had he known that the *Kearsarge* wore an armor of chain beneath her outer coverings. Thus was the *Alabama* lost by an error, if you please, but, it must be admitted, a *most pardonable* one, and not until "Father Neptune" claimed her as his own did she lower her colors.

The 11-inch shells of the *Kearsarge* did fearful work, and her guns were served beautifully, being aimed with precision, and deliberate in fire. She came into action magnificently. Having the speed of us, she took her own position and fought gallantly. But she tarnished her glory when she fired upon a fallen foe. It was high noon of a bright, beautiful day, with a moderate breeze blowing to waft the smoke of battle clear, and nothing to obstruct the view at five hundred yards. The very fact of the *Alabama* ceasing to fire, shortening sail, and hauling down her colors simultaneously, must have attracted the attention of the officer in command of the *Kearsarge*. Again, there is no reason given why the *Kearsarge* did not steam immediately into the midst of the crew of the *Alabama*, after their ship had been sunk, and, like a brave and generous foe, save the lives of her enemies, who had fought nobly as long as they had a plank to stand upon. Were it not for the timely presence of the kind-hearted Englishman and the two French pilot-boats, who can tell the number of us that would have rested with our gallant little ship beneath the waters of the English Channel? I quote the following from Mr. John Lancaster's letter to the London "Daily News": "I presume it was because he [Captain Winslow] *would* not or could not save them himself. The fact is that if the captain and crew of the *Alabama* had depended for safety altogether upon Captain Winslow, not one-half of them would have been saved."

When Mr. Lancaster approached Captain Semmes, and said, "I think every man has been picked up; where shall I land you?" Captain Semmes replied, "I am now under the English colors, and the sooner you put me with my officers and men on English soil, the better." The little yacht moved rapidly away at once, under a press of steam, for Southampton. Armstrong, our second lieutenant, and some of our men who were saved by the French pilot-boats, were taken into Cherbourg. Our loss was 9 killed, 21 wounded, and 10 drowned.

It has been charged that an arrangement had been entered into between Mr. Lancaster and Captain Semmes, previous to our leaving Cherbourg, that in the event of the *Alabama* being sunk the *Deerhound* would come to our rescue. Captain Semmes and myself met Mr. Lancaster for the first time when rescued by him, and he related to us the circumstance that was the occasion of his coming out to see the fight. Having his family on board, his intention was to attend church with his wife and children, when the gathering of the spectators on the shore attracted their attention, the report having been widely circulated that the *Alabama* was to go out that morning and give battle to the *Kearsarge*. The boys were clamorous to see the fight, and after a family discussion as to the propriety of going out on the Sabbath to witness a naval combat, Mr. Lancaster agreed to put the question to vote at the breakfast-table, where the youngsters carried their point by a majority. Thus many of us were indebted for our lives to that inherent trait in the English character, the desire to witness a "passage at arms."

That evening we landed in Southampton, and were received by the people with every demonstration of sympathy and kindly feeling. Thrown upon their shores by the chances of war, we were taken to their hearts and homes with that generous hospitality which brought to mind with tenderest feeling our own dear Southern homes in *ante-bellum* times. To the Rev. F. W. Tremlett, of Belsize Park, London, and his household, I am indebted for a picture of English home life that time cannot efface, and the memory of which will be a lasting pleasure till life's end.

4. The CSS *Florida*

Upon arrival in Liverpool on June 4, 1861, Commander James D. Bulloch began searching the docks and shipyards all over England for suitable vessels that could be converted into cruisers. By the end of June, Bulloch was frustrated in his search for the right vessel, and instead contracted with the shipbuilding firm of William C. Miller and Sons, of Liverpool, for the construction of the Confederacy's first foreign-built cruiser. (Hearn, *Gray Raiders of the Sea*, p. 53.)

The firm of Miller and Sons was a wise choice for Bulloch, for it had extensive experience building wooden ships for Her Majesty's government. Bulloch chose as the basis for his design a fast dispatch gunboat of the Royal Navy. The only changes he made were to lengthen the hull in order to accommodate additional coal, and her rigging was increased to allow her to carry more canvas. Fawcett, Preston and Company, also of Liverpool, was contracted to build the engines. Given the dockyard name of *Oreto* to forestall Union spies, Bulloch persuaded John Henry Thomas, the local agent of the firm of Thomas Brothers of Palermo, to oversee construction and to indicate that she was destined for his Italian-based firm. After her completion, the *Oreto* sailed on March 22, 1862, with no complications from British authorities. This was to change, however, when she reached Nassau in the Bahamas. (Owsley, *The C.S.S. Florida, Her Building and Operations*, p. 19.)

John Newland Maffitt was from North Carolina and had resigned his lieutenant's commission in the U. S. Navy on May 2, 1861. After commissioning in the Confederate navy, he served for a while at Savannah before being given command of the blockade runner *Gordan*. Bulloch requested Maffitt to command the *Florida*, and after the war in 1882, Maffitt wrote about the fitting out and operations of the cruiser for the *United Service* magazine. His essay, entitled "Blockade Running," is essentially written in three parts. Parts one and three deal with his experiences as commander of blockade runners, and part two, presented here, concerns the *Florida*. [RTC]

"Blockade Running, Part 2" by
Commander John Newland Maffitt, CSN
The United Service, Volume VII, July 1882, pp. 14–29

On the 10th of May, 1862, I arrived in Nassau with the steamer *Gordon*. When the usual swarm of newsmongers had dispersed, Lieutenant Low, of the Confederate navy came on board and presented me with a communication from Captain Bullock, our naval agent in Europe. The purport of his letter was to announce his having dispatched a gunboat to Nassau, and as the officer to whom Mr. Mallory had assigned the command had declined it, he requested that I would immediately take charge and hasten to sea before the government authorities became exercised as to her character and ultimate occupation. Lieutenant Low informed me that the *Oreto* had been anchored for some time at Cochran's anchorage, nine miles east of Nassau, where her position was daily becoming perilous and precarious. Fully appreciating the necessity for prompt action, I immediately surrendered the *Gordon*, and informed Adderly & Co., to whom the *Oreto* was consigned, that as a Southern officer it was my duty to become the custodian of the lone Confederate waif upon the waters until the pleasure of the Navy Department should be expressed. By a returning blockade-runner I informed the Secretary of the Navy of the course a sense of duty had caused me to adopt, and requested, should he confirm me in the command, that he would send without delay experienced lieutenants and other necessary officers, besides funds, to enable me to get the *Oreto* out of Nassau with promptness and dispatch, as her warlike construction and equivocal position were calculated to arouse suspicion, and through the agency of Federal spies cause investigation and consequent arrest.

The response to my communication brought three inexperienced young officers, strangers to the sea, with instructions for me (in the event of the non-arrival of Captain North) to assume command, equip, fit out, and immediately proceed to sea as a Confederate cruiser. From Lieutenant Stribling (who had just arrived from England en route for home) I learned that North had positively declined the command, consequently my status in regard to the *Oreto* became defined. The position immediately involved me in anxiety and trouble, as through the representations of the American consul the commander of Her Britannic Majesty's ship *Greyhound*, under the rulings of the "Foreign Enlistment, Act," had for the third time arrested the *Oreto* and had now placed her in the Court of Admiralty.

Trusting that the evidence would not be sufficient to condemn the steamer, I, with the intelligent assistance of Mr. I. B. Lafitte, of Charleston, South Carolina, then connected with the house of Frazier, Trenholm & Co., commenced (*sub rosa*, of course) to secure an armament and all the adjuncts that were requisite for the efficient equipment of a man-of-war. The complacent order to equip, fit out, and proceed on a cruise of aggression, as though a navy-yard and enlisting rendezvous were at my disposal, clearly indicated that the Navy Department had failed to properly consider the very many obstacles and difficulties that surrounded me at Nassau. In a British port, restrained by the "Queen's Neutrality Proclamation" and the stringent "Foreign Enlistment Law," with its severe penal enactments (not to mention Federal detective espionage), the want of officers, men, and money, all these hampers to my proceedings were constantly springing up from ambush like the armed men of Roderic Dhu.

Nevertheless, I hoped on, worked on, with a zealous determination that at all hazards I would faithfully guard the interests of the Confederacy in this its first constructed bantling of the billows. In my extremity the chivalric Stribling, who had served on the *Sumter* with Semmes, relinquished his leave of absence and gallantly came to the rescue by volunteering his services. Joyfully were they accepted, admirable was the succor, for no such could be obtained in Nassau. June and July passed in a wearisome state of uncertainty and secret labor. To multiply my discomfiture, malignant yellow fever became an epidemic. This created a demand for much of my time in attending on friends who were afflicted. At last the August term of the Vice-Admiralty Court arrived. The *Oreto* underwent her trial. It was clearly proven that she left England unarmed and unequipped, and had continued so during her stay at Nassau, and she was released from bondage. Without an hour's delay she was hastened out of the harbor, and at midnight, with a tender in tow that carried the equipments, we steamed quietly away from the scene of her troubles.

On the next day at noon the *Oreto* was anchored near a desolate, uninhabited islet called Green Cay, some ninety miles to the southward of New Providence. Then commenced a task more difficult and painfully laborious than anything my wide experience had heretofore encountered. Our crew consisted of twenty-two, all told, in place of the proper complement of one hundred and thirty. There was a deficit among the officers of two lieutenants, sailing-master, surgeon, paymaster, one engineer, five midshipmen, boatswain, and gunner.

Commander John Newland Maffitt (Library of Congress).

With this inadequate force two rifle 7-inch and six 6-inch guns, with carriages, powder, shot, shell, general equipment, and stores, were to be hoisted on board. However, no one murmured; officers and men stripped to the buff and went to work, while the broiling tropical sun of August blistered and burned their exposed persons. On the second day one of the men sickened, and in eight hours died. As he had while in Nassau dissipated to excess, this sudden winding up of his earthly career was attributed to that cause, though the yellow appearance of the corpse excited in my mind very grave misgivings. We buried him on the rocky islet, and resumed our Herculean task, which continued for seven days. On the eighth we rested from sheer prostration.

At length our task was finished, the guns mounted and in position, the anchor weighed, and with tender in tow we steamed away from the lone rock sentinel. After the establishment of general order the guns were run in for loading. An exclamation of despair from Stribling attracted my attention. "What is the difficulty?" I inquired.

"Good heavens, captain, we are ruined! In the haste and secrecy of loading, the tender, rammers, sponges, sights, locks, beds, and quoins have all been left in Nassau. The battery; sir, is impotent without these essentials, and we have no means of temporary substitution."

The misfortune was indeed deplorable, though slightly relieved by the completeness of our pivot guns.

When we passed through the Queen's Channel the tender was cast off, the English colors hauled down, and with loyal cheers for the *Florida*, we flung the Confederate banner to the breeze.

Alas! poor *Florida*. Beautiful in model, warlike in guns, the absence of important essentials despoiled the reality, and left her afloat the mere typical representation of what a gallant cruiser should be.

This, our first day of assumed nationality, proved wondrously beautiful. The bright tropical sun shone, but the softest of trade-winds cooled the atmosphere and invigorated all hands for judicious organization, and ingenious application of limited means into some tangible form of naval efficiency. These duties were not accomplished until night. Setting the watch, and directing the course to be steered, I obeyed the dictates of nature and retired to rest.

From uneasy dreams I was aroused at daylight to visit two of the men who were reported as ill. Premonitions of an approaching yellow fever epidemic cast its shadow over my mind. Nervously I paced the quarter-deck, vainly striving to conquer despondency, as I contemplated the overwhelming responsibilities that were charged upon my official position. The fact of being afloat I knew would excite extra extraordinary expectations, and to fail, under any circumstances, involved professional extinction. These gloomy reveries were interrupted by a delirious cry from the sick men. Hastening to their bedsides, I found them raving mad with fever. A survey of their condition confirmed my worst apprehensions, for it conveyed the dreadful intelligence that the pestilential tyrant of the tropics had invaded the *Florida*. Thus were we assailed by an element of impotence more terrible to encounter than all that was endured in our past physical struggle.

Intrusting to Stribling alone the melancholy information, we determined, if possible, to conceal the appearance of the epidemic, with the delusive hope that the cases might prove sporadic. In the absence of a regular physician, the medical duties of the steamer as a necessity devolved upon me, and throughout the anxious day the requisitions on my ability were constant. The trade-winds freshened, and the hope was indulged that the pure ocean air would disinfect the *Florida*, and relieve her from the malaria of the fell disease. Alas, "there was no balm in Gilead." By sundown more than half the crew, with two officers, were added to the sick list. The character of the affliction could be no longer concealed.

An epidemic on shore invariably produces a general panic. The well can obtain safety in flight, or at least free themselves from its constant terrible presence. But at sea, imprisoned, without the possibility of escape, within the narrow confines of the vessel, there is no relief from the howls of the delirious, the death-heralding black vomit, or the pinched and yellow countenances of those who have ceased to suffer and are reluctantly manipulated by their surviving shipmates as the hammock-shroud and ponderous shot are arranged for the final plunge into that ocean of rest, the seaman's uncoffined grave.

Reluctantly the idea of cruising was abandoned, a harbor of refuge had become a necessity. Cuba was in sight, and Cardenas, a familiar port, not far distant. Shaping the course in conformity with the obligations involved in my responsibility we eluded the numerous cruisers, and at midnight anchored at Cardenas, our force having been reduced by the epidemic to one fireman and two seamen.

Lieutenant Stribling was dispatched to Havana to obtain medical aid and nurses. By this time the quarter-deck had been converted into a hospital, where at all hours of the day and night my presence was required, for there were none to aid, none to relieve me from the exhausting demand upon my medical attention to the sick and dying. A communication was addressed to the governor of Cardenas, soliciting the aid of a physician. The response was couched in the most courteous of hyperbolical Spanish, but ingeniously equivocal. I was politely reminded of the queen's "neutrality proclamation," particularized by citing the injunctions against increasing military equipment, recruiting, or remaining in port longer than twenty-four hours.

Disgusted with this abnegation of the ordinary manifestations of humanity, I resolved to give no further heed to national laws or official mandates, but let fate do her worst, and battle with our misfortune, courageously to the bitter end.

The sun rose and set upon the beautiful *Florida*. At her peak the Confederate flag waved in solemn dignity, and no external spectator who gazed upon the outside symmetrical appearance could for a moment fancy that burning fevers and fatal vomitos were devouring the life-throbs of her scanty crew. There is a limit beyond which human ability is incapable of passing. The overwhelming duties and responsibilities that had been forced upon me reduced me physically to that terminus of endurance. This became painfully evident from the loss of appetite, nervous prostration, and inability to refresh myself with even a few moments of vital repose. Constantly inhaling the pestilential atmosphere of the quarter-deck had infected my system with the fell disease. The demon of Hades tarried not long in his approach, but came with a throbbing pulsation of the brain, accompanied by a dizzy blindness and shooting pains that produced excruciating agony, as if my bones had been converted into red-hot tubes of iron and the marrow in them boiling with the fervent heat. My tongue, mouth, and throat were blistered, as if molten lead had been poured down them. Unquenchable thirst that nothing could alleviate was accompanied by the most violent retching. There was no moisture in my eyes; the fountains seemed seared and parched, as if red-hot irons had branded the well-spring of tears. Every pore of my body seemed to be hermetically sealed with a burning fever from the furnace of my heart. This was succeeded by icy chills. At first the delirium of suffering ebbed and flowed, leaving brief periods of consciousness, which, with singular determination, were employed in directing the management of my case. At length a dreary blank enveloped my mind; the vital spark flickered in its unstable tabernacle as the battle of life was fought. Thus a week elapsed, when reason asserted a feeble sway. I awoke to a sense of reality, and discovered in the gloom of the cabin three somber-looking individuals, who, to my dreaming fancy, appeared like weird phantoms of the nether world. In a few moments I became conscious of their corporeal substance, and discovered that they were medical savants of Cardenas, whom some kind friends had summoned to my couch. Their consultation had ended, and the voice of the senior, in sepulchral cadence, enunciated, with the aid of his time-piece,

"It is now," said he, "twenty minutes after nine o'clock. I am convinced, from careful investigation, that the captain cannot survive beyond meridian."

The profound lugubriousness of their assent excited an irresistible impulse that caused me to exclaim, "You're a liar, sir; I have too much to do, and cannot afford to die."

The reverend medicos smiled at my excitement, and soon departed, without, however, revoking their opinion. This determination to live (for in sickness there is vitality in individual will) acted like a charm upon my system. By the interposition of divine Providence the messenger of death was arrested.

When my mind regained its normal condition, I expressed a desire to see the young gentlemen who had shared with me in the trials and dangers through which we had passed. The invitation was promptly accepted, and I was soon surrounded by these noble young men. Several had paid toll at the half-way house, but speedily retraced their steps on the road to health. There was one beloved form missing which in the early days of my illness was never absent from my couch. "Where," I nervously inquired, "is my beloved son, Laurens?" Every countenance saddened, and for a time only sobs responded to my interrogatory. Finally I learned that he had died the day before of the scourge that had so fearfully afflicted us, and had that morning been buried while I was unconscious and supposed to be passing into eternity. Appreciating the agony that oppressed me, the gentlemen soon departed and left me to regain composure.

John Laurens Read was a noble youth, a native of Charleston, South Carolina, and sixteen years of age. Well born (Henry Laurens, of Revolutionary fame, being his great-grandsire), he was the possessor of all those noble characteristics of the purest blood of the best and most patriotic days of the country, and was much beloved by his brother officers.

Stribling returned with a Georgia physician and fourteen non-enlisted laborers, the neutrality laws utterly precluding the possibility of procuring seamen.

Marshal Surano, the governor-general of Cuba, requested that the *Florida* would proceed to Havana, where she would be more secure under the guns of the Moro. In compliance with this friendly desire, at 9 PM on the 30th of August [1862] we weighed anchor and left the harbor of Cardenas, our reminiscences of the terrible sojourn being clouded with memories of our dead who slept beneath its sod. The passage was undisturbed by Federal cruisers, as we ran the land down, keeping within the tabooed marine limit of the Island of Cuba. To seaward an occasional blockader could be seen, alert as usual, not unfrequently halting suspected crafts that might perchance have dodged out of Dixie with sufficient cotton on board to reward the lynx-eyed cruiser with prize-money. Cotton under capture was certainly a kingly consideration in those times to the devoted blockader. At daylight we anchored in Havana, and were soon thronged with visitors, whose curiosity outweighed all dread of Yellow-Jack. We were kept under a strict surveillance, and all our ingenuity could not procure a piece of timber long and large enough to be molded into rammers and sponges.

It had become evident that the *Florida* would have to enter a Confederate port to be officered and properly equipped. This conviction determined me to sail for Mobile, which I learned had a smaller blockading force on duty than any other Southern port.

On the 1st of September, 1862, we steamed out of Havana and made a direct course for Mobile Bay. The voyage proved propitious, and at 3 PM on the 4th we sighted Fort Morgan, and two steamers, evidently blockaders, hastening to contest our entrance. Though still quite feeble, with assistance I was enabled to repair on deck and reconnoiter the situation. There was not a cloud in the sky, or zephyr breath on the sea, to disturb the serenity of the surroundings. But when the eye sighted the approach of the vengeful foe this poetry of view faded before the harsh and stern reality. Lieutenant Stribling suggested that under the circumstances of our crippled condition, and inability to offer resistance, it would be advisable to stand off again and defer the attempt to enter the harbor until darkness should mantle our movements. This proposition I rejected, as the draught of the *Florida* did not permit of dalliance with the shoals, nor was there any surety of finding the channel without the aid of the light-house, which had been dismantled. "But, sir," said Lieutenant Stribling, "in this attempt we cannot avoid passing close to the blockade-squadron, the result of which will be our certain destruction."

"The hazard is certainly very great, but it cannot be avoided. We will hoist the English colors as a 'ruse de guerre,' and boldly stand for the commanding officer's ship; the remembrance of the delicate Trent affair may perhaps cause some deliberation and care before the batteries are let loose upon us; four minutes of hesitation on their part may save us."

Moreover, having decided regardless of hazards to run the blockade, there was no time for hesitation, but dash ahead, trusting to fortune and a clean pair of heels.

The English colors were set, and under a full head of steam we boldly stood for the flag-ship. When about some eighty yards distant from her she fired a warning gun, and ordered us to heave to, evidently deceived by our general appearance and bold approach into the belief that we were English. We paid no attention to the signal or command, but continued to press vigorously on. A second shot passed over our bow, when immediately their whole broadside was poured into us, the effect of which was to carry away some of our hammock nettings and much of our standing and running rigging. Had their guns been depressed, the career of the *Florida* would have ended then and there. The example of the flag-ship, the *Oneida*, was instantly followed by the other two ships of the squadron, and their fierce fusillade was hurled with the resolute determination of destroying the Confederate. In truth, so terrible became the bombardment, every hope of escape fled from my mind. One 11-inch shell from the *Oneida* passed through the coal-bunkers on the port side, struck the port forward boiler, took off one man's head as it passed on the berth deck, and wounded nine men. If it had exploded, which it failed to do, I no doubt would have lost every man on the vessel except the two men at the helm, as I had ordered all the crew below, they being exposed to no purpose on the deck. The officers of course remained at their stations, and though subjected to constant storms of destructive missiles, they miraculously escaped. Immediately after this a shot from the *Winona* entered the cabin and passed through the pantry, and an 11-inch shell from the *Oneida* exploded close to the port gangway and seriously injured the vessel. The fire from this vessel, the *Oneida*, increased in warmth and destruction. I endeavored to make sail, and succeeded only so far as letting fall the topsails. Several men were wounded in the rigging; one had the whole bottom of his foot taken off by a shrapnel shot, and afterwards died from tetanus, and the sheets and tyes were shot away, so that I was not able to set the sails properly. At this moment I hauled down the English flag under which we were sailing, and gave the order to one of the helmsmen to hoist the Confederate flag. At that moment he was endeavoring to haul up the foot brail of the spanker, and lost his forefinger with a shrapnel shot, so that my order in regard to the flag could not be complied with. During all this time shell and shrapnel were bursting over and around us, the shrapnel striking the hull and the spars at almost every discharge. We made no effort at resistance, for though armed we were not at all equipped, having neither rammers, sponges, sights, quoins, nor elevating-screws. Properly manned and equipped, the excitement of battle would have relieved the terrible strain upon our fortitude, which nevertheless sustained us through the withering assaults of a foe who were determined upon capture or destruction.

The loud explosions, roar of shot, crashing spars and rigging, mingling with the moans of our sick and wounded, instead of intimidating, only increased our determination to enter the destined harbor. Simultaneously two heavy shells entered our hull with a thud that caused a vibration from stem to stern. The 11-inch shell from the *Oneida* which came in and passed along the berth deck entered three inches above the water-line, and if there had been any sea on our bilge pumps could not have saved the vessel from sinking. Everything depended upon the engineers, and in that department the duty was performed with efficiency and zeal.

Thus far we had borne the fierce assaults with the calmness that oft befriends the victims of desperation, and as nothing vital had been injured the gradual withdrawal from the close proximity of the guns of the enemy excited pleasurable hope. Finally we cleared the grouping circle, and the prospects of escape began to brighten. This the enemy observed, as more fiercely their efforts increased, more furiously roared their artillery, and denser became the black clouds from their smokestacks, as they fed their fires with rosin and other combustible material to increase their head of steam.

Vain were these excessive exertions; fate had carved out for the *Florida* a more extended career, and this baptism of fire christened the gallant craft as a Confederate torch-bearer on the ocean of public events. The shot and shell gradually fall short, a gentle northeast wind lifts the cloudy curtain and exhibits the indignant Federals hauling of from the bar, while in the channel-way, battered and torn, war worn and weary, with her own banner floating in the breeze, the *Florida* in safety is welcomed to her anchorage by hearty cheers from the defenders of Fort Morgan.

The dangers through which we had passed were unavoidable, our success a source of professional congratulation, and the reaction from overstrained anxiety to quiescent repose pleasurable beyond expression.

As the yellow fever still clung to the steamer, assailing both officers and men, very judiciously we were placed in quarantine. At noon of the second day after anchoring, on being called to Stribling's bedside, I was shocked to discover that this noble officer was afflicted by the fell disease that had already caused us so much misery. All that medical skill and devoted friendship could accomplish was rendered with a zeal that knew no tiring. Vain were human efforts. The fatal vomito announced the end of hope. Nothing remained to be done, apart from tender nursing and affectionate care. Lightly the rough seamen trod the quarter-deck, and the harsh coils of rope were flemished in their places as noiselessly as fall the gentle snow-flakes upon the bosom of our mother earth. All orders were issued in subdued whispers, that nothing might disturb the last moments of the dying officer. In unconsciousness his spirit seemed to wander, though he still held my hand that for twenty hours had never parted from his feeble grasp.

> "Sweet mother," he murmured, "take me to your heart of hearts
> "Lend, lend your wings; I mount, I fly!
> O grave, where is thy victory?
> O death, where is thy sting?"

These, his last words, were whispered with expiring breath, and the spirit of the chivalric Christian Stribling passed to that better land, "where the wicked cease from troubling, and the weary are at rest."

We buried him on the peaceful heights of Montrose, but not his memory, that was embalmed in our hearts, and every throbbing reminiscence of Confederate existence rewrites there the epitaph that had no carving on his grave.

For some length of time the poor *Florida* seemed haunted by ghosts as her ghastly crew slowly recovered from the baneful influence of the tropical epidemic. At last pratique is granted, the yellow flag disappears, and the din of workmen engaged in repairs arouses the lethargic into action. The repairs were multifarious, and vital to the efficiency of the vessel. The facilities were subordinate to the distance of twenty-eight miles from Mobile and its mechanical appliances. An extensive bay, subject to chopping seas in ordinary winds, operated against the efficiency of the ship carpenters who were employed to repair damages to the hull. In addition, the wire standing rigging was to be spliced, a most tedious and slow operation,—calking, under every disadvantage of rainy weather, besides hundreds of minor matters that nevertheless were important. Detail of officers and gathering together of a crew consumed time, as did the ordnance arrangements for the battery of the steamer. Three months were consumed from the date of pratique to the reporting of the vessel "ready for sea."

The Secretary of the Navy, in sending his cruising instructions, manifested extreme impatience at the long but unavoidable tarry of the *Florida* in port. In response, I stated that the blockade of the port had become so stringent, that the commanding officer had reported the *Florida* as "hermetically sealed up in Mobile Bay." I also added that the speed of the *Florida* had been vastly overrated, and as the entire responsibility of her safe delivery from thraldom rested upon me, I would not trifle with her safety, but be guided by my professional judgment, and select a northeast gale (due at this season) for testing my ability to carry the steamer in safety through the cordon of blockaders that clustered around the outlet of Mobile Bay.

The response to this communication was a telegram detaching me from command, and assigning it to Captain Barney. At this epoch in Confederate naval history President Davis arrived in Mobile, and Admiral Buchanan, who had indorsed all my views as correct and judicious, represented to the President that my detachment was decidedly a mistake, and might prove disastrous, etc., etc. Mr. Davis took decided action. Promptly the order of detachment was revoked, and I again reinstated, watched for the expected northeaster, determined to risk nothing until I had it at my heels.

In the mean time, Captain (now Admiral) Preble announces to Admiral Farragut the pain and mortification he experienced at the escape through his command of the "rebel" steamer, owing, as he officially stated, "to her speed and unparalleled audacity." The government, irritated by the escape of the steamer, disregarded Preble's earnest applications for a court-martial, and with unjust haste summarily dismissed him from the navy. Eventually he was honorably restored to his proper position.

As an enemy, Preble was consistent and honorable; as a. friend, faithful and true; even through all the vicissitudes of untoward events that erected barriers between old naval associates, who in by-gone days had buffeted together in happy unity the storms of old Neptune and hardships of the sea. The grand and gallant old knights of the navy, who inaugurated its reputation and emblazoned its history with a halo of glory, left as an heirloom a chivalry of brotherhood that purified friendship and exalted its sentiments above the factions of life and storms of adversity.

On the 14th of January, much to the delight of the ardent spirits of the *Florida*, the barometrical indications prognosticated stormy weather. Throughout the day it blew a gale from the southward and eastward, accompanied with gusts of rain. Feeling sure that my long expected northeaster was brewing, I determined to run down to Mobile Point and anchor, ready to face the music when in my judgment the propitious moment should arrive. About 5 PM the wind, as I expected, changed to the northward with clear weather, when the blockading squadron was revealed, and so aligned as to prevent, as they doubtless thought, my successful egress to the sea. Double reefs were taken in our topsails, and balanced reefs in the fore and main trysails. The topsails I caused to be mastheaded, and the gaskets replaced by split rope-yarns, which would give way when the sheets were hauled upon and the sail set without sending the top-men aloft. Everything was secured for bad weather, a double watch set, and the crew piped down. During the night the wind increased so violently that it was impossible to get under way until 2.20 AM, when the weather moderated. All hands were called, steam was up, and soon we were under way, heading for the bar. A night of bitter cold had doubtless caused the Federal lookouts to obtain partial shelter from the stinging blasts of winter, and consequently abate much of their acute vigilance. This was the presumption, as, to our astonishment, we passed quite near to a blockader inside the bar, and were not discovered until abreast of a third, when the alarm was given by drums beating the call, flashing lights, and general commotion, as cables were slipped, and, 'mid the confusion of a surprise, a general chase commenced in the wildest excitement. All the steam and canvas that could be applied urged us swiftly over the rugged seas, as half a dozen rampant Federals followed with intense eagerness on the trail of the saucy Confederate, that "rebel" craft whose escape from thraldom was sorely dreaded at the North, in visions of burning vessels and commercial disasters.

From stormy morn to stormy eve the chase is vigilantly continued, and the enemy, with a full appreciation of the magnitude of their duty, press on with unflagging zeal. From time to time a gunboat, more fleet than her companions, gains sufficiently on the *Florida* to increase the interest and excitement of the pursuit. As the day declines the pursuers one by one fade under the horizon, leaving but two with sufficient speed to hold their distance and flatter themselves with prospects of success.

High rolled the angry waves, and through its yeasty foam the Confederate plunges, regardless of the toppling seas that roll on board in cold blue waves from stem to stern. Heavy pitching springs the fore topsail yard; to fish and repair renders it necessary to unbend the sail and send the spar on deck. This is quickly done, but the reduction of canvas depletes our speed, and the enemy shorten their distance, with efforts to overhaul us. Their exertions are futile, for our damages repaired, the canvas again quickly swells to the storm, showing against the background of gathering darkness a white and fleecy guiding-mark for the persistent enemy.

Desirous of ending the chase, I determined to despoil them of their guiding facility for steering. All hands were called to shorten sail, and, like snow-flakes under a summer sun, our canvas melts from view, and is secured in long low bunts to the yards. Thus, shorn of her plumage, the engines at rest, between high toppling seas, clear daylight was necessary to enable them to distinguish the low hull of the "rebel."

In eager chase the Federals swiftly pass us, following with zeal the apparition of the Confederate, that to their deluded fancy looms up far in the distance. Satisfied with this successful maneuver, we jubilantly bid the enemy good-night and merrily steer to the southward.

Nautical correspondents from the squadron facetiously report "a vigorous pursuit of the *Florida* for a time, with every prospect of capture, but when the game was nearly in their clutches they were despoiled of the prize by stormy seas, that engulfed the rebel in its briny waters, never more to rise a pestilential source of annoyance to her enemies."

The morning of the 17th was ushered in by a bright sun and moderate northwest wind that betokened a cessation of stormy weather. By the log we had male a run of one hundred and fifty miles to the southward and eastward since parting with our persistent fellow-traveler of the previous evening. An officer reported from aloft, "Nothing in sight but sky and water," consequently the customary duties of the day were resumed.

The "sea orders" of the Secretary of the Navy were opened, and found to contain brief but distinct instructions in regard to the duties I was ordered to perform. The object of the Southern Confederacy was to cripple the commercial prosperity of the United States by destroying their merchant vessels captured upon the highways of the ocean. This predatory style of warfare had been pursued from time immemorial by all nations in their belligerent contests, and during the colonial struggle for freedom was resorted to by the colonies successfully and effectually.

Being interdicted by all governments from taking the captured vessels into any foreign port for adjudication, the only resort was burning or bonding, at the discretion of the commanders afloat. Prisoners were to be treated with humanity and kindness, their individual baggage respected and preserved from pillage. When opportunity offered these prisoners were to be released on parole, at the discretion of the commanding officer. Confederate cruisers were expected to subsist upon the enemy. As the Confederacy, especially in point of naval equality, was numerically no match for the United States, gratuitous combats with Federal cruisers were to be avoided, as even success would inflict no appreciable injury upon the enormous naval power of the enemy. The Confederate cruisers were armed for determined defense when battle cannot be avoided, but not for the indulgence of a quixotism that might deprive the South of the power of effectually wounding the mainsprings of the North. These instructions were brief and to the point, leaving much to the discretion but more to the torch.

At 4 PM overhauled the bark *Estelle*, of Bath; Maine, loaded with honey; burned her; brought officers and crew on board with their baggage; all made comfortable; put them on shore in Havana on the following afternoon.

We continued our cruise of destruction from the latitude of New York to 20° south of the equator. Many vessels of great value were disposed of according to our instructions, but we always extended humane consideration to those whom the misfortune of civil war cast athwart our pathway. This was particularly the case where ladies were the recipients of these misfortunes; then it was my invariable custom to surrender the comforts of my state-room and cabin, and court a brief and unrefreshing repose in one of the cutters, or between two guns on the quarter-deck. Sometimes this self-sacrificing courtesy was appreciated and acknowledged, but generally the desire for sensational statements in the public press ignored honesty and truth, and pandered sectional bitterness and hatred that hesitated at no exaggeration, however monstrous. Such pernicious inconsistencies are the unhappy off springs of bitter warfare, human nature in this respect being as barbarous as in the primitive ages.

There was not a Confederate naval officer who hunted up the Northern traffickers of the sea, and applied the torch as a secondary means of warfare, that did not experience a deep feeling of regret at the necessity that demanded his compliance with his strict official instructions.

It is presumed, on the score of humanity, that the officers of the Federal navy regretfully destroyed the poor Southerners' few bales of cotton, salt-works, agricultural implements, canoes, provisions, cattle, mules, etc. The humanities of war are very questionable quantities, and generally amount to an open-and-shut game, preponderance sweeping the board. On one side fortunes were accumulated. Nautical Confederates were the recipients of nothing, their captures were facetiously spoken of as prizes! Yes, prizes drawn in a blank lottery.

I have frequently been forced into humorous laughter when old friends have facetiously remarked, "You were very lucky during the late unpleasantness, and must have accumulated handsomely." Occasionally I have placed a copper cent in my funny friend's hand, and lugubriously remarked that that coin would more than purchase my share of the divide. With me confiscation swept the board. Luck scatters like a shot-gun, and I never bagged one feather.

The vicinity of Fernando de Noronha proved a successful locality, for the capture of Northern merchantmen. One of them, the *Lapwing*, was freighted with two hundred and sixty tons of anthracite coal; she was turned into a cruising-tender, and, as necessity required, met and delivered to the *Florida* a supply of fuel.

On the 13th of May, 1863, we anchored off the Rocas Island, near the coast of Brazil, awaiting the arrival of our tender with coal. A number of the officers visited the shore for recreation, among them our assistant surgeon, Dr. Grafton. On attempting to return the cutter was upset by the heavy surf that rolled upon the beach. The doctor obtained an oar, which, if retained, would have been the means of saving his life; but seeing a very young sailor, who was unable to swim, about to perish, he generously and heroically passed the oar to him, thus saving his life at the expense of his own. It was a self-sacrificing; heroic act, deeply affecting the hearts of all on board, who mourned his loss and affectionately honored his memory. Every effort was made to recover his body, but unsuccessfully.

Assistant Surgeon J. Dana Grafton, of Arkansas, entered the United States navy in the year 1858, having passed first on the list of many competitors for an appointment as assistant surgeon. He served with credit, enjoying the friendship of those with whom he associated, until 1861, when Arkansas, following in the footsteps of her sister Southern States, severed her compact with the United States, when he marshaled with her people among the unity of the Confederacy. Though devoted to the Union, and pained at the unhappy rupture, "blood was thicker than water," and he could not separate himself from the bonds of consanguinity and peculiar affection. He entered the Confederate navy; and in December, 1862, was ordered to the steamer *Florida*, then preparing for sea in the harbor of Mobile. His intelligence and manly traits endeared him to his messmates, and his kind attention to his duties won the respect and confidence of the crew.

Prior to sailing for the Rocas Islands, we captured a coffee-laden brig bound to Baltimore. I fitted her out as an armed tender, and dispatched Lieutenant C.W. Read, on his own application, on a roving mission to capture and destroy, in accordance with the orders dictated to the *Florida*. His successful career from the vicinity of Nantucket to Portland gave evidence of remarkable daring and ability. Capturing the schooner *Tacony*, and finding her faster and better adapted for the work in hand than the *Clarence*, he burned the latter, and made many captures in his new departure.

Entering the harbor of Portland at night in open boats, he surprised and took possession of the revenue cutter *Caleb Cushing*; putting her crew in irons, he towed her to sea. This daring act became immediately known, and produced intense excitement in the city.

Four fast steamers were chartered, manned, and equipped. The cutter was soon seen some miles from the harbor becalmed. Lieutenant Read endeavored to place his prize in a defensive condition, but after firing a short time without effect on the enemy, and finding that she would be carried by boarding, he set her on fire and deserted her. He then steered to join his command, the *Archer*, but was pursued, and being captured, had to submit to a long confinement in Fort Warren.

Coaling at Bermuda, the *Florida* continued her predatory warfare until a notification from the engineers stating that the *Florida's* shaft required relaying and her machinery overhauling; in consequence of the pressing character of her cruising, I determined to run her into the harbor of Brest and apply for permission to dock and repair. We made several captures in the English Channel, and then bore up for Brest where we were politely received by the authorities, who forwarded to the emperor my application for docking and repairs. An affirmative response being received, the *Florida* was docked.

5. The *Florida* Seized

When the *Florida* arrived at Brest, France, for repairs on August 23, 1863, it was not long before Maffitt began feeling ill, and by late September he was confined to his cabin with a searing pain in his chest. A specialist brought in from Paris diagnosed his condition as a possible heart attack and recommended a three-month rest. Taking his doctor's advice, Maffitt departed the *Florida* and a replacement, Commander Joseph N. Barney, was sent from Paris. Barney also became ill and in January of 1864, First Lieutenant Charles M. Morris replaced him.

With the *Florida's* repairs complete, she sailed from Brest on February 10, 1864. After eight long months at sea, Morris captured only thirteen prizes. The numbers are not a reflection upon him as a commander, however, for he had stopped as many vessels as did Maffitt who commanded before him. The scarcity of prizes was an indication of the great success of the Confederate cruisers, for at this stage of the war, there were few American registered vessels left. (Campbell, *Southern Fire: Exploits of the Confederate States Navy*, pp. 86.)

On the evening of October 4, 1864, the *Florida* dropped her anchor in the Brazilian port of Bahia. The career of the sleek cruiser as a Confederate commerce raider was about to come to an end. In February of 1865, Morris' executive officer, First Lieutenant Thomas K. Porter, wrote to his commander explaining what had happened to the *Florida*. [RTC]

"Capture of the Confederate Steamer Florida" by 1st Lt. Thomas K. Porter, CSN

Southern Historical Society Papers, Volume XII, 1884, Pages 40–45.

To Lieutenant-Commander C. M. MORRIS,
Confederate States Navy.

LIVERPOOL, *February 20th, 1865.*

SIR,—In obedience to orders I submit the following report of the capture of the Confederate States steamer *Florida* at Bahia, Brazil, on the 7th of October, 1864, by the United States steamer *Wachusett*, the treatment of the officers and crew while prisoners; and the manner of our release. But before commencing I beg to call your attention to the fact that before entering the harbor our shot were withdrawn from the guns; that after our being requested by the Brazilian naval commander to anchor in-shore of his squadron we let our steam go down and hauled fires.

At about 3 AM on the morning of the 7th October, the officer of the deck, Acting-Master T. T. Hunter, sent the Quartermaster down to call me, and tell me that the *Wachusett* was under weigh and standing towards us. I immediately jumped on deck, when I saw the *Wachusett* about twenty yards off, standing for our starboard quarter. A moment after she struck us abreast the mizen-mast, broke it into three pieces, crushed in the bulwarks, knocked the quarter-boat in on deck, jammed the wheel, carried away the mainyard and started the beams for about thirty feet forward. At the same time she fired about two hundred shots from her small arms, and two from her great guns. She then backed off about one hundred yard, and demanded our surrender. The reply from the *Wachusett* was to surrender immediately, or they would blow us out of the water. As more than half our crew were ashore, and those on board had just returned from liberty, I believed that she could run us down before we could get our guns loaded. But as I did not like to surrender the vessel without knowing what some of the other officers thought of it, I consulted Lieutenant Stone, the second officer in rank; and finding that he agreed with me that we could not contend against her with any hopes under the circumstances I would surrender the vessel. I then went on board, and delivered to Commander Collins the ship's ensign and my sword. He immediately sent a prize-crew on board the *Florida*, and towed her our of the harbor. During the day he transferred about two-thirds of those captured to the *Wachusett*. He then paroled the officers, and put the men in double irons. As there were so few men compared to the *Wachusett*'s crew, and those divided between the two ships, I tried to get Captain Collins to allow the irons to be taken off of all, or a part of them, during the day, but he refused to do so. Beyond keeping the men in double irons for nearly two months, there were but two cases of severity towards them that were reported to me. Henry Norman (cox.) was ironed to a stanchion with his hands behind him for having the key of a pair of the *Florida*'s irons in his pocket. He, as well as all the other men on the *Wachusett*, was ironed with the irons belonging to her (the *Wachusett*). John Brogan (fireman) was kept in the sweat-box. Dr. Emory reported to me that he was sick and could not stand such treatment. I asked Captain Collins to tell me why he was so treated. His reply was that Brogan was seen talking, and that when his master-at-arms came up he stopped. He also said that Brogan had, the day the *Florida* was captured cursed one of his engineers, who tried to get him to show him something about our engines. He said, though, that he had ordered his release two days before, and thought he had been taken out. This was about three weeks after our capture. Brogan informed me afterwards that he had been confined there for several days, and eighteen nights. A few days before going into St. Thomas, I went to Captain Collins and told him that on a previous occasion he had informed me that he was going to put our men ashore at Pernambuco, and that as we would be in port a few days, I would like to know if he still intended to put them ashore, at the same time telling him that I thought the *Florida* would be given up by his Government, and that I thought any honorable man would try to return the ship and crew as nearly in the condition in which he found her as he could. His reply was, "I have not thought of it—I have not thought of it to-day." After further conversation I left him, believing that he would not try to break that all of them who wished to go ashore could do so, and that Master George D. Bryan and other officer would meet them to look out for them. They asked what was to become of their money, which had been taken from them, and were told that Mr. Bryan would take it ashore for them. A number of them thought this was a trick to get rid of them, and would not go, but eighteen were foolish enough to believe it, and had their irons taken off on the berth-deck, and were put in a boat from the bow port, and allowed to go ashore. The first Mr. Bryan heard of his part of the affair was when we left *Wachusett* and had an opportunity of talking to the other men. After the men had time to get ashore, the commander of the *Wachusett* called away his boats, and sent an armed force after the boat in which our men had left. So anxious was he to get them ashore, that he sent them when the quarantine flag was flying at his fore in consequence of having the small-pox on board. The United States steamer *Keasarge* left St. Thomas while we were there, and Dr. Charlton and the eighteen men on the *Florida* were transferred to her. When we arrived at Fortress Monroe, we were sent up to Point Lookout Prison, and there the officers were separated from the men, and sent to the Old Capitol Prison in Washington. But in three or four days we were sent back to the *Wachusett* at Fortress Monroe to go to Fort Warren, Boston. On our return to Fortress Monroe, I heard that the *Florida*'s money-chest had been opened, and I went to Captain Collins and reminded him that soon after we were captured, I informed him that there were three hundred and twenty dollars in it which belonged to the wardroom mess, which I had given to the paymaster the evening before we were captured, to keep till the caterer, Lieutenant Stone, should return from shore. He told me that he had mentioned it to Rear-Admiral Porter, but that the Admiral refused to give it to us. We saw the *Florida* before we left. She had lost her jibboom by a steam-tug running into her. A Lieutenant-Commander told me that if the United States Government determined to give her up, the officers of the navy would destroy her. Several other of our officers were told the same. Whilst in Fort Warren we heard these threats were carried out.

1st Lt. Charles M. Morris (Naval Historical Center).

From Hampton Roads we were carried in the *Wachusett* to Boston, but before we were sent to Fort Warren, Lieutenant-Commander Beardsly went to the men and informed them that he was sent by Captain Collins to tell them that if they would take the oath of allegiance to the United States Government they would be released. He, meeting with no success, was succeeded by the master-at-arms of the vessel, and a sergeant from the Fort, who told them that all the men but five of those who had come from St. Thomas on the *Keasarge* had taken the oath. I do not know by whose orders this was told them; but we found on arriving at the fort that it had no more truth in it than the report they gave the men at St. Thomas, that Mr. Bryan was to meet them on shore. I am happy to say that but one of the crew deserted his flag, and he did it the day we were captured. When we arrived at Fort Warren, the men were all put in one room, and the eleven officers were put into one with thirty-two other prisoners.

These rooms were casemates, and were fifty feet long and about eighteen feet wide. At sunset we were locked up in these casemates, and released after sunrise, and allowed to promenade the extent of five such rooms. At 8 AM we were marched around to the cookhouse, and were all given one loaf of bread each, weighing fourteen ounces. After twelve we were marched around again, and were given our dinner, which consisted of about eight ounces of cooked meat, with half a pint of thin soup, three days, and two potatoes, some beans or hominy the other days. This was all we received each day. Many of the prisoners by economizing found this enough to appease their hunger, but a great many others were hungry all the time. If we had been allowed to buy sugar and coffee, and bread and cheese, a great many would have been able to do so, and divide with some of their friends who had no means, but we were allowed to buy nothing to eat without a certificate from the Post Surgeon that we were sick. There is an arrangement between our government and that of the United States Government now interprets this to mean that all boxes must come by a flag of truce. As half of the Confederate prisoners have their homes within what is now the United States military lines, this agreement works almost entirely for the Federals and against us. Half of the *Florida*'s officers were in this situation, and they were compelled to decline the offers of their friends. On the 24th December all the *Florida*'s officers except Dr. Charlton and fourteen other prisoners were locked up in a casemate, and kept in close confinement both day and night. We were not allowed to go out under any circumstances, except that for the first four days we were marched under a heavy guard to the cookhouse twice a day. After that our dinner was brought to us, and two of us were marched around to get the bread for all of those confined. This was for discussing a plan to capture the fort, which one of the prison spies, who pretends to be a Lieutenant-Colonel in our army, and a Lieutenant in the English army, revealed to the authorities. We were kept in close confinement until the 19th of January, when Lieutenant Woodman, of the United States army, sent for me, and told me that he had an order from the Secretary of the Navy to release the officers and crew of the *Florida* from Fort Warren, and that as such was the case he would release all of us from close confinement. He showed me the order from the Secretary of the Navy, which was that we would be released on condition that we signed a parole to leave the United States within ten days. I asked him if we would be given the money and our swords, and other articles captured on the *Florida*, which had not been sunk with her. He said that he knew nothing about them, but if I wished to write to Mr. Welles, he would send the communication. I then gave him a copy of the following note, which he assured me was sent the same day:

"To the Hon. GIDEON WELLES,
Secretary of the Navy:

FORT WARREN, *January 19th, 1863.*

SIR,—I have just been informed by the commanding officer of this fort that the officers and crew of the Confederate States steamer *Florida* will be released on condition of leaving the United States within ten days. We will accept a parole to leave at any time when we are put on board any steamer going to Europe, but we would prefer to go to Richmond. We would call your attention to the fact that there were somewhere about thirteen thousand dollars in gold on the *Florida* when she was captured, which was taken out of her by order of Rear-Admiral Porter. And to leave the United States it will be necessary to have that to take us out, unless the United States Government send us away as they brought us in. If you will give us our money we would prefer remaining here till a steamer leaves here for Europe, or we would ask for a guard till we are put on one in New York, as so many of us being together might be the cause of an unnecessary disturbance, of which we would be the sufferers.

"Very respectfully,
"Your obedient servant,

"THOMAS K. PORTER,
"First-Lieutenant, Confederate States Navy."

Mr. Welles made no reply to this. After waiting a week and finding that the United States Government neither intended to pay our passage away, nor to give us the money belonging to our government, and not even our private money, I sent Lieutenant Stone to Boston with directions to procure a passage in the British and North American steamer *Canada*, or if he failed in that, to get us out of the United States in any manner possible. He succeeded in getting passage for all of us on the *Canada*, by my giving a draft to be paid at Liverpool. And on the 1st of February we signed the following parole: "We, the undersigned officers and crew of the steamer *Florida*, in consideration of being released from confinement in Fort Warren, do jointly and severally pledge our sacred word of honor that we will leave the United States within ten days from date of release, and that while in the United States we will commit no hostile act," and I left the fort for the steamer *Canada*. It may be of importance to state that we were officially informed by Major Gibson, commanding the post part of the time we were there, that we could hold no communication with the Brazilian authorities.

Very respectfully,
Your obedient servant,

THOMAS K. PORTER,
First-Lieutenant, Confederate States Navy.

6. The CSS *Shenandoah*

The CSS *Shenandoah*, originally known as the *Sea King*, was the only Confederate cruiser to circumvent the globe. Commander Bulloch purchased her in Glasgow, Scotland, on September 30, 1864, as a replacement for the sunken *Alabama*. Destined to wage war against the Northern whaling fleet in the far off Arctic Ocean, the *Shenandoah* also wrote the final chapter in the history of the Confederate States Navy.

Her executive officer was First Lieutenant William C. Whittle, Jr., from Norfolk, Virginia. Whittle proved to be the real strength of the *Shenandoah*, for the cruiser's commander, First Lieutenant James I. Waddell, quickly learned to entrust all of the day-to-day operations to him. Whittle, a graduate of the United States Naval Academy at Annapolis, resigned from U. S. service on May 15, 1861, and after commissioning in the Confederate navy, served on the cruiser *Nashville* and the ironclad *Louisiana* at New Orleans. Taken captive upon the *Louisiana*'s destruction, he spent four months as a prisoner at Fort Warren in Boston harbor. After his exchange, and a brief period as commander of the gunboat CSS *Chattahoochee* in Georgia, he was ordered to Europe to await an assignment. (Campbell, *Fire & Thunder: Exploits of the Confederate States Navy*, p. 172.)

After the war the editors of the *Southern Historical Society Papers* prevailed upon Whittle to write a history of the *Shenandoah*'s cruise, and the following is his submission to the Society. [RTC]

"The Cruise of the Shenandoah" by Captain William C. Whittle, Jr., CSN

Southern Historical Society Papers, Volume XXXV, December 1907, Pages 235–258.

From time immemorial one of the most effective and damaging means resorted to in wars between nations and peoples has been an attack upon the commercial marine of an adversary. It is a mode of warfare legitimatized by being resorted to all through the ages. It was adopted by our colonial cruisers during the Revolutionary War, and during the War of 1812, 1813 and 1814 seventy-four British merchant vessels were captured by the United States Navy direct orders from their Navy Department and President Madison. Such depredations only became "piratical," in the minds of the Federal Government, when their own interests were jeopardized during our late war. Situated and conditioned as we were when that war began and during its continuance, such means of warfare were peculiarly alluring and suggestive of many and great results. The Southern Confederacy had no commerce and was at war with the United States, which had a large commercial marine. To attack it was not only to inflict heavy pecuniary loss from vessels destroyed, but to force upon them great expense in insurance against these ravages and marine war risks.

Nor was this all. The United States had a formidable navy with every facility to increase it; utilized most disastrously to the South by blockading its ports and closing the doors through which to receive, from the outside world, materials through its sea-board cities and towns. Every cruiser put on the ocean must and did have the effect to divert a force to protect as far as might be their threatened commerce.

But the South had no vessels of war, nor such as could be converted into cruisers. The quickest, best and well nigh only way to procure them was by purchase abroad, from the proceeds of sale of their cotton. Early in the beginning of the war this was seen and the course adopted. To manage this difficult and important work a man of professional ability, clear business capacity, wise judgment and discretion in selecting and dealing with men, a knowledge of maritime and international law, calm equanimity and great sagacity was needed. To find such a man meant such a measure of success as all the difficulties and counteracting efforts would admit of. To select the wrong man meant foreign entanglements, prejudice of cause and failure.

For this work the Confederate Government selected Captain James D. Bulloch, formerly an officer in the United States Navy, from Georgia, who, when the war began, commanded a merchant steamer running between New York and a Southern port. They might have searched the world over and would have failed to find another combining all the qualifications needed, as preeminently as he did. His heart was thoroughly in the cause and he threw his whole body and soul into his work. To his judgment, sagacity, energy and tact, was due the possession and fitting out of the *Alabama, Georgia, Florida, Rappahannock, Stonewall, Shenandoah,* and the building of the ironclad rams at Liverpool and the vessels in France.

Such of these vessels as took the sea, took it not as privateers, as they were called by some; not as pirates, as our enemies opprobriously spoke of us, but as armed government vessels of war, commanded and officered by men born in the South and holding commissions in the Confederate States Navy, of a government whose belligerent rights were acknowledged by the kingdoms of the earth—commissions as valid as those held in the United States Navy.

The Confederate States had, as I said, no naval vessels and none or very few that could be converted into cruisers. They had, however, a fine, loyal, able and true personnel, composed of officers educated and commissioned in the United States Navy before the war. They were Southern-born men, who represented their respective States in the United States Navy, just as their representative in Congress and other governmental branches represented them in their respective spheres. The expense of educating and qualifying them for their positions was borne from the general fund collected from all the States, their respective States bearing their just proportion for the qualifying of their quota. These men were not politicians, but when the war clouds gathered felt bound by every sense of duty, love and devotion, many of them against their judgment as to the judiciousness of disruption, and all of them against the professional hopes, aspirations and pecuniary interests, when their mother States withdrew, to rally to their standard, resigned and tendered their services. They were accepted and given commissions properly signed by the executive and confirmed by the Congress of the Confederate States. No more loyal men live on earth. Let no slanderous tongues or libelous pens impugn their motives. Let not their reputation for purity of purpose, as to their duty, be handed down to posterity with any stain, but let their children have perpetuated in their minds and hearts the fact that their fathers were neither knaves, fools, cowards nor traitors. These men were ready and anxious to serve their country in her hour of peril, in any honorable field that they might be called to by her. These men officered the cruisers of the Confederate States.

The Confederate States Steamers *Sumter, Alabama, Florida, Tallahassee, Nashville, Georgia,* and others, had gone out and done damaging service against the United States merchant marine. There was, however, one branch of that marine, a large and remunerative interest, prolific with gain and profit, against which no special expedition had been sent. That interest was the whaling fleet of the United States.

The conception of the judiciousness of such a special expedition came, I think, primarily from Lieutenants John Mercer Brooke and the late Robert R. Carter, two distinguished officers of the United States Navy, who, upon the secession of their native State, Virginia, had resigned and joined her cause. Captain Brooke is now, and has been for years, a professor at the Virginia Military Institute at Lexington. They had, as members of a scientific expedition fitted out by the United States, become acquainted with the extent and cruising grounds of the whaling fleet. Lieutenant Carter, afterwards associated with Captain Bulloch, talked the matter over with him, and to him it was due, from his knowledge of the field, that a comprehensive letter and general plan was formulated for such a cruise.

Of course it could only be an outline of an expedition which constant and unavoidable emergencies and exigencies must qualify, shape and control. But the sequel to its general observance by Commander Waddell, of the *Shenandoah*, proves with what masterly hand it was drawn up. Captain Bulloch also procured from the distinguished Commodore Matthew F. Maury, "the pathfinder on the ocean," who had likewise followed the standard of Virginia, a full set of "whaling charts." This expedition was to be the work of another vessel. It was to operate in distant and extensive fields and against vessels whose voyages were not finished until they were filled with oil. For such work, remote form every source of supply of coal or other stores, a cruiser of peculiar construction, etc., was needed. She must have good sail power and sailing qualities to economize coal, and she must have auxiliary steam power to carry her through calms of the tropic and to get her out of any peril in which Arctic ice might place her. She must have a propeller that cold be, when not in use, detached and hoisted out of water, so as not to impede her headway under sail. She must have a means of condensing steam into fresh water, for drinking purposes. She must have comfortable and healthy quarters for her crew and strength of construction to carry her battery.

The very vigilant professional eyes of Captain Bulloch and Lieutenant R. R. Carter, who was associated with him at that time, fell upon the trim new British steamship *Sea King*, when just on the eve of sailing from the Clyde for the East Indies on her first voyage. They, as far as circumstances permitted, possessed themselves of thorough knowledge of her. She was built for an East Indian trader, with capacity, etc., to carry government troops, if desired. They were greatly impressed by her fine lines, sail power, deck capacity, arrangement of machinery, her hoisting propeller, etc., and Captain Bulloch saw in her the very vessel he wanted to convert into a cruiser against the whaling fleet. He kept track of her, laid his plans for purchase and quietly awaited her return to carry them out, making, ad interim, all arrangements to speedily equip and dispatch her.

This end of all his work required great caution, tact and judgment, for a sharp system of espionage surrounded him all the time.

The *Sea King* was a composite built vessel. That is, had iron frame and teak wood planking about six inches thick. She was 220 feet long, 35 feet breadth of beam and was of about, 1,160 tons. She had a single, detachable and hoisting propeller. Direct acting engines; two cylinders of 47 inch diameter and of two feet nine inch stroke; of 850 indicated horse power. She had three masts, the lower masts and bowsprit being of iron and hollow. She was a full rigged ship, of full sail power with royals, rolling, self-reefing topsails and royal topgallant, topmast and lower studding sails, with all proper fore and aft sails.

By October 6, 1864, the officers of the Confederate Navy who were to go on her had been quietly collected at Liverpool, Eng., by Commodore Samuel Barron, commanding Confederate Navy officer abroad, to hold themselves in readiness, without a clear knowledge of for what, but simply at Captain Bulloch's call. On October 6, 1864, I was ordered by Captain Bulloch to take the 5 PM train from Liverpool for London, and on arrival to register at Wood's Hotel, Furnival Inn, High Holbron, as Mr. W. C. Brown. I was to appear the next morning for breakfast in the restaurant of the hotel, and while reading a morning paper to have a napkin passed through a button hole of my coat. So seated, I would be approached by a stranger with, "Is this Mr. Brown?" to which I was to reply, "Is this Mr.—?" Upon an affirmative reply I was to say "Yes," and Mr.— and I, after finishing breakfast, were to retire to my room.

All this was done, and on October 7 AM, Mr.— and I were in my room arranging for my getting on board the *Sea King*, which was then in port ready to sail. I went with Mr.—, and at an unsuspicious distance viewed the ship, and later, at a safe rendezvous, was introduced to her captain, Corbett. The ship was loaded with coal and cleared for Bombay by the captain, who had been given a power of attorney to sell her, at any time after leaving London, should a suitable offer be made for her. As I had been selected to be her executive officer after her transfer, naturally much, in every way, would devolve upon me, in the transportation of the vessel and her equipment, it was deemed expedient that I should observe her qualities, see her interior arrangements of space, etc., and formulate and devise for a utilization and adaptation of all the room in her. Captain Bulloch wisely deemed it best that I should thus have all opportunity of familiarizing myself with her, and hit on the plan of letting me join her in London.

On the early morn of October 8, 1864, I crawled over her side, at the forerigging, and the ship in a few moments left the dock and went down the Thames. To everybody on board except Captain Corbett, who was in our confidence, I was Mr. Brown, a super-cargo, representing the owners of the coal with which she was laden. We were fully instructed to proceed to Madeira, where we were to call, a fact only known on board to Captain Corbet and myself, and not to exchange signals with passing [vessels.] [With] Captain Corbett's assistance, I possessed myself of much information that served a good purpose afterwards. No one on board suspected anything out of the usual course.

By pre-concerted arrangement, on the same October 8, 1864, the propeller steamer *Laurel*, J. F. Ramsay, Confederate States Navy, commanding, sailed from Liverpool for Havana, with passengers and general cargo. The *Laurel* was to call also at Madeira and get there sufficiently ahead of the *Sea King* to enable her to coal up. The *Laurel* arrived at Madeira on October 15 and coaled all ready for moving, upon the appearance of the *Sea King*. The "general cargo" of the *Laurel* consisted, as afterwards found, of the guns, carriages, ammunition, etc., and stores for the future cruiser, and her passengers were the commander, officers and small nucleus for her crew. On the early morn of October 18, the *Sea King* arrived off Funchal, Madeira, and running in sight of the harbor, displayed a private pre-concerted signal. This was answered by her little consort and he two moved off successively to the Desertas, a rocky, uninhabited island not far from Madeira. There the *Sea King* anchored and her consort was secured alongside. It was perfectly smooth and a sequestered place, where there was little chance of observation or interruption. A rapid transfer of everything from the hold of the *Laurel* to the deck and hold of the *Sea King* was made, on October 19.

Her officers were: Lieutenant Commanding James I. Waddell, C. S. N., from North Carolina; W. C. Whittle, Virginia, first lieutenant and executive officer; Lieutenants John Grimball, South Carolina; Sidney Smith Lee, Jr., Virginia; F. T. Chew, Missouri, and D. M. Scales, Tennessee; Irvine S. Bulloch, Georgia, sailing master; C. E. Lining, South Carolina, surgeon; Matthew O'Brien, Louisiana, chief engineer; W. B. Smith, Louisiana, paymaster; Orris A. Brown, Virginia, and John T. Mason, Virginia, passed midshipmen, all regular officers in the Confederate States Navy, and F. J, McNulty, Ireland, acting assistant surgeon, and C. H. Codd, Maryland, acting first assistant engineer; John Hutchinson, Scotland, acting second assistant engineer; E. Mugguffiny, Ireland, acting third assistant engineer; Acting Master's Mate John F. Minor, Virginia; C. E. Hunt, Virginia; Lodge Cotton, Maryland; George Hardwood, England, acting boatswain; John L. Guy, England, acting gunner; H. Alcott, England, acting sailmaker; John O'Shea, Ireland, acting carpenter, were given the said acting appointments in the Confederates States Navy by proper authority. These twenty-three men were the officers who were transferred to the *Sea King*, all except myself and two engineers who joined from the *Sea King*, went out on the *Laurel*.

Captain Waddell read his commission and addressed both crews, calling for volunteers. Only nineteen men, including the small nucleus from the *Laurel*, volunteered, making, with the twenty-three officers, forty-two in all. Captain Waddell had the Confederate flag hoisted at the peak, received a bill of sale and christened the *Sea King* the C. S. S. *Shenandoah*. I do not know why the name *Shenandoah* was chosen, unless because of the constantly recurring conflicts, retreats and advances through the Shenandoah Valley in Virginia, where the brave Stonewall Jackson always so discomforted the enemy, causing, it is said, one of the distinguished Federal generals to say of that valley that it must be made such a waste that a crow to fly over it would have to take its rations. The burning there of homes over defenseless women and children made the selection of the name not inappropriate for a cruiser, which was to lead a torchlight procession around the world and into every ocean.

Guns, carriages and their fittings, ammunition, powder, shot and shell; stores of all kinds, all in boxes, were transferred from the *Laurel* to the *Sea King*. All was confusion and chaos. Everything had to be unpacked and stored for safety. No gun mounted, no breeching or tackle bolts driven, no portholes cut, no magazine for powder or shell room for shell provided. All was hurriedly transferred and in a lumbering, confused mass was on board. Every particle of work, of bringing order out of chaos and providing for efficiently putting everything in a condition for service, and of converting this ship into an armed cruiser at sea, admits wind and storm, if encountered, stared us in the face.

The entertained and expressed hopes, that from the two crews a suffi-

1st Lt. James I. Waddell (Naval Historical Center).

cient force would be induced to volunteer, were disappointed. Only nineteen men volunteered, which, with the twenty-three officers, made forty-two men for this stupendous work, and to man and care for a ship whose crew, with her battery, etc., as a cruiser, should be at least 150 men.

Captain Waddell, though brave and courageous, accustomed as a naval officer, to step on the deck of a man-of-war fully fitted and equipped at a navy-yard, where every facility aided to make everything perfect, was naturally discomforted and appalled. He conferred with Captain Corbett, late commander, and Lieutenant Ramsay, Confederate States Navy, who commanded the consort *Laurel*, both experienced seamen, and he told me that they both said they considered his taking the ocean, in such a condition, and so shorthanded, impracticable. As his executive officer, he naturally consulted me, saying that it was his judgment that he should take the ship to Teneriffe, communicate with Captain Bulloch and have a crew sent to him. I knew every one of the regular officers personally. They were all "to the manner born."

With the fate of the C. S. *Rappahannock* (which about a year before had gone into Calais, France, for some such object, had been held there inactive ever since) before me, and a positive conviction that our fate would be the same and result in ignominious failure, I strenuously advised against it. I said, "Don't confer, sir, with parties who are not going with us. Call your young officers together and learn from their assurances what they can and will do." They were called together; there was but one unanimous sentiment from each and every one, "take the ocean," and so it was, be it ever said with credit to them and to the zeal and courage of the now lamented Waddell, we did take the ocean, as we were, and steered clear of Teneriffe and every other port not in our cruise. Let those who hear the sequel judge of the wisdom of the decision.

The battery consisted of four eight inch smooth bore guns of 55 cwt., two rifled Whitworth 32-pounder guns and the two 12-pounder signal guns belonging to her as a merchant ship. The two vessels parted company at 6 PM, October 20, 1864, and left the Desertas, we on our southerly course and the *Laurel* for Teneriffe, to report progress. Every officer and man "pulled off his jacket and rolled up his sleeves," and with the motto "do or die" went to work at anything and everything. The captain took the wheel frequently in steering to give one more pair of hands for the work to be done. We worked systematically and intelligently, doing what was most imperatively necessary first.

In twenty-four hours we had mounted and secured for sea, two eight inch guns and two Whitworths, and the next day the other half of the battery was similarly mounted and secured. We cleared the holds and stored and secured everything below, and in eight days, after leaving the Desertas, had all portholes cut and guns secured therein. Under our instructions we had to allow sufficient time for Captain Corbett to communicate with England and have the custom house papers canceled and all necessary legal steps connected with the bona fide sale taken before any overt act.

On October 30, 1864, we captured the first prize, the bark *Alina*, Captain Staples, of Searsport, Maine, from Newport, Wales, for Buenos Ayres, with railroad iron. There was no notarial seal (required under law to establish ownership) to the signature of the owner of the cargo, and so she was, as and American vessel, with her cargo a legal prize. An order was given that nothing on any prize should be appropriated by any officers or man without permission from the commander through me. We determined to scuttle the prize, and after transferring her crew and effects and saving such furniture as saw on board, sorely needed for comfort, such as basins, pitchers, etc., we sunk her. Seven men of her crew of twelve shipped on the *Shenandoah*.

On November 5 we made our second capture, the United States Schooner *Charter Oak*, from Boston for San Francisco, Captain Gilman, who had his wife and wife's sister, Mrs. Gage, and her little son Frank on board. Captain Gilman surrendered $200 he had on board, which Captain Waddell gave to Mrs. Gilman and her sister. The schooner, after transferring a good supply of canned fruits and vegetables, was burned.

November 8, captured the American bark *D. G. Godfrey*, Captain Hallett, from Boston for Valpariso, which was burned. Six of her crew shipped on the *Shenandoah*.

November 9, overhauled the Danish vessel *Anna Jane* and sent the prisoners from the *Alina* and *Godfrey* on her, giving a full supply of provisions for them and a chronometer (captured) as a present for the Danish captain.

November 10, captured the American Brig *Susan*, Captain Hansen, of New York, with coal from Cardiff for Rio Grande do Sul, Brazil. This cargo was wanting in the notarial seal to the signature of the owner. She was sunk. Three men shipped from her on the *Shenandoah* (two seamen and one boy).

November 12, overhauled the splendid American ship *Kate Prince*, of Portsmouth, N. H., Captain Libby, from Liverpool for Bahia, Brazil, with coal. She had notarial seal to establish a neutral cargo, and we bonded the vessel for $40,000 and put on her all prisoners remaining with us. Captain and Mrs. Gilman and Mrs. Gage, of the *Charter Oak*, were profuse in their thanks for kindness while on board.

November 12, overhauled the bark *Adelaide*, Captain I. P. Williams, of Matthews County, Va. The vessel was under the Argentine flag, but there was everything to show a bogus sale. Learning, however, positively that she belonged to a Southern sympathizer, after preparations (crew and effects removed) to burn her, we bonded her.

November 13, captured and burned the schooner *Lizzie M. Stacey*, Captain Archer, from Boston for Honolulu. Four men out of the seven, shipped on the *Shenandoah*.

Crossing the Equator

On November 15, 1864, at 11:30 AM, we crossed the equator, or "crossed the line," and an amusing break in routine and monotony occurred. There were many officers and men on board who had never before gone into the Southern hemisphere, I among the number. I was approached, as executive officer to know if I had any objection to King Neptune's coming on board to look after and initiate those on board who had never crossed his domain before. I did not object. It was nearly clam. At 7:30 PM a loud hail was heard from under the bows and a brilliant light shone, asking permission from King Neptune to visit the ship. It was granted. A giant-like figure came over the bow, with an immense harpoon in his hand, and a chafing mat for a hat, and came aft, followed by a well disguised retinue or suite, to look after King Neptune's new subjects.

Lieutenant Chew was first seized. The first question was, "Where are you from?" Woe to the man who opened his mouth to answer. It would be filled with a mixture of soap, grease and molasses. If no answer was given your face was lathered with a mixture and you were shaved with a long wooden razor, and then the pump was started, which nearly drowned you, to wash it off. Dr. McNulty, on being asked where he was from, replied "Ireland," and his mouth was filled with the mixture. This was too much for his Irish blood and he knocked the barber full length on the deck. I, as executive officer, for that reason though I would be let off, particularly as I had given permission for the fun, but I was shaved also. The sport all went off very well and was a break in the shipboard life.

We now, from enlistments from our several prizes, had increased our crew from nineteen to thirty-nine, or, including the officers, had all told sixty-two souls, so that we felt quite comfortable. With such a mixture of nationalities the most rigid discipline had to be, and was, maintained, and the happiness of all was promoted by prompt punishment of all offenders. This, of course, devolved on me. Justice was tempered with humane and kind treatment, to the general good and as necessary to success.

On December 8, sighted the Island of Tristan da Cunha, and while sailing for it captured the first whaler, the bark *Edward*, Captain Worth, of New Bedford, Mass. Got from her a quantity of ship's stores, beef, pork, sea biscuits, etc., and after everything we needed at the time, or prospectively, was removed, the vessel was destroyed. Her crew consisted of captain, three mates and twenty-two men, or twenty-six all told. The whale ships, from the nature of their work, have very large crews. With three left of the crew of the schooner *Stacey* we now had twenty-nine prisoners on board, which, when the number of our own force and the manner in which it was made up, was considered, was more than we wanted to watch. So we landed them at Tristan da Cunha, sending off an abundant supply of stores form the last prize to maintain them until called for by some passing vessel.

The Island of Tristan da Cunha taken its name from the Portuguese discoverer. It was when Bonaparte was a prisoner at St. Helena, occupied by the British as a naval station. When we were there, there were thirty-five souls on the island, divided into seven families. The island is about seven miles each way and very high. One side of it, on the northwest, is productive and had fine beef cattle, chickens, eggs, milk, butter and sheep. It is a good point to call for such stores, but while the water is bold and deep, there is a "kelp," or sea weed, growing up from the bottom and so covering the surface, and so strong that it is hard to get through, and endangers the disabling of a steamer by winding up the propeller wheel. The island is under English protection. When we were there old Peter Green, a Dutchman from Holland, who was the oldest man on the island, had been there twenty-five years and seemed to be the leading man among them. The island is about 37 degrees south latitude and 10 degrees west longitude.

On December 29, while laying too in the Indian Ocean, after a heavy gale, which had lasted two days, and just before making sail, saw a trim bark running down towards us. As she passed she hoisted the United States flag and we fired a shot across her bow. She hove to and we sent a boat on board and captured the American bark *Delphine*, Captain Nicholas, of Bangor, Maine, from London for Akyab, in ballast. Going as she was, had the captain the nerve he could have saved his vessel and been out to reach of our second [shot and] beyond our power to catch her. The captain came on board with his papers. She was a legitimate prize, but he said his wife was on board and not in a good health, and that to remove her would be dangerous. It was suggested by me to Captain Waddell to let our surgeon look into that. The result was the she was found in splendid health. She came off in a boat, and as it was rough, a whip and a boatswain's chair was gotten from the yard arm, and she, with perfect self-possession, got into it and told men when to hoist. She was very irate with her husband and told him that he should have saved his ship by keeping on. We burned the ship.

An amusing incident I will here relate. Captain Nicholas was very much depressed at the loss of his vessel and was moodily pacing the deck. It was Lieutenant Chew's watch. Chew was a good, kind hearted fellow and he wanted to comfort the poor captain, and approaching said some cheering words. Poor Captain Nicholas was not to be confronted. Chew, very scientific, then said, "captain, upon what small actions important results depend. Just think that if at daylight this morning you had changed your course one-quarter of a point you would have passed out of our reach or sight." The captain turned and said, "That shows how darned little you know about it, for this morning at daylight I just did change my course 'a quarter of a point,' and that's what fetched me here." Chew retreated but it was heard, and it was a long time before he heard the last of that comforting conversation. Mrs. Nicholas and her little son, Phineas, six years old, with her husband, had a comfortable cabin, but she was always bitter and never appreciated our kindness.

January 25, 1865, arrived at Melbourne, Australia, and our prisoners, after being paroled, went ashore in shore boats with their effects. Mrs. Nichol's last words were to express a hope that we would come to grief. I cannot blame her much. The *Shenandoah* needed caulking and docking to repair the shaft bearings. We were given permission to do the work necessary for safety at sea. The population were generally kind and hospitable and treated us with marked courtesy. They came on board by thousands. Soon, however, enemies attempted to draw our men from us, but generally failed.

We had myriads of applications to enlist, but we had had notice given us not to violate the Queen's proclamation of neutrality, forbidding shipping men, and we refused all. Men of their own volition, or, as we were persuaded at the time, in many cases were secreted on board, to entrap us into some violation of neutral laws and get us into difficulty with the local government. We hauled out on the marine railway or slip, and at one time our enemies so far succeeded, despite our constant efforts to keep all men not belonging to the ship from getting on board, that one man was reported as on board and the authorities demanded to search the ship. This was positively and firmly refused, we saying that as a vessel of war we would not allow it, but would search her ourselves and send anyone, not on the vessel when we came in, ashore. This did not satisfy them, and pending reference to the law officer, the slip or railway was embargoed and all of her majesty's subjects forbidden to launch or work on the vessel.

A formal demand, in the same of our government, for the removal of the embargo was being drawn up when the law officer decided in our favor and our work continued. She was repaired and launched, and notice as requested given of when we would sail. At request of the authorities I was ordered to have her thoroughly searched for any stowaways. I selected several of the best officers, who made a conscientious search, and reported that they had examined carefully and could find no one not on the vessel when she came. In the meantime, however, when we gave our men liberty, the American consul or his emissaries persuaded several of our crew to desert. Application for assistance to arrest them was made to the authorities, but denied. Thus it is clear that the Victorian Government treated us badly.

We got some 250 tons of coal, and on February 18, AM, sailed. We had received an intimation of a suggested plot among some Americans to go on board, go to sea and capture the vessel, but we were on the alert and never saw anything to cause us to think that they did more than to talk of this desperate attempt. We were numerically weak, but it would have been fatal for all who had entered into any such plot.

Getting well to sea, outside the jurisdiction, after discharging the pilot, forty-two men, who had stowed themselves away, some in the hollow bowsprit and some in the coal, all where the officers of the ship could not find them, came on deck and wanted to enlist. We wanted men after our losses in Melbourne, but we were suspicious, after the intimated plot. The men were black with dirt. We drew them up in a line, took their names and nationally. Thirty-four claimed to be Americans and the other eight of various nationalities. We shipped them all, but watched them closely. They turned out to be good, faithful men. These gave us seventy-two men on deck. Some were from New England. One, George P. Canning, said he had been aide-de-camp to General (Bishop) Leonidas Polk, C. S. A., who had been discharged as an invalid. With him as sergeant, a marine guard was organized.

Sighted Drummond's Island and learned from natives in canoes that no vessels were there. Sighted Strong's Island and near enough to see no vessel in Charborl Harbor.

Sighted McAskill Island. Sighted Ascension (Pouinipete or Ponpai Island) of Carolina group, about six degrees north and longitude 160 degrees east, and on April 1, looking into "Lod Harbor" of that island, found four whalers there. Took a pilot (an Englishman, named Thomas Harrocke, from Yorkshire, who had been a convict, and had lived on this island thirteen years) and anchored in the harbor.

Sent off four boats and boarded each vessel and made prizes of American whalers *Edward Carey*, of San Francisco; *Hector*, of New Bedford; *Pearl*, of New London, and *Harvest*, from New Bedford, nominally form Honolulu, but really an American under false colors, having an American register, having no bill of sale, and being under her original name. All four of the captains had gone on a visit to a missionary post nearby. As they returned in their boat we intercepted them and brought them on board. It was no April fool for them, poor fellows. We transferred everything needed from the prizes, and taking them to a point indicated by the King where no harm could be done the harbor, destroyed them.

King Ish-y-Paw visited the ship with his suite in a large fleet of canoes. His royal highness drank freely of Shiedam Schnapps. He became very friendly and communicative through the pilot as interpreter.

Before firing the prizes we furnished the King with muskets and such things as he desired, and also sent ashore large quantities of provisions for the prisoners, who were, on the day of our sailing, set ashore with the King's permission. The prisoners preferred to be landed there. We shipped eight men from the prizes. Sailed on April 13, leaving the Ladrone Islands, Los Jardnes, Grampus and Margaret Islands to the westward, and Camira, Otra and Marcus Islands, to the eastward, we steered to intercept vessels from San Francisco and West Coast of South America for Hong Kong. We cruised in these tracks, but saw no sail. Before reaching the forty-fifth parallel of north latitude had heavy typhoons. Above that, the weather settled.

On May 21, passed Moukouruski Island, and going through Amphitrite Straits, of Kuril Islands, entered the Ohkotsk Sea. The most beautiful optical illusions I ever witnessed were in the mirage in this latitude, about Kamchatka. When not foggy the atmosphere was a perfect reflector. We saw prominent points seventy miles distant. We would see a snow clad peak direct, and above it, inverted, the reflection, peak to peak, with perfect delineation, or we would see a ship direct, and above it, the reflection of the same ship, inverted, masthead to masthead. Just as if you put your finger to a mirror you would see the finger and reflection, point to point.

We were in the Arctic and contiguous regions during their summer. It was most interesting, as we went north towards the pole, to mark the days grow longer and longer, and to experience the sun's being below the horizon, a shorter and shorter period each twenty-four hours in its diurnal circuit, until finally we went so far that the sun did not go out of sight at all, but would go down to the lowest point, and without disappearing would rise again. In short, it was all day.

In the Okhotsk we encountered thick fogs and heavy ice. On May 27, in latitude 57 north, longitude 153, captured the American whaler *Abigail*, of New Bedford, which was burned. We took her crew of thirty-five men on board. Went up as far as Ghifinsi and Tausk Bays, but could not enter for ice from fifteen to thirty feet thick.

June 10 and 12 twelve of the *Abigail's* crew enlisted. June 14 we went out of Okholtsk Sea, through Amphitrite Straits. June 16 two more men enlisted, and on same evening entered Bering Sea, through the Aletuiam Islands, going north towards Captain Navarin.

June 13, captured whalers *William Thompson* and *Susan Abigail*, which left San Francisco in April, and brought papers of April 17, giving correspondence between Generals Grant and Lee and a statement of the surrender of the latter to the former at Appomattox, but they also contained President Davis' proclamation from Danville, Va., stating that the surrender would only cause the prosecution of the war with renewed vigor. We felt that the South had sustained great reverses, but at no time did we feel a more imperative duty to prosecute our work with vigor.

Between June 2 and June 28, inclusive, we captured twenty-four whaling vessels, viz.: *William Thompson, Euphrates, Milo, Sophia Thornton, Jireh Swift, Susan Abigail, General Williams, Nimrod, Nye, Catherine, General Pike, Gipsey, Isabella, Waverley, Hillman, James Murray, Nassau, Brunswick, Howland, Martha, Congress, Nile, Favorite* and *Convington*, of which three, viz.: *Milo, James Murray* and *Nile*, were bonded and the others burned, and all prisoners put on board the bonded vessels, with ample provisions taken from the vessels destroyed for their support. Eleven of the enumerated vessels were captured on June 28. These were our last prizes. Some of the prisoners expressed their opinion, on the strength of the papers brought by the *Susan Abigail*, of General Lee's surrender, that war might be and probably was over, but as an evidence that such was not believed to be the case, eight men from these vessels enlisted on the *Shenandoah*.

On June 29, at 1 AM, passed the Bering Straits into the Arctic Ocean. At 10 AM, finding heavy floes of ice all around ahead of us, we turned to the southward and reentered, through Bering Straits, Bering Sea, being at noon, or two hours after we turned around, in 66 degrees 14 minutes north latitude. Encountered very heavy ice of July 1. On July 5 passed through Amukta Pass (172 degrees west longitude) of the Aleutian Islands, from Bering Sea into the Pacific Ocean. One of the islands by which we passed in coming out was volcanic, for smoke was seen coming out from its peak.

This was the last land which we were destined to see for a long time. Our course was shaped towards the coast of California, Lower California and Mexico, with the hope of falling in with some trans-Pacific vessels, or some of the steamships from San Francisco to Panama.

On reaching the 129th meridian of west longitude we ran down parallel with the coast. On August 2, when in latitude 16 degrees 20 minutes north, longitude 121 degrees 11 minutes west, we made out a vessel, a sailing bark, which we chased under steam and sail and overhauled and boarded at 4 PM. It proved to be the English bark *Barracouda*, from San Francisco for Liverpool, thirteen days out from the former port. The sailing master, I. S. Bulloch, was the boarding officer, and after he had examined her papers, to establish her nationally, he asked the captain for the news about the war. The English captain said "What war?" "The war between the United States and Confederate States," Bulloch replied. When the Englishman replied, "Why the war has been over since April. What ship is that?" "The Confederate steamer *Shenandoah*," Bulloch replied.

He then told of the surrender of all the Confederate forces, the capture of President Davis and the entire collapse of the Confederate cause, and when Bulloch returned he not only told all this, but, too, that Federal cruisers were looking for us everywhere and would deal summarily with us if caught. Files of recent papers confirmed everything. The information given by the captain of the *Barracouta* was appalling to the last degree. Coming as it did from an Englishman, we could not doubt its accuracy. We were bereft of country, bereft of government, bereft of ground for hope or aspiration, bereft of a cause for which to struggle and suffer.

The pouring of hirelings from the outside world had at last overpowered the remaining gallant Confederates. That independence for which our brave people had so nobly fought, suffered and died, was, under God's ruling, denied us. Our anguish of disappointed hopes cannot be described. Naturally our minds and hearts turned to our dear ones at home. We knew the utter impoverishment of those who survived, for surrender proved that, but what of the fate of each and all who were dear to us. These were the harrowing thoughts which entered into our very souls, the measure and intensity of which can never be portrayed. Then, too, by comparing dates, we found that most of our destruction was done, unwittingly, after hostilities had ceased at home. We knew the intensity of feeling engendered by the war, and particularly in the hearts of our foes towards us. We knew that every effort would be made for our capture, and we felt that if we fell into the enemy's hands we could not hope, fired as their hearts were, for a fair trial or judgment, and that the testimony of the whalers, whose property we had destroyed, would all be against us, and that the fact that we had been operating against those who had been nearly as much cut off from channels of information as we were ourselves, would count for naught. Even during the war we had been opprobriously called "pirates," and we felt that if captured we would be summarily dealt with as such.

These were disquietudes which caused no demoralization, or craven fear, however, but were borne by true men with clear consciences, who had done their duty as they saw it, with the powers given them by God. It was a situation desperate to a degree, to which history furnishes no parallel. Piracy is a crime, not against any one nation, but against all. A pirate is an enemy to mankind, and as such is amenable to trial and punishment, under the laws of nations, by the courts of the country into whose hands he may fall.

The first thing was to suspend hostilities and to proclaim such suspension. Captain Waddell promptly ordered me to disarm the vessel and crew. This was done immediately and our guns were dismounted and stowed and secured below in the hold of the ship. The captain addressed his crew and told them unreservedly the situation and declared all warlike operations stopped.

The next step was to go into the hands of some nation strong enough to maintain the rulings of the laws of nations and resist any demand, from our enemies, for our surrender, that we might have a full, fair trail. There were various opinions advanced as to the best course to pursue to promote the general safety. Our captain decided and made know his decision; that we would proceed to England, learn the true situation, and if all we heard was true, surrender to the British Government. We steered for Liverpool. Our coal supply was short and was needed for ballast and for emergency of pursuit, and for the last home stretch of our gauntlet of about 17,000 miles. So our long voyage must be under sail.

The admirable discipline, sedulously enforced and maintained all through, now, on our changed condition, brought forth good fruit. The crew, from here, there and everywhere, many being from our prizes, behaved splendidly and with a high loyalty to general safety. No serious disorders arose, but every man did his duty in the effort to safely reach our selected destination. It was a long, weary and anxious voyage, with its share of gales and storms. We rounded Cape Horn on September 16, 1865, under top gallant sails, but on getting to the eastward of it had heavy adverse gales, which threw us among icebergs. We passed many sails, but exchanged no signals—we were making no new acquaintances.

We crossed the equator, for the fourth time, on October 11, 1865. On October 25 PM, when about 500 miles southeast of Azores Island, we sighted a supposed Federal cruiser. Our courses converged. The stranger was apparently waiting for us, but to avoid suspicion we did not change ours, until night-fall, and then we made a short detour and the next morning nothing more was seen of her. We on that occasion got up and used steam, for the first time on a voyage of over 13,000 miles.

On November 5, 1865, we entered St. George's Channel, making Tuskar lighthouse, which was the first land we had seen for 122 days, after sailing 23,000 miles, and made it within a few moments of when it was expected. Could a higher proof of the skill of our young navigator, Irvine S. Bulloch, be desired? That night we took a Liverpool pilot, who confirmed all the news we had heard. He was directed to take the ship to Liverpool.

On the morning of November 6 the brave ship steamed up the river Mersey with the Confederate flag at her peak, and was anchored by the pilot, by Captain Waddell's order, near H. B. M. guard ship *Donegal*, Captain Paynter, R. N., commanding. Soon after a lieutenant from the *Donegal* came on board to learn the name of our vessel and advised us officially of the termination of the war. At 10 AM November 6, 1865, the last Confederate flag was hauled down and the last piece of Confederate property, the C. S. S. *Shenandoah*, was surrendered to the British nation by letter to Earl Russell, from Captain Waddell, through Captain Paynter, royal navy, commanding H. M. S. *Donegal*.

The gallant little ship had left London thirteen months before as the *Sea King*, and had, as a Confederate cruiser, defied pursuit, for twelve months and seventeen days, had captured thirty-eight vessels valued at $1,172,223, bonding six and destroying thirty two—second only to the C. S. S. *Alabama* in number; had circumnavigated the globe, carrying the brave flag around the world and into every ocean on the globe except the Antarctic; traveling over a distance of about 60,000 miles, without the loss of a single spar.

Captain Waddell's letter to Earl Russell set forth the unvarnished facts and work of our cruise and surrendered the vessel to the British nation. The *Shenandoah* was placed under custody of British authorities, the gunboat *Goshawk* being lashed alongside.

United States Minister Adams, on November 7 addressed a letter to the Earl of Clarendon, Secretary of State for Foreign Affairs, requesting that necessary steps be taken to secure the property on board, and to take possession of the vessel with view to her delivery to the United States. Minister Adams' letter, with that of Captain Waddell, with other documents relating to the *Shenandoah*, were referred to the law officers off the Crown on November 7, 1865, who advised in substance as follows:

"We think it will be proper for her Majesty's government, in compliance with Mr. Adams' request, to deliver up to him, in behalf of the government of the United States, the ship in question, with her tackle, apparel, etc., and all captured chronometers or other property capable of being identified as prize of war, which may be found on board of her.... With respect to the officers and crew ... if the facts stated by Captain Waddell are true, there is clearly no case for any persecution on the ground of piracy in the courts of this country, and we presume that his Majesty's government are not in possession of any evidence which could be produced before any court or magistrate for the purpose of contravening the statement or showing that the crime of piracy has, in fact, been committed.... With respect to any of the persons on the *Shenandoah* who cannot be immediately proceeded against and detained under legal warrant upon any criminal charge, we are not aware of any ground upon which they can properly be prevented from going on shore and disposing of themselves as they think if, and we cannot advise her Majesty's government to assume or exercise the power of keeping them under any kind of restraint."

The law officers who gave this advise and these opinions, and whose names were attached thereto, were Sir Roundell Palmer, Sir R. P. Collier and Sir Robert Phillmore.

In consequence of these opinions of the law officer of the Crown, instructions were sent to Captain Paynter, of her majesty's ship Donegal, to release all officers and men who were not ascertained to be British subjects. Captain Paynter reported on November 8 that, on receiving these instructions he went on the *Shenandoah*, and being satisfied that there were no British subjects among the crew, or at least none of whom it could be proved were British subjects, he permitted all hands to land with their private effects.

Thus ended our memorable cruise—grand in its conception. Grand in its execution and un-precedentally, awfully grand in its sad finale. To the four winds the gallant crew scattered, most of them never to meet again until called to the Bar of that Highest of all Tribunals.

The ship was handed over to the United States agents, a Captain Freeman was appointed to take her to New York, but going out and encountering high west winds, lost light spars and returned to Liverpool. It was not tried again. The noble vessel was put and sold to the Sultan of Zanzibar. She finally was lost on a coral reef in the Indian Ocean in 1879—fourteen years after the last Confederate flag was hauled down.

XII

Torpedo Bureau

1. Electric Torpedoes

The Confederate Torpedo Bureau was a division of the Confederate navy's Office of Ordnance and Hydrography, although the Bureau operated essentially as a separate entity. Organized in October of 1862, its importance grew as the reliability of the torpedoes (or mines as we term them today) improved. The Torpedo Bureau was first organized by Commander Matthew Fontaine Maury; however, he initially received little support from the Navy Department, for Secretary Mallory was skeptical concerning the use of torpedoes as a defensive weapon.

After Commander Maury demonstrated several successful tests in the James River and developed the torpedo into a useful weapon, the program stagnated because of a long-standing animosity that was carried over from the U. S. Navy between Maury and Mallory. Finally the naval secretary ordered Maury to Europe where he could continue his experiments.

The new commander of the Torpedo Bureau was First Lieutenant Hunter Davidson, and he brought with him into the Bureau R. O. Crowley, an experienced electrician. Little is known of Crowley, not even his first name, but he was very knowledgeable in the relatively new medium of electricity, and especially on how to use it to explode a weapon. After the war, in 1898, Crowley wrote extensively of his war experiences in the Torpedo Bureau for the Century magazine and his essay is presented here. (Campbell, *Hunters of the Night: Confederate Torpedo Boats in the War Between the States*, p. 94.) [RTC]

"The Confederate Torpedo Service" by
Electrician R. O. Crowley, CSN
The *Century* Magazine, Volume 56, Issue 2, June 1898

Organization and First Experiments

At the outbreak of the war, one of the most pressing needs of the Confederacy was some effective method of defending its water approaches, especially the James River, leading direct to, its capital city. The South had no ships of war, and the few old-fashioned brick-and-mortar forts located here and there were mostly armed with smoothbore iron cannon, relics of a past age, and rusty from neglect.

To look back now, it seems wonderful how very defenseless we were at the start, and how apparently easy it would have been for a single second-class war vessel to have steamed up to Richmond in the early days of the conflict. For the defense of the rivers men's minds turned toward torpedoes, which were then but little known in the military world. Scores of plans were submitted to the War and Navy departments, some advocating mechanical torpedoes—that is, those which exploded by contact or by timed mechanism—others strenuously urging electrical torpedoes. Those generally intended for use on land naturally fell into the hands of the War Department, while electrical torpedoes for use under water came within the province of the Navy Department. It is of the latter class that this article treats.

The idea of using torpedoes on the Confederate side originated, I believe, with the Hon. S. R. Mallory, Secretary of the Navy; and he directed the distinguished Captain M. F. Maury to make experiments, with a view to their general employment, if practicable. His work began in the spring of 1862, and continued for a few months only with electrical torpedoes. He had arrived at no definite conclusion from his experiments when he was dispatched on an important mission to Europe, where he continued to make experiments in electricity applicable to torpedo warfare, discovering an ingenious method of arranging and testing torpedo mines. The fact that there was no practical result from his experiments in the South was due simply to the want of time to organize his forces and collect material.

At that time the Federal government had no system of torpedoes; indeed, they did not consider it "honorable warfare." They had no necessity for submarine defenses, because early in the war we had no ships to attack them. Frequent reports reached us that they intended to hang or shoot any man they should capture who was engaged in the torpedo business. It was, therefore, a very risky business on our part, as we were constantly exposed to capture. As some slight security against being summarily executed by the Federals, in the event of my being captured, I was furnished with a document from our Navy Department, which read as follows, as near as I can remember:

> The bearer, R. O. Crowley, is in the service of the Confederate States Navy as electrician; and in case of his capture by the United States forces, he will be exchanged for any general officer of their army who may be in our hands.
>
> (Signed) S. R. MALLORY, Secretary of the Navy
> (Signed) JEFF'N DAVIS, President.

This document I always carried on my person, although I had no great confidence in its efficacy.

The experiments made under the supervision of Captain Maury consisted of placing a series of hollow spherical shells of iron, containing about fifty pounds of powder, and extending across the bottom of the river, and connecting them electrically by insulated copper wires leading to galvanic batteries on shore. Inside these shells fuses were placed, which were to be ignited by the passage of an electric current through a fine platinum wire.

It was confidently expected that the simultaneous explosion of these shells under a passing vessel would instantaneously destroy the vessel and all on board. Experiments soon demonstrated, however, that fifty pounds of powder in from ten to fifteen feet of water would scarcely do any harm; and very soon the whole plant was entirely disarranged, the wires broken, and the shells lost, by a heavy freshet in the river.

Captain Maury was succeeded by Lieutenant Hunter Davidson, and it was at this time that the writer was appointed electrician of the Torpedo Division. Our headquarters were on board a small but swift steam-tug called the *Torpedo*, and two Parrott rifles were put aboard of her for emergencies. In the cabin of this little steamer we studied, planned, and experimented for months with various fuses, galvanic batteries, etc., and finally we determined on a system.

Our first object was to prepare a sensitive fuse of fulminate of mercury, to be exploded by the incandescence of fine platinum wire by means of a quantity current of electricity. We succeeded in this, and our fuses were made by taking a piece of quill, half an inch long, and filling it with fulminate of mercury. Each end of the quill was sealed with beeswax, after fixing a fine platinum wire through the center of the quill and connecting the protruding ends of the platinum wire with insulated copper wire. Enveloping the fuse was a red-flannel cartridge-bag stuffed with rifle-powder. The fuse, thus prepared, was ready to be placed in a torpedo-tank containing cannon-powder.

I have been thus particular in describing the fuse because on it depends entirely the certainty of explosion. Our torpedo-tanks were made of half-inch boiler iron. There was an opening to pour in the powder and to receive the fuse. The opening was then fitted with a screw-plug, in which there were two holes for the passage of the wires, and packed with greased cotton waste to prevent leakage of water to the inside. There was a heavy ring by which the tank was slung into position, and through this ring was passed a heavy iron chain attached to a mushroom anchor about twenty feet distant. These tanks were generally manufactured at the Tredegar Ironworks, and subjected to a heavy hydraulic pressure to show any leaks or defects.

1st Lt. Hunter Davidson (Naval Historical Center).

Before we decided on the shape of the tank we prepared some ordinary copper soda-water tanks, capable of holding about one hundred to one hundred and fifty pounds of powder, and anchored them floating midway between the bottom of the river and the surface of the water. It was soon found, however, that, owing to their oscillating rotary motion, the electric wires became twisted and the electrical connection was broken. We also found that such floating tanks spent half their explosive force downward, and that copper was too soft to allow a fierce tearing power to the confined gases.

We experimented a long time with tanks of various sizes, and at various depths of water, and finally decided that a tank containing two thousand pounds of cannon powder was sure to destroy utterly a ship of any size at a depth of not more than thirty feet.

To give some idea of the many difficulties we encountered, I will mention, first, the scarcity of cannon-powder; secondly, we had only about four miles of insulated copper wire in the entire Confederacy; thirdly, we could obtain only about four or five feet of fine-gage platinum wire. Battery material was very scarce, and acids could be purchased only from the small quantity remaining in the hands of druggists when the war broke out.

In the autumn of 1862 we planted three of these copper torpedoes, each containing one hundred and fifty pounds of powder, in the Rappahannock, below Port Royal, the intention being to destroy any Federal gunboat passing up. Our plans, however, were disclosed to the enemy by a Negro, and no attempt was made to steam over the torpedoes. In December of that year, when Burnside was about to attack at Fredericksburg, it was deemed prudent to abandon our station near Port Royal, to avoid being cut off if the Federal army should succeed in making Lee retreat.

To this end, I was instructed to proceed without delay to Port Royal, to save all the wire possible, and bring off our galvanic batteries and other material. This was a hazardous undertaking, as our station was outside the Confederate lines, and the enemy was in strong force on the opposite bank of the Rappahannock. In pursuance of orders, I arrived at the station about sunset one evening, and after making due preparations for the transportation of our men and material, the galvanic battery was charged and the circuit closed, and a tremendous explosion took place, throwing up large columns of water, and arousing the inhabitants for miles around. We then began to retreat, and did not get inside our lines until near daybreak the next morning, being much delayed by the muddy roads.*

Such was the consternation of the few inhabitants of Port Royal at hearing the explosion, that the town was immediately deserted, and I understood that about forty persons slept that night in a small log hut on a hill about two miles distant.

Operations on the James River

Having our system now perfected, we established a torpedo station, some five or six miles below Richmond, by submerging two iron tanks, containing one thousand pounds of powder each, in twelve feet of water, leading the wires ashore, and connecting them with a galvanic battery concealed in a small hut in a deep ravine. From the battery-house the wires were led to an elevated position near by, where the man in charge could keep a lookout for passing vessels. The position of the torpedoes in the water was indicated by two sticks, planted about ten feet apart on the bluff, and in a line with each other and the torpedoes; and the watchman's instructions were to explode them by contacting the wires as soon as an enemy's vessel should be on a line with the two pointers. All this being prepared, we awaited the approach of a Federal gunboat. As was usually the case, one came when least expected, on a beautiful clear day, when our entire force except the man stationed as lookout was absent in Richmond, preparing other war material.

We were apprised by telegraph of the rapid approach of the gunboat, and immediately hastened toward our first station; but we arrived too late. The man in charge had not seen the United States flag for a long period, and never having previously seen a gunboat so near, lost his presence of mind, and fired one of the 1000-pound powder-tanks when the gunboat was at least twenty to thirty yards distant. A great explosion took place, throwing up a large column of water to a considerable height; and the gunboat by her momentum plunged into the great trough, and caught the downward rush of a wave on her forward deck. The guards were broken away, half a dozen men were thrown overboard, and other damage to the gunboat was caused. The steamer then turned about as quickly as she could, and prepared to retrace her route down the river, after picking up the men who had been

---

*On arriving at Milford depot, on the Fredericksburg Railroad, next day, I found immense numbers of sick and wounded soldiers retreating from Fredericksburg toward Richmond. I boarded the ambulance-train myself, in company with a lieutenant of engineers belonging to General Lee's staff, on his way to the War Department at Richmond, with plans of General Lee's intended route in the event of his being forced from Fredericksburg. When our train arrived at Ashland, we found the village in possession of Colonel Kilpatrick, of the Federal cavalry, who immediately summoned everybody to surrender and get off the train, which was then demolished and the engine run off the track. Here was a predicament, and I thought that the time had perhaps arrived when it would become necessary for me to show my document signed by Secretary Mallory. But, upon reflection, I concluded to keep as quiet as possible; so I went up to Colonel Kilpatrick, and said: "Colonel, what shall you do with citizens?" "Nothing," said he; "you may stand aside." "All right," I replied, and immediately vanished in the background. If he had only known what a nice capture he would have made of my friend the lieutenant, and also the aide-de-camp of the Governor of Virginia, who happened to be on the train with a large amount of money belonging to the State, which he was taking to Richmond! The next day I started for Richmond on foot, the railroad bridges and tracks having been destroyed by the Federals. We found their cavalry all along the route, even up to the very fortifications, which they could easily have entered, with scarcely any resistance.

washed overboard. There was a brilliant opportunity to accomplish her total destruction by firing the remaining torpedo as she passed back over it. But alas! the man had been so astounded at the first explosion that he had fled precipitately, without waiting to see what damage had been done, and the gunboat was thus enabled to return down the river in safety.

The partial success of this attempt at exploding torpedoes by electricity immediately established the reputation of the Torpedo Division, and created great excitement all over the South, it being an undisputed fact that but for this explosion a Federal gun-boat would have been moored at the wharf at Richmond that morning, and would have captured the city.

A description of the defenses of the James River would be incomplete that did not include the barricade at Drewry's Bluff. The river here is very narrow and deep. The right bank is a high, precipitous bluff, and the left low, flat land, so that the fort on the bluff commanded a wide sweep of country. The barricade was formed by driving piles, and then making square cribs of them, with the interior filled with broken granite, of which there were large quantities at Richmond. These cribs were stretched across the river in an irregular line, and were exposed a little at low tide. Between the cribs several steamboats and schooners were scuttled and sunk. No direct passage was left open, even for our own vessels, except a very labyrinthine route on the left bank, just large enough for small tugboats.

When the time came for our own ironclads to pass down the river, the Torpedo Division was sent to break up some of the cribs by exploding torpedoes on the top of them. In this manner a passage sufficiently wide was effected without damage to the remaining cribs. The barricade was left in such a shape that it could thereafter be quickly reconstructed so as to close the passage entirely.

Blowing up these cribs was great fun for our party, besides affording us practice in experiments. Numbers of fine fish were stunned by each explosion, and, floating to the surface, were speedily captured by us. There were no other barricades in the James River of any magnitude during the war. There was a slight one of stone cribs and sunken vessels at Howlett's Reach, but it was not considered effective. In fact, the main reliance on the barricades was that they would prevent a surprise movement by the enemy at night; and it was not believed that the one at Drewry's Bluff would do more than hold a determined enemy at bay for a few hours, while the shore batteries on the bluff could be pouring plunging shot on the decks of attacking vessels.

Immediate steps were now taken to establish other torpedo stations at several points lower down the river, using in every instance 2000-pound torpedoes. At our lowest telegraph station, which was located on General Pickett's Turkey Island plantation, opposite Presque Isle, we erected a lookout tower, about one hundred feet high, from which the Federal gunboats at City Point could be seen distinctly. At Presque Isle we stationed a scout whose duty it was to signal the man in the tower when anything suspicious occurred. Presque Isle is only a short distance from Bermuda Hundred, which is near City Point. The lowest torpedo station was at a place called Deep Bottom, about five miles above City Point by land, but more by water. As there were a good many free Negroes in the vicinity of Deep Bottom, we had to do our work with great secrecy, generally planting the torpedoes at night, in a position previously surveyed by day. At Deep Bottom we located the galvanic battery on the right bank of the river, in a pit about four or five feet deep, the top covered over with twigs and brush, and in another pit, some distance off, a place was prepared for the lookout; this pit was also concealed by twigs and brush.

We were duly advised of the advance of General Butler's army from Bermuda Hundred toward Drewry's Bluff, the entire Federal fleet also advancing up the river, covering his right wing. The Federals had been told by the Negroes that there were torpedoes at Deep Bottom, and used great caution in advancing. As soon as the fleet rounded the point below Presque Isle, the Federals began shelling our tower, and it was soon demolished;

but no one was hurt, as our men took away the telegraph instruments, and rapidly retreated up the river road. A force of marines was landed on both sides of the river, in order to discover the whereabouts of our batteries. A squadron of boats, heavily armed, went in advance of the fleet, dragging the river for wires and torpedoes. Their grapnels, however, passed over and over our wires, without producing any damage, our lookout, from his concealed station in the pit, noting all the movements of the men in the boats, and hearing every word of command. After a while the Federal commander, apparently satisfied that there were no torpedoes there, ordered the *Commodore Jones*, a double-ender gunboat carrying eight guns and manned by a force of two hundred men, to move up to Deep Bottom, make a landing, and report. This was done, the gunboat passing over our torpedoes; but our man in the pit kept cool, and did not explode them, because, as he afterward said, he wanted to destroy the ironclad, recently captured by the Federals from us near Savannah, Georgia.

The *Commodore Jones* steamed up to the wharf at Deep Bottom, and found our quarters deserted. This looked suspicious, and the order was then given for her to fall back. Our man now concluded that the entire fleet would retire, and he determined to destroy the *Commodore Jones*. As she retreated she passed immediately over one of the two torpedoes planted there. All at once a terrific explosion shattered her into fragments, some of the pieces going a hundred feet in the air. Men were thrown overboard and drowned, about forty being instantly killed. The whole Federal fleet then retreated some distance below.

The Federal marines on shore continued their explorations, and our man in the battery-pit suddenly jumped out, and was as killed by a shot from the marines. The small boats again began dragging for our wires, and finally caught them, and by under running them to the shore at length discovered the man in the lookout pit, who was immediately taken prisoner and carried on board one of the vessels composing the fleet. He was subsequently imprisoned at Fort Warren, but about a year afterward was exchanged. Both he and his assistant, when taken aboard the fleet, were securely placed in a conspicuous position on the wheel-house of a double-ender gunboat,—the foremost vessel—in order, as they were told, that if any further explosion took place they should share the consequences.

Thus was accomplished at one blow, and almost as quick as lightning, the complete destruction of a war steamer by submarine torpedoes. So far as I know, it was the first instance of the kind in the annals of war. Its effect astonished the world, and its immediate result was the safety of Richmond from a second peril. General Butler, finding his army completely uncovered on the right wing, was unable to accomplish anything by land, and retired to Bermuda Hundred.

Shortly afterward the land forces again advanced, and compelled us to abandon all our torpedo stations below Dutch Gap.

While we were busily engaged in perfecting our system of submarine defenses, making it necessary that we should have unobstructed navigation of the river, some mechanical torpedoes were planted, under the direction of army officers. As these were entirely unreliable as to certainty of explosion or contact, and were as dangerous to us as to the enemy, our chief, upon being advised of it, demanded their removal. The Secretary of War gave a reluctant assent to his demand that we should drag them up and put them out of harm's way. There was not much accord between the army and the navy in those days, however; and we were not fully advised in the premises, as will be shown herein. The steamer *A. H. Schultz*, formerly used as a passenger-steamer between Richmond and Norfolk, and commanded by Captain D. J. Hill, was at the outbreak of the war laid up as useless at the wharf in Richmond. Later she was taken possession of by the Confederate government for the purpose of transporting prisoners to and from Varina, on the James, the point of exchange. One day she started down the river, having on board four hundred and fifty Federal prisoners. She passed the barricades at Drewry's Bluff safely, and landed her prisoners at Varina, where they were duly turned over to the Federal authorities, and it was expected that she would then bring back to Richmond a like number of exchanged Confederates; but owing to some misunderstanding on the part of the commissioners of ex- change, no Confederates were brought up by the Federals to Varina, so she was obliged to start on her return to Richmond. When she reached a point just below the barricades at the bluff, she came in contact with one of these mechanical torpedoes, placed there by army officers, and an explosion followed, killing two firemen and two Confederate soldiers. The steamer sank in five minutes, and was a total loss. On the downward trip the torpedo probably swung downstream with the strong current, and for this reason the steamer did not come in contact with the percussion fuse; but on her return the torpedo, still swinging with the current, offered a fair mark for the steamer's hull coming up. It was a most fortunate thing for the South that the *Schultz* did not strike the torpedo on her downward trip, as the Federals, most of whom were just from the hospitals, and in a weak and sickly condition, would probably all have been drowned, and universal condemnation would have fallen upon the destruction of four hundred and fifty prisoners under a flag of truce.

Operations Near Wilmington, North Carolina

Nothing more of consequence took place on the James River, and we were transferred to Wilmington, North Carolina, to defend Forts Fisher and Caswell, at the mouth of the Cape Fear River, from any attempt of the Federal fleet to pass the forts. Here we were confronted with a new difficulty—that of laying torpedoes in the sea, in a wide channel; and our resources in the matter of copper wire and battery material were getting very scarce. We had plenty of cannon-powder only. The channel in front of Fort Fisher was about half a mile wide; but just at the bar, over which it was necessary for a vessel to pass to enter the channel, there was scarcely room for more than one or two ships to pass at a time.

We first planted in the regular channel near the bar seven torpedo-tanks, each containing two thousand pounds of powder. It was thought that at least one of these would be covered by a vessel in passing; and we knew from experience that if one vessel was destroyed by the explosion of a torpedo, no other vessel would dare to renew the attempt.

Of the electric wires, one from each torpedo connected it with a wire leading to one end of the battery, which was located in a bomb-proof comprising a part of the fortifications; another wire led from each torpedo to the opposite end of the battery, and hung disconnected until desired to be exploded. All these wires were entrenched in the sand from the shore-line to the battery. These latter wires were numbered from 1 to 7, and sights were placed showing when a ship covered any particular torpedo.

About this time we received a supply of wire, acids, battery, and electrical appliances through the blockade from Europe, and we intended to plant a torpedo right on the bar, the entrance there being very narrow. Everything was prepared for it; but the appearance of the Federal fleet put an end to the attempt, so we had to rest contented with the seven already planted.

Among the apparatus received from Europe was a lot of Wheatstone exploders and Abels fuses. With these we hastily prepared several copper tanks of a capacity of one hundred pounds of powder, and planted them about three feet deep in the sand on the land side of the fort, about three hundred yards in front, and led the wires in trenches to the traverses of the fort. This was done in expectation of an assault by the Federal land forces. The Federal fleet, however, proceeded to bombard that angle of the fort, and one by one our guns on that side were demolished. At the same time it was discovered that the heavy shells, plowing up the ground in front, had utterly destroyed all our wires, so that the plan of exploding the 100-pound tanks on shore failed entirely.

The result of the bombardment of Fort Fisher is well known. No attempt was made to pass our batteries until the fort was in the hands of the Federals.

As in former instances, our plans were betrayed. One or two nights before the attack, the writer was up at a very late hour, talking to his assistant about our preparations, plans, etc., in a room of a building occupied in part by the midshipmen and officers of the naval squadron doing land duty in Fort Buchanan, which commanded that part of the channel nearest the Cape Fear River. Our conversation was fully overheard by one of the ordinary seamen in the next room, who deserted in a boat that night, and went to the Federal fleet. But for the intelligence conveyed by this deserter, it is believed that the Federals would have made an attempt to pass our land batteries.

Above Fort Fisher, toward Wilmington, we had planted two submarine batteries of one thousand pounds of powder each, connected by electric wires with a Wheatstone exploder located in an old earthwork on the bank of the river. During a heavy thunderstorm the wires were struck by lightning, and both tanks exploded simultaneously, damaging nothing, but frightening the fleet, and causing great watchfulness in their slow advance toward Wilmington. The Cape Fear River could be entered by two channels, one leading up to Fort Caswell, and thence via Fort Campbell into the river, and the other leading up to Fort Fisher and via Fort Buchanan into the river.

The first-named route, via Fort Caswell, or the "old inlet," as it was called, was entirely undefended by submarine torpedoes, and probably would have been easy to turn with a small ironclad, as the two forts there were old brick-and-mortar constructions armed with old-fashioned smooth-bore guns; but the channel-way was comparatively shallow and tortuous. The other route, via Fort Fisher, was more commonly used by the blockade-runners, as there was no impediment to navigation except the bar in front of the fort.

I have previously noted the great scarcity of materials. To get up a battery without glass tumblers to hold the acid, and without platinum strips to immerse in the nitric acid, was a great difficulty. There was no glass manufactory in the South. Platinum strips could not be obtained. The only platinum suitable for that purpose was being used in the batteries in the telegraph offices. I finally arranged a battery as follows: with the zinc plates formerly used in the Wollaston battery in our early experiments, I had a number of zinc cells cast in the shape of an ordinary glass tumbler, having a projecting arm for a handle as well as to connect it with the next adjoining cell in the series. The inside of these zinc tumblers was amalgamated with mercury, and a solution of euphoric acid, composed of one part of acid and thirteen parts of water, was poured into each tumbler or cell. In this solution was placed a cylindrical porous cup, open at the top, and filled with nitric acid. In the nitric acid was immersed a piece of cast-iron having four projecting leaves and a projecting handle connected with a corresponding handle of the adjoining zinc cell by an ordinary brass clamp. It would appear, at a casual glance, that the nitric acid would almost instantly consume this cast-iron strip; but it did not, and we found that it would remain several hours without perceptible change, and then the nitric acid would become changed into probably a nitrous oxide gas, and effervesce suddenly. It was necessary, then, only to refill the porous cup with fresh, pure nitric acid. The composition of this battery had been suggested to the writer's mind from having seen, several years previously, a similar battery used by a Dr. Boynton, a public lecturer, to produce electrical phenomena.

This battery, as will be observed from its construction, would stand a great deal of rough usage. Its electrical heating-power was great, but its electromotive force was not sufficient to produce heat at a greater distance than two miles of a metallic circuit.

The operations of the Torpedo Division proper were confined principally to the James and the Cape Fear rivers. Our force was small, though sufficiently elastic to have extended to other points if we had had the necessary materials. It comprised the officer in charge, the electrician and his assistant, two men at each station, two or three telegraph operators, one or two scouts, and the crew of a tugboat, commanded by an executive officer—in all, about fifty men. Of the men at the stations, one was usually either a boatswain or a master in the navy, and the other a young man as a relief, generally a man who was incapacitated from doing active duty as a soldier in the field.

Submarine torpedoes containing powder could not be effectively used in the Mississippi River, principally on account of its great depth, varying from twenty to one hundred and fifty feet, the immense volume of water to be lifted offering too much resistance.

It would not do to calculate the weight of a perpendicular column of water, with a diameter of say three or four feet, in this connection, because powder, exploding equally in all directions, has a tendency to lift a column conically shaped—that is to say, with a lower diameter of about four or five feet and a diameter at the surface of from twenty to thirty feet. To lift a column sufficiently strong in its upward ascent to crush the hull of a passing vessel in water one hundred feet deep would require such an immense quantity of powder as to make it virtually impossible to handle it.

Again, the bed of the Mississippi River is continually varying by the unceasing deposit of accumulations of soil caused by the caving in of its precipitous bluffs, so that a torpedo, when planted in some localities, would in a few months be covered by an immense sandbar, and thus the effect of an explosion would be deadened. Submerged floating torpedoes, anchored in the channel of a swift current like the Mississippi, could not be depended on to maintain their position very long, and, as has already been explained, would soon part the electric wires by their continual oscillating rotary motion.

These objections—that is, the depth of the water and the difficulty of handling a large quantity of powder—do not, of course, apply in their entirety to guncotton torpedoes, which, being several times stronger than powder, and occupying much less space, could be used in many places to much more advantage. Guncotton is also much safer to manipulate than powder. One does not absolutely know when powder will explode accidentally, but guncotton cannot possibly explode, if kept moist with water to a certain degree, except by means of a detonating fuse of fulminate or other quick-flame material. But I am wandering from the subject. Guncotton was not practically known as an explosive during the war.

It is only the breaking or crushing of the hull of a vessel by the upheaving force of a column of water which makes torpedoes so destructive. It is not the flames of powder, or its suffocating or burning gases, which produce the awful death, in many instances, of all on board, but the instantaneous disruption of the hull, driven inward by the weight of the water, crushing everybody between decks, and instantaneously sinking the craft, and drowning those who are carried down by the rapid sinking of the wreck. An ironclad is more quickly and easily destroyed than any other class of vessel, for the reason that such an immense weight of metal armor carries down to the bottom everybody between decks the instant the hull is shattered by a torpedo, the heavy weight of the iron armor above causing the hull to oppose a more inert resistance to the upheaval of the water underneath, I believe several instances occurred in Southern rivers, during the war, where wooden vessels, coming in contact with mechanical torpedoes containing only a small quantity of powder, were simply lifted out of the water at the bows, without serious injury to the hull.

A review of the facts and experience here stated shows that a system of submarine defenses, to be effectual, should be protected by a small fortification and a land force sufficient to repel any attack by infantry for the purpose of breaking up the electric batteries and destroying the wires on shore, and, in addition to these, by a powerful electric-light reflector to light up the position at night; and the defenses should have one or two small steam-launches with a Gatling gun on board, and apparatus for striking the enemy's vessels with a spar torpedo while engaged in an attempt to drag for the wires under the water. Since the late war science has developed many improvements in this direction, but none that will prevent the passage of a land fortification by a swift iron-clad man-of-war except submarine torpedoes.

Offensive Torpedo Warfare

So far we had been acting on the defensive, and the torpedoes described might be called defensive torpedoes. It was now determined to apply offensive torpedoes; if the enemy would not come to us to be blown up, we would go to them.

The first thing to be done was to prepare a fuse which was not dangerous to handle, and which would explode quickly on contact with any substance.

To this end we made some sheet-lead tubes, the rounded end being of much thinner lead than the other part.

These tubes were about three inches long and one inch in diameter. Into this tube was inserted a small glass tube, of similar shape, filled with sulphuric acid, and hermetically sealed. The vacant space about the glass tube was then tightly packed with a mixture of chlorate of potash and pulverized white sugar, and the mouth of the lead tube was closed by fastening a strip of muslin over it.

Now, if the rounded end of the leaden tube is brought into contact with any hard substance, the thin lead will be mashed, the interior glass tube broken, and the sulphuric acid becoming mixed with the preparation of chlorate of potash and sugar, an immediate explosion is the result. We then prepared a copper cylinder capable of containing about fifty pounds of powder, and placed several of the leaden fuses in the head, so that no matter at what angle the butt struck the hull of a ship, one of the fuses would be smashed in, and flame from the potash and sugar ignite the powder. At the bottom of the copper cylinder there was a socket made to fit on the end of a spar.

We discussed the matter of exploding spar torpedoes by electricity, but the difficulty of arranging a contrivance to close the electric circuit when the torpedo came in contact with the hull of a ship, and want of conveniences for stowing a galvanic battery in the launch, induced us to adopt the fuses above mentioned instead.

This was a formidable weapon, and one extremely dangerous to handle. We first experimented with an empty cylinder fitted with leaden fuses. The copper cylinder was fastened to a spar attached to the bow of a small steam-launch. Thus prepared, we "rammed" an old bulkhead, or wharf, at Rocketts, in the lower part of Richmond, at first unsuccessfully. We then tried it loaded with twenty-five pounds of powder, and, lowering the spar torpedo about two feet under water, again rammed the bulkhead. The effect of the explosion shattered the old wharf and threw up a column of water, completely drenching the occupants of the launch.

Our steam-launch, or "torpedo launch," as it was called, was prepared for an expedition against the enemy's fleet snugly anchored off Newport News. Just at this time a new difficulty presented itself. The launch burned bituminous coal, the smoke from which could be discerned at a long distance, and the sparks from which at night would disclose its presence to an enemy. Some one suggested that we might obtain anthracite coal by dredging at the wharves and in the docks at Richmond. This was accordingly done, and we obtained a supply of the anthracite, for which an almost fabulous sum was paid.

Our launch was about twenty feet long, about five feet beam, and drew three feet of water. She was fitted with a small double engine amidships, and there was sufficient space in her bow for three men, and aft for an engineer, who also acted as fireman. An iron shield was then fixed on her, completely covering the men from plunging rifle-shots.

Thus equipped, and all being ready, we towed the launch down the James River, on a dark night, to a point about ten or fifteen miles below City Point, and then let her go on her dangerous mission.

There were only four persons on board of her, namely, the commanding officer, a mate, a pilot, and an engineer.

From reports afterward made, we learned that she steamed down toward Newport News until the approach of daylight, and then hid in a swamp until the next night, when the attempt was made to blow up the U.S.S. *Minnesota*, then the flag-ship of the Federal fleet, and the largest war vessel in the Union service. The launch steamed all through the fleet that night, being frequently challenged by the deck lookouts. Finally the *Minnesota* was seen looming up grimly in the darkness, and, letting down the spar torpedo in the water, the launch rammed the ship just below the water-line on her starboard quarter.

The effect was terrific, the shock causing the *Minnesota* to tremble from stem to stern. Several of her guns were dismounted and a big hole was opened in her side by the explosion of the 50-pound torpedo.

Owing to the strong tide prevailing at the time, and the violence of the ramming, the launch perceptibly rebounded, so that at the instant of the explosion, which was not simultaneous with the blow, a cushion of water intervened between the torpedo and the hull of the *Minnesota*, thus weakening the effect and probably saving the ship. She was so thoroughly disabled, however, as we afterward understood, that she had to be towed off, and underwent repairs in the docks. Our men were greeted with showers of bullets from the deck of the ship, but they struck harmlessly against the iron shield of the launch, which quickly steamed away under cover of darkness, and escaped.

This, I believe, was the first instance of successful ramming with torpedoes and the subsequent escape of the attacking crew, most other cases happening subsequently resulting in the death or capture of the attacking party. The effect of this daring attack exercised a great influence on the Federal fleets everywhere. It was necessary to double the watches and exercise untiring vigilance against any further attempts.

During the last year of the war arrangements had been perfected to secure a large quantity of insulated wire, cables, acids, batteries, and telegraph apparatus, etc., from England, an officer having been sent there for that purpose. Every material requisite for the extension of our torpedo system throughout the entire South was obtained, and a small advance shipment did actually reach us through the blockade at Wilmington. The remainder was put on board a swift steamer, with the intention of running the blockade and returning with a full cargo of cotton; but from stress of weather, or other causes, the steamer put into the port of Fayal, and, as I understood, was wrecked in that port, either from the stupidity of the pilot or from treachery. The entire cargo was lost, and it was impossible to duplicate our material before the war ended.

Torpedo Operations in Charleston

Perhaps there is no harbor on the Atlantic coast so well adapted for defense by submarine batteries as that of Charleston. All the requisite accessories for a successful defense by this method exist in a remarkably favorable condition. The main ship channel passes toward the city, between Morris Island on the one side, and Sullivan's Island on the other, with Fort Sumter between the two islands. Each of these points offers sure protection to galvanic batteries, and each is capable of being made the central point of independent systems. The submerged battery wires radiating from each position could not be destroyed by dragging in the daytime without coming under fire of the land batteries, and with the aid of calcium lights thrown on the position at night, any attempt at dragging would be extremely hazardous. Besides these natural advantages, the depth of water is not too great for effective explosions.

As previously stated in this paper, we were without the necessary material to extend our system to Charleston harbor; besides, the exigencies of the situation at Richmond and Wilmington were too pressing to permit us to think of Charleston. However, some attempts were made by the local military authorities to lay torpedoes in the harbor, and a large one was planted in the main channel, the wires being led into Fort Sumter.

On April 7, 1863, the Federal fleet commanded by Admiral Du Pont moved up the channel northward toward Sullivan's Island, the frigate *Ironsides* in advance, followed by the ironclad *Keokuk* and the wooden vessels. At a distance of about one thousand yards these powerful war-ships opened fire on Fort Sumter with terrific effect, and received, in return, a heavy fire from all the adjacent forts. The *Ironsides* passed over and over the torpedo before mentioned, and everybody awaited with intense anxiety the moment when it was expected she would be blown to pieces by its explosion. It failed to "go off," however. Several reasons were assigned for the failure, but probably the true reason was wet powder and want of system in properly testing the wires and the torpedo-tank.

The Federals believed that the harbor was thickly studded with explosives; and although this belief exercised a very considerable moral effect, it did not prevent them from advancing bravely to attack powerful forts, not knowing at what moment their ships might be destroyed.

The "Cigar-Boat" [*H. L. Hunley*]

In the "Southern History Society Papers," Colonel Olmstead gives the following account of an interesting episode in the service which did not come under my eye:

During the summer of 1863 there was brought to Charleston, South Carolina, by rail from Mobile, Alabama, a peculiarly shaped boat known as the "cigar-boat." Its history is linked with deeds of the loftiest heroism. This boat was one day made fast to the wharf at Fort Johnson, opposite Fort Sumter, preparatory to an expedition against the Federal fleet. It was built of boiler-iron, about thirty feet in length, with a breadth of beam of four feet, and a vertical depth of six feet. Access to the interior was had by two man-holes in the upper part, covered by hinged caps into which were let bull's-eyes of heavy glass, and through these the steersman looked in guiding the motions of the craft. The boat floated with these caps raised only a foot or so above the level of the water. The motive power was a propeller worked by the hands of the crew, cranks being provided in the shaft for that purpose. Upon each side of the exterior were horizontal vanes, or wings, which could be adjusted to any required angle from the interior. When it was desired that the boat should go on an even keel, whether on the surface or under the water, these vanes were kept level. If it was desired to go under the water—say, for instance, at an angle of ten degrees—the vanes were fixed at that angle, and the propeller worked. The resistance of the water against the inclined vanes would then carry the boat under. A reversal of this method would bring it to the surface again. A tube of mercury was arranged to mark the descent. It had been the design of the inventor to approach near to an enemy, then to submerge the boat and pass under the ship to be attacked, towing a floating torpedo to be exploded by means of electricity as soon as it touched the keel.

Insufficient depth of water in the harbor prevented this manner of using the boat, however; and she was then rigged with a long spar at the bow, to which a torpedo was attached, to be exploded by actual concussion with the object to be destroyed.

While the "cigar-boat" was at the wharf at Fort Johnson, with some of her crew on board, she was suddenly sunk by the waves from a passing steamer. Days elapsed before she could be raised. The dead bodies of the drowned crew inside were removed, and a second crew volunteered. They made repeated and successful experiments in the harbor, but finally they too went down, and, from some unknown cause, failed to come up. Once more a long time passed before the boat was raised, and then the remains of the devoted crew were taken from her; nevertheless, still another set of men came forward and volunteered for the perilous duty.

Finally the expedition started; but it never returned. That night the Federal sloop-of-war *Housatonic* was reported as having been sunk by a torpedo in the lower harbor; but of the gallant men who had thus accomplished what they aimed to do, at the risk of their own lives, nothing definite was ever known until after the war, when divers, in endeavoring to raise the wreck of the *Housatonic*, discovered the "cigar-boat," with the bleached bones of her crew, lying near the wreck of the noble ship she had destroyed!* [Since proven untrue]

Operations at Savannah

As in the case of Charleston, the torpedo operations at Savannah were without system, and were left entirely to the discretion of the local military authorities.

On March 3, 1863, three ironclads and two mortar-boats advanced up the Ogeechee River to attack Fort McAllister, and bombarded it for a whole day, without any practical results. During the action the ironclad *Montauk* came in contact with a mechanical torpedo, which exploded under her bow, but without serious injury.

Operations in Mobile

A great many mechanical torpedoes were planted in Mobile Bay and in the ship-channel, but none were operated by electricity. There was no regular system employed. Some of the torpedoes were merely cans of tin containing a small quantity of powder, with a trigger attachment for exploding them. Others were made of sheet-iron, with a fuse which exploded by pressure, the fuse being protected by a cap of thin brass covered with a solution of beeswax. This latter plan was known as the Rains patent—invented by Brigadier-General Rains—and was used in various places, both on land and water. Others were made of oaken kegs and barrels, well painted, and arranged to explode by mechanical contact. These barrels were firmly attached to heavy spars anchored at one end, and kept at the proper angle by chains passing through the spars, thus keeping the barrel torpedoes floating about five feet from the surface.

In the early part of August, 1864, Admiral Farragut, commanding the Federal fleet off Mobile, secured the military cooperation of General Canby for attacking and investing the forts in the harbor. On the morning of the 5th of August the fleet, numbering fourteen steamers and four monitors, carrying in all about two hundred guns, and manned by twenty-eight hundred men, made its entrance into Mobile Bay. In the early light of the morning the attacking fleet moved steadily up the main ship-channel, whereupon Fort Morgan opened on them, and was replied to by a gun from the *Brooklyn*. A moment later the Federal ironclad *Tecumseh* came in contact with a mechanical torpedo, an explosion followed, and she disappeared almost instantaneously beneath the waves, carrying with her

*Hunley was in fact not discovered for more than 140 years.

commander, T. A. M. Craven, and her entire crew, numbering nearly one hundred and twenty men, most of whom were drowned.*

No other casualties resulted from torpedoes, and it was a mere chance that the *Tecumseh* was sunk. No doubt the superincumbent weight of her iron armor carried her to the bottom so quickly, and it is probable that not more than fifty pounds of powder did the mischief.

Operations on the Yazoo River

Shortly after the fall of [?] the Federals advanced against Yazoo City, Mississippi, both by land and water. Anticipating such an event, a few rude mechanical torpedoes were planted in the Yazoo River, about three miles below the city. They were simply common acid carboys filled with powder and arranged to explode by contact with a trigger. On account of the frequent sudden rise and fall of the river, they required considerable attention to keep them in proper position. Here, again, as had frequently occurred at other points, the destructive force of a given amount of powder had been greatly exaggerated. A carboy would contain about twenty-five pounds of powder, and this quantity is insufficient to do more damage than knock a small hole in the hull of a vessel. On the occasion of the attack there was a sudden rise in the river, and some of the light-draft gunboats passed over the torpedoes safely; but the iron-clad steamer *De Kalb*, the flag-ship, mounting eight guns, and being of heavier draft, struck the trigger of one of the torpedoes, which exploded under her port bow, knocking a hole in her hull. The pilot, as soon as he felt the shock, ran her toward the shore, and she sank in twelve feet of water, close to the riverbank. No one was injured.

I have already stated that it was the common belief that summary execution would follow the capture of any person engaged in the torpedo service. Judge of my feelings, then, a few days after the capture of Richmond, to see a lieutenant of cavalry, accompanied by two orderlies, present themselves at my residence, with orders from General Terry to conduct me to his headquarters in the Capitol building! The very fact that it had so early been ascertained that I was in that service seemed to indicate prompt measures on the part of the Federals to justify common rumor in their intention to make an example of me. However, I went to the Capitol. I was much surprised, however. After a short conversation, General Terry informed me that I must report to Admiral Porter on his flagship, then lying at the wharf in Richmond. I started immediately, escorted this time by the lieutenant only. On arriving at the wharf, I went aboard the flagship—I think it was the *Malvern*—and walking into the cabin, found myself in the presence of President Lincoln.

After I had introduced myself, and stated the occasion of my visit, Mr. Lincoln called for Admiral Porter. When he came in, Mr. Lincoln said, "Porter, here is the young man you were expecting." This looked ominous to me. Why had I been expected?

However, in a few minutes we were all three pleasantly engaged in conversation.

Admiral Porter then informed me of his desire that, in company with some of the officers of his squadron, I should go down the river and point out where our torpedoes were located, so that they could be removed. "The war is ended," said he, "and we must clear the river for navigation." I told him there was no danger whatever to be apprehended from the torpedoes planted by the regular torpedo service, because they could be exploded

---

*One can never recount too often the heroism of Captain Craven on this occasion. As the vessel was sinking beneath them, he and the pilot, John Collins, met at the foot of the ladder leading to the top of the turret. Craven drew back, saying, "After you, pilot." "There was nothing after me," said Collins, who was saved. "When I reached the utmost round of the ladder, the vessel seemed to drop from under me." The Tecumseh *lies in the channel to this day.—EDITOR.*

only by electricity, and our galvanic batteries had been destroyed, and the connecting wires torn up and carried away; but that there were doubtless many others, planted under the direction of army officers, which were mechanical in their operation, and as likely to be fatal to friend as to foe, and of the location of these I knew nothing.

The next morning the *Unadilla* steamed down the river to the various stations where we had planted torpedoes, and took bearings of the positions. In a few days a regularly organized force had removed all the explosives, and all other obstructions to navigation, and the river was once more safe for travel.

2. Confederate Torpedoes

Matthew Fontaine Maury had served for over thirty-six years in the U. S. Navy when war came and his native state of Virginia seceded from the Union. By that time he had earned international recognition for his pioneering work in meteorology, hydrography, and navigation. His charts of the various ocean currents were published and used around the world. Appointed to the Virginia navy as a commander by Governor John Letcher, Maury retained that rank when the state's naval forces were transferred to the Confederacy on June 10, 1861.

Maury believed that the only way the new Southern nation could hope to impede the advance of Federal naval forces along the South's waterways was to mine those waters with hidden torpedoes. With this in mind, he set to work in Richmond experimenting with different methods of exploding cannon powder underwater. (Corbin, *The Life of Matthew Fontaine Maury*, p. 192.)

Lieutenant Colonel Richard L. Maury was the son of the commander and had served in the 24th Virginia Regiment during the war, where he was wounded at Seven Pines and Drewry's Bluff. After the war he became a prominent Richmond lawyer, and in 1904 he wrote an article for the Richmond *Times-Dispatch* concerning his father and the work he did with torpedoes. (Krick, *Lee's Colonels: A Biographical Register of the Field Officers of the Army of Northern Virginia*, p. 267.) [RTC]

---

*"The First Marine Torpedoes Were Made in Richmond, Va.,
and Used in the James River" by
Col. Richard L. Maury, CSA
(Son of Commander Matthew F. Maury, CSN)*

The Richmond, Virginia, *Times-Dispatch*, February 14 and 20, 1904.

Despite the study of this method of warfare, more was accomplished by the Confederate States of America than has been accomplished for many years since.

Colonel Richard L. Maury, a son of Commodore Matthew Fontaine Maury, has written for the *Times-Dispatch* an extremely interesting article on the invention and use of torpedoes, in which his father was the pioneer, and to the perfection of which he, himself, and other brave naval officers of the Confederacy devoted themselves with all the abandon which a devotion to a cause for the cause's sake can evoke. The interest caused by the destruction of Russian vessels by means of torpedoes gives increased interest to the article which is printed in full below:

The wonderful achievements of Japan, with her ironclad rams and torpedoes, should be specially interesting to your readers, because of the fact that these mighty engines of modern war, as successful appliances, had their origin in Virginia, were designed in Richmond and were first successfully used in the waters of James River. With them continually developed and improved by the fertile brain of her many clever officers, and by them operated with a daring and self-sacrifice never equaled, the Confederate navy totally revolutionized naval warfare, and, though barren of resources, of shops, machinery and experienced mechanics fully to avail of the many improvements and inventions they made, yet with her novel system of torpedoes accomplished more in her several years than with all the great advancement of scientific knowledge, improvements in mechanical construction and familiarity with electrical force during subsequent years, other nations have been able since to do.

In 1865 the Secretary of the United States navy reported to Congress that the navy had lost more ships during the war from Confederate torpedoes than from all other causes combined. Scharf's *History of the Confederate States Navy* gives as an incomplete list of forty, showing at one time ten were destroyed in less than three weeks, and General Rains, chief of the army torpedo department, says that the total number was fifty-eight, a number far in excess of what all other nations combined, with all their modern improvements and appliances, have effected, during the forty years since passed.

The first ironclad ram in actual conflict was the immortal *Virginia*, victoriously fought in Virginia waters, constructed in Virginia according to the design of Lieut. John M. Brooke, a Virginian, born near Fredericksburg, now an honored professor at the V. M. I. Her great achievement was her victory in Hampton Roads, especially her defeat of the Federal ironclad, an invention not of a naval officer or of an American, whereby the government at Washington was so alarmed, that preparation were made to the close the channel of the Potomac. The *Monitor* was ordered to be careful of herself, which she was, twice refusing the *Virginian's* offered battle, or to leave the protections of the guns of the fort, and the Secretary of the Navy, ignoring the "first army on the planet," and a navy as powerful as any afloat, called frantically upon a civilian of New York for protection, asking him to name his own price to destroy this Confederate terror, designed by Brooke and fought by Buchanan, Tatnall, Catesby Jones, Robert D. Minor, J. Taylor Wood, Hunter Davidson, Charles Simms and many another gallant Confederate.

Were Made Here

Torpedoes as a successful weapon in actual war were introduced into the Confederate navy by Captain Matthew F. Maury, also of Fredericksburg, and first placed by him in James River.

Hardly had he arrived in Richmond in April, 1861, in response to Virginia's call of her sons to come to her assistance, that his thoughts were turned to the realization of this means for the defense of the exposed rivers and harbors of Virginia and the South. Penetrated as the country was by innumerable navigable waters, and absolutely without vessels to defend them, he urged that the most effective way to keep off the enemy was to mine the channelways, and blow up by means of electricity when he attempted the passage.

At this time there was nothing save a few shore batteries to prevent any ship bold enough to run past them and ascend the river, shelling Richmond or any other water-side town in the South.

There was much prejudice against, or lack of appreciation of, this undeveloped system of defense by many of the Confederate authorities, who considered it ineffectual and unlawful warfare, but Captain Maury, undeterred by the lack of official support and opposition of many friends, proceeded at once to demonstrate its sufficiency as best he could without the use of proper mechanical resources.

His trial experiments to explode under water were made with minute charges of powder and submerged in an ordinary washtub in his chamber at the house of his cousin, Robert H. Maury, on Clay street, and the tank for actual use, with their triggers for explosion and other mechanical appliances for service, were made by Talbott and Son, on Clay street, under their ready and intelligent direction.

In the early summer of 1861 the Secretary of the Navy and the chairman of the Naval Committee of Congress and others, were invited to witness an explosion in James River at Rocketts. The torpedo was a small keg of powder, weighted to sink, fitted with a trigger to explode by percussion, to be fired, when in place, by a lanyard. The *Patrick Henry* gig was borrowed; Captain Maury and the writer got aboard with the torpedo, and were rowed to the middle of the channel just opposite to where the wharf of the James River Steamboat Company now is, whereon the spectators stood; the torpedo was carefully lowered to the bottom, taking great care not to strain upon the trigger, which was at full cock; the lanyard loosely held on board. The boat pulled clear, and the writer pulled the lanyard. The explosion was instantaneous; up went a column of water fifteen or twenty feet; many stunned or dead fish floated around; the officials on the wharf applauded and were convinced, and shortly after a naval bureau of coast, harbor, and river defense was created, and Captain Maury placed at its head with abundant funds for the work, and the very best of intelligent, able and zealous younger naval officers for assistants.

Commander Matthew Fontaine Maury (Naval Historical Center).

Mined the River

In a month or two he had mined the channel of the river just opposite Chaffin's Bluff, with fixed torpedoes to be exploded by contact, having then no insulated wire with which to explode by electricity, and during that summer and fall several attempts with floating torpedoes were made against the Federal squadron at Fortress Monroe, one of which he personally directed (July, 1861); another (October, 1861), by one of his skillful associates, Lieutenant Robert D. Minor, also of Fredericksburg.

He thus describes them:

"These torpedoes were in pairs, connected together by a span 500 feet long. The span was floated on the surface by corks, and the torpedo barrels, containing 200 pounds of powder, also floated at the depth of twenty feet, empty barrels, painted lead color, so as not really to be seen, serving for the purpose.

"The span was connected with a trigger in the head of each barrel, so set and arranged that when the torpedo, being let go in a tide way under the bows and athwart the hawse had fouled, they would be drifted alongside, and in so drifting tauten the span, and so set off the fuse, which was driven precisely as a ten seconds shot fuse, only it was calculated to burn fifty-four seconds, because it could not be known exactly in which part of the sweep along time the strain would be sufficient to set off the trigger. The torpedoes were launched at three fine frigates, the *Minnesota*, the *Roanoke* and the *Cumberland*.

"Finding that they all missed, I attributed it to the fact that such a fuse could not burn under a pressure of twenty feet of water. The conjecture was confirmed by experiment. The fuse could burn very surely at the depth of fifteen feet, never at twenty feet."

Some time afterwards those torpedoes were discovered by the enemy. Spans, barrels and barrages were soon got up, and carried off as relics.

The enemy prevented any further attack in this way by dropping the end of his lower studding sail boom in the water "every night, anchoring boats or beams ahead."

Grew in Favor

To obtain insulated wire an agent was sent to New York in secret, but failed, and as there was neither wire factory or insulating material in the South, the difficulties of preparing electrical torpedoes to which he attached the greatest importance and greatly preferred, seemed insuperable, until by a remarkable coincidence, in the following spring, it happened that the enemy attempting to lay a cable across Chesapeake Bay to Fortress Monroe were forced to abandon the attempt and left the wire to the mercy of the waves, which cast it up on the beach near Norfolk, where by the kindness of a friend, it was secured for Captain Maury's uses. With part of this he was enabled to mine James River below the obstruction with electrical torpedoes, which destroyed every Federal vessel that attempted to pass them, and kept their powerful fleet at bay during the entire war, and with part to enable other southern harbors to be similarly protected.

Meantime, torpedoes were rapidly growing in public favor, new designs and improvements, suggested by experience, were multiplied by the active brain of the many clever young naval officers, whose withdrawal from the United States navy left it paralyzed for years, and torpedoes of all kinds were left to be found in all our waters whenever Federal ships appeared.

Lieutenant Beverly Kennon, of Virginia, set them afloat in the Potomac, and later, was instrumental, he said, in procuring the first actual destruction of the *Cairo* in Yazoo River by Master McDaniel and Ewing, with a ground torpedo—a demijohn filled with powder and fired with a trigger by a string leading to the operator hidden on the bank. General Rains, chief of the army torpedo bureau, adopted the beer keg, filled with powder, and fitted with a percussion primer at each end, as the best form, and set hundreds of them afloat, to be carried by current and tide against the enemy's vessels below. Captain Francis D. Lee, of General Beauregard's staff, recommended the spar torpedo—i. e., a torpedo set upon the end of a twenty-foot spar, rigged upon the bow of a boat, to be fired by impact upon the sides of the vessel attacked; and with Captain Maury designed and constructed, at his own expense, a semi-submarine torpedo, called a "David," rigged with a star torpedo, with which at Charleston, Lieutenant Glassell struck and permanently disabled the *New Ironside*, the most powerful vessel then afloat. Shortly after, and with a submarine torpedo boat, the first ever used, designed and constructed with his private means by Mr. Horace L. Hundley, of New Orleans, but then living in Mobile, who was drowned in her, Lieutenant Dixon, of Mobile, of the army, with unsurpassable courage, attacked the Federal steamer *Housatonic*, and sunk her almost instantaneously; but Dixon and daring crew, and his pioneer submarine torpedo boat, all went to the bottom with their victim, where divers found them after the war lying side by side. [Maury here is in error. This myth gained much acceptance throughout the South after the war — RTC]

And John Maxwell, of Richmond, with matchless intrepidity, with his own hands handed a clock torpedo aboard a vessel at City Point, which blew her to pieces in a few moments, killing many and spreading consternation all around.

Went Abroad

By the fall of 1862 the importance of Captain Maury's work and its capabilities had become so highly appreciated that it was deemed best that he should go to England, that he might have every opportunity for the development and improvement afforded by the workshops and laboratories and facilities for experiment and construction. Accordingly he was ordered abroad in this service, where he remained, pursuing his researches, perfecting his valuable invention with great success, constantly reporting progress to the Navy Department at home for the instruction of the torpedo workers there, until just before the close of the war, which found him at sea, en route for home, with a most powerful, perfect and complete equipment of electrical torpedo material, perhaps never since equaled.

His valuable assistant in the James River defense was Lieutenant Hunter Davidson, who succeeded him in that charge, which he managed with unequaled skill until the end with electrical torpedoes, which, he says, he himself put down, Captain Maury's having been washed out by a severe freshet after he had gone. His operation crippled and destroyed two Federal vessels—the only ones, he says, destroyed by electrical torpedoes during the war. With a torpedo boat of his own construction and design, constructed here in Richmond, [the CSS *Squib*] rigged with a spar torpedo, he most courageously ventured a hundred miles and more down the river, into the enemy's lines, and rammed the frigate *Minnesota*, lying off Newport News. He exploded the torpedo, but the charge was too small, and but little damage was done or suffered.

Gallant Attacks

Besides these, numerous gallant attacks were made with torpedoes everywhere, despite the danger and death which often accompanied their use, and many of the older officers, who at first regarded them with disfavor, as Captain Parker said he did, were now torpedo mad. "Commodore Tucker and I," he said, "had torpedo on the brain." The destruction of the enemy's vessels increased so rapidly—in the last three weeks of the war ten were destroyed—that they were compelled to adopt our system, although at first denouncing it as barbarous and heathenish.

Captain Maury's experience and studies had now made him the chief authority upon the new weapon, so that when after the war he returned to Europe, he was requested by the Emperor Napoleon to explain to him its merits. He did so, and for the Emperor's benefit had an explosion in the Seine at St. Cloud, the Emperor himself firing the charge. Subsequently, by request of the several governments, he instructed and imparted his knowledge of torpedoes and their use to representatives of France, England, Russia, Holland and Germany, all of whom adopted his plan, and made the torpedo one of the chief branches of their armament. But, as yet with every advantage, with earnest desire and constant effort to excel, none have done as well with these Virginia weapons as did the Confederate States Navy forty years ago.

[An editorial in the *Times-Dispatch*, February 20, 1904, elicited the following communication which definitely settles the question in issue.—ED.]

SIR,—Your answer this morning to a recent article in the *New York Tribune* (which I have not seen), concerning torpedoes, stating that they were "only successfully employed two or three times by the Confederates," suggests additional facts in further refutation of a statement utterly erroneous. Two or three citations to the veritable records of the time abundantly show, save to those so blind that they will not see, that the writer of the article in the *Tribune* is altogether mistaken.

No matter when or by whom the idea of using torpedoes as weapons of war first occurred, and undoubtedly it has occurred to many, in one form or another—all practical for actual use—ever since the "engineer was hoist with his own petard," it cannot be successfully denied now that their use was introduced with the Confederate navy here in Richmond by Captain Matthew F. Maury, of Virginia, and that through his efforts and with the hearty and skillful assistance of many of his younger brother officers, who had been the very flower and life of the old navy, and were the best of sailors and patriots in the Confederate service, torpedoes were first successfully utilized in actual war by the Confederate navy, whose example in this and other respects has been imitated by every maritime nation.

The writer of the *Tribune* article in stating torpedoes were "Successfully employed but two or three times during the Confederate war" shows great ignorance.

They were successfully employed every hour of every day in every river and harbor in the South from the time Captain Maury first placed them in James River (1861) until the end of the war, in that their presence, successfully kept the Federal fleet from entering our many undefended rivers and harbors from Virginia to Texas. It suggested that a torpedo which successfully keeps away many ships is far more successfully used than if it had been successfully exploded and destroyed one.

But such was by no means the only successful use of Confederate torpedoes, for they were also successfully employed in the actual destruction of more (Federal) ships than all nations combined have since been able to effect in all the forty years since passed, and with all their improved modern facilities, knowledge and appliances.

Admiral Bradford, U. S. N., gives a list of forty. General Rains, C.S.A., says that the number was fifty-eight. No matter which is correct, for the smallest number of the United States admiral is more than sufficient to refute the "two or three" of the *Tribune*'s writer, and what will he say to the statement of the United States Secretary of the Navy in his report to Congress in 1865, "that the navy had lost more vessels from Confederate torpedoes than from all other causes combined?"

RICHARD L. MAURY,
Colonel 24th Virginia Infantry, Pickett's Division.

XIII

Blockade Runners

1. The *Robert E. Lee*

At the beginning of the war it was painfully evident in the South that the country would never be able to produce the materials necessary to maintain large armies in the field. While the Confederate government did work miracles in arming, clothing, and feeding its army and navy, it nevertheless depended heavily on the importation of war material by blockade runners. Confederate records alone show that 60 percent of the arms carried by her troops in the field were imported. The blockade runners brought in 30 percent, or roughly three million pounds, of lead for bullets, 75 percent or 2,250,000 pounds of the army's saltpeter, and nearly all of its cartridge paper. In addition, the runners brought in other essential materials such as food, cloth for uniforms, leather for shoes, accoutrements, chemicals, paper, and medicines. (Wise, *Lifeline of the Confederacy*, p. 226.)

Blockade runners were for the most part privately owned, though some were purchased entirely or in part by the Confederate government and operated by the Ordnance Bureau or the Navy Department. Regular officers of the Confederate Navy commanded the government-owned vessels, and the mostly English crews were usually shipped in Nassau or Havana.

In spite of the ever-tightening Federal blockade, the probability of a runner's reaching a Confederate port was very good. It has been documented that over 300 steamers tested the Union blockade during the war, and of the 1300 attempts made, 1000 were successful. The Federals captured 136 vessels and destroyed an additional 85, yet approximately 400,000 bales of cotton were safely carried out by the blockade runners, thus enabling the Confederacy to purchase munitions and supplies abroad. (Wise, p. 221.)

One of these government-owned blockade runners was the two-year old *Giraffe*, a sidewheel packet that was built in Scotland. She had operated between Glasgow and Belfast, but had lost money and her owners were forced to put her up for sale. Her iron hull was 258 feet long, and she was reputed to be very fast, though she would later prove that 13.5 knots was the best that she could do. Purchased by the Confederate government, the *Giraffe* was renamed the *Robert E. Lee* when she arrived in the Confederacy in late December of 1862.

Her commander was First Lieutenant John Wilkinson, who, along with John Newland Maffitt, became one of the Confederate navy's most famous blockade runner captains. Wilkinson was from Virginia, the son of a career naval officer, and had entered the U. S. Navy with an appointment as midshipman in 1837. He subsequently saw duty in both the Atlantic and Pacific squadrons.

When Virginia seceded, Wilkinson resigned and offered his services to the Confederacy. He served as executive officer on the ironclad *Louisiana* at New Orleans and with the destruction of that vessel, was captured and imprisoned at Fort Warren in Boston harbor. Upon his exchange on August 5, 1862, he was sent to England to purchase the *Giraffe*. (Campbell, *Gray Thunder, Exploits of the Confederate States Navy*, pp. 62–63.)

The following selection from his book *Narrative of a Blockade Runner* picks up the story of the *Robert E. Lee* in March of 1863. [RTC]

"We Sail for Wilmington" by
1st Lt. John Wilkinson, CSN

The Narrative of a Blockade Runner, 1877,
Chapter IX, pp. 149–158, Chapter X, pp. 159–168.

AFTER, discharging our cargo of cotton and loading with supplies for the Confederate Government, chiefly for the army of Northern Virginia, we sailed [the *Robert E. Lee*] for Wilmington in the latter part of the month of March. Our return voyage was uneventful, until we reached the coast near Masonborongh Inlet, distant about nine miles north of the New Inlet bar. The weather had been pleasant during the voyage, and we had sighted the fires from the salt works along the coast, but before we could get hold of the land, a little before midnight, a densely black cloud made its appearance to the north and east; and the rapidity with which it rose and enlarged, indicated too surely that a heavy gale was coming from that quarter. We had been unable to distinguish any landmark before the storm burst in all its fury upon us, and the rain poured in torrents. Our supply of coals was too limited to enable us, with prudence, to put to sea again; and of course, the marks or ranges for crossing the bar would not be visible fifty yards in such thick weather. Being quite confident of our position, however, I determined to run down the coast, and anchor off the bar till daylight. Knowing the "trend" of the land north of New Inlet bar, the engine was slowed down and the lead kept going on both sides. The sounding continued quite regular three and three and a quarter fathoms, with the surf thundering within a stone's throw on our starboard beam, and nothing visible in the blinding torrents of rain. I knew that if my calculated position was correct, the water would shoal very suddenly just before reaching the bar; but a trying hour or more of suspense had passed before the welcome fact was announced by the leadsmen. The course and distance run, and the soundings up to this point proved, beyond doubt, that we had now reached the "horse shoe" north of New Inlet bar. At the moment when both of the leadsmen almost simultaneously called out "and a quarter less three," the helm was put hard a-starboard, and the *Lee*'s bow was pointed seaward. We could not prudently anchor in less than five fathoms water, as the sea was rising rapidly; and that depth would carry us into the midst of the blockading fleet at anchor outside. It seemed an age before the cry came from the leadsmen "by the mark five." The *Lee* was instantly stopped, and one of the bower anchors let go, veering to thirty fathoms on the chain. The cable was then well stopped at the "bitts," and unshackled; and two men stationed at the stopper, with axes, and the order to cut the lashings, instantly, when so ordered; the fore-staysail was loosed, and hands stationed at the halliards; and the chief engineer directed to keep up a full head of steam. The night wore slowly away; and once or twice we caught a glimpse, by a flash of lightning, of the blockading fleet around us, rolling and pitching in the heavy sea. The watch having been set, the rest of the officers and crew were permitted to go below, except the chief engineer and the pilot. We paced the bridge, anxiously waiting for daylight. It came at last, and there, right astern of us, looming up through the mist and rain, was the "Mound." We had only to steer for it, to be on our right course for crossing the bar. The stoppers were cut, the engine started ahead, and the fore stay-sail hoisted. As the chain rattled through the hawse-hole, the *Lee* wore rapidly around, and the Confederate flag was run up to the peak as she dashed toward the bar with the speed of a greyhound slipped from the leash. The bar was a sheet of foam and surf, breaking sheer across the channel; but the great length of the *Lee* enabled her to ride over three or four of the short chopping seas at once, and she never touched the bottom. In less than half an hour from the time when we slipped our chain under the guns of the fleet, we had passed beyond Fort Fisher, and were on our way up the river to Wilmington.

The "Mound" was an artificial one, erected by Colonel Lamb, who commanded Fort Fisher. Two heavy guns were mounted upon it, and it eventually became a site for a light, and very serviceable to blockade-runners; but even at this period, it was an excellent landmark. Joined by a long low isthmus of sand with the higher main land, its regular conical shape enabled the blockade-runners easily to identify it from the offing; and in clear weather, it showed plain and distinct against the sky at night. I believe the military men used to laugh slyly at the Colonel for under taking, its erection, predicting that it would not stand; but the result showed the contrary; and whatever difference of opinion may have existed with regard to its value as a military position, there can be but one as to its utility to the blockade-runners, for it was not a landmark alone, along this monotonous coast, but one of the range lights for crossing New Inlet bar was placed on it. Seamen will appreciate at its full value, this advantage; but it may be stated, for the benefit of the unprofessional reader, that while the compass bearing of an object does not enable a pilot to steer a vessel with sufficient accuracy through a narrow channel, range lights answer the purpose completely. These lights were only set after signals had been exchanged between the blockade-runner and the shore station, and were removed immediately after the vessel had entered the river. The range lights were changed as circumstances required; for the New Inlet channel, itself, was and is constantly changing, being materially affected both in depth of water, and in its course, by a heavy gale of wind or a severe freshet in Cape Fear River.

1st Lt. John Wilkinson (Naval Historical Center).

The *Lee* continued to make her regular trips either to Nassau or Bermuda, as circumstances required, during the summer of 1863; carrying abroad cotton and naval stores, and bringing in "hardware," as munitions of war were then invoiced. Usually, the time selected for sailing was during the "dark of the moon," but upon one occasion, a new pilot had been detailed for duty on board, who failed in many efforts to get the ship over the "rip," a shifting sand bar a mile or more inside the true bar. More than a week of valuable time had thus been lost, but the exigencies of the army being at that time more than usually urgent, I determined to run what appeared to be a very great risk. The tide serving at ten o'clock, we succeeded in crossing the rip at that hour, and as we passed over New Inlet bar, the moon rose in a cloudless sky. It was a calm night too, and the regular beat of our paddles through the smooth water sounded to our ears ominously loud. As we closely skirted the shore, the blockading vessels were plainly visible to us, some at anchor, some under way; and some of them so near to us that we saw, or fancied we saw, with our night glasses, the men on watch on their forecastles; but as we were inside of them all, and invisible against the background of the land, we passed beyond them undiscovered, The roar of the surf breaking upon the beach, prevented the noise of our paddles from being heard. The *Lee*'s head was not pointed seaward, however, until we had run ten or twelve miles along the land so close to the breakers that we could almost have tossed a biscuit into them, and no vessel was to be seen in any direction. Discovery of us by the fleet would probably have been fatal to us, but the risk was really not so great as it appeared; for, as I had been informed by a blockade-runner who had been once captured and released, being a British subject, the vigilance on board the blockading fleet was much relaxed during the moonlit nights. The vessels were sent to Beaufort to coal at these times. My informant was an officer of the British Navy, and was the guest, for a few days after his capture, of Captain Patterson then commanding the blockading fleet off the Cape Fear. Speaking of the arduous service, he remarked to him, that he never undressed nor retired to bed, during the dark nights; but could enjoy those luxuries when the moon was shining. On this hint I acted.

It was about this time that I adopted an expedient which proved of great service on several occasions. A blockade-runner did not often pass through the fleet without receiving one or more shots, but these were always preceded by the flash of a calcium light, or by a blue light; and immediately followed by two rockets thrown in the direction of the blockade-runner. The signals were probably concerted each day for the ensuing night, as they appeared to be constantly changed; but the rockets were invariably sent up. I ordered a lot of rockets from New York. Whenever all hands were called to run through the fleet, an officer was stationed alongside of me on the bridge with the rockets. One or two minutes after our immediate pursuer had sent up his rockets, I would direct ours to be discharged at a right angle to our course. The whole fleet would be misled, for even if the vessel which had discovered us were not deceived, the rest of the fleet would be baffled.

While we were lying at anchor in the harbor of St. George's, during one of our trips, I was notified by the Governor of the island, that an officer of the Confederate Navy, then held as a prisoner on board one of H. B. M.'s ships of war at the naval anchorage, would be delivered up to me for transportation to the Confederacy, if I would assume the charge. This officer was charged with the murder of a messmate on board the Confederate States steamer *Sumter*, while lying at Gibraltar. The demand for his extradition, made by the Confederate Government, had been complied with by the British Government after much delay; and he was turned over to me for transportation to the Confederacy. Although the crime appeared to have been committed under circumstances of peculiar atrocity—it being alleged that the victim was asleep at the time he was shot—I so far respected the commission which the criminal bore, as to place him upon parole. Upon reporting his arrival at Wilmington to the Secretary of the Navy, the latter directed me to release him, upon the ground that it would be impossible to convict him by court-martial, all of the witnesses to the transaction being abroad. The man, Hester, was therefore released, and was never heard of again, I believe, during the war; but he has added to his evil reputation since its close, by plying the infamous trade (under the guise of United States Secret Service agent) of false informer and persecutor in several of the Southern States. The General Government failed to exercise its usual careful discrimination in making this appointment! The base renegades are many degrees worse even than the unprincipled adventurers from the North who have so long preyed upon the South. The latter are only thieves and robbers; the former are, in addition, unnatural monsters, who hate their own people and are guilty of the crime of Judas, who betrayed his Lord for thirty pieces of silver.

During the latter part of July 1863, the *Lee* was lying in the harbor of St. George's, when the Confederate States steamer *Florida* arrived there in want of coal, of which there happened to be a very limited supply on hand. The most suitable coal was procured with difficulty throughout the war, all of the British coals, although excellent for raising steam, making more or less smoke, and objectionable on that account. Exportation of the American anthracite, which would have been almost invaluable, was prohibited by the Government. This is, I believe, the only accessible, or at least available non-bituminous coal in the world; but the best substitute for it is the Welsh semi-bituminous coal, and this was chiefly used by the blockade-runners.

The *Florida* was in greater need of coal than ourselves, for the United States steamer *Wachusett* came into port a day or two after the former, and Maffitt, in command of the *Florida*, wished to get to sea first. When belligerent rights were accorded to the Confederate Government by foreign powers, the Confederate cruisers were admitted into their ports upon equal terms with the United States men of war, except that there was no interchange of social courtesies. In order to preserve strict neutrality toward the contending powers, a man of war under either flag was not permitted to follow out of a neutral port a ship under the enemy's colors within twenty-four hours of the sailing of the latter; and it was an equal violation of neutrality for a ship of war under either flag to cruise within a marine league of neutral territory.

When occasion required no one could be more resolute than Maffitt, as he had repeatedly shown in the management of the *Florida*; and especially when he ran the gauntlet in broad daylight through the whole Federal fleet blockading Mobile, and for which affair Preble, then commanding the fleet, was so harshly dealt with; but the chief object of the Confederate cruisers being to destroy the American commerce, an engagement with a United States ship of war was to be avoided, if possible.

The *Florida*'s deck, when the crew were at their meals, was a curious scene; the plain fare of the sailors being served in costly china, captured from homeward bound "Indiamen," and the scamps had become fastidious in their taste about tea. I had the pleasure to carry into Wilmington ten or twelve chests of the finest hyson, which were distributed among the hospitals; and a lot of silver ingots made a narrow escape from confiscation. But the law officers in Bermuda, whom Maffitt consulted, assuring him that they would be adjudged legal prize of war in the British courts, they were shipped to England, instead of the Confederacy, and there returned to the claimants.

Although there was no exchange of civilities between the officers of the two ships, the sailors harmonized amiably and got drunk together ashore with mutual good will. A jack tar is probably the only representative left of the old "free lance," who served under any flag where he was sure of pay and booty. The blue jackets will fight under any colors, where there is a fair prospect of adventure and prize money.

After the *Florida* had been coaled, there was scarcely a sufficient supply left to carry the *Lee* into Wilmington under the most favorable circumstances; but it was necessary either to sail at once, or to wait two weeks for the next moon. Our chief engineer had noticed a large pile of coal on one of the wharves rented by the Confederate agent; but the heap had been so long exposed to the weather, and trampled upon for so many months, that it appeared to be a mere pile of dirt. "Necessity having no law," however, we shoveled off the surface; and were surprised to find that it was of very fair quality. It made an abundance of steam, indeed, but burned with great rapidity; and although we took on board an extra supply, we were able to retain barely enough English coal in the bunkers to use in running through the fleet on our next outward voyage. The consequence was the narrowest escape from capture ever made by the *Lee* while under my command.

We were ready to sail for Nassau on the 15th of August, 1863, and had on board, as usual, several passengers. Indeed we rarely made a trip either way without as many as could be accommodated, and many ladies among them. My observation of the conduct of the fair sex, under trying and novel circumstances, has convinced me that they face inevitable dangers more bravely and with more composure than men. I have frequently seen a frail, delicate woman standing erect and unflinching upon the deck, as the shells were whistling and bursting over us, while her lawful protector would be cowering "under the lee" of a cotton bale. I pay this humble tribute of admiration to the sex, but a cynical old bachelor, to whom I once made the observation, replied that in his opinion their insatiable curiosity prevailed even over their natural fears!

On our outward voyage we had among our passengers ex-Senator Gwin and his daughter, and Dr. and Mrs. P. We passed safely through the blockading fleet off the New Inlet Bar, receiving no damage from the few shots fired at us, and gained an offing from the coast of thirty miles by daylight. By this time our supply of English coal had been exhausted, and we were obliged to commence upon North Carolina coal of very inferior quality, and which smoked terribly. We commenced on this fuel a little after daylight. Very soon afterwards the vigilant look-out at the mast-head called out "Sail ho!" and in reply to the "where away" from the deck, sang out "Right astern, sir, and in chase." The morning was very clear. Going to the mast-head I could just discern the royal of the chaser; and before I left there, say in half an hour, her top-gallant sail showed above the horizon. By this time the sun had risen in a cloudless sky. It was evident our pursuer would be alongside of us by mid-day at the rate we were then going. The first orders given were to throw overboard the deck-load of cotton and to make more steam. The latter proved to be more easily given than executed; the chief engineer reporting that it was impossible to make steam with the wretched stuff filled with slate and dirt. A moderate breeze from the north and east had been blowing ever since daylight and every stitch of canvas on board the square-rigged steamer in our wake was drawing. We were steering east by south, and it was clear that the chaser's advantages could only be neutralized either by bringing the *Lee* gradually head to wind or edging away to bring the wind aft. The former course would be running toward the land, besides incurring the additional risk of being intercepted and captured by some of the inshore cruisers. I began to edge away therefore, and in two or three hours enjoyed the satisfaction of seeing our pursuer clew up and furl his sails. The breeze was still blowing as fresh as in the morning, but we were now running directly away from it, and the cruiser was going literally as fast as the wind, causing the sails to be rather a hindrance than a help. But she was still gaining on us. A happy inspiration occurred to me when the case seemed hopeless. Sending for the chief engineer I said "Mr. S., let us try cotton, saturated with spirits of turpentine." There were on board, as part of the deck load, thirty or forty barrels of "spirits." In a very few moments, a bale of cotton was ripped open, a barrel tapped, and buckets full of the saturated material passed down into the fire room. The result exceeded our expectations. The chief engineer, an excitable little Frenchman from Charleston, very soon made his appearance on the bridge, his eyes sparkling with triumph, and reported a full head of steam. Curious to see the effect upon our speed, I directed him to wait a moment until the log was hove. I threw it myself, nine and a half knots. "Let her go now sir!" I said. Five minutes afterwards, I hove the log again, thirteen and a quarter. We now began to hold our own, and even to gain a little upon the chaser; but she was fearfully near, and I began to have visions of another residence at Fort Warren, as I saw the "big bone in the mouth" of our pertinacious friend, for she was near enough to us at one time for us to see distinctly the white curl of foam under her bows, called by that name among seamen. I wonder if they could have screwed another turn of speed out of her if they had known that the *Lee* had on board, in addition to her cargo of cotton, a large amount of gold shipped by the Confederate Government? There continued to be a very slight change in our relative positions till about six o'clock in the afternoon, when the chief engineer again made his appearance, with a very ominous expression of countenance. He came to report that the burnt cotton had choked the flues, and that the steam was running down. "Only keep her going till dark, sir," I replied, "and we will give our pursuer the slip yet." A heavy bank was lying along the horizon to the south and east; and I saw a possible means of escape. At sunset the chaser was about four miles astern and gaining upon us. Calling two of my most reliable officers, I stationed one of them on each wheelhouse, with glasses, directing them to let me know the instant they lost sight of the chaser in the growing darkness. At the same time, I ordered the chief engineer to make as black a smoke as possible, and to be in readiness to cut off the smoke, by closing the dampers instantly, when ordered. The twilight was soon succeeded by darkness. Both of the officers on the wheel-house called out at the same moment, "We have lost sight of her," while a dense volume of smoke was streaming far in our wake. "Close the dampers," I called out through the speaking tube, and at the same moment ordered the helm "hard a starboard." Our course was altered eight points, at a right angle to the previous one. I remained on deck an hour, and then retired to my state-room with a comfortable sense of security. We had fired so hard that the very planks on the bridge were almost scorching hot, and my feet were nearly blistered. I put them out of the window to cool, after taking off slippers and socks.

While in this position, Miss Lucy G. came on the bridge in company with her father. Tapping my foot with her hand, she said, "Ah, captain, I see we are all safe, and I congratulate you!." At one time during the chase, when capture seemed inevitable, the kegs containing the gold had been brought on deck, and one of them opened by my orders, it being my intention to distribute its contents among the officers and crew. Miss Lucy, who preserved her presence of mind throughout the trying scenes of the day, called me aside, and suggested that she should fill a purse for me, and keep it about her person, until the prize crew had taken possession, and all danger of personal search was over, when she would make an opportunity to give it to me; and I have no doubt she would have accomplished her intentions if occasion had required. The chaser proved afterwards to be the *Iroquois*. Feeling confident that she would continue on the course toward Abaco, and perhaps have another and more successful chase, I changed the destination of the *Lee* to Bermuda, where we arrived safely two days afterward.

2. The *Gordon*

In his article for the *United Service* magazine, Maffitt does not name the blockade runner in the first part of his narrative; however, he refers to her in Part 2 as the *Gordon*. It is reasonable to assume, therefore, that it is the same steamer he writes about here.

The *Gordon* was built in 1851 by the Lawrence Sneden, & Company of Greenpoint, New York. Originally designated the *Carolina*, her name was changed to *Gordon* before her launching. In August of 1861 the steamer was purchased by John Fraser and Company, of South Carolina, and her name changed to *Theodore*. Early in 1862, the Confederate navy purchased her and the name was again changed, this time to *Nassau*. (Wise, *Lifeline of the Confederacy: Blockade Running During the Civil War*, pp. 323–324.)

John Newland Maffitt, who continued to refer to his steamer as the *Gordon*, was assigned as her commander. Below is Part One of his essay for *United Service* magazine. [RTC]

"Blockade Running, Part 1" by Commander John Newland Maffitt, CSN

The United Service, Volume VI, June 1882, pp. 626–633

As the war between the States expanded into gigantic proportions, it became manifest that great as was the ingenuity and industry unexpectedly developed by the people of the South, they were nevertheless totally inadequate to supply the increased military demands. The pressure on the government at Richmond occasioned deep anxiety and uneasiness that could not be concealed.

At this important crisis the public-spirited mercantile firm of Frazier, Trenholm & Co., of Charleston, South Carolina, promptly came to the rescue. They possessed a number of swift steamers, which were employed in running the blockade for commercial purposes. Influenced by patriotic zeal, these vessels were immediately employed in introducing supplies for the support and equipment of the armies of the Confederacy. This relief was most efficient; nor was there at this period of the war any material difficulty experienced in departing from or entering the harbor of Charleston, the Federal government not having succeeded in inaugurating the stringent blockade established at a subsequent period. Following the prologue of Sumter, the bloodstained curtain rose upon the battle-field of Manassas, startling the audience of the world with the sanguinary performance of a tragedy that apparently threatened the disintegration of a colossal power. Nor was this amazed audience, though individually passive, affected only by its sympathy with the combatants of the arena. In England alone the interests of millions were jeopardized by the war. From Virginia to Texas every port was being blockaded by the Federal navy. The North was determined to dethrone "King Cotton," and nullify his ability to aid the Confederacy with credit abroad for the purchase of materials of war.

Commander John Newland Maffitt (Naval Historical Center).

This important Southern staple was bread to millions of Englishmen, who beheld with consternation its confinement to America. Prices were advancing, work falling off, and wages declining. The murmurs of the poor heralded the season of distress, that precursor of hunger and cold, with those attending diseases that are born of privation.

In the Confederacy cotton abounded; few could purchase with prospects of exportation. Here it sold for three pence the pound, and brought in England from two shillings and three pence to two shillings and eight pence,—realizing a gross profit of about fifty-eight or sixty cents. A steamer with the average capacity of eight hundred bales often netted on the round trip about four hundred and twenty thousand dollars. These fabulous profits, coupled with the increasing demand, excited not only the cupidity, but characteristic enterprise, of British merchants. In less than eight months after the inception of hostilities and closing of Confederate ports, the ship-yards of England and Scotland were actively engaged in the construction of suitable steamers for blockade-running. In a brief time the harbors of Bermuda and Nassau swarmed with sky-colored vessels, eagerly seeking pilots and adventurous seamen to assist in transporting desirable cargoes into Dixie. Thus as an institution blockade-running was established.

In the hands of foreigners it proved in some respects injurious. The in cargoes were usually paid for with Confederate currency, and by the blockaders changed into gold at enormous discount, thereby producing a perceptible depreciation in the status of our money.

Many adventurous speculators made fortunes, while others, again, came to grief. Notwithstanding the difficulties and extreme hazards attending these ventures, cotton, with its magnetic power, attracted constant supplies for the war, and enabled our armies to maintain a bold and oft successful opposition to the splendidly equipped men of the North.

The adroit evasion of the blockade greatly irritated the Federals, and determined their government, by extraordinary accessions to their navy, to annihilate the whole system. In addition, their minister to the Court of St. James was instructed to protest against the many facilities afforded the South both in Great Britain and its colonies. The trans-shipment of goods at Bermuda and Nassau direct to steamers bound for the Confederacy became a particular cause of complaint, and "was considered as an act of encouragement to a domestic, rebellion, with decided manifestations of discourtesy to a friendly power."

Lord John Russell failed to view the case through the diplomatic representations of Mr. Adams, consequently the facilities accorded to blockade-runners were not withdrawn, but continued in operation until the fall of the curtain.

In consequence of my knowledge of the Southern coast, I was ordered to command one of the steamers offered to the government by Frazier, Trenholm & Co. She was reported to be unusually fast, and could stow to advantage about seven hundred bales of cotton. With the cargo on board we departed from Wilmington, and before sunset anchored off the village of Smithville. Twilight afforded an excellent opportunity to reconnoiter the enemy. They were numerous, and assumed their stations with an air of vigilance that seemed to announce the channel as hermetically sealed for the night. The prospects afforded no joyful anticipations of a pleasant exit.

As it, was necessary to bide the movements, of the moon, her sluggishness in retiring for the night was regarded with considerable impatience. At last her royal majesty, over the margin of the western horizon, tips us a knowing wink and disappears. We improve the hint, and get under way. In silence Caswell is passed, and a dim, glimpse of Fort Campbell affords a farewell view of Dixie, as the steamer's head is turned seaward through the channel. The swelling greetings of the Atlantic billows announce that the bar is passed; over the cresting waves the good craft swiftly dashes, as if impatient to promptly face her trials of the night. Through the settled darkness all eyes on board are peering, eagerly straining to catch a view of the dreaded sentinels who sternly guard the tabooed channel. Nothing white is exposed to view; every light is extinguished, save those that are hooded in the binnacle and engine-room. No sound disturbs the solemn silence of the moment but the dismal moaning of the northeast wind and unwelcome, but unavoidable, dashing of our paddles.

Night-glasses scan the bleared horizon for a time in vain; suddenly an officer with bated breath announces several steamers. Eagerly pointing, he reports two at anchor and others slowly cruising. Instantly out of the gloom and spoondrift emerges the somber phantom form of the blockading fleet. The moment of trial is at hand; firmness and decision are essential for the emergency. Dashing between the two at anchor, we pass so near as to excite astonishment at our non-discovery; but this resulted from the color of our hull, which, under certain stages of the atmosphere, blended so perfectly with the haze as to render the steamer nearly invisible.

How keenly the grim hulls of the enemy are watched! How taut; like harp-strings, every nerve is strung, anxiously vibrating with each pulsation of the throbbing heart! We emerge to windward from between the two at anchor.

"Captain," whispered the pilot, "according to my chop logic, them chaps aren't going to squint us this blessed night."

Ere a response could be uttered a broad spread flash of intense light blazed from the flag's drummond, for in passing to windward the noise of our paddles betrayed the proximity of a blockade-runner. "Full speed!" I shouted to the engineer. Instantly the increased revolutions responded to the order. Then came the roar of heavy guns, the howl of shot, and scream of bursting shells. Around, above, and through the severed rigging the iron demons howled, as if pandemonium had discharged its infernal spirits into the air.

Under the influence of a terrible shock the steamer quivers with aspen vibrations. An explosion follows; she is struck!

"What is the damage?" I ask.

"A shell, sir, has knocked overboard several bales of cotton and wounded two of the crew," was the response of the boatswain.

By the sheen of the drummond-lights the sea is so clearly illuminated as to exhibit the perils of our position, and show the grouping around us of the fleet, as their batteries belched forth a hail-storm of angry missiles, threatening instant annihilation.

In the turmoil of excitement a frightened passenger, contrary, to orders, invaded the bridge. Wringing his hands in agony, he implored me to surrender and save his life and the lives of all on board. Much provoked, I directed one of our quartermasters stationed near me to take the lubber below. Without ceremony he seized the unhappy individual, and as he hurried him to the cabin, menacingly exclaimed, "Shut up your fly-trap, or by the powers of Moll Kelly I'll hould ye up as a target for the diversion of them Yankee gunners."

As perils multiplied, our Mazeppa speed increased and gradually withdrew us from the circle of danger. At last we distance the party. Spontaneously the crew gave three hearty cheers as a relief to their pent-up anxiety, and every one began to breathe more naturally.

This was my tenth episode in running the blockade; not always a hazard, but more frequent than seldom. During the night we were subjected to occasional trials of speed, to avoid suspicious strangers whose characters could not be determined. In fact, nothing in the shape of a steamer was to be trusted, as we entertained the belief that Confederates were Ishmaelites upon the broad ocean, the recipients of no man's courtesy.

Day dawned upon one of ocean's most beautiful mornings; the soft blue sky circled the bluer horizon, and over the broad expanse a profound calm settled upon the sleeping waters. It seemed difficult to realize that such serenity was ever tortured into the most wild and terrific commotion by the rude storms and hurricanes that often held high revelry, where now not a ruffled wave appeared or a gentle ripple bleared the mirrored surface. Solitary and alone we pursued our voyage, flattered with the hope that it would terminate without interruption. At four in the afternoon we were aroused from this felicitous reverie by the familiar cry from the mast-head of "Sail ho!"

"Can you make her out?" was the official interrogatory.

"Yes, sir; a large steamer, heading for us."

Our course was immediately changed; so was that of the stranger. When she was reported we were engaged in overhauling the engines and cleaning fires. Of course our speed under these circumstances was inconsiderable, and the steamer neared us without difficulty. Annoyingly soon the old flag was recognized,—in former clays a welcome banner,—and the chase commenced. Night approaches in a royal blazonry of gold and crimson, the sun sinks below the horizon, leaving a brief twilight to light up the scene of contest. Some derangement of our engines depletes our speed, and the unpleasant knowledge causes the thermometer of hope to fall below zero. Perplexed and annoyed, I debated the expediency of relieving the vessel by throwing overboard a portion of her cargo. Fortunately a happy thought came to my-mind: Promptly acting upon the mental suggestion, I sent for the chief engineer, and inquired if he had a quantity of coal-dust convenient. "I have, sir," was the response.

"Be ready in fifty minutes to feed with it, and have at hand clean fuel that will not smoke. The order will be given in due season."

In the darkness of night a chasing vessel is guided by the smoke of the fleeing craft.

This fact was familiar from experience, and at the proper moment I availed myself of the acquired knowledge. The enemy held his own, though at times we thought he gained upon us. At length I directed the engineer to give a liberal application of coal dust, and instantly dense volumes of sooty vapor rolled out of the funnels and traveled on the bosom of the northeast wind to the southward and westward. By the aid of good glasses we were charmed to observe that the bait had been swallowed, as the Federal steadily pursued our bank of smoke. When this became obvious, clean coal was applied that emitted no tell-tale evidence of our position. The course was changed to the northward and eastward, and the enemy left to capture the Confederate's shadow. This successful ruse excited much hilarity and considerable laughter over what was considered "a cute trick."

At sunrise, entering the friendly port of Nassau, we were warmly greeted by many friends, by none more vociferously than the sons of Africa. The cargo was promptly landed, and the return freight received on board.

We are ready to depart; friends bid us farewell with lugubrious indulgence of fears for our safety, as the hazards of blockade-running had recently increased in consequence of the accumulated force and vigilance of the enemy. Discarding all gloomy prognostications, at dusk we left the harbor. Before break of day Abaco light was sighted, a place of especial interest to Federal cruisers as the turning-point for blockade-runners. At the first blush of day we were startled by the close proximity of three American men-of-war. Not the least obeisance made they, but with shot and shell paid the early compliments of the morning.

The splintering spars and damaged bulwarks warned us of the urgent necessity for traveling, particularly as nine hundred barrels of gunpowder constituted a portion of our cargo. A chance shell exploding in the hold would have consigned steamer and all hands to tophet. We were in capital running condition, and soon passed out of range. Tenaciously our pursuers held on to the chase, though it was evident that the fleet Confederate experienced no difficulty in giving them the go by. In the zenith of our enjoyment of a refreshing sense of relief, the old cry of "Sail ho!" came from aloft. The lookout announced two steamers ahead and standing for us. A system of zigzag running became necessary to elude the persistent enemy. Our speed soon accomplished this object. In about three hours the Federals faded under the horizon, and our proper course for the Cape Fear was resumed. Those who needed repose retired for the indulgence. My relaxation from official cares was of brief duration, as a gruff voice called out,

"Captain, a burning vessel is reported from aloft, sir."

Repairing on deck, by the aid of a spy-glass I could distinctly see, some four miles ahead, a vessel enveloped in smoke. Though not ourselves the subjects of charity, nevertheless we were human, and as seamen cherished the liveliest sympathy for the unfortunate who came to sorrow on God's watery highway. Regardless of personal interest, your true Jack Tar scorns the role of Pharisee, and prides himself upon the Samaritan proclivities that fail not to succor the sufferer by the wayside.

Increasing our speed, we quickly ran quite near to the burning vessel. She proved to be a Spanish bark, with ensign at half-mast. Out of her fore hatch arose a dense smoke. Abaft were clustered a panic stricken group of passengers and crew. Among them several ladies were observed. An ineffectual effort had been made to hoist out the long-boat, which was still suspended by the yard and stay-tackles.

Sending an officer aloft to keep a sharp lookout that we might not be surprised by the enemy while engaged in succoring the unfortunate, the chief mate was dispatched in the cutter to render such assistance as his professional intelligence might suggest. He found the few passengers, among whom were four ladies, much calmer than the officers and crew; the latter, in place of endeavoring to extinguish the fire, which had broken out in the forecastle apartment, were confusedly hauling upon the stay-tackle in a vain effort to launch the long-boat. Our mate, with his boat's crew, passed the jabbering panic-stricken Spaniards, and proceeded at once to the forecastle, which he instantly deluged with water, and, to the astonishment of all hands, speedily subdued the trifling conflagration, which proved to have resulted from the burning of a quantity of lamp rags that had probably been set on fire by one of the crew who carelessly emptied his pipe when about to repair on deck. The quantity of old duds that lay scattered about Jack's luxuriously furnished apartment supplied abundant materials for raising a dense smoke, but the rough construction of the vessel in this locality fortunately offered nothing inflammable, and the great sensation, under the influence of a cool head, soon subsided into a farce.

The mate, who was much of a wag, enjoyed the general perturbation of the passengers, particularly on ascertaining that three of the ladies hailed from Marblehead, and were returning from a visit made to an uncle who owned a well-stocked sugar plantation near Sagna Le Grande, in Cuba. A Spanish vessel bound to Halifax had been selected to convey them to a British port convenient for transportation to New York or Boston, without the risk of being captured by Confederate "buccaneers," who, according to Cuban rumors, "swarmed over the ocean, and were decidedly anthropophagous in their proclivities."

A hail from the steamer caused our mate to make his adieus, but not before announcing himself as one of the awful Southern slaveholders they had in conversation anathematized. They would not believe that so kind and polite a gentleman could possibly be a wicked "rebel." "But I am, ladies, and also a slave-owner, as is your uncle,—farewell." Instead of manifesting anger at the retort they laughed heartily, and waved their handkerchiefs in kind adieu, utterly unsuspicious of having received kindness and courtesy from a blockade runner. We made the best of speed on our way to Wilmington.

The following day—our last at sea—proved undisturbed and pleasant. At sunset the bar bore west-northwest seventy miles distant. It would be high water at half-past eleven, the proper time for crossing. Sixty miles I determined to dash off at full speed, and then run slowly for meeting and disentangling ourselves from the fleet.

None but the experienced can appreciate the difficulties that perplexed the navigator in running for Southern harbors during the war. The usual facilities rendered by lighthouses and beacons had ceased to exist, having been dispensed with by the Confederate government as dangerous abettors of contemplated mischief by the blockaders.

Success in making the destined harbors depended upon exact navigation, a knowledge of the coast, its soundings and currents, a fearless approach, and banishment of the subtle society of John Barleycorn. Non-experts too often came to grief, as the many hulks on the Carolina coast most sadly attest.

Under a pressure of steam we rushed ahead, annihilating space, and melting with exciting fancy hours into minutes. Our celerity shortens the distance, leaving only ten miles between us and the bar. With guiding lead, slowly and carefully we feel our way.

"Captain," observed the sedulous chief officer, as he strove to peer through the hazy atmosphere, "it seems to me from our soundings that we should be very near the blockaders. Don't you think so?"

"I do," was my response. "Hist! there goes a bell,—one, two, three, four, five, six, seven,—half-past eleven,—a decidedly good calculation, and it is high water on the bar. By Jove! there are two directly ahead of us, and I think both are at anchor. Doubtless others are cruising around these indicators of the channel."

I ordered the helm put hard a-starboard, directing the wheels-man to run between the two blockaders, as it was too late to sheer clear of either. Through a bank of clouds huge grim objects grew distinctly into view, and necessity forced me to run the gauntlet, trusting against hope that our transit would not arouse their vigilance. They were alert weasels, for a sparkling, hissing sound was instantly followed by the fiery train of a rocket, succeeded by the dreaded calcium light, with a radiance so brilliant, though brief, as to illuminate distinctly an area of miles.

"Heave to, or I'll sink you!" shouted a gruff, imperious voice, so near that we could fancy his speaking-trumpet projected over the steamer.

"Ay, ay, sir!" was the prompt response, and to the horror of all on board I gave the order in a loud tone, "Stop the engine!"

Then was heard the boatswain's whistle, the calling away of cutters, and the tramping of boat's crews. Our impetus had caused the steamer to nearly emerge from between the Federals.

"Back your engine, sir, and stand by to receive my boats!" said the same stern voice. Affirmatively acknowledging the command, I whispered loud enough for the engineer to hear me,

"Full speed ahead, sir, and open wide your throttle-valve."

The movements of the paddles for a moment deceived the Federal commander into the belief that we were really backing, but speedily comprehending the maneuver, with very fierce execrations he gave the order to fire. Drummond-lights were burned, doubtless to aid the artillerists, but so radiated the mist as to raise our hull above the line—of vision, causing the destructive missiles to play hob with the sparse rigging, instead of shattering our hull, and probably exploding the nine hundred barrels of gunpowder with which General Johnston afterwards fought the battle of Shiloh. It certainly was a miraculous escape for both blockader and blockade-runner.

We paused not recklessly, but at the rate of sixteen knots absolutely flew out of unhealthy company, who discourteously followed us with exploding shells, and for some time kept up such a fusillade as to impress us with the belief that the blockaders had inaugurated a "Kilkenny cat muddle," and were polishing off each other, a supposition I subsequently learned was partially correct.

The breakers warned us of danger, and the smooth water indicated the channel, through which we passed in safety, and at one o'clock in the morning we anchored off the venerable village of Smithville. Then came the mental and physical reaction, producing a feeling of great prostration, relieved by the delightful realization of having passed through the fiery ordeal in safety and freedom.

> "If after every tempest come such calms,
> May the winds blow 'till they have wakened death;
> And let laboring barks climb hills of seas
> Olympus high I and duck again as low
> As hell's from heaven."

After sunrise we proceeded in all haste to Wilmington, where our cargo was quickly discharged. Having obtained our return cargo, in company with two other blockade-runners I started for Nassau, and although the sentinels of the bar presented me with affectionate souvenirs in the way of shot and shell, they did but little damage. My companions came to grief, thereby adding to the prize fund that was shared by the government with the officers of the blockade squadron.

3. The *Advance*

An important area of Southern blockade running operations, but less known than those controlled by civilian- and Confederate-owned blockade runners, were those conducted by vessels owned and operated by the states, with North Carolina being the most active. The people and government of North Carolina were determined that their state's soldiers would not have to depend on the Confederate government for their needs. As a result of a Herculean effort, North Carolina was the only state during the war to fully clothe and arm her own troops in the field. North Carolina's Adjutant General James G. Martin saw that local supplies would soon be exhausted and proposed to Governor Zebulon Vance in September of 1862 that the state purchase a steamer to bring in the needed raw materials from England. (Gordan, "Organization of Troops," *Histories of the Several Regiments and Battalions From North Carolina in the Great War 1861-'65*, vol. I, pp. 28–30.)

Vance dispatched John White and Lieutenant Thomas M. Crossen of the North Carolina Navy to England with instructions to purchase material, especially shoes and blankets, for the North Carolina troops, and a vessel to transport the supplies to the Confederacy. Crossen's instructions were to locate and purchase a steamer for the state that would be able to outrun anything that the Federals might have on blockade duty.

After much searching Crossen found the vessel that, in conjunction with several other North Carolina–owned vessels, would contribute significantly to the supply of all North Carolina soldiers with their arms, uniforms, and accoutrements. She was the *Lord Clyde*, an iron side-wheeler that had been traversing the route between Glasgow and Dublin. The price of the sleek vessel, plus extra fittings and equipment, cost the state of North Carolina $175,000 (£35,000), but she would prove to be worth every penny. (Vance, *The Papers of Zebulon Baird Vance*, vol. I, pp. 288–290, 360–363.)

Built by Caird and Company of Glasgow, she was 236 feet long, 26 feet abeam, and drew 10 feet of water when fully loaded to 902 tons. Two oscillating steam cylinders of 63-inch bore and 78-inch stroke turned her giant thirty-foot paddlewheels. With steam pressure in her boilers at twenty pounds per square inch, these powerful engines drove her forward at seventeen knots, and with pressure increased to thirty pounds, she clicked off twenty knots without difficulty, a phenomenal speed for that era. Crossen christened her the *Advance*. (Sprunt, "Blockade Running," *Histories of the Several Regiments and Battalions From North Carolina in the Great War 1861-'65*, vol. V, p. 361.)

James Maglenn of the North Carolina Navy was her chief engineer, and in 1901 he contributed an essay to the *North Carolina Regiments* series detailing several of his exciting trips on the *Advance*. [RTC]

"The Steamer Advance" by Chief Engineer James Maglenn, NCN

North Carolina Regiments 1861–65, Volume V, 1901, pp. 335–340

This steamer, formerly called the *Lord Clyde*, running between Dublin and Glasgow, was purchased by the State of North Carolina to carry out cotton and other Southern products, and bring in arms and supplies of clothing and medicines for the North Carolina State Troops, and was named the *Advance*.

I joined the ship on her first arrival in Wilmington, and was with her until captured September, 1864, with the exception of one trip made from Wilmington to Nassau and return, serving in different capacities; first trip as second assistant engineer, second trip as first assistant engineer, then as chief engineer, making several successful trips, one to Liverpool for repairs, returning to Bermuda in June, 1864, thence to Wilmington.

Some of her trips were very exciting and hazardous. On one occasion there were four steamers leaving St. George, Bermuda, including the *Advance*, for Wilmington. But two of these arrived in Wilmington. One put back to Bermuda badly disabled; the other was lost in the gale. On this occasion I was limited to twelve revolutions per minute for thirty-six hours, or during the severest of the gale, which was just enough for the ship to mind the helm, being head to the gale all this time and water increasing in the hold to such an extent that it got within six inches of the grate-bars. In fact, I thought our time had come and, therefore, informed Captain Wiley how matters were in the engine and fire room, and that "we could not hold out this way much longer." I suggested to him the importance of turning the ship around and running before the wind, to enable me to get the water out by working the engines faster. He remonstrated by saying that "to attempt such a thing in a night like this would be certain destruction to the ship and all on board, but do the best you can until morning and when the worst comes, I may attempt it in daylight, but I feel confident we will have a change for the better by morning. The barometer has commenced to rise and is going up rapidly. It is the first time it has made a movement in that direction for two days." Strange to say, by 8 o'clock the next morning, it was perfectly calm, but a tremendous sea was rolling, which knocked us about considerably. This was the heaviest gale we ever experienced. On our arrival at Wilmington, we made some improvement in bilge and other pumps, which was actually necessary to make her seaworthy in anything like heavy weather.

The ship was in critical and dangerous positions on divers occasions. Once on the shoals of Fort Caswell where she remained for two or three days in range of the enemy's guns, but was finally worked off and arrived in Wilmington without any serious damage. Again, coming from St. George, Bermuda, we expected to make Bald Head light about 12 o'clock at night. However, a light was seen ahead about this time, but it proved to be Cape Lookout, and, when this was thoroughly understood and consultation held, Colonel Crossen, Captain Wiley, the pilot Kit Moss and Chief Engineer, as to what was best to be done, it was decided that we should try to get in at New Inlet.

Failing to get in there, she was to be run on the beach, as we did not have coal enough on board to go back to Bermuda. However, we left Cape Lookout about 2 o'clock on a beautiful October morning, all excitement and ship working at full speed close in to the land, determined to go in or on the beach. It being a little hazy along the line, was something in our favor. Did not see any of the fleet until we passed Wrightsville and sighted Fort Fisher. As we approached the fort, the gunboats made for us, firing shot that fell short. At this time we were approaching them very rapidly; on account of a point of shoal, we had to turn to make the channel inlet. By this time their shot were going over us, and when Colonel Lamb's Whitworth guns, began their firing upon the fleet, one large steamer, supposed to be the *State of Georgia*, came rapidly towards us, and when in dangerous proximity, was about to turn to bring her broadside guns upon the *Advance*, but a well-directed shot from a 10-inch Columbiad from the northeast salient of the fort crashed into her bow, when she rapidly backed water and withdrew from the chase, enabling the *Advance* to get safely in, amid the shouts of the garrison and the cheers of the officers and crew and the waving of handkerchiefs by those on deck of the blockade runner. A number of officers came on board to congratulate us, and Captain Wiley and the Rev. Moses D. Hoge, who was on board bringing in a lot of testaments, Bibles and tracts for the soldiers, sent special thanks to Colonel Lamb and his garrison for their timely aid. This was considered one of the most daring and gallant feats performed by the blockade-runners during the war.

Her Last Trip and Capture

We left Wilmington about 9 September, 1864, Captain Wiley still in command, with a full cargo, principally of cotton, bound for Halifax, N. S., and anchored at New Inlet, near Fort Fisher, and in full sight of the Federal fleet of twenty-five or thirty vessels, who, of course, understood our designs and would be on the lookout for us that night. Although the night was not altogether favorable, we started as soon as the tide would permit. Of course, smoke, sparks and flames from the stack had to be kept down. This was very difficult to do, as our last shovel full of good coal was used shortly after crossing the bar and in plain sight of some of the fleet. Those that could see us would throw rockets, indicating the direction we were going. Then the dodging on our part and the frequent change of the ship's course to keep from running into them. The excitement at this time was very great. Yet all was as quiet as the grave on board and every man was at his post and doing his duty faithfully. The rocket firing and shooting were very heavy, and nothing but good management on the part of our officers could have pulled us safely through the fleet that night. At sunrise there was nothing in sight, yet our black smoke was giving us away. Some of the fleet were following it, and about 8 o'clock a vessel was discovered chasing us and appeared to be gaining. Everything possible was done to increase the speed of the *Advance*, but the steaming qualities of the coal were against us. We were using Chatham, or Egypt coal, which was very inferior; in fact nothing but slate or the croppings of the mine. Our good coal at Wilmington was taken for the Confederate cruisers, which accounts for our capture. We were in hopes we could evade the pursuing steamer in the darkness of the night, but, in our present condition, she was too fast for us and was able to throw some shot over us some time before sundown, which caused us to stop the ship and surrender. From the stopping of the ship to the boarding of the United States officers, some time elapsed, causing an accumulation of steam, which was blowing off very freely. The United States Engineer Corps, seeing the condition of affairs, asked me to have my men haul the fires and arrange to have the boilers supplied with water. I told him I had nothing more to do with the ship and considered him in charge. He then asked if my assistant engineers would go down and attend to this. I pointed them out to him, saying they would answer for themselves and, on their refusal, the Lieutenant ordered us on the bridge on top of the boilers, saying: "If she does blow up I will send you all to eternity." Imagine us sitting on top of the boilers waiting for the explosion. However, we knew there was no immediate danger, if they could succeed in getting the pumps to work, which they did in a short time, and we were relieved from our dangerous position and sent on board the *Santiago de Cuba*, which captured us. All were examined as to their nationality, many North Carolinians and Virginians on board claiming British protection. In fact, all on board except two, one from Connecticut and one from Virginia, claimed British protection and all could sound the letter "O" in "home" very broad. Mr. Carter, our purser, was the only one on board that was sworn, and this was on account of the clothing he wore, it being a suit of North Carolina home-spin. The Captain looked at him from head to foot and vice versa, saying that he was the first Englishman he ever saw with a suit of clothes of that kind.

On our way to Norfolk, with Cape Henry in sight, Sunday morning we were ordered on deck for prayer (Episcopal service). During the service our Captain Wiley called my

Chief Engineer James Maglenn (Clark, *North Carolina Regiments*).

attention to the Captain of the *Santiago de Cuba*, saying the prayers were doing him no good, from the fact that he was turning around every minute to see if the valuable prize, the *Advance*, was coming, and when satisfied that all things were well with her, would turn around again, giving a little more attention to the sermon for a few minutes. We arrived in Norfolk Sunday afternoon and had the freedom of the city, that is inside the Provost Marshal's limits.

We, however, wanted to go "ome," and had to appeal to the British Consul at Norfolk. We had some trouble at first, but the Consul finally took our case to heart and wrote a letter to Lord Lyons, stating the way her Britannic Majesty's subjects were treated. This did the work for us and we were permitted to find our way "ome" as best we could, without interruption.

This was the last I saw of the *Advance*, but I have been told by Colonel Lamb that she was turned into a gun-boat, The *Frolic*, and was in the second bombardment at Fort Fisher, and has been seen several times at Wilmington since the war.

Many of the North Carolinians made their way from Norfolk to Halifax, N. S., thence to Nassau, where I was appointed Chief Engineer of the steamer *Col. Lamb*, with Captain Thomas Lockwood in command. We were then ready to run the blockade again to Wilmington, but were informed by an incoming steamer that Forts Fisher and Caswell had been taken. This left no port open for us but Galveston. We then left Nassau for Havana, took on supplies and started for Galveston; on arriving off the bar, it was thought too risky to go in as the wind had been blowing unfavorably for several days, which caused low water in the harbor which would increase the risk of the steamer. On consultation with pilots it was decided not to take the risk; we then returned to Havana, all ports being now effectively closed, and after making some repairs to the machinery, we were ordered to Halifax, N. S., touching at Nassau and Bermuda, arriving at Halifax about 10 April, 1865.

While lying in the harbor, Captain Lockwood gave a dination to the Agents and Confederate friends on Saturday, 15 April, and at sun rise the ship was decorated with flags from stem to stern and the steamer *Col. Lamb* made a very handsome appearance, but they were not allowed to remain there long. About 9:00 or 10:00 AM, a British boat was seen coming towards us and pulled alongside. The officer in charge inquired for the Captain. When told he was ashore, he then ordered the flags to be taken down, as it was very unbecoming to be rejoicing over the death of the President of the United States in British waters. When told that they were displayed for another purpose, it made no difference. They had to come down at once. This was news to us and created quite a sensation in the city and the newspapers were full of it for several days on both sides, but it was claimed that the flags should have been allowed to remain, as the news of President Lincoln's death did not reach Halifax until about 9:00 o'clock that morning, and the flags were up at sunrise.

The surrender having taken place while we were here, it was decided to take the ship to Liverpool. We left here about 5 May and had a stormy passage all the way—in fact a gale of wind carrying away the foremast a few feet above deck, which came near swamping us; then came the remorse of conscience with those of us that belonged on this side of the Atlantic for not going home immediately after the surrender instead of taking this trip. However, we arrived in Liverpool about 1 June. We remained there a few days and then started for home in the Cunard steamer *China*. This being an ocean-going steamer, we felt much safer than in the *Advance* or *Col. Lamb*. We had a pleasant return trip, arriving in Halifax, N. S., on 4 July, 1865, from there to Charlotte, N. C., where my family resided during the last two years of the war. I found all well and was glad to be home with my family once more.

James Magleen.

Hamlet, N. C.,
10 September, 1901.

4. The *Owl*

Below is the third part of John Newland Maffitt's three part series entitled "Blockade Running" that appeared in the *United Service* magazine in 1882. He had just relinquished command of the cruiser *Florida* at Brest, France, where he was diagnosed with a possible heart attack. After a short season of travel and rest, he returned to the Confederacy and in December of 1864 was ordered to command the blockade runner *Owl*.

The *Owl* was a 230-foot sidewheel steamer built in Liverpool, England, in 1864, by Jones, Quiggin and Company specifically for the blockade-running trade. After her completion she was turned over to Fraser, Trenholm & Company which transferred her to the Confederate navy. She proved to be Maffitt's last command. (Wise, *Lifeline of the Confederacy Blockade Running during the Civil War*, p. 315.) [RTC]

"Blockade Running, Part 3" by Commander John Newland Maffitt, CSN
The United Service, Volume VII, July 1882, pp. 29–33

The demand on my physical ability had been excessive, nor had I entirely recovered from the effects of yellow fever, which still clung to me, and was militating against my general usefulness. For this reason I was compelled to apply for detachment, which being granted, Commander Barney became my successor. Consulting a distinguished physician in Paris, he pronounced my heart affected from tropical disease, and, after putting me through a course of severe treatment, started me off for Sweden, not to rest, but to travel for health. My health improving, I took command of a blockade-runner in England, and made my passage to Wilmington, and was soon afterwards ordered to relieve the gallant Captain Cooke from the command of the *Albemarle*, at Plymouth.

As the duty enjoined was more that of a river-guard than anything else, I was not sorry when the Secretary, of the Navy wrote that, having purchased in England several steamers for running the blockade for the government, he was under the necessity of employing my knowledge of the Southern coast by ordering me to the command of the *Owl*, daily expected from Bermuda. On the 21st of December, 1864, I received on board the naval steamer *Owl* seven hundred and eighty bales of cotton, and with three other blockade-runners ran clear of the Federal sentinels without the loss of a rope-yarn. Unfortunately, one of my companions, in this race for our destined harbor, met with an accident to her machinery and came to grief. Her cargo was not of material value, as it principally consisted of spirits of turpentine and rosin, cotton being scarce in the market.

Arriving in St. George, I found a number of steamers loaded and impatiently awaiting news from the Federal expedition under General Butler against Fort Fisher before resolving to make an attempt to enter Dixie. By the Halifax steamer the desired intelligence was obtained. The Northern press admitted that the assault had proved abortive. The *New York Herald* stated that the cargo of powder was gallantly anchored near Fort Fisher and touched off, produced an explosion so terrible as to absolutely arouse several fatigued and somnolent Dixie soldiers from their much-needed repose. Upon the receipt of this, to us, cheering news, six of us in company joyfully departed, anticipating a speedy reunion with Dixie.

We parted at sea and met not again. In two days I communicated with Lockwood's *Folly*, where they reported all serene and Fisher intact. Delighted with this information, I steamed for the Cape Fear. The moon was not expected to rise until eleven o'clock, and at eight o'clock we should meet high water on the bar, the time for crossing. Approaching the channel, I was surprised to find but one sentinel guarding the port. No difficulty was experienced in eluding him. A conflagration at Bald Head and no response to my signals excited some apprehensions, but as Fort Caswell looked natural and quiet, I decided to venture in, and passing on, came to anchor off the fort wharf. We were immediately interviewed by two officers from the fort, who confirmed my most gloomy apprehensions. A second attack, under General Terry and Admiral Porter, had been successful, and Fisher and the Cape Fear were in possession of the enemy.

To instantly depart became an imperious necessity. Gunboats were approaching; Fort Caswell was doomed; the train, already laid, only awaited the match. In poignant distress I turned from the heartrending scene, my sorrowing mind foreshadowing the fate of Dixie. The solitary blockader awoke from his lethargy and pursued me furiously. His

Commander John Newland Maffitt (Naval Historical Center).

artillery palled under the reverberation of an explosion that rumbled portentously from wave to wave in melancholy echoes that enunciated far at sea the fate of Caswell.

The history of the five steamers in whose company I sailed from the harbor of St. George's is briefly told. Captain Wilkinson, the late gallant commander of the *Chickamauga*, was too experienced and keen a cruiser to be caught in a trap. Convinced from observation there was "something rotten in the state of Denmark," he judiciously returned to Bermuda. The remaining three were decoyed into New Inlet by the continuance of the Mound light, and became easy prey under the following circumstances. First the *Stag*, with several English officers on board as passengers, deceived by Admiral Porter's cuteness, crossed the bar, and, as was customary, anchored under the mound, there to bide the usual visit of inspection from the boarding officer of Fort Fisher. Waiting for some time without receiving the official call, the captain naturally concluded it had been deferred until daylight. He therefore directed the steward to serve the entertainment that had been elaborately prepared to celebrate their safe arrival in the Confederacy. The gastronomic hidalgo flourished his baton of office, and escorted his guests to the festive board. In shouts of revelry and with flowing bumpers the jocund party huzzahed for Dixie, and sang her praises in songs of adulation that made the welkin ring, and aroused the sea-mews from their peaceful slumbers. A pause from exhaustion having occurred in their labor of justice to the luxurious repast, gave to an English captain a desired opportunity to ventilate in appropriate sentiments his appreciation of the joyful occasion. Mysteriously rapping to enjoin attention, in the silence that followed he solemnly arose. At a wave of his dexter the steward, all alertness, replenished the glasses.

"Gentlemen," said the captain, "after a successful voyage, fraught with interesting incidents and excitements, we have anchored upon the soil of battle-worn, grand old Dixie. We come not as mercenary adventures to enlist under the banner of the Confederacy, but, like true knights-errant, to join as honorable volunteers the standard of the bravest lance in Christendom, that of the noble, peerless Lee. (Cheers, hear, hear.) In gaining this Palestine of our chivalrous aspirations we have successfully encountered the more than ordinary perils of the sea, in storms, the lingering chase, and hazards of the blockade. Through all vicissitudes there was a mind to conceive, a hand to guide, a courage to execute. Gentlemen, I propose the health, happiness, and speedy promotion of the officer who merits these commendations,—our worthy commander."

Mingled with vociferous applause came the customary hip! hip! hussah! hip! hip! huz——-

The half-uttered huzzah froze like an icicle on the petrified lips of the orator, who,

> "With wild surprise,
> As if to marble struck, devoid of sense,
> A stupid moment, motionless stood,"

as the apparition of a Federal midshipman appeared upon the cabin stairway.

"Who commands this steamer?" was the Federal's interrogatory.

"I am that unfortunate individual," groaned the unhappy commander, as reminiscences of a long confinement came painfully to his mind.

"You are a prize to Admiral Porter's squadron, and I relieve you from all further responsibility. Gentlemen, as paroled prisoners, you are at liberty to finish your repast."

The withering enunciation of capture blighted like a black frost the hopeful blossoms that had, under the inspiring influence of the sparkling Epherney, bubbled into poetic existence. One by one the lights soon faded in this banquet-hall deserted, their last glimmer falling mournfully on the debris of the unfinished congratulatory repast.

Ere an hour elapsed two more unfortunates, lured by the channel lights, entered and likewise anchored off the mound, and became a prey to Admiral Porter's fleet.

My cargo being important, and the capture of Fort Fisher and the Cape Fear cutting me off from Wilmington, I deemed it my duty to make an effort to enter the harbor of Charleston, in order to deliver the much-needed supplies.

I had been informed that the blockade of that port was more stringent and numerically guarded than ever before since the inauguration of hostilities. The *Owl's* speed was now accommodated to the necessary time for arriving off the bar, which was 10 PM. Throughout the day vigilant steamers were seen along the shore, inspecting inlets and coves regardless of their want of capacity for blockade purposes. This spirit of inspection and watchfulness was most assiduous, as if an order had been issued to overhaul even the coast gallinippers, to see that aid and comfort in the shape of muskets and pistols were not smuggled into the needy Confederacy. Occasionally one of these constables of the sea would fire up and make a dash after the *Owl*; a little more coal and stirring up of the fire-draft was sufficient to start the blockade-runner off with such admirable speed as to convince the Federal that he was after the fleetest steamer that ever eluded the guardians, of the channel-ways.

Seasonably making the passage, nine o'clock PM found us not far from the mouth of Maffit's Channel. Anticipating a trying night and the bare possibility of capture, two bags were slung and suspended over the quarter by a stout line. In these bags were placed the government mail, not yet delivered, all private correspondence, and my war journal, including the cruise of the *Florida*, besides many other papers. An intelligent quartermaster was ordered to stand by the bags with a hatchet, and the moment that capture became inevitable to cut adrift and let them sink.

When on the western tail-end of the Rattlesnake Shoal, we encountered streaks of mist and fog that enveloped stars and everything for a few moments, when it would become quite clear again. Running cautiously in one of those obscurations, a sudden lift in the haze disclosed that we were about to run into an anchored blockader. We had bare room with a hard-a-port helm to avoid him some fifteen or twenty feet, when their officer on deck called out, "Heave to, or I'll sink you!" The order was unnoticed, and we received his entire broadside, that cut away turtle-back, perforated forecastle, and tore up bulwarks in front of our engine room, wounding twelve men, some severely, some slightly. The quartermaster stationed by the mail-bags was so convinced that we were captured that he instantly used his hatchet, and sent them, well moored to the bottom; hence my meager account of the cruise of the *Florida*. Rockets were fired as we passed swiftly out of his range of sight, and drummond-lights lit up the animated surroundings of a swarm of blockaders, who commenced an indiscriminate discharge of artillery. We could not understand the reason of this bombardment, and as we picked our way out of the melee, concluded that several blockade-runners must have been discovered feeling their way into Charleston.

After the war, in conversing with the officer commanding on that occasion, he said that a number of the steamers of the blockade were commanded by inexperienced volunteer officers, who were sometimes overzealous and excitable, and hearing the gunboat firing into me, and seeing her rockets and signal-lights, they thought that innumerable blockade-runners were forcing a passage into the harbor, hence the indiscriminate discharge of artillery, which was attended with unfortunate results to them. This was my last belligerent association with blockade-running. Entering the harbor of Galveston, and finding it in the possession of the Federals, I promptly checked progress and retreated. The last order issued by the Navy Department, when all hope for the cause had departed, was for me to deliver the *Owl* to Frazier, Trenholm & Co., in Liverpool; which I accordingly did.

XIV

The CSN in Europe

1. The CSS *Stonewall*

Convinced that it would soon become impossible to build war vessels in England, Commander Bulloch on July 16, 1863, signed an agreement with the shipbuilding firm of Lucien Arman based in Bordeaux, France, to build two formidable ironclads based on Secretary Mallory's stipulations. (Spencer, *The Confederate Navy in Europe,* p. 155.)

The 1,390-ton ironclads were 171 feet, 10 inches long, and 32 feet, 8 inches in beam. The most interesting aspect of them was their twin stern-posts and twin screws that could be operated independently. Driven by four engines of 300 horsepower each, the reversing of one screw enabled the vessel to turn within its own length. Each ship was armed with one twelve-ton 300-pounder rifle manufactured by Armstrong, and housed in a fixed armored turret that formed the bow. The gun was fixed and positioned to fire directly forward in line with the keel, for the operation of the twin screws allowed the pointing of the entire vessel. Two smaller 70-pounder Armstrong rifles that could be fired rearward, broadside, and forward to within 25 degrees in line with the keel were mounted in a fixed turret aft. Armor was 4.75 inches of iron backed by teak amidships, tapering to 3.5 inches at either end. A speed of 12 knots in smooth seas was guaranteed, but the best that the *Stonewall* would ever see was 10.5 knots. (Melton, *The Confederate Ironclads,* p. 267.)

In the fall of 1864, Arman applied to the marine ministry for permission to arm the ironclads and represented them as the *Cheops* and the *Sphinx,* both of which were destined for the viceroy of Egypt. When the two ironclads were completed the French Marine Department, in February of 1864, detained them, and Emperor Napoleon ordered all ships being built for the Confederacy to be sold. The *Cheops* was sold to Prussia and the *Sphinx* to Denmark. Due to the termination of the Schleswig-Holstein War, however, the Danes no longer wanted the *Sphinx,* and she was, through a series of intermediaries, transferred to the Confederacy.

For the ironclad ram's commander, Bulloch chose Captain Thomas Jefferson Page, a native of Virginia. Born on January 4, 1808, Page was a commander in the U. S. Navy when he resigned his commission upon the outbreak of war. He had served briefly in the Virginia Navy until that service's personnel were transferred to Confederate service. He was in command of the Gloucester Point battery on the York River until the army's evacuation of the Peninsula during Major General George B. McClellan's advance on Richmond in the spring of 1862. Later, he commanded the forces manning the guns on Chaffin's Bluff on the James River below Richmond, and in 1863 he was sent to Europe to await assignment. (Moebs, *Confederate States Navy Research Guide,* pp. 246–247.) [RTC]

"The Career of the Confederate Cruiser Stonewall" by Captain Thomas J. Page, CSN

Southern Historical Society Papers, Volume XII, 1879, pp. 263-280

In presenting this blurred picture of the *Stonewall,* its imperfections should be attributed more to the shortcomings of the artist than to the absence of intrinsic worth in the subject represented.

The *Stonewall*, a small twin-screw ironclad man-of-war, was built in France by the then most eminent constructor in the Empire. Her tonnage, twelve hundred; armament, one three-hundred pounder and two seventy-pounder guns, and crew about forty men.

Thus equipped, this little craft was seen one fair morning, after much negotiation, bearing the beautiful Confederate flag in place of the Danish, under which she had arrived from the region of the North sea. She was built with the knowledge and sanction of the late Emperor of France, and on the eve of her completion and readiness for delivery it was rumored that she was designed for the Confederate Government. Every ship then being built in Europe acquired this reputation. This rumor reached the ears of the Emperor, and he was officially informed, from high authority, that if this or any other such vessel should be permitted to leave France and fall into the possession of the Confederate Government, Mexico would be made untenable ground for French troops. However impotent such a threat may have been at that time, it had the desired effect. The Emperor was truly sensitive on this Mexican question. His policy there was unpopular in France, and he was not the man to long debate which of the two to choose when compliance with his word pointed to the right and self-interest to the left.

He ran no risk in laying an injunction on his friend and ship builder, that no vessels, under his construction, should pass into the hands of the Confederate Government. Whatever may have been his sentiments individually, policy constrained him to consult those of the French people, who may not have comprehended his aim and object in measures of such remote bearing. He had been challenged to a game of "brag," in which he was no proficient. Astute, sagacious, far-seeing as he was, he could not see into his adversary's hand—he was bluffed—he revoked the permission he had given the constructor.

A similar diplomatic game had already been successfully played in England, in the case of the Berkenhead rams—as two vessels built on the Mercey were called; for a like issue had been made on the charge that they were designed for the Confederate Government. Had all the vessels charged to the Confederate account so actually belonged, that Government would have been the most formidable of all naval powers.

This case could not be so summarily disposed of in England, where all questions involving the rights of the people had been up to this time invariably adjudicated and decided according to law—the English people being pre-eminently conservative and law-abiding. This case was adjudicated, and all the powers of Government brought to the investigation in order to establish the charge that these vessels were built for the Confederate Government. The prosecution exerted a degree of energy unparalleled in the accumulation of evidence from every hole and corner; for there were consequences involved in the decision so momentous as not to be weighed in the balance with tens of millions of pounds sterling, or any other sum of money—the life of a nation was at stake.

Notwithstanding the disposition on the part of the Government, the earnest hope that the investigations of the Attorney-General would discover evidence to sustain the charge, that learned jurist, after a laborious search, was obliged to report that there was no evidence to show that the Berkenhead rams were built for the Confederate Government. This was too important a measure to be given up because the law was impotent, or even after the failure of the desperate efforts that had been resorted to. It was a case of life or death. If the law were not strong enough, some other course must be adopted. A threat was made—it would be a "casus belli" if the vessels in question should come into the possession of the Confederate Government. Impotent as was this threat, it prevailed. The Government succumbed, did what had never before been done—violate their own laws and take peaceable possession of the vessels; that the law could not condemn—the surest course by which to satisfy the complainants. This occurred previously to the action of the French Emperor—in the case before mentioned—an example he conceived worthy of his following.

The *Stonewall* had not, at this time, been baptized with the ever memorable name she subsequently bore, for she was not then a Confederate vessel; and, after much circumlocution, fell into the hands of the Danish Government, at the time, be it remembered, while Prussia and Austria were at war with Denmark. How this occurred is not pertinent to this narrative. We can only conjecture that Prussian spies were not so wide-a-wake as had been some other detectives. She was taken to Copenhagen under the direction of Danish naval officers, in order to witness and test her capacity as a sea-going vessel. Her performance in the North sea somewhat dampened the ardor of these hardy seamen of the North, for they looked upon her as being more of the amphibian kind than of that class of vessels in which they had been accustomed to navigate the ocean.

It is true she had no very great respect for the heavy waves of the sea—she defied them—and if they did not permit her to gracefully ride over, she would go through them—protruding her long elephantine proboscis as the seas receded; and, rising from her almost submerged condition, would shake the torrent from her deck and again walk the water like a thing of like. She was not so dangerous. She was dangerous only when coming in conflict with one of her own kind; and even in this respect her reputation subsequently grew to vast proportions—far exceeding her capacity to do damage.

Arrived in Copenhagen, the report as to her sea-worthiness was not favorable. Her good qualities were ignored, and her disposition to act the part of the leviathan exaggerated. Moreover, the war in which Denmark was engaged was speedily brought to a close and the services of such a vessel were no longer required. In a word, that Government wished to get rid of her; and after much discussion, deliberation, investigation, &c., as to compliance with contract, it was finally determined to return the little craft to the builders. Their agent received her, and under charge of a Danish merchant captain and crew, she was dispatched to France.

Before leaving port a Confederate navy officer, who was curiously interested in all such naval architecture, had been often on board and inspected the vessel throughout—her armament, gun-gear, projectiles, naval stores, &c.—for in her construction, equipment, &c., she was quite unique. Pleased with the appearance of the vessel and all on board, he accepted the invitation of the builder's agent and took passage in her for France. She had scarcely got fairly into the North sea when the weather, always boisterous in those latitudes in the winter season, became so bad that the captain conceived it prudent to put into Christians and in Norway. Time was precious—for there were pressing obligations pending. Moreover, the captain and crew were to be discharged after the lapse of a limited time. Under these circumstances, the passenger, Mr. Brown, whose status on board was known only to the captain, urged him to put to sea on the least abatement of the gale. They had been out in blue water only a few hours when the vessel began to exhibit her powers of diving and coming up, after the fashion of the porpoise, as if for the amusement of all on board. But the engineers and crew, not amused by these fantastic tricks, as they were neither ducks nor fish, petitioned the captain to put back into port. He, quite of their opinion, proposed the same to Mr. Brown; but the latter, though in a minority of one, declined to accede to the proposition of the majority—the rule of the sea being the reverse of that on land under republican government—and expressing his entire confidence in the sea-worthiness of the vessel, advised the captain to assure the engineers that turning back was always attended with danger; that there was bad luck in it; that the only danger lay in stopping the engines; that, in a word, the safety of the vessel and all on board depended entirely on the continuous movement of the engine, and the watchful care of it by the engineers.

She weathered that gale and arrived off the coast of France in clear weather and a smooth sea, where—a very singular coincidence—a steamer had taken up her anchorage, as though there had been some preconcerted arrangement for their meeting, for this was neither a port nor harbor. The agent of the builders, who had been up to this time the ostensible owner of the vessel, concluding it would be as well for him to land on the nearest point of the coast, took his departure accompanied by the captain and crew, and went on shore, indulging the pleasing remembrance of an adventurous passage from the North sea, and the still more pleasing anticipation of the fruitful results he was about to realize.

Captain Thomas J. Page (National Archives).

This procedure would seem inhospitable and unkind towards the little craft that had borne them safely through the tempestuous weather of the North sea, thus to be left with one solitary man on board. But she had not long to remain in this un-peopled state. Boats came, crowded with men, from the steamer that lay close by, not only curious to see, but perhaps, to minister to the wants of the little craft in her deserted condition and to offer their services, which sailor men are prompt to render when duty calls; for "old salts" are proverbially kind, and will often risk their lives in an adventure. It turned out, however, that these visitors were not actuated solely by curiosity, for they consisted of officers and sailors prepared to cast their lot, to do their duty, under the Confederate flag, come weal or woe.

The spar deck of the vessel presented, on that bright, sunny morn, a busy scene. The Confederate flag was run up at the peak, and the pennant at the main-mast head, when the commander, surrounded by the little band of officers and men, with caps in hand, pointed to the pure emblem at her peak, the token of the nationality of the vessel, and announced her "The *Stonewall*"—ever to be remembered name, given at the baptismal font of the Bay of Biscay.

Certain preliminaries, the shipping of men, assignment to specific duties, &c., having been gone through with, the deck was soon cleared of the various articles, so generously presented and as gratefully received from the steamer in company, which, having been stowed in their appropriate places, all was made snug for the cruise. The anchor was hove up under the inspiration of that joyous music, familiar to every sailor man, when the boatswain "calls all hands up—anchor for home"; for that is music, though it comes from nature's roughest cut, whose melody touches the soul and causes a responsive vibration of the tenderest chords of the heart.

The Bay of Biscay, whose normal condition is that of a boisterous sea, lay like a mirror, reflecting the bright rays of the sun; while balmy air, fanned into the gentlest of breezes by the headway of the vessel, promised a happy entrance into the broad Atlantic. "Man proposes but God disposes." The night was not half spent ere the wind blew and the storm arose, and at the dawn of day the *Stonewall* was contending against a gale and heavy sea, well calculated to test the sea-worthiness of the little craft, and try the faith of the stoutest heart in their capacity to weather the storm. Battened down, she was water-tight, and, although she was no "Mother Cary's chicken" to gracefully dance on the crest of waves, would, in her lazy way, receive them over her bows, in cataract form, and give them free exit through the quarter ports to their mother ocean. Romantic as this may seem, though not comparable to the grandeur of the Falls of Niagara, it was neither exhilarating nor agreeable; for, apart from these too frequent and overwhelming visitations, the officers and men began to look upon them as an imposition, in compelling them to appear on deck booted up to the knee. This round of amusement continued for three days to the monotonous music of the howling of the storm, and the contention of the sea with the skies; when the *Stonewall's* friend—the steamer that had befriended her at the anchorage, and now anxiously watched her performance in this terrific gale, in order to render other assistance if needed—telegraphed or signaled to know "how she was getting on"; for at times when the *Stonewall* would be in the "through of the sea," partly submerged, there could be nothing seen of her. Knowing that her friend had some other important duty to discharge, with a heavy heart she replied, "all right, so ahead." The steamer went on her way; in her construction she was better constituted to resist the gale.

Only a few hours had elapsed when it was discovered that all was not right, that water was flowing into the captain's cabin from abalf in a very unusual manner; and, although men were set to bailing with buckets, the water gained on them. The storeroom for the men's clothing and other purser's effects was abalf the cabin, whence came the water. On opening this apartment a very discomforting spectacle met the eye. The caps over the two rudder heads were, by the force of the sea, as the *Stonewall* would occasionally dive beneath, being gradually lifting, the bolts yielding to the pressure, and the water gushing in every direction with great force. Had these blocks been suddenly fitted from their places there would have been opened two holes of ten inches diameter each below the water line, apertures well calculated to endanger the safety of the vessel. A temporary repair was soon made by nailing the blocks into their places, and the rush of water partially arrested.

This disaster rendered it necessary to put into the nearest port for repairs; although the great consumption of coals would alone have caused this course to be taken, as but little headway had been or could be made in the face of such a gale. No observations for determining the geographical position of the vessel had been made for more than two days. The sun, moon and stars—those beacons by which the mariner shapes his course mid the trackless ocean—were obscured by the lurid clouds that spanned the firmament. With exhausted bunkers and paralyzed engine the *Stonewall* would have been a prey to the raging storm; she was not capable of contending under sail alone against a several gale. To run the risk of being wrecked on the iron-bound coast of Spain, should the hoped for port not be reached, was preferable to being swamped in the Bay of Biscay. From the best data available, under the circumstances, an imaginary position was assigned the vessel and a course determined upon, which it was hoped would lead into some safe anchorage; for any port in a storm is a sailor's snug harbor.

Trusting to "that little cherub that sits up aloft and keeps watch on poor Jack," the helm was put hard up, the close-reefed fore topsail sheeted home, and the little craft went off before the wind like a thing of life and proudly said to the foaming seas, "follow me." They did follow, as though frantic to get on board, but however given to taking them in over the bows, the *Stonewall* refused them admittance over the stern. To scud so small an ironclad so little above the water's edge was a dangerous evolution, but necessity makes its own laws, and this was one of those cases in which success proved the propriety of adopting the exceptional rule.

The coast of Spain lay ahead, but what part of it was the doubtful question soon to be solved. The pulsations of every heart beat quickly, and every eye was anxiously strained to descry, midst the obscurity of the atmosphere, the crescent shaped contour of the coast, in which lay the port hoped for. Not more joyously did the cry of "land Ho!" find an echo in the hearts of Columbus' crew, than it did in the hearts of the *Stonewall's* on this occasion, when the anxiously looked for haven was seen directly ahead. None but the wearied mariner, after days of doubtful contest with the angry elements, can appreciate such deliverance from the dangers of the sea. This was the happy lot of the *Stonewall*, as she steamed into the snug harbor, leaving the raging of the gale behind, and dropped anchor in the placid, hospitable waters of Ferrol.

The usual visits of ceremony were made and on calling on the Captain-General, who was an old salt holding the rank of Admiral, the character of the *Stonewall* was stated, and the object of her visit to have certain repairs made and to procure a supply of coals. Permission was politely granted, and authority to employ such hands from the dock-yard as might be required.

Ferrol is one of Spain's principal naval stations. I should not pass over the admission of the *Stonewall* into this port without expressing the obligation under which she lay for this very courteous, hospitable reception at the hands of the Captain-General and others, of which there remains a pleasing remembrance not soon to be forgotten.

Ship carpenters were immediately at work repairing damages, and at the same time a supply of coals was being taken on board. These operations has scarcely gotten fairly under way when it became known that there were other difficulties and dangers than those she had just escaped that beset the *Stonewall*. The intelligence of her arrival was not to be confined to Ferrol. There were here, as in every other part of Europe, curious gentlemen, whose avocation was to find out other people's business. The wires soon flashed the news of this arrival, under a novel flag, to the American Minister at Madrid, who forthwith protested to that Government that the admission of such a vessel—a pirate, an enemy to all mankind, a reckless rover of the sea—was an infringement of international law, a violation of the rights of nations, and that the Government should effect here from that port and prohibit her entering another, though she might go to the bottom—the only port the hospitalities of which she was entitled to. Now, it had been supposed that this unpretending little craft had come into the world all right; had been baptized in accordance with the strictest tenets of received public creed, and that she did not come under that class designated by such harsh epithets. She was aware that she was not exempt, in the eyes of some, from the imputation of having been conceived in sin, but, as she had been baptized in the purest of salt water, she intended to take upon herself the responsibilities of her sponsors, to strive hard to do her duty, and to this and she had sought while in distress the hospitable haven of Ferrol.

When a grave complaint is laid before a Government by a foreign minister, it is supposed to be actuated by important considerations and sustained by truthful arguments, in accordance with the dignity of the high position from which such complaint issues. It necessarily commands that respectful consideration demanded by international courtesy. The Government at Madrid was unwilling to believe that their trusted official, the Captain-General, had been delinquent in the discharge of the important duties assigned him, but it became necessary that they should be officially advised as to the status of this stranger in the port of Ferrol, thus denounced by such authority as a pirate and all the rest of it, for the pride of the nation would be compromised in extending hospitality to such an enemy to mankind.

The Captain-General was therefore required to furnish the Government with positive evidence as to the nationality of the *Stonewall*. There was no difficulty in doing this. The commanding officer's presence was requested at the office of the Captain-General; the information required by the Government stated, with the pleasing assurance that he was satisfied as to the status of the *Stonewall* but inasmuch as the American Minister had officially made grave charges against the vessel, it became the duty of the Government to place themselves in a position to rebut such charges, if erroneously made; or, if true, to withhold their national hospitality. The required evidence was at hand. The commanding officer presented his commission, showing the authority under which he acted, and the evidence that he was no pirate, nor was the vessel under his command a lawless rover of the sea. He went farther, in order to satisfy the inquiry of the Government—he exhibited a document, bearing the signature of authority—his instructions—stating what the Captain-General, an Admiral in the Spanish navy, very readily appreciated, "that his instructions were for his guidance solely, and that he would be recreant to his trust were he to submit them to the perusal of another." The Admiral considered the evidence sufficient to satisfy the requirements of his Government, and transmitted the same to Madrid. Orders came to permit the continuance of the repairs that had been suspended.

It is eminently proper here to state the ground on which rested the nationality, not only of the *Stonewall*, but of every other Confederate man-of-war, because it was not an uncommon assertion in high places, and eagerly embraced in some quarters, that inasmuch as these vessels under the Confederate flag had been neither built, nor fitted out, nor commissioned in some Confederate port, they were not, in view of international requirements, men-of-war; and consequently not entitled to the hospitality usually accorded to belligerent in neutral ports. It is sufficient to set at rest all quibbling as to the legal status of the *Stonewall*, to quote a few extracts from the very authorities on this point, as laid down in the British Counter Case before the Geneva Convention, and sustained by learned writers on international law: "Where either belligerent is a community or body of persons not recognized by the neutral power as constituting a sovereign state, commissions issued by such belligerent are recognized as acts emanating, not indeed from a sovereign government, but from a person or persons exercising de facto in relation to the war, the powers of a sovereign government.

"Public ships of war, in the service of a belligerent, entering the ports of waters of a neutral, are, by the practice of nations, exempt from the jurisdiction of a neutral power. To withdraw or refuse to recognize this exemption without previous notice, or without such notice to exert or attempt to exert jurisdiction over any such vessel, would be a violation of a common understanding which all nations are bound by good faith to respect.

"A vessel becomes a public ship of war by being armed and commissioned—that is to say, formally invested by order or under the authority of a government with the character of a ship employed in its naval service, and forming part of its marine, for purposes of war. There are no general rules which prescribe how, when or in what form the commissioning must be effected, so as to impress on the vessel the character of a public ship of war. What is essential is that the appointment of a designated officer to the charge and command of a ship likewise designated, be made by the Government or the proper department of it, or under authority delegated by the government or department, and that the charge and command of the ship be taken by the officer so appointed. Customarily, a ship is held to be commissioned when a commissioned officer appointed to her has gone on board of her and hoisted the colors appropriated to the military marines."

The doctrine set forth in the above extracts clearly and incontrovertibly establish the claim of the *Stonewall* to the right and title of a Confederate man-of-war. This claim was immediately recognized by the Government at Madrid, so soon as counter representation was presented, and that international comity usually extended to belligerent was not denied the *Stonewall*. Neither was it withheld from the powerful man-of-war *Niagara*, for she too had put into Ferrol, not crippled nor it want of repairs, but simply to pay a visit, to enjoy the hospitalities of the port, or, as was said, to look after the *Stonewall*. On the same errand arrived the man-of-war steamer *Sacramento* in the port of Corunna, situated in the same crescent of the coast and distant from the entrances to Ferrol only a few miles; so near that the departure of a vessel from the latter would be seen from the former.

The telegraph wires had been brought into requisition, and these two powerful men-of-war summoned to seek out and arrest the mad career of this "rebel rover." They found her, but what then? If actuated simply by curiosity to see and learn something of this novel specimen of naval architecture, their subsequent course would indicate that they had become perfectly satisfied. The *Niagara*, after remaining a day or two in Ferrol, got under way and proceeded to Corunna, where both she and the *Sacramento* remained until after the departure of the *Stonewall*. This was assumed as prima facie evidence that they designed to attack the *Stonewall* immediately on her leaving Ferrol and having got beyond Spanish jurisdiction. Had the *Niagara* remained in Ferrol, she could not, under the international rule, have sailed until the lapse of twenty-four hours after the sailing of the *Stonewall*; but from Corunna she could have sailed on the same day and hour, for every movement of this little vessel was promptly telegraphed to the *Niagara*.

That this procedure is inadmissible in public law is clearly laid down by publicists, and that the international hospitality of the port of Corunna was in this instance violated is clearly deducible from the recognized doctrine as to the treatment of belligerent in neutral ports. It cannot be doubted that the *Niagara* and *Sacramento*, while lying in the port of Corunna, were making that neutral port a "base of naval operations"—a point of departure—where they lay in wait for and whence they designed to issue and attack the *Stonewall* on her going to sea. This is clearly prohibited to belligerent, and a violation of the hospitalities usually extended by the neutral power to the vessel in distress. These two men-of-war had not put into port wanting either repairs or provisions. A striking instance of the argument of "meum and tuum' is here illustrated. It was urged upon the Government at Madrid to eject the *Stonewall* from the port of Ferrol without repairs, without coal or provisions; while the *Niagara* and *Sacramento*, wanting neither, were not only to enjoy the hospitalities of the very near port, but be permitted to make that port a "base of naval operations." It seemed, however, that the "bases" was not suited to the operations for which these vessels had been summoned.

The repairs had been finally completed, the *Stonewall* stripped to lower-masts and standing rigging, in order that neither spars nor running rigging, if shot away, should entangle her propellers—when the commanding officer called to make his acknowledgments to the Captain-General and others, for the hospitalities extended in the work of making her again seaworthy. It was kindly suggested, in view of the great odds against her, that the *Stonewall* should avail herself of the obscurity of the night to make her escape from the superior force supposed to be lying in wait in Corunna. The suggestion was the prompting of gallant, generous spirits, who invariably sympathize with the weaker party in all conflicts. It was gratefully acknowledged, but the *Stonewall* had been built to fight, not to run—especially in this case, where the pursuer would have the speed of two to one of the pursued. Her boats, save one at the stern, had been sent on shore, lest they should obstruct the free use of the after-guns in time of action, for if sunk or captured the boats of her kind friends would be amply sufficient to rescue from a watery grave those who might be on the surface. The gallant spirits on board of the *Stonewall* were not dismayed in the face of this superior force; but trusting in the Omnipotent Ruler, and in the justice of the cause represented by that emblem at the peak, they were of one mind to do their duty. The small sum of Government money on hand was sent on shore, and the officers sent, each one, his watch—a memento of his last gallant deeds—to some dear relative.

One bright spring morning, after the men had broken their fast, the *Stonewall* put to sea, to face the momentous ordeal awaiting her, as it was supposed. She was followed by a very imposing Spanish frigate, whose object—doubtless coupled with a little curiosity to witness a fight—was to see that in the impending conflict between the belligerent there should be no violation of Spanish territory. A few minutes only served to put them both in blue water. Doubtless the anticipations of the frigate's officers were wrought to the highest pitch of interesting excitement; but they were destined to disappointment. When the *Stonewall* had passed beyond the marine league from the Spanish coast, the frigate fired a gun, from which the inference was that she had got beyond Spanish jurisdiction. Assuming an imaginary line between the headlands of the crescent-formed coast, the *Stonewall* stood on that line, to and for, taking care not to approach either headland within three marine miles. The *Niagara* and *Sacramento*, lying in Corunna, were plainly in sight, with steam up and issuing from the steam pipe.

The sloping of the mountains, both north and south, presented a beautiful panoramic spectacle. Curiosity had led thousands of persons from both Corunna and Ferrol, as one some gala occasion, to assemble on these mountain slopes to witness the anticipated conflict; but they, too, were destined to disappointment, and as the day waned, convinced that no performance would come off, they retired to their homes, as it was reported, giving went to their feelings in no measured terms, against those actors who were to come from Corunna and without whom there could be no performance.

The dinner hour of the crew had come, while the *Stonewall* stood on the line she had taken back and forth, her screws slowly revolving, seeming to think there was a screw loose in Corunna. The men had been at quarters—that is, at their several stations in time of action—for some hours since an early breakfast, sitting, standing, walking by the side of their respective guns, chatting in low tones among themselves as cheerfully as though they were going into some home port. They ate their dinner at quarters, for the distance between the *Stonewall* and here anxiously looked for friends from Corunna was too short to admit of the usual formalities of a set dinner. They imagined that after the settlement of the "slight unpleasantness," should any of them happen to turn up alive, they would be invited to a more formal dinner on board of the *Niagara* or *Sacramento*.

Thus passed the day, in hopeless anticipation. The spectators on the mountain side had disappeared, and the Spanish frigate, seeing there would be no violation to Her Majesty's territory, had returned to Ferrol, while the *Stonewall*, at the close of the day, abandoning all hopes of meeting her fellow-travelers of the sea, for they evidently desired none of her company, stood on her course for Lisbon. It became necessary to put into this port, though so near, because the *Stonewall* had taken on board in Ferrol only a limited quantity of coals. This was done in order to enable her to carry the bow gun as high as possible above the sea, and thereby be more efficient. She conceived the chances of victory greatly against her, and that she would not require coals if captured or sent to the bottom.

Arrived in Lisbon, and while in the act of taking on board a supply of coals, the *Stonewall* was honored with an official visit, the object of which was to ascertain when she was going to sea. The tone and nervous manner accompanying this inquiry were strongly indicative of an earnest desire that she should leave the port without delay. This Portuguese reception, in contrast with that of the Spanish, was very sticking. The official was given to understand that the *Stonewall* had availed herself of the hospitalities of Lisbon only with the view of procuring coals, and that if he would kindle expedite the delivery of them on board she would hasten her departure. The truth was the authorities on shore had received information of the sailing of the *Niagara* and *Sacramento* from Corunna, and, doubtless, the phantom of a naval engagement in the Tagus floated before their eyes. Before the setting of the sun on that mild, calm day, these two men-of-war appeared off the entrance to the port. This, in no small degree, added to the nervousness on shore. It had certainly the appearance, if not confirmation strong, of a pursuit, and seemed as though these vessels had not seen enough of the *Stonewall*. But this idea was dispelled by their coming into the port and anchoring. By so doing they subjected themselves to the international rule—prohibiting them from leaving the port until the lapse of twenty-four hours after the departure of the *Stonewall*. The weather was good, the sea was smooth, and it was argued that if they desired to meet the *Stonewall* in action they would have remained outside. Perhaps the weather was too good, the sea too smooth—conditions most favorable to the *Stonewall*, for in a heavy sea she could not have fought her guns at all, while the *Niagara* could have not only fought hers, but, towering above, could have run over her, provided she had not run "afoul" of her most salient point, the spur at the bow. It is not, however, my purpose to express an opinion as to how the *Stonewall* might have been destroyed.

The coaling of the vessel was not finished until after the night had set in, when the pilot of the port refused to take her out to sea, as he did not consider it safe to attempt doing so. Although the quiet of the night, for all was calm and still, had not brought peaceful rest to the slumbers of the Lisbon officials while these belligerent lay in their port, relief came at early dawn when they saw this troublesome little craft turn her bow towards the ocean and proceed down the river. On passing the *Niagara* and *Sacramento* (they had anchored about a mile below), the commander of the *Stonewall* was pleased to see on the quarter-deck of the *Niagara* his quondam shipmate and friend, bearing the rank of commodore. They had cruised in the West Indies on board of the same ship, the "old *Erie*," when one was sailing master, the other a green midshipman. This midshipman, ere the end of the cruise, had seen some service, had passed some dangers during the three years spent in those boisterous latitudes. When the *Erie* was visited by that dire disease, the yellow fever, it pervaded the ship from cabin to forecastle, striking down the captain, most of the officers and forty of her crew in the course of a few days. The captain, ere he became too ill, gave this midshipman orders, with the appointment of an acting lieutenant, to take the ship into Norfolk. This was safely done after a stormy passage, and anchoring off the navy hospital the sick were sent on shore. It may be asked, what this little episode has to do with the *Stonewall*? Nothing, save that this midshipman, after the lapse of years, became the commander of the craft whose short life and shortcomings are here treated of.

Taking an unceremonious leave of her friends lying quietly in the Tagus, for they seemed to think here unworthy their steel, the *Stonewall* stood out to sea, touched at Tanariffe, the most eligible point from which to cross the Atlantic, and filling up with coals, shaped her course so as to reach the latitude of the trade winds in the shortest possible time, where her sails would come into requisition. It was advisable to avail of those winds in order to economize coals, as she could not carry enough to steam the whole way across. It was also important to have enough on board for the emergency of falling in with any of those cruisers that it was supposed were keeping a sharp lookout for her. But the lookout could not have been very much on the alert, inasmuch as no man-of-war was seen throughout the entire passage to Havana, although the conclusion was inevitable that she must call either at Bermuda or Nassau to replenish her bunkers. That her departure from Lisbon was speedily made known in the United States cannot admit of a doubt. Her arrival at Ferrol had been made the subject of diplomatic correspondence with the Government at Madrid, and before here departure from Lisbon she was honored with a visit from a gentleman attached to the American Legation at Madrid, who availed himself of the privilege granted all persons wishing to visit the vessel, but omitted the observance of the usual courtesies on such occasions and presented his card at the gang-way from his boat, only when in the act of going on shore in company with many other visitors. He doubtless satisfied his curiosity, saw all that he cared to see, perhaps a little more, for there was nothing to conceal on board of the *Stonewall*, and boasted on shore of the gallantry of his conduct; though it was closely akin to that of a spy—a character recognized by the laws of war as entitled, if caught, to hanging; but the dignity of his position should have deterred him from the commission of an act of vulgarity. There was a low bravado in boasting of the accomplishment of a design in which there could be no detection, unbecoming the office he held and the gentleman he assumed to be. His acquaintance would, doubtless, have been politely acknowledged by the commanding officer, and quarters suited to his rank assigned him.

On the slow, monotonous passage across the Atlantic, nothing worthy of note occurred, save the appearance of a clipper-built bark, bound from Baltimore to Rio the Janeiro, laden with flour. She was under all sail, going rapidly through the water, with a free wind. There is but one object, either in nature or art, given to the eyes of man to behold more beautiful than the ship under full sail. The French flag was hoisted at the peak of the *Stonewall*, and immediately the American flag was flown by the bark. When she had come within a suitable distance, the French flag was hauled down, the Confederate hoisted in its place, and a nine-inch shell thrown across her bow. The music of such a projectile, flying through the air with ignited fuse, is not that of the Aeolian harp. With flowing sheets, the bark came up into wind as gracefully as are the movements of the swan when gliding through the waters of a placid lake. Here was presented an unpleasant conflict of duty and inclination. To destroy such a craft was repulsive; and yet duty might demand it. The commander of the *Stonewall* would gladly avail himself of a justifiable excuse to avoid such an alternative. The captain of the bark was brought on board. His troubled appearance may be more easily imagined than described. In great anguish he declared that he had been in that trade many years, and this was the first time he had brought his wife and little daughter with him. Here was an appeal that added to the embarrassment of the situation, not easily disregarded. The *Stonewall* had no accommodations for such passengers, and moreover this was not the kind of game she was in pursuit of. The captain of the bark was given to understand that a bond would be required of him for the release of his vessel, and that he should assure his owners they were indebted solely to his wife and daughter for the rescue of their vessel and cargo from the flames. A heavier oppression was never lifted from the human breast, and his countenance beamed with all the kindly feelings the human heart is susceptible of. He begged that he might be allowed to present to the *Stonewall* some of the luxuries with which his pantry was supplied. His offer was gratefully acknowledged, but declined. The bark went on her way rejoicing, and the *Stonewall* pursued her course to Nassau, a convenient port at which to procure coals.

She did not enter the harbor, but received the coals outside—an unpleasant indication, for there were rumors on shore, though not authentic, which made the *Stonewall* an unwelcome visitor. She was permitted to take on board coals sufficient for the passage to Havana.

Arrived at Havana, the usual visits of ceremony made, the vessel was admitted to the customary hospitalities of the port, with no limitation as to the time she would be permitted to remain. Mark the difference of the *Stonewall's* reception here and that at Nassau! The sad intelligence here received, which I need not describe, was not to be questioned, and the feelings of both officers and men many be imagined, but not expressed.

The little craft that had so bravely breasted the storms of tempestuous seas, to do her duty in a holy cause, found herself a useless hulk, an encumbrance.

The political state of affairs in the Confederacy had not been as yet officially announced to the authorities of Cuba. When that shall have been done, the *Stonewall* would no longer be entitled to the flag she so proudly bore off Ferrol.

Negotiations were entered into with the authorities of Havana, which resulted in the acceptance of the *Stonewall* as a present, subject to the decision of the Queen of Spain. By the terms of the agreement, there was advanced to the *Stonewall* the sum of $16,000 in order to pay the officers and crew what was due them, as set forth in the books of the paymaster. A much larger sum would have been advanced, and was suggested, but her commander was in honor bound to the crew for the payment of what was due them—the vessel being fully responsible—and he would receive nothing more.

An Admiral, with his attendant staff of officers, came on board to formally receive the *Stonewall*. The delicacy and courtesy of this distinguished officer on this occasion will ever be remembered. He appreciated the painful position of the commanding officer, and before proceeding to the details involved, remarked to him, "My barge is at your service, and Captain—- will attend you to the arsenal, and thence to your quarters on shore." Officials of some governments would have avoided a Confederate officer at that time as they would have done a contagious pestilence. Captain—performed the duty assigned him with all that courtesy for which the Spanish race has ever been pre-eminently distinguished.

Thus terminated the career of the *Stonewall* under the Confederate flag.

What was her ultimate fate? It is said she came into the possession of the United States Government, was sold to the Japanese Government, and was wrecked during a severe typhoon while lying at anchor.

It may be proper to mention, as a pertinent episode in the last days of the *Stonewall*, that among the arrivals which soon followed her into Havana was an imposing looking American man-of-war steamer. She anchored only a very short distance off. One morning a letter was handed to the commander of the *Stonewall*, which bore the signature of an old acquaintance—the captain of the man-of-war close by. The purport of this communication was suggesting the propriety of a surrender of the *Stonewall* to him. Its receipt was promptly acknowledged, and although its kind suggestions were fully appreciated, they were politely declined.

The *Stonewall* was in a position to present herself to the Captain-General, or, through him, to the Queen of Spain; but she was not the craft to surrender on demand or solicitation.

2. European Warships

An unsung and mostly unknown naval hero of the Southern war effort was James Dunwoody Bulloch. Without his untiring efforts waged far from his beloved native land's embattled shore, there would have been no *Alabama*, no *Florida*, no *Shenandoah*, and no *Stonewall*. Numerous blockade-runners and hundreds of tons of war material would never have arrived at Southern ports. The decision to appoint Bulloch as naval purchasing agent in Europe was probably one of the best decisions that Secretary Mallory ever made.

James D. Bulloch was born near Savannah, Georgia, on June 25, 1823, and entered the U. S. Navy in 1839, where he served briefly in California during the Mexican War. He then commanded several naval and commercial mail steamers, and after a career spanning approximately fourteen years, he resigned his commission in 1854 for personal reasons. By the outbreak of the War Between the States, he was a competent and seasoned naval officer. When Georgia seceded, he offered his services to the Confederacy, and soon after the firing on Fort Sumter, Mallory sent him to Europe to "buy and build" a navy overseas. (Moebs, *Confederate States Navy Research Guide*, p. 282.)

Commander Bulloch was very diligent in keeping the naval secretary informed of his actions in England and France. Following is a selection of his correspondence to Mallory that is preserved in the *Official Navy Records*. [RTC]

Letters from Commander James D. Bulloch, CSN, to Secretary of the Navy Stephen R. Mallory

Official Records Navy, Series II, Volume II, pp. 222–226, 235–239, 423–425, 588–590,

LIVERPOOL, *July 21, 1862.*

SIR: The cipher appointed to be used in my communications with the Navy Department is such as not to admit of lengthy correspondence, and I have therefore been compelled to set it aside in most instances and to adopt instead a somewhat vague mode of expression in the various reports I have had the honor to make to you, except when, as in the present instance a private messenger has enabled me to be full and explicit.

The duties assigned me when I left the Confederacy in February last, were not, however, of a complicated character, and did not involve much obscurity in the mode by which their progress could be explained. In brief, I was directed to complete the second ship contracted for by me in Europe for the C. S. Navy and to equip her as a cruising man-of-war whenever I might find the attempt feasible, operating afterwards against the enemy in whatever sea and in whatever manner my judgment might indicate as most effective to injure or cripple his resources. These instructions were written in a manner so kind and flattering that I did not hesitate to express my gratitude to you personally, nor to add that you had excited "ambitious hopes" I had reasonable expectations of realizing. Almost at the moment of departure from Wilmington, I was directed, on my arrival in England, to examine into the subject of armorclad ships, and to assist Commander North (who had been previously sent to England to buy or build a vessel of that description), either by advice or otherwise in the object of his mission. Finding on my arrival that Commander North had, as he informed me, specific orders to buy or build a frigate and that he had already made arrangements to contract for such a vessel as soon as the necessary funds arrived, I devoted myself to the especial duties assigned me, but as vessels capable of acting efficiently either in the attack or defense of our coast and its estuaries must necessarily be of light draft, I put myself in communication with an eminent iron shipbuilder, whose position enabled him to obtain the official reports of all experiments, with the view of determining the minimum draft compatible with seaworthiness and invulnerability. It resulted from a close calculation of weights and form of model that by using turrets instead of broadside batteries, whereby the sides would be relieved of much strain and the heavy weights be thrown near the center, a vessel might be built of about the following dimensions: Length, 220 feet; extreme breadth 42 feet; draft, with crew and stores for three months, 15 feet; engines, 3:50 horsepower, nominal; speed, 10½ knots; tonnage, 1,800 tons. I immediately directed the plans and scale drawings of such a ship to be made, and reported to you by letter that I would forward them as soon as they were ready and an opportunity offered. While this was going on, I think about the middle of May, Commander North received a remittance of $150,000, unaccompanied by any letter of advice, and supposing it to be for the uses mentioned in his original instructions, he prepared at once to close up a contract for an armored frigate and notified me of the fact.

I advised him of the fact that a ship of less size, cost, and draft could be built, but he deemed his orders specific and peremptory as to class of ship and contracted for a frigate of 3,200 tons accordingly.

About the 10th of June I received your letter of April 30, in which you say, "I write to Commander Semmes to take command of the largest of the two vessels built by you," and "I write also to Lieutenant North to take command of the other vessel," and you direct me to furnish these officers with funds for cruising expenses. As to myself you say, "I hasten to urge upon you the necessity of having at least two armored vessels built and equipped at the earliest moment. Act upon your own judgment to save time. British enquiry and experiments and your own knowledge of the bars and waters of our country will enable you to act advisedly." To render these instructions possible of fulfillment you inform me that $1,000,000 has already been placed to my credit with the house of Messrs. Fraser, Trenholm & Co., and that you hope to increase the amount to two millions very soon. Fortunately, I was in a position to act promptly upon these instructions. The drawings and plans ordered were nearly finished, and on the day after the receipt of your letter I requested the parties who had been assisting me all along to make a tender for the contract, having previously provided myself with the estimates of other builders who competed for the Admiralty contracts. In a few days the price was agreed upon and I gave a verbal order for two vessels, so that no time should be lost in contracting for the large quantity of armor plates required, while the actual contract could be formally drawn up, stamped, and signed.

By giving the order for both ships to the same builder I got the advantage of a reduction of £1,250 on the cost of each, while by adopting the same size and model of ship and a like form of engine they could both be completed in very nearly the same time. Besides this, experience has taught me that it is far safer to keep our business as little extended as possible, as otherwise the chance of our transactions being ferreted out by the Federal spies, who abound even in this country, is greatly increased. For full descriptions of these vessels I beg to refer you to the drawings.

The internal arrangements for officers and crew, position of magazines and shell rooms, and some other details are drawn as now proposed, to give a finish to the plan; a clause in the contract gives me the right to modify or alter them as experience during the progress of the work may suggest.

To illustrate the drawings I will give a brief explanation: Each ship will be plated from 3½ feet below the water line to the waterways of the upper deck. For 120 feet of the midship section covering the entire engine space and the principal magazine, the armor will be 4½ inches thick, and will taper very gradually to 4, 3½, 3, etc., until where the plates join the stem and stern posts the thickness will be 2 inches. This tapering of the plates is necessary to keep the displacement within bounds, and is not, I think, too great, as the cant of the frames at the extremities and the angles of the bow and stern will render it impossible for a shot to strike squarely upon any portion of a plate. To provide, however, against such a contingency, the two ends will be cut up into a number of water-tight compartments, the bulkheads being of light and thin, but tough Low Moor iron. The armor plates will be backed by 12 inches of teak amidships, tapering to 6 at the ends, both resting upon a shelf, as shown in the drawing, and bolted through the inner skin of the ship. All through the midship section on each side will be a strong bulkhead about 16 feet from the center line, the end of which will be riveted to athwartship bulkheads, thus making, as it were, an inner ship. The space between these fore-and-aft bulkheads and the sides of the ship proper will be divided into a number of water-tight compartments, so that if a shot should break the outside plating or a blow from an opposing ram should crush in the outer side, only one or more of these compartments would be filled, and it is calculated that filling the whole of them on one side would only list the ship a few inches. Upon each ship will be three fixed turrets, very nearly in the positions shown, made of 5½-inch iron, backed with 12 inches of teak.

The bottom, or floors, of these turrets will be of iron, with smooth upper surfaces for bearing the guns, either mounted upon turntables or otherwise, as may hereafter be determined, the whole shored up by a series of stanchions resting upon the keelsons and frames of the floor. The decks will rise gradually from the sides to the center and be plated with iron five-eighths of an inch thick at the waterways, increasing to three-fourths at the base of the turrets, and there will be an open watercourse all around the upper deck, as shown in the drawing. It is known that five-eights iron plates will break up shells and hollow shot (Admiral Halsted, R. N., on iron-cased ships), and as no vertical fire can be thrown from one ship upon another it is thought that this deck covering will be sufficient. The bulwarks will be made to drop outboard abreast of the turrets for a sufficient distance to give the required sweep of the guns in training, and the ports will be so constructed as to allow sufficient fore-and-aft range and vertical movement of piece with the smallest possible external opening. I have had suggested to me by one of the firm who are to build the ships a very ingenious plan for fitting "port shields," which I have reserved for consideration. The great difficulty is in handling them, if of sufficient weight really to protect the ports. It is proposed to let them slide up and down in grooves, to have under each shield (and in a turret-armed ship there will not be many) a small cylinder and piston, the rod connecting with the lower part of the shield. The process is simple. Open a steam valve, the shield rises and covers the port; open an exhaust valve, the shield slides down by its own weight and opens the port.

Commander James D. Bulloch (Scharf, *History of the Confederate States Navy*).

I propose to rig these ships as barks, with iron lower masts, supported by three large wire shrouds on each side. The lower yards will be trussed in their proper places, and the lower topsail yards will be trussed to the heads of the lower masts as in Rowe's rig. The topmasts will be of wood so fitted that in action or steaming head to wind they can be lowered into the hollow of the lower masts, the upper topsail rolling up as the yard is lowered, after the manner known as "Cunningham's patent." The gaffs will be of iron, also fitted to the masts, with joints admitting of their being eased over as the wind may require or being dropped up and down the masts when the sails are not in use. The object of making the spars of iron is that should a mast be shot away its weight will carry it down at once with the topmast inside of it, and the danger of fouling the screw be avoided. The bowsprit will be fitted with a hinge so as to be turned inboard when the ship is to be used as a ram.

The apartments for officers and the quarters for crew will be lighted and ventilated from the deck above, as shown by the circular spots in the deck plan. You will perceive that the quarters for firemen and stokers are entirely distinct from the berthdeck of the seamen and marines, and are in direct proximity to the engines. The athwart ship bulkheads are continuous from the floors to the spardeck, but each will have a sliding water-tight door, so that there can be communication from one end of the ship to the other on the accommodation deck, if it should be necessary. In conclusion, there will be an inside water-tight bottom or floor about 2½ feet above the outer plates, upon which the engines, boilers, etc., will rest, forming a tank or compartment which can be filled at pleasure, to preserve the proper immersion of the armor plating when the ship is light from the consumption of fuel. The floor frames will be the full depth of this space.

The above is a mere outline sketch of what the ships are intended to be; a detailed description would be too lengthy for our limited mode of communication. As the work progresses I will make reports in cipher, which I trust you will be able to understand by reference to the drawings. I am fully aware of the superior advantages of the revolving turrets, but the admiralty have bought Captain Coles' patent and have not yet decided whether private builders will be allowed to use it. I have all the plans and drawings, however, and it will not be too late to make the change three months hence.

The first of these ships will be ready for sea in March and the second in May, 1863. Cost of each fully equipped, except battery and magazine fittings, £93,750. The parties of the first part of these contracts have shown great faith in the stability of the Confederate Government, as well as great confidence in me personally, and I sincerely hope that the remittances will be such as to admit of the installments being regularly paid. I have at present about £140,000, out of which is to be taken £20,000 as a cruising fund for Commander Semmes, as you direct in your letter of May 3d. I am looking most anxiously for the arrival of Captain Semmes. His ship is all ready, and the American minister is besieging the Foreign Office with demands to stop her.

I am, very respectfully, your obedient servant,

JAMES D. BULLOCH,
Commander, C. S. Navy,

Hon. S. R. MALLORY,
Secretary of the Navy.

LIVERPOOL, *August 11, 1862.*

SIR: I have already informed you by letter, as well as by private messenger, that the *Alabama* is safely clear of British waters and that another vessel, with her battery and ordnance stores, had previously sailed for a concerted rendezvous. I have now the satisfaction to report that Commander Semmes, with his officers, has arrived here and will sail to-morrow in a steamer chartered for the purpose to join the *Alabama*. It has been deemed advisable that I should go with Commander Semmes as far as the rendezvous to smooth away as much as possible his embarrassments and difficulties in assuming the command of an entirely new ship with a strange and untried crew. My absence will not be prolonged beyond one month, and I have arranged all other business so that there will be no delay or interruption in the progress of other work. As soon as it would be safe to allude to the movements of the *Alabama* in detail you shall have an account of her escape from the *Tuscarora* and the manner in which a crew was got on board. Suffice it for the present to say that the United States consul neither by the strictest espionage nor the most shameless false witnesses has been able to prove any violation of the foreign enlistment act or of her Majesty's neutrality proclamation. When finally armed the *Alabama* will have a battery consisting of a 7-inch 100-pounder rifled gun, Blakely pattern, 84 cwt.; one 8-inch solid shot 68-pounder, smooth bore, 108 cwt.; and six 6-inch 32-pounder guns, 55 cwt. each. The 8-inch gun is of course provided with shell as well as shot, and I have provided seventy 42-pound spherical shot for the rifled gun in addition to the elongated shell and shot peculiarly adapted to its character. It will give me the greatest satisfaction to know that Commander Semmes is fairly afloat in the *Alabama* and confident of his ability to do good service with her. I shall watch with pride her coming success, although I can not overcome the feeling of disappointment I experienced when first informed I was not to command her myself. The papers necessary to show all the plans, equipments, etc., of the ship are too bulky to be sent by any means now offering, but you shall have all these points as soon as possible.

I have now to call your attention to a subject of so personal a character that I regret the necessity of alluding to it at all, but I should be wanting in self-respect and in consideration for the commission I hold if I did not make some comments upon the peculiarities of my position. When in February last you did me the honor to send me a commission as commander in the Navy I felt fully aware that your act would be criticized and the traditional ideas of naval officers on the subject of relative rank would be shocked, and I therefore promptly expressed to you my reluctance to accept that particular commission. My knowledge of human nature, furthermore, instructed me that the criticisms of the service would not be confined to the supposed offense against the traditions, but would in some way or other find vent in detractions or perhaps only insinuations more or less personal to myself. In the letter acknowledging the receipt of my commission as commander I requested you to change it to that of lieutenant and to place me in the list where I should have been had I never resigned from the old service. It mattered not to me one iota by what title I was called. I felt sure that a Government just struggling into existence, and necessarily dependent upon the united exertions of its adherents for success, would not irretrievably bind itself to a system of promotion in the military and naval services such as existed under the old Government of the United States, a system which proved itself, even in time of peace, so destructive to the efficiency of the Navy that it resulted in the forced removal of many officers from the active list by the action of the well-known "Board of Fifteen." The history of this event is familiar to you. The officers composing the board were personally and collectively abused both in and out of the service. Congress almost wholly reversed their action, and the Navy was divided into two acrimonious parties which never could have become reconciled. In view of such experiences I felt sure that however the Army or Navy list might be arranged in the beginning zeal and merit would be left to find their proper level during the progress of the war and that the higher grades of the service would be fairly opened to all who entered it in any rank. I was willing to compete upon this understanding for naval advancement. I regret to learn from a few officers who have been or are now in Europe that much feeling has been evinced on the subject of my being in the naval service at all, and I learn with surprise that I am by some regarded as an interloper. Private advices inform me that influence has been used to prevent my being employed in the active duties of the sea, it seeming to be thought by a certain class of naval men that I should be sufficiently rewarded by the appointment of Navy agent or constructor in Europe. These gentlemen seem willing to grant me the ability necessary to build and equip ships, but are unwilling that I should be put to the test of proving my ability to command them. Now, sir, I appeal with confidence to you to bear me out in the assertion that I have never sought reward of any kind for services rendered; I simply requested to be placed anywhere upon the Navy list, that I might serve our common country in the sphere which education and habit rendered me most fit to occupy. It never entered my mind to imagine that the employment of any man in the service could or would give offense, nor that an effort would be seriously made to keep anyone in the background. For myself I would rather be a private in one of the numerous regiments of my native State than to hold the highest commission in the Navy if I am never to exercise its legitimate functions. One or two naval officers have told me that Congress had pledged itself to give any officer who resigned from the U. S. service the same pay and the same relative rank that he held in that service, and that this relative rank, etc., should be perpetuated. This would imply a bargain, and I am sure that the majority of the officers in the C.S. Navy did not sell their allegiance. I have the satisfaction to know many who have seemingly followed their natural impulses in joining the cause of justice and their native land.

Having already built two ships for the Navy, the second of which is as fine a vessel of her class as any service can show, and which I was to have commanded myself, I am, as you have been informed, busily at work upon two armor-clad ships of entirely new design. In no event and under no circumstances of action upon your part will I relax my efforts to complete them in an efficient state, but I earnestly beg leave to urge my claim to command one of these ships in person. I desire, if you approve the designs sent you, to be allowed to complete these ships without interference on the part of others, and to select the one for my own command. Whoever you may appoint to command the other shall receive my cheerful assistance in equipping her for sea, but as I can alone be responsible for the character of the ships, I respectfully request to be untrammeled in the completion of their designs. I trust I shall never be called upon to be more explicit in what I have said relative to my position in the Navy, but if it ever becomes necessary my correspondence and the information I have received from others will convince you that I am not without just cause of complaint. In concluding this disagreeable subject, I wish to emphatically declare that my disappointment in not commanding the *Alabama*, as you originally designed, is only the natural regret at parting with a piece of handiwork which had come to completion under my own eye and the future career of which I had allowed my imagination to foreshadow, and that it has no reference whatever to the officer you have appointed to the actual command. Commander Semmes was the first officer to show the Confederate flag upon the high seas, and his services in the *Sumter* entitle him to a prominent place. Recognizing this claim, when we first met in England I freely offered him the command of the ship and expressed my readiness to serve under him in any capacity. He declined this offer, wholly, I believe, from generous motives to myself; indeed, he said as much to me at the time. I shall, therefore, follow his career in the *Alabama* with unalloyed interest, and shall hear of his successes with pleasure, on private as well as public grounds. I wish equally to declare that I do not complain of your individual action toward myself. I gratefully acknowledge the continued confidence you have placed in me and the flattering manner in which you have left important transactions to be managed at my discretion. What I deprecate is the position a certain clique of naval officers seem desirous to assign me, and my simple appeal to you, as the head of the Navy, is that I shall not be debarred from entering into competition fairly for its honors. If I had no ambition beyond that of a private agent to do the work assigned him properly, I should be content to labor in a quiet sphere, but I aspire to purely professional distinction, and I feel that to toil here, as it were, in exile and then to turn over the result of my labors for the use of others is willingly to consign myself to oblivion. To retain the commission of commander and yet never to command a ship seems to me a mockery. I have no fear but that you will do me justice in the duties I am now performing, and that you will appreciate the difficulties I have had to overcome and which still confront me, but my real profession is that of the sea, and I have many friends who will be seriously disappointed if I am never heard of upon that element. Trusting that you will not misunderstand the spirit of this appeal, I close the subject.

The vessel which has sailed with the battery, etc., for the *Alabama* has also on board 250 tons of coal. I have bought her for the Navy Department, especially to run as a transport, and Commander Semmes can employ her regularly to carry coal from point to point as he may require, sending her back to me for additional supply when required. I have furnished Lieutenant Sinclair with minute drawings and specifications and the identical contract under which the *Alabama* was built, and he desires to duplicate her, but until the funds necessary to complete the contracts now under way have been received it will be out of my power to do anything more for him. The armor-clad ships are getting on finely, and I have great hopes that I shall be allowed to use the revolving turrets. On my return I hope to find this point settled. If the war continues until spring these vessels may yet have important and perhaps conclusive work in the question of the blockade. The difficulty of getting them fairly to sea will be very great, however, and I confess that thus far I can not see clearly the means to be adopted. The means I adopt for sending my letters render it unnecessary to disguise them in cipher, yet I refrain from mentioning names as much as possible and from speaking of events until they have some time transpired. I shall continue to avail myself of every opportunity to write you.

I have the honor to be, very respectfully, Your obedient servant,

JAMES D. BULLOCH.

HON. S.R. MALLORY,
Secretary of the Navy.

LONDON, *May 16, 1863.*

SIR: Having been detained here last night, I avail myself of the time thus gained to add something to my hurried dispatch of yesterday.

You have doubtless learned from the Northern press, as well as from my cipher dispatches, that the British Government is now enforcing the provisions of the foreign enlistment act in a manner most injurious and damaging to us. I long since reported to you that it would not be advisable to attempt any further operations in England, and that I would go to France to build the additional screw ships you had so frequently requested me to put in course of construction. There has been no delay in this matter except such as has arisen from the lack of money, for I have all along had approved plans and specifications, and have made many efforts to induce builders to take contracts; but have not succeeded except in the one instance I have already reported to you, because I have neither had means to make the first payments nor such securities as would be taken in pledge. The drafts for $1,000,000 each you sent me some months since could not be used, inasmuch as no Treasury bonds have been sold, and the cotton certificates have thus far proved the only source from which money could be raised. You informed me some time since that $1,000,000 in such certificates would be sent me, and, depending upon their receipt, I went to France to push forward new ships. I felt quite at ease because I had understood, and Mr. Slidell was under the impression, that French builders, being anxious to establish business connections with the South and to compete with England for the custom of the Confederate States after the war, would be willing to deal with us largely upon credit. Under this impression, I contracted with two firms, one at Bordeaux and one at Nantes, for four corvettes, which can not fail from their designs to be very fast and which, for obvious reasons of policy and convenience, I have proposed to arm with the French "Canon Rayé de Trente," equivalent to the English gun of 6.4, a most formidable gun, the shell particularly so. Each ship will be capable of carrying 12 of these guns.

The contract being duly made, I found that French builders, like the English, wanted money, and were not willing to lay down the ships unless I could give security in the shape of cotton certificates for the two first payments. I have sought through our financial agent to arrange for other modes of procedure, and he thinks he will be able, now that General McRae has arrived, to furnish me the means of going on with two of these ships; but unless you have arranged for me to receive a portion of the loan through Mr. McRae, or the promised $1,000,000 of cotton certificates reaches me, the progress of this work will be indefinitely delayed. I think it essential that our financial affairs in Europe should be put upon a more settled footing, and that there should be some one with authority to regulate them. At present each agent of the Government is very naturally struggling to get possession of such funds as are required for his own immediate operations, and the deplorable spectacle of a competitive struggle between officers and other agents is presented. I beg here, very respectfully, to suggest that when an order is sent to any agent of the Navy Department, the source from which he is to draw the means of executing it be at the same time pointed out, and the money or its equivalent security be at once placed at his disposal. Then would be avoided a repetition of what has lately occurred, namely, one officer buying a ship for cash in one yard, while payments were overdue upon a ship building in an adjoining yard, under, contract with another officer of the same department. It is essential to the credit of your department that actual engagements should be provided for, or if advisable suspended, with satisfactory compensation or forfeit to the contractor before new engagements or operations are entered into. A creditor will not be satisfied to wait indefinitely for payment when he finds his debtor making purchases elsewhere for cash. These French ships are larger than the *Alabama*, in order to get greater speed, as you urged me to accomplish if possible. The builders have agreed to complete one in eight months and to have them all at sea in ten months. Four or five weeks have already passed since the completion of the contracts, and there will be further delay unless I get money from Mr. McRae. The time is not, however, wholly lost, as models are being made and material collected. I only now fear that for want of power to direct, or control other expenditures I may find some new contract made, with money supplied to another officer which will eventually lag as these are doing. In fine, I respectfully suggest that you direct existing contracts to be either completed or set aside, as you may deem proper, and furthermore, that your appoint the order of precedence which shall be assigned to the various proposed operations of your department, so that when there is a scarcity of money, it may be applied to the best interests of the country, and not be indefinitely divided among several undertakings, whereby none can be fully, accomplished.

I fear to write even by the hands of so gallant and intelligent an officer as will carry this, on the subject of your letter of the 12th instant. Be sure that I will give the matter my most earnest attention. The matter must be arranged with the greatest prudence and caution, an indiscreet remark or boast would be ruinous, and I shall therefore mention the subject to none but Mr. Mason and Mr. Slidell, unless it be necessary to employ them in the management of the affair. The necessity of this move, has, of course, created delay, but if my plans, which thus far look favorably, succeed, we will make up this lost time. The officers you mentioned have arrived. Please send more lieutenants, not here but to the Continent. Discretion is most essential, and I should feel rather embarrassed by having any more midshipmen. We can get this class of officers bye and bye in a manner I will hereafter suggest. As soon as I feel safe you shall have further-particulars. Our efforts will, I think, be successful if our tongues can only be kept quiet.

In view of the subsequent operations you suggest it may be necessary for me to send an officer to communicate plans to you, as some additional men will be required. Offensive operations require greater preparation and organization than those which are simply desultory or defensive, and besides the expedition you now propose will require a combined movement of other forces in order to secure the results of success.

I must pray you to excuse the untidiness of this dispatch. I am writing in great haste to leave for Paris by the next train.

I am, sir, very respectfully, your obedient servant,

JAMES D. BULLOCH

Hon. S. R. MALLORY,
Secretary of the Navy.

LIVERPOOL, *February 18, 1864*

SIR: I have the honor to enclose herewith duplicate of my dispatch of November 26, 1863, on the subject of the ironclads and corvettes building for us in France wherein I ventured to express some apprehension as to the policy the Imperial Government would pursue when the ships approached completion. That policy has been pronounced sooner than I then anticipated and the Emperor, through his minister of foreign affairs and of marine, has formally notified the builders that the ironclads can not be permitted to sail, and that the corvettes must not be armed in France, but must be nominally sold to some foreign merchant and dispatched as ordinary trading vessels. I believe that Mr. Arman, the builder of the ironclads, has acted in a perfectly loyal manner throughout these transactions, and sincerely regrets the present turn of events. He has proposed that a nominal sale of the vessels should be made to a Danish banker, as if for his own Government, and that there should be a private agreement providing for a redelivery to us at some point beyond the jurisdiction of France. This would simply be substituting France for England, Denmark for France, and the Danish banker for Messrs. Bravay, and if the two most powerful maritime nations in the world have not been able to resist the importunities of the United States, it would be simply absurd to hope for success through the medium of Denmark, a weak nation at best, and just now struggling almost hopelessly for her very existence. The proposition was therefore declined as it only involved an increased and useless expenditure of money without a hope of profit, and the ironclads will be sold if possible as you will perceive from the enclosed letter marked B and dated 8th February, 1864. This case may be summed up in a very few words; it is one of simple deception. I never should have entered into such large undertakings except with the assurance of success. I was, not individually, but as an agent of the Confederate States, invited to build ships of war in France, and so far at least as the corvettes are concerned received every possible assurance that they might be actually armed in the ports of construction. During three or four months after the contracts were made the work advanced very rapidly, but latterly there has been a gradual falling off which caused me to fear that the builders had received some discouraging intimations from the Government. I am not satisfied on this point, but the result would seem to indicate that my suspicions were not unfounded. By affording refuge to our ships at Calais, Cherbourg, and Brest, the Imperial Government has shown us more favor than that of her Britannic Majesty, and I presume that the Emperor, trusting to the chances of war and diplomacy, hoped that before the completion of the ships, affairs both in America and Europe would be in such a condition as would enable him to let them go without apprehension. He now favors us so far as to tell us frankly to sell out and save our money, but this can scarcely ameliorate the disappointment. The corvettes have already been nominally transferred to other owners, and their construction will be continued, but I have little hope of getting them to sea in efficient fighting condition, as they are marked ships, and when about to leave, the pressure of the United States minister will be very strong upon the Imperial Government to prevent their departure.

The two Bordeaux ironclads together with the four corvettes would have made a formidable attacking squadron, and would have enabled its commander to strike severe and telling blows upon the northern seaboard. The loss of the ironclads changes the whole character of this force and deprives it of its real power of offense. It is difficult to predict what may be the state of Europe even a month hence, and how the progress of events may affect the chances of getting the wooden ships to sea. I shall, however, make every effort to get at least two of them out to supply the places of our present cruising squadron, should accident or the casualties of the sea reduce their number. There really seems nothing for our ships to do now upon the open sea. Acting Lieutenant Commanding Low of the *Tuscaloosa* reports that in a cruise of several months during which he spoke over 100 vessels only one proved to be an American, and she being loaded entirely on neutral account, he was forced to release her after taking a bond. The *Alabama*, too, only picks up a ship at long intervals, although she is in the Indies, heretofore rich in American traffic. Nevertheless if all our ships should be withdrawn the United States flag would again make its appearance at sea, and it is therefore necessary to provide the proffer relay of vessels. There is, however, no resisting the stern logic of accomplished facts. I am now convinced beyond a doubt that we can not get ironclads to sea and unless otherwise instructed, I shall make no more contracts for such vessels, except with such a pecuniary guarantee for actual delivery upon the ocean as will secure us against loss. Several propositions of this tenor have been made and I have one under negotiation now, but heretofore they have all fallen through when the agreement was reduced to practical working shape, and I have little hope of being able to make any arrangement of the kind in the future. For the present there is lack of money for fresh operations, as I shall have to continue the payments upon all vessels until actually sold, and when this is accomplished the purchase money will probably be paid by installments. I will hand you a statement of cotton received and money remaining to my credit in a, separate letter.

Although sorely disappointed in reference to ironclads, from which we were justified in expecting so much, there are means at hand by which the enemy can be greatly annoyed and harassed. If the Navy Department would take the blockade running business into its own hands it might soon have a fleet of formidable, swift, light-draft screw and paddle steamers at work, so constructed as to have their engines and boilers well protected either by coal when the bunkers were full or cotton when they were empty. The beams and decks of these steamers could be made of sufficient strength to bear heavy deck loads without exciting suspicion, and then if registered in the name of private individuals and sailed purely as commercial ships they could trade without interruption or violation of neutrality between our coasts and the Bermudas, Bahamas, and West Indies. When three or more of the vessels happened to be in harbor at the same time a few hours would suffice to mount a couple of heavy guns on each, and at early dawn a successful raid might be made upon the unsuspecting blockaders. From time to time two or three of them might be filled with coal and sent out for short cruises off Hatteras, and in the Gulf of Mexico, from Mobile, to pick up transports, etc. After a raid or cruise the vessels could be divested of every appliance of war, and resuming their private ownership and commercial names, could bring out cargoes of cotton to pay the cost of the cruise, or to increase the funds of the Government abroad. Such operations are not impracticable, and if vigorously carried on without notice and at irregular periods, would greatly increase the difficulty of blockading our harbors, and would render hazardous the transportation of troops along the line of our coasts and through the Gulf of Mexico.

I have no dispatch from the department of later date than December 3, 1863, and am looking anxiously for comments or instructions based upon my latter reports. I hope the department will deem it advisable to send monthly couriers as suggested in my letter of January 24, 1864, a duplicate of which is enclosed.

I am, very respectfully, your obedient servant,

JAMES D. BULLOCH.

Hon. S. R. MALLORY,
Secretary of the Navy.

XV

The Marine Corps

1. The CSMC

The Confederate Marine Corps, similar to its counterpart in the U. S. Navy, was an integral part of the Confederate navy. The Confederate "Leathernecks" were active on many warships and participated in numerous engagements. Midshipman J. Thomas Scharf, in his book *History of the Confederate States Navy*, devotes a short chapter to the Confederate Marines. [RTC]

"The Confederate States Marine Corps" by Midshipman J. Thomas Scharf, CSN
History of the Confederate States Navy, Chapter XXIV, pp. 769–773

BY act of Congress of the Confederate States, March 16th, 1861, the establishment of a Corps of marines was provided for, and subsequent legislation of May 20th enlarged its numbers and elevated the rank of its principal officers. It was, in fact, organized under the second act, whose provisions were that it should consist of: "1 colonel, 1 lieut. col., 1 major, 1 quartermaster with rank of major, 1 adjutant with rank of major, 1 serg.-major, 1 quartermaster-sergeant, 10 captains, 10 first lieutenants, 20 second lieutenants, 40 sergeants, 40 corporals and 840 privates, 10 drummers, 10 fifers and 2 musicians."

The pay and emoluments were the same as those of the army, except that the paymaster and adjutant received the same as the quartermaster, and seamen's rations were allowed to enlisted men. Enlistments were for three years or the war; recruits to receive a bounty of $50 and re-enlisted men $40. An act of Sept. 24th, 1862, authorized the addition of 20 sergeants, 20 corporals, 20 drummers, 20 fifers and two principal musicians; and by an act of Oct. 2d, 1862, men enrolled for the army were permitted to choose service in the marine Corps or the navy.

Previous to the war the U.S. marine Corps was an exceptionally fine and well-disciplined body of men, and from it came the nucleus of the corresponding establishment of the Confederate service. Its headquarters were at the Washington navy-yard, and the following officers resigned and tendered their swords to the Confederate Government: Maj. Henry B. Tyler, of Va., adjutant of the Corps; Capt. and Brevet Maj. Geo. H. Terret, of Va.; Capt. Robert Tansill, of Va.; Capt. Algernon S. Taylor, of Va.; Capt. John D. Simms, of Va.; First Lieut. Israel Greene, of Va.; First Lieut. John K.H. Tatnall, of Ga.; First Lieut. Julius E. Meire, of Md.: First Lieut. Geo. P. Turner, of Va.; First. Lieut. Thos. S. Wilson, of Mo.; First Lieut. Andrew J. Hays, of Ala.; First Lieut. Adam N. Baker; Second Lieut. George Holmes, of Fla.; Second Lieut. Calvin L. Sayre, of Ala.; Second Lieut. Henry L. Ingraham, of So. Car., and Second Lieut. Baker K. Howell, of Miss.

Most of these officers arrived in Richmond by the time that the seat of the Confederate government was transferred from Montgomery to that city; and, with the exception of Capt. Tansill and Lieut. Turner, they thenceforth served in the C. S. Marine Corps. They met at Richmond, in May 1861, more than a hundred men of their former command in the Federal service, who fully shared in their enthusiasm for the Confederate cause and had left their comfortable berths under the old flag to risk their lives and fortunes in the yet untested possibilities of the success of the South.

There had been no concert of action by which so many of the former men and officers of the U. S. Marine Corps were assembled at Richmond, but it was not an unfortunate accident for the Confederacy that they did come together at that time. They formed the skeleton of the organization that it was desired to establish, and brought it into order and being with a celerity that would have been impossible to unskilled hands.

The organization of the Corps, which had begun at Montgomery, was completed at Richmond. Col. Lloyd J. Beall, a former officer of the U. S. Army, was appointed commandant with the rank of colonel. A commission as paymaster, with the rank of major, was issued to Richard Taylor Allison, who had held similar rank and office in the U. S. navy.

Other commissions issued at Richmond, made Henry B. Tyler lieut. colonel of the Corps; Geo. H. Terret, major; Capt. Greene, who captured John Brown, at Harper's Ferry, when the U. S. marines attacked his fortress in the engine-house at the arsenal, was made adjutant, with the rank of major; Lieut. Taylor became quartermaster, with the rank of major; and Simms, Tatnall, Holmes, Meire, Wilson and Hays, were appointed captains. Sayre and Howell were made lieutenants, and the lists of that rank were subsequently filled up by appointments made from time to time. Capts. Thom and Van Benthuysen, and all the lieutenants, except Sayre and Howell, were appointed from civil life, or from the army and navy, while the other officers, with the exception of Col. Beall, came from the U. S. marine service.

The Corps remained in and around Richmond, practically unbroken, until the summer of 1862. It was engaged in the battle with the Federal iron-clads *Monitor*, *Naugatuck* and *Galena*, at Drewry's Bluff, on May 15th, when its service at the guns assisted the artillerists of the army and navy in the repulse of those vessels. Major Terrett commanded the Corps on that occasion, and soon after detachments from it were ordered to other stations, and to vessels preparing for sea, or for the coast defence. Because of the great lack of trained seamen in the Confederacy, the veteran marines were of inestimable value on board the ships to which they were attached, and they were made use of in numerous capacities that embraced the duties of sailors. One squad of marines that fought at Drewry's Bluff had previously formed a part of the ship's company of the *Virginia*, and had helped work her guns in the battles in Hampton Roads. They were under the command of Capt. R. Thom, and remained with the ship until she was destroyed. Other detachments served on the *Sumter* and the *Alabama* during their cruises, and were commanded by Lieut. B. K. Howell, who was highly commended by Capt. Semmes. Lieut. James Thurston commanded the marine guard on the *Atlanta*, during her brief and ill-starred career in the waters around Savannah, and had charge, with his men, of a division of the guns, in the short engagement in the Ogeechee that ended with her surrender. When Adm. Buchanan took the *Tennessee* out to fight Farragut's fleet in Mobile Bay, he had on board a marine guard, under the command of Lieut. David G. Raney, which was assigned to one of the gun divisions, and was largely instrumental in the quick and efficient work with her battery that inflicted such great damage upon the enemy. In the same battle a detachment of marines, under the command of Lieut. J. R. T. Fendall, served on the gunboat *Gaines*, and escaped to Mobile with the crew, after the vessel was beached under the guns of Fort Morgan. At the defence of Fort Fisher, Dec. 24th-25th, 1864, and Jan. 5th, 1865, a body of marines participated. They were commanded by Capt. A. C. Van Benthuysen, and Lieuts. Henry N. Doak and J. Camp-

Marine Encampment at Drewry's Bluff (*Illustrated London News*).

bell Murdoch. Finally, such companies and detachments of the Corps as were not isolated at Mobile, or were not away at sea, or had not been captured, were gathered around Richmond in Feb. and March, 1865, and were then assigned to the former positions of the marines in the fortifications on Drewry's Bluff. Then they made up a part of the naval brigade, under Com. John R. Tucker, and with the sailors held out at the battle of Saylor's Creek, after Gen. Ewell had surrendered.

This mention is to be taken only as a scant index of the services of the marines. Their inadequacy in numbers to the tasks required of them necessitated the breaking up of the Corps into small detachments, and hence they participated in many actions their share in which has not been recorded. The report of Col. Beall, dated Oct. 30th, 1864, shows that the aggregate strength of the Corps then was but 539 men, of which number two captains, three lieutenants, and sixty-two privates were prisoners in the hands of the enemy, and thirty-two recruits had recently been received at the Charleston naval station from the conscript camp near Raleigh, N. C. The report continues:

"The Marine Corps is distributed at the following naval stations: Mobile, Savannah, Charleston, Wilmington, and at Drewry's Bluff; also on board of the three iron-clad steamers in the James River, and as guards at the Richmond navy-yards. Marine guards have been assigned to the armed steamers *Tallahassee* and *Chickamauga*, destined to operate against the enemy's commerce on the sea.

"Since my last report the marines have been under the enemy's fire at Drewry's Bluff and on the James River; also in the land and naval engagements near Mobile, on the 5th and 6th of August last. A marine guard under the command of Lieut. Crenshaw was attached to the Confederate steamship *Tallahassee* during the late cruise, when much damage was inflicted upon the enemy's shipping at sea.

"Upon all occasions when the marines have been called upon for active service, they have displayed the promptness and efficiency of well disciplined soldiers."

[Scharf note] Colonel Beall, now approaching fourscore years, is a resident of Richmond. His books and papers were destroyed by fire about the close of the war, and in that disaster were lost many of the most valuable records of the Corps.

"The Corps," he says, in a letter to the author, "was composed of enlisted men, many of whom were old soldiers and commissioned officers, a number of whom had seen service before in the U. S. Marine Corps and elsewhere. The Corps was thoroughly trained and disciplined, and in all encounters with the enemy the officers and men were conspicuous for their courage and good conduct."

2. Marine Correspondence

Colonel Lloyd T. Beall was born on October 19, 1808, at Fort Adams, Rhode Island. He was appointed to West Point from Maryland in 1826, and was graduated in 1830. Rising from second lieutenant to captain, he subsequently served with the 2nd Dragoons of the U. S. Cavalry. Promoted to major on September 13, 1844, he was stationed at St. Louis, Missouri, when war came and he immediately resigned and headed South. Beall was appointed colonel-commandant of the newly authorized Confederate States Marine Corps by Mallory, and he remained in that position until the end of the war. (Donnelly, *The Confederate States Marine Corps*, pp. 200–201.)

Colonel Lloyd T. Beall (Scharf, *History of the Confederate States Navy***).**

Most of the Marine Corps records were burned when Richmond was evacuated in April of 1865. All that were saved are the following series of reports to Secretary Mallory from Colonel Beall that are preserved in the *Official Navy Records*. [RTC]

*Official Correspondence of
Colonel Lloyd T. Beall, CSMC*

Official Records Navy, Volume VIII, p. 842, Volume IX, pp. 453–454, 808

HEADQUARTERS C. S. MARINE CORPS,
Richmond, Va., September 20, 1862.

SIR: The bleak and exposed condition of Drewry's Bluff makes it necessary, in order to preserve the efficiency of the marines stationed at that point, that they should be protected from the inclemency of the weather during the approaching winter by temporary buildings. Besides contributing greatly to the health [and] comfort of the men, placing them under such shelter would render them more contented with their condition and thereby have a tendency to prevent desertion.

The estimated cost of putting up the buildings required is $16,000, for which sum an appropriation by Congress is needed.

The principal item of expense in the estimate is lumber, which would be useful for public purposes should the buildings not be required beyond the winter.

Very respectfully, etc.,

LLOYD T. BEALL,
Colonel Commandant C. S. Marine Corps.

Hon. S. R. MALLORY,
Secretary of the Navy.

HEADQUARTERS C. S. MARINE CORPS,
Richmond, Va., April 28, 1864.

SIR: I have the honor to submit herewith a return of the Marine Corps, showing its strength and disposition on the 31st ultimo. Since that date some addition has been made to its strength by recruits, with a fair prospect of further increase.

The marines are on duty with the naval forces at Mobile, Savannah, Charleston, Richmond, and at Drewry's Bluff; on the James River. There is also a marine guard at sea on board of the C. S. S. *Alabama.*

The discipline and efficiency of the corps are such as to reflect much credit upon the captains and subordinate officers. In this connection, I beg leave to enclose herewith a copy of a letter addressed to me by Colonel J. Taylor Wood, who commanded the expedition which boarded and captured the U. S. armed steamer *Underwriter* off New Berne, N. C., under the fire of the enemy's shore batteries. Captain [Thomas S.] Wilson therein referred to commanded a detachment of marines, and in boarding the *Underwriter* had 1 man killed and 3 wounded.

Very respectfully, your obedient servant,

LLOYD J. BEALL,
Colonel, Commanding C. S. Marine Corps.

Hon. S. R. MALLORY,
Secretary of the Navy.

[Copy of letter]

HEADQUARTERS C. S. MARINE CORPS,
Richmond, Va., February 16, 1864.

SIR: It gives me pleasure to report to you the fine bearing and soldierly conduct of Captain Wilson and his men whilst absent on special duty. Though their duties were more arduous than those of the others, they were always prompt and ready for the performance of all they were called upon to do. As a body they would be a credit to any organization, and I will be glad to be associated with them on duty at any time.

Respectfully, etc., your obedient servant,

J. TAYLOR WOOD

Colonel L. BEALL,
Commanding Marine Corps.

XVI

The Naval School

1. The Confederate Naval School

In the summer of 1863, a most unusual institution opened its doors to a group of fledgling naval officers. It was unusual in that it was inaugurated during the midst of a violent war in which the country it represented was struggling for its very existence. Unlike its counterpart, the U. S. Naval Academy which moved to Rhode Island for the duration of the war, the Confederate Naval Academy existed for two years at the very vortex of the swirling battles that eventually tore the Southern nation apart.

Midshipman James Morris Morgan was assigned to the school in early 1864, which surprised him because he was already a seasoned naval officer, or so he thought. Morgan had served on the CSS *McRae* at the Battle of New Orleans and then had transferred overseas where he served a tour of duty on the commerce raider CSS *Georgia*. On returning from England to the Confederacy, the seventeen-year-old was told to report to the Academy. In his book, *Recollections of a Rebel Reefer*, Morgan described his experiences at the naval school. (Campbell, *Academy on the James, the Confederate Naval School*, pp. 68–69.) [RTC]

"A Realistic War College" by
Midshipman James Morris Morgan, CSN

Recollections of a Rebel Reefer, Chapters XXIV and XXV, 1917, pp. 204–219

"PRIDE goeth before a fall." I fear that the dignity of being an engaged man caused my chest to enlarge disproportionately to my rank. I received my orders, and instead of being sent to an ironclad I was ordered to report on board of the school-ship *Patrick Henry* to be examined for promotion [1864]. Most of my classmates had been nominally taken out of active service and put to school while I was at sea, and they were now passed midshipmen. I had not opened a schoolbook since I had left Annapolis, and the result was that I failed to pass. But I was given another chance and had to begin school again. Although I did not know it, if there was one thing that I needed more than anything else, it was a little schooling.

The *Patrick Henry* was a small sidewheel seagoing steamer with a walking-beam engine and a brigantine rig. She had formerly belonged to the "Old Dominion" line running between New York and Norfolk. She had been converted into a man-of-war by having ten guns put on board of her and she had played quite a conspicuous part in the naval battles in Hampton Roads. She had now become the most realistic war college that ever existed. She was anchored in front of Drewry's Bluff, Richmond's principal defense on the James River, which is situated seven miles below the city. The reason for her being located there was that the "school" was expected to sink itself in the channel between the obstructions in case the enemy's ironclads tried to force a passage by the land batteries. One always associates a collegiate institution with peace and quiet, but this naval college was located in the midst of the booming guns. Below Drewry's Bluff, on the south side of the river, were the naval land batteries of Wood, Brooke, Semmes, and Howlett, and on the other side of the river were the Federal batteries of Bohler, Signal Hill, Crow's Nest, and the Dutch Gap batteries; and when they all broke loose together the din they made was not conducive to that peaceful repose so prized by all students.

There were about sixty young midshipmen on the *Patrick Henry*, varying in age from fourteen to seventeen. Their jackets were made out of very coarse gray cloth and the food they had to eat was, at first, revolting to me. The menu offered little variety. If it was not a tiny lump of fat pork, it was a shaving of fresh meat as tough as the hide which had once covered it, with a piece of hardtack and a tin cup of hot water colored by chicory or grains of burned corn, ground up, and brevetted *coffee*. But no one kicked about the food, as it was as good if not better than that the poor soldiers in the trenches received. The James River furnished a capital article of chills and fever not malaria, but the good old-fashioned kind with the shivers which made the teeth chatter and burning fever to follow. On an average about one half of the midshipmen went through this disagreeable experience every other day. No one was allowed to go on the sick-list on account of chills and fever; one was, however, allowed to lie down on the bare deck while the chill was on, but had to return to duty as soon as the paroxysm was over.

Lieutenant William H. Parker, who had been a professor of seamanship at Annapolis, was the superintendent of this extraordinary naval academy, and he was assisted by two or three navy lieutenants and a like number of civilian professors. There were on the hurricane deck and between the paddle boxes two little recitation rooms, and on top of these rooms were posted signalmen who from daylight to dark wigwagged to, and received messages from the batteries. The scenes in the recitation rooms were frequently exciting and interesting. The guns on shore roared and the shells burst, and the professor would placidly give out the problem to the youngster at the blackboard, to be interrupted by the report of some gun which his practiced ear told him was a newcomer in the fray. He would begin by saying: "If $x-y$—One moment, Mr. Blank. Would you kindly step outside and find out for me which battery it is that has opened with that Brooke gun?" The information obtained the recitation would be resumed, only to be again interrupted by a message from the captain that a certain battery was short of officers and a couple of midshipmen were wanted. It was useless to call for volunteers, as every midshipman clamored for permission to go: so these details were given as rewards. It was from among these midshipmen that the men came who steered the boats when the gunboat *Underwriter* was boarded and captured in the night, and it was in the fight that Midshipman Palmer Saunders had his head cloven to his shoulders by a cutlass in the hand of a big sailor. Saunders was only seventeen years of age. It was in that same boarding expedition that Dan Lee, another midshipman from the *Patrick Henry*, called out to his would-be rescuer, when a sailor had him down and was trying to kill him, not to shoot, as the man on top of him was so *thin*! Lee and Saunders were of the same age. This *Patrick Henry* may have been a unique institution of learning, but the "Confederate States Naval Academy" turned out men who afterwards became United States Senators, members of Congress, judges, successful bankers, and successful business men as well as sailors.

The *Patrick Henry*, besides being a naval academy and stopgap for the river obstructions, also served as a receiving ship. Steamboats under flags of truce, carrying Northern prisoners to Harrison's Landing for exchange, had to stop alongside of her to get permits to continue their trips, and returning frequently discharged their human freight of Confederate prisoners on board the school ship while they went again down the river for more.

One day, while I was assisting the officer of the deck in receiving these poor, forlorn fellows, I was trying to hurry them forward so that they would not block the gangway; this was necessary, as with few exceptions they were so glad to be once more under their beloved Confederate flag that those who did not succeed in embracing the officer of the deck at least wanted to swap congratulations with the gray-coated midshipman. I was continually interrupting them by begging them not to block the gangway, but to pass forward, and that I would attend to their wants as soon as the rest could come aboard, etc. Suddenly the shabbiest, the raggedest, and most unkempt of the lot, with his matted hair reaching to his shoulders and looking as though it had never known the caress of a comb, shambled across the gang-plank, in a rather peremptory manner demanded the name of my captain. I replied with the usual advice, "Go forward, my man: go forward!"—when to my amazement the human wreck drew himself up and rather sternly said, "Little Morgan, I will apply for you as soon as I get a command and I will then show you, sir, who goes forward!" The man was Commander Beverly Kennon, who had rammed and sunk the U.S. sloop-of-war *Varuna* when Farragut passed the forts below New Orleans. I thought I should faint when I became aware of his identity. Here was I, a poor devil of a midshipman, ordering forward a man who ranked me so far that I would hardly be able to see where he passed along! It was not fair. Kennon was last seen by his compatriots in the fight at the forts standing on the paddle box of his ship while the *Hartford*, *Brooklyn*, and the frigate *Mississippi*, with their tremendous broadsides, were shooing him ashore, when suddenly they blew him up, set fire to him, and sunk him almost simultaneously. By all the rules of the game he was a dead man, and had no right to come back and scare a poor innocent midshipman out of several years' growth. Several years afterwards Kennon served in the Egyptian Army where he was a full colonel and I was again his junior. He seemed to take a delight in telling his brother officers how, as he described it, he had once been "ordered forward by a d—d midshipman!"

Midshipman James Morris Morgan (Naval Historical Center).

From the *Patrick Henry* we could see the constant movement of troops, both Union and Confederate, on the north side of the river, where they frequently clashed in skirmishes; but this sort of thing was so common that to break the monotony two of the midshipmen got permission to go ashore, and improved the time by fighting a duel with muskets.

One morning we saw our soldiers hastily constructing a pontoon bridge on the river a short distance above where we were anchored. We soon learned that the cause of their activity was that General Grant's troops had surprised and captured Fort Harrison during the night, and that Fort Harrison was the key to our advanced line of defenses on the north side of the stream. The bridge was no sooner completed than Hoke's North Carolina division were rushed across it. These were the best-dressed and best-cared-for troops in the Confederate Army, as the State, with commendable paternalism, owned its steamers and had gone into the blockade-running business on its own account.

Believing that the object of the sudden movement was to retake the fort, Midshipmen Carter, Hale, Wright, and myself asked and received permission to go ashore and see at close range the coming fight. Following the troops we saw them form their line of battle in front of the fort and its outlying breastworks, while the shells of the enemy were bursting over their heads as well as in front, behind, and among them. Soon we heard the rumble of the wheels of gun carriages and caissons, as our light batteries came, at the gallop, from the rear and dashed through the spaces between our brigades and regiments, and wheeling and unlimbering a short distance from our front, they opened a rapid fire. There was no wind stirring, and soon the enemy's position, as well as that of our light batteries, was obscured from view by the dense smoke. Then their firing ceased, and so did that of the enemy's heavy guns. All at once our artillery was seen to burst through the bank of smoke and rapidly come back to us, dashing through our infantry line again, wheeling and unlimbering just in their rear: this maneuver was followed by complete stillness, the most trying time in the life of a soldier, that two or three minutes, which seem unending, while waiting for the order to charge.

The infantry moved forward, at the double-quick, under cover of the smoke which lay close to the ground in the heavy atmosphere. Nothing could be heard save the tramp of hurrying feet. Fort Harrison maintained an ominous silence. As our men neared the fortifications suddenly from twenty thousand throats burst forth the famous rebel yell which fairly rent the air. When within about a hundred yards from the coveted works there arose a long line of blue-coated soldiers, seemingly from out of the ground, who poured a deadly volley into the oncoming ranks of the North Carolinians and at the same time the heavy guns of the fort sprinkled them with shrapnel, grape, and canister. The fight was fast and furious for a time, and then we saw some slightly wounded men going to the rear; these were followed by the more seriously injured, each accompanied and assisted by two or three unhurt men, who, moved by compassion (?) assisted them. We then knew what was coming, and soon saw the whole line fall back, but not in any great disorder. We had been repulsed, but the enemy was not following us.

When we reached the line, from which we had started to make our unsuccessful assault, the troops re-formed and waited. Suddenly from the left of the line we heard cheering and wondered what it was for. It was not the rebel yell, which once heard could never be mistaken for any other sound; the sound we now heard was evidently a burst of enthusiasm, which was taken up by regiment after regiment until the whole line was adding to its volume. It was not long before we discovered the cause of the manifestation—for there, with his silvery head uncovered, hat in hand, was seen riding down the line—General Robert E. Lee. He was a picture of dignity as, mounted on his famous gray Charger "Traveler," he spoke seriously to his unsuccessful troops. As he passed in front of where we were standing, we could plainly hear what he was saying—he was telling the men how important Fort Harrison was to our line of defense, and that he was sure they could take it if they would make another earnest effort. Their answer was given in deafening cheers.

Again they went forward to the assault, and again were they repulsed, this time with worse slaughter than had been their lot on the first attempt. The second retreat was much more disorderly than the first, but again they reformed and waited—and again General Lee rode down the line.

I had always thought General Lee was a very cold and unemotional man, but he showed lots of feeling and excitement on that occasion; even the staid and stately "Traveler" caught the spirit of his master, and was prancing and cavorting while the general was imploring his men to make one more effort to take the position for him.

Again they went forward and again they came back—this time in great disorder. In fact, it was a sprinting match on a big scale. I had heard a great deal about the marvelous marching powers of the Confederate infantryman, and I was only a poor "webfoot," temporarily off his element, but I do not recall having seen any infantrymen pass me on the way to our second line of defense.

When the troops re-formed, General Lee again rode down the line trying to comfort his men by telling them they had done all that men could do, and that anyhow the place was not of as much importance as he had first thought it was. This talk cheered them men, and they, although worn out with fatigue, replied by cheering their beloved general.

After the battle a surgeon pressed me into service and made me hold a soldier's shattered leg while he amputated it. I would have preferred to be shot myself. Medicines were scarce in the South and that particular surgeon had neither chloroform nor ether in his medical kit.

Disgusted, tired, and weary, I returned to my school and my studies.

Shortly after the fall of Fort Harrison I passed my examination for promotion and arrived at the dignity of being a passed midshipman. I was immediately ordered to the naval battery called Semmes, situated on a narrow tongue of land formed by the river. It was the most advanced of our defenses on the river, and was the nearest of any of our batteries to the Dutch Gap canal which was then being dug by General B. F. Butler.

Our seven heavy guns, rifled and smooth-bore, were mounted in pits dug on the brow of a gently sloping hill—the battery was only thirty feet above the river. Between each of the guns was a bomb-proof which protected our ammunition. The guns were mounted on naval carriages so that our sailors could handle their accustomed blocks and tackles.

On the opposite side of the river, and forming a semicircle around the peninsula on which Semmes was located, were the heavy Union batteries called Bohler's, Signal Hill, Crow's Nest, the Dutch Gap batteries, and the Howlett House batteries, and when they all opened fire at once they made a perfect inferno out of Battery Semmes. It surely was a hot spot.

Some six hundred yards in front of Battery Semmes, on the land side, we had four little Cohorn mortars in a pit, and with these we tossed shells constantly into the canal to interfere with its construction. General Butler put a number of Confederate prisoners to work in his canal, and very thoughtfully sent us word that we were only killing our own men with our mortar shells. About the same time that we received this considerate message, Jeff Phelps, a midshipman who had been one of the "Brood of the Constitution," and who was one of the prisoners compelled to dig in the canal, in some way managed to get a note to us telling us that we "were doing fine" and to "keep it up." We only kept some eight or ten men at a time in the mortar pit and between the pit and our battery were a number of rifle pits. When the mortars aggravated General Butler too much, he would send a force across the river to charge the mortars. Seeing them coming, our men would hastily beat a retreat, and like prairie dogs tumbling into their holes, they would disappear. The Union soldiers would, of course, capture the mortars and spike them, but when we thought that as many of them as the pit could hold were well in it, we would cut loose with the heavy guns of the big battery behind us which were trained on it. Then the Federal soldiers would hasten back to the river, and before they could get across, our men, who were provided with bows and drills, would have new vent holes bored and would be again tossing shells as though nothing had happened to interfere with their day's work. Why General Butler's men never carried off the mortars with them we could never understand—two strong men could have lifted any one of them, they were so small and light.

General Butler had built a lofty lookout tower out of timber. It was very open work, and on the top of it he placed a telescope. I met a member of his staff after the war who told me that they could see every movement we made, and that on one occasion he had distinctly seen a man in our battery cut off a chew of tobacco and put it into his mouth.

There was a mystery as to the way in which privates would come to a tacit agreement with the enemy about not doing any sniping on certain parts on the line. I knew of one stretch of breastworks where our men could expose themselves with perfect impunity up to a spot on which stood an empty barrel, and on the other side of that barrel, if a man showed an old hat on the end of a ramrod, it was instantly perforated with bullets.

The Union soldiers craved tobacco of which the Southerners had an abundance and the "grayback" longed for coffee or sugar. At some points on the line trading in these commodities went on briskly without the knowledge of the officers. Their dealings were strictly honorable. A man, say from the Southern side, would creep outside the works, and when he reached a certain stump he would place a couple of large plugs of tobacco on it and then return to his companions. After a time he would again creep to the stump to find that his tobacco was gone, but in its place was a small quantity of the longed-for coffee and sugar. We always carried one or two long plugs of tobacco in our inside breast pockets, as it was a common belief that if a man was captured and had tobacco it would insure him good treatment.

One foggy night I was on duty and had visited our outposts. While returning to the battery on a path close to the riverside, I distinctly heard oars slapping the water—the rowlocks were evidently muffled. Although I could not see the boat I felt that it must be very near the shore, and I hailed it with a "Boat ahoy! Keep farther out in the stream!" The answer came back: "We don't do any picket firing on this line." I told the spokesman that I knew that, but we didn't want him to bunk with us, and hardly were the words out of my mouth when the bow of the boat was rammed into the mud at my feet. I felt sure my time had come, and hastily jerked my pistol out of the holster intending to fire so as to give the alarm, when I heard a voice say, "For the love of Mike, Johnny, give me a chew of tobacco." The tone was so pleading and earnest that I could not resist it and handed the fellow my plug. In return he gave me a canteen full of whiskey. We entered into conversation, and I discovered that he was an old classmate of mine at Annapolis who had "bilged" and was now a master's mate in charge of a picket boat whose duty was to give warning if our ironclads descended the river. I warned him about the folly of his act, and he shoved out into the stream and disappeared forever out of my life. When I produced my canteen before my messmates they fairly went wild with joy, but nothing ever could induce me to tell how I had come into possession of the liquor.

Muskrats or rabbits, when caught, which was rarely, were a welcome addition to our menu. Pickett's division supported our battery and was encamped about half a mile from us. One day we thought that those thousands of men had gone crazy—there was the wildest commotion among them. Men rushed to and fro in the wildest confusion, falling over one another in every direction—it looked like a free fight. We sent over to find out the cause of the riot and were informed that one poor little "cotton-tail bunny" had jumped out of a bush in the center of the camp and that some ten thousand men had given chase in hopes of having him for supper.

The winter of 1864–65 was an intensely cold one. Snow from three to six inches in depth lay constantly on the ground keeping the trenches wet and muddy, and the consequent discomfort was great. Lieutenant Bradford, our commander, and Lieutenant Hilary Cenas and the surgeon had two log huts to live in. Becoming envious I got several of the men to assist me in building a cabin for myself, with the chinks all stuffed with mud and with a beautiful mud chimney of which I was very proud. I had had it located in a little gulch behind the battery and it did look so comfortable, but alas, work had gone on very rapidly in the construction of the canal despite our continual mortar fire, and on the afternoon of the day on which my house was finished a monitor fired several eleven-inch shells through the canal, and with the whole State of Virginia to select from, one of these projectiles could find no other place to explode in but my little cabin, which it scattered to the four winds.

Some days there would be a lull in the artillery fire, and we could walk about exposing ourselves to the enemy's fire with perfect impunity, and on other days the most trifling movement on our part, such as the moving of an empty water barrel, or a few men chasing a frightened and bewildered "cotton-tail" would bring upon us a storm of projectiles from the enemy's guns. Constant practice had made the artillery firing very effective, so much so that it was not an uncommon thing for us to have one or more of our guns knocked off their carriages. Lieutenant Cenas seemed to have a tacit understanding with the gunner of a rifled piece in the Crow's Nest Battery whose marksmanship he admired very much. Cenas would go outside of the works and place an empty barrel or tobacco box on top of a stump, and then, stepping to one side, he would wave his arms as a signal to his favorite gun-pointer on the other side, and immediately we would see a puff of smoke and the projectile would always tear up the ground very close to the stump and frequently both stump and barrel would be knocked into smithereens.

One afternoon a monitor fired a shell through the canal which landed a few yards in front of our battery. A sailor, in pure dare-deviltry, went outside to pick it up. Just as he got to it I saw a thread of smoke arising from the fuse, and I yelled to him to jump back—but too late. The sailor gave it a push with his foot and it bounded into the air taking off the man's leg; the shell then landed in one of our gun pits and exploded killing and wounding several men. It must have been spinning with great rapidity on its axis and only needed the touch of the sailor's foot to start it again on its mission of destruction.

We flew no flag, as it was useless to hoist one; the enemy would shoot it away as fast we would put it up. A wonderfully accurate gun was a light field piece, a Parrott gun, which would come out from behind the Bohler Battery, take up a position in the bushes, and shoot at any man bringing water from a near-by spring, and he was frequently successful in hitting him. One day General Lee was inspecting the line and stopped for a few moments at our battery. He ordered us to drive this fellow away, and then looking at his watch added, "Give him a shot in fifteen minutes." Then the general on his gray horse rode away. At the expiration of the fifteen minutes we let go our seven heavy guns into the bushes where we supposed the fellow to be with the result that he limbered up and hastily took refuge behind his works, and from fifty to seventy-five guns in the batteries which enfiladed Semmes cut loose into us and kept it up for three days and nights, dismounting three of our guns, killing and wounding a number of our men.

We could shoot just as well at night as we could in the daytime, as from constant practice we had the ranges of all of the enemy's batteries, and had marked the trunnions of our guns for range and the traverses for direction. Such firing was accurate, as was proved on several occasions by our discovering at daylight that we had dismounted some of the guns of our antagonists.

In the latter part of January, 1865, our supply of ammunition was running short, and as a consequence we were ordered to be sparing with it, so we would only fire a gun when the enemy's fire would slacken up a bit to let them know that we were still there. This seemed to encourage our opponents and they hammered us all day with their big guns, and all through the nights they dropped mortar shells among us. These shells, with their burning fuses, resembled meteors flying through the air; they made an awful screeching noise as they tore the atmosphere apart when coming down before we heard the thud of their striking the ground and the terrific explosion which would follow, and then would come the whistling of the fragments as they scattered in every direction. We were so accustomed to these sounds that we did not allow them to interfere with our slumbers, as wrapped in our one blanket we slept in the bomb-proofs or magazines.

The end of the Southern Confederacy was near at hand, although we at the front little realized the fact. The authorities in Richmond determined to make a daring attempt to capture or destroy General Grant's base of supplies at City Point on the James. Late on the afternoon of January 23, 1865, we received notice to be ready, as our three ironclads, the *Virginia Number 2*, the *Richmond*, and the *Fredericksburg*, would come down that night, run the gantlet of the Federal batteries, and try to force their way through the boom the enemy had placed across the river (at Howlett's) in anticipation of just such an attempt. I happened to be officer of the day. The night was very dark, and suddenly I heard a sentry challenge something in the river. I ran down to the edge of the water and arrived there just in time to see a rowboat stick her nose into the mud at my very feet, and was much surprised to see my old shipmate, "Savez" Read, step ashore. He was in a jolly mood, as he told me that our ironclads would follow him in a couple of hours, and that he was going ahead to cut the boom so that they could pass on and destroy City Point. "And now, youngster," he said, "you fellows make those guns of yours hum when the 'Yanks' open, and mind that you don't shoot too low, for I will be down there in the middle of the river." And then he put his hand affectionately on my shoulder and added: "Jimmie, it's going to be a great night; I only wish you could go with me: a sailor has no business on shore, anyway;" And laughing he stepped back into his boat and shoved out into the stream.

The enemy must have had some information as to our plans, for Read had not proceeded very far before the bank of the river looked as though it was infested by innumerable fireflies as the sharpshooters rained bullets on his boat which was proceeding with muffled oars. They completely riddled it, but Read kept on while bailing the water out of her, and strange to say he reached the boom and successfully cut it.

About two hours after Read left, our so-called ironclads noiselessly glided by the battery. The stillness was unbroken for so long a time that we began to congratulate ourselves that they had safely got by the enemy's batteries without being discovered. But our exultation was premature—they did get by the Bohler and Signal Hill batteries unobserved, but unfortunately the furnaces of the leading boat were stirred, and a flame shot out of her smokestack which instantly brought upon her a shower of shot and shell, and instantly the big guns on both sides were in an uproar. My! but that was a thunderous night; the very ground quivered under the constant explosions.

The next morning we learned that our demonstration against City Point had resulted in a most mortifying failure. The smallest of our ironclads, the *Fredericksburg*, passed safely through the obstructions, but the *Virginia*, which steered very badly, ran aground and blocked the passage to the *Richmond*. The wooden gunboat *Drewry* also missed the channel and ran ashore. The *Fredericksburg* was recalled and the big monitor *Onondaga* with her immense guns arrived on the scene shortly after daylight. With one shot she smashed in the *Virginia's* forward shield. The *Virginia* got afloat again and presented her broadside, which was also perforated as though it was made of paper. She then brought her after gun into action and a shot from the monitor also smashed her after shield. They all returned that night under a rain of projectiles from the shore batteries similar to that they had been exposed to the night before, and on that occasion our ironclads, on which we had based such high hopes, fired their last hostile shot. The end was near.

2. Report to the Academy

When the Confederate Naval Academy was established, one of the first cadets to be assigned to it was Hubbard T. Minor. Born near Spotsylvania Court House, Virginia, on

July 7, 1845, Minor painstakingly penciled daily entries into a pocket diary from the time that he was appointed to the school until the end of the war. Each cadet at the Academy was required to keep a journal of his studies and daily activities, which had to be presented at the time of final examination. Minor's diary is a product of this directive, and one of only two that are known to have survived the conflict.

Although the Confederate Naval Academy's "official" opening has most often been recounted as occurring in October with the move to Drewry's Bluff, in reality midshipmen were onboard and working diligently on their studies as early as July of 1863. At that time the school ship was moored at Rocketts Landing on the Richmond waterfront while the finishing touches were being applied to her living quarters and recitation rooms.

Government facilities on the James River had, by the summer of 1863, turned the Confederate capital of Richmond into a bustling and strategic naval center. The navy yard referred to as Rocketts was situated around a landing on the city side of the river and housed several wharves, dock equipment, storage sheds, and numerous warehouses. Here, while the finishing touches were being applied to the *Patrick Henry*, the ironclad CSS *Fredericksburg* had been completed and was now awaiting only her armament prior to being commissioned. In addition, sprawled across the river was the navy facility known locally as the "yard opposite Rocketts." Another ironclad, the CSS *Virginia II*, was nearing completion there, and a fourth, the CSS *Texas* (the *Richmond* was already in service), was in the beginning stages. It was here in August of 1863, among this thriving center of naval activity, that Acting Midshipman Hubbard T. Minor reported aboard the school ship *Patrick Henry*. (Coski, *Capital Navy*, p. 13–14, 153.) [RTC]

"I am Getting a Good Education" by Midshipman Hubbard T. Minor, CSN

Richmond, Virginia
Friday, August 7, 1863

Reported for duty & got permission to remain on shore until Wednesday when I will go to hard study. Today has been quite a warm one & I have suffered a good deal from the heat & oppressiveness of the atmosphere today. I was fortunate enough to meet with Hack Wilkensen from Mo. & spent quite a pleasant time with him. Now good-night.

Saturday, August 8

All of this day I have spent in looking for the articles I was to send Henry [Henry Minor, Hubbard's brother] with some I was successful with others not. I am now very much fatigued after my walk & will lay down & take a nap. So goodbye.

Sunday, August 9

Went to Hollywood [Cemetery] before church & then went to [Saint James] Church & sat in the old place & heard one of the best sermons I ever listened to. Shook hands with Mrs. [Joshua] Peterkin & saw & spoke to Judge Meridith & his wife. Late this evening called to see Mrs. Marshall & spent quite a pleasant time with her & Miss Ellen who is beautiful but I do not intend to fall in love with her. Now Good Night.

Tuesday, August 11

Not quite as warm a day as yesterday tho' quite disagreeable. Have spent it quite lazily most all of the evening asleep. Saw about the making of my uniform and furnished buttons for same. The whole suit will cost $100.00. It will be made at Mr. Spece's. Late in the evening called on Judge Meridith & family. Miss Ella was out & I did not enjoy her music as I had anticipated. Spent altogether quite a pleasant evening.

Wednesday, August 12

Succeeded in getting Hen's [Henry's] Articles off By the express Co. & whilst there was seized with a fainting fit & did actually faint & became utterly senseless. Wrote to Aunt Betts in Lexington, Va. Finished my letter to my brother & will mail it at the first opportunity. Reported for duty & left shore as I had no right to remain longer in enjoyment of idleness. Also wrote a letter to my friend S. A. Cowley. When I got on board of the [schoolship] *Patrick Henry* it was quite late & I now am a little disappointed, but I hope [everything] will be all right soon. I sleep tonight in a hammock.

Thursday, August 13

My sleep was a little interrupted last night for the boys tied ropes to my hammock & swung me all night nearly. In the evening of this day I went up to my assigned watch for four hours with sad thoughts.

Friday, August 14

Last night my thoughts were quite sad & if I had been allowed I should [have] written some thing to while away the weary four hours [in] which I had to watch a bad man in prison who no doubt will be shot or hung ... [His crime] is that of attempting to strike an Officer. This day I have been busy studying & will if possible catch up to the first class [a number of cadets had begun their studies in 1862 prior to the establishment of the Academy]. I was on duty again today & will be on every other four hours until 8 o'clock Sunday morning.

Saturday, August 15

Was relieved from watch for four hours from 12 to 4 [p.m.] & spent them in town & got my uniform which was quite well made & impresses me much. I got on this day $50.00 from Uncle Will Hart & am in his debt now for the amount of $100.00. Just after 3 o'clock took a nice bath & had a good row in our fastest boat.

Sunday, August 16

Went on watch at 4 o'clock & came off at 8 for about a week. Went to church at about 20 minutes past ten but failed to hear Mr. [Joshua] Peterkin. Saw his son Guy at church also Mr. Claiburne who invited me to come & see him & told me he would think [it] strange of me if I did not do so. Returned from church & took Dinner with Uncle Will. Exchanged some little tales in the Southern literary class & at 5 o'clock [ran] into a fellow Middy & had a pleasant walk. Went [past] the President's house & saw my old school & house [&] returned by the Baptist college. Also, I called to see Cousin Rob Minor [Lieutenant Robert D. Minor, CSN] but he was absent. Saw at his [house] the poet [James Barron] Hope who is staying with him. Had a warm

Midshipman Hubbard T. Minor (author's collection).

walk down to the vessel & soon went to supper & then smoked my Powhattan pipe that Uncle Will gave me.

>Robert D. Minor, Hubbard's cousin, was born in Virginia, and was formerly a lieutenant in the United States Navy. He resigned his commission, however, upon the secession of Virginia, and served briefly in the Virginia Navy during April of 1861. He was commissioned a first lieutenant in the Confederate States Navy on June 10, 1861, and promoted to first lieutenant on October 23, 1862, to rank from October 2, 1862. During 1861 and 1862, Minor served as director of the Bureau of Ordnance and Hydrography, and participated in the capture of the United States steamer *St. Nicholas* on June 29, 1861. He also served on the ironclad CSS *Virginia* where he acted as flag lieutenant to Admiral Buchanan. He was severely wounded during the battle of Hampton Roads, Virginia, on March 8, 1862, and after his recovery, served on ordnance duty at Richmond during 1862 and 1863. Here he was in charge of the Naval Ordnance Works at Richmond through most of 1864. Robert D. Minor was paroled at the end of the war on May 3, 1865, at Richmond, Virginia. (Moebs, Confederate States Navy Research Guide, p. 242.)
>
>James Barron Hope was a prestigious Virginia poet who in 1857 published, in Philadelphia, his first volume, "Leoni di Monota, and Other Poems." In this appeared his spirited "Charge at Balaklava," which was widely admired. The same year, acting as the poet at the two hundred and fiftieth anniversary of the settlement at Jamestown, he began to deliver those memorial poems which gained him the sobriquet of "Virginia's laureate." Hope was the nephew of Captain Samuel Barron, CSN, and served as a captain in the Confederate army during the war. (Trent, Southern Writers: Selections in Prose and Verse, pp. 295–296.) [RTC]

Monday, August 17

Studied hard all day long and will in a day or two catch up with the class for which I am now studying. This morning went in & had a nice swim & also got a single drawer cut large enough to [fit] the few clothes I have & put most of them in it together with [my] smoking tobacco which I find it quite difficult to keep under lock & key. We have it a great deal worse on board that I expected & sometimes I wish I were still in the army, but then when I think that here I am getting a good education & at the same time serving my country I am content.

>Minor's class was seven months ahead of him, and during the next week he worked hard in order to catch up with them. Studying did not seem to interest him, however, for according to his diary, he applied the next week for a leave of absence in order to visit his relatives and friends. He finally returned to the *Patrick Henry* on August 30, 1863. [RTC]

Sunday, August 30

Went to St. Paul's [Episcopal] Church with Miss Savage & had quite a good sermon from Mr. Menegerrode [Reverend Charles Minnigerode] & late in the evening called to see Cousin Bob Minor & his wife & he promised to get me orders for sea if I could skimp one year. After tea returned to the vessel & reported for duty.

>Founded in 1845 by members of Monumental Church, St. Paul's was at the center of Confederate Richmond, counting numerous soldiers and leaders among those in attendance, especially General Robert E. Lee and President Jefferson Davis. The Rev. Dr. Charles Minnigerode stood out among nineteenth-century rectors because of his leadership of the church during the war. [RTC]

Monday, August 31

Have been studying all day & have written as I said some distance behind from the 18th up to the present time. Went down just a moment ago to see how much pay was due me & found that I was in debt but not as much as I expected. I succeeded today in catching up with the class in everything except algebra. Now good night.

Wednesday, September 2, 1863

Succeeded in having my teeth fixed & returned to the ship & went steadily to work. I have still one tooth to plug for which will cost me 12 dollars & this will make 37 dollars in all for fixing my teeth. Tomorrow I will go up by ten o'clock & have the above job done.

Friday, September 4

Went uptown in the morning & in the evening took a delightful sail in one of our large boats. Jams. Minnegerode [Midshipman James G. Minnigerode who most probably was the son of the Episcopal bishop] & another young man was with me.

Saturday, September 5

Went uptown & saw as much as possible of Aunt Vinnie & all before the leave which will be over Monday. In the evening called to see Miss Mary Savage & spent quite a nice time with her, then came back to my boat & rolled into my hammock.

Sunday, September 6

Again went up town & went to Centenary Church to hear Mr. Duncan one of the finest preachers in the city, then met with Theodore Martin who was wounded at Gettysburg, also with William Maben & with Miss Savage with whom I walked home. Took dinner with Edgar Hill & in the evening came back to my boat.

Monday, September 7

Studied hard & did very well & in the evening read some few pages in Bulwer's "What will he do with it" & became intensely interested though I had read some portion of it before.

Tuesday, September 8

After study hours took another good sail in the glorious James & enjoyed myself very much for I had a good wind for the most of the time & besides was with two agreeable companions.

Wednesday, September 9

Studied hard all day & feel quite tired on this day. I also heard from Stephen A Cowley who writes in a very despondent mood of the Army of which I was a member. With his letter was enclosed one to me from my brother which was written before he saw me at Chattanooga. Mr. Cowley informed me that my transfer had arrived all safe & approved & now I perhaps might have occupied a good position & among troops less noble than none in the field. He speaks of the enemy's having reached the door of the Confederacy, Chattanooga, & says that he thinks that they are unable to force an entrance.

Friday, September 11

Don't recollect what I did on this day so you must excuse me if I do not interest you. I recollect that being on watch at midnight & thinking of my first boyish love & its object my love returned with full force, & I resolved to write Rosalie & ascertain my fate, but recollecting that Bulwer who I have been reading all along says that when we see the object of our affection after an absence of many years that we love no longer & wonder that we could ever have loved such a personage, but in Darrel that was false for he looked at the object of his earliest love & felt that he could love no other but his whom he first loved for he never loved his wife. At any rate I resolved to await until I had again seen Rosalie before I in any way committed myself, but how long that resolve will last I do not know.

Saturday, September 12
All of this day I spent on board ship & wrote a long letter to Edward Rivers & in the evening was put in charge of a boat to convey the secretary of the navy, Mr. Mallory [Stephen R. Mallory] & his wife, across the river to the gunboat. After that I copied in my little book of original poetry a piece I had written in Cousin Lou Scott's album.

> Stephen R. Mallory was born at Port of Spain in 1811 or 1812 (records are unclear). In 1820 his family moved to Key West, Florida. There he grew to manhood, and in 1850, he was elected to Congress as a United States Senator. During much of the next ten years, as the nation slipped perspicuously down the slope toward civil war, Mallory served as chairman of the Naval Affairs Committee. After Florida's secession from the Union, young Mallory resigned his Senate seat, and on February 25, 1861, President Jefferson Davis appointed him Secretary of the Confederate States Navy. [RTC]

Tuesday, September 15
After study hours took another sail with same boat & same companions as the last time. The wind was fairer this time than either of the others & our only fault was in getting too far down the river & the wind dying away with the sun we were forced to pull back to our quarters.

Wednesday, September 16
On this day studied hard & have been at the head of my class for some days.

Thursday, September 17
I will skip from this day to the 28th of this month which is today Monday. On Thursday, 24th I learned that Cousin Robert Minor was going to sea & went up in the evening of the following day to see him, but he was absent from town so I wrote to him & have not yet received an answer to my letter. I asked him to take me to sea with him & I am in hopes that he will be able to do so. Today is a beautiful one & I have just come out of a lecture room.

On Board Steamer *Patrick Henry*
Richmond, Va., Sept. 24th, 1863

Lieutenant Robt. Minor, C. S. N.
Dear Cousin:
    Having learned that you were going to sea, I am anxious to go with you, & went, last night, to Capt. Parker, & asked permission to go up town & see you. He told me that you were not in town, that he had written to you; & that his letter, would be delivered, to you as soon as you returned; when he thought you would come on board, but that I might go up in the morning, & inquire when you would return. I went up town this evening, & found that John, & yourself also, were out of town, & not likely to return until the day of starting from this point. I therefore obtained your address, & have taken this mode of communicating writing. You told me some time ago that you could arrange to get me orders to sea & if you could manage to take me with you, I shall be much obliged to you. I had rather establish a reputation under you, than anybody I know of; for should I do so, it would surly be deserved; & then, too if I do not first enjoy the good opinion of one who takes more than a common interest in me, how can I hope to enjoy that of others who do not. Besides, I prefer you, as do many others, with whom to serve. Should Mr. Mallory object to my going to sea, because I am in the fourth class, I am willing, at any time, to stand an examination for the third, without the fear of the results. I asked Capt. Parker if it would not be of advantage to me, to go to sea now, if possible, & he said that it would be, & I think he will approve any application for orders you think it necessary to make. Mr. Brit-

tingham, the gunner, made application to be sent with your party, and his application was approved by Capt. Parker. Mr. B. thinks that he will be able to go if you ask for him. Remember me to Mrs. Minor whom I suppose you are with. I hoped to have the pleasure of hearing her sing before she left Richmond, but could not get off ship for a single day she was here. I am very tired of staying here, & would like very much to go with you, & promise to do my duty as well as I am able, & to study hard all the while. Now goodby.

Very respectfully,

Your Obt. Servant,
Midn. H.T. Minor, Jr.
Steamer *Patrick H.*
Richmond, Va.

Tuesday, September 29

All of this day have been spent in hard study & onerous duty. Nothing of any importance has occurred, so I will close until tomorrow. At night had a fight with midshipman [unintelligible, probably Lewis Levy] & got the best of it. Was suspended & so was he.

Wednesday, September 30

This is the day in which Cousin Robert Minor was to return & having been released from suspension I obtained permission to go uptown & see him. He had not received my letter for which circumstances I was sorry, for he was very busy & would have paid more attention to it than to myself, & besides I wished him to see it. He said that there would be no chance for me [to go to sea] until I had graduated, so I have made up my mind to get through as soon as possible, then come what will I am prepared for it.

Thursday, October 1, 1863

Spent like the most of my days here in hard study & duty on this day. While reading over the [Richmond] *Inquirer*, I saw the death of Cousin Joe Pannell announced & quite a beautiful tribute attached to it. I have the tribute with the announcement of his death now & will preserve it. It is signed "W." I intended to have gone over to Petersburg tomorrow & had asked for permission to do so which was refused, & when I saw the notice of Cousin Joe's death, which took place on Monday, I was reconciled to the refusal.

Friday, October 2

Went on watch at midnight & stood until four in the morning. On this day we had quite a hard lesson in algebra, in which I stood quite a good examination.

> The cadets at the Academy were required to be enrolled in one of four classes. Minor studied, besides algebra, practical seamanship, gunnery, artillery, infantry tactics, geometry, plane and spherical trigonometry, physical geography, history, and French. [RTC]

Saturday, October 3

Will go on watch again today from 12 to 4 & then shall go up town. Was paid off also on this day & the amount I received is not sufficient to pay my mess bill. I hope this evening to get some letters from uncle Will & to have a good game of billiards.

Sunday, October 4

Went up to church & heard quite a good sermon from Mr. Peterkin then went round to church to see whom I knew, & as I expected, met Miss Mary Savage & walked home with her, then called on Miss Anna Dean & Frank who arrived here from the army 2 days ago. After that, took dinner at the American Hotel & then returned to the ship. As I was coming down Main Street I overtook the funeral procession of a soldier & the band was playing one of the sweetest tunes I ever heard. 'Twas soft, sad, & sweet. It forcibly reminded me of the first funeral tune I heard since I left home to join the army & which I mentioned sometime ago at the time I heard it.

Monday, October 5

Came off duty this morning & have been demerited for smoking during study hours. Saw this evening Miss Mary Savage, her sister & several other ladies & expect to see them again tonight. They have gone down to Drury's [Drewry's] Bluff & will return by dusk.*

Tuesday, October 6

All of this day has been spent in hard study & nothing of importance has occurred. The days all slip swiftly by here in the same monotonous way.

Friday, October 9

Was informed that we would go to this Bluff [Drewry's] tomorrow evening & that in the meantime, all who were not on duty were at liberty to go to town, so I went up & told all of my friends good-by & also wrote a letter to Cousin Ellen Jackson by flag of truce she was to forward it to Pa. Left the letter with Uncle Will & returned to the ship.

Saturday, October 10

Again went uptown & returned by twelve o'clock. left at 2 o'clock & with our huge craft started for the Bluff where we arrived safely.

Sunday, October 11

Obtained permission to go on shore & look around & was charmed with the place, & only wish that I was in command of a piece of heavy ordnance & stationed here on the bluff. There is quite a little village here now & two churches in one of them. Bishop Johns preached today but as it was a very small one, I did not get in but stood on the outside of the door for some time & at length went away. I walked around the fortifications & was charmed with their appearance also. Took dinner on the Bluff with some midshipmen who are stationed there & in the evening walked down with them to the shore & hailed the *Patrick Henry* which is lying out in the river opposite the Bluff. A boat was sent for us & we all went on board, & later in the evening I was sent in charge of a boat to bring Mrs. [William H.] Parker aboard who had remained on shore after church.

Monday, October 12

On this day while at the black board there was one of the strangest things happened to me I ever saw. I was unable to do anything at all & I could not reason one bit.

Wednesday, October 14

Studied here all day & will try to take a sail this evening with some members of the [CSS] *Nansemond*.†

Drewry's Bluff was the principle fortification on the James River seven miles south of Richmond. It was here on May 15, 1862, that Union warships were repulsed, and it would later become the anchorage of the Patrick Henry *and the living quarters for the midshipmen attending the Academy. [RTC]*

†*The CSS* Nansemond *was a small wooden steamer built at Norfolk, Virginia, in 1862. The 166-ton gunboat was armed with two 8-inch guns and was assigned to duty with the James River Squadron under Flag Officer Samuel Barron, CSN. With Lieutenant John Rutledge, CSN, in command, she sailed from Norfolk with the other vessels of the squadron on May 4, 1862, just prior to the evacuation of the Gosport Navy Yard. The* Nansemond *continued on active duty in the James River until the end of the war. Her commander in November of 1863 was Lieutenant James H. Rochelle, CSN. (Dictionary of American Fighting Ships, "Confederate Forces Afloat" Vol. II, Appendix II, p. 275.) [RTC]*

Thursday, October 15

Studied hard & got good marks. This evening will review all I have been over lately & perfect myself for the coming examination.

Friday, October 16

Read today a letter from Grand Pa Minor forwarded by Uncle Will stating that he would be in Richmond on the 15th which was yesterday & that I must come up & see him. I applied for permission to do so but cannot go until tomorrow. I then have permission to stay until Monday morning until 9 o'clock.

Saturday, October 17

Awoke by 4 o'clock & then walked two miles, after being put on shore, to the Petersburg railroad when I took the cars for Richmond.... I arrived at 7 o'clock took a good Breakfast at a restaurant & then sat about finding my grand father, but did not succeed until dinner time. Spent the evening with him & then we both went to Mrs. Hills & took supper where he stayed all night. A little while after supper we called upon Mrs. Herndon & family & then separated to meet in the morning.

Sunday, October 18

Today Grand Pa left. He came around to uncle Wills soon, with whom I staid, & fixed up his bundle of purchases & told us good by. Sometime latter I dressed myself & went down to the Spotswood Hotel & got breakfast. I then went to St. James Grammar School & saw Miss Savage, Miss Meridith, & Mr. Christian, & several others. Then to St. Paul's & heard Mr. Minnigerode & after church went home with James Dunlop & took dinner with him & was invited to come up at any time & make myself at home there. After dinner lit my segar & walked out to Camp Lee & then returned by way of Grace St. & called on the Miss Savage but they were out. I then left word that I would call that night & take them to church. Took supper at the American & then proceeded to fulfill my promise. I spent quite a pleasant time with Miss Mary, Miss Parker being too unwell to accompany us. After I had sat a little while when I had returned from church told her good-by & went to uncle Wills soon & stayed all night with him.

Monday, October 19

Awoke early & walked to Rocketts [Rocketts Landing] to be in time for the boat which ought to have left at eight o'clock but did not do so until after 9 some time & in consequence I was too late for the morning duties but was excused as I had done all I could to get here.

Tuesday, October 20

Studied hard all day & have done pretty well. Today has been a sad one with me. Late this evening I was ordered to hold myself in readiness to take charge of the boys for Richmond & am now ready & must bid you good-by until the morrow when I will tell you of my trip to the city.

Wednesday, October 21

Last evening I had a crew of six men & the Capt. & Mrs. Parker went with me to the city. We went up on the *Nansemond*, a screw steamer, & got to Richmond at about 20 minutes to seven & the Capt. then told me that he would be there at 9 o'clock. I then allowed all of my crew to go on shore well knowing that they would all be quite intoxicated but determined never the less to gratify them knowing I could easily control them no matter in what state they were. I remained on board not caring to go uptown for so short a time of [on] the steamer along side of which I had ordered the barge to be lashed. At five minutes to 9 o'clock the Capt. came on board & asked if I was there & I immediately advanced & recd him & informed him that all was ready my crew having returned as I had ordered some minutes before nine & assisting the Capt. & his wife in the boat gave the orders to shove off & pulled rapidly down the river beneath the silvery light of the moon. Along the way I conversed with Mrs. Parker for some time. I found that she knew both my father & mother. I pulled that night against a flood tide 7½ miles in an hour & 25 minutes & then went to rest. All of this day I have spent in hard study.*

Thursday, October 22

Today I have been looking over my last volume of memorandum & have been making out there from an account against the government which I will collect if possible on Saturday coming. On this day I wrote to Miss Rosalie Rives & hope that she will answer my letter.

Friday, October 23

Spent the morning in study & in the evening took a walk of three miles over to Stark's [Major Alexander W.] Battalion of Artillery & inquired for Mr. Rives & William Harrison, but they had left his battalion & I understand are now with Col. Lightfoot [Lieutenant Colonel Charles E.] on the other side of Richmond. I expect to go up to tomorrow & will call & see them.

Saturday, October 24

Got permission to go up in town to collect my account against the government & return the following morning, so I arose early & started in the rain for the cars & got to Richmond & stopped at the Spotswood House & it being raining I played billiards nearly all day & not being able to collect my account without my orders, which I had forgotten to bring, had to get the proprietor of the hotel to credit me which he readily did knowing me well. Mrs. Betts & Uncle Will, being out of town, I could do nothing but go to him.

Sunday, October 25

Went to St. James grammar school & was asked to teach a class of young ladies but not feeling my self capable of doing so declined. I borrowed from Mr. Dashids a book on confirmation by Bishop McIlwaine & intend to prepare myself for confirmation at the earliest opportunity. At 20 minutes to eleven o'clock left for the wharf to come down on the *Schultz* [CSS *Schultz*], but the boat starting as I believe before her schedule time 1/2 past eleven, I was left & had to remain until the following morning. [I] then went to St Paul's church & after dinner went out to see Mrs. Rives & Wm. H. & was surprised to find Edward Harrison a lieutenant of the battery. William was out but came before I left & walked into town with me. We then called to take the Miss Savage to church but they

---

*Lieutenant William H. Parker, superintendent of the Naval Academy, was a son of Commodore Foxhall Parker, USN, and brother of Commander Foxhall A. Parker, USN. While one brother went with the South, the other remained in the Federal navy during the war, and attained distinction. William H. Parker entered the U.S. Navy in 1841, when he was only 14 years old, and was graduated at the head of a class at the Naval Academy that gave to the United States and Confederate States service more distinguished officers than any other single class. Previous to the War Between the States, he had attained a high reputation as an officer and instructor, and held the position of assistant professor of mathematics at the Annapolis Institution. In the Confederate Navy he had taken part in the battles in the North Carolina Sounds, had commanded the gunboat Beaufort *at the battle of Hampton Roads, and was executive officer of the iron-clad* Palmetto State *at Charleston in the breaking of the blockade. His professional writings were used as textbooks at Annapolis and in the Confederate Naval Academy. They were "Elements of Seamanship," "Harbor Routine and Evolutions," "Naval Tactics," "Naval Light Artillery Afloat and Ashore," and "Remarks on the Navigation of the Coasts between San Francisco and Panama." (Scharf,* History of the Confederate States Navy, *p. 773.) [RTC]*

had already gone so we went ourselves to St Paul's & then I told him good-by, promising to meet him at the Spotswood Hotel next Saturday. I also [saw] Mr. Rives who is now married.*

Monday, October 26

As I said above I was forced to remain in the city until this morning & when I got on board I was quarantined for two weeks & cannot now leave the vessel for any purposes whatsoever & though I have promised to meet William Harrison at the Spotswood House on the coming Saturday I fear I shall disappoint him, but not if I can help it for I shall ask permission to go up on Saturday.

Tuesday, October 27

This day, like many, has passed swiftly away & I do not know anything of importance that has occurred except that I have all the day that I could call my own been reading the Scottish Chiefs & have been intensely delighted.

Wednesday, October 28

Again I have passed those hours which my duty allowed me in perusing Mrs. [Jane] Porter's matchless production of the Scottish Chiefs. I read of the noble deeds of Wm. Wallace, [and] I feel myself elevated to something beyond my finer self & think that it is one of the most beneficial works to inoculate the principals of virtue, but one ought not read it until he is able to appreciate it in its true spirit. Most persons read this volume too soon.

Thursday, October 29

Was put on duty for a little while but I was relieved & again, when opportunity afforded, have followed Miss Porter as she forcibly attracts me with a heaving bosom & attentive interest.

Friday, October 30

On this day I have felt quite gloomy & have walked the deck for my hours in communing with myself. Ah! how I long to be once more at home among those who love me so well & who now mourn over my wearisome stay. I feared I cannot get off to see my friend but intend to ask the Capt.'s permission to do so to night. Now farewell.

Saturday, October 31

Nearly all of this day it has been raining & I have been unable to go uptown on account of the rain, but intend doing so this evening, rain, hail, or shine. As I intended I go uptown this evening & it has cleared off beautifully & I shall enjoy myself much. I have permission to remain in town until Monday morning & then I must again betake myself to my duty here. On this day I was released from my quarantine & feel in quite a good humor.

Tuesday, November 3, 1863

All of this day I have been studying & also finished the Scottish Chiefs & was quarantined for ten days again, & I think quite unjustly, by the Capt. as there were many committing the same offense at the time with myself & not one of them in any way was punished. I fear that I will have to be at eternal war with Lt. Hall [Lieutenant Wilburn B. Hall, Commandant of Midshipmen] the executive officer as long as he or I remain aboard, for I was bound by duty to report him one day & he has taken outrage at my having done

---

*The CSS Schultz, *also known as* A.H. Schultz, *was built at New York, New York. She served the Confederates in the James River, Virginia, as a flag-of-truce boat, and was probably armed.* Schultz *was accidentally blown up in the James River by a Confederate torpedo which may have drifted from its original position.* [RTC]

so & now looks for every opportunity in his power to get me into trouble. He has a contemptible disposition & no chivalric feeling or he would not use such petty revenge. I feel almost at times like it would do me good to humble his mean spirit.*

Wednesday, November 4
On this day we were drilled in the launch with a boat howitzer & I was one of the stroke oarsmen & was not like a good many obliged to jump overboard when we landed the howitzer. On this day I was again reported & very unjustly. I am getting into a snare with everybody, but know not why. I look every day for an answer to my letter from Miss Rosalie Rives, but have begun to despair of ever hearing from her. Now good-by.

Thursday, November 5
Drilled in small arms & I fear that I will be reported for being late at drill, but did not know that it was time or I would have been there. Today has been a beautiful one, & there was a party of young men & I was invited to be one of them who chartered the steamer *Schultz* & brought a nice party of young ladies, most of whom I knew down to the Bluff. I should like to have been with them but owing to my quarantine could not.

Friday, November 6
All of this day has been a beautiful one & in the evening we were drilled in the launch with the howitzer & I was one of the stroke oarsmen a place given to good oarsmen. I no longer expect to hear from Miss Rives nor will I again trouble her with my correspondence. I am not allowed to leave the ship except on duty being still under quarantine.

Saturday, November 7
Today all on board was quiet for almost all of the midshipmen have gone away on liberty & those who have not are with the boardroom offices or in the cutter sailing. I stood some time & watched the noble little vessel plough the white cap waves & not able to bear my disappointment at not being one of those who [rode] in her came below & and now writing my disappointment down.

Sunday, November 8
This is another beautiful day & again some are out & enjoying it but I, besides being debarred pleasure of even liberty, am on duty on board.

Monday, November 9
Again all is bustle on board for all are now present & ready for the duties of the day

---

Born and reared in South Carolina, Wilburn B. Hall was also graduated from the United States Naval Academy at the top of his class in 1859. He served one year on the sloop USS Constellation before the outbreak of war. Having only recently been graduated from the academy at Annapolis, Hall was still a midshipman when he resigned from the U.S. service on March 7, 1861. His first appointment, July 24, 1861, was that of a master, but he quickly proved his worth and was commissioned a lieutenant on September 19, 1861. Hall served on the Confederate steamers CSS Resolute and CSS Savannah with the Savannah Squadron during the latter part of 1861 and into 1862. Next Hall went to Charleston where he was assigned for a short time to the CSS Huntress. He also saw duty on the CSS Tuscaloosa at Mobile and at the naval station in Selma, Alabama, during 1862. From there, Hall was transferred west of the Mississippi River to Galveston, Texas, where he joined the officers on the CSS Harriet Lane. At this time the Red River Squadron at Shreveport, Louisiana, was desperately short of officers and men, and on April 21, 1863, Hall led a contingent of forty men to Shreveport to reinforce the depleted squadron. By October he was on the Patrick Henry where he assumed the duties of Commandant of Midshipmen. (Register of Officers of the Confederate States Navy, 1861–1865, 1864.) [RTC]

& I too am relieved of duty & ready to do my part in what takes place on every week day. Today we drilled at the great guns & I was first sponger of the gun to which I was attached.

Tuesday, November 10
Hard study is the order of the day & I have struggled hard to do my part in carrying it out. We had today a hard lesson in algebra & I think that I got through it quite well. Nothing of much importance has occurred. I think it quite strange that uncle Will Pannell has not answered my letter & must write & find if possible a list of Pa's Law Book's which was among Cousin Jos Pannell's papers. Must also write to Grand Pa, & all.

Wednesday, November 11
Again have gone through my daily routine of duty & study & am now at leisure not knowing what to do. On this day we again drilled in launch & I had my old place of stroke oarsman. We fired blank cartridges & they made quite a noise & a great many were unable to keep the stroke for jumping when she fired, but I have gotten used to them & had as soon hear them as not. But don't like them with balls.

Monday, November 15
Awoke early from a comfortable sleep & walked down to the cars & got off to the Bluff & have gone through my duties with a heavy heart. In the evening I asked permission to go to Petersburg on business but was not allowed to do so. Today we drilled at great guns & shot some rounds at a target & most of the shots struck.

Tuesday, November 16
Drilled in launch & fired some shrapnel & shell but only burst one or two of the former.

Wednesday, November 17
All of this [day] have been studying & this evening drilled with small arms.

Thursday, November 18
Drilled in launch & fired shell & shrapnel again & bursted most of them all.

Friday, November 19
Been hard at study & will drill again in the launch this evening.

Saturday, November 20
I do not know what occurred on this day nor on any of the succeeding ones of this month so I shall skip up to the period on which I do recollect. Today is the 7th of December, 1863, Sunday, & I shall commence on the 1st of December, Tuesday, 1863.

Tuesday, December 1, 1863
On this day I was challenged to a duel which I accepted knowing that nothing would come of it & such was the case.

Wednesday, December 2
On this day I asked permission to go to Petersburg but did not get it.

Thursday, December 3
On this day went to Richmond & there met Willie Harrison & promised to come & see him before I was ordered off from the state & he told me that he had something nice to tell me. I spoke to him of going up in Albemarle Co. [County] before I left the state.*

---

*Midshipmen who had passed their examinations would most likely be ordered to active duty with the various squadrons within the Confederacy. [RTC]

Tuesday, December 8

On this day they examined my class in mathematics & I passed in a class of 50 or more No 2 or 3. I will now prepare for the examination on grammar tomorrow.

Wednesday, December 9

Today I passed the examination on grammar & think that I am entirely through & still retain the same study as on my mathematical examination. On this day a great many of the graduates left for their respective stations & we are expecting our orders everyday as it is determined not to give us the above mentioned leave of absence but to assign us immediately to duty.

Thursday, December 10

On this day some of my class received their orders but they were all ordered to Mobile Ala. & we still await ours. I went up town today & saw uncle Will & got from him the sum of 40 dollars which makes 310 dollars in all that I have gotten from him.

Friday, December 11, 1863

I returned onboard of the ship in time to get my orders to Savannah Ga. & immediately set to work to pack up my things in order that I might go up to Richmond for I had no idea of going directly off but intended to apply for a two weeks leave of absence which I did but only got three days leave to visit my Grand Pa in Caroline Co. This was on Saturday that I applied for the leave & I intended to go up on Sunday Dec. 13th 1863, & this I did, but did not see my Grand Father but spent the few days I stayed there quite pleasantly.*

3. Confederate Treasury

On April 1, 1865, General Grant's army, which greatly outnumbered the Army of Northern Virginia, outflanked General Lee's thin lines southwest of Petersburg at the Battle of Five Forks, and Grant ordered an all-out assault along the trenches for the next day. Union batteries shelled the Confederate lines all night, and at first light the storm broke. Ragged Southern soldiers fought savagely all day, but little by little they were forced out of their positions. That night Lee began his withdrawal. (*Civil War Naval Chronology, 1861–1865*, p. V-75.)

By this same day, Lieutenant William H. Parker had spent two and one-half years as commandant of the Confederate Naval Academy. His duties there, and those of his midshipmen, were about to change; a change that would lead to their finest hour. [RTC]

Although Minor had passed his initial exams, he was not considered a "passed" midshipman, but still a student of the Academy. His next course of training involved assignment to an operational unit, and he was now directed to report to the Savannah Squadron at Savannah, Georgia. (Campbell [ed.], Confederate Naval Cadet: The Diary and Letters of Midshipman Hubbard T. Minor, with a History of the Confederate Naval Academy, *2006.) [RTC]*

"The Gold and Silver in the Confederate States Treasury" by
1st Lt. William H. Parker, CSN

Southern Historical Society Papers, Volume XXI, 1893, pp. 304–308.

I was an officer of the United States Navy from 1841 to 1861. In the latter year I entered the Confederate Navy as lieutenant. During the years 1863-'64-'65 I was the superintendent of the Confederate States Navy Academy. The steamer *Patrick Henry* was the school-ship and the seat of the academy. On the 1st day of April, 1865, we were lying at a wharf on the James river between *Richmond* and *Powhatan*. We had on board some sixty midshipmen and a full corps of professors. The midshipmen were well drilled in infantry tactics, and all of the professors save one had served in the army or navy.

On Sunday, April 2, 1865, I received about noon a dispatch from Hon. S. R. Mallory, Secretary of the Navy, to the following effect: "Have the corps of midshipmen, with the proper officers, at the Danville depot to-day at 6 PM; the commanding officer to report to the Quartermaster-General of the army."

Upon calling at the Navy Department I learned that the city was to be evacuated immediately, and that the services of the corps were required to take charge of and guard the Confederate treasure.

Accordingly at 6 o'clock I was at the depot with all my officers and men—perhaps something over one hundred, all told—and was then put in charge of a train of cars, on which was packed the Confederate treasure, and the money belonging to the banks of Richmond.

About Half a Million

I will here remark that neither the Secretary of the Treasury, nor the Treasurer were with the treasure. The senior officer of the Treasury present was a cashier, and he informed me, to the best of my recollection, that there was about $500,000 in gold, silver, and bullion. I saw the boxes containing it, many times in the weary thirty days I had it under my protection, but I never saw the coin.

Sometime in the evening the President, his Cabinet and other officials left the depot for Danville. The train was well packed. General Breckenridge, Secretary of War, however, did not start with the President. He remained with me at the depot until I got off, which was not until somewhere near midnight. The General went out of the city on horseback.

Our train being heavily loaded and crowded with passengers—even the roofs and platform-steps occupied—went very slowly. How we got by Amelia Courthouse without falling in with Sheridan's men, has been a mystery to me to this day. We were unconscious of our danger, however, and took matters philosophically. Monday, April 3d, in the afternoon, we arrived at Danville, where we found the President and his Cabinet, save General Breckenridge, who came in on Wednesday. On Monday night Admiral Semmes arrived with the officers and men of the James River squadron. His was the last train out of Richmond.

We did not unpack the treasure from the cars at Danville. Some, I believe, was taken for the use of the government, and, I suspect, was paid out to General Johnston's men after the surrender, but the main portion of the money remained with me. The midshipmen bivouacked near the train.

In the Mint

About the 6th of April, I received orders from Mr. Mallory to covey the treasure to Charlotte, N. C., and deposit it in the mint. Somewhere about the 8th, we arrived at Charlotte. I deposited the money-boxes in the mint, took a receipt from the paper officials, and supposed that my connection with it was at an end. Upon attempting to telegraph back to Mr. Mallory for further orders, however, I found that Salisbury was in the hands of the enemy—General Stoneman's men, I think.

The enemy being between me and the President (at least such was the report at the time, though I am not sure now that it was so), and the probability being that he would immediately push for Charlotte, it became necessary to remove the money. I determined, on my own responsibility, to convey it to Macon, Ga.

Mrs. President Davis and family were in town. They had left Richmond a week before the evacuation. I called upon her, represented the danger of capture, and persuaded her to put herself under our protection. A company of uniformed men, under Captain Tabb, volunteered to accompany me. These men were attached to the navy-yard in Charlotte. Most of them belonged to the same little town of Portsmouth, Va., and a better set of men never shouldered a musket. They were as true as steel.

Having laid in, from the naval storehouse, large quantities of coffee, sugar, bacon, and flour, we started in the cars with the treasure and arrived at Chester, S. C. This was, I think, about the 12th of April.

Formed a Train

We here packed the money and papers in wagons and formed a train. We started the same day for Newberry, S.C. Mrs. Davis and family were provided by General Preston with an ambulance. Several ladies in our party—wives of officers—were in army wagons; the rest of the command were on foot, myself included.

The first night we encamped at a crossroads "meeting-house." I here published orders regulating our march and made every man carry a musket. The Treasury clerks, bank officers, and others made up a third company, and we mustered some one hundred and fifty fighting men. Supposing that General Stoneman would follow, we held ourselves ready to repel an attack by day and night.

At sunset of the second day we went into camp about thirty miles form Newberry, S.C., and breaking camp very early the next morning, we crossed the beautiful Broad river on pontoon bridge at noon, and about 4 PM arrived at Newberry. The quartermaster immediately prepared a train of cars, and we started for Abbeville, S.C., as soon as the treasure could be transferred.

Always Ahead

On the march across the state of South Carolina we never permitted a traveler to go in advance of us, and we were not on a line of telegraphic communication; yet, singular to say, the news that we had the Confederate money was always ahead of us. [See Sir Walter Scott's remark on this point in "Old Mortality."] We arrived at Abbeville at midnight, and passed the remainder of the night in the cars. Mrs. Davis and family here left me and went to the house of the Hon. Mr. Burt, a former member of Congress. In the morning we formed a wagon train and started for Washington, Georgia. The news we got at different places along the route was bad; "unmerciful disaster followed fast and followed faster." We "lightened ship" as we went along—throwing away books, stationery, and perhaps Confederate money. One could have traced us by these marks, and have formed an idea of the character of the news we were receiving.

From Abbeville to Washington is about forty miles, and we made a two days' march of it. The first day we crossed the Savannah River about 2 PM and went into camp. The next day we arrived at Washington. Here we learned that General Wilson, United States army, with 10,000 cavalry, had captured Macon, and was on his way north.

After a day's deliberation and a consultation with some of the citizens of Washington, I determined to go to Augusta.

Heard of the Surrender

On the 18th of April, or thereabouts, we left in the train, and at the junction, while we were waiting for the western train to pass, we heard of General Lee's surrender. This we did not at the time credit. We arrived at Augusta in due time, and I made my report to General D. B. Fry, the commanding general. General Fry informed me he could offer no protection, as he had few troops, and was expecting to surrender to General Wilson as soon as he appeared with his cavalry. However, Generals Johnston and Sherman had just declared an armistice, and that gave us a breathing spell. The money remained in the cars, and the midshipmen and the Charlotte company lived in the depot. While in Augusta, and afterwards, I was frequently advised by officious persons to divide the money among the Confederate, as the war was over, and it would otherwise fall into the hands of the Federal troops.

The answer to this was that the war was not over as long as General Johnston held out, and that the money would be held intact until we met President Davis.

Declined to Disband

While waiting in Augusta I received a telegraphic dispatch from Mr. Mallory directing me to disband my command; but under the circumstances I declined to do so.

On the 20th of April, General Fry noticed me that the armistice would end the next day, and he advised me to "move on." I decided to retrace my steps, thinking it more than probable that President Davis would hear of Mrs. Davis being left in Abbeville. Accordingly we left Augusta on the 23d, arrived at Washington the same day, formed a train again, and started for Abbeville. On the way we met Mrs. President Davis and family, escorted by Col. Burton N. Harrison, the President' private secretary. I have forgotten where they said they were going, if they told me.

Threats Made to Seize It

Upon our arrival at Abbeville, which was, I think, about the 28th, we stored the treasure in an empty warehouse and placed a guard over it. The town was full of paroled men from General Lee's army. Threats were made by these men to seize the money, but the guard remained firm. On the night of May 1st I was aroused by the officer commanding the patrol, and told that "the Yankees were coming." We transferred the treasure to the train of cars which I had ordered to be kept ready with steam up, intending to run to Newberry.

Just at daybreak, as we were ready to start, we saw some horsemen descending the hills, and upon sending out scouts learned that they were the advance guard of President Davis.

About 10 AM May 2, 1865, President Davis and his Cabinet (save Messrs. Trenholm and Davis) rode in. They were escorted by four skeleton brigades of cavalry—not more than one thousand badly-armed men in all. These brigades were, I think, Duke's, Dibrell's, Vaughan's, and Ferguson's. The train was a long one. There were many brigadier-generals present—General Bragg among them—and wagons innumerable.

Turned Over to General Duke

I had several interviews with President Davis and found him calm and composed, and resolute to a degree. As soon as I saw Mr. Mallory he directed me to deliver the treasure to General Basil Duke, and disband my command. I went to the depot, and there, in the presence of my command, transferred it accordingly. General Duke was on horseback, and no papers passed. The Charlotte company immediately started for home, accompanied by our best wishes. I have a dim recollection that a keg of cents was presented to Captain Tabb for distribution among his men, and that the magnificent present was indignantly declined.

The treasure was delivered to General Duke intact so far as I know, though some of it was taken at Danville by authority. It had been guarded by the Confederate midshipmen for thirty days, and preserved by them. In my opinion this is what no other organization could have done in those days.

A Gallant Corps

And here I must pay a tribute to these young men—many of them mere lads—who stood by me for so many anxious days. Their training and discipline showed itself conspicuously during that time. During the march across South Carolina, footsore and ragged as they had become by that time, no murmur escaped them, and they never faltered. I am sure that Mr. Davis and Mr. Mallory, if they were alive, would testify to the fact that when they saw the corps in Abbeville, way-worn and nearly after its long march, it presented the same undaunted front as when it left Richmond. They were staunch to the last, and verified the adage that "blood will tell."

The officers with me at this time were Captain Rochelle, Surgeon Garrleson, Paymaster Wheliss, and Lieutenant Peek, McGuire, Sanxay, and Armistead. Lieutenants Peek, McGuire, and Armistead are living, and will testify to the truth of the above narrative.

Immediately after turning the money over to General Duke I disbanded my command. And here end my personal knowledge of the Confederate treasure.

What Become of the Money

On the evening of May 2d, the President and troops started for Washington, Ga. The next day the cavalry insisted upon having some of the money (so its is stated), and General Breckinridge, with the consent of the President, I believe, paid out of them $100,000. A least, that is the sum I have seen stated. I know nothing of it myself. It was a wise proceeding on the part of the General, and it enabled the poor, worn-out men to reach their homes.

Its Disposition

The remainder of the treasure was carried to Washington, Ga. Here Captain M. H. Clark was appointed assistant treasurer, and in a frank and manly letter to the Southern Historical Society Papers, for December, 1881, he tells of the disposition of a portion of the money. Some $40,000, he says, was entrusted to two naval officers for a special purpose—to take to England, probably—but I happen to know that this was not done, and this money was never accounted for, and moderate sums were paid to various officers, whose vouchers he produces. Thus, it seems, he paid $1,500 to two of the President's aids, and the same amount to my command. That is, he gave us who had preserved the treasure for thirty days the same amount he gave to each of the aids. I do not know who ordered this distribution, but we were very glad to get it, as we were far from home and penniless. It gave us each twenty days' pay.

President Jefferson Davis (National Archive).

Never Accounted For

In my opinion a good deal of the money was never accounted for, and there remains what sailors call a "Flemish account" of it.

The Mysterious Box

Several years ago I read in the papers an account of a box being left with a widow lady who lived, in 1865, near the pontoon bridge across the Savannah River. It was to this effect: The lady stated that on May 3, 1865, a party of gentlemen on their way from Abbeville to Washington, Ga., stopped at her house, and were a long time in consultation in her parlor. These gentlemen were Mr. Davis and his Cabinet beyond a doubt. Upon leaving, they gave the lady a box, which, they stated, was too heavy to take with them. After they were gone the lady opened the box, and found it to be full of jewelry. Somewhat embarrassed with so valuable a gift, the lady sent for her minister (a Baptist) and told him her circumstances. By his advice, she buried the box in her garden secretly at night. A few days after, an officer rode up to the house, inquired about the box, and said he had been sent back for it. The lady delivered it up, and the man went off.

Now, I believe this story to be true in every respect, and I furthermore believe that the box contained the jewelry which had been contributed by patriotic Confederate ladies. The idea had been suggested some time in 1864, but was never fully carried out. Nevertheless, some ladies sacrificed their jewels, as I have reason to know.

As for the man who carried off the box, whether he was really sent back for it or was a despicable thief, will probably never be known, but to say the least, his action was, as our Scotch friends say, "vara suspicious."

Capture of President Davis

Mr. Davis was captured on the morning of May 9th, just a week after my interview with him at Abbeville. There were with him at the time Mrs. Davis and three children; Miss Howell, her sister; Mr. Reagan, Postmaster-General; Colonels Johnston, Lubbock, and Wood, volunteer aids; Mr. Burton Harrison, secretary, and, I think, a Mr. Barnwell, of South Carolina. There may have been others, but I do not know. Of these, all were captured save only Mr. Barnwell.

It is not my intention to write of this affair, as I was not present, and besides, Colonels Johnston and Lubbock, Judge Reagan, and others have written full accounts of it. I only intend to tell of the escape of my old friend and comrade, John Taylor Wood, as I had it from his lips only a few months ago in Richmond. It has never appeared in print, and I am only sorry I cannot put in the graphic language of Wood himself.

But this is what he told me, as well as I recollect:

Colonel Wood's Escape

The party was captured just before daybreak on the 9th of May. Wood was placed in charge of a Dutchman, who spoke no English. While the rest of the Federal troops were busy in securing their prisoners and plundering the camp, Wood held a $20 gold piece (the universal interpreter) to his guard, and signified his desire to escape. The Dutchman held up two fingers and nodded. Wood gave him $40 in gold, and stole off to a field, where he laid down among some brushwood. The Federals (under a Colonel Pritchett, I think), having finished their preparations, march off without missing Colonel Wood.

Started for Florida

After they were out of sight, Wood arose and found a broken-down horse, which had been left behind. He also found an old bridle, and mounting the nag, he started for Florida. I have forgotten his adventures, but somewhere on the route he fell in with Mr. Benjamin, Secretary of State, and General Breckinridge, Secretary of War. Benjamin and Breckinridge owed their escape to Wood, for Wood was an old naval officer and a thorough seaman. On the coast of Florida they bought a row-boat, and in company of a few others they rowed down the coast, intending either to cross to Cuba or the Bahamas.

A Close Call

Landing one day for water and to dig clams they saw a Federal gunboat coming up the coast. Wood mentioned as an evidence of the close watch the United States vessels were keeping, that as soon as the gunboat got abreast of them she stopped and lowered a boat. Thinking it best to put a bold face on the matter, Wood took a couple of men and rowed out to meet the man-of-war's boat. The officer asked who they were. They replied: "Paroled soldiers from Lee's army, making their way home." The officer demanded their paroles, and was told the men on shore had them. It was a long distance to pull, and the officer decided to return to his ship for orders. As he pulled away Wood cried to him: "Do you want to buy any clams?"

Upon the return of the boat she was hoisted up, the gunboat proceeded on her way, and our friends "saw her no more." Proceeding on her way to the southward, the party next fell in with a sail-boat, in which were three sailors, deserters from United States vessels at Key West, trying to make their way to Savannah. Wood and party took their boat, as she was a seaworthy craft, put the sailors in the row-boat, and gave them sailing directions for Savannah.

Wood then took the helm and steered for Cuba. In a squall that night he was knocked overboard. There was but one man in the boat who knew anything at all about managing her, and it looked black for him. Fortunately he caught the main sheet, which was trailing overboard, and was hauled in. It was providential, for upon Wood depended the safety of the entire party.

After suffering much from hunger and thirst they arrived at Matanzas (I think) and were kindly cared for by the Spanish authorities, from whom they received most respectful attention as soon as they made themselves known.

WILLIAM H. PARKER.
Richmond, Va.

Some Final Thoughts

When the Civil War ended, most Confederate naval officers found themselves completely destitute. Not only had they lost their commands, they had also lost their country. As a result, a few went to South America where they served in the navies of Brazil and Argentina during the War of the Triple Alliance. Some, along with several army officers, moved to Egypt, while still others remained overseas in England or France. For the most part, however, former Confederate naval officers took up some civilian pursuit within the devastated South. It was from within these situations that many of the preceding selections were written.

It is unfortunate that so many of the naval records of the Confederacy were destroyed at the end of the war. This is particularly true of the Marine Corps records, for none survived. It is understandable that this happened, for there were many threats emanating from the North indicating that Southern naval officers would be tried for treason or piracy. The thought at the time was that it would have been foolhardy to leave available to an enemy records that could then be used as evidence to prosecute those that might be arrested. In fact, Admiral Semmes, in spite of having been given his parole, was arrested but later released.

It is, therefore, to the credit of these Southern officers that when requested by the U.S. Navy Department and the editors of various publications they were more than willing to share their copies of official correspondence and to write about their recent experiences. It is through these essays that we are able to gain a better understanding of just what challenges and obstacles that these men faced. While this adds "color" to our understanding, one must be careful in accepting their accounts as being absolutely accurate. Except for the "Official Records," most selections here were written many years after the cessation of hostilities. As enumerated earlier, memories fade and some veteran's accounts may not reflect the true picture of an engagement. Yet, it is only human nature to try to recount one's actions in a positive light. The serious student of the war must take into account many reports of a particular engagement (both North and South) to reach a fair conclusion as to exactly what happened.

As with many aspects concerning the epic saga of the Southern states' bid for independence, the desperate struggle endured by Southern naval forces was long, bitter, painful, and sometimes humiliating. The selections presented here attest to that. But, with all of the disasters during those four long years of terrible war that befell the Confederate armies, it should be remembered that behind them, it was Confederate naval units that defended the harbors and the coastline, brought in supplies stuffed in the holds of blockade runners, and destroyed the Northern merchant marine with European built cruisers. Without this naval force, the armies of the Confederacy, and the nation as a whole, could not have survived as long as it did.

Voices of the Confederate Navy has, hopefully, given the reader a better understanding of this struggle.

Bibliography

Alexander, William H. "The Work of Submarine Boats." *Southern Historical Society Papers*, vol. XXX, 1902.

Biggio, William. "Running the Blockade on the Mississippi." *Confederate Veteran*, vol. XXII, no. 1, January 1914.

Brown, Isaac N. "The Confederate Gun-Boat Arkansas." *Battles and Leaders of the Civil War*. 4 volumes. New York: Century, 1884–1888.

Campbell, R. Thomas (editor). *Southern Naval Cadet*. Jefferson: McFarland, 2006.

_____. *Southern Service on Land and Sea: The Wartime Journal of Robert Watson, CSA/CSN*. Knoxville: The University of Tennessee Press, 2002.

_____. *Academy on the James: The Confederate Naval School*. Shippensburg: White Mane, 1998.

_____. *Confederate Naval Forces on Western Waters*. Jefferson: McFarland, 2005.

_____. *Fire & Thunder: Exploits of the Confederate States Navy*. Shippensburg: White Mane, 1997.

_____. *Gray Thunder: Exploits of the Confederate States Navy*. Shippensburg: White Mane, 1996.

_____. *Hunters of the Night: Confederate Torpedo Boats in the War Between the States*. Shippensburg: White Mane, 2000.

_____. *Sea Hawk of the Confederacy: Lt. Charles W. Read and the Confederate Navy*. Shippensburg: White Mane, 2000.

_____. *Southern Fire: Exploits of the Confederate States Navy*. Shippensburg: White Mane, 1997.

_____. *Southern Thunder: Exploits of the Confederate States Navy*. Shippensburg: White Mane, 1996.

_____. *Storm Over Carolina: The Confederate Navy's Struggle for Eastern North Carolina*. Nashville: Cumberland House, 2005.

Carter, Jonathan H. *Letter Book of Lt. Jonathan H. Carter*. Washington: War Records Branch, Record Group 45, National Archives.

Civil War Naval Chronology 1861–1865. Washington: Naval History Division, U.S. Navy Department, 1971.

Clark, Walter. *North Carolina Regiments*. Goldsboro: Nash Brothers Book and Job Printers, 1901.

Conrad, Daniel B. "Capture of the USS Underwriter." *Southern Historical Society Papers*, vol. XIX, January, 1891.

Corbin, Diana Fontaine. *The Life of Matthew Fontaine Maury*. London: S. Low, Marston, Searle, & Rivington, 1888.

Coski, John M. *Capital Navy*. Campbell: Savas Woodbury Publishers, 1996.

Crowley, R. O. "The Confederate Torpedo Service." The *Century* Magazine, vol. 56, issue 2, June 1898.

Dictionary of American Fighting Ships. "Confederate Forces Afloat." Washington, D.C., Navy Department, vol. II, appendix II.

Donnelly, Ralph W. *The Confederate States Marine Corps*. Shippensburg: White Mane, 1989.

Elliott, Gilbert. "The Career of the Confederate Ram *Albemarle*." *The Century Magazine*, volume 36, issue 3, July 1888.

Glassell, William T. "Reminiscences of Torpedo Service in Charleston Harbor." *Southern Historical Society Papers*, vol. IV, 1877.

Gordan, A. "Organization of Troops." *Histories of the Several Regiments and Battalions From North Carolina in the Great War 1861–'65*, Goldsboro: Nash Brothers, Book and Job Printers, 1901.

Hearn, Chester G. *Gray Raiders of the Sea*. Camden: International Marine Publishing, 1992.

Johnson, Robert U., and Clarence Clough Buel: *Battles and Leaders of the Civil War*. 4 volumes. New York: The Century Company, 1884–1888.

Johnston, James D. "The Ram *Tennessee* at Mobile Bay." *Battles and Leaders of the Civil War*. 4 volumes. New York: Century, 1884–1888.

Jones, Catesby ap R. "Services of the *Virginia* (*Merrimac*)." *Southern Historical Society Papers*, volume XI, January 1883.

Kell, John McIntosh. "Combats of the *Alabama*." *Battles and Leaders of the Civil War*. 4 volumes. New York: Century, 1884–1888.

Krick, Robert K. *Lee's Colonels: A Biographical Register of the Field Officers of the Army of Northern Virginia*. Dayton: Morningside, 1991.

Luraghi, Raimondo. *A History of the Confederate Navy*. Annapolis: Naval Institute Press, 1996.

Mabry, W. S. *A Brief Sketch of the Career of Captain Catesby ap R. Jones*. Published privately, Selma, Alabama, 1912.

Maffitt, John Newland. "Blockade Running." *The United Service*, vol. VII, July 1882.

Maglenn, James. "The Steamer *Advance*." *North Carolina Regiments 1861–65*, vol. V, 1901.

Maury, Richard L. "The First Marine Torpedoes were made in Richmond, Va., and Used in the James River." Richmond, *Times-Dispatch*, February 14 and 20, 1904.

Melton, Maurice. "First and Last Cruise of the CSS *Atlanta*." *Civil War Times Illustrated*, November 1971.

_____. *The Confederate Ironclads*. New York: Thomas Yoseloff, Publisher, 1968.

Miller, Francis T. *Photographic History of the Civil War*. New York: The Review of Reviews, 1911–1912.

Moebs, Thomas T. *Confederate States Navy Research Guide*. Williamsburg: Moebs, 1991.

Morgan, James Morris. "The Pioneer Ironclad." *Proceedings*, vol. 43, no. 176, October, 1917.

_____. *Recollections of a Rebel Reefer*. New York: Houghton Mifflin, 1917.

Myers, Henry. "Cruising With the *Sumter*." *Confederate Veteran*, December 1923.

Official Records of the Union and Confederate Navies in the War of the Rebellion. 31 volumes. Washington, D.C.: Government Printing Office, 1894–1927.

Owsley, Frank Lawrence, Jr. *The C.S.S. Florida, Her Building and Operations*. Tuscaloosa: The University of Alabama Press, 1987.

Page, Thomas J. "The Career of the Confederate Cruiser *Stonewall*." *Southern Historical Society Papers*, vol. XII, 1879.

Parker, William H. "The Gold and Silver in the Confederate States Treasury." *Southern Historical Society Papers*, vol. XXI, 1893.

_____. *Recollections of a Naval Officer*. New York: Charles Scribners' Sons, 1883.

Porter, Thomas K. "Capture of the Confederate Steamer *Florida*." *Southern Historical Society Papers*, vol. XII, 1884.

Read, Charles W. "Reminiscences of the Confederate States Navy." *Southern Historical Society Papers*, vol. I, no. V, May 1876.

Register of Officers of the Confederate States Navy, 1861–1865. Richmond: Navy Department, 1864.

Robinson, William Morrison. *The Confederate Privateers*. New Haven: Yale University Press, 1928.

Scharf, J. Thomas. *History of the Confederate States Navy*. New York: Crown, 1877.

Semmes, Raphael. *Memoirs of Service Afloat*. Baltimore: Kelly, Piet, 1869.

Shingleton, Royce G. *John Taylor Wood: Sea Ghost of the Confederacy*. Athens: University of Georgia Press, 1979.

Shippey, W. Frank. "A Leaf from my Log-Book." *Southern Historical Society Papers*, vol. XII, 1884.

Spencer, William F. *The Confederate Navy in Europe*. Tuscaloosa: The University of Alabama Press, 1983.

Sprunt, James. "Blockade Running." *Histories of the Several Regiments and Battalions from North Carolina in the Great War 1861-'65*. Goldsboro: Nash Brothers, Book and Job Printers, 1901. Vol. V.

Still, William N., Jr. *Iron Afloat, the Story of the Confederate Armorclads*. Nashville: Vanderbilt University Press, 1971.

Symonds, Craig L. *Confederate Admiral, the Life and Wars of Franklin Buchanan*. Annapolis: Naval Institute Press, 1999.

Taylor, Richard. *Destruction and Reconstruction*. New York: Longmans, Green and Co., 1955.

The War of the Rebellion: A Compilation of the Official Records of the Union and Confederate Armies. 130 volumes. Washington, D.C.: Government Printing Office, 1880–1901.

Trent, W. P. *Southern Writers: Selections in Prose and Verse*. New York: MacMillan, 1905.

Turner, Maxine. *Navy Gray: A Story of the Confederate Navy on the Chattahoochee and Apalachicola Rivers*. Tuscaloosa: The University of Alabama Press, 1988.

Vance, Zebulon B. *The Papers of Zebulon Baird Vance*. Raleigh: State Department of Archives and History, 1963.

Warley, Alexander F. "The Ram *Manassas* at the Passage of the New Orleans Forts." *Battles and Leaders of the Civil War*. 4 volumes. New York: Century, 1884–1888.

Whittle, William C., Jr. "The Cruise of the *Shenandoah*." *Southern Historical Society Papers*, vol. XXXV, December 1907.

Wilkinson, John. *The Narrative of a Blockade Runner*. New York: Sheldon & Company, 1877.

Wise, Stephen R. *Lifeline of the Confederacy*. Columbia: University of South Carolina Press, 1988.

Index

A.H. Schultz, CSS 264, 265, 343–345
Abbeville, South Carolina 349, 350, 353
Abercrombie, Lieutenant Colonel L.A. 193
Abigail 255
Adela, USS 100, 101
Adelaide 252
Advance 99, 100, 291–295
Alabama, CSS 199–205, 224–231, 246–248, 257, 311, 315, 317, 319, 320, 323, 326
Alabama River, Alabama 105
Alabama Secession 3
Albatross, USS 13
Albemarle, CSS 39, 44–51, 155, 296
Albemarle Sound, North Carolina 30–39, 45
Alcot, Sailmaker Henry 250
Alexander, 1st Lieutenant Joseph W. 10, 16–17, 19, 25, 31
Alexander, Lieutenant William H. 75–82
Alexandria, Louisiana 147–152
Algiers, Louisiana 119, 139
Alina 251
Allison, Major Richard T. 323
Amelia Courthouse, Virginia 348
Anderson, Midshipman Edwin M. 226, 229
Anderson, Major General Richard H. 27
Anna Jane 252
Apalachicola, Florida 96, 99, 100
Apalachicola River, Florida 96, 101
Appomattox, CSS 31
Appomattox River, Virginia 29, 44
Archer, CSS 241
Arkansas, CSS 44, 144, 173–182, 185
Arkansas Post, Arkansas 144, 182
Arkansas River, Arkansas 144, 182
Arledge, 1st Lieutenant George H. 55
Armant, Colonel Leopold L. 139
Armstrong, 1st Lieutenant Richard F. 212, 225
Arnold, Lieutenant Thomas 136
Assyrian 110
Atchafalaya River, Louisiana 139, 141
Atlanta, CSS 83–85, 323

Augusta, USS 65, 68
Augusta, Georgia 350

Bacot, 2nd Lieutenant Richard H. 175
Bagby, Colonel Arthur 190–199
Bahama 224
Bahia, Brazil 242
Baker, 1st Lieutenant Adam N. 322
Baldwin, Captain Charles H. 227
Baltic, CSS 104
Banks, Assistant Paymaster John S. 64
Banks, General Nathaniel P. 199
Barbot, 1st Lieutenant Alphonse 84, 175
Barclay, Master's Mate A.H.E.W. 86, 87, 185
Barney, Commander Joseph N. 10, 15, 238, 242, 296
Barracouda 256
Barron, Captain Samuel 249, 337, 341
Bassett, Henry D. 104
Batesville, Arkansas 182
Baton Rouge, Louisiana 139, 181, 182, 209
Battery Beaulieu, Georgia 86–88
Battery Bohler, Virginia 328, 331, 333, 334
Battery Brooke, Virginia 328
Battery Buchanan, North Carolina 53, 54, 56, 93, 266
Battery Dantzler, Virginia 22
Battery Howlett, Virginia 328, 331
Battery Lamb, North Carolina 56
Battery Marshall, South Carolina 80–82
Battery Semmes, Virginia 328, 331, 333
Battery Wood, Virginia 328
Bay of Biscay 303, 304
Baylor, Governor J.R. 196
Bayou City, CSS 190–199
Bayou Teche, Louisiana 140–144
Beall, Colonel Lloyd J. 323, 324–326
Beaufort, CSS 10–21, 30–39, 343
Beaufort, Sailmaker W.P. 212
Beauregard, General Pierre G.T. 62,

68, 73, 78, 80, 81, 90, 93–95, 164, 165, 167
Beck, Master Charles 137
Bell, 2nd Lieutenant Thomas P. 24, 25
Belle Algerine 129, 134
Benjamin, Secretary of State Judah P. 353
Bennett, 1st Lieutenant John W. 107, 110, 115
Benton, USS 158, 162
Bermuda Hundred, Virginia 263, 264
Berwick Bay, Louisiana 139–144
Bestwick, Acting Carpenter Chester 152
Biggio, Quartermaster William 185–189
Birkenhead, England 224
Black Warrior, CSS 31–39
Blackwater River, Virginia 26–29
Blake, Lieutenant Homer C. 201–205, 227
Blanc, Midshipman Samuel P. 101, 159
Blountstown, Florida 96
Bombshell, CSS 48
Bordeaux, France 300
Bowen, 1st Lieutenant Robert J. 64, 136
Bradford, 1st Lieutenant William L. 332
Brady, Pilot James 176, 178
Brand, Lieutenant Colonel F.B. 168–173
Brandywine, USS 14
Brasher City, Louisiana 139
Breckenridge, Major General John C. 348, 353
Brent, Major Joseph L. 139, 168–173
Brent, Commander Thomas W. 93–95, 145
Brest, France 242, 296
Brincker, USS 32
Britannia, USS 51, 52
Brogan, Fireman John 243
Brooke, Commander John M. 7, 44, 248, 274
Brooklyn, USS 107, 120, 135, 157,

359

201, 202, 210, 213, 215, 217–219, 271, 329
Brooks, 1st Assistant Engineer William P. 212
Brown, Lieutenant Commander George 168–173
Brown, Commander Isaac N. 173–182
Brown, Midshipman Orris A. 250
Brownsville, Texas 191
Brunswick 255
Bryan, Master George D. 243
Buchanan, Admiral Franklin 8, 12–15, 104–118, 146, 238, 274, 323, 337
Buchanan, Commander Thomas McKean 143
Budd, Lieutenant Commander William 102
Bulloch, Master Irvine S. 225, 250, 256
Bulloch, Commander James D. 83, 224, 225, 231, 232, 246–248, 300, 311–321
Bunicum, 2nd Assistant Engineer John 145
Burbank, Gunner F.G. 142
Burdett, Pilot O.S. 142
Bureau of Ordnance and Hydrography 259, 337
Burke, Captain John H. 163, 164
Butt, 1st Lieutenant Walter R. 13, 24, 25

Cadiz, Spain 220, 221
Cairo, USS 158, 276
Cairo, Illinois 158
Caldwell, Engineer George W. 86
Caleb Cushing, USS 241
Calhoun, CSS 155–157
Cambridge, USS 14
Cameron & Company Shipyard, South Carolina 62
Campbell, 1st Assistant Engineer Loudon 13, 64, 101
Canada 246
Canandaigua, USS 65
Cannon, Pilot J.A. 72
Cape Fear River, North Carolina 51–53, 265, 266, 281, 289, 296
Cape of Good Hope 227
Capitol, CSS 174
Cardenas, Cuba 234, 236
Carondelet, USS 158, 164, 165, 176, 177
Carter, Midshipman J.A. 330
Carter, 1st Lieutenant Jonathan H. 144–152
Carter, 1st Lieutenant Robert R. 248
Cary, Midshipman Clarence 64
Cassidey, James 51
Castle Pinckney, South Carolina 92
Catherine 255
Cayuga, USS 135

Cenas, 1st Lieutenant Hilary 175, 332, 333
Ceres, USS 32, 48
Chaffin's Bluff, Virginia 21, 23, 275
Chapman, 1st Lieutenant Robert T. 56, 155, 209, 212
Charleston, CSS 92
Charleston, South Carolina 53, 62–82, 91, 153, 269–271, 286, 298, 326
Charleston Squadron 62
Charlotte, North Carolina 349
Charlton, Assistant Surgeon Thomas J. 245
Charter Oak 251
Chattahoochee, CSS 34, 96–100, 103, 246
Chattahoochee River, Georgia 96
Cheops 300
Cherbourg, France 227, 230
Cherr, Carpenter Virginius 137
Chesapeake and Albemarle Canal 35
Chester, South Carolina 349
Chew, 1st Lieutenant Francis T. 64, 137, 250
Chickamauga, CSS 297, 324
Chickasaw, USS 108
Chicora, CSS 62–70
Cincinnati, USS 158, 164, 165
City, 1st Assistant Engineer George W. 175–182
City Point, Virginia 25, 44, 110, 263, 277, 334
Clarence, CSS 241
Clayton, 2nd Assistant Engineer Anderson 147
Clifton, USS 192–199
Codd, 1st Assistant Engineer William H. 250
Collins, Commander Napoleon 243–246
Colonel Lamb 295
Colonel Lovell 163–167
Columbia, CSS 92
Columbus, Georgia 34, 96–99
Columbus, Kentucky 158
Commodore Barney, USS 32
Commodore Hull, USS 48
Commodore Jones, USS 264
Commodore Perry, USS 32, 37
Comstock, 1st Lieutenant John H. 118, 159
Conestoga, USS 182
Confederate Marine Corps 322–326
Confederate Naval Academy 85, 327–354
Confederate Point, North Carolina 54, 93
Confederate Torpedo Bureau 259, 260, 263, 266
Congress 255
Congress, USS 8–21, 153
Conrad, Surgeon Daniel B. 39, 109
Convington 255

Cook, Colonel J.J. 193–199
Cooke, Commander James W. 31, 38, 45–51, 296
Coons, Acting Master I.C. 141
Copenhagen, Denmark 302
Corbett, Captain G.H. 249, 251
Corinth, Mississippi 166
Corpus Christi, Texas 191
Corunna, Spain 307, 308
Cotton, CSS 145
Cotton, Master's Mate Lodge 250
Cotton Plant, CSS 48
Couronne 228
Cowley, Stephen A. 338
Craig, Master William J. 13, 97, 98
Crain, Lieutenant Walter O. 145–147
Craney Island, Virginia 13, 15, 18
Crenshaw, Captain Edward 27
Crenshaw, Lieutenant Edward 324
Croatan Sound, North Carolina 31
Crossen, Lieutenant Thomas M. 292
Crowley, Electrician R.O. 259–273
Crow's Nest, Virginia 328, 331, 333
Cuddy, Gunner Thomas C. 212
Cumberland, USS 8–21, 153, 276
Cummings, 3rd Assistant Engineer Simeon W. 212
Curlew, CSS 31–39
Curtis, James O. 119
Curtis, General Samuel R. 182
Cushing, Lieutenant William B. 49, 74, 155

D.G. Godfrey 252
Dahlgren, Rear Admiral John A. 74
Dallas, Pilot Moses 86–88
Danville, Virginia 348, 351
David, CSS 69–75
Davidson, Commander Hunter 13, 259, 260, 274, 277
Davis, Captain Charles H. 164
Davis, President Jefferson 39, 149, 159, 208, 238, 256, 337, 339, 350–353
Davis, Varina Howell 348–350, 353
DeBlanc, 3rd Assistant Engineer A. 101–103
Debois, 2nd Assistant Engineer Edward 113
Debray, Colonel X.B. 195
Deep Bottom, Virginia 263, 264
Deerhound 230
Defiance 129, 134
Delaney, Captain James C. 163, 164, 167
Delaware, USS 32
Delphine 253
Department of Texas 190
Diana 134
Dismal Swamp Canal 13, 14, 35
Dixon, Lieutenant George E. 79–82, 276, 277
Doak, Lieutenant Henry N. 323
Dr. Beatty, CSS 168–173

Dorning, Private Henry 142
Drewry, CSS 21–25, 334
Drewry's Bluff, Virginia 13, 26, 44, 263, 323–328, 335, 341
Duke, Brigadier General Basil W. 351
Duncan, Brigadier General Johnson K. 123, 125, 126–138, 211
Dunnington, 1st Lieutenant John W. 23, 25, 159, 183–185
Dupont, Admiral Samuel 65, 67
Durning, 2nd Assistant Engineer James 137
Dutch Gap, Virginia 21, 23, 110, 438

Eads, James B. 158
Eason, James 62
Edward 253
Edward Cary 254
Eggleston, 1st Lieutenant John R. 13, 159
Eliza G. 183
Elizabeth City, North Carolina 30, 35, 38
Elizabeth River, Virginia 14
Elliott, 1st Lieutenant Gilbert 45–51
Ellis, CSS 31–39
Empire Parish 216
Enoch Train 119, 154
Enrica 224
Equator, CSS 51
Essex, USS 158, 180–182
Estella 240
Estrella, USS 142
Euphrates 255
Evans, Lieutenant William E. 212
Ewing, Master Francis M. 276

Fabian, Engineer James L. 86
Fagan, 2nd Assistant Engineer Henry 96–99
Fairbanks, Master Charles B. 129, 132
Fanny, CSS 31–39
Farragut, Admiral David G. 104, 120, 124, 127, 137, 157, 163, 271
Farrand, Captain Ebenezer 110
Fashion 96
Favorite 255
Fear Not, USS 187
Fendall, Lieutenant J.R.T. 323
Ferrol, Spain 305–307
Firefly, CSS 86, 91, 94
Flag, USS 65
Flake, 3rd Assistant Engineer William 146
Flemington, North Carolina 54, 92
Florence, South Carolina 92
Florida, CSS 122, 159, 226, 231–248, 282, 283, 296, 298, 299, 311
Florida Coast Guard 53
Florida Secession 3
Fluery, Gunner William J. 151

Flusser, Captain Charles W. 48, 50
Folly 296
Fontaine, Captain S.T. 193–199
Foote, Admiral Andrew H. 158
Ford, Assistant Surgeon Marcellius 97, 101
Foreman, 1st Lieutenant Ivy 14, 17
Forrest, CSS 31–39
Forrest, Captain French 15, 18
Fort Anderson, North Carolina 60
Fort Bartow, North Carolina 31
Fort Campbell, North Carolina 57, 266, 287
Fort Caswell, North Carolina 265, 266, 287, 293, 295, 297
Fort Fisher, North Carolina 25, 51, 53, 54, 56, 57, 72, 93, 265, 266, 281, 295–299, 323
Fort Forrest, North Carolina 31, 33
Fort Gaines, Alabama 106
Fort Harrison, Virginia 330, 331
Fort Hindman, Arkansas 182
Fort Huger, North Carolina 31, 33
Fort Jackson, Georgia 85, 90, 91
Fort Jackson, Louisiana 123–138, 156, 163, 211
Fort McAllister, Georgia 90, 271
Fort Monroe, Virginia 223, 244, 275
Fort Morgan, Alabama 106, 107, 111, 112, 236, 237, 271, 323
Fort Moultrie, South Carolina 66, 68
Fort Pickens, Florida 106
Fort Pillow, Tennessee 144, 163–167
Fort Point, Texas 193
Fort St. Philip, Louisiana 120, 121, 123, 125–138, 156, 163, 211
Fort Sumter, South Carolina 66, 68, 72–74, 269, 270
Fort Taylor, Louisiana 168
Fort Warren, Massachusetts 74, 137, 223, 241, 244, 246
Foute, 1st Lieutenant Robert C. 13
Frazee, Master's Mate Carman 101
Frazier, Trenholm & Company 232, 285–287, 296, 299
Fredericksburg, CSS 21–25, 75, 334, 335
Freeman, Master's Mate Arthur C. 86
Freeman, 1st Assistant Engineer Miles J. 212, 226
French, Lieutenant C.A. 50
Frolic, USS 295
Fry, Brigadier General Birkett D. 350
Fry, 1st Lieutenant Joseph 157, 158, 183–185
Fulham, Master's Mate George T. 229
Fulkerson, Captain Issac D. 163, 164
Fuller, Captain Emelious W. 139–144

Gaines, CSS 105–116, 323
Galena, USS 13, 323

Galt, Surgeon Francis L. 212, 225, 229
Galveston, Texas 148, 190–205, 226, 295, 299
Galveston Bay, Texas 191
Garnett, Assistant Surgeon Algernon S. 13
General Beauregard 163–167
General Bragg 163–167
General Earl Van Dorn 163–167
General Lovell 129, 134
General M. Jeff Thompson 163–167
General Pike 255
General Polk 163
General Quitman 129, 133
General Sterling Price 163–167
General Sumter 163–167
General Williams 255
Georgia, CSS (Cruiser) 247, 248, 327
Georgia, CSS (Ironclad) 51, 85, 90, 95
Georgia Secession 3
Gibbs, Midshipman Paul H. 97, 99
Gibraltar 220, 221, 282
Gift, 1st Lieutenant George W. 40, 100, 101, 136, 175–182
Gipsey 255
Giraffe 279
Glasgow, Scotland 246
Glass, Acting Master John 137
Glassell, Commander William T. 69–75, 276
Golder, Master's Mate Hamilton 86, 87, 97–99
Goldsborough, Rear Admiral Louis M. 32
Goldsborough, North Carolina 61
Gordon 232, 285–291
Goshawk, HMS 258
Gosport Navy Yard, Virginia 46
Gossamer 142
Governor Moore 123, 124, 129, 131, 132, 137
Grafton, Assistant Surgeon J. Dana 241
Grand Era, CSS 168
Grand Gulf, Mississippi 168
Grand Lake, Louisiana 140, 141
Granite, USS 32
Grant, Captain Alexander 129
Grant, 1st Lieutenant Alexander, Jr. 145, 151
Graves, 1st Lieutenant Charles I. 25
Green, Colonel Thomas 190–199
Greene, 1st Lieutenant Israel 322, 323
Greenwood, Mississippi 173, 174
Grenada, Mississippi 181
Grey, Master's Mate Thaddeus S. 86
Grey Cloud, USS 142, 143
Greyhound, HMS 232
Grimball, 1st Lieutenant John 175–182, 226, 250

Guthrie, 1st Lieutenant John J. 96–100
Guy, Gunner John L. 250
Gwin, Lieutenant William 176, 177

H.L. Hunley, CSS 75–82, 153, 270, 271
Hale, Midshipman William K. 330
Halifax, North Carolina 45
Hall, 1st Lieutenant Wilburn B. 24, 344, 345
Hamilton, Master William P. 64
Hamilton, North Carolina 47
Hampton, CSS 21, 23, 113
Hampton Roads, Virginia 12–13, 20, 26, 153, 244, 274, 323, 327, 337
Handy, Lieutenant T.H. 171
Hanleiter, Captain Cornelius 86
Hardee, Lieutenant General William J. 93–95
Hardeeville, South Carolina 91, 93, 94
Hardwood, Boatswain George 250
Harmony, CSS 15, 18
Harriet Lane, CSS 192–199, 345
Harris, Master Frank M. 31, 122, 136
Harrison, Colonel Burton N. 350, 353
Harrison, Commander George W. 113–116
Harrison, 1st Lieutenant Thomas L. 107, 115, 116
Harrison, Surgeon William D. 25
Hart 140
Hart, 3rd Assistant Engineer Theodore 137
Hartford, USS 69, 107, 108, 111, 113, 115, 117, 120, 135, 157, 178, 179, 187, 329
Harthorne, First Officer J.E. 163, 164
Harvest 254
Harvest Home 222
Hasker, 1st Lieutenant Charles H. 13
Hatteras, USS 199–205, 226, 227
Hatteras Inlet, North Carolina 32
Havana, Cuba 234, 236, 310, 311
Haynes, Gunner William H. 137
Haynes' Bluff, Mississippi 176
Hays, 1st Lieutenant Andrew J. 322, 323
Head of the Passes 153–158, 215
Hearn, Assistant Paymaster William A. 149
Hector 254
Henderson, Texas 147
Herring, 1st Assistant Engineer Benjamin S. 13, 146
Hetzel, USS 32
Hicks, Midshipman William A. 212
Higgins, Brigadier General Edward 123, 126
Hillman 255

Hindman, Brigadier General Thomas C. 182, 185
Hodges, Chief Pilot John 176
Hoge, Reverend Moses D. 293
Hogue, Midshipman William S. 101
Hoke, Major General Robert F. 47–51
Holden, Midshipman John F. 210
Holland, Colonel D.P. 101
Hollins, Captain George N. 53, 119, 122, 153, 155–163, 182
Hollyhock, USS 188, 189
Hollywood Cemetery, Richmond 335
Holmes, 2nd Lieutenant George 322, 323
Hoole, 1st Lieutenant James L. 31, 33
Hope, James Barron 336, 337
Hornet, CSS 21
Housatonic, USS 65, 68, 75–82, 153, 271, 277
Houston, Texas 147, 191
Howell, 1st Lieutenant Becket K. 212, 226, 322, 323
Howland 255
Howquah, USS 52
Hudgins, 1st Lieutenant Albert G. 55, 56, 212
Hudgins, Lieutenant William E. 92, 94, 95
Huger, Major General Benjamin 35
Huger, 1st Lieutenant Thomas B. 120, 124, 126–138, 159
Hulse, Acting Master Albert F. 137
Hunchback, USS 32
Hunley, Horace 75, 78, 79, 276
Hunt, Master's Mate C.E. 250
Hunter, Lieutenant James M. 176
Hunter, Acting Master Thomas T. 31, 33, 35, 243
Hunter, Captain William W. 85, 89, 190
Huntress, CSS 345
Hurt, Captain James H. 163, 164
Hutchinson, 2nd Assistant Engineer John 250
Hutter, Midshipman William C. 19

Iglehart, Passed Assistant Surgeon Osborn S. 113
Indian Chief, CSS 80, 91, 92
Indianola, USS 167–173, 186
Ingraham, Captain Duncan N. 62, 65, 70, 94
Ingraham, 2nd Lieutenant Henry L. 322
Ino, USS 222
Iroquois, USS 120, 135, 221
Isabella 255
Island No. 10, Missouri 123, 127, 144, 158–163
Isondiga, CSS 91, 94, 95
Ivy, CSS 155–159, 213, 214

J.A. Cotton, CSS 139–144
Jack, 1st Assist Engineer E. Alexander 13
Jackson, CSS 128, 130, 134, 155–157, 215
Jackson, Midshipman William C. 38
Jackson, Mississippi 182
James Murray 255
James River, Virginia 10–13, 15, 26, 44, 51, 75, 110, 223, 259, 263, 268, 274–278, 324, 326, 335, 341
James River Squadron 15, 17, 21–25, 113, 348
Jamestown CSS 10–13, 15, 19, 113
Jireh Swift 255
John F. Carr, CSS 190
John Laird & Sons 224
Johnson, David S. 96
Johnson, Lieutenant John H. 30, 33, 34, 36
Johnston, Commander James D. 104–110
Jones, Commander Catesby ap R. 7–13, 19, 96–100, 105, 274
Jones, 2nd Assistant Engineer F.P. 147
Jones, 1st Lieutenant J. Pembroke 51, 52, 97
Jones, Acting Boatswain Samuel 137
Jones, Assistant Surgeon William C. 86

Kansas, USS 52
Kate Prince 252
Kearsarge, USS 227–231, 244
Kell, Commander John M. 23, 25, 211, 224–231
Kelly, Quartermaster James 186, 187
Kennett, Midshipman Ferdinand B. 25
Kennon, 1st Lieutenant Beverly 24, 123, 129, 132, 137, 157, 276, 329
Keokuk, USS 270
Key West, Florida 53, 354
Keystone State, USS 65, 68, 69
Kilty, Commander Augustus H. 182
King, Lieutenant E.T. 142
Kingston, Jamaica 227
Kingston, North Carolina 43, 45

Labadieville, Louisiana 139
Lackawanna, USS 187, 188
Lady Davis, CSS 62
Lafourche River, Louisiana 139
Lamb, Captain W.W. 163, 164
Lamb, Colonel William 281, 295
Lancaster, John 230
Landis 129, 134
Lapwing 241
Larmour, 2nd Lieutenant Robert B. 149
Launch No. 1, CSS 140, 141
Launch No. 3, CSS 129, 130, 134

Launch No. 6, CSS 129, 132, 136
Laurel 249, 250
Lawrence Sneden & Company 285
Lea, Major A.M. 194
Lee, Midshipman Daniel M. 328
Lee, Captain Francis D. 70, 276
Lee, General Robert E. 75, 330, 331, 333, 337
Lee, 1st Lieutenant Sidney Smith, Jr. 136, 250
Leonard, Captain William H.H. 163, 164
LeRoy, Captain William E. 67
Lewis, 1st Lieutenant Henry H. 27–29
Lexington, USS 182
Lincoln, President Abraham 272, 295
Lindsey, Carpenter Hugh 13
Lining, Assistant Surgeon Charles E. 250
Lisbon, Portugal 308, 309
Little Rebel 163–167
Little Rock, Arkansas 144, 182
Littlepage, 1st Lieutenant Hardin B. 13
Liverpool, England 224, 231, 249, 257, 258, 295, 299
Livingston, CSS 159, 162
Lizzie M. Stacey 252
Llewellyn, Assistant Surgeon David H. 225, 229
Lockwood, USS 32
Lockwood, Captain Thomas 295
Long, Master James C. 13
Lord Clyde 292
Louisiana, CSS 44, 123–138, 144, 246, 279
Louisiana, USS 32
Louisiana Secession 3
Louisville, USS 158
Lovell, Major General Mansfield 129
Lowe, Alfred 92
Lowe, 1st Lieutenant John 225, 232, 320
Loyall, Commander Benjamin P. 31, 33, 40, 42
Lubbock, Captain Henry S. 151, 190–199
Lucien Arman Shipbuilding 300
Luck, Pilot John 47, 48
Lucy Gwin, CSS 190
Lynch, Surgeon Arthur M. 64
Lynch, Captain William F. 30–39, 52
Lyons, Thomas B. 75

Macon, Georgia 349
Madrid, Spain 306
Maffitt, Midshipman Eugene A. 226, 229
Maffitt, Commander John Newland 231–242, 283, 285–291, 296–299

Magleen, Chief Engineer James 292–295
Magruder, Lieutenant George A. 196
Magruder, Major General John B. 146, 147, 149, 190–200
Mallory, Midshipman Charles K. 17, 20, 34, 97, 98
Mallory, Secretary of the Navy Stephen R. 7, 44, 85, 104, 113, 127, 138, 144–152, 185, 232, 238, 240, 259, 260, 311–321, 326, 339, 348–351
Malvern, USS 272
Manassas, CSS 119–138, 153–159
Mangum, Captain James W. 172
Manhattan, USS 186, 187
Manly, Lieutenant Colonel J.H. 193
Marmaduke, 1st Lieutenant Henry H. 13, 153, 159
Marques de la Habana 122, 155
Marsh, 3rd Assistant Engineer George R. 145
Martha 255
Martin, Adjutant General James G. 292
Mary Patterson 183
Mason, James M. 319
Mason, Midshipman John T. 250
Masonborough Inlet, North Carolina 280
Massachusetts, USS 116
Mattabesett, USS 48
Maurepas, CSS 182, 183, 184
Maury, Commander Matthew F. 248, 259, 260, 273–278
Maury, Lieutenant Colonel Richard L. 273–278
Maury, Robert H. 275
Maxwell, John 277
McAdam, 1st Lieutenant Sidney H. 93
McBlair, Lieutenant Charles 173
McCarrick, 1st Lieutenant Patrick 31
McCasky, Boatswain Benjamin P. 212
McClintock, James 75
McCloskey, Captain James 168, 169, 171, 172
McClosky, 3rd Assistant Engineer T.O. 95
McDaniel, Master Z. 276
McDermott, 2nd Lieutenant Edward J. 137, 146
McIntosh, Commander Charles F. 123, 131, 133
McKean, Assistant Paymaster Edward 147, 149
Mclaughlin, 1st Lieutenant Augustus 96–100
McNulty, Assistant Surgeon F.J. 250, 252
McRae, CSS 120–138, 153, 155–163, 185, 215, 327
Meads, Naval Constructor Richard P. 146, 148–150

Medford, Massachusetts 119
Meire, 1st Lieutenant Julius E. 322, 323
Melbourne, Australia 253, 254
Memphis, USS 65, 67, 68
Memphis, Tennessee 144, 165–167, 173
Mercedita, USS 65–68
Merrimack, USS 7, 14–21, 62
Metacomet, USS 107, 115, 117
Miami, USS 48–50
Milliken, Master Samuel 175
Milo 255
Minnesota, USS 9–13, 14, 17, 19, 72, 210, 269, 276, 277
Minnigerode, Reverend Charles 337, 342
Minnigerode, Midshipman James G. 338
Minor, Henry 335, 336
Minor, Midshipman Hubbard T. 85–88, 334–347
Minor, Master's Mate John F. 250
Minor, 1st Lieutenant Robert D. 10, 13, 19, 274, 275, 336, 337, 339
Mississippi, CSS 125, 127, 144
Mississippi, USS 120, 125, 135, 157, 329
Mississippi River 122, 127, 144, 149, 153–189, 267
Mississippi Secession 3
Mississippi Sound 116
Missouri, CSS 144–152, 185
Mitchell, Captain John K. 21–25, 123–125, 127–138
Mobile, Alabama 104–118, 236–242, 270–272, 326
Mobile River, AL 105
Mobile Squadron 116
Monarch, USS 167
Monitor, USS 11–13, 153, 274, 323
Monroe, Louisiana 191
Montague, Lieutenant E. 140, 143
Montauk, USS 271
Montgomery, Captain James E. 163–167
Montgomery, Alabama 3
Moore, Acting Carpenter Charles 152
Moore, Pilot Edward 22
Moore, Brigadier General John C. 172
Moore, Thomas 144
Morgan, CSS 105–110, 113–116
Morgan, Midshipman James Morris 153–163, 327–354
Morris, 1st Lieutenant Charles M. 242–246
Morris, Lieutenant George 16
Morris Island, South Carolina 72, 73, 269
Morse, USS 32
Mosher 129, 132, 156
Mosquito Fleet 30–39

Index

Mound City, USS 158, 164, 165, 182
Mount Pleasant, South Carolina 80
Mouton, Brigadier General Alfred 140, 142, 143
Mt. Vernon, USS 14, 52
Mugguffiny, 3rd Assistant Engineer E. 250
Murdoch, Lieutenant J. Campbell 324
Murphy, 1st Lieutenant Peter U. 107, 110, 116–118
Murray, Master's Mate John R. 118
Muscogee, CSS (*Jackson*) 99, 100, 103
Musgrave, Master Linus 146, 151
Music 129, 139, 156
Myers, Paymaster Henry 212, 220–224

Nag's Head, North Carolina 31
Nahant, USS 83–85
Nansemond, CSS 341, 342
Nansemond, USS 52
Nashville, CSS 110, 111, 246, 248
Nassau 255, 285
Nassau, Bahamas 232, 289
Natchez, Mississippi 168
Naugatuck, USS 323
Nausemond, CSS 21, 23
Naval Ordnance Works, Richmond 7, 337
Neapolitan 221
Nelson, Assistant Paymaster Albert A. 145
Neptune, CSS 190–199
Neuse, CSS 39, 51
Neuse River, North Carolina 39, 40, 44, 45
New Bern, North Carolina 13, 30, 39, 326
New Inlet, North Carolina 51, 280, 284, 297
New Ironsides, USS 56, 65, 72, 73, 270, 276
New Madrid, Missouri 123, 127, 159–163
New Orleans, Louisiana 104, 113, 119–139, 182, 186–189, 206–220, 246
Newport News, Virginia 14, 16, 268, 269
Niagara, USS 210, 307–309
Nile 255
Nimrod 255
Niphon, USS 52
Nitre & Mining Bureau 148
Nolan, 3rd Assistant Engineer James 137
Norfolk, Virginia 13, 14, 30, 35, 294, 295
North, Commander James H. 312
North Carolina, CSS 72, 73
Nye 255

O'Brien, 2nd Assistant Engineer 212, 250
Offutt, Gunner Z.A. 113
Old Point, Virginia 14, 17
Oliver, 1st Lieutenant Charles B. 13
Oneida, USS 135, 236, 237
Onondaga, USS 334
Oreto 231–233
O'Shea, Carpenter John 250
Ossabaw Sound, Georgia 85, 86
Ossipee, USS 109
Ottawa, USS 65, 74
Owasco, USS 192–199
Owl 296–299

Page, Captain Thomas Jefferson 300–311
Page, Surgeon William M. 150, 152
Palmetto State, CSS 14, 62–69, 343
Pamlico Sound, North Carolina 30–39, 45
Park, Thomas 75, 78, 80
Parker, 1st Lieutenant William H. 10–20, 30, 31, 37, 62–69, 328, 339, 340, 343, 347–354
Parks & Lyons Machine Shop 75, 78
Pasquotank River, North Carolina 35
Passe a l'outre, Louisiana 154, 210, 214–216
Patrick Henry, CSS 10–13, 15, 19, 85, 275, 327–330, 335–348
Payne, 1st Lieutenant John A. 78, 113
Pearce, Constructor Henry 105
Pearl 254
Pelot, 1st Lieutenant Thomas P. 85–88
Pendergrast, Lieutenant Austin 17, 18, 88
Pensacola, USS 135
Pensacola, Florida 106
Petersburg, Virginia 26, 44
Petrel, HMS 200
Philippi, USS 115
Phillips, Surgeon Dinwiddie 13
Phillips, 1st Lieutenant John L. 146, 150–152
Phoenix 129, 134
Pickett, Major General George 40
Pierce, Captain Charles 168, 170, 172
Pinola, USS 135
Pittsburg, USS 158
Plum Point, Tennessee 163–165
Plymouth, North Carolina 47–51
Point Lookout Prison, Maryland 244
Pontchartrain, CSS 159, 182, 183
Pope, Captain John 153–158
Pope, Major General John 160–163
Porcher, 1st Lieutenant Philip 64
Port Hudson, Louisiana 144
Port Royal, South Carolina 62, 68

Porter, Admiral David D. 272, 297, 298
Porter, Chief Constructor John L. 44, 45, 173
Porter, Constructor Thomas 106
Porter, 1st Lieutenant Thomas K. 242–246
Porter, Commodore William D. 180
Powhatan, USS 68, 213–215
Pratt, 2nd Lieutenant Thomas S. 95
Preble, USS 155, 156
Preble, Commander George H. 238, 239
Presque Isle, Virginia 263
Price, 1st Lieutenant Joseph 85–88
Putnam, USS 32

Quaker City, USS 65, 67, 68
Queen of the West, CSS 168–173, 176–177

R.J. Breckinridge 129, 134
Radford, Commander William C. 16
Rains, Brigadier General Gabriel J. 271, 274, 276, 278
Raleigh, CSS (Gunboat) 10–13, 15–19, 25, 31–39
Raleigh, CSS (Ironclad) 51–53
Ramsay, 1st Lieutenant John F. 249, 251
Ramsey, Chief Engineer H. Ashton 13
Raney, Lieutenant David G. 323
Rappahannock, CSS 247, 251
Rappahannock River, Virginia 261, 262
Rattler, USS 149
Read, 1st Lieutenant Charles W. 21–29, 122–126, 132, 151, 159, 161, 175–182, 185–189, 241, 334
Read, Assistant Paymaster John Laurens 234
Red River, Louisiana 139, 144, 167, 185, 186, 200
Reily, Colonel James 192
Renshaw, 1st Lieutenant Francis B. 128, 134
Renshaw, Commodore William B. 178, 190
Resolute 124, 125, 129, 134
Resolute, CSS 89, 345
Rice, Lieutenant H.A. 172
Richmond, CSS 21–25, 334, 335
Richmond, USS 111, 135, 153–158, 179, 188
Richmond, Virginia 26, 75, 149, 259, 262, 263, 268, 272, 273–278, 323, 326, 335
Riley, 3rd Assistant Engineer James H. 137
Rio Grande River, Texas 191
River Defense Fleet 144, 165–167
Roanoke, USS 9, 14, 16–17, 276

Index

Roanoke Island, North Carolina 14, 30–39
Roanoke River, North Carolina 45–51
Robert E. Lee 279–285
Robinson, Carpenter William 212
Roby, Midshipman Francis M. 183, 185
Rochelle, 1st Lieutenant James H. 15, 341
Rocketts Landing, Richmond 268, 275, 335, 342
Rodgers, Captain John 84
Rogers, Acting Master J.M. 140
Rootes, Midshipman 13
Rosler, Master's Mate John A. 86
Rowan, Commodore Stephen C. 36, 37
Russell, Lord John 287
Rutledge, 1st Lieutenant John 62, 64, 66, 341

Sabine River, Texas 190, 191
Sachem, USS 192
Sacramento, USS 307–309
Saffold, William O. 96
Saffold, Georgia 96
St. Charles, Arkansas 182–185
St. George, Bermuda 282, 292, 293, 296
St. George's Sound, Florida 101, 102
Saint James Church, Richmond 335
St. Lawrence, USS 9, 10, 14, 17
St. Louis, USS 158, 182
St. Nicholas 153
Saint Paul's Episcopal Church, Richmond 337, 342, 343
San Antonio, Texas 191
Sanders, Midshipman Palmer 40, 45, 328
Sangster, Captain William H. 190–199
Santiago de Cuba, USS 294, 295
Saratoga, USS 122
Sassacus, USS 48, 49
Satartia Bar, Mississippi 175
Savage, Mary 337, 338
Savannah, CSS 51, 53–61, 85, 89–95, 98, 99, 345
Savannah, Georgia 53–61, 83–95, 271, 326, 354
Savannah River, Georgia 85, 98, 350, 352
Savannah Squadron 85
Sayre, 2nd Lieutenant Calvin L. 322, 323
Scales, 2nd Lieutenant Dabney M. 175–182, 250
Scharf, Midshipman J. Thomas 4, 51, 52, 100–103, 322–326
Scorpion, CSS 21–25
Scott, Midshipman Henry H. 27
Screven's Ferry, Georgia 90, 91, 94, 95

Scurry, Brigadier General William R. 193–199
Sea King 246, 248, 249
Seabird, CSS 31–39
Seger 140
Selma, CSS 105–110, 116–118, 159
Selma, Alabama 105
Semmes, Rear Admiral Raphael 75, 199–220, 224–231, 312, 315, 317, 348
Semple, Paymaster James 13
Sevier, Midshipman Charles F. 64
Sewell Point, Virginia 11, 15, 17, 18
Seymour, USS 32
Seymour, Boatswain Lester 86, 87
Shacklett, Pilot James R. 176
Shaw, Colonel Henry M. 31, 35
Shawsheen, USS 32
Shenandoah, CSS 246–258, 311
Shepperd, 1st Lieutenant Francis E. 23–25
Shippey, Master W. Frank 25–27
Shirley, John T. 173
Shreveport, Louisiana 144–152, 185, 345
Shryock, 1st Lieutenant George S. 64, 136, 137
Signal Hill, Virginia 328, 331, 334
Simms, 1st Lieutenant Charles C. 13, 31, 32, 38, 274
Simms, Captain John D. 322, 323
Sinclair, 1st Lieutenant Arthur, Jr. 13, 225
Sinclair, Midshipman George T. 226
Slidell, John 319
Smith, Lieutenant General Edmund Kirby 146, 149
Smith, Commander Joseph B. 10, 17
Smith, Major Leon 190–200
Smith, Captain Melancton 48, 116
Smith, Peter E. 47
Smith, Master Peter W. 25
Smith, Captain's Clerk W. Breedlove 212, 250
Smith, Captain William 17, 18
Smith, Master William 185
Smith, 2nd Assistant Engineer William 146
Smoker, John 144
Somerset, USS 100, 102
Sophia Thornton 255
Sotheron, Paymaster Marshal 101
South Carolina Secession 3
Southfield, USS 32, 48–50
Southwest Pass, Louisiana 154, 156, 213–215
Sparks, Midshipman George W. 101
Sphinx 300
Spotsylvania Court House, Virginia 334
Squib, CSS 277
Stag 297
Stanard, Lieutenant H.M. 196
Star 129, 134

Star of the West, USS 209
Stars and Stripes, USS 32
State of Georgia, USS 293
Stellwagen, Captain Henry S. 66
Stettin, USS 65
Stevens, Lieutenant Henry K. 143, 174–182
Stevenson, Captain John A. 119, 123, 129–131, 134
Stone, Midshipman Sardine G. 159, 243, 244, 246
Stonewall, CSS 247, 300–311
Stonewall Jackson 124, 129, 134
Stoney, Theodore 72
Stribling, Lieutenant John M. 212, 214, 232–238
Stuart, James 72
Sullivan's Island, South Carolina 80, 269, 270
Sumter, CSS 155, 206–220, 226, 248, 282, 317, 323
Sunflower River, Mississippi 175
Susan 252
Susan Abigail 255, 256
Susquehanna, USS 65
Swan 91
Swift, 2nd Assistant Engineer John W. 147

Tacony, CSS 241
Tallahassee, CSS 248, 324
Tangier, Morocco 220–224
Tansill, Captain Robert 322, 323
Tar River, North Carolina 45, 51
Tarboro, North Carolina 45
Tatnall, 1st Lieutenant John K.H. 322, 323
Tattnall, Captain Josiah 12, 13, 274
Tayloe, Midshipman James L. 19, 31
Taylor, Captain Algernon S. 322, 323
Taylor, Major John 31
Taylor, Lieutenant General Richard 139, 146, 200
Taylor, Captain William R. 65
Teaser, CSS 10–13, 16, 19
Tecumseh, USS 106, 107, 271
Tennessee, CSS (Memphis Ironclad) 166, 173
Tennessee, CSS (Mobile Ironclad) 104–118, 323
Tennessee, USS 152
Terret, Major George H. 322, 323
Texas, CSS 335
Texas Marine Department 190–199
Texas Secession 3
Theodore 285
Thom, Captain Reuben 13, 323
Thomas, Assistant Surgeon C. Wesley 86
Thompson, Brigadier General M. Jeff 160, 165–167, 175
Thurston, 1st Lieutenant James 84, 323

Tift, Asa F. 83
Tift, Nelson 83
Tilford, Acting Master Robert H. 129
Tiptonville, Tennessee 162, 163
Tomb, Chief Engineer James H. 72
Torpedo, CSS 21, 23, 260
Trans-Mississippi Department 144
Tredegar Iron Works, Richmond, Virginia 8, 46, 261
Trenholm, George A. 70
Trent River, North Carolina 39
Trent's Reach, Virginia 21–25
Trimble, Midshipman John D. 85, 86
Trinity River, Texas 190
Tucker, Captain, John R. 10, 15, 19, 67, 71, 73, 75, 94, 324
Turner, 1st Lieutenant George P. 322, 323
Tuscaloosa, CSS 226, 320, 345
Tuscarora, CSS 155, 156, 159
Tuscarora, USS 220
Tyler, USS 176, 177
Tyler, Midshipman Clarence W. 175
Tyler, Major Henry B. 322, 323
Tynan, Acting Chief Engineer John W. 13

Unadilla, USS 65, 273
Underwriter, USS 32, 39–44, 326, 328

Valley City, USS 32
Van Benthuysen, Captain A.C. 323
Van Dorn, Major General Earl 176, 181, 182
Vance, Governor Zebulon 292
Vanderbilt, USS 227
Varuna, USS 135, 329
Vaughan, Midshipman Henry L. 101
Vernon River, Georgia 86
Vicksburg, Mississippi 144, 167, 173–182, 186
Vincennes, USS 155–158
Virginia, CSS 7–20, 44, 46, 153, 159, 274, 323, 337
Virginia II, CSS 21–25, 334, 335
Virginia Point, Texas 191

W. Burton 129, 134, 135
Wabash, USS 65, 80
Wachusett, USS 242–246, 283
Waddell, 1st Lieutenant James I. 246–258
Wainwright, Lieutenant Jonathan M. 192
Walke, Captain Henry 176, 177
Wall, 1st Lieutenant William H. 25, 27
War of the Triple Alliance 355
Ward, 1st Lieutenant William H. 136
Warley, 1st Lieutenant Alexander F. 49, 119–122, 128, 131, 132, 136, 155, 156, 159
Warrior 129, 131, 134
Washington, Georgia 349, 350–352
Wasp, CSS 21–25
Wassaw Sound, Georgia 83, 94
Water Witch, USS 85–88, 94, 155–157
Waters, 3rd Assistant Engineer James 137
Watson, Baxter 75
Watson, Seaman Robert 53–61, 89–93
Waverley 255
Weaver, 2nd Assistant Engineer George J. 122
Webb, Commander William A. 10, 15, 19, 83–85
Weehawken, USS 83–85
Weitzel, Brigadier General Godfrey 139–144
Weldon, North Carolina 45
Welles, Secretary of the Navy Gideon 3, 20, 137, 203, 245
Wells, Acting Master William N. 50
West, Pilot Tim 187
Westfield, USS 178, 192–199
Wharton, 1st Lieutenant Arthur D. 146, 175
Wheeler, Major General Joseph 94
White, 3rd Assistant Engineer Elsberry V. 13
White, John 292
White Hall, North Carolina 39, 45
White River, Arkansas 144, 182, 183
Whitehead, USS 32, 48
Whiting, Commander William D. 74

Whittle, Commander William C. 127, 129, 136, 226
Whittle, 1st Lieutenant William C., Jr. 226, 246–258
Wier, Captain A.R. 191
Wilcox, 2nd Assistant Engineer A.H. 137
Wilkinson, Private F.D. 142
Wilkinson, 1st Lieutenant John W. 133, 136, 279–285, 297
William C. Miller & Sons 231
William H. Webb, CSS 145, 146, 151, 167–173, 185–189
William Thompson 255
Williamson, Midshipman John A.G. 27
Wilmington and Weldon Railroad, North Carolina 39
Wilmington, North Carolina 45, 51, 53, 56, 57, 61, 92, 99, 151, 265–268, 280–295, 312
Wilson, Gunner James 137
Wilson, 1st Lieutenant Joseph D. 25, 212, 225
Wilson, Paymaster's Clerk Joseph L. 113
Wilson, 1st Lieutenant Thomas S. 322, 323, 326
Winnebago, USS 108
Winona, USS 135, 237
Winslow, Captain John A. 227, 228, 230
Wise, Brigadier General Henry A. 31
Wissahickon, USS 135
Wood, Captain John Taylor 13, 39–44, 274, 326, 353, 354
Wood, Pilot Samuel 22, 24
Wragg, Master Thomas L. 84
Wright, Chief Engr. Henry X. 23
Wyalusing, USS 48

Yadkin, CSS 51
Yazoo City, Mississippi 174, 272
Yazoo River, Mississippi 173–182, 272, 273, 276
Young 97
Youngblood, Chief Engineer Wilson 136

www.ingramcontent.com/pod-product-compliance
Lightning Source LLC
Chambersburg PA
CBHW081536300426
44116CB00015B/2644